MAJORITARIAN STATE

ANGANA P. CHATTERJI, THOMAS BLOM HANSEN
and CHRISTOPHE JAFFRELOT
(*Editors*)

Majoritarian State

*How Hindu Nationalism
is Changing India*

HURST & COMPANY, LONDON

First published in the United Kingdom in 2019 by
C. Hurst & Co. (Publishers) Ltd.,
41 Great Russell Street, London, WC1B 3PL
© Angana P. Chatterji, Thomas Blom Hansen, Christophe Jaffrelot
and the contributors, 2019
All rights reserved.
Printed in India

The right of Angana P. Chatterji, Thomas Blom Hansen, Christophe Jaffrelot
and the contributors to be identified as the authors of this publication is asserted
by them in accordance with the Copyright, Designs and Patents Act, 1988.

A Cataloguing-in-Publication data record for this book
is available from the British Library.

ISBN: 978-178738-147-6 *hardback*

This book is printed using paper from registered sustainable
and managed sources.

www.hurstpublishers.com

CONTENTS

CONTENTS

PART III
THE SANGH PARIVAR: A NEW 'DEEP STATE'?

PART IV
ECONOMIC POLICIES AND 'MODINOMICS'

PART V
THE OTHERED 40 PER CENT: THE HINDU NATION AND ITS MARGINS

PART VI
DIPLOMACY AND GLOBAL ASPIRATION

CONTENTS

PART VII

WHAT RULE OF LAW?

PART VIII

GENDER AND NATION

ACKNOWLEDGEMENTS

This volume was made possible by the contributions of many. We thank them for shaping the intellectual and political contours of the project with critical insight, urgency, and discernment.

We are especially thankful to Michael Dwyer for committing to this book, and to him, David Lunn and the incredible team at Hurst for publishing it in record time.

Our grateful thanks to the peer reviewers. We thank our authors for their knowledge and commitments: Flavia Agnes, Paola Bacchetta, Pranab Bardhan, A.K. Bhattacharya, Ian M. Cook, Parvis Ghassem-Fachandi, Abdul R. JanMohamed, Pralay Kanungo, Ratna Kapur, Arkotong Longkumer, James Manor, C. Raja Mohan, Suhas Palshikar, Jyoti Puri, Mridu Rai, Tanika Sarkar, Nandini Sundar, Paranjoy Guha Thakurta, and Sukhadeo Thorat.

Angana thanks the Center for Race and Gender at the University of California, Berkeley, especially Leti Volpp and Pamela Mutsuoka, and Alisa Bierria, for their generosity of spirit and support of this work. Her grateful thanks to student research associate, Pei Wu, for her skillful assistance with copy editing, and with indexing. To Richard Shapiro, for his generative feedback on some of the essays in their formative stages.

We are appreciative of the various collaborations and solidarities that made this volume possible. The disciplinary and personal genealogies that inform this project, and the work and experiences that bring us to it, can be recorded on multiple registers. At its intersections, this book is born of a deep and shared concern for the majoritarian present, and the formative role of Hindu nationalism, in India today.

And, of course, we accept responsibility for the book, including its limitations.

Angana P. Chatterji, Thomas Blom Hansen, Christophe Jaffrelot
January 2019

ACKNOWLEDGMENTS

LIST OF ACRONYMS

ABISY	Akhil Bharatiya Itihas Sankalan Yojana
ABVP	Akhil Bharatiya Vidyarthi Parishad
AFSPA	Armed Forces Special Powers Act
AGP	Asom Gana Parishad
AIDWA	All India Democratic Women's Association
AIUDF	All India United Democratic Front
ASDC	Autonomous State Demand Committee
BJP	Bharatiya Janata Party
BMS	Bharatiya Mazdoor Sangh
BPF	Bodo People's Front
CM	Chief Minister
CPI	Communist Party of India
CRPF	Central Reserve Police Force
DHAC	Dima Hasao Autonomous Council
FIR	First Information Report
GOI	Government of India
HJV	Hindu Jagarana Vedike
HRA	House Rent Allowance
ICHR	Indian Council of Historical Research
IPC	Indian Penal Code
ISI	Inter-Services Intelligence
KAAC	Karbi Anglong Autonomous Council
LGBTQ	Lesbian, gay, bisexual, transgender, queer
MIM	Majlis-e-Ittehadul-Muslimeen
MLA	Member of Legislative Assembly
MNS	Maharashtra Navnirman Sena
NASA	National Aeronautics and Space Administration
NCERT	National Curriculum of Education and Research Training

LIST OF ACRONYMS

NCP	Nationalist Congress Party
NDA	National Democratic Alliance
NDTV	New Delhi Television Limited
NEZ	Natural Economic Zone
NPCC	Nagaland Pradesh Congress Committee
NPF	Naga People's Front
NSCN-IM	National Socialist Council of Nagalim—Isak Muivah
NSCN-K	National Socialist Council of Nagaland—Khaplang
OBC	Other Backward Class
POTA	Prevention of Terrorist Activities Act
PPA	People's Party of Arunachal
PUCL-K	People's Union for Civil Liberties—Karnataka
RSS	Rashtriya Swayamsevak Sangh
SC	Scheduled Caste
SEZ	Special Economic Zone
ST	Scheduled Tribe
TADA	Terrorist and Disruptive Activities (Prevention) Act
UN	The United Nations
UP	Uttar Pradesh
US	United States
VHP	Vishva Hindu Parishad
VK	Vivekananda Kendra

INTRODUCTION

Angana P. Chatterji, Thomas Blom Hansen and *Christophe Jaffrelot*

This book is about the contemporary ascendance of Hindu nationalist dominance to establish a majoritarian state in India. The 2014 elections witnessed the culmination of the Bharatiya Janata Party's (BJP's) longstanding efforts to rule India. This second ascent of the BJP to power in New Delhi was markedly different from its first under the prime ministership of A.B. Vajpayee (1998–2004). The triumph of the BJP in 2014 brought about two unprecedented events: never had the Hindu nationalist movement won an absolute majority in the Lok Sabha, the lower house of parliament, and never had this movement, known for its hostility to the personalisation of power and for its collegial governance, been so influenced by one politician, Narendra Modi.

The new dispensation combined four features that have also emerged in other countries in recent years, including in Donald J. Trump's America: populism, nationalism, authoritarianism, and majoritarianism. The majoritarian dispensation in India combines two further elements: the implementation of a more unvarnished pro-corporate and pro-upper caste compound of policies than ever before, paired with the normalisation of anti-minority rhetoric, routine assertions of the imminent danger posed by internal as well as external enemies to the nation, and a systematic deployment of false claims and partisan facts. The vision of a Hindu majoritarian polity held by the Rashtriya Swayamsevak Sangh (RSS) and the BJP combines cultural nationalism and political strategies aiming at

1

flagrant social dominance by the upper castes, rapid economic development, cultural conservatism, intensified misogyny, and a firm grip on the instruments of state power.

Modi's rhetoric, his authoritarian style of governance and his electoral support from the elite and the urban middle class suggests many parallels with other populist strongmen across the globe. However, the circumstances and processes that made the BJP's victory possible and sustains its power are historically complex and in large measure unique to India, as we sketch below. This volume is an attempt at assessing the diverse aspects of the policies and politics that shape the Modi government in the present, with particular focus on to how its Hindu nationalist, majoritarian ideology functions and modifies institutions and social relations. As the title of the volume suggests, we are interested in mapping and exploring if, and how, the political and social dominance of the BJP and the plethora of Hindu nationalist organisations are shifting the relationship between the Indian state and its diverse peoples and communities.

Modi's neo-sultanism

The four 'isms' noted above—populism, nationalism, authoritarianism, and majoritarianism—resonate with the notion of 'sultanism', that Max Weber introduced a century ago to describe situations when power 'operates primarily on the basis of discretion' under the aegis of a strong man.[1] Analysing 'sultans' of the twentieth century, Juan Linz and Alfred Stepan have complexified this model to define it as a regime in which 'all individuals, groups and institutions are permanently subject to the unpredictable and despotic intervention of the sultan, and thus all pluralism is precarious'.[2] This suggests that sultanism has affinities with our four 'isms', including populism, a concept that to this day remains analytically 'elusive', according to Gellner and Ionescu.[3]

Populist leaders are primarily characterised by the way they claim to speak in the name of the people against the elite. Populists project themselves as new men against old political establishments, despite the fact that they often are seasoned public figures, but typically not centre stage. In 2014, Modi, in spite of being chief minister of Gujarat for thirteen years, presented himself as an alternative for and of the people because he came from a plebeian background, had never had any major role in Delhi, and could stand in stark contrast to the Gandhi family because of his modest origins.[4] While he had not very often referred to this pedigree in Gujarat, he successfully projected himself as an ordinary man from humble origins during the 2014 election campaign. Castigating Rahul Gandhi as *shahzada* (Mughal princeling), Modi highlighted his low social background (in belonging to an OBC caste) and that he had to work in his father's tea shop on the railway platform when he was a child.

The second major trait of a populist leader pertains to his communication techniques. He relates directly to 'his' people, short-circuiting his own political party to some extent, touring the country and using diverse media. In 2014, Modi saturated the public sphere, taking the country by storm, behaving like a muscular rock star on stage (endowed with a '56-inch chest'), and resorting to TV, social media, holograms, etc. His image was everywhere.[5] In terms of content, his campaign promised everything to everyone, but more importantly he repeated ad nauseam catchy and vague slogans that emerged as powerful, though 'empty signifiers', the trademark of populists according to Ernesto Laclau.[6] One of these formulas, '*Acche din anewalle hein!*' can be translated as a vaguely hopeful, 'Good days are coming!', a slogan that became representative of many forms of aspiration across the country.

Nationalism is the bedrock of most populists and Modi is no exception. A member of the RSS since his childhood, and later a full time *pracharak* (preacher or propagator), he has been deeply influenced by Hindutva ideology. Since its codification by Savarkar in 1923, this ideology looks at Hindus not primarily as practitioners of a diverse faith tradition, but as a people descending from ancestral sons of the soil, the 'Vedic fathers.' In the ideological repertoire of Hindutva, the people are not defined only as the victims of the elite but in cultural terms as the true autochthons and owners of the land. This politics gives rise to what Gino Germani named national populism,[7] which is a distinct repertoire of the right. The populism of the left (that Indira Gandhi epitomised in the 1970s for instance) does not rely on ethnic or religious exclusion, even as Gandhi's policies contributed to the systemic marginalisation of religious and ethnic groups, for example, Sikhs in Punjab, Muslims in Kashmir, and Mizos in the Northeast. These policies and practices of marginalisation, ironically, impacted the projection of the BJP into national politics.[8]

Modi is a product of the RSS and has clearly shown his deep commitment to the Hindutva doctrine, but he did not emphasise this aspect of his personal convictions during the 2014 campaign.[9] He hardly needed to. The organized mass violence of 2002 in Gujarat, which had resulted in a pogrom against Muslims when he was chief minister, had already earned him with the status of a '*Hindu Hriday Samrat*' (Emperor of the Hindu Heart).[10] His commitment to Hindu nationalism was also evident from the fact that the BJP nominated a very small number of candidates from the minorities (especially from the Muslim community) in order to signal that the party intended to represent a Hindu(ised) people. Following the pogrom in Gujarat in 2002, Hindu majoritarianism was further consolidated across various states; through orchestrated attacks on minorities in Orissa in 2007 and 2008 and in Muzaffarnagar in 2013.[11] The legitimacy of such Hindu domination harked back to their autochthony, while also augmenting their numbers. Hence, the third 'ism' on our list, majoritarianism, which is inherent to Modi's populism because the people he claims to represent are made up of Hindus only. This is evident from the fact that in 2014, the BJP nominated only a handful of Muslim candidates, and that, consequently, for the first time in India's history, the winning party in the general elections had no Muslim in its parliamentary group in the Lok Sabha. The main goal of the BJP is to 'defend' the interests of Hindus first and foremost, at the expense of the rights of the Othered/minorities in the country.

Majoritarian national-populists are authoritarian by definition, since they claim that they embody the people and as the people can only be one/singular, there is no room for pluralism.[12] This explains their tendency to disqualify their adversaries as 'anti-national' or even traitors, and even reject the multiparty system of democracy. The BJP has made it clear that no other party should compete with it, or is even needed, as indicative from its slogan of a *'Congress Mukt Bharat'* (a Congress-free India). This formula reflects its views of competitors not as adversaries, but as enemies. The BJP routinely (and falsely) claims that Congress relies on the vote of 'anti-national' elements (such as members of the minorities) and that the party is 'soft on Pakistan'—a country that figured prominently as an existential threat in every election campaign of Narendra Modi and the BJP, both at the national level and state level.

While Modi exemplifies the authoritarian, majoritarian, national-populists of today,[13] his regime is not merely sultanistic as those described by Linz and Stepan. India continues to organise reasonably free and fair elections; its government interferes with the appointment of judges but cannot prevent the most independently-minded lawyers from attempting to do their jobs; the government and the BJP influence and curtail the media but indirectly, not via official censorship. If anything, Modi is a 'neo-sultan' who observes some facets of democracy while pushing India further towards an illiberal ethnic democracy.

Illiberal democracy is one of the by-products of the proliferation of populist styles of politics. In fact, populism generally develops within democracies, because populist sentiment requires an open public space within which to articulate itself. But populism can also be a threat to the democratic regime itself. Democratic regimes are based on a demotic pillar that implies regularly held elections, but also on a liberal pillar, upheld by the rule of law and guaranteed by an independent judiciary—without which elections cannot remain free and fair. The populist sentiment hypertrophies the demotic aspect of democracy at the expense of the liberal aspect, that is undermined in the name of the people. The liberal dimension relies on institutions legally sanctioned by the constitution. But the populist politician claims that they represent something higher because they draw their legitimacy from the mandate they have received from the people. As a result, as Edward Shils showed as early as the 1950s, populism undermines liberal institutions because it 'identifies the will of the people with justice and morality'.[14] India saw this dynamic play itself out to disastrous effect in the 1970s culminating in the imposition of a national emergency rule by Indira Gandhi between 1975 and 1977. Gandhi claimed to act in the best interest of the Indian people and to protect the nation from 'anti-national elements' and social division within. The restoration of democracy in the late 1970s left the supreme court greatly strengthened but the centralisation of political authority, personalistic rule by charismatic leaders, and attempts at circumventing civil liberties and the rule of law in the name of popular majorities have remained central elements of the political culture in India ever since, at the central level as well as in many states in the union.

National-populism can turn 'conflicted democracies'[15] illiberal as well as ethnic. The notion of 'ethnic democracy' was theorised by Sammy Smooha as the product of ethnic nationalism, an identity that goes along with a rejection of the Othered, generally perceived as a threat to the survival and integrity of the ethnic nation.[16] Smooha considers that many countries have gone down the road of ethnic democracy but that the archetype of this political system remains Israel, a state that endeavours to combine an ethnic (Jewish) identity and a parliamentary system drawing its inspiration from Western Europe. The two sides of this coin are the Jewish nature of the nation-state and the restrictions imposed on the rights of minorities, primarily the 'Israeli Arabs,' and, further, the subjugation of Palestinians. For Smooha, one of the conditions for the emergence and persistence of an ethnic democracy is 'the existence of a threat (real or perceived) to the ethnic nation that requires mobilisation of the majority in order to preserve the ethnic nation'.[17] Conjuring a constant political, social and demographic threat from Muslims, whether in Pakistan, Kashmir or as India's Muslim minority, is the constitutive feature of the ideology of Hindutva. It is no coincidence that many members of RSS and BJP express strong admiration for the state of Israel and regard Zionism as something of a political ideal.[18]

The allure of the strong leader

The 'neo-sultanism' we have just described marks a rupture with the traditional political culture and practices of India. Except under Indira Gandhi—before, during and after the Emergency—the country has never experienced before such a personalisation and centralisation of power. Most of the time, since the 1950s, it has cultivated parliamentarism, observed a certain multiculturalism in the name of secularism, and generally respected federalism. While Modi's predecessor, Manmohan Singh, has been described by one of his former collaborators as an 'accidental Prime minister',[19] the question remains why India's electorate embraced Modi in 2014 and why he is not considered an aberration.

The BJP won partly because of the Congress' limitations in 2014. First, there was a fatigue with the same prime minister for ten years: anti-incumbency is very strong in such a context. Second, Singh's last term did not evince a clear sense of direction, as the rate of reforms slowed markedly compared to the first term. Third, the image of the ruling party was tainted by corruption cases—which gave rise to the Anna Hazare campaign in 2011,[20] a movement Modi exploited fully. Fourth, Rahul Gandhi lacked political experience since he had never been part of any government and was not even president of his party. Clearly, the BJP won, to some extent, by default in 2014 and its victory was not due to a wave but to the concentration of its 31 per cent of valid votes in northern and western India.

However, the BJP benefitted from important supports too. First, the RSS and its front organisations mobilised their activists in favour of the party even more intensely than before.[21] This was largely because the new RSS chief, Mohan Bhagwat, did not want to see the BJP losing for the third time in a row. Second, the business milieu shifted from Congress to the BJP to a large extent, primarily because of some of Manmohan Singh's policies, including those perceived as protecting the peasantry at the expense of industry.[22] This shift explains the huge monetary resources the BJP could command during the 2014 election campaign—and its correlative ability to saturate the public sphere with its message, greatly aided by open support from most of the major privately-owned media houses in the country. Third, saffron-clad religious figures also contributed to the BJP's victory. In addition to the old guard, represented by Sakshi Maharaj, a controversial[23] and provocative[24] *sadhu* (Hindu ascetic) who was already elected as a member of parliament in 1991, newcomers contributed to make this support base more diverse. Baba Ramdev and Yogi Adityanath are two cases in point. The former is not only popular because of his yoga lessons on TV, but also because he is a very successful businessman.[25] The later is not only the head of the monastery cum temple of the Nath in Gorakhpur, but also the founder of an actual militia.[26]

Modi succeeded not only because of these powerful supporters; his voters also chose the BJP for 'positive' reasons. First, Modi appeared as a 'development man', *vikas purush*, because of the image of continuous economic growth in Gujarat under Modi's tenure. Second, he had made promises on the economic front that met the aspirations of many Indians who were badly affected by the slowdown in 2013–14. Of these, the promise of jobs in a burgeoning private sector for millions of young people across India was the most potent and effective. Third, and perhaps more imperceptibly, Modi's political style and message—forcefully masculinist/majoritarian and strongly anti-minority—was in tune with the general atmosphere of increasing polarisation, and the anti-minority, heteronormative and gendered politics that Hindu nationalists had generated over several decades in the context of resurgent islamism (see jihadist attacks in 2001–2008).

However, this normalised majoritarianism and hostility to minorities was the result of more than one man's authority and growing ethno-religious exclusivism. There has always been a substantial support for authoritarian rule in India, including the period of emergency rule, and the hostility towards democracy has been growing in the Indian public for at least twenty years.

In 2017, the Centre for the Study of Developing Societies (CSDS) report on 'The State of Democracy in South Asia' showed that the percentage of the interviewees who supported democracy has dropped from 70 per cent to 63 per cent between 2005 and 2017. The 2017 Pew report reconfirmed the trend: 55 per cent of the respondents backed 'a governing system in which a strong leader can make decisions without interference from parliament or the courts', while 53 per cent supported military rule. Commenting upon this result, the Pew team added: 'Support for autocratic rule is higher in India than in any other nation surveyed', 38 per cent in total, and India is 'one of only four nations where half or more of the public supports governing by the military'. An even larger proportion—two thirds—say 'a good way to govern the country would be experts, not elected officials, making decisions according to what they think is best for the nation'. Interestingly, the BJP supporters and the urban dwellers are over represented in the three groups—of those who support personal rule, military governance and a technocratic regime.[27]

The demand for a strong leader is related to an acute feeling of vulnerability. According to the Pew survey, while 'Crime takes the top spot on the list, with 84 per cent of Indians seeing it as a *very* big problem', 'terrorism' comes immediately next for 76 per cent of the interviewees (before corruption and unemployment).[28] This is well in tune with the idea that ISIS appeared as the main threat to India according to 66 per cent of the interviewees, ahead of every other threat.[29] Correlatively, 64 per cent of the interviewees have a 'very unfavourable' view of Pakistan (a percentage that was rising since 2014). The need for a strong state further arises from the drive to stifle unresolved issues and conflicts, as evident from the fact that a '63 per cent majority believes the government should be using more military force' in Kashmir.[30] This is in alignment with the popularisation of national metanarratives, such as the reassertion of Kashmir as integral to India or the movement to revoke Article 35A of the Constitution of India.[31]

If one goes by surveys, Kashmiris are not the only Muslims viewed with suspicion. Tensions between a putative Hindu majority and minorities, premised on evermore asymmetric relations of power, have a long history and are on the rise. Surveys show that Hindus are less and less prepared to have Muslim neighbours.[32] While this estrangement reinforces the ghettoisation of the Muslims and mutual ignorance that prepared the ground for the Modi vote of 2014, it is also the consequence of the Hindu nationalist propaganda and the polarisation effect of religion-based, communal, gendered, and racialised violence. Hindu–Muslim clashes tend to take place below the radar since the 2002 Gujarat pogrom, but they have continued to spread. In Uttar Pradesh, Sudha Pai and Sajjan Kumar have shown that since the defeat of the BJP in 2004, the Sangh Parivar group of Hindu nationalist organisations have opted for low intensity riots which have almost systematically resulted from the exploitation of minor issues, often relating to economic and cultural matters.[33]

Another major reason why Modi received the support of new voters in 2014 has to do with class. In many countries where new populist leaders have taken over, they have been supported by middle class conservative voters who resented the growing assertiveness of plebeians (including ethnic minorities) and pro-poor schemes. Barack H. Obama's policies in favour of underrepresented minorities and the famous Affordable Care Act (routinely called 'Obamacare' by its detractors) are a case in point. In India, the UPA government also provoked a sense of elite revenge because of the extension of positive discrimination schemes (27 per cent of the university seats have been reserved for the OBCs, for instance) and because of pro-poor policies like the Mahatma Gandhi National Rural Employment Guarantee Act (MGNREGA). These policies have fostered anger among the upper and middle castes who resented the transformation of a social order they had tacitly benefitted from for decades if not centuries.[34] For those who longed for some elite revenge and the restoration of some social conservative status quo, national populism was a very useful instrument: it conveyed the idea that the relevant unit of society was neither caste nor class, but the ethnic nation, a nation made of the ethnic majority which could rally around a common cultural identity against a new scapegoat, the internal enemies that are the minorities. In India, Narendra Modi could mobilise not only the middle class, but also what he called the 'neo' middle class, a social category that had emerged from two decades of growth. These were mostly OBCs, like himself, who had migrated from the countryside and hoped to get a good job in the city—not a job in the public sector where the reservations had reached the saturation point, but in the industry that Modi was supposed to promote like he had allegedly done in Gujarat.

Table 1: The 2009 and 2014 Lok Sabha Elections: class-wise support for BJP and Congress—all-India (all figures are in percentages)

Class	INC		BJP	
	2014	2009	2014	2009
Poor	20	27	24.0 (+8)	16
Lower	19	29	31.0 (+12)	19
Middle	20	29	32.3 (+10)	22
Upper	17	29	38.0 (+13)	25

Source: Lokniti-CSDS, *National Election Survey (NES)*, 2014. Adapted from C. Jaffrelot, 'The Class Element in the 2014 Indian Election and the BJP's Success with Special Reference to the Hindi Belt', in 'Understanding India's 2014 Elections' *Studies in Indian Politics*, 3, 1 (June 2015), pp. 19–38.

To sum up: if the standard explanation for Modi's success in 2014 is 'development', the subtext is Hindu nationalism. This explanation too needs to be qualified because while this ideology is particularly popular among certain social categories, its unevenness suggests a sub-subtext in terms of class. Not only the middle class and the neo-middle class appreciated Modi's national populism, but also his authoritarian leanings. In 2008, the CSDS survey on the 'State of Democracy in South Asia' showed that in India 51 per cent of the respondents from the 'elite' 'strongly agreed' and 29 per cent 'agreed' with the proposition: 'All major decisions about the country should be taken by experts rather than politicians'.[35] The interviewees from the 'mass' were 29 per cent to 'strongly agree' and 22 per cent to 'agree'. The 'illiberalism' of the Indian middle class,[36] a group over-represented among the supporters of Narendra Modi, is part of what Suhas Palshikar calls the middle class's 'search for sanitised politics' in which the state would 'reduce the chaos and noise'.[37]

With the 2014 elections, the needle moved decisively towards a consolidation of a Hindu nationalist-majoritarian polity. The centre of gravity transitioned from traditionalists within the BJP and the RSS to a new generation of activists invested in a more agile and flexible notion of the Hindu nation. In practice, this energised a transformation of the erstwhile fixation on cultural purity to put in place a social hegemony that meets the complex realities and demands of India's ascendance in a politically fraught South Asia within a rising Asia.

Now written upon a much larger national canvas, distinct divisions of labour organise the relationships between the BJP, Modi, and the Sangh Parivar. The most remarkable shift is perhaps that the Modi government has reframed the force of modernity in a new and compelling way. The promises of modernity, national strength and development were for decades the predominant rallying points in national politics for the left and Congress, with inclusiveness, social justice and a measure of austerity as secondary components. For Modi, the focus is on operationalising mega-development in India via globalisation to position the country as an emergent, modern world power and, simultaneously, a well-defined Hindu state. This change signals major shifts in governance, ideology, identity and social relations between the local and the national.

The citizen patriot and the security state

The sense of a Hindu majority being the dominant force at the heart of the Indian nation has been evolving throughout the twentieth century and has also found support among Congress leaders even as they refrained from speaking of it openly. The change brought about by the BJP, through repeated, remodelled experimentations in electoral politics, is an unfettered social articulation and acceptability of majoritarianism, now at the highest level of the state. The Modi campaign combined this broad, tacit political common sense of a majoritarian nation with the energetic, widespread power and appeal of imminent change and success, a sentiment desired by many but rarely experienced. A Modi rally became a place to experience this feeling of strength, rage and possible dominance, not unlike the emotions of a resurrected American greatness conjured up at Trump rallies. Among the active supporters attending Modi's meetings and taking part in the most militant sections of the Sangh Parivar, including the Bajrang Dal, were lumpenised 'angry young men'.[38] Some of them are resentful, jobless, upper caste members who epitomise a new political culture based on the quest for self esteem.[39] Their aesthetic is well exemplified by the figure of the 'angry Hanuman',[40] who has replaced the 'angry Ram' of the 1990s.[41]

The BJP seeks to amalgamate national pride and long-held aspirations of the global recognition of India as a world power. Bolstered by innumerable allies among people of the Indian Diaspora across the world, the BJP seeks to project India's heritage, power and potential in the world. A critique of the BJP is often viewed as a critique of India with the potential to negatively impact the gross domestic product. The strength of the BJP, here, rests in its capacity to allow ultra-nationalists into the mainstream and frontline positions in national and state government while permitting non-state actors to implement militant cultural policing and other forms of vigilantism.

The BJP's plan of action is focused on winning elections and using the existing provisions of law and administrative decrees to impose a more restrictive but not fully authoritarian regime. The exception to this norm lies in unleashing, in a more aggressive form, the full force of India's illiberal security state in the tribal belts, in the Northeast and in Kashmir. We note that the process of securitisation of state in India also delimits the state's constantly shifting relations to its internal and external enemies,[42] and 'builds and fortifies the national collective and protects state sovereignty'.[43] The BJP's stratagem deploys the existing security state more aggressively to weed out dissenting bureaucrats, put pressure on the judiciary and bureaucracy, restrict progressive civil and political society,[44] and intellectual life, and enforce rules and economic regulations that benefit large corporations who support the Modi program.[45] Many of the suppressive clampdowns on NGOs, such as on foreign funding, on access to sensitive areas, or on conversions from Hinduism, often required nothing more than a stricter implementation of pre-existing rules, many of which were crafted during Indira Gandhi's most repressive years.

Modi's leadership of the BJP has rendered porous the associations between government and ultra-nationalist groups. In India today, a plethora of organisations and outfits disburse violence, intimidation and the enforcement of morality and majoritarian 'standards'. These outfits operate quite freely under the gaze of the police, possibly colluding with the BJP and institutions of law enforcement, or, at a minimum, banking on the inability and the hesitation of the state authorities to restrain and constrict them. This project of weaponising and militarising society through organisation, vigilance and a capacity for violence has been an objective of the Sangh Parivar through the many decades during which Hindu nationalists were distant from elected office.[46] This form of vigilante violence, or the threat of it, is executed through the capillaries of the RSS-led Sangh Parivar's vast network, and generally reinforce already existing caste, gender, class, and communal-racial attitudes prevalent among upper caste Hindus and aspirational lower caste groups. The result is a broad nationalist and communal majoritarianism that targets liberal elites, castigated as excessively emancipated, immoral, westernised and pro-minority, and of course the country's minority communities. Persistently gender/hetero-normative and deeply xenophobic, these inequitable relations between majority and minority/Othered can no longer be viewed as an aberration or a fringe phenomenon.[47] They now occupy centre stage in government and within public discourse, impacting policy, law, and the everyday functioning of marginalised lives as well as institutions such as universities and the media. The minority/Othered is now officially reconfigured as an obstacle to development, a drain on resources, an alien and socially divisive element that weakens cultural cohesion, a primitive, non-modern and unassimilable remnant of the past.

Unparalleled turn: Interpreting present effects and future impact

The complexity of the emerging conditions named above calls for scholarly recognition and explication. Through a wide-angle and in-depth examination of (post)colonial India's present authoritarian turn, *Majoritarian State* delimits the ascendance of Hindu nationalist dominance in India via the institutions of state and within civil and political society. The volume presents an interdisciplinary collection of articles spanning the humanities, social sciences, and law, bringing together diverse scholars of/on India to interpret the unparalleled turn, trace the continuities and discontinuities, and deliberate on its present effects and future impact. The contributors inquire into the ways in which the systemic arousing of public fear targets dissenting individuals, groups, and institutions, and if and how this majoritarian ethos is being contested from the streets to the courts. Organised under different thematics, the essays delve into the politics, representations, and aspirations, the aspects and events, and the traumas and dislocations of the seemingly continuous yet structurally reconstituted experiment to establish a majoritarian state in India.

Elaborating on the theme 'Majoritarianism as Democracy', Thomas Blom Hansen discusses how the possibilities for intellectual freedom and civil liberties have diminished under BJP rule, a reality produced through the combination of vigilante violence by groups aligned with Hindu nationalism and the inequitable application of existing laws, policies and policing that target non-elites and minority peoples. Christophe Jaffrelot uses the analytical frame of 'ethnic democracy' to describe India's tiered society, which is structured by vigilantism and a decrease of minorities in government fuelled by Hindu majoritarian ideologies based on cultural characteristics that imply a sense of superiority and a rejection of minorities. Ian M. Cook examines the context and function of ongoing moral and cultural policing of young people and minorities in Mangaluru by vigilante Hindu groups with government complicity, arguing that the violence is fuelled by more than electoral politics and performs as an intervention against the liberalism within neoliberalism toward shaping behaviour in contemporary India. Parvis Ghassem-Fachandi discusses the social mechanism of delegation in connection to the 2002 anti-Muslim pogrom in Gujarat. In this case, a group of Hindus transmits power to a chosen delegate, Narendra Modi, to act on their behalf and to make meaning of the pogrom and the future of Hindu majoritarian politics.

Under 'Debates on Hegemony', Suhas Palshikar focuses on the emergence of the new party system in India and its consequences, arguing that in addition to the electoral rise of the BJP, political developments also indicate the gradual shaping of a new hegemony, and the attendant dominance of new ideas and sensibilities, in India. In contrast, James Manor analyses the limitations of the key elements of Modi's strategy in his drive for supremacy, including dramatic promises and the efforts to fulfil them, theatrics and projection of himself as a compelling personality, an anti-corruption drive, and the polarisation between the Hindu majority and religious minorities, especially Muslims.

The next thematic focuses on 'The Sangh Parivar: A New "Deep State"?' Here, Pralay Kanungo discusses the leadership dynamics between the Sangh Parivar and Narendra Modi, demonstrating how the RSS leadership has mentored India's governance, while dividing the areas of influence with Modi: Modi rules the economy, commerce, foreign affairs and security, while the

RSS determines the social, cultural and educational agenda of the nation. Tanika Sarkar analyses what Hindu nationalist groups want to project as history in general, and Indian history in particular, toward unmasking nationalist rhetoric and pedagogy and majoritarian organisational networks and institutions via which 'history' circulates at multiple social levels and is disseminated in multiple ways, including through ideological texts and textbooks.

In 'Economic Policies and "Modinomics"', Pranab Bardhan provides an evaluation of the policies and programmes of the current BJP regime, categorising them as hoaxes, public relations coups, continuities with UPA policies, newer policies in the right direction, and regressive policies. A.K. Bhattacharya and Paranjoy Guha Thakurta detail how the current government, though it claims that the incidence of corruption has decreased since the end of UPA rule, continues to face critics that argue that opaque electoral financing and crony capitalism remains strong in India under the Modi government.

In the section on 'The Othered 40 per cent: The Hindu Nation and its Minorites', Sukhadeo Thorat discusses the BJP's attempts to appropriate the Dalit leader, B.R. Ambedkar, and assesses the BJP's Dalit-related policies and their outcomes by using information that has been made available by the government itself. Abdul R. JanMohamed approaches the 2016 suicide of Dalit student and activist Rohith Vemula in India through a viewpoint informed by the phenomenology of the 'touch', as elaborated by Edmund Husserl, Jacques Derrida, and by JanMohamed's own work on the political economy of death in the formation of slavery. Nandini Sundar examines the conditions and discursive strategies utilised by the BJP to contribute to building an extensive Adivasi (tribal) voter base that continues to support the BJP despite its alignment with industrialists who displace rural and tribal communities, and whose ruling ideology marginalises and devalues Adivasis. Mridu Rai discusses the location of Kashmiri Muslims in India after the election of the BJP in 2014, identifying how Kashmiri Muslims are made to serve as contrapuntal symbols for constructing a mythical Hindu nation, dissipating the possibility of resolving the Kashmir question under the Modi-led BJP. Arkotong Longkumer provides an ethnographic and media-based examination of the ways in which the BJP has been able to negotiate its status with regard to national-regional tensions, through the use of a dynamically structured political machine and the adoption of an agenda that sweeps across religious, social and cultural boundaries.

In 'Diplomacy and Global Aspiration', C. Raja Mohan focuses on the broad movement of Indian diplomacy under Modi's rule and the kind of challenges it has had to confront, reviewing Modi's inheritance and principal contributions and setbacks in guiding India's international engagement. Jyoti Puri examines Hindu nationalism's traffic in a popular strand of yoga, one aimed at enhancing health and wellbeing, which has become popular in India and internationally, and while many 'yogas' coexist, the article enquires into the Hindu Right's mobilisation of this iteration of yoga in representing India as Hindu.

In 'What Rule of Law?', Flavia Agnes scrutinises the triple *talaq* issue in the context of an aggressive Hindu nationalism, to provide the intersectional and historical context for the overemphasis on triple *talaq* and the lack of reporting on the progress in Muslim women's rights, and to challenge popular misconceptions surrounding Muslim personal law. Ratna Kapur illustrates how the Indian judiciary, through mobilising a politics of 'belief', has endorsed the identity of the Indian state as a Hindu nation through the discourse of rights and has underscored such practice through the constructed opposition between Islam and gender equality in the advocacy of the Hindu Right.

In the closing section, 'Gender and Nation', Paola Bacchetta describes Hindu nationalist examples of national and transnational strategies of social inclusion and exclusion that mobilise gender and sexuality, including strategies that valorise some queer categories and de-valorise others while targeting the Hindu nation's Others (such as Muslims) through complex social operations that draw upon, in part, colonial queerphobic legacies. Angana P. Chatterji excavates the contemporaneous practices of majoritarianism in Uttar Pradesh that preceded and followed the 2014 elections led by the parliamentary BJP and the grassroots Sangh Parivar and the emergent relations between Hindu cultural dominance and nationalist Hinduism, inducing and deepening cultural anxiety, xenophobia, misogyny, hate and violence, and examines their imprint on minority/Othered subjects.

PART I

MAJORITARIANISM AS DEMOCRACY

1

DEMOCRACY AGAINST THE LAW

REFLECTIONS ON INDIA'S ILLIBERAL DEMOCRACY

Thomas Blom Hansen

The shrinking space for intellectual freedom and the threat to civil liberties have been key concerns since the BJP won an absolute majority in Lok Sabha in 2014. However, since coming to power, the BJP has not passed any significant new legislation that curtails liberal freedoms. The actions by the Modi government have relied on applying the rather voluminous body of existing legislation, and police protocols, that can limit free speech, assembly, movement and funding of those deemed to be 'anti-national' or otherwise a threat to public order and safety. Some of this legislation has colonial roots but most of it came into being as elements of the extensive security state that successive Congress regimes have built since the 1960s in the name of protecting national unity and sovereignty.

The other threat to civil liberties has emerged from cultural and social vigilantism by outfits that are ideologically aligned with the BJP and the RSS. The frequency and gravity of such extra-legal action, backed up by mob violence, has increased significantly in the last few years. Violence is indeed a foundational element of Hindutva—as ideology and as political action. But the routinisation of violence in Indian public life is not only the making of the BJP and its allies. Hindu nationalists have amplified and systematised a longer-standing trend towards accepting public anger, and collective violence, as legitimate means of political expression and legitimate means of exercising political power.

Here, I want to probe into some of the conditions of possibility that made possible the current political climate in India. I propose that political forces that emerged in the 1980s and 1990s, and were celebrated as deepening Indian democracy—such as the regional movements, lower caste mobilisation and also Hindu nationalism—also reflected an entrenched 'non-liberal' underside of Indian politics. These forces all deployed languages of deprivations and anger, and a politics of passion claiming to represent hitherto voiceless majorities. Their languages of strength and popular sovereignty were rarely based on a commitment to liberal values of the constitution but, rather, a realist belief in political power, strong partisanship and violence as a legitimate expression of anger and political will.

In what follows I will try to elucidate these points from two angles. First, I will briefly discuss the obvious discrepancy between the liberal language of rights in the constitution and the largely illiberal and often violent ways in which the 'force of law' is visited upon non-elite Indians by the country's police powers. Secondly, I argue that the thriving vernacular publics across India enabled an intensified sense of intimacy and also injury that, in turn, facilitated the rise of a popular politics of passion and action that has made displays of public anger, and public violence, into some of the most effective means of political expression in the country. These sentiments and techniques of what I call 'the law of force' have been honed and perfected by the Hindu nationalist movement over the past decades.

Taken together, these two developments indicate that India's democracy indeed is deepening but also turning less liberal, more antagonistic and more violent.

Liberal norms—for whom?

On the face of it, India is a liberal democracy with incredibly dynamic electoral politics at all levels, a judiciary that still retains a measure of independence, and a constitution that guarantees fundamental rights and liberties as well as the rule of law. It is also a fact that the Indian constitution is a capacious and farsighted document that has been able to creatively accommodate group rights[1] and has been appropriated by many groups in Indian society in their quest for inclusion and fuller citisenship,[2] giving the constitution a social and political life of its own.[3]

But it is equally true that the liberal norms that pervade this seventy-year-old document have neither penetrated everyday political life, nor substantively changed the social and cultural norms among the vast majority of Indians. It is by no means self-evident that the Indian constitution, as it stands, would find favour in the Lok Sabha and Rajya Sabha in 2018. There are deep reservations about several elements of the constitution among many in the BJP and the RSS as evidenced by calls from senior BJP ministers for removing the term 'secular' from the constitution.[4]

Over many decades, neither Congress nor the mainstream Left parties deployed the promise of liberties and the rule of law as major campaign planks. Many on the Left were skeptical of the value of the 'negative rights' guaranteeing individual and collective freedoms enshrined in the constitution. These negative rights were seen as emblems of a bourgeois ideology of liberal freedoms. Instead, both the Congress Party and the parliamentary Left promoted 'positive rights'—to development, education, and social upliftment.[5] Centrist and left of center forces in India built themselves as defenders of India's sovereignty against the ubiquitous 'foreign hand', as guarantors of pluralism, social reform, modernity and development. In everyday political discourse, it was progressivism (*pragativad*), emphasising equality, reform and modernity that became the unifying rallying point, rather than the more contrived and 'rightist' notion of liberalism (*udaravad*), understood as economic freedom and individual rights. The only exception to this general tendency was the activism in defense of civil rights during and after Indira Gandhi's imposition of Emergency Rule that led to the imprisonment of thousands of opposition leaders and activists in 1975–76.[6]

Apart from a very vocal activist community, including feminists and LGBTQ groups, the only larger communities in India that today consistently appeal to the constitution and consistently advocate the rule of law and protection of human rights are the country's recognisable minorities—Dalits, tribals, Muslims, and several groups coming out of Northeastern India. Those groups appear akin to an Indian version of what Habermas and other theorists of democracy call 'constitutional patriotism'.[7] But even that is a problematic label, considering that each of these groupings emphasise and defend only particular aspects of the constitution's provisions—such as secularism, freedom of religion, reservations, etc. Few of these socio-political formations or communities can be said to embrace the liberal and democratic spirit of the constitution in their own community practices. For whatever it is worth, a recent Pew Research poll asked people across the world about their faith in democracy and related questions. The responses from India—mainly urban and educated as is the norm for Pew polls—make for interesting if confusing reading: 75 per cent of those asked in India supported representative government (the lowest in all of the Asian countries polled); 65 per cent supported direct rule by experts (one of the highest in all the countries polled); and more Indians supported auto-cratic rule by a 'strong leader' (55 per cent) than in any other country polled, surpassing Russia by 7 points, and Turkey by 15 points. (55 per cent of Americans thought such arrangement to be 'very bad'.) Curiously, as many of 53 per cent of Indians also thought military rule to be a good idea.[8]

So how does one explain what can only be called a general diffidence about the constitution and its basic values in political discourse in India? How does one explain that a deepening democracy that has allowed previously excluded and denigrated groups a role in the electoral process, has been accompanied by a concomitant weakening of liberal norms, such as respect for rights, equal-ity, the rule of law, and cultural difference? One key element, I will argue, lies in the disjuncture, if not discrepancy, between the promise of the constitution and the functioning of India's administrative apparatus, especially its law enforcement agencies.

It would be very difficult to argue that the various branches of the Indian government function in a way that is consistent with principles of a liberal and accountable government. A very substantial part of basic laws in India are still derived from colonial legislation and administrative principles: notably the Indian Penal Code (which I shall return to), a large part of the administrative law that governs the inner workings of the Indian state—such as transfer and promotion policies, the revenue system, the police services and much more. Colonial legislation had multiple rationales: securing the colonial state, main-taining an often tenuous public order, creating and protecting private property and reforming and codifying social practices, to mention the most prominent. Some of those legal forms had liberal elements and intentions just as promi-nent public figures in nineteenth- and early twentieth-century India espoused what could be called a liberal agenda.[9] Decades of scholarly work has docu-mented the how the liberal political orders in the Western hemisphere were enabled by a simultaneous despotic and authoritarian rule in the colonies.[10] Similarly, colonial India was governed through several parallel regimes and configurations of sovereignty. The force of colonial law was always applied in a deeply unequal manner that exposed the poor, lower caste majority of the population to the most despotic and harsh dimensions of governance and punishment.[11] Gradual incorporation of elite segments into representative institutions from the early twentieth century went hand in hand with violent police practices in popular neighborhoods,[12] with multiple formulas of indirect rule in the princely states,[13] and paternalistic inclusion and violent suppression of tribal groups in special zones.[14]

The formal construction of a unitary Indian nation state from 1950s onwards changed only little of this substantively. In practice, the Indian state continued to work through several, parallel regulatory regimes, calibrated according to class, caste and region. It also retained and expanded a very extensive regime of secrecy and classification of files and archives. By the 1970s, the Congress had all but abandoned its commitment to liberal principles in favour of a populist reform agenda that reconfigured the political landscape in India. Its main elements were rhetorical embrace of vague socialist Third World-ism, a deep commitment to state sovereignty coupled with several redistributive pro-poor policies, but also harassment of opponents, violent suppression of insurgencies and the systematic building of a large security state, with more than a dozen different paramilitary services ranging from central forces such as Central Industrial Security Force, Border Security Forces to the Armed Provincial Constabulary and many armed police forces in each state in India.[15] This emergent security state waged violent wars and put large populations under permanent emergency laws such as the Armed Forces Special Powers Act (AFSPA) that has granted extensive powers and immunity to the armed forces in so-called 'Disturbed Areas' in the North East since 1958 and Jammu and Kashmir since 1990.[16] The Unlawful Activities Prevention Act (UAPA) was passed in 1967 and was used to violently suppress Naxalite activity in West Bengal in 1971. After it was amended in 2011, UAPA is applied in the so-called 'red corridor' in central India, as well to deal with less specified 'terrorist activity'.[17] The long and violent suppression of Khalistani militants in Punjab was enabled by the application of Terrorist and Disruptive Activities (Prevention) Act (TADA), probably the most stringent and sweeping security measure ever passed in India.[18] The 'cleaning up' of the Punjab in the 1990s was overseen by K.P.S. Gill, a senior officer who was subsequently lionised by the Indian mainstream media.

Most political forces in the country, including the mainstream left, have tacitly supported this policy of large-scale, perpetual human rights violation in the name of national sovereignty and fending off 'anti-national' forces within the country.[19] Critiques of such policies and violations by international human rights organisations or international multilateral agencies have for decades been dismissed by the Government of India as undue interference in the domestic affairs of a sovereign nation.

At a more everyday level, the Indian police and security forces have over decades developed an infamous record of systematic brutality, disappearances, systemic corruption and a chronic lack of investigative capacity[20] that is strangely at odds with the celebrations of India as a democracy. This everyday violence is almost exclusively visited upon poor and vulnerable populations, the social and religious minorities in particular. In these communities, the police force is seen as a major danger and a source of routine harassment, extortion and unpredictable violence. It remains one of the major paradoxes of Indian political life that despite a strong presence of left and progressive political formations and lower-caste movements over many decades, no major political formations have ever found it important to promote police reform, or effectively address the daily human rights violations by the Indian police force that disproportionately affect poor and lower-caste populations across the country. The public debate about the endangered independence of the judiciary rarely includes the state of the lower courts where most cases are settled by touts and political operators outside the courthouses, and where the quality of public prosecution is so low and biased that India has one of the lowest conviction rates in the world.[21]

The educated middle classes rarely face the force of law in India—except if they belong to minority communities. For most members of the middle class, the police remain abstract and distant, or appear in the form of traffic officers that can be easily bribed, or as ordinary constables that most members of the middle class treat assertively, or condescendingly, as their social inferiors. Any encounter with the police will be sought to be remedied by phone calls to relatives or friends in the bureaucracy or the police force—fellow members of the middle class—and such measures often prove rather effective. The general incompetence of the police force is widely acknowledged but normally blamed on the poorly educated and underpaid constables. Upper level officers, drawn from the middle class itself, are often lionised and admired for their capacity to navigate the gritty world of crime and corruption, as if those with education and social status can stand above a murky reality. What accounts for such systematic blindness to how the force of law is actually administered in India?

Let me provide some vignettes from marginal communities in India that point to a possible answer: 'the force of law' has been subverted by the 'law of force', that is, the extremely widespread belief across caste and class in India that the application of the law, and by extension the police force itself, is nothing but an instrument of larger configurations of social and political power that manipulate law and policing at their will.

The force of law in practice—three ethnographic vignettes

1.

On a sweltering monsoon evening in July 2011, an elderly man called the local police station in central Mumbai to report what seemed to be a burglary in progress. He and his wife heard men trying to break through their bedroom window. Two constables arrived ten minutes later to find the couple in their bedroom staring at an open window. The men had fled and nothing was stolen and the couple could only give a vague description of the suspects—one had a full beard, the other one a mustache. Now that an FIR existed, the sub-inspector thought it prudent to have the constables pursue the suspects in the nearby slum area. Twenty minutes later they had apprehended three boys, two with full beards and a thin young boy with a mustache. After interrogating them roughly for some hours, the constables took photos of the swollen and bruised faces of the suspects and returned to the elderly couple the next morning to ask if these boys were the intruders. The elderly people were not sure about the identity of the suspects but thanked the sub-inspector for his diligent efforts. Later in the day the boys were released and no charges were laid.

This story was related to me by the elderly couple who were relatives of a friend. The uncle and aunty were happy with the outcome of and praised the police. But what if these were not the guilty ones, I asked. Uncle was unconcerned with this finer point: 'Well, it is good that the police teach these people a lesson—surely these boys will think twice about breaking the law, no?'

Afterwards my friend shook his head in despair. 'This is what passes as policing, and justice in this country', he mumbled. For years he had been helping young people from this slum prepare for exams and tests and get jobs. He knew one of the boys who lost his job and had walked with a slight limp for months after. My friend continued, 'We talk to these boys about their rights (*haq*), justice (*insaf, nyaya*) and all that, then this happens. How will they ever believe me?'

My friend was right. Trust in the police or in due process was not easy to find in Muslim-majority areas that often have a higher density of police *chowkis* and visible policing than Hindu areas. Police arrest mainly young men, often on flimsy tips or pretexts, and the young men are normally subjected to harsh and violent interrogation before they are released, normally well before the limit of twenty-four hours. Most of this violence is never reported, never shows up in any statistics, as the police refuse to accept complaints or FIRs about violence committed by police officers. It is a regime of low-intensity terror. As a former corporator from a Muslim-majority area with older slums told me:

> The police call this a 'notorious area'. Whenever anything happens, they come rushing in and arrest people, mostly charge-sheeters and notorious characters but also innocent boys. ... Crying mothers would come to my office. I had to go to the police station at least three times a week to plea with them, to ask them to let these boys go.

During the years of multiple bomb blasts in Mumbai between 2002 and 2008, it became standard procedure in the wake of bomb blasts or incidents somewhere in the city that platoons of constables, often fired up by anger and shouting anti-Muslim invective, would rush through such 'notorious' Muslim neighborhoods, forcing every Muslim male they could find to sit in long rows in the streets. I personally witnessed this on one occasion in the busy Maulana Azad Road in central Bombay. Hundreds of men were made to sit for hours in the sun, hands on heads, while being forced with batons or rifle butts to give up the names and addresses of themselves and their family members. No arrest was made, and there were no particular charges, not even specified targets. Some handful of men were taken away in police vans. After three hours the police just left, while the Muslim men would get on their feet, gingerly, quickly walking off, wary of another potential action by the police. The day after, I met an inspector I had befriended in the local police station. When I asked him why the police had rounded up these men, he shrugged and said:

> Well, it is a security precaution. We are trying to find people who know something. These people have so many secrets, we know that. ... When you let them sit like that for some hours, people crack, you see. Those who hide something tend to sweat and be nervous, or they ask to talk to us. We get a lot of information this way.

2.

In the summer of 2017 the debate about the public use of *Vande Mataram*, the Indian national anthem, reached Aurangabad city politics. A young

Muslim corporator elected for AIMIM refused to stand as members of the General Body in the Municipal Corporation sang *Vande Mataram*. He was physically attacked by Shiv Sena members and in the ensuing scuffle furniture and equipment was damaged. The AIMIM corporator was suspended for disrespect for the elected body and then arrested and charged with disturbing public order and destroying public property. Hundreds of his avid followers took to the streets near the Municipal Corporation building and the police came out in strength to control the situation. The protests gathered force as the corporator was denied bail, and the day after the local court relented and granted bail. In the months after the event, the case has moved to the higher court which was not keen to deal with the matter. The corporator told me: 'If they grant me bail they admit it is not a serious case; if they arrest me again or prosecute me, all the MIM supporters in this city will come out on the streets. ... The police don't want this situation so the case will be pending for a long time.' In our many conversations, the young corporator would often cite the exact number of votes he received in his ward as a proof of his standing and legitimacy. 'The majority of the people are with me, they support me so what right do they have to charge me with any crimes? I am just speaking for what my people feel.'

One of his followers described this as a political battle where the Indian Penal Code was nothing but an instrument used to violate a more basic right: 'They [Shiv Sena and the police] used some law to charge him but nowhere in the Constitution does it say that you must stand and sing *Vande Mataram*. This is his right (*haq*). ... Muslims know that in Arabic *haq* actually means truth.' At the same time, the Indian Penal Code also provided a measure against which the success of a political agitation could be measured when another young supporter asserted 'We were so many that they had to put a 141 [IPC 141—unlawful assembly] on us!' This was said with some measure of trepidation, as all the activists were aware of the Aurangabad police's well-known propensity to use deadly force against assemblies of Muslims.

A few months later the higher court took on the case. I asked the corporator if he was worried about the outcome: 'Not at all,' he said in his signature, *filmi* bravado style:

> How can I lose this case? We have learned one thing from Shiv Sena, you see. If you respect the people's feelings and use their strength, you can never lose. If the court goes against me, it goes against all Muslims and we have already shown our 'nuisance value' [in English] here in the city. This is what Thackeray always said, 'nuisance value'.... So even if they win in court, they will lose.

3.

Some weeks later, I was invited for a rally called by Muslim organisations to commemorate the twenty-fifth anniversary of the demolition of the Babri Masjid on 6 December 1992. The organisers had announced that they would congregate on the public space in front of the Divisional Commissioner's office but the police forced the meeting onto the side of a busy street making it impossible for the crowd to stand in front of the stage. Heavily armed police in full riot gear almost outnumbered the crowd at the rally. Speeches and slogans proceeded, defiantly, against these heavy odds.

The contrast with the happenings on 19 February, *Shivaji Jayanti*—the official holiday where the birth of Shivaji, the seventeenth-century founder of the Maratha Empire, is celebrated—could not be greater. On that day, bands of boys were roaming the city on their two-wheelers with saffron flags fluttering from the vehicles along with loud music, cheering. The boys seemed to take particular pleasure roaming through Muslim neighborhoods, always in large groups, though nobody entered the Muslim heart of the old city. There were many smaller gatherings and celebrations, disrupting traffic on major streets, taunting those who did not join in. This assertion of political muscle was protected, escorted and supported by the police. Sitting in a traffic jam caused by the celebrations, I asked a policeman what the fuss was all about. 'Oh, it is a celebration for Hindus' he told me. I must have looked somewhat skeptical so he added with a big smile 'Hindu *dharma*'.

What do these vignettes tell us?

Firstly, for those who are marginal and vulnerable, the police and legal procedure are experienced as a constant possibility of random and overwhelming violence. Across India, slum areas, and areas with high concentrations of Muslims, SCs and STs, experience regular police raids during which young men are arrested and beaten. These young men can either confess to be implicated in crimes they never committed, or be subjected to severe physical punishment, often both.

Secondly, and most importantly in this context, the only possible antidote and protection from the police, and from the force of the law that may be unleashed by one's adversaries, is some form of political power and the potential of mobilising sufficient numbers to disrupt public order. The second vignette shows that while charging an opponent with a criminal offense is a common political weapon, the force of law can be countered, possibly neutralised, by the force of numbers and the potential for disruption of public order. The proof of such a force lies in forcing the police to 'give us a 141' as the young activist stated. As we will see below, the various sections of the IPC have certainly entered political vernaculars across the country. Such incidents of public disorder can in turn reflect negatively on the local police force and possibly result in transfer of officers.

Finally, it seems that interpreting an evanescent 'public' or 'people'— whether as a physical crowd or an imputed mass sentiment—is a very important factor in how laws are enforced and public goods are distributed. A retired city commissioner put it succinctly to me:

> As a government servant, your best ally is always the public. If you do your job, show your face and make sure that people see that you are doing your job, you are safe. The chances of being transferred are much lower. No politician wants to go against the people.... If you have the support of the public, all the politicians want to be your friend, they want to be seen with you, as if it is they, and not you, who are doing the work...it is quite simple.

Yet, this public is elusive, multiple and often fickle. And, as we saw, not all publics are equal.

The law of force and segmented publics

Majoritarianism commonly refers to the idea that pre-existing ethnic, racial or religious majorities have a natural right to dominate a certain political entity. But in reflecting on how this sentiment became acceptable to so many Indians, it may be worth probing a bit deeper into how the very idea of a majority became the ultimate arbiter of political right, might and legitimacy.

Postcolonial India inherited a rich repertoire of political actions and rituals from the nationalist movement. At the heart of this new political vernacular was the notion that the people are always right and that every effective political action must stage this 'people' or a community in significant numbers to make a point. Crowds—angry, mobilised, determined or disciplined—became an evermore powerful currency of political transaction in India. The bigger the crowd, the stronger the argument. In an important article, Dipesh Chakrabarty argued that in the first decades of the new Indian nation state, senior bureaucrats, against all their instincts, had to appear from time to time in front of angry crowds in order to apologise for the non-delivery of some government service.[22] As Indian democracy matured and multiple opposition forces arose this political vernacular of numbers, and the performance of public anger, became more complex.

From the 1990s onwards, the idea of mobilising, or representing, majorities—in states, in elected bodies, as caste coalitions, as religious communities—became an evermore powerful idea. It gradually began to challenge the older ideal of political parties attracting votes across different communities and minorities in order to consolidate a legitimate political majority. The notion of majority itself—*bahumat*—began to acquire a stronger affective and moral force. In Sanskrit, *bahumata* literally means 'esteemed by many' and it seems that by the 1990s this aspect of *bahumat*/majority as something that in and of itself has a moral force began to acquire an ever more effective and visceral reality on the ground. The moral force of a majority—whether defined as a pre-given cultural entity or understood as an electoral proof of the superior force and truth represented by a political formation—emerged in no small measure from regional politics across India.

The linguistic movements of the 1940s and 50s had mobilised powerful sentiments on the assumption of an inherent superiority, and naturalness, of a polity based on the linguistic affinities of a majority as well as the strength of emotional bonds this indexed and made possible. It is no coincidence that prior to the rise of Hindutva most of the morally charged rhetoric of sacrifice, of 'treason', of emotional outrage and attachment, often accompanied by physical attacks on newspapers and public figures, emerged in states where strong linguistic and regional polities had emerged since the 1950s.

Powerful language ideologies drove the movements for the purification and re-invention of modern vernaculars in the latter half of the twentieth century in much of India. These ideologies promised to overcome traditional social and caste-defined diglossia, and to overcome the sense of inferiority *vis-à-vis* English that was reproduced on a daily basis in the vernacular press and in institutions of government, science, the national press and higher learning.[23] Most importantly, the language movements enabled flourishing vernacular publics to be experienced as culturally intimate in historically unprecedented ways. The vernacular was now that which could be shared and mobilised with many strangers as a medium of intimacy and solidarity *vis-à-vis* outsiders, as in the case of the regional movements in Andhra Pradesh, Maharashtra and Tamil Nadu. It could also be the medium of less restrained and more nakedly majoritarian sentiments, a 'split public' divided between a more formal English-speaking public and a more intimate vernacular sphere.[24]

The vernacular language itself, its grammar, the joy of speaking it, the sharing of references and the sense of community it enabled, became a medium of condensed emotions and a thick sense of community.[25] For Maharashtra, Clare Talwalker posits that the sharing of both modern and classical Marathi among middle-class Hindus generated a certain 'kin-fetishism'—an imagined world of familial intimacy and commensality where everyone becomes uncle, sister, brother, etc. This world thrives, she argues, on its supposed contrast to what is perceived to be a more alienating world of stranger sociality in metropolitan areas or in national spaces.[26] This 'kin fetishism' has distinct limits and vulnerabilities insofar as it is founded on a preexisting if unstated premise of social and ritual compatibility among upper-caste Hindus.[27]

Some of the most inventive and irreverent writers in Marathi in the past decades are Dalit writers and public intellectuals such as Baburao Bagul, Namdeo Dhasal, Arun Kamble, and Urmila Pawar who both are, and are not, included in the intimacy of modern Marathi. For these figures, some of whom are now included in the Marathi literary canon, mastery of the vernacular was both a platform for critique and a claim for recognition. This happened not through cultural intimacy but through the creation of a parallel Dalit public sphere, marked by festivals, institutions and symbols that are neither generally known, nor recognised by many caste Hindus in the state.[28] Like many other segmented publics, the Dalit public sphere is perfectly knowable but not generally known. It is technically public in a linguistic sense but not a general public in any wider social sense. This became very clear after militant Hindus in early January 2018 attacked the annual celebration of the valour of the Mahar soldiers in the defeat of the Peshwa empire in 1818 at Bhima Koregaon. The attacks led to widespread protest by Dalits across the state and made a key element in the annual calendar of events in the Dalit public sphere visible to a much larger audience. What holds such publics together is rather a shared experience of stigmatisation, a shared moral universe, and a claim for recognition as full citizens and humans that cannot be fully captured through a conventional idea of a public sphere as a network of institutions, texts, and linguistic performances. The Dalit public sphere, like other emerging lower caste 'counter publics', asserts the democratic and constitutional rights of the community against the cultural and social hegemony of upper-caste Hindus.[29]

These intensified, segmented and vernacular publics are crucial in understanding the steady deployment of 'routine' public violence, such as the destruction of public property—buses, police vans, offices, schools—by protesters of many kinds, acts that are often recorded in police records as acts of 'public vandalism' rather than political events or riots, and mostly classified merely as disturbance of public order.

As I indicated above, for the Indian police, the actual prosecution of crime is at best a secondary objective, always subordinated to the maintenance of a semblance of public order which is given inordinate attention in the Indian Penal Code (IPC), that was promulgated in 1860 and since has grown very substantially. Chapter 8 of the IPC is entitled 'Offences against Public Tranquility' and it has slowly grown over the decades to consist of as many as eighteen sections ranging from the milder 'unlawful assembly' (141) to 'rioting with a deadly weapon' (148) all the way to sections 153A (promoting enmity between different groups) and 153B (assertions prejudicial to national integration), the latter carrying more severe punishments, especially if they involve 'places of worship or religious ceremonies'. Most of these sections reference groups and communities as those being 'incited' or 'offended' or harboring 'feelings of ill will' while the legal term 'person' is only invoked in the sections referring to those who stand to 'benefit' from riots (sections 154–156) or those being 'hired' to commit public violence (sections 157–159).

If we look at the official crime statistics since 1960 (and we can be sure these numbers are very under reported) the aggregated number of public offenses against public order (all the eighteen sections of the IPC) stood at less than 30,000 across India in the 1960s, climb to above 90,000 in 1980, and above 95,000/year in the early 1990s. After a dip during the early 2000s to under 60,000 per year, the number has been rising since 2012 reaching 73,000 in 2016.[30]

In the last decade, the Crime Bureau has started detailing the specific category of riot—as caste (2,500 in 2016), communal (1,200 in 2016), student, or political (1,800 in 2016). The rest of these disturbances—well over 60,000—fall in the category of 'other riots', defined as 'Civil Unrest, Community dispute, Attack on Police, dispute over Water supply'.[31]

What are we to make of this? Firstly it is clear that staging a riot or a protest of some sort, either against a public institution or another community/hostile neighbours is a very widespread phenomenon indeed. We actually have no idea what these tens of thousands of incidents registered are about and how they get classified as 'other riots'. We know that police personnel have a vested interest in putting as many incidents as possible in this category as they are seen as less serious than the specified caste or communal incidents. We also know that getting a case registered as a public disturbance is a relatively light and bailable offense, low-risk and yet high-profile. It is a way of showing anger, and demonstrating that a group or community is willing to publicly perform this anger and make a point that makes news of some sort.

Secondly, it is obvious that the very provisions of the Indian Penal Code in some ways structure the forms that political and social protest and expression will take. The IPC defines the perceived injury of religious sentiments of a group/community as an criminal offense (295A) and it bans the incitement of enmity among groups and communities (153A and B). Since such collective offense is banned, it becomes imperative that the effect of the offense is demonstrated, not as individual sentiments but as a mirror of the spirit of the law itself—as a collective sentiment that threatens public order. As a result, being booked under one of the IPC 140s or 150s becomes in itself a form of proof of a collective sentiment and anger, and indeed a part of a political vernacular, a measure of success—something has happened (*kuchh to huaa hai*).

Protesters describe such events as the inevitable effect of pent up anger and outrage, as if the scale of physical destruction is an index of the depth and intensity of their rage. Protesters often blame the offenders for provoking such anger—such as when vigilante groups in Karnataka or Maharashtra routinely blame 'immoral youth' for the anger that wells up in themselves, vigilantes, the urge to protect Hindu values that is provoked in them and leads them to beat up and molest middle-class youth.[32] The protesters or vigilantes want the government and various publics to take note but the audience is rarely a general public. The main audience for many protests is more often than not a more segmented caste or community public that is directly affected by certain policies or events.

Such language of outrage and hurt pride has today become the predominant modality justification of public violence in India.[33] However, there is little doubt that Hindu nationalism has played an exceptionally important role in this process. The Shiv Sena was a particularly radical heir to this politics of popular emotion of the linguistic movements. The Shiv Sena developed fury (*raag* in Marathi) and anger (*gussa* in Hindi) into a public virtue, a increasingly legitimate style of politics whose forceful directness (*seeda marpeet*) against authorities and perceived enemies of the ordinary Marathi speaker indexed its authenticity and association with a rougher plebeian world.[34] This sentiment was directly relayed by the name of Shiv Sena's newspaper *Saamna* (confrontation) which has been pivotal in making a coarser style of colloquial Marathi acceptable and legitimate, if often dismissed as poor taste among the traditional upper-caste and middle-class communities.

Hindu communal politics has historically been framed as militant self-defense against perceived Muslim aggression. However, since the 1980s Hindutva discourse increasingly adopted a style of forceful anger that foregrounded hurt sentiments—such as the presumed historical humiliation of Hindus by the very existence of the Babri Masjid on the birth place of Lord

Ram—or the theme of a Hindu pride (*Hindu gaurav*), presumably resurgent after centuries of humiliation, that was so prominent during the 2002 anti-Muslim pogrom in Gujarat.[35] The success of the BJP has been based on its capacity to instigate anti-minority violence and then reap the electoral benefits of the emotional wave of aggression and fear that communal riots tend to generate.[36] It is also clear, as Amrita Basu has demonstrated, that there is a direct correlation between the incidence of communal riots and attacks and the growth and importance of Hindu nationalist organisations in different parts of India.[37]

In these public actions, even excessive and cruel violence is purified and made just and moral by the imputed injury to a community or a collective emotion that provoked it in the first place. Violence is purely reactive, spontaneous and therefore inherently just. It is '*natural nyaya*' as a Shiv Sena activist in Mumbai put it to me many years ago, something that is inherent in a brave and self-respecting man: 'if someone slaps me, my hands come out and I slap him. It is natural *nyaya* (justice)'. In this light, the contemporary *gaurakshaks* (self-proclaimed cow protectors) and the lynching of mostly Muslim men suspected of transporting beef in 2016–17 appear as less of an aberration than they are extensions of an existing grammar of action whereby righteous anger—especially that of the putative majority community—is already justified and legitimate.

Violence, I propose, has become a 'general equivalent' in India's multiple publics, akin to Marx's notion of money as the general measure of value of otherwise disparate objects (commodities, capital, debt, etc.). Acts of public violence generate wildly disparate experiences and interpretations of violence—avenging, retributive, sacrificial, or victimising, etc. Often, the experiences of violence are entirely incommensurate with one another, as in the reckoning after major communal riots and other crowd violence. At other times, violence is invisible and incomprehensible to an adjacent public and social world, as in routinised atrocities against Dalits, or the systematic violence visited upon Muslims by police forces across India.

Yet, these experiences and real events are invariably presented, and performed, as public violence—that is extralegal, excessive and exceptional—in order to become visible and intelligible across deeply segmented and antagonistic public worlds. While the thick social context and experience of violence may be impossible to translate, the figures of victims, outraged crowds, or the self-sacrificing activist, or the brutal police action against a crowd, are general equivalents that have the potential to transcend otherwise deeply segregated social and cultural worlds.

Violence is conventionally seen as the limit, if not negation, of political life and civil political discourse. However, violence has become a completely routinised and integral part of the political life in India's many diverse publics. Public violence, or the threat thereof, demands attention and it generates reaction. Violence has become deeply intertwined with the more formal, mediated and institutional aspects of India's modern publics such as newspapers, news channels and social media. As Francis Cody has shown in compelling detail, newspaper reporting and op-eds in the Tamil press always factor in the possibility of violent reprisals in the wake of controversial statements.[38] Similarly, *Saamna* and other right wing newspapers are open about their reporting bias (or 'truth', as its reporters insist), and they routinely taunt their readers to take 'direct action' against their enemies, including offices of newspapers critical of the movement. The street and the editorial office are not categorically different in contemporary India, one civil and objective, the other partisan and rogue, but rather parts of the same vernacular publics where the public performance of anger and fury is every bit as legitimate as a sarcastic op-ed. This indicates that violence is no longer politics by other means but the heart of political life itself. This, I submit, is a deeper and long-term process that must be factored into our understanding of how Indian democracy works.

Public violence as popular sovereignty

In a dialectical loop of history, the seemingly spontaneous anger and violence of 'frenzied' mobs that colonial officers feared and loathed as deep 'oriental irrationality'[39] are now back, carefully staged as a deep emotional truth, and instrumentalised as the most legitimate expression of popular anger and political will. Today, the mightiest socio-political force in India today is neither the state nor the law but deeply embedded vernacular ideas of popular sovereignty. Notions of the right to rule by the people (*svatantra rajya*, or *lokshahi*) have taken deep hold. But unlike the specificity of precisely delineated caste and religious communities that play such a large role in everyday life, 'the people' or the majority that are invoked in public performances remains a more open category and never entirely pre-given. It needs to be continuously filled and performed in order to remain potent.

One of the crucial enabling conditions making public violence so common to invocations of popular sovereignty is the application of the force of law in the face of such exertions of 'the law of force'. Violent crowd action—destroy-

35

ing public property, beating up and attacking opponents—is to this day rarely prosecuted with much vigour.

Colonial policing suspended the principle of individual culpability in the context of crowd violence. This practice was continued by the police in independent India. Countless reports and inquiries since the 1960s have depicted crowd violence as a mere symptom of social or communal tension, and rarely as concrete action perpetrated by identifiable actors. The state of Maharashtra still retains a legal provision, 'The Maharashtra Prevention of Dangerous Activities of Slumlords, Bootleggers, Drug offenders and Dangerous Persons Act' promulgated in 1981 (by a Congress government) and amended in 2009, that allows the police to detain 'notorious characters' when the police feel that communal or other tension is building up in an area.[40] After riots, police and public figures have conventionally attributed these riots to the 'handiwork of criminal elements'—though these always remain unnamed, and unidentified.[41] If we look at the National Crime Statistics how many individuals were charged under IPC 153A and 153B—that is the incitement of enmity between groups—between 2014 and 2016 fluctuate between 400 and 600/ year under each, and these are often overlapping charges. Probing a bit deeper in these numbers, one finds, interestingly, only thirteen cases led to conviction in 2016.[42]

Another interesting pattern emerges when one looks at the conviction rate for 'rioting' and other offenses against public order. The police claim a 16 per cent conviction rate in such cases in 2016, which in any case is low, but when one looks at the numbers of people arrested and charged (around 300,000/year in about 30,000 cases/year) one sees an exceptionally high 'pendency' rate. The number cases that are pending each year is around 95 per cent—mostly cases carried over from previous years.[43] What does this tell us? Purely on the basis of the official and undoubtedly somewhat 'cooked' figures: that at the very highest, a few per cent of those charged with disturbing public order are ever convicted. Most of those charged (more than 2 million individuals reported in 2014)—and we cannot assume their guilt—are on bail for years, even decades.[44]

This means that in practice, the only punishment for disturbing public order takes place not after the events but as they unfold. But here too, the application of force is calibrated according to which communities and classes are in the street. Until about a decade ago, the Indian police used mainly extremely forceful *lathi*-charges or live ammunition as a means of crowd control. The multiple injuries and deaths caused by these blunt methods have rarely been questioned mainly because such violence has been disproportionately targeting the poorer minority communities. Let me give a few examples.

The active complicity of the Bombay police force in targeting Muslims while protecting Shiv Sena activists during the riots in 1992–93 was assiduously documented by the Srikrishna Commision.[45] The pattern has repeated itself many times since then. In July 2012, Raj Thackeray and his MNS movement staged a march through Mumbai to protest a demonstration by Muslims at the city's Azad Maidan. That day, I witnessed fully armed police blocking all main thoroughfares leading into the dense Muslim areas in central Mumbai. In the name of maintaining public order, the police faced the Muslim *mohalla* while protecting the 60,000 militant and belligerent Hindus marching through the city behind them.

After the brutal killing of a Dalit family in Khairlanji in Maharashtra in 2007, Dalits protests erupted across the state. The police came down heavily on these protesters, detaining and beating up thousands of activists. The police also launched what became known as 'combing operations' in Dalit neighborhoods, arresting and detaining hundreds of young men charged with 'disturbing public order'. After the state wide protests following the attacks on Dalit celebrations at Bhima Koregaon on 1 January 2018, the same techniques were deployed on an even more intensive scale, now aided by video footage and targeting individual protesters. Police would search Dalit slum areas, destroy two-wheelers, kick down doors and beat up any able bodied male they could find.[46] At the time of writing, hundreds of young men are still languishing in jail in Maharashtra, most of them draconically charged under IPC section 307 with the intent to murder police officers, a charge that can carry severe sentences.

This rather extraordinary imposition of the force of law upon minority communities has scarcely been reported in the mainstream press. The Dalit movement in the state successfully managed to impose a state-wide *bandh* on 3–4 January 2018—a feat that no other political force has been able to achieve since the Shiv Sena's *bandhs* of the 1990s. These actions produced very little sympathy or attention among general caste Hindus. 'These people have no right to disturb the peace like that', my Shiv Sena-supporting middle class neighbour told me, while in the same breath assuring me that Shiv Sena's vigilante-style politics had provided 'justice for Hindus'. The dividing line seems, in other words, no longer to be whether public violence is legal or not but, rather, a question of who has the right to violently dominate public space claim to be 'the people'.

Such tacit legitimacy of violence is arguably the most pervasive effect of politics in India having been increasingly organised as assertions of popular sovereignty, along lines of the friend/enemy distinction that Carl Schmitt defined as the essence of all political life.[47] At the same time, this deepening friend/enemy distinction also makes such violent street politics a site of deep and enduring jouissance and excitement. As I have alluded to in previous work,[48] ordinary politics in India is often fueled by outrage and scandal—the corruption, the transgression, the bending of power, the cynicism—all these things outrage voters, and motivate them to vote differently. But the shame-lessness and routine violence of electoral politics is also a distorted mirror of people's selves, a source of 'perverse' entertainment and, at times, furtive enjoyment. Such surreptitious endorsement and excitement during times of riots—the feeling that murderous mobs are exacting a form of magical justice beyond procedure and law; the middle class voters' fascination with the eros of naked power and the audacity of political operatives—these are all richly and disturbingly documented by ethnographers of violence.[49]

Is India's democratic revolution devouring democracy?

The deepening of India's democracy in the 1980s and 90s seemed to suggest that formal equality in the sphere of political representation would lead to a questioning of hierarchies of caste and community and an assertion of lower-caste identities and communities.[50] Lower-caste communities were politically empowered and they managed to mobilise educational and economic oppor-tunities through reservations and new economic networks. Key elements of liberal democracy—individual and equal rights to vote, to access public goods, to claim reservations, the (nominal) rule of law, etc.—were all crucial condi-tions of possibility that enabled the mobilisation of lower-caste communities. But the result was not a questioning of caste practices within, or among, these communities. Instead, a new 'substantialisation' of caste communities took shape along with a renewed emphasis on myths of origin, ritual life, marriage prestations and kin-alliances that have all acquired new importance in a quest for consolidating the social respectability of politically mobilised OBC com-munities.[51] Democracy in a caste society is essentially organised as collective mobility, as a fight to level the political playing field and claiming recognition and visibility that often reifies the caste communities that are mobilised and strengthens the illiberal and patriarchal practices within these communities, now justified in the name of honour, collective strength and respectability. The BJP's victory in 2014 owes a lot to the party's systematic recruitment of aspirational leaders from lower-caste communities who saw the BJP as a possible vehicle for further inclusion, mobility and respectability of their communities. This suggests that the deepening of democracy in India has produced ever-stronger assertion of the legitimate power of majorities, popular power and popular sovereignty, but without any concomitant percolation of liberal-democratic values, and without any stronger assertion of the rule of law as a value in and of itself. Electoral politics and mobilisation are at the heart of popular worlds across India, often performed as ludic rituals of war in a polarised atmosphere where hurt sentiments, outrage and public violence have more legitimacy than a few decades ago. In these milieus, it is neither the embrace of liberal rights, nor the defense of entitlements and access to public goods and government services that seem to be strongest driver of political mobilisation. It is, rather, 'the law of force', i.e. the idea that political power and popular mobilisation provides an umbrella that protects against the force of law and promises its supporters a certain room for manoeuvre and a measure of impunity. Herein lies perhaps the answer to why there seems to be no contradiction between a strong support for democracy—understood as the will of the people—as a form of government, and support for authoritarian styles of governance ruling in the name of this people.

A *DE FACTO* ETHNIC DEMOCRACY?

OBLITERATING AND TARGETING THE OTHER, HINDU VIGILANTES, AND THE ETHNO-STATE

Christophe Jaffrelot

After the euphoria of 'the third wave'[1] of democratisation, since the late 1990s, the political scientists who admitted that liberal democracy was not the only game in town have been striving to qualify democratic regimes that do not abide by the principles of the genre.[2] These 'hybrid' democracies are thus sometimes tagged with epithets such as 'illiberal' or even 'authoritarian'.[3] India is not immune to this trend. Under Narendra Modi, 'the world's largest democracy' has taken on the features of a certain electoral authoritarianism stoked by national-populism. But the present chapter will explore another aspect of India's democratic regression, and that is the 'majoritarianism' promoted by the Hindu nationalist Bharatiya Janata Party (BJP—Indian People's Party) as the dominant ideology since it came to power.

The theoretical framework that proves most useful to this analysis is that of 'ethnic democracy' (another epithet for wayward democracies). This model was constructed by Sammy Smooha, who defines it on the basis of a broad but precise set of criteria. Ethnic democracy is first the product of ethnic nationalism, the ideology of a majoritarian group based on racial, linguistic, religious or, more generally speaking, cultural characteristics, that implies a strong sense of belonging and often of superiority. This identity goes along with a rejection of the minorities, generally perceived as threats to the survival and integrity of the ethnic nation. For Smooha, one of the conditions for the emergence and persistence of an ethnic democracy is 'the existence of a threat (real or perceived) to the ethnic nation that requires mobilisation of the majority in order to preserve the ethnic nation'.[4] Smooha considers that many countries have gone down the road of ethnic democracy but that the archetype of this political system remains Israel, a state that endeavours to combine an ethnic (Jewish) identity and a parliamentary system drawing its inspiration from Western Europe. The two sides of this coin are the Jewish nature of the nation-state and the restrictions imposed on the rights of minorities, primarily the Palestinians/Israeli Arabs.

Ethnic democracy implies two-tiered citizenship, the majority enjoying more rights than the minority, both *de jure* and *de facto*. In Israel, Jews have more rights because the state officially recognises their religion. Hence the Judaisation of symbols of identity: 'Israel's titular name, calendar, days and sites of commemoration, heroes, flag, emblem, national anthem, names of places, ceremonies and the like are all Jewish'.[5] But Jewish dominance at the expense of Muslims is also exercised *de facto*, in contradiction with the law. Smooha moreover adds:

> Most of the discrimination is, however, rather covert. The extensive use of military service as a criterion for the allocation of benefits is very striking, because most Jews serve in the army, whereas most Arabs do not. … Unfair allocation of funds and provision of unequal services by governmental offices are quite common. For example, the subsidies received by Arab local councils from the Ministry of the Interior average only about one-third of the subsidies granted to comparable Jewish local councils.[6]

Majority public opinion contributes to legitimating these practices, given that Muslims 'are regarded as potentially disloyal to the state and placed under security and political control',[7] not to mention the fear generated by their demographic growth.

Illegal practices that basically treat Israeli Arabs routinely as second-class citizens under security or other pretenses take a wide variety of forms.[8] The discriminatory practices visited upon Israeli Arabs were explicitly recognised by the Or Commission—named for Theodore Or, the former supreme court Justice who presided over it. Appointed by the government to investigate police repression, which in October 2000 claimed thirteen Arab and Palestinian lives at the start of the Intifada, the Commission found that 'Israeli democracy is not democratic towards the Arabs to the same extent that it is democratic towards the Jews'.[9]

If I have presented in detail how Israel illustrates the type of regime labelled ethnic democracy, it is because I believe India under Narendra Modi has moved toward this model over the 2014–19 period, while exhibiting a specific variant of it. The main difference lies in the lack of any major legal reform, as evident from the fact that the 1950 constitution continues to embody the ideals of secularism (and therefore multiculturalism) and equal citizenship for all. But while the *de jure* aspect of ethnic democracy is virtually absent, the *de facto* aspect on the other hand is omnipresent due to the vanishing of minority representation in elected assemblies and the role that vigilante militias play in conducting Hindu nationalist cultural policing with the blessing of the law enforcement agencies. Of all the minorities, the principal victims of this trend are Muslims, the traditional target of Hindu nationalists on which this chapter will primarily focus.

The institutional occultation of the Other

Muslims have remained on the sidelines of some of India's institutions since 1947, which has led Gurharpal Singh to consider that India has been an ethnic democracy from its inception.[10] But this analysis in fact holds true only for the administration, the army and the police. In elected assemblies, Muslims remained somewhat represented up until recent years, despite extensive regional variations.

The database I compiled with the help of Shweta Bhutada shows that in the 1950s, the percentage of Muslim officers in the Indian Police Service (IPS)—the elite leadership body for national policing—was already lower than 5 per cent, less than half the proportion of Muslims in Indian society according to the 1951 census.[11] While the share of Muslims in the population subsequently rose, reaching 14.25 per cent in 2011, the proportion of Muslims in the IPS dwindled, falling beneath the 3 per cent mark in 2016, and even as low as 2.5 per cent of the whole service if Jammu and Kashmir is excluded from the calculation. Never had the gap between the share of Muslims in the population and their share in the IPS been so wide. For a long time, Muslims were able to take advantage of the parallel track offered at the state level, through which police officers recruited by the state administration could join the IPS (partly through seniority). But this recruitment channel has dried up: while they were 7 per cent to be promoted in 2006, the number of Muslims fell to 3.8 per cent in 2016.[12]

The situation is less unfavourable to Muslims if the analysis is broadened to include police officers in the lower echelons. In 2013—the last year for which these data were compiled[13]—Muslims made up 6.27 per cent of police officers in India. But their strength was on the wane, as in 2004 they still comprised 7.1 per cent, then 7.5 per cent in 2005, 9.1 per cent in 2008 (year for which statistics are skewed due to lack of reporting by Madhya Pradesh), and 6.5 per cent in 2011.[14] The remarkable investigative work of the Centre for the Study of Developing Society and the NGO Common Cause that appears in the *Status of Policing in India Report 2018* has led to the creation of an indicator of sociocultural diversity within the Indian police forces. It shows that between 2006 and 2013, Muslims were particularly underrepresented in these law enforcement agencies. While the average index was 0.31 (compared to 0.50 for women), it varied between 0.08 in Assam and 0.69 in Andhra Pradesh, with only 0.09 in Rajasthan and 0.18 in Uttar Pradesh.[15]

Figure 1: Muslims in the Indian population and among the IPS officers (1951–2016), in per cent

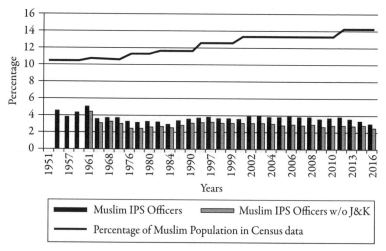

Sources: Ministry of Home Affairs (Government of India), *The Civil List of Indian Police Service*, New Delhi.

This state of things is one of the reasons why Muslims fear the police more than any other community. According to the *Status of Policing in India Report, 2018*, 64 per cent of them are 'highly' or 'somewhat' fearful of the police.[16] The main reason for this fear appears to be the fact that the '[p]olice often implicates Muslims under false terrorism charges'.[17] Indeed, there are many cases of young Muslims who have been to jail and even spent years behind the bars for this 'reason', before the judiciary, at long last, released them: 21 per cent of those in prison awaiting trial are Muslim.[18] Yet the Muslim share of those sentenced in 2015 (15.8 per cent) is nearly the same as the proportion of Muslims in the general population, a sign that many of those arrested are cleared at trial.[19] But the Indian justice system is so notoriously slow that being arrested can itself mean a long prison term before any trial.

The situation is even more critical within the army, and this since independence in 1947. That year, Partition led to the departure of virtually all of the Muslim officers to Pakistan.[20] Nehru himself expressed concern over the situation in 1953, the year in which his defense minister confirmed that the percentage of Muslims in the Indian army had gone from 32 per cent in 1947 to 2 per cent: '...in our Defence Services, there are hardly any Muslims left.... What concerns me most is that there is no effort being made to improve this situation, which is likely to grow worse unless checked'.[21]

In fact, Muslims no longer made up more than 1 per cent of higher-ranking officers (colonels and above) in 1981 according to Steven Wilkinson's reckoning,[22] a figure confirmed in 1999 by former Defence Minister Mulayam Singh Yadav.[23] The man who succeeded him in this position under the Vajpayee government, George Fernandes, bluntly explained the situation: 'The Muslim is not wanted in the Armed Forces because he is always suspect—whether we want to admit it or not, most Indians consider Muslims a fifth column for Pakistan'.[24] In 1985, an opinion poll showed that the majority of Hindus interviewed believed that Muslims should not be allowed to join the armed services.[25]

The situation there is once again less unfavourable if the analysis is not limited to senior officers but instead broadened to take into account the armed services as a whole. In the Army, Muslims made up 2.5 per cent of the people in uniform in the years 1990–2000, particularly thanks to the Jammu and Kashmir Rifles, the Jammu and Kashmir Light Infantry and other companies such as the Rajput Regiment.[26] Similar figures are found in the Navy (1.9 per cent of Muslims in the higher-ranking categories and 3.2 per cent in the others) and the Air Force (3.1 per cent of Muslims, including 0.9 per cent senior officers).[27]

These data were recently updated by Ali Ahmed's study on officers trained at the Military Academy. From 2005 to 2011, 2 per cent of them were Muslims, a figure still below the one the Sachar Committee had found for the previous period, 2.62 per cent.[28] Figures for so-called 'paramilitary' forces, which form an intermediary category between the police and the army, are in the same ballpark. The Assam Rifles had 2.5 per cent of Muslims in 1995–96, the Border Security Force 4.5 per cent, the Central Industrial Security Force 3.7 per cent, the Central Reserve Police Force, 5.5 per cent, the Indo-Tibetan Force 1.8 per cent, and the Rapid Action Force, 6.9 per cent.[29]

The public sector counts scarcely more Muslims but their under-representation remains more substantial and is more significant because the Indian state is a big employer and an even bigger one than the private sector due to nationalisations made long ago (in the banking sector, for instance) and increasing use of temporary contracts by private-sector Indian companies. In 2011–12, there were 17.61 million government employees, as opposed to only 12.04 million in the private sector,[30] but very few of them were Muslims, as the Sachar Committee Report has shown fifteen years ago.[31] The elite corps of the bureaucracy, the Indian Administrative Service (IAS), is a case in point. While the proportion of Muslims in the IAS rose slightly between 2006 and 2016, going from 3 to 3.3 per cent,[32] this share did not show any improvement when compared to the Muslim population in India, which is also on the rise. Moreover, the share of Muslims entering via the parallel track (enabling state civil servants to enter the IAS) partly explains these results: in 2016, only 2.7 per cent of Muslims in the IAS entered by passing the Union Public Service Commission exam for civil service jobs. In 2017, the situation had improved somewhat, with the share of Muslims among the candidates who passed the UPSC (Union Public Service Commission) exam for jobs in the administration rising to 5.1 per cent. But this figure fell to 4.5 per cent in 2018.[33] Such under-representation is partly due to the fact that many Muslims do not sit for the civil service exam. According to Amitabh Kundu's estimate, they make up only 8 per cent of the candidates on average.[34]

At the level of the states, each with its own civil service, the situation is rather variable. In Maharashtra, for instance, although Muslims make up 11 per cent of the population, only five individuals passed the Maharashtra Civil Services exam out of 435 candidates (or 1.14 per cent) in 2015.[35] In spite of this, in 2015 as it so happens, the new coalition government formed by the BJP and Shiv Sena decided not to defend in court the previous Congress government's plan of reserving for Muslims 5 per cent of the regional civil service by decree,[36] which would have brought the sum total of quotas over the 49 per cent mark that the courts set as a limit not to be exceeded.[37] Only some states in the south continue to follow an affirmative action policy for Muslims. Aside from Kerala and Karnataka, where the policy is longstanding,[38] Telangana is also striving to bring the quota reserved for Muslims in the civil service up to 12 per cent despite BJP opposition.[39]

While the proportion of Muslims in the civil service has never been very large, their political representation was far more significant up until recent years.

Table 1: Muslim MPs in the Lok Sabha

Year	% of Muslims according to the 10-year census	Total number of seats	Number of Muslim MPs	% of Muslim MPs
1980	11.4 (1981)	542	49	9
1984	11.4 (1981)	542	46	8.4
1989	11.4 (1981)	543	33	6
1991	12.6 (1991)	543	28	5.1
1996	12.6 (1991)	543	28	5.1
1998	12.6 (1991)	543	28	5.1
1999	12.6 (1991)	543	32	5.8
2004	13.4 (2001)	543	35	6.4
2009	13.4 (2001)	543	30	5.5
2014	14.2 (2011)	543	20	3.7

Sources: Z. Hasan, *Politics of Inclusion. Castes, Minorities and Affirmative Action*, Delhi: Oxford University Press, 2008, p. 257 for 1980–2004 and Election Commission of India for 2009 and 2014.

Between 1980 and 2014, the number of Muslim MPs in the lower house of the Indian parliament—and hence their percentage—diminished by more than half. This evolution is all the more significant as the share of Muslims in the Indian population rose during the same period. Consequently, the gap between their proportion of the population (which rose from 11.1 to 14.2 per cent) and that of their elected representatives in the Lok Sabha (which dropped from 9 to 3.7 per cent) increased fivefold, jumping from two to ten percentage points. Responsibility for this trend lies primarily with the BJP, which has only ever endorsed very few Muslim candidates, and this in constituencies where the party had a slim chance of winning, even as its group in parliament continued to increase in numbers.

In 2009, the BJP fielded four Muslim candidates, or 0.48 per cent of the total, and only got one elected. In 2014, it fielded seven Muslim candidates out of 428 (or less than 2 per cent) and none were elected. For the first time in India's history, the winning party in the general elections had no Muslims in its parliamentary group in the Lok Sabha and therefore, in states such as Uttar Pradesh, India's largest state, where Muslims make up over 18 per cent of the population and where the BJP won seventy-one out of eighty seats, did not have a single Muslim MP (compared to six in 2009 and ten in 2004).[40]

The BJP decision not to field any Muslim candidates aimed to liberate the party entirely from the 'Muslim vote'[41] that other parties in UP in 2017 were accused of wooing for electoral gain at the expense of the Hindu majority. During the 2017 state election campaign in Uttar Pradesh, one BJP leader admitted:

> Everyone was wooing the Muslims. We told the Hindus—they will unite, will we always remain divided? Trump in the US showed that it is not blacks and Hispanics and Muslims who will decide who becomes US president. It is whites. Here too, it is not Muslims who will decide who rules UP. It is all other Hindus. They want to defeat us. We want to defeat them and their parties. It is a battle.[42]

The formation of a Hindu vote bank by the BJP, which in particular aimed to sideline minorities in the political arena, prompted other parties as well no longer to nominate Muslim candidates, except in areas with a high Muslim proportion. This tactic was especially clear in the Congress' case, which the BJP accused of cultivating a Muslim vote bank by showing concern for their social and economic condition—a false claim if one goes by the impoverishment of Muslims under the UPA regime.[43] In 2009, the Congress, unwilling to embrace its traditional secularism, only endorsed thirty-one Muslim candidates (or 3.7 per cent of the total), among which only eleven won seats. That year, the parties that fielded the most Muslim candidates and got them elected were regional parties, starting with the Bahujan Samaj Party.[44] Five years later, the Congress fielded twenty-seven Muslim candidates out of 462 (less than 6 per cent of the total). Among non-Muslim parties, only the Rashtriya Janata Dal, the Samajwadi Party, the Trinamool Congress in West Bengal and the CPI(M) fielded a percentage of Muslim candidates higher than the share of Muslims in the population (see Table 2). But in many cases, the candidates in question were in constituencies far from the areas where these parties were strongest.[45]

Table 2: Muslim candidates in the 2014 general elections, by party

Party	Muslim candidates	Total number of candidates	%
AAP	41	427	9.6
AGP	1	12	8
AIADMK	5	40	12.5
AIFB	5	39	12.8
AITC	21	131	16
AUDF	10	18	55.5
BJD	0	21	0
BJP	7	428	1.6
BSP	48	501	9.6
CPI	2	68	2.9
CPM	14	93	15
DMDK	0	14	0
DMK	2	35	5.7
INC	27	462	5.6
INLD	1	10	10
IUML	22	25	88
JD(S)	2	33	6
JD(U)	8	93	8.6
JKNC	3	3	100
JMM	2	22	9
LJP	1	7	14
MDMK	0	6	0
MNS	0	10	0
NCP	3	35	8.6
Others	23	305	7.5
PMK	0	9	0
Peace Party	24	51	47
RJD	6	29	20.7
RLD	0	10	0
SAD	0	10	0
SHS	1	58	1.7
SP	36	195	18.4
TDP	2	30	6.7
TRS	1	17	5.9
Total	320	3 245	9.9

Source: SPINPER (The Social Profile of India's National and Provincial Elected Representatives), CNRS, Sciences Po, Ashoka University and Bordeaux University.

Not only did parties of all political stripes field fewer than 10 per cent of Muslim candidates for the Lok Sabha in 2014, but above all, few of them were elected. Muslim MPs finally made up about 4 per cent of elected representatives in the lower house. This under-representation, linked to the boom in Hindu majoritarianism, was reflected at the government level by an unprecedented situation. Only two members in the first Modi government—or less than 3 per cent—were Muslims in 2014. Both had come from the Rajya Sabha (the upper house), given that there was none among the BJP MPs in the Lok Sabha and that only MPs can be appointed as government ministers in India. In July 2016, the minister of Minority Affairs, Najma Heptulla, resigned but was replaced by another Muslim minister in this position, Mukhtar Abbas Naqvi (minister of state prior to that).[46] A second Muslim MP was then appointed in the government, M. J. Akbar, who became minister of state for External Affairs. Inventorying the loci of power in the Indian republic, veteran journalist and media personality Shekhar Gupta concluded, 'India's minorities have never been so out of the power structure. They are justified in having a sense of unease about it.'[47]

However, an examination at the level of the states of the Indian Union is necessary to make a full appraisal of the situation. Aside from the fact that there is no longer a single Muslim chief minister at the time of writing (2018), the presence of Muslim representatives in state assemblies (as Members of Legislative Assemblies—MLAs) and governments (as Ministers or Ministers of State) is on the wane. In January 2018, out of 1,418 BJP elected representatives in these assemblies, only four were Muslim and only two members of the BJP state governments (coalition governments are not taken into account here) were Muslim.[48] This situation holds true as much in states where the BJP has been governing for a long time (such as Gujarat, where the party did not endorse a single Muslim candidate in 2007, in 2012, or in 2017)[49] as for those it recently conquered, such as Assam (30.9 per cent Muslims), where out of sixty-one MLAs (enabling it to win the elections in 2017), it has only one Muslim elected representative.[50]

In general, when the BJP conquers a new state that was ruled by a regional party, the number of Muslim MLAs drops. The most spectacular example is found in Uttar Pradesh where, in 2017, their proportion went from 17 to 6 per cent. While the figure of 17 per cent, achieved in 2012 mainly thanks to the success of the Samajwadi Party,[51] had brought the share of Muslim MLAs closer to their share of the population in Uttar Pradesh—that is, according to the 2011 census, 18.5 per cent—the figure of 6 per cent, associated with the

BJP landslide victory, reflects an under-representation comparable to that of 1991, when the party had already taken control of the state.[52]

A similar diminution in the number of Muslim representatives was not noted systematically when power changed hands from the Congress to the BJP, simply because the Congress never fielded very many Muslim candidates, especially in northern and western India where the Hindu nationalists traditionally have the greatest influence. In Maharashtra, whatever the winning party, the portion of Muslims among the MLAs has never exceeded 5 per cent (i.e. half the proportion of Muslims in the state), including when the Congress won, because it never endorsed more than 7 per cent of Muslim candidates. In Gujarat, Muslim assembly members already made up no more than 1 per cent of the assembly in 1990, prior to when the BJP came to power—and they have remained at this level, as the Congress never fields more than a half-dozen Muslim candidates in the elections. The situation is comparable in Madhya Pradesh and in Karnataka (see Table 3). In Rajasthan, by contrast, the Congress has always fielded the same number of Muslim candidates since the 1990s, despite the rise of Hindu nationalism. More interesting still, this number—between 13 and 14, or at least 8 per cent of the candidates, a proportion close to the share of Muslims in the population, 9 per cent in 2011—is higher than it was in the 1960s to 1980s, a trend found, moreover, in Maharashtra.

As evident from Table 3, the only state where the percentage of Muslim MLAs continues to grow is West Bengal, because of the Trinamool Congress.

To sum up, while Muslims have traditionally been underrepresented within the institutions of the Indian Republic, this phenomenon, which was primarily salient in the police, the army and the administration, has extended to elected assemblies owing to the rise to power of the BJP. But that is only one aspect of Indian-style ethnic democracy. Majoritarianism has also developed with the rise of a new Hindu nationalist cultural police that seeks to control and put down minorities. Muslims are once again the main victims of this trend, which has strengthened since the years 2014–15 and of which the primary actors are vigilante militias generally working with the tacit agreement of the states' police forces.

Vigilantes as state actors?

Vigilantism can be defined as 'a range of collective coercive practices, which are often violent and usually illegal, that aim to keep order and/or mete out justice, in order to enforce legal or moral norms.'[53] Indeed, vigilantes, since Charles

Table 3: Muslim candidates and MLAs in a selection number of state assemblies (per cent)

States	1962	1967–69	1969–71	1972–78	1980–83	1985–87	1989–91	1993–96	1996–01	2002–06	2007–11	2012–16	2017–18
Gujarat	**2.9**	**1.6**	**3.3**	**4.5**	**4.1**	**4.1**	**5.7**	**6.7**	**4.6**	**4.5**	**6.6**	**9.0**	**6.7**
	5.1	*2.3*	*1.8*	*2.2*	*6.0*	*4.9*	*1.0*	*0.5*	*2.7*	*1.6*	*2.7*	*1.0*	*1.6*
	8.1	8.1	8.1	8.4	8.5	8.5	8.5	8.7	8.7	9.0	9.0	9.7	9.7
Karnataka	NA	NA	NA	**7.5**	**6.7**	**6.5**	**5.7**	**5.8**	**6.6**	**5.8**	**6.8**	**6.8**	**9.5**
				7.1	*1.3*	*4*	*4.9*	*2.7*	*5.3*	*1.8*	*2.7*	*2.7*	*3.1*
		10.6	11	11	11	11.6	11.6	12.2	12.2	12.9		12.9	
Madhya Pradesh	**1.5**	**1.9**	**2.5**	**2.8**	**3.5**	**4.6**	**5.4**	**4.7**	**3.1**	**4**	**4.1**	**4.9**	NA
	2.4	*1*	*2.7*	*0.9*	*2.1*	*1.5*	*0.9*	*0*	*1.8*	*0.9*	*0.4*	*0.4*	*0.8*
	4	4	4	4.4	4.8	4.8	4.8	5	5	6.4	6.4	6.6	6.6
Maharashtra	**3.8**	**2.2**	**4.6**	**4.7**	**4.9**	**7**	**8.9**	**7.6**	**7.8**	**8.7**	**10.3**	**9**	NA
	4.2	*2.6*	*5.2*	*3.8*	*5.2*	*9*	*2*	*2.4*	*4.9*	*3.5*	*3.8*	*3.1*	*3.1*
	7.7	7.7	7.7	8.4	9.2	9.2	9.2	9.7	9.7	10.6	10.6	11.5	11.5
Odisha	NA	**0.6**	**0.5**	**0.7/1.6**	**0.9**	**1.2**	**0.8**	**1.2**	**1.1**	**1.5**	**1**	**1.2**	NA
		0	*0.7*	*1.4/0.7*	*2*	*2.7*	*1.4*	*1.4*	*0.7*	*2*	*0*	*0.7*	
		1.2	1.2	1.5	1.6	1.6	1.6	1.8	1.8	2	2	2.2	
Rajasthan	**3.6**	**2.9**	**5**	**5.3**	**6.4**	**7.8**	**7.2**	**8.9**	**5.8**	**6.4**	**6.2**	**7.2**	NA
	1.7	*3.2*	*3.2*	*4.5*	*5*	*4*	*4*	*2*	*6.5*	*2.5*	*6*	*1*	*4*
	6.5	6.5	6.5	6.9	7.3	7.3	7.3	8	8	8.5	8.5	9.1	9.1
Uttar Pradesh	**7.7**	**9.1**	**9.7**	**10/12**	**10.8**	**10.2**	**12.7/10.7**	**10.6**	**8.7**	**10.6**	**11.3**	**12.8**	**10.3**
	6.7	*6.8*	*8.2*	*9.7/11.5*	*11.7*	*12.2*	*9.6/5.5*	*7.5*	*11.7*	*11.7*	*13.9*	*16.9*	*5.6*
	14.6	14.6	14.6	15.5	15.9	15.9	15.9	17.5	17.5	18.5	18.5	19.3	19.3

West Bengal	10.4	7.4	11.6/11.1	11	11.6	11.3	11	10.6	11.4	12	11.2	10.7	NA
	11.1	*13.6*	*13.6/13.6*	*14.7*	*14.6*	*12.9*	*14.6*	*15*	*14.3*	*14*	*20*	*20*	
	20	20	20	20.5	21.5	21.5	21.5	23.6	23.6	25.3	25.3	27	

Source: SPINPER (The Social Profile of India's National and Provincial Elected Representatives) (1919–2019), CNRS, Sciences Po, Ashoka University and Bordeaux University.

N.B.: The percentage of Muslim candidates are in bold characters, that of Muslim MLAs in italics and the percentage of the Muslims in each state according to the Census preceding the election is below.

In some columns, there are two figures because there have been two elections during the period under review.

Lynch (1736–96) in America,[54] have acted as 'outlaw law enforcers' (to borrow a formula from Favarel-Garrigues and Gayer), whether they are self-defence groups or ideological militias and whether they set up people's courts or hand their victims over to the police. When they come from the ethnic majority and focus on cultural policing, these groups operate in two different ways: for one, vigilantes attack ethnic groups whose customs are perceived as deviant and/or who arouse fear among the local majority, and second, these same groups (and others) go after members of their own community on the pretence that they are betraying its traditions (be they religious, cultural, social or other) and must therefore be brought in line by force. In both cases, the method used involves a degree of physical and symbolic coercion.[55]

The RSS as a vigilante group?

Vigilantism is inherent in the mission that the Rashtriya Swayamsevak Sangh (RSS, National Volunteer Corps) assigned itself from its inception, its aim being to work at the grassroots level to organise the Hindus and defend their interests. The founder of RSS in 1925, K.B. Hedgewar, told the *Swayamsevaks* once: 'Remember, we have to organise the entire Hindu society from Kanyakumari to the Himalayas. In fact, our main area of operation is the vast Hindu world outside the Sangh.'[56] He developed the *shakha* technique to this society-oriented end, as *shakhas* are the local branches of the RSS where volunteers meet in uniform every day for physical and ideological training. Hedgewar's successor, M.S. Golwalkar, confirmed in the 1930s–40s that the RSS, in contrast to the Hindu Mahasabha of V.D. Savarkar, was not interested in playing a political game in order to conquer state power. In *We, or Our Nationhood Defined* (1938) he explains that the priority is to build the Hindu nation from below, not to capture the state: 'We are out to understand the Nationhood of Hindusthan, which done, all questions regarding the form of "state" shall be worth entrusting to the "Nation" as we find it to exist.'[57] To build this Hindu *Rashtra* primarily implied not only to persuade Hindu society to adhere to the worldview of Hindutva (including the interpretation of history and the depiction of the minorities propagated in the *shakhas*), but also to enforce traditional rites and practices.[58] One of the mainstays of this orthopraxy was the caste system, which Hindu nationalist ideologues defined on the basis of the antiquarian *Varna Vyavastha*. The most influential one, Deendayal Upadhyaya, emphasised the need to restore this organic social arrangement because in the Hindu 'concept of four castes, they are thought of as analogous to the different limbs of Virat-Purusha ... These limbs are not only complementary to one another, but even further, there is individuality, unity. There is a complete identity of interest, identity of belonging.'[59] To promote such unity, the RSS did not turn to the state which, according to Updhyaya, never played a major role in India's history: only a grassroots organisation like the RSS could achieve it in a long-term perspective.

While the RSS relied on social work and persuasion to implement this agenda, it never ruled out the use of constraint and violent means. In fact, the *Swayamsevaks* not only wore a paramilitary uniform and observed quasi-military discipline, but they were also trained to ply the *lathi* in the *shakhas*. This other face of the Janus-like organisation that is the RSS reflected another dimension of its mission:[60] it had to defend Hindus against other groups comprising Indian society, starting with the Muslims, and even the Hindus who would interfere with the organisation's agenda. This aspect of the RSS' story asserted itself at the time of crisis. After Partition, M.S. Golwalkar, leader of the RSS, gave an enlightening speech in this regard—transcribed by the intelligence services, whose report can be consulted at the Nehru Memorial and Museum Library:

> On 8.12.47 at 5 P.M. about 2500 volunteers of the Sangh collected in their camp on Rohtak Road. After some drill, M.S. Golwalkar, the Guru of the Sangh addressed the volunteers. He explained the principles of the Sangh and said that it was the duty of every individual to be prepared for facing the coming crises with full force. Very soon they would be placing a complete scheme before them. The time for mere playing had gone. Our volunteers should enrol new volunteers in every house, and should install in them the essence of Hinduism. Referring to the Government he said that law could not meet force. We should be prepared for guerilla warfare on the lines of the tactics of Shivaji. The Sangh will not rest content until it had finished Pakistan. If anyone stood in our way we will have to finish him too, whether it was Nehru Government or any other Government. The Sangh could not be won over. They should carry on their work. Referring to Muslims he said he had that no power on earth could keep them in Hindustan. They shall have to quit this country. Mahatma Gandhi wanted to keep the Muslims in India so that the Congress may profit by their votes at the time of election. But, by that time, not a single Muslim will be left in India. If they were made to stay here, the responsibility would be Government's, and the Hindu community would not be responsible. Mahatma Gandhi could not mislead them any longer. We have the means whereby such men can be immediately silenced, but it is our tradition not to be inimical to Hindus. If we are compelled, we will have to resort to that course too.
>
> After this the address finished and fruits were distributed among the volunteers and then the meeting dispersed.

No outsider was admitted into this meeting.[61]

Golwalkar's speech of 8 December 1947 in Delhi indicates the RSS modus operandi. Its preferred method was to win over Hindu minds by persuasion. This approach, which dates back to the movement's inception, is revealing of its agenda in terms of societal and cultural transformation from below and shows that the conquest of state power was not its priority. But the movement has displayed a tendency to fight Muslims physically, to show its strength to Hindu opponents and to stand up against the government if it tries to get in its way, particularly when the organisation targeted Muslims. Golwalkar made clear that following the establishment of Pakistan, India had to be rid of them. Violence, however, was legitimate not only against Muslims, but also against all those protecting them—such as Mahatma Gandhi, whom Golwalkar claimed was motivated by petty electoral intentions.

Gandhi's assassination in January 1948, as it happens, would prompt the RSS leader to alter his course of action. After the government banned the RSS in reaction to the assassination, Golwalkar tended to confine the movement to its initial repertoire of action—conquering Hindu minds by active persuasion—so as to prevent it from being outlawed, which would have had disastrous effects. RSS chiefs had to negotiate twice with the government for having a ban lifted, in 1948–49 (successfully) and 1975–76 (unsuccessfully).[62] But the use of force remained an option. Starting in the 1980s, the RSS began to outsource coercive action to some of its affiliates, in particular the Bajrang Dal, so as not to put the parent organisation in the front line.[63] But they remained cautious because the state could still intervene against them, like in 1992, when the VHP and the Bajrang Dal were banned in the wake of the demolition of the Babri Masjid.

Since 2014, the RSS' activation of its militias has entered a new phase owing to the state protection it enjoys, as seen in the tacit agreement, when not the active participation, of the police during operations against minorities conducted by these militias—which, as a result, tend to become quasi state actors.

In the social science literature on vigilantism, the relationship between state authority and vigilante groups is subject to intense discussion.[64] Some authors, such as Les Johnston, define vigilantism as a citizens' movement whose actions are undertaken without the state's authority or support.[65] Others, such as R.M. Brown[66] and R. Abrahams,[67] do not rule out the existence of ties between such groups and state institutions, starting with the police. The motivations behind these relationships can vary in nature: ideological affinity, convergence of interests, compliance with a political diktat when rulers impose biased behaviour on law enforcement, and so on. Such dynamics can lead to establishing a continuum (the police outsources its dirty work to vigilantes) or overlapping functions (men in uniform assist vigilantes in the field or join them when their workday is finished). The variety of interpretations partly reflects the diversity of practices, as some vigilantes take the law into their own hands (historically, this is the case especially in the United States), whereas others simply turn their prey in to the police. Moreover, not only is the state not a monolith, but within an institution such as the police, the lower echelons sometimes act with considerable autonomy.

In the case of India after 2014, I will argue that the converging interests and concerns of the RSS and the BJP government explain the rise of Hindu vigilantism: on one hand, the government remained 'clean', exterior to illegal forms of cultural policing of society which were in tune with its ideology, and on the other, the Sangh Parivar could resort to its favourite modus operandi for disciplining society, at the grassroots level, without fearing state intervention.[68]

Between 2014 and 2019, the Parivar launched various types of campaigns—first in succession and then largely overlapping—against what the movement has named 'love Jihad', against conversions to Islam and Christianity, against Muslim occupation of the urban space (also known as 'Land Jihad') and against cow slaughter, of which Muslims were also the primary victims. Each time, more or less ad hoc groups in the RSS nexus have been found in the front lines and have enjoyed state protection, if not help from the police. Evidence of this will be shown by focusing on the first and the last of these campaigns.

Resisting 'Love Jihad'

The first campaign in this series set out to resist so-called Love Jihad, in other words a strategy allegedly deployed by Muslims to woo young Hindu women.[69] According to adherents to Hindutva, this strategy involves marrying these women with the aim to convert them. In September 2014, a few months after Modi was voted into office, two weekly magazines put out by the RSS, one in English, *The Organiser*, the other in Hindi, *Panchjanya*, devoted their cover stories to 'Love Jihad', one showing the photo of a Hindu 'victim', the other an Arab wearing a keffiyeh and dark glasses beneath which read the title, '*Pyar andha ya dhanda?*' (Is love blind or is it a business?).[70] *The Organiser* in particular explained, 'There are examples of feigning love, followed by devastating tales of pain, suffering, blackmailing and torture for conversion.'[71]

In reaction to what the Hindu nationalists presented as a dire threat to the survival of their community, they launched a counter-offensive that involved forming special groups such as the *Hindu Behen Beti Bachao Sangharsh Samiti* (Save Hindu sisters and daughters committees). Activists offered to help parents who lamented their daughter's marriage to a Muslim, but they sometimes also undertook pre-emptive action owing to a vast network of informers in police stations and courts where parents might go to report a missing daughter (when she runs away to marry) or file a complaint for abduction. Once on a case, warriors against Love Jihad resorted to all sorts of methods, ranging from disinformation to intimidation to coercion. Their methods were revealed by journalists for two investigative news websites, *Cobrapost* and *Gulail.com*. Posing as students sympathetic to the Hindu nationalist cause, they recorded their conversations with activists using hidden cameras.

According to these investigations, the first task of the Hindu nationalists was to convince young Hindu women—whom they systematically claimed were 'vulnerable'—to go back on their decision to marry a Muslim. Sangeet Som, a BJP MLA from Sardhana, in the district of Muzaffarnagar (Uttar Pradesh), emphasises the importance of moral pressure on each young woman targeted:

> We make her see the reason that this is not good for her. We tell her that they are Muslims, they never settle for one woman, whereas a Hindu boy will be automatically sent to jail if he does so. On the other hand, a Muslim can marry up to four women and those women can adjust among themselves. [...] Most importantly we exert on her emotionally (saying) that her mother will die, her father will die and brother might even commit suicide as he would not be able to face the society.[72]

If persuasion failed, other techniques were brought to bear. An RSS leader from Muzaffarnagar, Omkar Singh, thus described how he 'rescued 125 girls "from the clutches of Muslims" and remarried them to Hindu men. Usually, a rape and kidnapping case is filed against the Muslim youth with whom she has eloped.'[73] As the accusations are entirely fabricated, vigilantes need testimony from the women who have married, dated, or eloped with Muslims in order to press charges against the young men. Sanjay Agarwal, a Hindu activist who ran in the Muzaffarnagar municipal elections under the BJP banner in 2014, admitted to having forced false testimony out of a Hindu girl who was going out with a Muslim boy so as to file fake rape and kidnapping charges against him.[74]

Hindu nationalists claim to be working with the police throughout the entire process, but it is when the time comes to collect false testimony that collaboration with the police is the most essential. Agarwal explains that if a girl is not prepared to give false testimony, then:

> We don't let the girl appear in court for days. We say that the girl is not listening. They [police] say it's alright, we will see her tomorrow. If she isn't listening even tomorrow, they say it's alright. They help us a lot. They send her mother to us to talk. We are not allowed to do that. They help us a lot. Judges help us, so does the SSP (senior superintendent of police) [...] The judge gives the girl to us in his judgment. He hands her over to her parents. Once she is under her parents' control, we can get her married in three days.[75]

Militant Hindu nationalists and policemen work together not only to combat 'love jihad'. Collusion has been even closer in the cow protection campaign.

Attacking Muslims in the name of cow protection

The sacred cow is an identity symbol that Hindu defence organisations have used to galvanise crowds since the nineteenth century. In the 1950s, the Jana Sangh, precursor of the BJP, campaigned for a ban on cow slaughter. Several states passed such laws, in most cases at the Congress' initiative. When the BJP came to power, it systematically made them more stringent, as seen in the laws passed in 2015 in Haryana and in Maharashtra after the party took the helm of their state governments.

Over and above this new legislation, the cow has become the focus of intense activism on the part of Hindu vigilantes who have made protection of this sacred animal the centrepiece of their anti-Muslim agenda. The issue is well chosen, as not only can they accuse Muslims of eating bovines and offering them in sacrifice during the Eid celebration, but some Muslims ply the trade of butcher. Breeders, who are greater in numbers, are even more targeted than butchers, however.

Between 2015 and 2017, northern India was the theatre of a series of lynchings of Muslims, following a near identical pattern each time: the Muslims accused of cattle smuggling or consuming beef were attacked and, in dozens of cases, died of their wounds. The series began with the murder of Mohammad Akhlaq on 28 September 2015 in Dadri, a village in Gautam Buddha Nagar district, located in Uttar Pradesh, but adjacent to the state of Delhi. That day, a group of young Hindus gathered near Akhlaq's house at 10 p.m. Among them was the son of the local BJP leader and his cousin. The mob talked the temple priest into announcing over the loudspeaker that Akhlaq ate beef. They stormed his house and exhibited meat taken from his refrigerator, claiming it was beef. Akhlaq was savagely beaten and later died of his injuries in hospital in Noida, while his son, Danish, who had intervened, was grievously wounded.[76]

The lynching of Pehlu Khan is sadly even more typical. Khan, a breeder specialised in dairy cows, was on his way home to Haryana after having purchased cattle in Rajasthan when his truck was intercepted on National Highway 8. Some fifty Hindu youths forcibly searched it, accusing him of taking his animals to slaughter. He produced proof that his activity was perfectly legal, including the sales receipt showing he had paid 50,000 rupees for the cow, and was therefore unlikely to sell it for 6,000 rupees for butcher meat. He was nevertheless beaten severely, as were his sons. He died shortly thereafter, but not before giving the police the name of his assailants when they arrived on the scene, but the police never troubled the suspects.[77]

Muslim cattle transporters (who sometimes raised cattle as well) have become favourite targets for self-appointed Hindu nationalist cow protectors. Others have been lynched in Rajasthan,[78] West Bengal,[79] Assam,[80] Haryana,[81] Jharkhand, and so on.[82] The phenomenon took on such proportions that it ended up becoming banal[83] and certain publications compiled databases. IndiaSpend[84] estimates that in 2017 there were 34 bovine-related incidents, compared to 25 in 2016, 13 in 2015, 3 in 2014, 1 in 2013 and 1 in 2012. Twenty-four out of the twenty-eight victims during the period ending in June 2017 were Muslim.[85]

Press reports often present these lynchings as spontaneous reactions of the mob. Certainly, some ordinary people took part in them—and the Hindutva forces cultivate the dominant narrative according to which society itself is defending its values. But the perpetrators' ideological orientation could be surmised from the fact that they often insisted that their victims shout '*Gau Mata ki Jai*' (Hail the cow-mother!') or '*Jai Hanuman!*' (Hail Hanuman!),[86] slogans which are dear to the Sangh Parivar. That the choice of victims for assault had less to do with cow protection than with underlying hostility toward Muslims is clear in the way Hindu cow breeders and transporters were spared—like Pehlu Khan's truck driver who got away with merely being slapped, whereas the others, all Muslims, were beaten (one of them to death) for the same 'crime'.[87] More importantly, most of the lynchings noted between 2015 and 2017 were perpetrated by vigilante militias or were the result of the atmosphere they created.

The most visible Hindu nationalist organisation in this domain, the Gau Raksha Dal (GRD—The Cow Protection Association), has chapters in

Punjab, Uttar Pradesh, Rajasthan, Himachal Pradesh, Gujarat, Madhya Pradesh, Maharashtra, Goa, Delhi and Haryana. In Punjab, one of the movement's strongholds where it claims 5,000 activists, the GRD emblem is none other than a cow's head flanked by two AK-47s. Elsewhere, daggers replace firearms on the movement's coat of arms. In practice, its members use cruder instruments: cricket bats, hockey sticks, *lathis*, and so on.

The organisation works in close conjunction with the police, as a body of investigative reporting has revealed. Ishan Marvel, in *The Caravan*, recounts how he managed to be accepted into a GRD group in Haryana patrolling the highway linking Chandigarh and Delhi. Armed with field hockey sticks, *gau rakshaks* (cow protectors) search trucks likely to be transporting cows and beat up the drivers when they are Muslim (Hindus merely receive a reprimand). The GRD existed before the BJP came to power in Haryana in 2014,[88] but the situation changed in 2015 with the formation of the new government and the passing of a law making cow slaughter and sale of beef non-bailable offences:[89] the GRD's schemes were no longer considered illegal—and even if they still acted illegally, the authorities did not find fault with them. On the contrary. In practice, the GRD and the police have arrived at a division of labour. Ishan Marvel explains that the night he joined the *gau rakshaks* for their nocturnal highway patrol—on the pretence of helping them—their SUV was already parked near police vehicles. One of the policemen (who preferred not to be named) explained to Marvel:

> We put up checkpoints and wait. The volunteers—the GRD vigilantes—keep driving around, and call us when they find something. See, we have a hundred other things to think of beside cows. These guys do the job. It's good, right? Prashasan bhi poora saath de raha hai ab—now, the administration is also supporting them fully.[90]

In fact, during their patrol, one of the 'volunteers' described how the 'beef ban' law passed by the new BJP government of Haryana in 2015 had changed their activity: 'Before the BJP brought in the new law against cow-slaughter, the vehicles were returned to the owners. So we used to get angry and burn the trucks. Now, we don't have to. The vehicles become government property. So we just hand them over to the police.'[91] One of the leaders even declared, 'The Chief Minister is happy with our work, and we have his blessings and full support.'[92]

The osmosis between vigilante groups and the state goes well beyond this. The president of the Haryana branch of the GRD, Yogendra Arya, who is also national vice-president of the GRD, sits on the board of the Gau Seva Aayog, a Haryana government institution devoted to cow welfare—along with ten other people who like him are longstanding members of the Sangh Parivar, including the chairman, Bhani Ram Mangla.[93] Some of these people are at the interface of the GRD and the state. There is a continuum between the two, so much so that this vigilante group is a quasi-state actor. Arya himself outlines the terms of GRD collaboration with the authorities: 'We have a huge network of volunteers and informants. [...] As soon as someone sees something fishy, they call us up, and we then inform the volunteers of the relevant district, and the local police, who then set up joint nakas—checkpoints—to catch the smugglers'. He added that GRD activists usually reach the spot before the police. 'Police can't do what we do, they have to follow the laws. They don't have the resources and network we have,' he said. 'Besides, our boys work with great religious zeal.'[94] The GRD thus acts as a community cultural police, with its members closely monitoring the deeds of those who deserve not only to be reported, but also to receive the punishment meted out by them.[95]

In Haryana, the convergence of two types of policing—unofficial and official—was strengthened by the creation of a 'cow task force' within the state police force itself. A female police officer, Bharti Arora, from the Indian Police Service was appointed to head this network, which now has specialised officers in each district. These officials work together with the GRD, deeming that they outsource the most thankless tasks to the organisation, as a local policeman admitted: 'There are uncountable trucks. Who can check them all? So, we provide supervision while the GRD boys use their fervour to do the job.'[96] In some respects, the state subcontracts policing tasks to non-state actors, turning them into a para-state force.

The other Indian state that criminalised beef consumption by law in 2015, Maharashtra, took even more radical steps: the state government appointed Honorary Animal Welfare Officers to implement this new law, hiring former *gau rakshaks* for these jobs.[97] They now have an official status with which to undertake their activities.[98] Never has the lack of distinction between non-state actors and government authorities been so great, in spite of the fact that the former sometimes indulge in clearly illegal activities: not only is the role devolved to *gau rakshaks* to enforce laws against cow slaughter illegal, but these activists have also gone after Muslim breeders who had no intention of slaughtering their animals or who were transporting poultry or sheep. They aim to impose vegetarianism in defiance of the law.[99] Beyond that, such activists sometimes prefer extortion to the purity propounded by their leaders: instead of confiscating the transporter's cargo, they extract payment of often very large sums of money.[100] Satish Kumar, who was at the helm of the Punjab chapter of the GRD is a case in point. Because of this kind of people, Narendra Modi, in early August 2016, broke the silence he was observing till then on any vigilante act. He 'urge(d) the state governments to prepare a dossier on such self-proclaimed volunteers and big cow protectors. It will be found that 70 to 80 per cent are such people who commit such bad deeds which society does not accept. To hide their bad activities, they don the mantle of cow protectors.'[101] Soon after, on 20 August, Satish Kumar was arrested for 'rioting, extortion and unnatural sex' (because he had been accused of sodomy).[102] Modi was immediately criticised by the RSS[103] and *gau rakhshaks*. Some of the GRD leaders even composed a poem saying:

> The hopes of one billion people
> Got you the PM's seat
> The country's cow-devotees
> Had all put in the effort
> There is still time, apologise
> Or else, from the country's throne
> Now you shall be uprooted.[104]

Modi, corrected himself immediately, replacing the previous figures ('70 to 80%') he had mentioned by 'a handful'.[105] A couple of months later, Mohan Bhawgat, the chief of the RSS congratulated the *gau rakshaks* for their action during his annual speech on the occasion of the Hindu festival of Vijaydashami.[106] This episode is revealing of the balance of power between official and unofficial power centres which, usually, work together but epitomise two faces of the state.

From the building of the Indian state to the formation of a Hindu *Rashtra*

Since 2014, Hindu militias and the BJP government have triggered a new dynamic in the relationship between state building and state formation, as defined by Bruce Berman and John Lonsdale. These authors aptly distinguish the formation of the state as a social institution and state building as an administrative process.[107] Reasoning solely in terms of state building, as we usually do, tends to reduce power relations to official agents and their actions. Berman and Lonsdale's analysis, on the other hand, takes into account the role of private actors in their understanding of state trajectories. As the authors point out all kinds of groups systematically work their way into the process of state formation to exert some authority through a process that they call the 'vulgarisation of power', which involves commandeering public authority to further private ends.[108] This approach has obvious heuristic advantages for the analysis of Hindu vigilante groups and their relationship to the state. It helps to put the *prima facie* anti-state aspect of these private armies in perspective and to consider their contribution to state formation through two different modes and in two opposite directions: on one hand, violence is outsourced to 'society' by certain state building-related actors, including the police and politicians; and on the other, these state patronages are flaunted by violence entrepreneurs for ideological or economic ends.

Collusion between the police and Hindu nationalist movements is indeed evidence of the start of a transition from a state-building process, in which the administrative and coercive apparatus is supposed to treat all citisens equally, to a state-formation process through which the social and cultural order is imposed by non-state actors. What adds a layer of complexity to Berman and Lonsdale's model is the fact that these non-state actors enjoy the protection of state-builders because of ideological affinities and enjoy also some support from society in the majoritarian logic: while the authority the cow vigilantes are exercising is illegal, it is nevertheless legitimate in that it is inspired by the values and interests of the dominant community to which the BJP government is accountable. In that sense, the Sangh Parivar is more India's deep state than a parallel government, all the more so as the BJP is part of the Parivar. This shift from a neutral state to an ideological Hindu *Rashtra* well illustrates a form of violent majoritarianism that can be observed in all countries where vigilantes bring minorities to heel with the more or less tacit agreement of shadow forces that share their biases if not their ideology (the relationship between white militias and the police in the United States could provide other examples).

However, India's case is specific[109] because non-state actors impose not only their religious norms on religious minorities, but also their social norms on 'deviant' individuals in their community—such as young women who seek to marry outside their religion or even outside their caste. This reflects the initial RSS project: the militias in charge of cultural policing help to bring about a Hindu nation primarily based on social structures drawing from the sources of Hindu orthopraxy.

The Hindu *Rashtra* is therefore indeed underway. This label in fact perfectly describes the ambivalence of the process at stake as 'Hindu *Rashtra*' refers as much to a people united by blood ties, a culture and community codes as to a political framework; it is at once a society, a civilisation, a nation and a state. In this way, the Sangh Parivar's work partakes of a new formation of the state, the formation of a *de facto* if not a *de jure* Hindu Rashtra on the basis of an unofficial, societal type of regulation benefitting from the protection of the state building-related institutions.

Conclusion

Over the past five years, India has moved further away from the multicultural model set forth in its secular constitution. While its prescriptions have never been followed to the letter, as seen in the underrepresentation of minorities—Muslims in particular—in the administration, the police and the military, as of 2014, Muslims also began to vanish from elected assemblies, where this minority is hardly represented anymore.

Not only are Muslims marginalised in major institutions and the public sphere, but they are targeted by Hindu nationalist militias as well. These groups are trying to rid the public space of this minority by (re)converting its members to the dominant religion, preventing them from praying in the open and prohibiting them from acquiring real estate in mixed residential areas. They are also trying to cut the majority community off from the Muslim minority by preventing interfaith marriages. Over and beyond this, the vigilantes attack Muslims, accusing them of eating beef or taking cows to slaughter, which is against the law. Not only do these accusations sometimes result in perfectly illegal lynchings, but in many cases vigilantes also enjoy police protection.

The fact that vigilantes and police work hand in glove has several explanations. Firstly, not only is Muslim presence in the police very weak, but also, Hindu nationalists endeavour to infiltrate this pillar of law enforcement. A BJP Member of the Legislative Council (upper house of a state legislature) from Karnataka interviewed by *Cobrapost* and *Gulail.com* journalists at party headquarters in Mangalore thus explained, 'We have tried to send some of our boys into police. When I talk to students I tell them to join the police. So, when we need help there are a lot of karyakartas [militants of the] [RSS]. Sixty percent of the young constables are our students.'[110] Secondly, while the conduct of Hindu militias is illegal, they enjoy a degree of legitimacy in the eyes of the majority because they claim that they are acting in defence of the dominant religion. Thirdly, and correlatively, vigilantes enjoy popular support and neutralise opponents, not only because they promote Hinduism, but also because of their sense of organisation, their penetration of society and the weapons they carry. Sangeet Som, mentioned above, thus explains:

This is Hindustan and it does not matter which party is running the govern-ment. In a democratic country like this, there are many other ways to get things done. The police know it well that we will do picketing, hold demonstration and all this will lead to rioting. So, they perforce co-operate with us.[111]

This ability to enforce its version of the law no matter what party is in power, and thus independently from the state, demonstrates the success of the RSS project, which since 1925, has endeavoured to win Hindu society over to its cause rather than to conquer political power directly. The attitude of those in government is of course important, but more than anything else, the RSS expects them not to interfere with its work and even to facilitate it. It does not expect the state to operate in its stead, as no state can transform minds from above. That is a long-term task that can only be accomplished through action at the grassroots level—and which is compatible with a cer-tain form of democracy.

In Som's above-quoted remarks, he indeed speaks of India's democratic nature as a good thing. The country can thus continue to enjoy a positive image abroad, and majority rule—at the heart of the democratic system—is naturally appreciated by proponents of Hindu majoritarianism.[112] Once the majority is won over to Hindutva, its champions are bound to benefit from this regime. This is indeed the position of proponents of an ethnic democracy, a concept I will return to in closing this chapter.

This notion is a contradiction in terms because it divides the 'demos' into two categories: some citizens do not have the same rights as others simply because of their faith. But majority communities living in ethnic democracies do not see things this way. Israeli Jews, for instance, claim to support the prin-ciples of democracy, as the supreme court moreover stated in a 1988 decision denying the right of the Progressive List for Peace to participate in elections because the party refused to recognise Israel as a Jewish state in essence: 'there is no contradiction whatsoever between these two things: The state is the state of the Jews, while its regime is an enlightened democratic regime that accords rights to all citizens, Jews and non-Jews.'[113] The judges even went so far as to consider that 'the existence of the State of Israel as a Jewish state does not negate its democratic nature, any more than the Frenchness of France contra-dicts its democratic nature.'[114]

This approach does not pertain only to institutions, as, according to Smooha, 'Jewish public opinion not only condones constraints imposed on Arabs, but also endorses preferential treatment of Jews.'[115] An opinion poll taken in 1995 among Israeli Jews showed that 74.1 per cent of them expected the state to give Jews preferential treatment over Arabs—who, for 30.9 per cent of the respondents, should not even have the right to vote, or be hired in civil service jobs according to 32.2 per cent.[116] Smooha adds, underscoring the scope of the problem: 'Most Jews do not even perceive the above differential practices as discriminatory against Arabs, but consider them rather as preferences rightfully accorded to them as Jews in a Jewish state.'[117]

Paradoxically, Smooha concludes, 'The Israeli case demonstrates the viability of an ethnic democracy as a distinct type of democracy in deeply divided societies.'[118] He considers on the whole that, 'As a mode of conflict regulation, it is superior to genocide, ethnic cleansing, involuntary population transfer and systems of non-democratic domination.'[119]

Such an approach resonates as an invitation to minorities to accept a status as dominated, second-class citizens—the plea of Arabs of Israel. In India, a similar evolution may one day result in constitutional amendments transforming a *de facto* Hindu *Rashtra* into a *de jure* one.

3

IMMORAL TIMES

VIGILANTISM IN A SOUTH INDIAN CITY

Ian M. Cook

On the evening of 28 July 2012 activists belonging to the nationalist militant group Hindu Jagarana Vedike (HJV) stormed the Morning Mist homestay at the edge of Mangalore, a smaller city in coastal southern Karnataka. The HJV found seven men and five women, all unmarried, who were celebrating a birthday party. The vigilantes had been alerted by locals, some of whom had previously complained about loud 'rave parties' and drinking taking place in the homestay. Upon entering the property, the attackers beat and partially stripped the party goers before locking some of them in one of the rooms, sporadically hitting them as they awaited the arrival of the police.

A journalist was tipped off about the attack, and his video of women in 'western' clothes and shirtless men attempting to cover their faces whilst fending off blows made Mangalore the topic of national and regional news for a few days. The morality of Mangaloreans—both the attackers and the attacked—became a discussion point well beyond the city limits. The Hindu nationalist Bharatiya Janata Party (BJP) was at the time in power at the federal state level and the then chairperson of the Karnataka State Women's Commission, C. Manjula, suggested that the birthday party was in fact a rave with drugs and trafficked women.

After the event, the local organisation Forum Against Atrocities on Women produced a fact-finding report in English, gathering statements from those at the party and their parents.[1] One of the men whose birthday it was describes the attack:

> At that time I heard loud noises downstairs. The girls were screaming in confusion. I came outside. All of them were hitting the girls. By the time I started climbing downstairs, around 5 or 6 people were behind me. I ran upstairs and closed the door behind me. They broke open the door, pulled me out, stamped me, pulled off my tee shirt and gave me a good beating. Then they brought me down. All this is not shown in the video. Even downstairs they gave me a good beating. I said, 'This is my and her birthday. This is not a rave party.' They said, 'you are celebrating a rave party' and started abusing me using bad words. They pulled off the girls' clothes and fingered their bodies.
>
> The camera-man was familiar by sight. I asked him, 'Don't you know me?' He did not say anything. 3 or 4 more people came and started beating me. 'Do you need only girls to celebrate your party?' they asked me. They locked me in the room to the right and took photographs of me. The girls' dresses were torn. I did not have my tee shirt. They made me sit on the bed and took photographs of me. Till then no policemen had arrived there. For 10 to 15 minutes they had been beating us.[2]

The above-mentioned journalist described the immediate aftermath:

> Shocked by the events inside, I had stepped out for a breather. I saw...the area Corporator [local politician] talking to others in the group of aggressors in the compound, right in front of the house. After the assailants had completed one stage of their planned action... [the police] arrived at the spot.... Whenever the police is called to attend to a group that is unruly it arrives carrying *lathis* [long wooden canes]. But this group of policemen did not carry a single *lathi*. It appeared as though the police had had previous contact with the assailants. For over half an hour the police were immersed in conversation with the assailants. I was surprised that the policemen instead of arresting the attackers were conversing with them. Even the Corporator...was part of the group, apparently taking pride in the actions of the assailants. While they were conversing, one of the boys who had been present at the party tried to escape but was caught by the police. The assailants thrashed this boy in the presence of the police.[3]

Aside from the fear and shock, the statements reveal a sense of smaller city intimacy, and a seemingly close relationship between the attackers, the policemen and the local elected representative. The attackers (and the journalist) were eventually arrested and jailed, and locals, including many students, held a series of protests against the attacks and the government's response in the weeks that followed.[4]

After the protests the Forum Against Atrocities on Women received a typed letter in English through the post:

My Dear So Called Women Protector,

...You have a lot of concern to women. You have full confidence your boys and girls in Morning Mist enjoying Bday party with least or no dress, of course per your they have the right to do whatever they want. Bloody because of you people these things happen and you provoke Sangh Parivar [family of Hindu nationalist groups] people and boys with hot blood will sure attack and trash. You people too deserve that sooner or later. Don't think you have huge support. This is Mangalore dear madams remember. We will not hide or hesitate to act. Please stop your ugly comments and activities inside four walls. Otherwise you too get same treatment however without media. This is warning to each one of you and think about this. You will better stop all your anti hindu activity before you realize the taste of slap or something else which will be done in well planned manner.

FROM SANGH PARIVAR[5]

It is important not to overstate the importance of this particular event. It was just one of many incidents termed 'moral policing' in India, where vigilante groups attempt to ethically discipline others, often with violence or threats.[6] Mangalore, since renamed Mangaluru, has become famous for such moments of moral policing. The three most well-known cases are the Morning Mist homestay attack,[7] the 'pub attack' in 2009,[8] in which a group of women who had met in a city-centre bar were assaulted, and finally an attack in 2015 when a Muslim man was stripped and tied to a post in the street, before being whipped for allegedly trying to seduce his female Hindu colleague.[9] These cases gained traction in the wider public's imagination, in part, because they were all filmed, but they were not particularly shocking to locals for whom news of such acts is fairly common. For instance one analysis of newspaper reports reveal forty-five instances in seven months in the district,[10] whilst another analysis of 'communal incidents' includes a breakdown of moral policing: 17 cases in 2010, 31 (2011), 34 (2012), 46 (2013), 53 (2014), 47 (2015), 22 (2016), 23 (2017).[11] Such moral policing is not the exclusive preserve of Hindu outfits, with both Muslim and Christian groups attempting to control the behaviour of those in their community (for instance cases of Muslim moral policing accounted for a third or more of instances each year between 2013–15 and there are complaints relating to pressured conversions by some

Christian groups), however Hindu vigilantism has asserted itself as a powerful structurer within Mangalorean society.

Amongst most locals I spoke with who complained loudly about 'communalism', the obvious, commonly applied, and yet misplaced analysis has been to suggest that the rise of vigilante attacks is a direct consequence of the electoral success of the increasingly Hindu majoritarian BJP under Narendra Modi, especially since he led the party to victory at the centre in 2014.[12] In recent years there have been a number of high-profile attacks against those accused of eating beef or transporting cows, and against those accused of 'love jihad' (the supposed phenomena in which Muslim men seduce Hindu women with the aim of conversion). Modi and other BJP leaders have remained silent in the aftermath of the attacks, leading many to suggest that they enable a climate within which such attacks take place. However, to not look beyond this is to ignore deep-rooted tendencies for mob violence as a competing claim of sovereignty in India,[13] skip over the times when the centrist Indian National Congress (henceforth referred to as Congress Party) has operationalised communal violence for its own ends, and apportion immense power to actions in a narrowly defined political realm—suggesting that the Prime Minister can affect law and order across state federal lines with immense ease—something that glosses over incidents that happen when the BJP is not in power at the federal state or central level or the complex ways in which politics and public debate take place in India. Political actors do, of course, ferment and shape communal incidents like moral policing, not least because they help stoke the emotionally and morally contoured public manifestations of outrage, which have a long history in India as both an affective and often effective way of engaging in the public sphere.[14] What this all suggests is that we must look beyond electoral politics when trying to understand this articulation of cultural policing.

One other possible way of situating these attacks would be to view them within majoritarian sacred claims over national space. Satish Deshpande has argued that through 'spatial strategies'—such as the destruction of the Babri *masjid* (mosque) in Uttar Pradesh or the fight over raising a flag over Idgah Maidan (open space) in Hubli-Dharward in northern Karnataka—groups have attempted to construct a Hindu geography into the national space.[15] They have found room to manoeuvre, he goes on to argue, in the gaps left by a waning Nehruvian economic nationalism: the planned economies of the decades following independence, where hegemonic notions of national 'socialist' secular development temporarily displaced religious claims from the public sphere. If we accept this argument however, then we must also accept that such an analysis is as much about time as it is about space. Yes, Hindutva-inspired groups are staking claim to spaces in cities and pilgrimage sites as part of a wider claim over the national space, but they do so with the temporal assertion that now is their moment.

This assertion feeds from the economic changes wrought over the last three decades, though of course has an older and independent history. There is a narrative that in 1991, when India took its neoliberal economic turn, the country was 'unbound', finally set free from socialist constraints,[16] allowing it to develop from its dark past into its 'shining' present,[17] finally arriving on the global stage as an enterprising, prosperous and technologically adept country.[18] This economic 'freedom' saw a concomitant rejection of secularism and rise of Hindu assertion by groups inspired by or involving members of the Rashtriya Swayamsevak Sangh (RSS)—from the militant Bajrang Dal to the mainstream political manoeuvres of the BJP. The state-led development programme of the secular Congress Party-led governments had failed, they claimed, and it was now time for an unabashedly Hindu majoritarian market-led country. As such 'Hindu assertion...is deeply connected with structural transformation and new modes of social aspiration. It reflects not only a changing alignment of upwardly mobile and dominant classes. It also points to a reaction against the erstwhile paradigm of postcolonial development, a paradigm that buckled under the pressures it was subject to.'[19]

However, the joint rise of Hindu nationalism and increasing pro-market/anti-state policies in India has a complicated relationship that goes back to before the watershed moment of 1991. The relationship is both occasionally complementary and occasionally contradictory, but always, I suggest, with the need to order and control not far from the surface. The upper middle classes and elites started to fear the way the state changed in the 1970s; it moved from being one in which 'democracy and secularism meant protection and extension of social privileges to the educated Hindu middle classes, and condescending paternalism vis-à-vis lower-caste groups and minorities', to one in which popular figures from poor backgrounds could gain mass followings through the amoral vocation of politics, and thus 'the "softness" of the secular state became the target of the Hindu nationalist critique of a "pseudo secularism" that was "pampering minorities"'.[20] Hindu nationalism offered an order against the disorder of a state captured by subaltern elements.[21] More recently, the BJP has garnered immense electoral support amongst the elite and aspirant sections of the 'middle classes' by projecting themselves as CEO-type governors, free from the corrupt politics of the Congress party.[22]

Neoliberalism and right-wing Hindu nationalism further complement one another as they both see divisions within society as unnecessary, if not pathological, and create bounded internal and external realms (e.g. the Muslim other, or the welfare agency) in their rhetoric of ongoing revolutionary transformation.[23] However, and here we turn towards the source of trouble on Mangaluru's streets, whereas the individualism celebrated by economic liberalism offers 'freedom' (whilst holding the market supreme and punishing those who disrupt it), the individual within a majoritarian vision is always subordinated to the good of the Hindu community.[24] This entwines with a perceived loss of national sovereignty with the deepening penetration of global capital, leading to attempts at controlling 'national culture', more often than not in ways that uphold rigid conceptions of gender and sexual identities.[25]

As such, and as I will detail below, there is an ethical tension at the heart of this Hindu majoritarian and market-led development project: the continuing 'opening-up' of the Indian economy has also opened up ethical questions. The same groups who celebrate 'India's moment' after centuries of national impediment due to Muslim, colonial and then 'socialist' rule are also often those who are deeply troubled by the effects of these changes in terms of cultural purity, gender norms, and youthful experimentation. Moral policing, I argue, is one of the ways in which this ethical tension reveals itself. I will make this argument based on material gathered during twenty months of ethnographic fieldwork undertaken between 2011–16.[26]

Ill-disciplined times

Every now and again I played cricket (badly), with a group of young men from the neighbourhood where I lived in Mangalore. Once in a while I used to stay and chat with Lokesh, a college educated man a bit younger than myself. During the time I knew him he was in the process of sitting entrance exams at different companies around the city. He was always forthright with his opinions, whatever we talked about. I always thought he found me naïve, no matter if I was deliberately trying to be naïve or not.

Once some girls were staring at us as we stood talking. 'It's a pity you're married', he said, 'the way all these girls look at you.'

'They only stare at me because I'm big and white. Like seeing something in the zoo. Anyway', I ventured, 'Indian girls aren't so forward.'

'Ho! Let me tell you about Indian girls!' he stopped me. 'Today, it's a fashion for girls to have sex. A trend. Girls want to have sex, or go around telling people they are having sex.'

'You know', he went on to say after a moment of pause 'girlfriends are too expensive, you have to spend money on them. Taking them to the cinema and so on.'

Talk of the cinema brought up an act of moral policing that had taken place earlier in the week. Members of the Bajrang Dal had stormed a local multiplex where, in their words, 'a Hindu girl was doing "bad things" with two Muslim boys'. They beat up the trio with glass soda bottles, filming the event on their mobile phones. It turns out Lokesh was in the cinema at the same time and saw the attack. I was a little surprised when he told me that he thought it was right for the group 'to intervene, but not to thrash girls... [Because] we don't want Hindu girls going around flirting here and there. We don't want to have American culture, where a girl can spend two days with one guy and then two days later switch.' Lokesh's general opinion on moral policing was representative of many people that I spoke with. Such people would say that the violence was 'bad' or 'too much', especially against the girls, however, in general it was good that someone stopped the immoral behaviour. For instance, the most commonly voiced opinion about the Homestay Attack—the above-mentioned incident where young people were attacked at a birthday party in a lodge—was that hitting the girls was wrong, but if it was a birthday party, then why weren't the parents there?! Lokesh's approval of the attacks had surprised me, because I had wrongly put him into the category of those young students who embraced and celebrated the rapid changes the city was undergoing.

Mangaluru has been a port for millennia, and thus has long entertained outside populations and large numbers of religious minorities. Demographically, the city region shares similarities with the state of Kerala to the south: most inhabitants are Hindu (69 per cent), but there are sizable Muslim (17 per cent) and Christian (13 per cent) communities. However, it is also a culturally secluded area, surrounded by hills to the east, the sea to the west and different cultural-linguistic regions to the north and south. A majority of the Hindu population consider themselves Tuluva, and thus do not speak the state language of Kannada as their mother tongue, but rather Tulu, and have distinct religious, cultural and social traditions such as matrilineal inheritance and *bhuta* (spirit) worship. The largest *jati* (caste) group is Billava (estimated around 18 per cent in the wider Tulu region) and though they had untouchability practiced against them in the past (their *jati* profession is toddy tapping), they are a strong and upwardly mobile group. The traditional feudal landowners in the district, Bunts—sometimes referred to as 'Shettys' due to the prominence of the surname amongst the community—did lose some influence after the land reforms of the 1970s, but remain a dominant caste in terms of land holding, rituals and political influence. The largest Christian denomination, Catholics, and the powerful trading community Gowda Saraswat Brahmins, both speak Konkani having migrated from Goa due to Portuguese oppression during the colonial period and still live in clusters within the city region to this day. Most Muslims belong to the Beary *jati*, speak their own language of the same name, and have traditionally been involved in trade (*byara* means trade or business in Tulu).

The city is small by Indian standards, around half a million people, or around 650,000 including the metropolitan region and this has increased steadily over the decades with populations of 539,390 in 2001, 426,340 (1991), 309,490 (1981) and 217,040 (1971).[27] However, this relational small-ness feeds into feelings of intimacy and perceived lack, when compared to larger cities.[28] Such comparative framings by locals is enabled by a long history of out migration to cities such as Mumbai or Dubai. What might surprise a visitor from one of India's larger cities, are the number and size of the shop-ping malls which, when opened, often feature in the ever changing 'top ten largest malls in India' lists, and a skyline filled with ultra-luxury high-rise apartments. These displays of new wealth do not sit in such stark contrast to poverty as is often the case in the country's metropolitan centres. There are only a few small slums in Mangaluru and the region is comparatively wealthy, gender balanced and literate. However there has been a decline in labour intensive industries such as tile-making and *beedi* (leaf cigarette) production, with the new industries that have opened-up around the all-weather port north of the city employing fewer and more highly qualified people. The result is a substantial group of young people who are neither extremely poor nor rich, but have quite a bit of time on their hands. These are, for the most part, quite a distinct group from the large and growing body of both local and outsider students.

The city, or more precisely the joint districts of Dakshina Kannada and Udupi, are increasingly imagined as an 'education hub'. Commission agents (who make money by bringing fee-paying students to colleges) boast that they can bring in young people from north India on just the promise of a place 'at a college in Mangalore', without specifying the institute. A lot of these colleges draw from the fame of St. Aloysius College (set up by the Jesuits in 1880), a National Institute of Technology north of the city, and the prestigious Manipal University near Udupi. This last institute was something of a trailblazer for the current slew of private colleges marked by local *jati* and community identity that dominate the local 'education market'. Set up as Kasturba Medical College in 1953 it was the first self-financing and fee-paying medical college in the country. The brainchild of local banker and doctor TMA Pai, he used his status as a Gowda Saraswat Brahmin and thus a minority language speaker (Konkani) to claim minority privileges. This allowed more autonomy in running the college, including avoiding the ban on admission fees that applied to 'regular' education institutes. As mentioned above, Tulu is also a minority language in the state of Karnataka (albeit the local *lingua franca* of the street), and this allowed Tulu-speaking communities to do the same— although this was mostly done post economic liberalisation, after changes in the law. It is now clear, at least to locals, which colleges and schools 'belong' to each community. Indeed some, such as Bearys College of Education, bear the *jati* name (Bearys are a Muslim community). This particular college is similar to many others in that it is built on money made elsewhere, in this case real estate, something that is important to keep in mind because, whilst education institutions are entwined with caste and/or religious community pride and advancement, they also can be an extremely profitable business—a motivation many make no secret of. Importantly, whilst some of the less prestigious and some of the Muslim colleges see an over-representation of students from the same communities, the better-established colleges are highly mixed. The Deputy Dean of a government college believes that 'at the end of the day, most parents will send their children to what they believe will be the best college, regardless of [religious] community or caste'.

The relatively large student body can, during the day, give the city a youthful feel.[29] There are numerous new public places in Mangaluru for students to socialise outside, and sometimes during, school hours. Six shopping malls, a smattering of the popular chain Café Coffee Day, ice-cream parlours and multiplexes compete with more long-standing choices such as parks and beaches as places for groups of students to hang out, often in groups that cross *jati*, gender and religious community lines.

The region's students also come from a diverse number of places within and occasionally outside India. Most of the graduates from outside the region leave upon completing their studies in part due to the lack of skilled jobs. This transitory attachment to the place may also play a role in a feeling of otherness, with some of the students from outside the city expressing an exasperation with the local 'culture' which they claimed should be more tolerant of their 'cultures'.

The feeling of mutual distrust was also evidenced in an interview with an area leader from the Hindu Yuva Sena. The local organisation was formed by members of the RSS in 1989, but became separate as the RSS were 'not involved in conflicts'—i.e. physical confrontations—and is now 'under them but not completely, we follow the same aims, but we are separate.' Currently, they are relatively small and insignificant with the violent acts that were previously their 'role' undertaken by the Bajrang Dal, who are officially affiliated with the RSS and who were founded in north India in 1984 before spreading south. The Hindu Yuva Sena area leader told me:

> Nowadays the girls who go to college, most of their parents are rich, so before college they give them money—maybe 500 rupees. Their parent's main idea is to give them education, but girls will roam here and there, taking alcohol and drugs. They are addicted. Parents are irresponsible.... In the Morning Mist case [the Home Stay attack], the students were from rich backgrounds. So they closed [solved] the case very quickly. If they were poor then nothing would have happened.

Whilst there are exceptions, broadly it can be said that many of those involved in the vigilante attacks are from so-called 'lower' or 'backwards castes'. Meanwhile those in other branches of the Sangh Parivar, such as the RSS, are from the 'upper castes'. I met some of those from Bajrang Dal who were involved in the above-mentioned attack in the cinema, all of whom were from the 'backwards' Billavas *jati*. At first, they were extremely open, proud and fearless about their activities and began showing me photos on their phones, until the second-in-command told them to stop. Meanwhile, when I asked older Brahmin RSS workers about their thoughts on the violence, they either excused the 'hotness' of the violence as a symptom of the attackers' young age, or switched topic to the violent actions of Muslim groups relating to cows—or women—'love jihad is their plan to take over the world by having more children than anyone else'. Against such attacks, it was either implicitly or explicitly suggested that violence was justified.

Whilst it is wrong (both factually and, I would argue, politically) to label those who carry out the attacks with the insult 'jobless', as many do in Mangaluru,[30] it is true that most of those I spoke with were in non-prestigious and irregular work. In keeping with such classed understandings, Tambe and Tambe suggest in relation to the above-mentioned 'pub attack' that in Mangaluru, because the divide between the working classes and the 'upper-middle' classes is not so sharply spatially marked as in India's metropolises, and because '[t]he young women in the pub, [are] perceived as visual signifiers of the new wealthy consumer, [they] were viewed as a potential influence on women from other social strata because of the closer contact between classes.'[31] As such, the attacks were done in a way to be seen by as many people as possible: a warning to women in the city. The need to warn women in the city is, as I argued before, related to a tension between economic and social liberalism as expressed in contemporary India—a tension that 'traditional' forms of disciplining cannot control.

Ethical openings

During a roundtable discussion that I organised at one of the more prestigious local colleges, I asked a group of fifteen students (aged 19–20) what they thought 'Westernisation' meant. The word was often used by those from the religious right, and indeed a local Muslim organisation had recently leafleted at the college gates warning students about the dangers of 'western culture' in relation to premarital relationships. I brought along my wife (also an anthropologist), to help ease any gendered issues relating to asking young women about 'unethical' behaviour. The students were a mix of different religions and came from different parts of India, with just under half from Mangaluru.

The students of course had a variety of views, but one of the common threads was that moral policemen will disappear once the region becomes more 'developed'—some further suggested that the Bajrang Dal and others were a reaction to a fast-changing city in which local culture is disappearing. They equated development, to a large degree, with increased freedoms akin to those they see in 'The West'. Indeed one even said that '[being western] means to be free. Not to be questioned in terms of what to wear, how to behave. In terms of religion'.

In a very different setting, the anthropologist Robbins argues that during moments of intense cultural change moral conflicts arise.[32] He suggests moral codes are smoothly socially-reproduced in cultures that have a dominant value from which ethical norms can derive. At times of rapid cultural change however values come into conflict, and people have a heightened sense of freedom as they are pushed into reflecting on (moral) decisions. Whilst there was not a single strong value around which Indian society has traditionally been organised (and we should be wary of suggestions that there was), in the past there was, nevertheless, a stronger sense that, within communities, certain ethical considerations were not open to question.

This argument chimes with Kapur's suggestion that there is a heightened awareness of the 'politics of time' with concomitant shifts in moral norms emanating from the state in contemporary India.[33] She argues that whereas the early post-colonial state in India had a certain moral imperative based on the struggle for freedom, the contemporary neoliberal state has abolished many of the past notions of collective responsibility. Moreover, she suggests that contemporary global capitalism positions certain places as being characterised by systematic under-development, which in turn helps ferment an often individualistic and precarious race against time (a sort of catching up). This all takes place within a system that simultaneously abstracts time into exchangeable units—i.e. a person's time has a price that she can sell as labour. Building on this, she further argues that contemporary India is marked by a fragmented time consciousness, with the present, past and future experienced as if they were cut from each other. Within this environment youthfulness, novelty and 'living for the moment' are celebrated (as evidenced especially strongly in adverts and films) and an increasingly individualistic morality in which future consequences are brushed aside is on the ascendency.

Drawing from this, I suggest that because in contemporary urban India there is no one coherent and dominant value system, for some young middle-class students there is a feeling of ethical 'freedom'. Freedom here is understood as the freedom to ethically cultivate oneself through various techniques drawn from a diverse range of moral exemplars (streams or processes, some strong some weak, variously pulled together).[34] Kapur identifies a number of such exemplars in popular culture—commercials that celebrate newness and youth, self-help 'business guru' books that draw on a reading of the *Mahabharata* that suggest one should do one's duty without worrying about the consequences, and films in which vigilantes administer summary justice. Crucially, she suggests that such exemplars, engendered by the fragmented experience of time, are conducive for cultivating a self as a packageable commodity in competition with others. Taken together this produces a feeling of helplessness for many as they struggle to assemble a coherent self under such conditions.

Here is where the link between neoliberalism and the appeal of authoritarian movements makes itself apparent. It is not only the case, as is sometimes simplistically argued in the popular press, that violent Hindu nationalist groups have a strong appeal for those 'losers' of economic change. Rather the type of moral ordering offered by vigilante groups is accepted and quietly supported by many in Mangaluru because, at a time when cultural change has led to an explosion of ethical values and the opening-up of new possibilities for ethical self-cultivation, the actions of vigilante groups offer both a coherent narrative and a sense of control for many who feel helpless to stop the decay of morality. The Bajrang Dal's motto, as they reminded me when I met them, is 'service, safety and culture'; they saw their service to Indian culture in their provision of protection to Hindus, especially Hindu women, from the dangers of western influences and Muslim men. In practical terms, this means a careful observation of people's timings (for example, to catch interreligious couples) and the controlling of times, realised through attacks on late night parties, or the reporting of women on the street after dark.

Conclusions: A new discipline for a new India?

Each and every day in Mangaluru, as in many other places across India, a group of men dressed in khaki meet on a public ground and perform games, sports and synchronised actions with long sticks. The drill, known as the *sangh shakha*, aims to instil virtuous behaviour and ideals, as the local RSS *Vibhag Sharirik Pramukh* (trainer) explained:

> The main thing is personality development.... The most important thing is one programme, every day, uninterrupted. It's a *tapasu* [meditation]. There is no syllabus, it's not written, yet the procedure is the same everywhere. How to start, the games, the end—the one hour programme. The main thing is to bring changes in the man. So, what type of changes? That he loves his country, his motherland.

The *shakha* has been performed in Mangaluru since 13 September, 1940, when around twenty or so people gathered. Since then, the *shakha* has grown from place to place in the region and, by 2013, 100,000 uniformed RSS members gathered outside the city for a one-off extended performance of various martial drills. However, despite its militaristic overtones and large numbers of attendees, such gatherings do not provide a moral exemplar to the students I spoke with. Rather, for the most part, the students found the often middle-aged Brahmin men in shorts as figures of fun. I also got the same impression from the vigilantes' wry smiles when I probed them on along these lines, although they would not voice such opinions openly to me. Such activities are not, in short, 'cool', and they certainly lack the dangerous edge palpable at some Bajrang Dal actions. As a moral exemplar, the *shakha* sits alongside activities such morality camps for young girls organised by RSS-supporting dance schools, in failing to bring order to the ethically disorderly city.

If the khaki-clad men gathered for drills on open land resemble, or want to resemble, a parastatal army, then the vigilantes are the guerrilla urban street fighters: groups that blend in and out of the city's flows appearing, when needed, to attack. As we saw above, such groups are not always above the law, and the vigilantes I met were keen to point out the number of cases filed against them. However, very often their actions remain unreported and many of the attackers are happy to openly talk about what they do and why they do it. When I went to meet some of the Bajrang Dal on Valentine's Day they were crowded round a computer screen, laughing and joking with one another. The source of their entertainment was a news report on the English site Daiji World, in which they were the stars. They had spent the morning burning (blank, purchased) Valentine's Day cards outside Besant Women's College. Their behaviour at that moment reminded me of any group of friends looking back together at photos from a trip or celebration.

The public sphere in India, and indeed elsewhere, is not only constituted by transparent debate and discussion—rather image and spectacle proliferate, with seemingly spontaneous yet highly organised acts of mass violence framed by political actors as the will of the people,[35] and both the number of debaters as well as the quality of the debate important, guided by the knowledge that protest, force and agitation are a means for getting their demands met.[36] Within such an arena, the public nature of the attacks moves beyond a reaction to perceived immoral behaviour, and becomes a proactive intervention into the shaping of behaviour in contemporary India. A further example of how anger and violence function as a legitimate mode through which to realise political aims.[37] Moreover, via traditional media, such as print news and television, and increasingly via new media such as WhatsApp groups, the actions of the street reverberate throughout the city, region and country.[38]

As the majoritarian Hindu state project continues with its pro-market development model, attacks against those who experiment with multiple streams of ethical cultivation in public urban settings will continue to serve as a reminder of one of its contradictions. Moral policing is, in part, a response to the wider ethical-temporal tension between India's time on the global stage and the concurrent time of 'immorality'. It has resulted in an increased disciplining within the immediate times of the city: an attempt to hold time still on moral transformations and curtail the liberalism within neoliberalism. As long as the tension remains unresolved, such violence is set to continue.

4

REFLECTIONS IN THE CROWD

DELEGATION, VERISIMILITUDE, AND THE MODI MASK

Parvis Ghassem-Fachandi

Delegation

In *La délégation et le fétichisme politique*, the French sociologist Pierre Bourdieu analyzed the mysterious mechanism by which power is transferred between individuals when forming larger social orders.[1] A group achieves permanency in the act of representation through a deputy (a leader, a mandatory, a spokesperson). In India one finds ministers, members of parliament, political leaders, a president and a prime minister. Delegation constitutes that extraordinarily complex social act by which a group brings itself about through its proxy. The power of proxy, in turn, is based on a tacit authorisation given by each mandator to the delegate (the plenipotentiary, the minister) to speak and act on his behalf. This transmission of power locates the proxy in a privileged position *vis-à-vis* his mandators to usurp this power, the meaning through which the group constitutes itself. He writes, '*in appearance* the group creates the man who speaks in its place and in its name..., [while] *in reality* it is ... the spokesperson who creates the group.'[2] How did this tacit mechanism function during and after the Gujarat pogrom of 2002? How did an increasingly invulnerable Narendra Modi, who was first Chief and then Prime Minister, relate to his growing electoral majorities?

Political turmoil

Narendra Modi, who served as chief minister of Gujarat from 2001 to 2014, did not initially assume political office through an ordinary election. Instead, he was appointed chief minister by the NDA-led coalition government at the centre in Delhi. The man who would later be celebrated for his formidable ability to run political campaigns and win elections entered through a political back door—one that was left wide open. Heaved into a prominent position, Narendra Modi replaced Keshubhai Patel, the previous Chief Minister of Gujarat. Patel was a failed CM who had resigned, officially due to ill health. In reality he had mishandled relief work after the Bhuj earthquake in January 2001. Accused of corruption and abuse of power, Patel was blamed for the losses of BJP seats in recent by-elections. Modi had been one of his staunchest critics within the *Sangh Parivar* (the family network of Hindu organisations). Rejecting the idea of becoming Patel's deputy, Modi insisted instead on replacing Patel in a state often labeled 'the laboratory of *hindutva*'. Hindutva means, literally, Hindu-ness, or the essence of the Hindu. Patel never quite recovered from this humiliation nor did he ever forgive Modi.

Having led the BJP to their very first victory in Gujarat in the 1995 assembly elections, Keshubhai Patel had modeled himself a political leader of the Patels, a community considered economically successful and influential in the state. While certainly a Hindu nationalist by affiliation and persuasion, his public appeal relied more on familiar themes such as caste-based patronage—i.e. what many would describe as local corruption or 'politics as usual'. His main rival had been Shankersingh Vaghela who forced Patel to resign in 1995, after only seven months in office, and who would himself assume the post of Chief Minister in 1996. Vaghela was associated with groups considered Kshatriya—traditional rivals of the Patels.[3,4]

All three men—Keshubhai Patel, Shankersingh Vaghela, and Narendra Modi—were native to the state of Gujarat and former RSS members (*pracharak*, literally a Hindu propagandist). While Patel and Vaghela had been active in parliament at least since the late 1970s, Modi was their junior and a newcomer. He nonetheless distinguished himself quickly from his predecessors.

Not identified with a particular community or caste constituency that provided a local power base, Modi rather placed his hope in an appeal to *hindutva*, the ideology of Hindu nationalism. For a long time he had been active in Hindu nationalist organisations, whose various branches reach deep into Gujarat's civil society. If initially some had seen Narendra Modi as an unambitious and humble administrator, they quickly realised that appearances can be deceiving as these adjectives do not properly describe the man.[5]

Between Modi's appointment as Chief Minister in October 2001 and his first proper election to the legislative assembly on 24 February 2002, there were two important events which provided an affect-laden context for what was to follow: the 11 September 2001 attacks in New York and the terrorist attack on Indian Parliament on 13 December 2001. It was in the aftermath of these two events that only three days after Modi's entrance into the legislative assembly, on 27 February, an ill-fated Sabarmati Express reached Godhra railway station and the train burning took place. The immediate context of Modi's political tenure was hence on the one hand an incessant rivalry between political leaders who were influenced by the same ideology, had a similar biography, held the same political posts and yet represented different social constituencies in the state. On the other hand, Modi's ascension to prominence was under new conditions, as there emerged simultaneously the new international spectre of Islamic terrorism. After becoming visible abroad, the new spectre reached Delhi. Modi made sure that it was also to arrive in Gujarat.

If, by this time, many Gujaratis had been suspicious and hesitant to affirm vitriolic *hindutva* rhetoric, this was to change soon. Gujarat was a state strongly identified with Gandhi and *ahimsa* (nonviolence). Yet, political leaders appeared to replicate the divisions within society by close links to their respective political constituencies, which essentially blocked political progress. The chief ministership was the top prize in an endemic War of the Roses. Simultaneously, there were also strong undercurrents of mutual suspicion and animosity between communities, which had been part of central Gujarat for a long time and were regularly confirmed by repeated rounds of communal violence and simmering neighborhood tensions. These included conflict between Hindus and Muslims in the late 1960s, between Dalits, Muslims and Hindus in the mid 1980s and clashes between Muslim and Hindus in the 1990s. Although political leaders derided communal violence in the past as unfortunate aberrations, such incidents nonetheless occurred frequently.[6]

A general prejudice circulated that Muslims, although a minority, were more prone to the use of violence, with Hindus frequently at the receiving end. Such misrepresentations—stereotypes with no basis in historical fact—were typically accompanied by bland statements such as 'The typical Muslim is a bully and the typical Hindu is a coward.'[7] Such enunciations had acquired the quality of proverbs (*kahevat*); they emerged in the mind of the speaker to automatically complete a picture already prefigured.[8] And yet, even if mere projection, such enunciations gave expression to how intimacy between Muslims and Hindus was experienced and hence to what problem the Gujarat pogrom implicitly provided an answer. Nor are such perceptions limited to Gujarat. Rather, they form part of a larger story of religious and sectarian division on the subcontinent.

Stimmung and verisimilitude

The Gujarat pogrom of 2002 was accompanied by a *Stimmung*, a collective mood, that cannot be adequately captured by 'collective anger' or 'revenge'.[9] The fractured nature of experience does not allow a rationale such as revenge or an emotion such as anger to take the place of an explanation. We are confronted here with a problem of language in analysis because our common-sense notion of 'event' suggests a completeness prior to experience. Rather, an event is always already the abstraction from a narrative.[10] The narrative organises contradictory and fragmentary experiences into an order that suggests a particular meaning. In this way various elements are enlisted as links indexing the Godhra incident preceding the pogrom. We have to be careful here because narratives formed part of the pogrom itself in which the *krodh hindu* (the angry Hindu) was invoked as a historical subject who, once awoken to his anger, cannot be stopped. What is left for the ethnographer is to allude to the ways in which what occurred might not be equal to this narrative or might even contradict it.

After the Godhra incident in the morning of 27 February it took the city of Ahmedabad an entire day and night to awake to violence. In this bracing period, the city was full of discussion and fearful premonition about what was most likely going to come. Yet in my observation in the inner areas of the city, Muslims did not have to hide and barricade themselves in their neighborhoods.[11] Muslims walking the streets were not yet occasions for hunting and killing.[12] In the evening of that same day, however, the official government press release defined the Godhra incident as a 'preplanned inhuman collective violent act of terrorism'.[13] This authoritative characterisation of a communal incident as 'preplanned' (*purvayojit*) and as 'a terrorist action' (*traasvadi kru-*

tya), before any investigation was on its way, served the purpose of invocation of a sense of conspiracy and urgency that achieved parity with events that had recently been witnessed in the news, namely the terrorist attack on the Indian Parliament by Pakistani terrorist outfits such as Jaish-e-Mohammad and Lashkar-e-Taiba, as well as Al-Qaeda, which had organised the 9/11 attacks in the United States.

On the morning the next day, the ruling BJP together with the VHP declared a strike (*bandh*, literally a closure) inaugurating the pogrom. What a vitriolic rhetoric of militant Hindu nationalist organisations (like the Bajrang Dal, the VHP, and the RSS) had claimed for years now seemed confirmed as fact and proven to be correct: India was under attack by superlative forces (the Pakistani ISI); there was more to this train burning than meets the eye ('the tale of the missing women');[14] the neighbourhood Muslim with whom one daily rubs shoulders can no longer be trusted ('terrorists'). This was not merely about so-called bullies and cowards, nor about communal violence as usual. This was extraordinary. In such an atmosphere 'violence is in the air' (*hinsa havama chhe*).

What characterises the pogrom most distinctly is that it began more or less contemporaneously (*zeitgleich*) with an explosion in fantasy. The debris of these fantasies became visible in speech, reveries, rumours, and some strange behaviours. Fantasies are threshold phenomena that commingle one man's desire with another's and with elements of the real world. They are intersubjective in a deep psychoanalytic sense, always implicated in a relation with an Other who is both an internal and external object. Fantasy blooms in and through human relationships. During the days of pogrom violence in Ahmedabad, people only progressively realised what exactly was unfolding. Isolated happenings were not linked to one another. The facticity of events became only gradually known, while imaginations were already abundantly full and widely shared. For me, the initial indication that something exceptional was occurring was based on this incongruence between the factual and the phantasmatic—a singular observation. Preceding the media reports of massacres, words were spoken in an unfamiliar register by relatively uninvolved bystanders or small-time street actors. Various rumours that sounded absurd to me (and were later found to be false) were sternly believed. People's attention was focused on gruesome specifics that distracted from the official line of anger and revenge. Violence was articulated as if under a microscope, applying a sharp focus that zoomed in and savoured brutal actions in slow motion.

Important here is that while these enunciations were excessive of the acts alleged to have been witnessed at that time, the excess in language did not misrepresent the real acts that were to be perpetrated (or were already being perpetrated in various locations). The murders, rapes, and mutilations of the pogrom were real, while these articulations added more material to an unfolding context. In other words, imagination anticipated and accompanied violent action. Language had no detached vantage point anymore from which to offer a description, but itself participated in a violent acting-out. It thus became a conduit for fantasy while it simultaneously accounted for some of what was factually happening. There was a fascination at work that circumvented all censoring and made manifest latent material. In this way, the pogrom revealed dimensions of an intersubjective relationship that usually remains submerged: something was happening between how Hindus relate to the Muslim as an inner object, divorced from any actual Muslims, and Muslims could be said to partake in the same circumvention of the censorship of reality.

Many articulations during the pogrom appear like the material of a dream, or perhaps it would be more proper to say, the material of a nightmare. This material reveals layers of an unconscious and it suggests the work of the pleasure principle exactly in a moment where one would expect only the reality principle at work.

If the latter demands deferral of immediate gratification, the script unleashed during the pogrom suggested the opposite. Pregnant with pornographic imagery and themes, actions on the street frequently took a festival-like atmosphere. The pleasurable dimensions of this violence, where the imagination is given free license to act, are what have become most difficult to acknowledge today. I suspect this is the reason why many participants do not care to remember, or are unable to account properly for their own actions, emotions, and identifications at the time. These aspects of the pogrom were submerged under the narrative of 'Hindu anger'. If anger authorises violent action and authenticates the *krodh* (angry) Hindu, pleasure risks obscuring this. The figure of the angry Hindu makes sense as a response (if not 'solution') to the proverbial cowardice of the Hindu as invoked in the Mahatma's own words.[15]

After three days, on March 2, the Chief Minister named the pogrom a 'natural reaction' (*svabhavik pratikriya*) to the Godhra train-burning incident. Once the expression 'natural reaction' was authoritatively employed in an affect-laden context to name still unfolding events, it became a legitimation and spontaneous affirmation for collective retribution.[16] The expression combines the theme of revenge and retribution with the image of an automatic mechanism, suggesting the detachment of ritual or of legal procedures. By stressing detachment and automaticity in the context of organised violence, however, agency is seriously obscured. Who authorised this reaction? As re-action, emphasis is laid on the actions preceding the pogrom (i.e. the Godhra incident for which Muslims were solely held responsible). And by 'natural' a sort of inevitability is suggested as if organised collective violence was akin to a twitch following a pinch, an unavoidable and almost innocent reflex. While the expression captured well what many Gujaratis told themselves about the violence, it entirely misrepresented the facts of the pogrom. With this triad of conspiracy, automaticity, and inevitability, the pogrom unfolded more or less unhindered.

After the pogrom, the attempts to legally prosecute the instigators and leaders did not receive the wide public support one might have expected. This concerns especially the many members of organisations who had visibly sprung into action on the street in droves (RSS, VHP, Bajrang Dal, and Shiv Sena). Human-rights activists, by contrast, were not heralded as heroes but more often strongly denounced as 'politically motivated'. Attempts at legal retribution were frequently deemed 'inauthentic' because they were not driven by a striving for truth, but the desire for political gain by specific actors. In short, the violence unleashed had expressed a certain kind of truth that escaped all indignation or empathy. It expressed the legitimacy of a *pratikriya*, after having been attacked in Godhra and this logic of reaction had been enunciated by Modi and the Sangh Parivar, repeatedly and openly. The power of these enunciations, however, really lay with the echo they received from large parts of an urban Gujarati public. It is here where a tacit act of delegation can be found.

Modi became the embodied purveyor of that truth, the spokesperson who although he had not yet run a political campaign as chief minister, came to speak the meaning of the pogrom. I believe that Narendra Modi's success in Gujarat is fundamentally connected to a moment of verisimilitude: a congruence between his enunciation and the general mood at the time. Modi offered an acceptable form to the collective reverie that many Gujaratis experienced in this re-actionary violence. The complicity was widely shared in thoughts and emotions, and sometimes even in specific actions during the days of violence. By speaking in the voice of this public *pratikriya*, Modi seemed not only authentic as an ideologue of *hindutva* but also truthful to the resentful mood compared to the contortions of political leaders of other parties, who on the one hand regularly engaged the moralistic discourse of Gandhi, blamed their political opponents for violence, and on the other hand engaged in communal provocation whenever it suited their immediate political needs.

And yet, this truth was merely the truth of the pleasure principle, which, after the violence ebbed, could only continue its existence through a decisive negation (*Verneinung*). On the one hand, there followed a widespread denial and even disavowal of involvement in the collective attunement to violence during the pogrom, and, on the other hand, Modi absorbed the national and international fallout of the pogrom. He stood accused (the US even refused him a visa), but he skilfully avoided commenting on that matter, or revealing any specific knowledge of what had gone on. One cannot really say it in any nicer way: he got away with murder.

After the pogrom, Modi defended the Gujaratis against the accusations of being violent ('five crore Gujaratis'), partly in self-defence, as he was the very one who proved unwilling or incapable of stopping the violence and bringing the perpetrators to justice. Instead of a public debate to understand what had gone on, Modi remained completely silent about the violence itself. In a second step, he shifted the rhetorical register to the economic agenda that had been neglected in the years preceding his tenure. Development became the currency linking everyday relations with Modi as political leader.

Negation, according to Freud,[17] can be a way to attain the permanency of an affirmation that can no longer be made openly, directly, or consciously. Whenever Modi seemed to consciously disavow violence he was actually affirming the effectiveness of the violence he had rendered legitimate through inaction and proclamation. The term *ahimsa* lends itself to such obfuscation and curious reversal as nonviolence is nothing but the negation of an already present violence (*himsa*). Violence is invoked every time nonviolence is being enunciated.[18] This negation continued within weeks after the pogrom, when the Gujarat government announced plans to open an 'Ahimsa University' and to develop 'Ahimsa tourism'.[19] Modi understood that the 'truth' of Hindu cowardice had to be overcome without straying too far from established norms. The pogrom provided that possibility. The Hindu had to awake to his violent possibilities in the name of nonviolence. Only someone who has the power and the courage to mete out violence can then decide to be nonviolent. This then is the political project of *hindutva*, which is about the rearrangement of affective experience to allow for resentment, ambivalence, and anger to become available for the machinations of power.

A chief minister who had mismanaged the Godhra incident then failed to stop the pogrom and again failed to provide proper care to the victims afterwards had become the guarantor of future peace and stability in the state.

Through this absurd triumph, for which the Gujarati electorate is entirely responsible, Modi successfully appropriated the means of violence. To Gujaratis he has shown that he can do both, orchestrate and administer violence as well as rule a state without any major clash or communal conflagration. He has indeed proven to everyone that an identification with nonviolence (*ahimsa*) can become the means by which to instantiate violence (*himsa*). There is no longer a reason to feel vulnerable just because one is identified with nonviolence. Indeed, whether violent or nonviolent is no longer a question of truth, but a question of proper leadership and skill: the abilities necessary in wielding political power. It would have been preferable if Gujaratis would have denied him at least that final hat trick.

This act of delegation made it unnecessary for Gujaratis to acknowledge and confront their own propensities for violence and contributed to shielding the chief minister from any legal accountability. One way to conceptualise this is to ask how, in everyday life, people came to see themselves mirrored in Modi, who no longer remembered what he did or didn't do, what he said or didn't say, who he called or didn't call, and what he felt or did not feel during those dark days of spring in 2002. They, too, did not remember and did not want to. To sustain this form of not-knowing, they found it useful to wear the Modi mask at public rallies.

Reflection in the people

During fieldwork in 2011–14 and again in 2016, I began to see political supporters of Chief Minister Narendra Modi engaging in the curious practice of collective masquerade. In various public venues at the time, still visible today on countless photographs and in video recordings, large groups of people gather in which every single individual makes the same face. They all wear a Modi mask. The photos seem eerie for what they lack: individual facial expressions. The mask, one of which I purchased, is a rubber contraption that depicts the face of the Indian politician not as parody but in typifying detail. The practice started around 2007 when Modi had not yet entirely overcome major legal and political hurdles linking his administration to the Gujarat pogrom. It had, for Modi, a brilliant effect: the sea of masks made every photograph of a crowd gathering in his name a permanent visual advertisement for his face. Crowds of every kind are ubiquitous in India. In linking name and face via the crowd, Modi's face became iconic beyond Gujarat. With his mass appeal and popularity steadily increasing, the Modi mask soon became an item *en vogue*.

Several types of masks circulated in various periods of electoral and public agitation leading up to the general election in 2014. Street workers, Modi supporters, and sometimes accidental bystanders, wore these masks during mass events. Some were made of stiff plastic, others of colored paper, but the most popular one was made of a soft, pliable rubber—the type one finds in Halloween stores in the US. It reminded me of the masks worn in the famous British comedy series *Spitting Image*. The soft rubber is produced by an India-based company and when worn causes heavy perspiration. It also smells strongly of the petrol chemicals with which synthetic rubbers are made. This most popular version of the Modi mask, covering only the front part of a wearer's face, depicts the politician's facial features most accurately. During his national campaign in 2013–14, it far outnumbered the others. It faithfully depicts Modi's distinctive features: smoothened white hair, high forehead, light skin tone, small ears, rimless eyeglasses, thick, full lips framed by a white mustache that blends seamlessly into the edges of his beard. The soft rubber material is of a kind that allows adjustment to any head size or shape while also minimising distortion of facial features. For an Indian today, it is impossible to doubt who this mask presents.

These masks acquired an unintended humorous quality at times by transferring the politician's increasingly familiar features into strange social televisual contexts: dark-skinned tribal women as Modi-versions in interviews espoused economic development in their own unique tongues and voices; dusty rickshaw-drivers looked like Modi clones as they stuttered awed excitement about the prospects of a decent living wage into a reporter's microphone; an athletic muscle-man in a T-shirt stretched his pecks into the TV camera, impersonating the somewhat plump and more humble politician while speculating about the future of health in the nation. And then there were countless children hidden behind a single overlarge adult face with white hair—all of them sweating profusely under the soft plastic in the incredible heat. In the mask their voices resounded hollowly through its orifices articulating their hopes for a better India, all hiding behind the rubber contraption.

The popularity of Modi masks can be contrasted with the popular disenchantment with the Congress system. There is no face in the Congress Party today that could do the work that Modi's face does for the BJP. It's former leader, the Italian-born Sonia Gandhi, represents a cosmopolitanism that is popularly disparaged as 'Western'. Rahul Gandhi, its current leader, after winning his father Rajiv's old seat in Amethi, UP, in 2009, did very badly in 2014 by bestowing on Congress one of its worst defeats. Congress has other problems relevant to representation and delegation: a very complicated mechanism of segmented representation; and the internal layering of dynastic rank, primogeniture, and traditional power as against the promise, however naive, of a singular strong authority. While Modi was able to oust his immediate predecessors, Rahul can ill afford to show disrespect to his mother. The Congress umbrella doesn't open properly any longer. Such a decisive identification with a political leader like Modi is a phenomenon that has not taken place at a national scale in India at least since the days of Indira Gandhi. The Modi mask is the plastic symbol of a new political formation that the BJP came to dominate. By presenting a single face and focusing all attention on only one man's features, some degree of definite clarity in appearance was achieved which in the election attracted many voters.

A crowd is usually understood to be a faceless phenomenon, but these political crowds found their face in Narendra Modi's. This identification through masking becomes more intelligible when placed alongside the context of how people used them for the ubiquitous Indian ritual of *tilaka*: putting a mark of red vermillion on the center of their foreheads in order to honour the receiver.[20] By putting a *tilak* on the rubber mask instead of one's actual face, it suddenly became unclear, who was being honoured by this habitual act. Is it the anonymous individual wearing the mask or is it the important persona depicted by the mask's surface features? The convergence of the anonymous member of the crowd with their designated leader was now complete: the politician as the representative face of the group and the group as the embodiment of the man.

A mask is an object that depicts and conceals at the same time. While the facial features depicted in and through the mask are shown, the face beneath it remains hidden. There is something strange happening when someone puts on a mask. Something breaks in the air. There enters a new presence, a supplementary address by a third, and this address becomes interrupted once it is taken off again. Masked supporters of Modi never seem to want to take off their masks while cameras are rolling or while photos are being shot. This, despite the fact that it was highly unlikely they would ever again be on live TV. I found the insistence on remaining concealed surprising, because I assumed that one way to emphasise the authenticity of one's opinion is to add one's individual features to it—i.e. to take off the mask. It reminded me of veiled Muslim women in Gujarat, who will often tie a *niqab* tightly when cameras are rolling for the duration of what they have to say, only to relax the practice a moment later, when they hail their rickshaw and drive home. The women want to become visible to an anonymous public only as pious and veiled and without their individual facial features. The Modi supporters similarly did not want to add something that might disturb the smooth surface of their leader's rubber replica. Instead of becoming visible as who they were, they made themselves invisible as members of his crowd.

And yet, it is insufficient to understand this practice, the wearing of a mask of the leader by political supporters, as a unidirectional affair. The mirror works both ways. In India, politicians, too, wear the coverings of their potential voters. Election campaigns include elaborate tours through regions and the countryside, as well as cities in the Indian union during which candidates engage in spectacles of costuming that sometimes approximate a veritable carnival of sorts. Enveloped by playful accoutrements, such as coats and shawls, they pose bearing typifying swords, and especially colourful turbans or other headgear originating from various ethnic, regional, and caste communities. Sometimes the head coverings make them even look silly. Such productions are a remnant of a once much more elaborate ceremonial logic of honouring the stranger as a visiting guest.

For electoral candidates, sartorial styles, wearing garments and displaying other regalia, are symbolic strategies, especially while on the campaign trail. They offer token recognition to particular identities of which there are many in India. The practice of wrapping oneself in unfamiliar clothes is indexical of the inclusion and mutual consideration demanded in the world's largest and by far the most diverse democracy. Nowhere can one find such a density of kitsch and superficial yet also endearing symbolism as when Indian politicians take on the garbs of their respective audiences, offering studied postures and making bland, complementary statements. Yet, the exchange always remains reciprocal: the attention the people give to the candidate (the guest) is reciprocated by the attention the candidate gives to the regional specificities and particularities of the hosts. Wearing the Modi mask marks a dramatic break with this customary reciprocity: under the mask, the people do not become present except in the leader's image.

For all their efficacy, these routine acts of mutual consideration in interaction at political rallies are deemed interesting for a wider audience only when something goes wrong during the stage-managed choreography. When a failure plays out in front of a large audience—not infrequent given the current technologies of communication like television, mobile or smart phone, and internet—the botched ceremony becomes read and interpreted in overdetermined ways. Such an accident indeed occurred by chance recently in a widely reported incident. Narendra Modi resisted putting on a white Muslim skull cap, what is locally called a *topi*, during his *Sadbhavna* ('Goodwill') mission launched in 2012 in preparation for his electoral run for prime minister of India. The *Sadbhavna* mission was intended to reconcile the chief minister with his many audiences, including skeptical and recalcitrant Muslims, who had soured since 2002.

An unknown Muslim official, said to be a heterodox Sufi Pir, offered Modi a *topi* on stage before rolling cameras and recording mobile phones. The idea to offer Modi an opportunity to wear a *topi* seems to have been more or less a spontaneous idea by the witty man. The chief minister, unperturbed and polite in what equally appears to be a spontaneous gesture, decisively declined to wear the *topi*, even if only for the short duration of a camera's click. Modi's sudden recalcitrance created somewhat of a stir. He is known for his piety, and this could have been interpreted as an appeal to that. Yet it looked strange for a man interested in portraying himself as finally above and beyond all communal division to refuse to wear a *topi* now, since he had been identified for his entire political career with divisive Hindu nationalism. Modi acted petty the way some Muslims might act, when they refuse to wear the *tilak* on their foreheads or if they claim to feel bothered by visual depictions of Hindu gods and god-desses because they represented polytheism or idolatry—*shirk*.[21] In this refusal to mirror the community he was to represent, Modi, a Hindu, acted like the bad version of a Muslim, steering his religion down a rapid descent into com-munalism, which rendered the simplest gestures of respect complicated.

After members of the public later demanded an apology, Modi commented that he never saw other national leaders like Mahatma Gandhi, Jawaharlal Nehru, or Vallabhai Patel wear a Muslim skullcap. Why should he have to prove his credentials as a neutral arbiter? This is a typical Modi answer in how his comments obfuscated instead of clarified what issue was at stake. Instead of an apology, the chief minister showed indignation. He appealed to a notion of sheer equivalence that revealed, embarrassingly, an arrogance: his comparison suggested he had the stature of the founding political leaders. Unlike himself, these national leaders were not Hindu nationalists, nor were they implicated in fomenting or tolerating mass violence as he did. After all, during the Gujarat pogrom, Narendra Modi was the ruling chief minister of Gujarat as well as the state's home minister. He was well aware of the violence, and who inflicted it on whom, in the pogrom. The question at the moment, rather, was about the appropriate gesture of a symbol of recognition that might serve as a sign of reconciliation. For Modi, however, such gestures risked becoming interpreted as a symbol of 'appeasement', an impossibility for him and his followers. Despite the semblance of a conciliatory future, there was in fact no willingness to depart from the past.[22] If Modi refuses the *topi*, even if only for the short duration of a camera's click, why should Muslims not refuse his mask?

The mask and the *topi* seem similar yet asymmetric in their relation to one another and to the crowd they seem to address. The rejected *topi* was, to my knowledge, the only piece of clothing the chief minister and prime ministerial candidate effectively refused to wear during the entire election campaign. The rationale of the mission, in turn, was largely due to Modi's ambiguous role in the 2002 anti-Muslim pogrom. Can a mask be understood as part of a sartorial style? And can the *topi*, the Muslim skullcap, in turn, be understood to be a sort of mask?

One interpretation of why Modi did not put on the *topi* was because he risked becoming an object of incorporation as Muslim. He would no longer be himself: a Hindu however enhanced and multiplied by many masks. It would have allowed members of that aggregate community to reproduce and enlarge a photograph of the politician and to hang the picture up wherever they wanted to in order to express his honourary membership in their respective natal communities, as was done with so many other communities on the campaign trail and during the *Sadbhavna* mission. The chief minister would have become vulnerable to how Muslims might incorporate him into their own symbolic registers for their own purposes. The future leader of the country would have shown his vulnerability to the volition of his subjects, to appear in their likeness, in accordance to their ideas and wishes. Candidate Modi resisted this danger of incorporation that all masks pose, and thus rejected wearing the *topi* altogether. In other words, Modi treated the Muslim skullcap indeed as if it were a mask, making him similar to a people from whom he wanted to remain distinct.

His honorary appearance as a Muslim would have repeated an experience that he, as a Hindu nationalist, must be very familiar with. Namely, the moment of in-distinction when one is confronted with a familiar face wearing a *topi*. Modi's face looks ultimately like the face of an Indian. It is similar to other Indians, including those that happen to be Muslim. Islam by contrast, is often emphasised as coming originally from elsewhere. Modi's beard is a common feature for a Muslim in India. Wearing the beard with the addition of the *topi* might have accentuated even further the possibility of being similar. It would have denied his iconicity as someone who stands apart from Muslims. The recognition of the familiarity of the Muslim face was probable enough that it posed a danger to the future prime minister. Such mimesis risks obscuring the authenticity of the conservative (*rudhichust*) Hindu.

Conclusion

When Modi spoke to the crowds in his most recent national campaign spectacles, the distinctive masks that were frequently worn quite literally incarnated him. Thus he faced time and again on stage, posters, screens, in the newspapers, his own reflection (*pratibimba*) in the people. The BJP propaganda machinery produced a campaign of a scale and tenor new to the Indian context.

How must it feel to be confronted with a crowd that wears your face? The mask is a hollow shell behind which there lies another face hidden behind the rubber version of yourself. Compared to ceremonial costuming, the mask does not entail an expectation of reciprocity. The people Modi represents in all their individual particularity disappear behind his own face. As a delegate, he is the receiver of their votes, their mandate, their will. Yet in the crowd, they become visible to him only as a reflection of his own face. More recently, Modi tattoos in various forms also have appeared on forearms, legs, and backsides, despite the fact that in Indian public life skin is much less frequently shown than in Western countries. The tattoos depict the now entirely familiar features of the new prime minister of India and again emphasise the special link between the citizen and leader. Such a need to re-present the representative, the proxy of the group, on one's skin is a symptom of the complex and tacit process of what Pierre Bourdieu tried to capture by the word *délégation* and the subsequent fetishistic idealisation of the leader.

The *topi*, if worn, would have confronted Modi with a collapse of distinction between aggregate religious categories. He would have had to articulate a Hindu face while wearing a Muslim skullcap. The embarrassment could have been charming, eliciting a shy smile. There are so many beautiful smiles adorning India. But apparently the prime minister found nothing amusing or pleasurable in this chance opportunity for sartorial play. In this way, Modi was true to himself proving again that he possesses no musicality whatsoever for what he so ardently defends: religion. He has none of the tact that constitutes in India the large field of religious sensibility. This is in stark opposition to many of the people who he represents and who wear rubber masks of his own liking. These followers frequently do have a great sense of tact and sublimity when traversing religious boundaries.

While the Modi mask eliminates all distinction under a single face, the *topi* confronted Modi with his own need for distinction, the need to make or have a Hindu face. Resisting this incorporation while simultaneously encouraging the wearing of his mask is as strange as it is revelatory. Modi might as well be a Muslim, because, after all, he looks exactly like them. All that makes a difference is the skullcap. With the skullcap, the future prime minister could have represented a fine Muslim indeed. In that way he could have reciprocated for the alienation each mandate must experience when in the act of delegation the mandatory appropriates the means of production of the meaning of the group. Modi would have triumphed as the leader who constitutes the group as Indian and not merely as Hindu.

PART II

DEBATES ON HEGEMONY

5

TOWARD HEGEMONY

THE BJP BEYOND ELECTORAL DOMINANCE

Suhas Palshikar

This chapter proposes to discuss the consequences of emergence of the new party system in India and the politics of shaping 'new India'.[1] It is argued here that besides the electoral ascendance of the Bharatiya Janata Party (BJP) (the steadiness of which is rather incontrovertible), political developments also indicate the gradual shaping of a new hegemony in India. Thus, the 'second dominant party system' is more than mere party system; it is a moment of rise of a new set of dominant ideas and sensibilities that would provide ideological sustenance to the dominant party system. It is of course true that electoral politics is bound to replace existing governments and prop up new majorities in politics from time to time. But it is argued here that electoral uncertainties notwithstanding, the recent rise of the BJP has contributed to the emergence of a new ideological framework within which India's democracy and public life in general seem to be operating. This framework might be better understood when it is seen as the crafting of hegemony. Five years since the initial appearance, the newness of the hegemonic aspects emerging in the polity are clearer.

This politics of crafting a new hegemony did not emerge all of a sudden. While this chapter primarily looks at how this project has developed since the last leg of the second term of the United Progressive Alliance (UPA),[2] it is useful to keep in mind the broader context that has made the emergence of a new hegemony possible. Beyond the immediate context of the rise of the BJP, this phenomenon needs to be understood in the broader political context that has been shaped since 1989. If one were to move beyond electoral performance, the post-1989 period is marked by the absence of an ideological theme that could bind politics together. In the backdrop of the defeat of the Indian National Congress (INC) party in the 1989 elections, we have also witnessed the inability of the INC to command any control over the narratives that constituted the key reference points for political contestations.[3] This has been variously described as a decline of the Congress party,[4] or the 'third life' of Congress marked by the challenge of survival.[5]

Decisive restructuring of the party system

In 2014, the BJP emerged as the dominant party not merely in numeric terms; it expanded its political presence to a large number of states, received support from a cross section of society, placed the leadership factor at the centre of competitive politics, and above all, set the tone for the political debates. Since then, but also during that election, the BJP and Narendra Modi made every effort to set aside the state-specific factors, make them less relevant, and bring about an all-India imagination that dominated the electorate. Throughout the nineties, in spite of the initial success of the *Ramjanmbhoomi* mobilisations, the growth of the BJP was arrested by the then existing state-specific nature of politics wherein not just electoral contests but the language of politics and issue framing were mostly state-specific. But in the 2014 elections, the BJP managed to break this barrier and present an all-India imagination. This feature of the BJP's politics went against the established pattern of state-dominated competition.[6] Besides the fact that BJP was the first party to gain a clear majority since 1984, the 2014 outcome underscored its dominance in terms of the near-lethal defeat inflicted on the main competitor, the INC (which received only 19 per cent of the vote and forty-four seats). Thus, the distance between the BJP and all other parties who were separately opposed to it (or as part of the UPA, which polled 23 per cent of the vote and won fifty-nine seats), constitutes the core of its dominance. The BJP's capacity to frame issues and project an image at the all-India level distinguished it from the politics of the previous decade and a half.

After coming to power in 2014, the BJP alternated between acquiescing to the dynamics of state-specificity and further strengthening an all-India paradigm of politics. The 'Modi factor' continued to push state-specificity aside. The Bihar Assembly election of 2015 was a rude reminder of the importance of state-specificity, but the BJP still persisted with its strategy of countering state-specificity with national or all-India factors. The 'crusade' against black money and the hype over nationalism are both instances of this strategy. Modi's address to the party after the election results to the Uttar Pradesh (UP) Assembly indicates this turn most explicitly. After UP, he was not talking only—or even primarily—about UP.[7] The vision he talked about was the vision of new India. This shift away from the states may pose a serious crisis for state parties.

To slightly restate my earlier argument about the emergence of the 'second dominant party system,'[8] this means that: a) Congress is unlikely to strike back in the near future; b) any coalition led by the Congress will remain only weak and nominal (together, both these points mean that there won't be a single node around which 'opposition' to BJP can take shape); c) one by one, state parties that stood their ground in 2014 are likely to fall;[9] d) most social sections, in terms of class, caste and location, would support the BJP in large proportions making it difficult to argue that the BJP is a sectional party,[10] thus making its social profile flat but robust; e) in the short term, there would be a delinking between its performance and electoral support because the voter would be willing to posit trust in promises rather than checking on actual performance; f) Modi would continue to be the central force within the BJP for winning elections, controlling the party, and acquiring popular acceptability.

Dominance in the terrain of ideas

But more than dominance in terms of the structure of competition, it is the ideological terrain where the emergent dominance needs careful attention. In tune with the true implication of the idea of a dominant party system, the rise of the BJP as the dominant force underscores the emergence of a new politics. While the BJP has yet to truly emerge as a dominant party by getting re-elected in 2019, the party is already busy ushering in a new dimension of dominance. The idiom and import of this new dominance are complex. The new politics of Modi's BJP is going to be a blend of new Hindutva and the political economy of a new variety.[11] Newspaper columns and unsolicited counsels to Modi keep hoping and advising that this moment be used by Modi to rein in Hindutva elements and focus on the economy (and governance). Indeed, a whole lot of the commenting crowd in India loves Modi as the messiah of development and governance and thinks that the other Modi would fade into the background. What they conveniently ignore is the fact that it is unthinkable that the BJP and Modi have given up, or for that matter would ever give up, Hindutva.

New Hindu nationalism

Hindutva is a century-old project. To be sure, it has travelled a long way from the ideas of Golwalkar. While opposition to Muslims (and minority religious groups in general) and the idea of homogenisation constitute the bases of Hindu nationalism, under Deoras during the seventies and later in the late eighties under Advani, Hindutva's approach to religion and its social composition have changed quite substantially. This transformation has been variously described as neo-Hinduism[12] and the vernacularisation of Hindutva.[13] Modi and contemporary Hindu nationalism are products of that transformation.[14] While Modi has never pretended to proffer a new vision of Hindutva (much of his approach originates in the Savarakarite view of Hindutva that percolated to the Rashtriya Swayamsevak Sangh or RSS *pracharaks* through Deoras), his politics and that of his party have the ability of shaping the Hindutva rhetoric and also shaping the popular imagination about what Hindutva constitutes.[15]

Modi's Hindutva exhorts the followers to become Hindu politically and become 'religious Hindus' by way of public manifestation of religiosity. Both of these are gifts of the Advani-era which unfolded during the Ayodhya agitation. The conflation between nationalism and Hindutva has been the backbone of the new ideological dominance. This is why the BJP has been so happy with intellectuals trying to problematise the idea of a nation. Such an ideological/intellectual stance places the BJP in a position of immense advantage and ensures that 'anti-BJP' would necessarily be equated with the 'anti-national'. Even without getting into the debate about Hindutva, the BJP has been able to discredit critiques of the idea of nation by creating an atmosphere of nationalist excitement. From there, it is not very difficult to implicitly suggest that being a nationalist is equivalent of being a Hindu and vice versa. That is precisely what the RSS chief's speeches did. The mixing of the registers of nationalism and Hindutva adroitly strengthens the BJP's new hegemonic project because while many people may not have any emotional connection with the idea of Hindutva, a majority certainly has emotional investment in the idea of nation. Because the BJP succeeds in conflating these two, for the new recruits to Hindutva who come from a cross section of the society, being a staunch Hindu becomes a vehicle that expresses their nationalism.

Of course, from the beginning, Hindutva has claimed to be coterminous with nationalism. But since he appeared on the national scene, Modi has spoken less about Hindutva and more about nationalism. This tactical shift has helped him in generating enormous support to not only his personal leadership but also to the overarching nationalist narrative—a narrative that encompasses development, national power and Hindutva. This move, beyond all else, has been characteristic of a hegemonic project nearly achieved. Since coming to power, almost every single step of the Modi government has been presented as constituting the grand narrative of nationalism. In the early phase, two critical episodes erupted that placed a seal of public approval on the emergent hegemony and the new nationalism that was being presented. One was the 'Jawaharlal Nehru University (JNU) issue'. It is not necessary to go into 'facts' here. The key point is that sections of the JNU students could be projected as challenging India's nationalism and the response from opponents of the BJP could be dubbed as anti-national. While intellectual circles were aghast at the arrogance of nationalist fervour, ordinary citizens did not find anything wrong in privileging nationalism over everything else. A related issue that emerged then, was freedom of expression when the Modi regime argued that freedom of expression is subject to the idea of nation. In the normative register of a majority of the citizens, this resonated: freedom of expression could not supersede nation and nationalism; it could be only next to and subservient to the idea of a nation. Thus, the debate on nationalism was appropriated by the BJP to bring home the point that its opponents are 'anti-national' in their approach.

But besides name-calling and stigmatisation of opponents, the Modi regime has found it possible to slowly begin redefining Indian nationalism. While it has boldly begun to bring Savarkar's ideas to the centre stage of nationalist discourse, it has also introduced controversial elements in the nationalist discourse at the level of practice. For long, the slogan *vande mataram* has been a bone of contention. To that, the contemporary debates have added the slogan *Bharat Mata ki Jai*. The supreme court ruling[16] on the national anthem in movie theatres became a useful ploy for the BJP to highlight the need to assert national sentiments and national symbols. The cow is added to this as a matter of national pride and concern. Together, these newly assertive symbols have changed the discourse on the question of nation and nationalism beyond recognition. In a short span of a couple of years, the BJP has successfully shifted the meaning and importance of the idea of nationalism. This new nationalism is firmly and multiply rooted in new symbolisms, supposed economic advance, the status of the country in the international arena, and the militaristic policy articulated by the publicity accorded to 'surgical strikes.' For ordinary citizens, each of these has become incontrovertible aspect of nationalism and hence, it is easy to stigmatise those who oppose these measures and contest this particular variant of nationalism.

New developmentalism

The other key component of the ideological dominance consists of the idea of development. The INC was the initial architect of this component but does not have the political courage and ideological sophistication today to capitalise on it. Thus, development as an idea emerges from a certain amount of consensus. However, throughout the decade since the late 1990s, the popular expectations fanned by globalisation and inadequately satiated by India's political economy remained unattended. The BJP faltered in making haste on the platform of 'shining India', but no other party really took note of the potential of that politics of hope and expectation. Ironically, the INC did have the past record of similarly tapping hope and expectation: through the audacious '*Garibi hatao*' (remove poverty) slogan. But the party has ceased to allow any political imagination and therefore, while it came close to capturing the public imagination through its '*aam admi ka saath*' (with the common man) slogan, it failed in tapping the energy of hope. By then, the INC had completely lost the capacity to appropriate ideas and slogans for building a durable ideological apparatus that would ensure diffuse support beyond mere votes. Instead of seizing the initiative, it continued hoping that the voters would be willing to support it solely on the basis of a discourse of palliatives.

Modi took over from where Pramod Mahajan[17] had left the politics of hope and received enough response for it to turn it into an integral element of his ideological offering. The second key element of the ideological dominance was thus carved out from the utterly innocuous but eminently evocative term of 'development'. The BJP's emerging ideological dominance seeks to deploy new shades of meaning to the idea of development and while these are as yet unarticulated the efforts are visible to redefine development. Though during the campaign for the Lok Sabha elections Modi equated development with nationalism, after coming to power he floated three non-controversial elements to speak about development. Many observers were (at least in the first year of this rhetoric) impressed by the possibilities that Modi's developmentalist rhetoric appeared to contain. These were the ideas and slogans associated with *Swachh Bharat* (Clean India), Make in India, and Skill India (to which Digital India was added).[18] Subsequently, the imagination of 'new India' is being developed in which the emphasis is on opportunity and achievement, thus replacing key reference points such as welfare and redistribution. This direction is not entirely new—sections of policymakers have been pushing the country into this direction during the past couple of decades and the Modi-regime has taken this forward.

The narratives of both Hindutva and development are presented as parts of the larger and more influential 'grand narrative' of nationalism. Independently, both ideas—Hindutva and development—are potent political discourses. By weaving them together with nationalism Modi has bound them into an arsenal of his political and ideological offensive.

Crafting discursive dominance

The crafting of a new hegemony is a complex challenge related to both the production of ideas and their dissemination. In this sense, it is a task comprised of repackaging the old along with packaging the controversial in an acceptable form. The dominant forces always need to ensure that elements acceptable both to a large cross section of society and to sections of the intelligentsia and media are given a place of prominence. The more controversial ideas get acceptability through association with these accepted ideas, besides, of course, concerted efforts on the part of the dominant powers. But equally, it is important that in crafting hegemony, new ideas are floated in the public domain which might generate only limited controversy and have the potential of becoming acceptable to a cross section of the population. The Modi regime did this with remarkable skill. In an effort to strengthen the hegemonic project, Modi and the BJP needed to combine the acceptable and the controversial. The years of BJP rule since 2014 are characterised by this exercise. In most cases, the idiom is from the repertoire of accepted ideas and labels but the connotations and implications are new.

We can take a quick look at the debates and subsequent acceptance of some of the ideas that the new regime has sought to float.

Cashless: The prime minister unveiled 'demonetisation'[19] by addressing the nation and arguing that this was a move necessary to dig out black money.

Subsequently, he even lamented the sufferings of the ordinary citizen on this account but appealed to their sense of national duty. In the course of the bizarre developments that continued to unfold, the arguments kept changing; the objectives varied from black money to terrorism to digital/cashless economy, to broadening the tax base. While economists have wondered at the economic wisdom behind the move, political commentators have wondered about the near-suicidal political wisdom (or lack of it) behind the move. But the fact remains that Modi has shown the capacity to shift the discourse from a defensive argument to an aggressive one that involved nationalism and made the idea of the digital/cashless economy acceptable (or at least 'fashionable'). Taking off from the talk about black money that began with the 2011 anti-corruption agitation,[20] the new hegemony seeks to introduce a set of new values in terms of cashless transactions and the marginalisation of the informal economy in favour of a corporate-driven economy affectionately welcomed by the middle classes. The demonetisation discourse also legitimised a strong state-centred and vigilance-/surveillance-driven exercise of authority. So, through the anti-corruption agenda a new structure of the economy and a new turn toward regulation-centred state authority actually emerged as elements of the new hegemony.

Electoral Reforms: Right from the early days of the Modi-regime, Modi has often talked of 'electoral reforms'. Again, this is a beautifully consensual platform. That it can become part of the new discursive space is evidenced from the willingness of the INC to also engage in discussion of 'change in the electoral system'.[21] A host of civil society organisations have regularly initiated debates over this issue. Modi latched on to that term, though he added his own meaning to it: holding elections to national and state legislatures simultaneously is his key electoral reform (remarkably, a pithy slogan has emerged: 'one nation–one election', thus connecting the initiative to the nationalist motif) and the Election Commission of India (ECI) has dutifully subscribed to the wisdom of this move. The apparent argument is boldly populist in that such a move would reduce election expenditure. With all its robustness, India's democracy is always seen by many as an expensive affair and this idea of reducing expenses quickly sets off a string of support among the larger public. It is also argued that simultaneous elections would improve 'governance' because of the reduction in restrictions for the governments in taking policy decisions. On the margins of this discussion of electoral reforms, there is occasional mention of the the monetary aspect of election campaigns, and restrictions on it. Election funding and political funding in general is a key issue for democracy in India but that is buried under the new initiative to start 'bonds' for political funding which can only make funding more hazy.[22] Thus, a new idea gets floated, it overshadows the core issues, and in fact, sets out to change the basic principle of the parliamentary system without raising any public debate on that aspect—and yet the space for arguing against it remains almost non-existent.

EPI vs VIP: A third instance is the popular decision to 'end Very Important Person (VIP) culture'. This is in reference to a decision of the Government of India to do away with red beacons on VIP vehicles which has generally been welcomed even by the grudging media. It is another matter that this is not exactly the initiative of the Modi regime—it flows from a court case. But the way it has been appropriated showcases the capacity of the architects of this new hegemony to accommodate factors that would make the emergent set of new ideas morally superior, acceptable to the general public, and politically difficult to counter. In fact, Modi has shown an extraordinary agility in connecting his own discourse to the removal of red beacons. When Modi was campaigning in 2014, and even after he became the prime minister, he often referred to not only his austere background, but the fact that he was an 'outsider' to Delhi's power circles. This claim replaced Arvind Kejriwal's[23] claim against the 'political class' in general. Modi's claim was promptly endorsed by some commentators, shifting attention from the political class to Lutyens' Delhi.[24] It has been argued that Modi intended to not only break that power grid in Delhi but ensure that the state apparatus works for the ordinary citizen.[25] In his characteristic manner, Modi coined a term for this: *Pradhan Sevak* (Prime Servant). So, using the red beacon ban, he reminded the public of his resolve to remain only a servant and that he upholds a new culture wherein 'Every Person is Important' (EPI) as against the 'VIP' culture. It is necessary not to discount these merely as gimmicks or cosmetic measures or wordplay, but to note that such 'small' measures do resonate with the popular imagination and expectation. Initiatives such as discarding red beacons show that there is a basis of public resentment, a context in the form of anti-corruption mobilisation, a skilful political appropriation of the anti-elite (or anti-establishment) sentiment and more sophisticated explanations of what Modi symbolises—all contributing to a crafting of a new dominant discourse.[26]

'Secularism': Alongside these ideas with greater and easy acceptability, the dominant set of ideas also includes ideas that draw their sustenance more from prejudices of the majority than from their actual connotation. The Modi-regime has always assured that it would not treat the minority in an unjust manner and in fact the regime prides itself on the question of 'equal treatment' of majority and minority. The BJP has always—from Advani's time—claimed that while it seeks to enforce true secularism, the INC and most other parties indulge in pseudo-secularism.[27] True secularism, according to this view point, entails strictly equal treatment of all religious communities. Modi gave expression to this narrow construction of secularism when, during the UP electoral campaign, he said that true secularism meant that whether Eid or Diwali, both communities would receive equal treatment in terms of uninterrupted power supply.[28] Similarly, Modi and the BJP hijacked the progressive and reformist agenda on the question of triple *talaq*[29] both during the hearing of the case and the SC ruling subsequently. In insisting on reforming Muslim personal law, the BJP sought to attract the Hindu community on the basis of strict equality, believing that this is a path to true secularism and justice for women. The government's drive to push for a ban on triple *talaq* naturally added to the popularity of the Modi regime among the majority community. At the same time, the claim that this was a measure to give justice to Muslim women indicated the larger acceptability that the government sought to gain for the measure.

Organisational Network: While relatively more acceptable ideas constitute the outer appearance of discursive dominance and ideas addressing the majority community's prejudices constitute the popular elements, the real core is drawn from the most controversial elements—controversies surrounding the issues of cows and conversions are instances of these. Contestation over these ideas and issues has become tough partly because of vigilantism that seeks to suppress debate and partly because public support is building up in favour of the Hindutva arguments on these matters. This intervention in the discursive domain and a shift in the public attitudes have been possible because of the complex alignment of leadership, party, government and allied organisations.

While as a party the BJP is indeed busy coining new ideas and slogans and engaging in continuous campaign beyond merely electoral considerations, the real strength of the new ideological offensive lies in the realm of civil society. As I have argued,[30] it is necessary to understand the contributions being made by the huge network of organisations allied with the RSS and also functioning independently of it. Critics of the BJP (and RSS) have often mentioned the Hindutva link between the two. However, it is necessary to appreciate the value and utility of the convenient arrangement of being 'separate and yet connected'. Even the latest speeches (referred to above) by Mohan Bhagwat underscored this when Bhagwat distanced himself from the idea of 'Congress-*mukt*' Bharat (India free of Congress) and even went on to underline the contribution of the INC. In an exercise of shaping the discursive domain, mere electoral support is not enough. The battle unfolds mainly in the arena of civil society and it is here that the large number of RSS-linked organisations matter. Even a cursory look at the Sewa Bharati website[31] should acquaint us with the vast social territory occupied by the organisations that are either floated by or take inspiration from the larger Hindutva viewpoint generally and the RSS more specifically.

This unique organisational arrangement helps the ideological interventions in two different ways. One is to build diffuse support (as pointed out by Tariq Thachil),[32] and the other, to intervene in public debates more directly. These 'aligned' organisations come forward as and when necessary to extend support to the various decisions of the BJP government. Even in order to skilfully use social media and media in general, the regime requires not just money and a battery of employable trolls, it also requires independent interventions by social actors with their own base, legitimacy and identity. The Modi regime faced three critical moments, different in scale, intensity and context. One was the controversy surrounding the returning of awards by eminent intellectuals and artists, the second was demonetisation, and the third the Kashmir failure. At each of these times, many voices 'outside' of the party have emerged from this larger organisational network and joined the debates on behalf of the regime. Sensing that the media, particularly the English-language media, is not adequately enamoured with all the aspects of the Modi-regime, a slew of new writers and columnists is thrusting itself forward into the public domain just as many persons not directly associated with the party have been occupying the cultural space. The entire arena of the public sphere is being increasingly occupied by the new entrants from various organisational backgrounds belonging to the larger Sangh network. The BJP government has been able to sustain ideologically, generate, and receive support for many of its risky initiatives through a range of pre-existing organisations and activists belonging to those organisations.

The second feature of this structure is the way in which many organisations of the Sangh and beyond[33] are 'independently' raising many issues and shaping public debates. Just as the Sanatan Sanstha does not have any direct links to RSS, so also, the Hindu Yuva Vahini is not connected with the RSS. Nevertheless, during the years of the Modi regime, many issues have been brought to the forefront steering the debate unmistakably to the idea of Hindutva. Thus, for instance, 'Love Jihad' or *Ghar Wapsi* were not formally pursued by the party in power, and for the record, the prime minister assured all minorities full protection yet at the same time, public debates revolved around these sensitive issues because there was enough organisational space within Hindutva for such a 'fringe' to exist and push its own agenda. The vigilantism associated with *Gau Raksha* (cow protection) is also an instance of the same space and confusion between the mainstream and the fringe. Again, the prime minister has chastised the vigilantes, but street action and the shrill rhetoric both persist because of the organisational space available to them.

In other words, there is a very happy and convenient situation for the BJP. The party has a ready-made apparatus of voluntary organisations which supplies manpower and generates support for the regime, while at the same time raises issues that the party may not formally want to be seen to be raising. The formal electoral battle will be fought by the party where the organisational network will chip in, but the real battle is ideological and for that, the network is all the more important for expanding and complicating the agenda and thus overcoming the limits of the party.

Towards hegemony?

Given the combination of electoral strength and dominance in the field of ideas, is the BJP heading toward enjoying a hegemonic position?

Ever since the INC began facing difficulties in the aftermath of Indira Gandhi's landslide victory of 1971–72, India has not experienced the hold of any hegemonic ideology in political and cultural realms. The constitutive elements of the previous hegemony had already begun to crumble by then. The post-independence hegemony had helped the INC gain a position of political dominance in the electoral arena. The intervening period of the 'decline of Congress' witnessed not only an era of multi-party coalitions but also a phase where caricatures of old hegemonic ideas and glimpses of many newly emerging ideas (including that of social justice) co-existed without any decisive confrontation. In other words, while the previous hegemony was crumbling, there was not necessarily any great war of ideas but an atmosphere of confusion and ideological chaos. Nevertheless, both electoral dominance and ideological ascendancy presided over by the INC had come to an end.

The BJP seems set to fill both these vacuums. The electoral dominance of the BJP has created conditions for hegemony to take shape. That India may be headed toward a new hegemony is indicated by the strength gained by new values that are not necessarily in consonance with the foundational values on which democracy in India was built. This shift away from the foundational values is displayed more than anywhere in the field of diversity. The public approach to question of diversity is marked by an uneasy acceptance of the value of diversity at best and normative reservations about it at worst. The heightened debate on nationalism represents this approach. Instead of the healthy coexistence of democracy, nationalism and diversity, new binaries are being posited: democracy vs nationalism and nationalism vs diversity. In other words, the present political situation is not merely marked by the relative electoral success of one party or the rise of a popular leader alone. Both these factors are indeed present, but they are leading to something more than mere electoral victory.

In all probability, a new political idiom, a new political elite, and a new political culture are shaping in contemporary India. As the societal arena goes through more and more changes, the possibility of the present moment turning into a new hegemony becomes stronger. And if we take into account the complete absence of a political counter and an ideological counter to the emerging discourse, its hegemonic portents become more visible.

Modi's steadfast pursuit of a new idea of development makes the current discourse all the more hegemonic because then, it does not remain only a political project of one organisation, nor does it remain restricted to the agenda of one political party. While majoritarianism and the changing political culture sustain the dominant ideas and promise their durability, the associated idea of development makes sure that they would receive tacit (and even open) support from both the middle classes and corporate interests. What the current regime is set to do is to acquire approval of corporate interests separately (i.e., unconnected from the cultural agenda) for its economic agenda and at the same time, acquire approval for its socio-political agenda from the larger public by linking it to the economic agenda. The corporate classes are expected not to be interested in or concerned with the emerging debates in the arena of public political culture believing that irrespective of what political culture emerges, the economic agenda would be implemented vigorously and the erosion of diversity would not hurt the material interests of the corporates. On the other hand, the ordinary citizen is sought to be convinced that economic wellbeing is primarily a function of a strong nation and therefore, the hurdles in becoming a strong nation (such as social schisms, minority appeasement, anti-national use of freedom of expression) need to be overcome.

This is where the ability of Modi to bring together the middle classes and corporate interests becomes crucial. This alliance is critical not only to his electoral prospects, but more so for the hegemonic project. Modi emerges as the extraordinary leader because of skilfully marrying an aggressive corporatised economy with an assertive majoritarian politics. This marriage is predicated on the acceptance by or turning of the proverbial blind eye by corporate interests as far as majoritarian logic is concerned. To what extent and how long the marriage remains happy will determine whether the new hegemony will take root and become a durable force. But at the same time, the political agency of Modi and shifts in political culture may convince corporate interests to live happily with majoritarianism. Therefore, India is at a historic juncture where direct support of corporate interests to majoritarian logic might not be required if there is a substantial shift in public opinion. Modi knows this and therefore strives hard to create a discursive domain where the logic of Hindu majoritarianism is skilfully camouflaged by impressive yet shallow ideas of 'new India'.

After the UP victory, Modi felt assured to inaugurate his idea of 'new India'—a land of opportunities rather than handouts.[34] Modi's 'chale jao' (leave)' message[35] similarly represents the determination to dictate the terms of discourse and win acceptability in the fields of ideas and ideals. There are gaping holes in the new set of dominant ideas that are gaining ground and surely, there is bound to be deep unease at the fundamentally inegalitarian and anti-pluralist populism informing these ideas. But the fact of the arrival of this hegemony is not easy to contest.

There will be many factors determining how this project will take shape. Concerns of formal power may circumscribe the BJP's zeal for pursuing the grand narrative; centralisation of powers within the party too may impose hurdles on the ability to build hegemony; tensions may build between the RSS and the party over critical aspects of the hegemony; overexposure of Modi may result in Modi fatigue, resulting in limitations to his ability to function as the architect and builder of the new hegemony. Moreover, the Modi regime would need to handle a deeper challenge. Ideas and normative regimes become hegemonic only when they penetrate larger sections of the society and also sizable sections of the intelligentsia. The Modi regime may falter on two counts. One, not only has it had an awkward relationship with the intelligentsia and institutions of knowledge production, but the regime often prides itself on its anti-intellectual stand as articulated by Modi in his juxtaposition between 'Harvard experts and hard work'.[36] Two, whether the Modi regime will be successful in extending its acceptability—of the norms it upholds—to geographic peripheries (as in the North East, in Kashmir or in Tamil Nadu and Kerala) and social margins (Dalits and Adivasis, not to speak of Muslims) will be a more critical factor in the onward march of the hegemonic project. But these limitations and caveats notwithstanding, the change that came about in 2014 is a regime change, a change in the nature of party competition and above all, a decisive move to craft hegemony that would ensure long term changes in the tenor and texture of democratic politics in India.

Hegemonies have a complex relationship with democracies. Hegemony represents the continuing battle between democratisation—expansion of democracy—and elite efforts to keep the radical aspects of democracy limited. Thus, the co-existence of democracy and hegemony, though consisting of tensions, is not extraordinary. Most democracies often experience this co-existence and the tensions involved in it. In the case of India, the emerging hegemony also holds the possibility of altering the nature of India's democracy as it was imagined and at least partially practised so far. In this sense, the emerging hegemony portends a distortion of democracy.[37] The new hegemony may usher in a new 'normal' as far as our collective imagination of what democracy means and what it should do is concerned. Just as the hegemonic project is bound to penetrate popular imagination, competitive politics too could shape the success and intensity of the hegemonic project. That is what makes both the politics of hegemony and the politics of petty electoral competition so intertwined and so exciting to watch.

Paradoxical as it may appear, while electoral upsets might not easily forestall the shaping of the new discursive terrain, electoral defeat alone can puncture the BJP's resolute march toward crafting a new hegemony.

6

CAN MODI AND THE BJP ACHIEVE
AND SUSTAIN HEGEMONY?

James Manor

Narendra Modi's Bharatiya Janata Party (BJP) dominates India's political system at the time of writing in December 2017. It is likely to win the next national election in 2019, and seeks to go further, to achieve hegemony—overwhelming supremacy.[1] It wants India to be not just 'Congress-*mukt* (free)', but also 'opposition-*mukt*'. It aims to rule 'for at least 50 years'[2] and to usher in a new political order that will transform India's culture and social relations.

This chapter analyses the promise and limitations of key elements of Modi's strategy in his drive for hegemony. It assesses features of the new order that may make hegemony hard to achieve, and even harder to sustain. Because Modi needs mass support in this quest, several changes which are scarcely noticed by ordinary voters are omitted here: eroding the authority of parliament;[3] pressuring the courts;[4] harassing or expelling independent non-governmental associations;[5] treating independent media outlets as if he 'has declared war' on them;[6] banning or censoring inconvenient films;[7] takeovers or assaults on universities;[8] raids on rivals by investigative agencies;[9] hyper-nationalism and the extravagant use of charges of sedition.[10] Impediments posed by laws, the constitution and institutions of state are also left for another occasion.

Let us first consider three devices used in the pursuit of hegemony: dramatic promises and efforts to fulfil them; theatrics and the projection of Modi as a compelling personality; and an anti-corruption drive. A further instrument and a core element of the new order—polarisation between the Hindu majority and religious minorities, especially Muslims—is then discussed before longer term issues are examined.

Stirring promises and government performance

During the 2014 election campaign, Modi won broad support by appealing to popular aspirations—offering voters better times (*achhe din*) and two more specific promises. First, vast amounts of illicit funds stashed overseas would be repatriated, and every bank account would receive 1.5 million rupees (US$23,400). They have received nothing. The government must recover 9,000 times more than it has retrieved to honour that pledge.[11]

His more crucial promise—massive job creation—was compelling among younger voters. It has not occurred. Modi promised to create 250 million new jobs in a decade. He is way behind—'with each passing year, we are adding to the backlog'.[12] The Labour Bureau found that 2015 saw the fewest jobs added since 2008.[13] Growth in organised sector employment fell by 60 per cent in 2015.[14] Modi's 'much-hyped "Make in India"' campaign to increase manufacturing jobs is 'drifting'[15] and 'seems hardly to have worked'.[16] Annual growth in manufacturing was a mere 1.6 per cent in the five years to 2016, and in the next nine months it contracted by 0.5 per cent.[17] In the first quarter of 2017, 1.5 million jobs were lost.[18] An eminent economist argues that Modi's demonetisation 'may have broken the back of small and new enterprises' which create 80 per cent of jobs.[19]

The *Global Competitiveness Report* revealed a 'miserable performance' on indicators that might enable job creation: 'technological readiness, higher education, training and skill development'. A government committee issued 'a damning critique of its flagship skill development programme'.[20] Rankings remained low on life expectancy and infant mortality because of a weak public health sector—on which spending has been cut. On the global hunger index, India lagged behind Myanmar, Bangladesh and Nepal.[21] This explains alarming figures on irreparable childhood stunting which undermines people's capacity to find and retain jobs.[22]

Some eminent analysts note mitigating trends,[23] but overall, the evidence indicates severe disappointment for job seekers. Popular doubts have risen. In one 2017 survey, 63 per cent saw joblessness as a problem—up from 43 per cent in 2016.[24] Two others found that it was voters' greatest concern.[25] A third identified it as Modi's 'Achilles heel'. Anxiety was most acute among the 'aspirational "neo-middle class"', his core base.[26] One account speaks of government 'panic' on the issue, and a 'gathering storm' amid worrying signs for the economy.[27] A distinguished economist fears that Modi will turn to 'diversionary tactics...the polarising, majoritarian, poison-fuming Hindutva machinery....'.[28]

His stirring speeches about retrieving illicit money and job creation have become what Indians call 'tall promises'. But instead of damping down high expectations when these over-ambitious pledges go unmet, Modi—who relishes their dramatic impact—has offered yet another: farmers will soon 'be rich', their incomes will double by 2022. Doubts have already arisen. Farmers in the Gujarat state election preferred Congress to the BJP by 51 per cent to 40.[29] The BJP won that election partly because Gujarat is highly urbanised, but in most states, a decline in rural support would gravely damage the party. If unfulfilled, that promise could rival the jobs issue in undermining the drive for hegemony.

Farmers' incomes might double in 'nominal' terms—which 'means very little because offset by inflation'.[30] But doubling them in 'real' terms 'would be a miracle of miracles'[31]—requiring annual agricultural growth of 15 per cent after less than 2 per cent over the last four years.[32]

Government efforts to assist farmers have stuttered. It trumpeted a major investment in irrigation, but in 2015–16, less than a third of those funds were released. Much, possibly most of the millions of rupees for rural credit will go to agri-business.[33] Most initiatives to strengthen vocational education for farmers 'have hardly had any positive impact on the actual creation of employment opportunities...', and demonetisation damaged agricultural incomes from late 2016 onward.[34] The 2017 budget was presented as pro-farmer, but a careful analysis shows it to be a 'big prank...a washout'.[35] The ban on beef sales has hurt and alienated even those 'backward' castes who oppose cow slaughter—because they depend heavily on livestock sales.[36] This is another tall promise in the making.

Some government initiatives—for improved roads and power supplies,[37] and free gas provisions for poor households—have made headway. But the exclusion of many poor people from lists of beneficiaries of poverty programmes—300,000 in Rajasthan alone—as a result of faulty implementation of the universal ID system is a potential time bomb.[38] Overall, government performance is 'patchy, if not floundering'.[39]

Theatrics, projecting Modi's personality

Modi's dramatic promises are a key element of his extravagant—and often effective—theatricality. But the impact of his formidable communication skills is already waning. When promises go unfulfilled, he responds with distractions: more promises and stirring inaugurations of new initiatives—glitteringly depicted by many compliant media outlets.[40]

They sometimes produce gains, but can boomerang. As a former supporter, Arun Shourie, notes 'drama is not achievement'. As soaring expectations turn to disappointments when people experience little material change from 'the 99-odd schemes'[41] he has introduced, they tire of this. Continuing theatrics threaten to turn Modi into 'a caricature of the riveting speaker' of 2014—with 'grotesque comic effect'. In 2016, he claimed that by introducing demonetisation, he had put his own life at risk. This was so implausible that it provoked laughter.[42] He also claimed that he was a mere *fakir*—a penniless, half-dressed mendicant—seeking only to help people. An opponent asked how Modi—a fashion icon who changes clothes four times daily—could be a *fakir*. More laughter ensued. If he becomes a figure of fun, the hegemonic project will be in jeopardy.

His limited theatrical repertoire also poses dangers. '[H]eaping humiliation on his adversary is central to all Modi's campaigns'. But that is not appropriate in all circumstances. '[H]e will have to unlearn some of his tactics... Uninstalling mockery from his arsenal is top of the list'.[43] But he seems unable to do that. For example, he began a major speech in Parliament in 2015 with soothing words to win cooperation from opposition parties, but then could not help himself from ending with his customary caustic denunciations that defeated his purpose.[44] Scathing attacks on rivals often worked when they held power, but now that the BJP governs in New Delhi and many states, it will become the focus of popular discontent.

Indian voters are sophisticated enough to see the ironic contrast between dazzling theatrics and the drab realities that they face. As inevitable ambiguities overtake BJP governments, a shrewd leader might de-dramatise, to make expectations more realistic,[45] but Modi's repertoire is dangerously limited to high drama. He has made some adjustments. As disbelief in *achhe din* mounted,[46] the BJP systematically avoided the phrase. But promises and pageantry continue unabated.

He often adroitly eludes debates on troubling issues by changing tack. When opponents try to 'pin him down', he has already 'skated away'.[47] When embarrassments arise, orchestrated 'forced trending' on social media interprets them as successes.[48] But such tactics have become less effective as failures mount. A central bank report suggested that demonetisation probably knocked '2.3 percentage points' off economic growth,[49] and destroyed 'almost 1.5 million jobs'. After 'record-high train accidents' left the government 'squirming for answers', Modi's strange attempt to blame Pakistan flopped.[50]

After his predecessor, a wooden public speaker, he still seems refreshingly dynamic. Many who are disappointed say that at least he is trying. But note a remark by an Uttar Pradesh farmer during the 2017 state election campaign. He saw no change for the better. He would vote for Modi this time, but if things did not improve soon, he would turn on him.[51]

Tackling corruption

Modi's personal popularity remains high, partly because of his aggressive efforts to address corruption.[52] He has had some success at the national level. But corruption is more rampant at the state level which has more impact on ordinary people's lives, and is largely beyond any prime minister's reach.[53] If citizens feel little change in everyday corruption, popular appreciation for Modi's anti-corruption drive may wane.

The ferocity with which he has attacked corruption at the national level has also produced a damaging result. Civil servants avoid making decisions or even annotating files, lest they (like several famously honest colleagues) be wrongly charged with malfeasance. Buck-passing is rife, paralysing much of the administration.[54]

That and bureaucratic sclerosis have damaged delivery on government programmes. For example, its 'Housing for All' scheme was supposed to construct 1.2 million homes by 2017–18, but only 149,000 have been built. The government also failed to make adequate preparations to vaccinate people at high risk of the H1N1 virus, which has spread widely—despite the memory of a 'pandemic' in 2009 and severe problems in 2015.[55]

Outrages by Hindu extremists

Hindu zealots' mostly violent, often murderous actions are often reported individually, but no cumulative picture reveals the immensity of this trend. So for the record, here is an account of most such incidents since 2014. Note the many regions affected and the rising tide.

2014: Extremists mounted a campaign against so-called 'love jihad' (allegedly to rescue Hindu women from the clutches of Muslims), and prioritised religious conversions of minorities, and efforts to glorify the Hindu fanatic who murdered Mahatma Gandhi. In Gujarat, an extremist organisation, abetted by the police, committed violent attacks on Muslims.[56] Elsewhere, amid numerous 'attacks on Christians and their places of worship', it warned to police not to intervene.[57] In Maharashtra, five communal clashes occurred which police said were 'pre-planned'.[58]

2015: Early in the year, two communal riots occurred in Uttar Pradesh.[59] Attacks on churches continued. In September, a Muslim in Uttar Pradesh, accused of killing a cow thirty years earlier, was beaten to death by Hindu vigilantes and his son was left in a coma—after 'generations of harmony' in that village where land for a mosque had been donated by Hindus. One attacker stated that Muslims 'want to destroy the country'.[60] The incendiary Hindu Yogi Adityanath demanded action against the murdered man's family for eating beef.[61] This was an example of a trend noted by Pratap Bhanu Mehta: 'The victim...is presented as the criminal, while ideologies that justify this killing enjoy the patronage of the state'.[62] In October, a nineteen year old Muslim in Himachal Pradesh was 'attacked by a mob and set on fire inside his truck' for 'allegedly slaughtering cows'.[63]

2016: Outrages gained momentum. In January, 'Hindu Right-wing activists...allegedly assaulted a Muslim couple on a train...on the suspicion of carrying beef, which was in fact buffalo meat found in another passenger's luggage'.[64] In March, two Muslim cattle traders in Jharkhand—one aged thirteen—were 'lynched and hanged from a tree by a mob'.[65] Later that month in Delhi, three Muslim boys were beaten for refusing to chant a Hindu nationalist slogan.[66] The BJP chief minister of Maharashtra stated that those who do not recite it have no right to stay in India.[67] This was an example of 'coerced displays of nationalism by private armies of vigilantes. They have all the freedom. Citizens have only duties... The state seems happily complicit in allowing them a free run.'[68]

In March, fifteen Hindu extremists trashed a church in Chhattisgarh and beat the worshippers.[69] A Muslim was killed in Haryana while transporting newly bought bullocks to work his fields. Then police threatened his family instead of investigating the murder.[70]

Even government officials were not spared. On two occasions, dairy and animal husbandry department officials transporting cows with valid documents were severely injured by mobs. A Muslim policeman was beaten, paraded down a street and forced to chant a Hindu nationalist slogan.

In July, two Muslim women were brutally beaten for allegedly carrying beef.[71] Seven Dalits (ex-untouchables) were thrashed and urinated upon in Una, Gujarat for performing their traditional occupation, skinning a dead cow. A video of the event went viral. A similar incident in Chikmagalur District, Karnataka went largely unnoticed.[72]

Soon thereafter, Modi broke the long, studied silence[73] with which he had greeted these attacks, regretting the Una attack on Dalits—whose votes the BJP needed. He said nothing about attacks on Muslims, despite the murder in that period of a Muslim plumber in the constituency of his tourism minister who called it an 'accident'.

In Uttar Pradesh, an activist from the BJP's affiliate, the Rashtriya Swayamsevak Sangh (RSS), dressed in a *burqa* 'was caught running away after throwing beef into a temple'. In Chhattisgarh, 'pork was thrown into two mosques and beef into two temples on the same day'.[74]

In October, policemen charged an RSS leader for an anti-Islam post on social media. Their relatives stated that '(a)bout a 1,000 strong mob' of Hindu militants 'threatened to burn the police station down and warned of riots'. Extremists then told the police 'You don't know who you have dared to touch... We can make or break governments. You are worthless'. The policemen, charged by the BJP state government with 'attempt to murder, robbery, trespass and criminal intimidation' went into hiding.[75]

2017: In April, a Muslim dairy farmer was beaten to death by a mob in Rajasthan while transporting cows.[76] The BJP state home minister blamed the victim, saying 'It is illegal to transport cows, but people ignore it and cow protectors are trying to stop such people from trafficking them'.[77] Elsewhere in Rajasthan, six people transporting cows to a cattle fair were stopped by vigilantes. One, a Hindu, was released. The five Muslims were 'severely beaten', one fatally. The same home minister claimed that both sides were to blame, and the chief minister was 'surprisingly quiet'. India's commerce minister stated—inaccurately—that 'cow protection was the spirit behind India's freedom movement'.[78]

Also in April, in Jammu and Kashmir, five Muslim nomadic herders including a nine year old girl taking animals to new pastures were attacked by 'a frenzied mob'. Some were later hospitalised. When police took the victims into their post, the rioters attacked and destroyed it. Later, police transporting the animals were attacked and accused of smuggling cows.[79] In the same period, in Delhi, three Muslims transporting buffaloes with a legal permit were beaten by Hindu extremists.[80]

Three Muslim youths were attacked in an argument over seats on a train. One died while his brother survived despite eighteen stab wounds. Passengers reportedly egged on the assailants with cries of 'they eat meat, kill them'.[81]

The BJP's new Uttar Pradesh Chief Minister, Yogi Adityanath, promised firm maintenance of law and order and his senior policeman warned of 'tough action' against vigilantes. But then a group of them, including members of Adityanath's organisation, beat a Muslim to death 'on suspicion that he had helped a Muslim neighbour elope with a Hindu woman'.[82] Others from that organisation attacked a police station and slapped a deputy superintendent after police filed a case against fellow activists who had beaten and robbed a Muslim vegetable vendor. The local BJP MP had first brought the mob to his house, 'incited them to vandalise the place', and watched the attack.[83] Members of that organisation also 'thrashed' a Muslim man and a woman in their home on suspicion of 'immoral activity' and distributed a video of it.[84]

These incidents persuaded one columnist who had supported Modi to denounce 'hunting Muslims...the madness and murderous barbarism that have been unleashed on the pretence of saving cows...'. She dismissed senior BJP leaders' bizarre claims that these attacks were carried out by secular parties' infiltrators into Hindu organisations.[85]

In that period, civic activists in Rajasthan protested the lynching of Muslim dairy farmer, saying that 'an atmosphere of terror was being created' and vigilantes have a 'free run'. Twenty-three retired civil servants wrote to the BJP chief minister complaining about government inaction.[86] Then in June, a Muslim was beaten to death when he tried to stop a group from photographing women defecating. The chief minister called his murder a 'demise'.[87]

Mere rumours fuelled an estimated 52 per cent of the attacks catalogued here. In Jharkhand during May and June, a Muslim dairy farmer was attacked on a 'rumour' that he had slaughtered a cow. Then false rumours of child lifting led to the lynching of two people and, ten days later, seven Muslims and tribals were beaten to death as police stood by. One Muslim said the BJP 'administration wants to rule us by fear'. The BJP's president in Uttar Pradesh concurred: 'we want to instil fear'.[88] There and elsewhere, the National Security Act was invoked, linking cow protection to India's security.[89]

Vigilantes interpreted Modi's refusal to criticise assaults on Muslims as tacit approval. He only broke his silence on 16 June 2017, after the *New York Times*[90] condemned the atrocities, damaging his image in the West. But then and later, by stressing that state governments in this federal system managed law and order, he deflected blame onto them.

His words rang hollow since he had chosen Yogi Adityanath to govern India's most populous state. Mehta wrote that the appointment 'signals that minorities will now face cultural, social and symbolic subordination'. The BJP would now stress 'resentment rather than hope...hate rather than reconciliation, and violence rather than decency. The party believes it can get away with anything.'[91] He later added that 'A monstrous new moral order is unfolding, irrigated by the blood of our citizens.'[92]

Attacks on Muslims continued apace after Modi's criticism.[93] August saw sixty-six reports of beatings and murders. In Uttarakhand, which had been peaceful before the BJP took power there, numerous violent incidents occurred. In one, Hindu extremists ransacked a shop and forced shops to close after accusing a Muslim of having sex with a cow. In another, they beat a Muslim for his attentions to a woman who turned out to be his wife.[94]

Only when the supreme court ruled in September that vigilantes should be 'prosecuted with promptitude' within one week did state governments, facing punishment from the court, take swift action so that the violence finally ebbed.[95] They plainly had the power to stop the carnage. That had long been evident from the minimisation of atrocities by several state governments headed by opposition parties—and even by the BJP government in Madhya Pradesh which was led by a moderate chief minister. Some therefore asked why it took others so long—and why the prime minister had not pressed them to end the barbarity.

Modi and polarisation

Modi has adopted five different postures amid this mayhem. First and strangely, since he comments constantly on many issues, he has remained silent for long periods. Second, he has then made vague, 'roundabout'[96] or mild comments about outrages, as when he described the widely reported murder of a Muslim as 'unfortunate'.[97] Such remarks do little to curb brutalities, and he sometimes adds qualifying comments that undermine these statements.[98] Third, after many months when his silence appeared to imply approval, he specifically condemned violence by cow devotees—but only against Dalits, not Muslims. His eventual criticism of assaults on Muslims in June 2017 only came after securing his election victory in Uttar Pradesh, after that *New York Times* condemnation threatened his international image, and as rival parties planned loud protests in parliament.[99] But even these belated comments were undermined by a fourth tendency: sly remarks suggesting continued commitment to religious polarisation, more blatant provocations such as the communalist rhetoric that he used in the Uttar Pradesh state election campaign,[100] and the appointment there of Adityanath. Finally, during the state election in Gujarat, he largely abandoned references to development and offered a toxic combination of 'communal poison' and 'unhinged conspiracy theories'—alleging that Pakistan was seeking to influence the result, and that opponents' actions were 'bordering on treasonous'.[101]

That marked a change from an earlier pattern of encouraging efforts by Hindu zealots to keep communal antipathy 'simmering'[102] but on a low boil, lest atrocities make BJP governments appear unable to maintain order. That was often difficult to achieve. Many extremists believe that they need not restrain themselves now as when the more moderate Atal Behari Vajpayee led the BJP. He would have been embarrassed by the atrocities listed above, and by the glorification of Godse, Gandhi's assassin. But as one BJP leader tellingly stated, 'Unlike Vajpayee, Modi personifies the Hindutva ideology. You cannot embarrass Modi by using...Godse.'[103]

Many militants believe that Modi's long silences imply that beatings and murders have the blessing of higher authority. They disregard his occasional criticisms as statements that a prime minister must make. This is especially true in BJP-ruled states where most outrages occurred. In Bihar after the BJP was drawn into the state government in 2017, vigilantes using a WhatsApp network that included a local policeman, beat a Muslim 'on suspicion' of transporting beef—claiming that they had 'our own government now'.[104] RSS men there 'feel bold enough to declare that they are now empowered' to undertake extreme acts 'as the state is now under their rule'.[105]

Modi's silences, his early complaint about vigilante violence against Dalits but not Muslims, his long delay in criticising attacks on Muslims, and his blatant communalism during recent state election campaigns strongly suggest that he shares the views of the extremists. That impression is reinforced by an astonishing foreign policy decision. He left India isolated by echoing the Myanmar regime's grotesque description of the (Muslim) Rohingyas as terrorists—an especially egregious example of victim blaming.

His actions may also be partly motivated by 'fear...[of] the serious risk of being outflanked from the right' by extremists whom he and associates 'have unleashed' but 'can no longer control'.[106] That partly explained his hard-line approach as chief minister of Gujarat, where he successfully saw off challenges from the right.

What of the BJP's longer term prospects at achieving and sustaining hegemony? We must consider the role of communal polarisation since it will remain a major theme, but let us begin with two other issues.

Leaders' skills, the BJP organisation and party competition

Since its 2017 victory in Uttar Pradesh, the BJP's president Amit Shah has been lauded in India's media as a genius, 'a Colossus'.[107] But Shah and Modi designed and dominated state election campaigns in Delhi where the BJP was humiliated, and in Bihar where they began the campaign leading in the polls but blundered their way to a thumping defeat.[108] Shah is working assiduously at organisation building, but he is a genius only some of the time.

Despite many strengths, the BJP's organisation often lacks the capacity to penetrate beyond cities and below the district level.[109] It is especially frail in several important states: West Bengal, Andhra Pradesh, Telangana, Tamil Nadu and Kerala—where other parties are formidable. Recent surveys suggest that it may make significant gains in Odisha in the state and national elections in 2019,[110] but in the 2014 election there, its organisation and performance were wretched.[111]

Many rival parties look bereft at the time of writing. But opposition parties have often revived unexpectedly because of disappointing performances by ruling parties. The BJP has inserted RSS leaders without experience of the complexities of governing as chief ministers in several states. This has led to severe problems in Gujarat where the initial appointee had to be replaced, and in Haryana. It appointed Vasundhara Raje Scindia in Rajasthan even though in an earlier spell as chief minister she alienated many interests (including most in the BJP and the RSS), and there are signs of a similar trend now. Such problems could turn poor BJP performance into rival parties' secret weapon.

The BJP may also find that after constructing multi-caste coalitions during election campaigns, the groups which take control after victories shatter those alliances. One glaring example is Uttar Pradesh where Thakurs have mounted many violent attacks on Dalits who voted for the BJP in substantial numbers in the 2017 state election.

From aspirations to resentments

Soaring aspirations are double-edged. By stimulating them with what turn out to be 'tall promises', Modi incurs popular disillusionment over the longer term. Extravagant new promises can buy him time, but far from solving the problem, they compound the risk.

His main alternative is to stress not aspirations but resentments. He has already de-emphasised aspirational appeals: nothing has been heard for over two years of the coming of *achhe din*. But as he stokes resentments, Modi faces a painful irony. Since the BJP now rules in New Delhi and most states, rival parties can no longer be blamed. The very success of the BJP ensures that it will be the main focus of popular discontent over unfulfilled promises and poor government performance. As he shifts from aspirations to resentments, Modi is left with only one main target: religious minorities, especially Muslims.

That is another dangerous game—dangerous to social cohesion, but also to the BJP. If citizens become angry over joblessness, farmers' problems[112] and other thwarted aspirations—year after year when the BJP holds power—can they really be expected to see Muslims as the culprits? That is as implausible as Modi's blaming Pakistan for railway accidents. Indian voters are highly sophisticated. They have thrown out most state and central governments since 1977. Stoking resentments may ultimately scuttle the BJP's drive for hegemony.

Communal polarisation over the longer term

Preliminary findings from a reliable recent survey in four states found that polarisation has—despite some ambiguities—influenced popular perceptions. More than one-third of Hindu respondents have a Muslim close friend, but in three states, Muslims are considered less patriotic than other religious groups. And while most respondents see Muslims as peaceful, a third of them perceive them as mostly violent. Majoritarian attitudes predominate strongly over liberal views.[113]

But over the longer term, will communal polarisation—which Modi increasingly stresses—help to achieve and then sustain hegemony? This is dubious. First, consider regional variations. Polarisation helped the BJP win the 2017 Uttar Pradesh election,[114] but in the 2015 Bihar election, it backfired. One Bihar BJP leader said 'hard Hindutva didn't work in Bihar'. Another added, 'Bihar is not Uttar Pradesh'.[115]

It also backfired when the BJP governed Karnataka before 2013. Hindu zealots ran amok in coastal districts there. '[C]ommunal riots took place... with unusual frequency and ferocity...'. Muslim boys were assaulted merely for talking to Hindu girls. Extremists stormed a pub where young women were 'slapped, beaten and chased out' for 'violating "Hindu culture and tradition" by drinking publicly'. 'Indiscriminate looting and atrocities against minorities were the order of the day.'[116] But then in the 2013 election on the coast, long a BJP stronghold, voters reacted against these outrages and against a fiercely communal campaign speech by Modi—giving rival candidates fourteen of the seventeen seats there.[117]

Across much of India, communalism has found little traction. The BJP has won re-election in several states not by polarising but by governing adroitly, pursuing development and maintaining public order which extremist outrages disrupt.[118]

Many on the Hindu Right nonetheless welcome and provoke clashes with minorities to sow communal enmity. But as noted above, these tend to be useful to Modi only as long as they keep tensions on a low boil. And as the extensive list of atrocities above indicates, it is difficult to prevent extremists from going too far. Where the BJP governs, this can alienate many voters because the authorities appear not just unable to maintain order, but even complicit in the brutalities.

The BJP's drive for hegemony, in which communal polarisation looms large, faces one last massive impediment. Indians have a diverse array of identities available to them: national, regional, sub-regional, linguistic, class, urban/rural and gender identities—plus three kinds of caste identities, and not just broad religious identities (Hindu, Muslim, etc.) but narrower sectarian identities within each religion. Many of these identities cut across and undermine one another. And crucially, polls over recent decades show that people tend to shift their preoccupations from one identity to another, and then another, in response to recent events—often and with great fluidity. They do not fix tenaciously upon one identity. So tension and conflict do not build up along a single fault line in society. This is bad news for leftists who focus on 'haves' versus 'have-nots', and for the Hindu Right which foments enmity between Hindus and minorities.[119] Sustaining communal polarisation will be excruciatingly difficult—and on past evidence, impossible.

The BJP has achieved dominance by winning elections against incumbent governments, and by appealing to popular aspirations. Hereafter, it will usually be the incumbent, and aspirations are being overtaken by disappointments. The party still lacks mass support across much of eastern and southern India.

Ironically, the same theatrics that swept the BJP to dominance by stimulating aspirations can become a liability. The performance of Modi's central government has been disappointing on many fronts, and has turned his most inspiring pledges into 'tall promises'. Dismal showings by several BJP state governments compound the problem. Its inept Gujarat chief minister had to be changed, its Haryana government has repeatedly bungled, discontents from diverse quarters have arisen in Rajasthan,[120] and its chief ministerial candidate in the 2018 Karnataka state election is a proven incompetent.[121]

To sustain the drive for hegemony, Modi must overcome these daunting problems. He needs to adjust his grand narrative. Dramatic visions of a glittering future lack credence as earlier promises go unfulfilled. Caustic denunciations of rival parties that are now powerless ring hollow.

His limited repertoire leaves him with one toxic option—shifting emphasis from aspirations to resentments. But can Muslims and allegedly seditious forces be credibly blamed for unemployment, mass poverty, the agrarian crisis, etc. India's voters are too canny to accept such patent implausibilities for long. Polls indicate that many currently harbour suspicions of minorities. But given decades of voters' fluid shifts among their multiple identities, this recent sentiment is likely to wane amid the next mood swing. Modi's drive to achieve and then sustain hegemony is open to serious doubt.

PART III

THE SANGH PARIVAR: A NEW 'DEEP STATE'?

7

SANGH AND SARKAR

THE RSS POWER CENTRE SHIFTS
FROM NAGPUR TO NEW DELHI

Pralay Kanungo

When India's President Pranab Mukherjee's tenure was coming an end and the search started for his successor, the Shiv Sena proposed RSS chief Mohan Bhagwat as the presidential nominee. Was the Sena really serious? Though the Shiv Sena's public rationale was that Bhagwat's nomination as president of India would be a befitting tribute to Hindu *Rashtra*, the common ideological mission of both the Sena and the RSS, it would be hard to ascertain what it really thought in private as the Sena-RSS relationship, since the days of Bal Thackeray, has been complex; moreover, the Sena's notoriety in making sarcastic and provocative statements was common knowledge. Anyway, Bhagwat did not entertain this offer and played a political master-stroke by sending a Dalit and RSS loyalist Ramnath Kovind to the Rashtrapati Bhawan.

But when one listened to Bhagwat's 2017 Vijaya Dashmi speech,[1] it was very much like a presidential address—applause for the government's action, caution for its omissions and directions for the future. Of course, with some differences: first, the script was not written by the government and it was delivered in Nagpur, not in Delhi; second, the tone and tenor were more assertive than that of any Indian president. Thus, the speech demonstrated more autonomy and authority than Bhagwat, though not technically the constitutional head, had any prerogative to display, in stocktaking as the conscience keeper or the moral custodian of the present government. In the present context, this empowering role is certainly more substantive than the mere procedural powers enjoyed by the president of India.[2]

Only barely a month before his Nagpur address, Bhagwat had a breakfast meeting with fifty diplomats in Delhi which even the president of India would envy.[3] With the backdrop of rising intolerance, he spoke at this august gathering about the RSS's disapproval of aggression and trolling on social media, and also issued a standard clarification on the RSS's relationship the Bharatiya Janata Party (BJP): '[The RSS] does not run BJP; BJP doesn't run [the RSS]. As Swayamsevaks we consult and exchange notes but are independent.'[4] Obviously, behind such clarifications, his major objective was to send a message across the world that the RSS mattered in India's present governance and the world had to engage with the RSS as well.

Thus, in hindsight, it seems that the Shiv Sena had logic and seriousness in its proposal; it was well aware that as *Sarsanghchalak*, Bhagwat would in any case monitor the former RSS *pracharak* Modi's governance and assert his mentorship. Then why not legitimise this extra-constitutional arrangement by making him the president of India? Further, ideologically, his elevation would usher in a full-fledged Hindu *Rashtra* expeditiously rather than wait for a truncated and protracted one which is being promoted by Modi.

In this context, this chapter illustrates the dynamics of the relationship between the RSS and the Modi government, showing how the top RSS leadership, including the *Sarsanghchalak*, has been mentoring and monitoring India's governance, not from a long distance or the RSS headquarters at Nagpur, but from very close quarters in New Delhi, India's seat of political power. While acknowledging Modi as the supreme leader of the government and the party—standing by him firmly—the RSS strategically intervenes in some key spheres of governance with mutual consent. Thus, as per this *quid pro quo*, while Modi's undisputed writ runs through major areas like the economy, commerce, foreign affairs and security, the RSS gets a free hand in determining the social, cultural and educational agenda; besides, the RSS chief extends his role as the 'philosopher and guide' beyond the RSS by legitimising and expanding Hindutva in a larger public sphere.

The Modi-RSS power-sharing pact

Modi understands that his mission of achieving *Congress-mukt Bharat* (an India free of the Congress party)[5] and building a 'New India' would be fulfilled not just by defeating and decimating the Congress Party electorally, but also by wiping out the Nehruvian idea of India from the minds of Indians. To achieve both these objectives, Modi needs the RSS. While the RSS organisational machine will help in achieving electoral victory, its ideological machine will de-Congress-ise and Hindutva-ise India simultaneously. Hence, Modi, while retaining his supreme control over the governance of the state and keeping the party machinery under his close confidant Amit Shah, has strategically left the organisational apparatus of the BJP and educational and cultural apparatus of the state to the RSS.

The rationale of this power-sharing arrangement needs to be understood in the context of a new symbiotic relationship between the RSS and Modi. The RSS gracefully acknowledged that it was Modi's charisma that brought the BJP back to power at New Delhi. Modi also understood that without the RSS machinery, his charisma alone could not have achieved such an astounding victory. For the RSS family of organisations, the 2014 victory was unique, being much different from the past experiences of 1977 and 1998: while in the former, the political front was only a coalition constituent in the ruling government; and in the latter, lacking a majority, the BJP led a coalition with constraints. In contrast, in 2014, no more did it have to be contented with limited or constricted maneuverability as the BJP got an absolute majority on its own. Both the RSS and Modi conceded that this accomplishment was not an outcome of a solo mission, but of a joint enterprise. Though Modi smartly brought in his confidant Amit Shah as the party president to control the distribution of tickets for the Lok Sabha and to control the party apparatus, at the same time, Modi let the RSS micro-manage the elections as his national outreach was limited. This complementarity continued even after Modi became the Prime Minister.

Sarsanghchalak: the mentor and monitor

No doubt, while Modi has emerged as the most popular leader and powerful prime minister, he has been a protégé of the RSS, which has nurtured him for this position. Recognising the political potential of this committed '*pracharak*', the RSS brought him to the national political arena where he demonstrated his skill, first as Advani's navigator in the 1990 *Rath Yatra* and later as the BJP's key organiser and point-man in Delhi. When the Keshubhai government in Gujarat fell, he was asked to take over to rescue the BJP. The 2002 Gujarat riots not only resurrected the RSS family of organisations, but also firmly put Modi in Gujarat's political saddle. He soon became an icon of Hindutva and an unchallenged leader by offering a new paradigm—*Moditva*, or Modi-ism—which weaved Hindutva with Gujarati *asmita* (identity). With his soaring popularity, Modi started ignoring the RSS family and alienated many of its constituents and leaders. Though the RSS family felt marginalised, yet it could hardly help. When Modi won the 2007 Assembly elections despite the indifference of the RSS family, the RSS had no alternative but to make amends with Modi. Later, a pragmatic Bhagwat, despite being aware of the Modi-RSS contradictions in certain spheres, settled the BJP's leadership issue with his vote for Modi.

A vigilant Mohan Bhagwat, as *Sarsanghchalak*, the supreme leader and the 'guide and philosopher' of the RSS (per Article 12 of the RSS Constitution), then obviously would not play second fiddle to Modi. As the supreme authority of the RSS, he has to play a special role *vis-à-vis* the Modi regime. His moral authority entitles him to play the role of the mentor to the Modi government as well the monitor of the governance of the nation. Moreover, it was Bhagwat's unequivocal support of Modi which made him the BJP's choice for prime minister, setting aside the claims of veterans like L.K. Advani, and it was the RSS machinery which worked day and night to make Modi's victory possible. Hence, Bhagwat's clout over the Modi government was unquestionably a foregone conclusion.

Bhagwat gave Modi time to settle down. In his Vijaya Dashmi address in October 2014, Bhagwat certified that, though the government had not even completed six months, yet positive signs had already started emanating. He hoped that Bharat would emerge on the international horizon and 'the people's desire of a life, secure and progressing in all its aspects, will soon start reflecting in the governance.'[6] He applauded the policy initiatives of the Modi government on the economy, national security, international relations, and other areas, and expected the government to 'now ensure that these policies maintain their momentum in a determined and well organised manner. We need to wait for some more time, with a sense of hope and faith.'[7] Meanwhile, he had already secured some major gains from the Modi government.

Top political appointments

Political appointments in the key government positions has always been crucial to the RSS from the days of the Janata experiment to the Vajpayee government. In the Morarji Desai government, Vajpayee and Advani headed crucial ministries like External Affairs and Information and Broadcasting respectively. When Vajpayee became the prime minister, the then-RSS chief K.S. Sudarshan reportedly barged into his office to appoint RSS nominees to the cabinet. Contrary to his predecessor's open intervention, Bhagwat did not even visit Delhi during those days and the RSS publicly announced that it would have no role in the government formation. As he was aware of Modi's caution and compulsion to meet the high expectations of the watchful nation in the cabinet's formation, Bhagwat apparently did not bargain for an all-RSS cabinet allowing Modi to pick some talent from outside the RSS fold. In any case, he was sure that most of them by default would be connected to the RSS family of organisations in some ways and all the BJP nominees, for sure, would remain indebted to the RSS for their electoral victory; even outsiders, who came from other parts of the political spectrum or a purely professional background, would compete to swear by the RSS ideology even more than a RSS loyalist. This proved very much true when Najma Heptullah, Minority Affairs Minister, after swearing in, came out with a startling statement that Muslims must not be considered as minorities in India as they were 'so large in number', going far beyond her ministerial mandate and responsibility.[8]

While exercising his prerogative and pledging his commitment to merit and efficiency, Modi still accommodated some trusted RSS nominees, though in a few cases, like the allocation of the Human Resources Development Ministry to Smriti Irani, he created resentment in the RSS. While the first cabinet formation was a cautious exercise, in the subsequent reshuffles in 2016 and 2017, the RSS's quota in the cabinet got a substantial hike. While RSS choices like Nitin Gatkare, Ram Prasad Katheria, Radha Mohan Singh, Mahesh Sharma, Hansraj Ahir, Bandaru Dattatreya, Giriraj Singh and Sadhvi Niranjan Jyoti got cabinet berths in the first round, the subsequent rounds brought many more nominees of the RSS to the Modi government, like Faggan Singh Kulaste, Anil Madhav Dave, Mahendra Nath Pandey, Mansukh Mandaviya, Parshottam Rupala and P.P. Chaudhary. Modi also placated the RSS by replacing Smriti Irani with Prakash Javdekar to facilitate the RSS agenda in education and culture, and she also went the extra mile to convert herself into a RSS loyalist. The RSS also did not object when Modi asked some RSS confidants to tender their resignations from the cabinet on account of poor performance. This accommodative relationship signalled a perfect understanding and coordination between the RSS and the Modi government.

As the BJP repeated its 2014 electoral victory in different states, RSS *pracharaks* and nominees were rewarded with appointments as chief ministers and cabinet ministers. In most cases, the choice showed a convergence between Modi and the RSS. While RSS *pracharaks* like M.L. Khattar and Trivendra Singh Rawat became chief ministers of Haryana and Uttarakhand, the RSS nominee Devendra Fadnavis became the chief minister of Maharashtra and a former ABVP full-timer Jai Ram Thakur became the chief minister of Himachal Pradesh. It was not Yogi Adityanath but Manoj Sinha, who was known for his competence in governance, who was Modi's choice for UP's chief minister. When the powerful RSS *sah-sarkaryavah* (Joint General Secretary) Krishan Gopal resisted Sinha's appointment, Modi back-tracked and then an agreement was reached around Yogi Adityanath as a perfect Hindutva mascot to win UP in the 2019 election.[9] Tripura chief minister Biplab Deb was also under the RSS tutelage for a couple of years.

Old RSS veterans were appointed as governors of states: Balramji Das Tandan (Chhattisgarh), Ram Naik (UP), Om Prakash Kohli (Gujarat), Keshri Nath Tripathi (West Begal), Kalyan Singh (Rajasthan), Vidya Sagar Rao (Maharashtra), Vaju Bhai Bala (Karnataka), Padmanabha Acharya (Nagaland), Jagdish Mukhi (Assam), and Tathagat Roy (Tripura). With their long political experience, these leaders were expected to play not just active constitutional roles, but also complementary roles in promoting Hindutva wherever the constitution and the august office leave scope to do so. For instance, when Lenin's statue was demolished by enthusiastic BJP workers after the party got an unprecedented victory over the Marxist government in the 2018 assembly elections, Tripura Governor Tathagat Roy tweeted to rationalise the demolition. Similarly, UP Governor Ram Naik instructed the Uttar Pradesh government to officially change the name of Dr Bhimrao Ambedkar in all official documents to Dr Bhimrao Ramji Ambedkar; Ramji, which was the name of Ambedkar's father, would connect Lord Ram with Ambedkar and Dalits symbolically.

Ideological control of cultural and educational institutions

Control of key cultural and academic institutions has always been the prime agenda of the RSS, again from the Janata years to the Vajpayee government;

controlling institutions for re-writing history textbooks, reinterpreting Indian history, and redefining Indian culture remain a major bone of contention between secularists and Hindu nationalists. The 2014 electoral victory gave an opportunity to the RSS family of organisations to go in full throttle to appoint their trusted followers. H.V. Sudarshan Rao of the RSS family's Akhil Bharatiya Itihas Sankalan Yojna (ABISY; All-India History Collection/Compilation Project) was appointed as the head of the Indian Council of Historical Research (ICHR). The RSS's history research organisation ABISY, set up in 1984 and reportedly having a national network of 500 professors and 350 publications, aims to bring out the *vastavik itihaas* (real history) of India. In October 2014, ABISY organised a symposium in Delhi's national museum to pay tribute to Hemchandra Vikramaditya, or Hemu, the last Hindu emperor of Delhi, who was defeated by Akbar. The union Minister of Culture and Tourism Shripad Yesso Naik and RSS affiliates participated in this symposium. ABISY's secretary stated, 'Henceforth, every time you talk of Akbar, you have to mention Hemu' and also complained about how history books had not given due space to national warriors like Maharana Pratap and Shivaji. Instead, 'they teach students about cricket and about the Monalisa in world civilization.'[10] The ICHR's governing council was also filled with historians with RSS backgrounds or leanings. Another institution where the change of guard became crucial was Nalanda University, a prestigious global project; Nobel laureate Amartya Sen, a strong critic of the RSS family of organisations, resigned as the University's chancellor as the government was not keen to give him a second period of tenure.

Other key institutions were brought under control from the nominees of the previous regime; the record of these replacements was mixed. Noted Sanskrit scholar and linguist Dr Lokesh Chandra became the president of the Indian Council for Cultural Relations (ICCR). Though Chandra was nominated to the Rajya Sabha twice by Indira Gandhi, he became closer to the BJP subsequently. Incidentally, Chandra's father Dr Raghuvir was president of the Bharatiya Jana Sangh (BJS). Ram Bahadur Rai, former ABVP organising secretary, who was jailed during the Emergency, was appointed to the Indira Gandhi National Centre for Arts (IGNCA). Baldev Sharma, former editor of the RSS Hindi mouthpiece *Panchajanya*, was rewarded with the chairmanship of the National Book Trust (NBT). Shakti Sinha, a former bureaucrat and private secretary of Atal Behari Vajpayee, was brought in as the Director of the Nehru Memorial Museum and Library; this was a key appointment intended to wrest control the intellectual hub of the Nehru-Gandhi legacy. Kapil

Kapoor and Makarand Paranjape, two scholars from Jawaharlal Nehru University known for their anti-left positions, were picked as chairman and director, respectively, of the Indian Institute of Advanced Study (IIAS) in order to change the research orientation of this prestigious institute.

But when a small-time actor Gajendra Chauhan was appointed as the chairman of the Film and Television Institute of India (FTII), it created a furore among Institute students and faculty, and the Institute remained turbulent for quite some time. Later, the veteran cinema actor Anupam Kher, who has a strong Hindu nationalist inclination, was given this responsibility. Pahlaj Nihalani's appointment as the head of India's Central Board of Film Certification (CBFC) became contentious. Nihalani's controversial decisions included the banning of *Lipstick Under My Burkha*, and his objection to the word 'intercourse' in Imtiaz Ali's *Jab Harry Met Sejal*, starring Shah Rukh Khan. He also asked for an unprecedented eighty-nine cuts for *Udta Punjab*, a Hindi thriller about the drugs problem, which decision was overturned by the court, and the film was released with just one cut. Before his term ended, he was replaced by renowned lyricist and screenwriter Prasoon Joshi.

As educational institutions are key for ideological dissemination, the RSS pushed its nominees as vice chancellors and directors in universities and research institutions. As a result, RSS leaders gained entry to prominent educational, research, and cultural institutions of higher learning. Bhagwat addressed over fifty vice-chancellors and 700 academics from across the country in a two-day conference on the Indian perspective in education in Delhi called *Gyan Sangam* (Confluence of Knowledge), organised by *Prajna Pravah*, an RSS affiliate.[11] Bhagwat said: 'This is not an alternative but a real attempt to develop Bharatiya [Indian] perspective.' The conference discussed how to decolonise education and use Indian tools and terminology in academic pursuit. The academicians resolved to introduce 'Bharatiya perspectives' in education in their respective states.

All such appointments no doubt enabled the RSS family of organisations to extend its sphere of ideological influence to the educational and cultural sphere and determine their agenda and activities. But undoubtedly, the RSS's appointments were compromised in terms of merit in many cases, thus poorly reflecting on the image of Modi's governance and damaging the institutions in the long run. The RSS's rationale was clear: it was their government and they had every right to make appointments. Moreover, educational and cultural institutions had been under the left's control for decades and it was the time to bring them under Hindutva.

Expanding and intensifying Hindutva ideology and networks

The RSS intervention was not limited to education and culture alone. After the installation of the RSS government in New Delhi, Bhagwat thought it was the right opportunity not only to expand and consolidate the organisation, but more importantly to carry out the Hindutva mission beyond the RSS and the government in order to give it more legitimacy and credibility in a larger public sphere encompassing new regions and social groups which were yet to embrace Hindutva. Bhagwat started touring the states to propagate Hindutva, particularly the ones where the RSS had been organisationally weak and the BJP had been struggling to find a strong foothold. At Cuttack, Odisha, he said: 'Hindustan is a Hindu nation. Hindutva is the identity of our nation and it [Hinduism] can incorporate others [religions] in itself.'[12] He continued: 'The cultural identity of all Indians is Hindutva and the present inhabitants of the country are descendants of this great culture.' In Kolkota, where he was initially denied permission by the Mamata Banerjee government to speak, Bhagwat said that 'Muslims in India must realise that their forefathers were Hindus who converted to Islam.'[13] His predecessor, K.S. Sudarshan had earlier made similar claims. He also expressed his opposition to the Sachar Committee Report; the RSS has always interpreted it as communal in nature and an act of appeasement. Bhagwat addressed mega Hindu congregations in places like Tripura in 2017 which mobilised large numbers of tribal people and launched an ideological war against the Marxist regime; these activities paid dividends after some months, when the BJP displaced the Marxist government.

While ensuring key appointments, disseminating Hindutva ideology across the country and in media, and keeping ideological control on institutions, Bhagwat did not forget the primary focus of the RSS—the organization. He had been careful not to allow the attainment of political power to create complacency on the organisational front; rather, he used the pull factor of the Modi government to expand the membership RSS exponentially. As a result, one could see how the *shakhas* (local branches) grew rapidly since Modi became the prime minister. To manage the growing number of members and activities, in 2018, the Akhil Bharatiya Pratinidhi Sabha (All-India General Body) of the RSS increased the number of joint-general secretaries from four to six, Dr Manmohan Vaidya and C.R. Mukunda being the new additions.

The RSS is not only focusing on growing its membership. It has also taken up some concrete programmes like *Parivar Prabodhan* (Family Awakening), *Grama Vikas* (Village Development), and *Samarasata* (Social Harmony) in around 450 villages. *Kutumb Prabodhan* (Kin Awakening), which was initiated in Karnataka in early 2000, became a pan-Indian project to bring in a 'good change' in the family value system.[14]

Table 1: Growth of RSS *shakhas* (2014–17)

Year	Places	Shakha	Milan (Weekly)	Mandali (Monthly)
2014	29,624	44,982	10,146	7,387
2015	33,222	51,330	12,847	9,008
2016	36,867	56,569	13,784	8,226
2017	36,693	57,233	14,650	7,790

Source: Annual Reports presented by the General Secretary (*Sar-karyavah*) of the RSS before Akhil Bharatiya Pratinidhi Sabha (ABPS). Note: in the absence of any other corroborating source, the author has relied on RSS sources, which are unverified.

Some illustrations may help to grasp Bhagwat's networking skill. Connecting with the key personalities and leaders from diverse professions is not unusual for *Sarsanghchalaks*. But Bhagwat made his meetings more extensive and intensive than a routine affair. In 2014–15 he met several media persons, judges, educationalists, bureaucrats, religious leaders, littérateurs and many other distinguished personalities and had special meetings with the chief of Mangalyaan (India's Mars Orbiter Mission space program), Mylswamy Annadurai, Nobel Prize-winner Kailash Satyarthi, Acharya Mahashraman, Bhante Rahul Bodhi, Swami Dayananda Saraswati, and the Maharaja of Puri, Shri Gajapati.

In 2015–16, Bhagwat had personal meetings with more than sixty prominent persons and dignitaries like President Pranab Mukherjee, Saint Devsingh Adwaiti of Valmiki Samaj, Shri Chandra Swami of Udasin sect, Mahant Devendranath of Dehradun, Swami Chidanand Puru of Kerala and Swami Gyananand of Ramkrishna Math of Bhagyanagar (Hyderabad). He also had meetings with industrialists Venkat Krishnamurthy of the G.V.K. group, Venu Srinivasan of T.V.S. motors, and Samir Somaiya from Mumbai. Among the media persons, Pratapsinh Jadhav of the Marathi daily, *Pudhari*, Shanta Kumar of *Kannad Daily*, Shobhana Bhartiya of *Hindustan Times*, Arun Puri of *Aajtak*, Rantidev Sengupta of the *Vartman*, Kolkata and Shri Ranga Raj of Tanthi TV were some of the notable persons. Bhagwat also visited Justice Shri Kanakraj and Shri Balsubramhanyam and Maharaja of Jodhpur Shri Gajsinghji. In addition to these meetings, he had conversations with about

600 prominent persons in twenty different meetings. While many were sympathisers of the RSS, others were potential sympathisers.

Bhagwat's outreach and networking were not mere courtesy calls; it was a well thought-out political strategy. He pulled out a political master-stroke when he got Pranab Mukherjee to speak at the RSS headquarters. Thus, Bhagwat's interaction with politicians, media, judiciary, industry, religious leaders and civil society clearly signalled that the RSS would not be content simply to control the Modi government, but it was keen to extend its hegemony to larger political, societal, and non-governmental spheres. Bhagwat made a *faux pas* when he stated that the RSS 'will prepare military personnel within three days which the Army would do in 6–7 months. This is our capability. Swayamsewak will be ready to take on the front if the country faces such a situation and Constitution permits to do so.'[15] The RSS has always cultivated and courted the military by invoking nationalism, patriotism, security and terrorism, and had attracted the top brass of the military to join the BJP post-retirement. But an over-zealous Bhagwat clearly overstepped the line while demonstrating his desire to control the overall state apparatus, including the Army.

Connecting RSS-party-sarkar: key pracharaks

While Bhagwat, as RSS chief, spelt out a broad ideological agenda for the government and secured the RSS's key interests *vis-à-vis* the government, he left the micro-management of the day to day coordination between the RSS, the party and the *sarkar* (government) to his lieutenants. Traditionally, since the Jana Sangh days, the RSS controlled the party by appointing a *pracharak* as an organising secretary (*Sangathan Mantri*) at every layer, from national to local. But the BJP's coming to power with an absolute majority and Modi's appointment as prime minister offered a new challenge. Bhagwat would not just restrict the RSS to monitor the party but would like to intervene in the spheres of governance as well. Hence, the organisation decided to entrust the task of influencing governance to its top trusted leaders.

When Sudarshan advocated a generational change in the BJP, the RSS had already initiated that process in its family, including in the RSS hierarchy. Bhagwat's anointment as the chief, when he has not even reached sixty, was a testimony to this. The process speeded up with the appointment of Dattatryea Hosabale and Krishna Gopal as joint general secretaries. As Bhagwat's exalted position as the 'philosopher and guide' of the RSS demanded distancing from the day to day governance of the Modi government, some dynamic RSS office-bearers were deputed for the job, who would play key roles in the party as well as the government. A few illustrations will give some clarity.

Dattatreya Hosabale, the *sah-sarkaryvah*, a *pracharak* from Karnataka, with a postgraduate degree in English literature, had been the organising secretary of the Akhil Bharatiya Vidyarthi Parishad for almost two decades since the late 1980s. He showed his astute leadership by steering the students' wing of the RSS quite successfully. Under his tutelage, many ABVP leaders graduated to the BJP. Hosabale is intelligent, amiable, mature and a master strategist; he was likely to be elevated to the position of RSS general secretary in 2018, which was deferred for some organisational reasons. As he enjoyed a good relationship with Modi, the RSS assigned him to coordinate with the government on behalf of the RSS. Hence, in some sense, among the six *sah-karya-vahs*, he enjoys the prime position to deal with the Modi government. Hosabale played a key role in the 2017 Uttar Pradesh Assembly polls, from the selection of candidates to booth-level mobilisation and management.

The RSS-party interface is another crucial area. The RSS was careful not to depute someone with whom Modi would not be comfortable. Hence, a high-profile *pracharack* and *sah-karyavah* Suresh Soni, who had been liaising between the RSS and the BJP for a decade, but became controversial, was sent on 'sabbatical'.[16] Soni, incidentally, played a key role in isolating L.K. Advani and favoured Modi's selection as the BJP's prime ministerial candidate. Soni was replaced by one of *sah-sarkaryavahs* (joint general secretaries), Dr Krishna Gopal, who usually kept a low profile. Hailing from the city of Hathras in UP and having earned a doctorate in botany from Agra University, Sharma became a *pracharak* in the 1970s. He once worked as a personal assistant to H.V. Sheshadri, the late RSS general secretary, and was also in charge of eastern UP and later the northeast, where he showed his organising strategy and networking skills. While in eastern UP he launched an innovative rural health initiative 'Dhanvantari Project', which sent healthcare professionals, and medical students, to serve in remote, tribal areas for a few weeks; the project became a success and enhanced his reputation in the RSS. Considered an intellectual and a good orator, Krishna Gopal had written a book on Ambedkar. The RSS elevated him to the position of joint general secretary in 2012 and strategically deployed him in UP before the 2014 elections; Gopal stitched together various caste alliances with the BJP, mobilised the RSS family's cadres, and played an important role in the allocation of tickets in Uttar Pradesh and Uttarakhand where the BJP had a spectacular performance. Krishan Gopal maintains and coordinates the RSS-party relations and has a say in key appointments.

The next crucial area is the party-government relationship. Ram Lal, who had been the organising secretary of the BJP, was allowed to continue with the job. As the BJP became the ruling party and had grown enormously, it needed more efficient functionaries to manage the party-government coordination. Hence, the RSS sent Ram Madhav, a suave *pracharak* and a former spokesperson of the RSS, as the general secretary of the BJP. Madhav had a big advantage as both the RSS and Modi trusted him. Years ago, when the Modi-RSS relationship was running through a rough patch in Gujarat, it was Ram Madhav who successfully mediated and brought them onto the same page. He reportedly played a key role in ending the European Union's boycott of Narendra Modi over the 2002 anti-Muslim violence in Gujarat. Besides, Madav had been widely travelled and well exposed to the outside world with a sharp understanding of India's foreign affairs. A China analyst, he authored *Uneasy Neighbours: India and China after Fifty Years of the War*, and had set up a think tank, the India Foundation. Madhav showed great skill by organising Modi's interface with the Indian diaspora from Madison Square to Sydney quite successfully.

Ram Madhav was entrusted with the hard task of looking after the BJP's affairs in Jammu and Kashmir and the Northeast. To everyone's surprise, he successfully stitched together the BJP's alliance with the Peoples Democratic Party (PDP) to form a coalition government despite the two being ideologically opposed to each other. Madhav also showed an unusual political shrewdness in steering the BJP's electoral success in the Northeast by winning Assam and Tripura hands down and forming coalition governments in Manipur, Nagaland, and Meghalaya. The BJP also formed a government in Arunachal Pradesh as the Congress legislators switched their loyalty to the BJP *en masse*. After the Telugu Desam Party's withdrawal from the National Democratic Alliance coalition, Ram Madhav was assigned to Andhra Pradesh.

These three illustrative cases of top RSS *pracharaks* suggest that aside from coordinating the RSS and government quite efficiently, the *pracharaks* have also carved out ideological space for Hindutva and political spaces for themselves. For instance, the Jaipur Literary Festival, once considered a 'secular' hang-out, forbidden for RSS acolytes, has invited Hosabale. Similarly, in a short span of time, Ram Madhav's India Foundation has become an influential Indian think tank with strong international connections. In fact, many *pracharks*, former *pracharaks*, and RSS activists have been proactive in the media and public sphere disseminating Hindutva and defending the Modi government unequivocally, in contrast to the intellectual vacuum of the right a few years ago. Thousands of big and small RSS activists have fanned out across the country setting up voluntary organisations and intervening in different spheres of civil society with a pro-Hindutva and pro-Modi agenda.

Rewarding affiliates and resolving contradictions

Affiliates are integral to the RSS system. They provide oxygen and energy for mobilisational programmes of the RSS family. Hence, their aspirations need to be fulfilled. As the student affiliate played a key role in mobilising students and youth in support of Modi, and the wing would continue to have an important role in the Modi regime, the ABVP received due recognition and reward. In fact, it completely overshadowed the party's youth wing, Bharatiya Janata Yuva Morcha (BJYM) and became an extended arm of the party as well as the government. First, many former ABVP leaders, namely Arun Jaitley, Vijay Goel, J.P. Nadda, Dharmendra Pradhan, Anantha Kumar, and others became ministers in the Modi government. Jai Ram Thakur became the chief minister of Himachal Pradesh and notably, five out of eleven ministers in his cabinet, namely Suresh Bhardwaj, Vipin Parmar, Virender Kanwar, Bikram Singh, Govind Singh Thakur and Rajiv Saijjal, were ABVP activists. The ABVP organising secretary, Sunil Ambekar, came to enjoy a big clout in universities and higher educational institutions. The ABVP threw challenges to the left and other students unions and organisations in college and university campuses and became an aggressive champion of Hindu nationalism.

While the ABVP enjoyed patronage, a few dissenting voices in the Parivar came primarily from the RSS's strong grassroots organisations like the Bharatiya Mazdoor Sangh (BMS), Swadeshi Jagaran Manch (SJM), Bharatiya Kisan Sangh (BKS). These affiliates were earlier opposed to the Vajpayee-led NDA government's economic policies; the confrontation between the RSS's veteran trade union leader Dattopant Thengdi and the Vajpayee government had reached a boiling point. The tussle got carried forward to the present regime as well, which has decided to pursue neo-liberal policies with full vigour. If the hike of foreign direct investments (FDI) in some sectors has been a big issue earlier, now there is hardly noise as key sectors of the economy have been opened up without any cap for foreign investors.

Obviously, the Modi government has got the RSS's nod to pursue this economic agenda to make India into a 'global economic superpower'. Moreover, as per the *quid pro quo* arrangement, governance of the economy remains under Modi's discretion. Hence, the RSS reportedly has issued a diktat:

'Affiliates can speak on [economic] issues, but must not pursue with them.'[17] As a consequence, the affiliates mellowed down their expression of resentment. For instance, Vrijesh Upadhyaa, the general secretary of the BMS, who earlier threated to mobilise civil resistance, suddenly discovered that the Modi government's initiatives were 'in the interest of the workers'. Similarly, the co-convener of SJM, who earlier demanded the inclusion of a Social Impact Assessment in the land bill, conceded that land acquisition was 'needed for development' though farmers' consent should be sought. The national secretary of the BKS Mohini Mohan Mishra, who earlier rejected the Land Acquisition Bill categorically, later argued in favour of passing it.

This ambivalence and dilution put the grassroots affiliates in an awkward position to try and mobilise their constituencies, which span a wide spectrum from retail, banking and insurance to agriculture and industry. These affiliates also opposed demonetisation and the Goods and Services Tax (GST) as they would adversely impact the poor, marginal farmers, small industrialists, and petty traders. However, the affiliates have remained silent under pressure even though this decision brought India's Gross Domestic Product (GDP) down by 2 per cent or so. They felt slighted as the negative economic impact on their constituencies did not adversely impact Modi politically; rather, the BJP was rewarded with a huge victory in the 2017 UP Assembly elections, interpreted to be an endorsement of Modi's economic policies by the common man. The RSS is in a dilemma as well; though it understands that the concerns of its grassroots affiliates are genuine, it does not want to unsettle the Modi government by raising any sharp criticisms. After all, Modi's failure would be construed as its own failure. Pravin Togadia's marginalisation and decision to walk out of the VHP, though unthinkable, clearly indicates how the RSS could ruthlessly dump even one of its most diehard loyalists for the sake of Modi.

The RSS unbound: Hindutva governance

Knowing well that their own family of organisations is the lifeline of the Modi government, over-zealous Hindutva organisations and activists have crossed the boundary line of the rule of law to embarrass the Modi government. Blatantly communal remarks by Union ministers Giriraj Singh, Sadhvi Niranjan Jyoti, anti-constitutional remarks by another minister Anantha Hegde, the anti-Muslim rhetoric of the UP chief minister Yogi Adityanath and Members of Parliament Sakshi Maharaj and Vinay Katiyar are some examples. The very idea of developmental governance which Modi had promised during the 2014 election campaign was dented when Hindutva groups raised communal issues like '*ghar wapasi*', '*gau raksha*', and 'love jihad', resulting in mob lynchings of Muslim minorities on the pretext of punishing cow slaughter and beef eating; a Muslim youth was even forced to utter '*Bharat Mata ki jai*' and then killed. Though Modi criticised these actions, the warning came late and there was no follow-up; this was obviously intended not to antagonise the hardline Hindutva groups. As a result, Modi's governance received a negative international perception.

Even Bhagwat crossed the line on some occasions by issuing provocative statements which put the party and the government in difficult situations. On the eve of state assembly elections in Bihar, he talked of reconsideration of the reservation issue. The BJP issued clarification of its position as Bhagwat's statement threatened the party's political prospects in the state. While addressing a huge gathering of the RSS volunteers at Muzaffarpur, Mohan Bhagwat announced with exuberance and pride that RSS volunteers were so disciplined that they could be mobilised in a matter of days, should the constitution and the laws of the country so demand. The government underplayed this statement as it was a great embarrassment for the army and it was also seen as an interference in the security matters of the state. But the RSS's influence over the state's security apparatus has substantially increased over the years, as Vivekananda International, a RSS security think tank located right next to Raisina Hill, has roped in many retired top defence personnel and is now advising the Modi government on security matters. More significantly, while the former army chief Gen. V.K. Singh joined the BJP and became a cabinet minister, the present army chief's occasional unprofessional statements show his leaning toward the Hindu Right.

Conclusion

The RSS does not have any pretensions of being 'cultural' any more. Now the RSS bureaucrats run India from New Delhi through the organisation's *pracharaks* and *swayamsevaks* and determine the agenda of the nation's governance. The BJP also does not have any pretensions of being 'autonomous' of the RSS any more. Now the RSS leaders are party leaders and ministers. This was clear when the RSS called for a 'review meeting' in September 2015 to assess the BJP's government's performance, in which many Union ministers presented their report cards; though for the RSS, this was a meeting only for 'exchanging ideas' and 'sharing inputs.' The RSS joint-General Secretary Dattatreya

Hosabale however unhesitatingly stated: 'We have every right to ask ministers, who are also swayamsevaks. Where is the question of secrecy? Swayamsevaks have become ministers.'[18]

Thus, the top hierarchy of the RSS, the *Sarsanghchalak* and his team, who claim to stay away from formal political power, exert enormous influence, not only moral but also political, in the Modi government. If Modi has charisma and leadership, Bhagwat has organisation and authority. As both understand each other's strength and weaknesses, they make India's governance a joint-enterprise by sharing power. As the RSS would still like to appear 'pure' by retaining its public image only as 'guide and philosopher' or '*Rajarshi*', Bhagwat's refusal of the presidential nomination makes sense.

8

HOW THE SANGH PARIVAR WRITES
AND TEACHES HISTORY

Tanika Sarkar

Let me begin with two Muslim names—Junaid Khan and Afrazul Mohammad—who have been flogged and hacked to death respectively. A fourteen year old filmed Afrazul's murder and posted it on social media for general enjoyment. Their killers were 'respectable' men of some substance and education: not at all the stuff that mobs are usually made of.[1] I have plucked their names at random out of many others who have met the same fate in recent years.

Both were killed by perfect strangers, in public places, and neither victim was accused of any wrongdoing, real or imagined. They were killed, not during riots, but in normal times: or let us say, in times when a new normal is being made. They were killed simply because they were Muslims.

Muslim bodies have become legitimate arenas where the most gruesome violence can be freely, joyfully, performed, with perfect impunity. Irrespective of electoral fortunes, such events do indicate a tectonic shift in Hindu popular common sense. Irrespective, again, of who does what in the coming elections, this shift, I think, will be irreversible for quite some time. How is such hate produced and sustained, how does it become hegemonic? More importantly, what does it hope to achieve, in the broadest sense?

Much can be explained, I think, by the critical role of the historical lessons that the Sangh conglomerate produces. What the 'science' of race difference was to Nazi ideology, the discipline of history is to Hindutva:[2] a claim to 'formal knowledge', which exalts political mission as accredited Truth. But whereas Nazi power lasted twelve years, the Hindu Right has been pursuing knowledge-production and dissemination for ninety-three years now.[3] Restricted till independence to the core organisations of the Rashtriya Swayamsevak Sangh (RSS), plans for installing an RSS version of the past at official and popular levels were systematically put together in 1973.[4] RSS schools started to teach it even earlier, from the early 1950s, while daily *shakhas* have propagated it from 1925.[5]

Its own particular representation of the past is both the medium and the message for Hindutva's ideological apparatus and political agenda. It is important, therefore, to grasp what Hindutva wants to project as history in general, and Indian history in particular. This involves an understanding of its rhetorical and pedagogical strategies, and its organisational networks, through which history lessons circulate at multiple social levels.

I begin with their foundational ideological texts, written by V.D Savarkar and M.S Golwalkar. Then I track their refractions in school textbooks prepared by the RSS, whenever and wherever its electoral front, the Bharatiya Janata Party or BJP, has been in power.[6]

Some textbooks were prepared for the RSS Vidya Bharati schools[7] and some were published in 2002 under the National Curriculum of Education and Research Training (NCERT) for central government schools when an earlier BJP government was in power.[8] For more advanced levels, I look at a recent course of lectures organised by the prestigious University of Delhi. Delivered to college teachers from different states, these 'Orientation' and 'Refresher' courses usually acquaint participants with new developments in their fields. In 2017, lecturers were hand-picked, largely from among BJP and Sangh functionaries, and many were not academics.[9] Finally, I will also analyse the RSS journal of history[10] and their research projects.[11]

RSS pedagogues

It is important to remember that RSS history is not taught in educational institutions alone. A simpler version is preached by the religious front or the

Vishwa Hindu Parishad (VHP), by Hindu sectarian leaders, and even by the RSS trade union or the Bharatiya Mazdoor Sangh (BMS).[12] Priests at Delhi temples told us that the most sacred event for them was Vijaya Dashami Day, 1925: when the Sangh was founded.[13] The sacred and the human are strangely conflated, and historical time gets pride of place in the sacred calendar. Similarly, Sanatan Dharm Temple functionaries in Delhi in 1991 discoursed, not about divine or spiritual themes, but only about past Hindu-Muslim conflicts, to justify the ongoing *Ramjanambhoomi* movement which eventually demolished a sixteenth-century mosque at Ayodhya in 1992, claiming— without any historical-archeological basis—that since the Mughal emperor Babur had demolished an ancient Ram temple in the sixteenth century, a new temple should rise on the ruins of the mosque. That 'history' of Mughal oppression led to massive anti-Muslim violence at that time, spearheaded by the BJP and VHP.[14]

RSS history teachers are legion. The Sangh trains myriad mass fronts, affiliates and sub affiliates on a daily basis. They seep into minute pores of Indian society: forming cells within religion, charity, culture, education, leisure: among women, students, Adivasis/tribals, Dalits/untouchable castes, urban and rural workers, Army personnel and lawyers. It is creeping hegemony, facilitated, but not really created by electoral victories. The RSS prioritises 'man making' as the first step to 'nation making'.[15] All affiliates, moreover, convey an identical sense of the past.[16]

This history is prepared by and for a Hindu vernacular elite, but it is now becoming mandatory for would-be scholars as well. It is not the work of trained historians, and it is dangerously easy to ridicule it: as naïve and plainly wrong, devoid of minimum academic standards. But it is propagated through multiple grassroots institutions, beyond the formal academic sphere. It is taught by thousands of cadres who have worked tirelessly for decades. Its strength and reach are, therefore, unparalleled.

Let me cite an example of how various pedagogic methods come together and how they are internalised. Thomas Blom Hansen[17] describes how he found Bombay slum boys happily building sand and mud castles to depict Shivaji's forts. They learnt about Shivaji's brave struggles against Muslims in their classes and their teachers inspired them to recreate his forts with the humble and humdrum material resources at hand, making classroom history a creative process. It is a competitive one too, which lends a keener edge to their historical enterprise. Their fort would be displayed at local Shivaji Jayanti festivals, along with the works of other schoolboys. Hansen demonstrates the integration of classroom teaching, self enterprise and religious festival into a deeply communal project. Young boys are inexorably drawn into the mythicised Shivaji histories by their own recreative act, and a wide floating historical common sense trumps actual historical research in the process. When a historian tried to prove, on the basis of hard research, that Shivaji was not implacably anti Muslim, even the Congress vehemently condemned him along with the Shiv Sena.

The content of historical pedagogy

Their basic historical narrative is best told in the words of V.D. Savarkar, who coined the term Hindutva in 1923. He later wrote a history of India in terms of its glorious epochs: a book that reveals his historical methods and purposes.[18] He claims that Indian history began five to ten thousand years back, as proved by both 'modern research' and by ancient chronicles which are histories proper, 'clothed in the poetical garb of mythology'. Puranas, he says, are 'are the pillars supporting the edifice of our ancient history'. We need to note that modern research, though smoothly appropriated, is nowhere substantiated. Sometimes exact statistics are cited of Muslim wrongdoing, making the historical claims appear precise: 50,000 Hindus courted martyrdom when Muslims attacked the Somnath Temple, he says, for instance. While numbers lend credibility to his narrative, he cites no sources for them. Myths are similarly presented as poetical rendering of actual historical truth: again, a claim that remains just that. He does cite the name of a Dr Jaiswal, a member of the Abhinav Bharat, a revolutionary group that Savarkar had joined in his early youth. He offers no credentials for him as a historian.[19] He also claimed that he inspired the renowned historian Sardesai to write the definitive history of the Marathas in English, and that Sardesai read his historical writings and came to meet the man who not only makes history but also writes it. The anecdotal, proving his influence on a major historian, simultaneously underwrites his own historical skills.[20]

How are 'glorious epochs' defined? They are the history of 'the warlike generation and the brave leaders and successful warriors who inspire and lead it on to a war of liberation in order to free their nation from the shackles of foreign domination.'[21] History, then, is national glory, and glory is earned in wars alone. His own historical practice, as we shall see, introduced habits of thinking that die hard.

Savarkar made Hindu and Indian synonymous, to reserve the nation for Hindus alone. He rendered each a seamless, monolithic unit. Undeniable caste inequalities, however, problematise the vision of an organic Hindu *volk*. He finds a solution in the motif of shared blood: despite caste endogamy among Hindus, he says, blood of all castes has mingled over the centuries through miscegenation, making Hindus one people. At one stroke, then, caste inequality is invoked and also left behind.

Identity is, above all, an act of exclusion:

> [...] we Hindus are bound together not only by the tie of the love that we bear to a common fatherland and the common blood that courses through our veins, but also by the common homage we pay to [...] our Hindu culture [...].We are one because we are a nation, a race and own a common Sanskriti [...] in the case of our Mohammedan or Christian countrymen [...] though Hindustan to them is Fatherland [...] yet it is not their Holyland too. Their mythology and Godmen [...] are not the children of this soil [...] their names and their outlook smack of a foreign origin [...].[22]

The ultimate tests of belonging are faith and language. They commingle as Sanskrit is the language of Hindu sacred texts. Its script being carried into modern Hindi, the latter claims to be the national language.[23] 'Hindi, Hindu, Hindustan' was a slogan that he coined.[24]

How did India become the land of Hindus? Savarkar glorifies 'Aryan'—often invoked as 'racial'—conquests of indigenous people. Aryans founded:

> new colonies [...] At last, the great mission [...] of founding a nation and a country [...] reached its geographical limit when the valorous Prince of Ayodhya [the mythological hero Ram: a striking alchemy, transmuting the mythical into the historical] made a triumphant entry into Ceylon and actually brought the whole land from the Himalayas to the Seas under one sovereign sway [...] that day was the real birth-day of our Hindu people [...].

Imperial wars and colonisation lie at the root of Hindu India, and acts of conquest are supremely valued.[25] Buddhism emasculated Hindus and all Buddhists, guilty of 'high treason', embraced Islam. So did 'low castes' as well, he admits, due to pressures of caste taboos. But, he warns, they must understand that 'change of religion means change of nationality'.

At this point, there is an extremely important engagement with the caste problem, as well as a resolution. He abundantly acknowledges that caste divisions bred disunity and weakened Hindus, though he says nothing about caste in terms of social injustice. He also admits that these were fetters that Hindus devised for themselves, they were not imposed by foreign invaders. At the same time, caste also led to remarkable cohesiveness: 'stupendous consolidation and remarkable stability of Hindu society'. Ancient Hindus voluntarily created this to 'protect their racial seed and blood, preserving their caste-life and tradition and keeping them absolutely free from any contamination.' Moreover, it has survived for centuries, so it did provide the 'life blood' that unified Hindu society 'with a certain consciousness of itself'.[26]

Savarkar denounced Ambedkar who converted to Budhhism, as 'a man burning with hatred against Hinduism': 'Pushyamitra [...] [was] forced [...] to hang the Buddhists who were guilty of seditious acts and to pull down the monasteries which had become centres of sedition. It was a just punishment for high treason [...]'.[27] Buddhism held yet another danger: that of peace. Peace destroys martial valour and exposes the nation to foreign attacks: so said VHP supremo, B.L. Sharma Prem in 1991. He had similar revulsion against medieval devotional sects, even though several belonged to the Hindu fold.[28] Their otherworldly mysticism enervated, he said, hyper-masculine Hindus. A BJP minister, Ananthakumar Hegde, has recently tweeted: 'If not for Buddhism, we would have had an Akhand Bharat.'[29]

Savarkar treats some invasions lightly: 'For the Greek, Saka, Huna and other invaders [...] their raids had never been occasioned by any cultural or religious hatred [...]'.[30] But when Mohammed of Ghazni invaded India, 'that day, the conflict of life and death began'[31] Muslims have many sins. First, abominable strength: 'Nations and civilizations fell before the sword of Islam [...]'.[32] Curiously, strength becomes a sign of Muslim viciousness, even though Aryan conquests are described as civilisational triumph. Second:

these new Islamic enemies not only aspired to crush the Hindu political power [...] but they also had [...] a fierce religious ambition [...]. Intoxicated by this [...] many times more diabolic than their political one, these millions of Muslim invaders from all over Asia fell over India, century after century with all the ferocity at their command to destroy the Hindu religion which was the lifeblood of the nation [...].[33]

There is absolutely no evidence that medieval Muslims were religious fanatics without territorial ambitions, and there is every evidence that these dynasties became fully Indianised quite soon. Histories of Muslim royal patronage to Hindu religious establishments are eschewed whereas occasional depredations of religious places are highlighted in garish colours: 'Muslim demons were demolishing Hindu temples and breaking to pieces their holiest of idols [...]'.[34]

A complex history of multifaceted intercommunity exchanges and intimacies, as well as royal conflicts,[35] cedes place to perpetual war: that being the leitmotif of RSS history. Indian Muslims—artisans, peasants, beggars, men, women, Muslims under Muslim rule as well as Muslims in Hindu-ruled areas—are all dissolved into the figure of the invader.[36] There is, moreover, total identity between nation/community/people (as synonymous, inter-changeable terms) and rulers.[37]

The Muslim becomes an open, floating signifier on which any kind of Hindu communalised histories can be freely inscribed. At the same time, he is also a closed category, representing fanaticism and oppression alone. The paradoxical logic makes the living Muslim stand in for the historical, the pseudo-historical and the mythological: sometimes as Babur who initiated Mughal rule (in the 1990s, all Muslims were called *Babur ki aulad* or Babur's children); sometimes as an earlier Sultan, Alauddin Khalji, who apparently ravished a Rajput queen who actually did not even live in the same century, if she lived at all;[38] and some-times for a mythological demon whom Ram, divine incarnation and epic war-rior-king, killed, because he abducted Ram's wife.[39] A glorious medley of referents, a universe of magical realism calling itself history.

The worst and the most persistent sin of this generic Muslim is rape:

> It was a religious duty of every Muslim to kidnap and force into their own reli-gion on non-Muslim women. This incited their sensuality and lust for carnage and while it increased their number, it affected the Hindu population in an inverse proportion. [...] Muslims [...] considered it their highly religious duty to carry away forcibly the women of the enemy side as if they were commonplace property, to ravish them, to pollute them, and to distribute them to all and sundry [...] and to absorb them completely in their fold [...] which increased their number [...].[40]

Rape tales circulate decade after decade, with fresh embellishments, drawn from different temporal contexts, where epic, medieval and partition times mingle effortlessly with recent allegations of Muslim conspiracies to abduct Hindu women. A timeless popular historical memory is born, justifying Hindu communal violence in the present.[41] It is this function that explains the centrality of history in Sangh politics: to provide an endlessly elastic pool of past villains since the vulnerable, cornered Muslims in the present cannot possibly offer adequate offences that can merit the bloodthirstiness that they face now at individual and collective levels. Political needs, beliefs and mem-ory-work assert privileges against investigative history: claiming something like 'your history' comes in the way of 'my memory'.[42]

In a sense, it seems, that Savarkar apportions blame even-handedly: for Hindus, too, suffered from a 'suicidal morbidity'. But their flaw lay in an excess of virtue, just as the Muslim's lay in absolute monstrosity. Hindus let go of the vanquished enemy too soon, without extracting sufficient humiliation from him. They are born noble-hearted and generous, too trusting, and always betrayed by enemies they forgave. Muslims and Christians, on the other hand, are born vicious and intolerant in the same measure.[43]

Savarkar blamed the iconic Hindu warrior king Shivaji for not abducting Muslim queens. 'The souls of those millions of aggrieved women might perhaps have said, "Do not forget, O Your Majesty, [...] the unutterable atrocities and oppression and outrage committed on us [...]. It was the suicidal Hindu idea of chivalry to women which saved the Muslim women [...]".'[44]

Partition was accompanied with monstrous violence against women in which Hindus and Muslims were equally complicit. But Hindutva chooses to excise Hindu rapes altogether from public memory. Savarkar prepared the notion of 'just and necessary rapes'. His biographer wrote: 'He said that Pakistan's inhuman and barbarous acts such as kidnapping and raping Indian women would not be stopped unless Pakistan was given tit for tat.'[45] So, 'Day after day, decade after decade, century after century, the ghastly conflict [between Hindus and Muslims] continued, and India single-handedly kept up the fight morally and militarily [...].' For Hindutva, past is but present-continuous, and Muslims of today represent invaders of yester-year. Revenge becomes the preeminent lesson of history, to be realised through ceaseless wars. The motif of war is all pervasive. Even classrooms—as a lecturer at the Delhi orientation course emphasised—must teach us how and why to go to war. For so did Krishna, 'the ideal teacher' and incarnation of god, in the sacred epic *Mahabharata*, teach a reluctant prince about the necessity of war, and transforming the battlefield into a classroom.[46]

Having constructed an awesome enemy figure, Hindutva then commands Hindus to refashion themselves in the image of the enemy—infinitely fanatical, cruel, lustful—so as to worst the imagined Muslim at his own game. The first step, therefore, is to create a serviceable image of the Other, and then recast the Self in that mold. Inaugural offence is always ascribed to the enemy, and everlasting benediction is, thereby, bestowed upon all subsequent aggression inflicted by the Hindutva self, however ruthless or unilateral.

The RSS never joined anti-colonial movements nor ever faced British repression. Savarkar, however, had been a heroic revolutionary extremist before he turned to Hindutva. He wrote an account of the 1857 anti-British uprising: representing it as the heroism of kings, rather than as subaltern resistance. He exulted in its bloodshed: the supposed beheading of British mothers by sepoys in front their infants, and vice versa.[47] The killing of innocents becomes patriotism and history functions as a spur to, and a celebration of, inhuman cruelty.

He was exiled to the Cellular Jail on the Andaman Islands in 1911 where he completely changed his tune. He pleaded with the British to let him go, so that he could serve their 'Aryan Empire', stretching between Ireland and India. The British obliged, and he remained unflinchingly loyal to the Empire, all through subsequent massive anti-colonial popular movements. Why the change of heart? He was alarmed, he says, by Hindu-Muslim unity that the contemporary Non-Cooperation-Khilafat upsurge had unleashed. Unless the 'Yavana (Muslim) snakes' could be tackled, India and the Empire faced a common crisis.[48]

If Savarkar genuflected before colonialism and if present-day Hindutva courts western leaders and commodities avidly, the West poses, nonetheless, a political-cultural problem for his successors today: as purveyor of dangerous ideas about social justice, constitutionalism, socialism and secularism. Above all, as progenitor of Christian missionaries who convert Hindus and educate Dalits and tribals.

However, just as Hindu-Muslim anti-colonial unity became a real possibility in the early 1920s, the representation of Hindus as a single organic substance began to crumble. This was a peak period for 'low caste' movements and organisations, especially in western and southern India.[49] That made the highlighting of a hostile 'Other' even more essential for managing Hindu unity.

Savarkar was admirably candid:

Nothing makes Self conscious of itself so much as a conflict with non-Self. Nothing can weld people into a nation and nations into a state as the pressure of a common foe. Hatred separates as well as unites. Never had Sindhusthan [Hindustan] a better chance and a more powerful stimulus to be herself forged into an indivisible whole as on that dire day when the great iconoclast [Mahmud of Ghazni] crossed the Indus [...].[50]

It is the external foe who creates the nation, the anti-national always predates the national. The nation, moreover, is not a modern political construct. It is primordial, everlasting and unchanging: actualisation of a singular cultural essence, defined by what it is not.

Savarkar's perspective has proved to be remarkably tenacious, composed though it was nearly a century back. He also laid down the groundwork for Hindutva's typical arsenal of rhetoric and arguments. His multi-volume history is free of verified source material. It is a string of assertions which double up as proof positive, simply because he said them—and said them with such rhetorical force. His is a battle against modern historical methods even as he overturns the substance of authenticated academic histories.

Savarkar inherited his building blocks from several nineteenth-century ideological writings:[51] stray fragments, which he assembled into a coherent whole. M.S. Golwalkar, second supreme leader of the RSS, added another contemporary inspirational model.

In 1938, Golwalkar wrote:

> To keep up the purity of the nation and its culture, Germany shocked the world by her purging the country of the semitic races [...]. Race pride at its highest has been manifested here [...] all the constituents of the Nation idea have been boldly vindicated in modern Germany and that, too, in the actual present, when we can for ourselves see and study them [...] a good lesson for us in Hindustan to learn and profit by [...].

The Nazi lesson for India was, 'they [non-Hindus] may stay in the country wholly subordinated to the Hindu nation, claiming nothing, deserving no privileges [...] not even citizen's rights.'[52] No Sangh constituent has ever retracted this profusely reprinted and much-used statement.

Nazi-worship persists. In 1998, when the ABVP was celebrating its fiftieth birthday, I was astonished to see their Hyderabad camp calling itself 'Blitzkrieg'. In 2004, the social studies textbook for Grade X in Modi-ruled Gujarat said: 'Hitler lent dignity and prestige to the German people'. It had nothing negative or critical about Nazism.[53] The admiration has wider and older sources, Nazi enmity against imperial Britain being one. But the real affinity with Hindutva has different roots. Savarkar prescribed fierce violence against vulnerable 'enemies': women, children, minorities. Hitler was a consummate exemplar of that.

Sites of historical pedagogy: RSS history in schools

A lot of this history is taught through extra-curricular activities. BJP-ruled Rajasthan compulsorily sends students from Jaipur government and private schools to 'spiritual' camps, to learn about Muslim violence and 'Love Jihads'.[54]

Their first RSS primary school—Saraswati Shishu Mandir—came up in 1952: middle and secondary level schools were added later. The RSS now runs the largest school chain, next to government schools, teaching a total of 3,206,212 students across the country: even in most inhospitable places.[55] West Bengal, for instance, which the BJP has never ruled so far, possessed twenty-one RSS schools in 1990, when the Left Front government looked invincible.[56] At Naxalbari in North Bengal, where tea gardens have shut down for a long time, and there are no affordable schools for the poor, a primary school was set up in 1999, taught by *pracharaks* earning Rs. 500 a month, and by part time *vistaraks* earning Rs. 250. Now grown into a formidable secondary-level school, it sends out its students among unemployed workers to distribute charity as well as spread 'moral education' about Hindutva.[57]

The nature of education is stratified. While mainstream schools are meant for the urban middle classes, there is abbreviated schooling for remote areas where *Ekal Vidyalays* meet once a week with one teacher and offer a basic education. *Vanvasi Kalyan Ashrams* provide rudimentary learning to tribal children and so do *Seva Bharati* schools[58] in slums.[59] Hundreds of *Samskar Kendras* disseminate 'moral education' in remote, inaccessible areas. Their minimal educational content is offset by the sheer absence of other educational channels for these children. In BJP-ruled states, Vidya Bharati decides the curriculum for government schools.[60] All implant an aggressive Hindu supremacism and hatred for the non-Hindu. All exalt Hindu heroes who fought against Muslims.[61]

Vidya Bharati schools for middle-class students use NCERT textbooks, in order to academically compete with government schools. When I visited them, the first NDA government was not yet in power and they were forced to teach out of nationalist-secular textbooks. To allay its effects, a whole host of supplementary aids had been instituted to align students to the Hindutva historical message. Visual icons, for instance, abound all over school premises: of Hindu kings who fought against Muslims—Shivaji, Rana Pratap. The Indian map, prominently displayed, is one of undivided India or *Akhand Bharat*, which also included Nepal, Afghanistan, Burma, Sri Lanka. Headmasters lecture about Muslim oppression at school assemblies. History teaching, thus, is non-stop, and it is an audio-visual spectacle, not confined to the classroom, the syllabus, or to fixed school hours. It pervades all times and spaces within the school.

Most important are the compulsory '*Bharatiya Sanskriti*' (Indian Culture) courses which are a combination of Hindu ethnic pride and ethnic hatred.[62] There are 'Know-your-Culture' booklets (*Sanskriti-jnana*) to cover standards IV to XII, to prepare students and teachers for annual in-house national examinations. Examinees memorise the one correct answer to each question. Instead of historical processes, then, we have a catalogue of names and the quiz substitutes for analysis. 'Who set up the five sacred mathas of Hinduism across India?'—Adiguru Shankaracharya. 'Which tyrant got Guru Gobind Singh's two sons buried alive for refusing to give up Hinduism?'—Aurangzeb.[63] No explanation of who they were and what they did.

In 2002, the BJP-led central government replaced existing NCERT text-books with its own set. Glaring factual mistakes were immediately detected but they are far too numerous to dwell on. I will discuss their historical logic instead.

The Class XI textbook on Ancient India presents 'the overall personality of the society and the people': implying both are singular. History helps us appreciate our 'nation', it said. History thus becomes a biography—or hagiography—of the nation.[64] Patriotism—defined as self-pride—is the sole purpose of history-learning. There is no doubt whatsoever that this is exclusively Hindu patriotism. The book is an epiphany to Hindu sages, including Manu, who had actually prescribed harsh caste and gender discipline. They were, apparently, more humane and scientific than savants from other parts of the world. It refers to western scholars—Voltaire, Schelling, Kant and numerous others—whose acknowledgement of Hindu greatness seems crucial for self esteem.[65] Even though Western thought is persistently denigrated, western approbation for Hindu civilisation is, nonetheless, continually referenced. When not found, the admiration is invented. Whenever western sources are critical of Hindu practices or customs, they are immediately excoriated: as is Marx, a 'shallow thinker', pro-British and racist.[66] Antiquity carries supreme value, and India must always stand out as the first and the best of civilisations. Borders between myths and historical sources vanish as Puranic chronologies are presented as precise historical sources and mythological figures become historical actors.[67]

Pedagogical methods are interesting. 'In 1600 A.D., the English East India Company was established in India', the textbook on contemporary history says, without explaining what a company was in the first place.[68] The French Revolution gets cursory mention: it 'destroyed the monarchy but ended in the dictatorship of Napoleon', 'and it used slogans like Liberty, Equality and Fraternity'.[69] The narrative organisation is puzzling. After a brief mention that Europeans were conquering the world—without the whys and the hows—we are abruptly told that 'Steamer [sic] was introduced in India in 1835': no connection is made with previous points, nor is the 'steamer' or its significance explained.[70] Disjointed, abrupt sentences mark the writings, and no term is clarified. They have a hectoring tone, they announce their 'facts' as axiomatic givens: 'Trade led to political power and political power was used to propagate Christianity.'[71]

'Popular Revolts' against British rule describes royal, and not subaltern resistance. No Adivasi-peasant-worker struggles against oppression, Indian or British, are mentioned. The students, therefore, will not connect past heroism and anti-colonial activism with present-day subalterns. Economic developments are discussed scantily and confusedly. Surprisingly, it connects the 1857 revolt with 'the famous theory of evolution by an English thinker Charles Darwin [...] through a long process of natural selection [unexplained] man had descended not from Adam but from Ape. The theory also propounded the idea of continuous struggle for existence leading to the survival of the fittest.'[72] Since students have been told nothing about Darwin's theory of evolution, it is difficult to know what they are to make of this. Understanding, clearly, is jettisoned in favour of rote learning, and intellectual interest or curiosity find no purchase.

The facts that are thrown down at students are chosen very selectively, leaving the account of modern times highly fractured. Moderate nationalists are dismissed as pro-British without a word about their economic critique of British rule. Gandhian *satyagrahis* are mentioned without clarifying the *Satyagraha* concept. Revolutionary terrorists are, indeed, glorious martyrs, being votaries of violence. But Bhagat Singh's socialist perspective, or his later turn to atheism are excised. The demand for Dalit separate electorates becomes a sinister British divisive plot and Ambedkar enters only as the author of the constitution, not for his critique of caste. There is nothing at all on liberal social reformers, women rebels like Pandita Ramabai or 'low-caste' protests. Critiques of caste and gender are embarrassing pointers to power lines among Hindus: they are best forgotten. History is stripped of processual content, of analytical imperatives, of thick descriptions, even of causal links.

In March 2018, a modified plan for NCERT books came up, without as yet a comprehensively revised National Curriculum programme. No doubt when that is done, textbooks will be overhauled more thoroughly. For the moment, the spatial distribution has been significantly altered to highlight national hero worship: of Rana Pratap, Shivaji, Vievkananda Aurobindo—Hindu warriors, Hindu sages, all. Hindu 'science' has been given pride of place in science textbooks and Hindu scripture and sacred commentaries are presented as scientific treatises and historical accounts.[73] Human Resources Minister Javadekar promised that Indian history would henceforth correspond to 'India's glorious past', so there is nothing left to history apart from epiphany. The realm of history, moreover, is made truly imperial since it colonises science, geography, and language textbooks.

My sense is that the really virulent anti-Muslim messages are, as yet, delivered orally in schools, camps and *shakhas*. For the present, the intention is to steadily expand the empire of Hindu greatness.

Sites of historical pedagogy: RSS history for college teachers

Despite their elementary grammatical and factual mistakes, these textbooks are still superior to what was taught as history to college teachers. They—intellectuals themselves, forming the thinking habits of young students—were repeatedly told that too much thinking is pernicious, one should follow prescribed action instead. RSS *Margdarshak* (guide; shower of the path) Lajja Ram Tomar's notions of history clearly provided the content. I will cite a few gems from him at random:

> Europe and the US are filled with the ruins of ancient Hindu empires. Molten gold flowed in rivers for six months after the British sacked Bhonsle's Nagpur palace. The Rig Veda calculated the speed of light. A sleepless Mussolini was lulled to sleep by Indian classical music. Paris set up Manu's statue with the caption [in English!]: 'First Lawgiver of the World'. The Upanishads described earth's rotation on axis as causing day and night. Sanskrit is the perfect computer-science language. Only the sacred pipal tree and tulsi plant produce oxygen.[74]

All these are faithfully reproduced in most lectures and Hindutva's account of India's cultural past becomes the ground for every subject that college teachers teach. A lecture on chemistry consisted entirely of the health properties of sacred plants and the excellence of ancient scientific treatises. The point is to demonstrate the superiority of ancient Indian science.[75] NASA scientists heard the sun uttering the Hindu holy sound, '*Om*'. Ancient Hindu medical treatises taught advanced plastic surgery skills; Chinese civilisation learnt everything from ancient Hindus though they now deny the debt; ancient Hindus reached the highest peaks of modern mathematics, astronomy, chemistry, physics; India was the first country to make oil and cotton.[76] Western authorities, again, are invariably cited/miscited for all civilisational claims.[77]

But western ideas are evil because they preach excessive individual freedom. A supreme court advocate said that the freedom to oppose one's employer is a dangerous privilege and that Gandhi always spoke of duties rather than rights. Equality before the law is not an absolute right: there should be a reasonable classification of individuals as some are more equal than others.[78] Another supreme court advocate said that democracy is an irrelevant western concept whereas Hindu monarchy provided an absolutely just form of governance. *Varnashrama*—the concept of caste and the stages of life—provided social equality and Hindu texts and social practices bestowed perfect gender equality.

The party slant is blatant and ubiquitous. A BJP functionary said that ancient *Gurukuls* or Hindu schools educated all but, in medieval times, Muslims blocked women's education. Modi is now reviving the *Gurukul* tradition of female education and empowerment.[79] Leftists are definitionally antinational, being inspired by Marx's contempt for Hanuman worship. Kapil Kumar (professor of history, Indira Gandhi National Open University) and Monica Aurora (supreme court advocate) heaped abuse on Marx and on leftist students and professors like Nivedita Menon of Jawaharlal Nehru University, who allegedly want to divide the country.[80] (Professor Menon currently faces several legal suits for her critique of the government's policies towards the Northeast and Kashmir.)

How did caste originate? Kapil Kumar explained that Turks introduced commodes to India. Hindus who refused to convert to Islam were forced to clean them and, thus, they became untouchables. Kumar twists the arguments of anti-RSS historians to support his points. He cites Dipesh Chakrabarty's work on Jadunath Sarkar to claim that since Chakrabarty thinks Sarkar was a great scholar, the latter's condemnation of Muslims carries absolute truth: though Chakrabarty had made it quite clear that Jadunath was no crude Muslim-hater, and that he himself does not share Sarkar's politics.[81] Kumar totally and flagrantly misquotes Sumit Sarkar to make Gandhi appear as the maker of partition.[82] The illicit appropriation of their Others, in all likelihood, emerges from a deep cultural envy for cosmopolitan scholarship. A couple of known names of opponents are cited for academic credibility, to simulate a shared perspective with, and entry into, a wider scholarly world.

RSS historical pedagogy: new research

The RSS has ambitious plans for advanced historical research, having now packed the Indian Council of Historical Research with its own functionaries. The agenda is 'Indianising' and 'nationalising' research, and—more significant—to take it to the common man. They plan to establish the historical authenticity of Puranic sources and to date them precisely.[83] The latter exercise being already done by scholars; the purpose, obviously, is to claim enhanced antiquity for them.

The research agenda was envisioned in 1973 by Morepant Pingley, RSS full-timer, and further developed by Balmukund Pandey, present Organising

Secretary of the Akhil Bharatiya Itihas Sankalan Yojana (ABISY). The purpose, according to its 'Visions and Perspectives' document, is to correct distortions introduced under the British Raj which 'perverted the traditional heroes, culture, literature and languages'. The West also transformed the minds of historians who forgot to admire the Self, and denied that Hinduism is the bedrock of Indian culture.[84]

Indianisation involves rejecting the globally accepted dating system, and adopting *Kaliyugabda*, instead—a laborious mythological chronology that is never used by historians. Time is calculated in *Itihas Darpan*[85] according to *Kali Yuga*[86]—the last and darkest of ages in the four-age temporal cycle used in myths. The new dating, however, is deeply problematic:

> In reality, Kali Yuga is an artificial creation of astronomers, fabricated at a much later date to provide a convenient chronology base for astronomical and calendrical calculations [...] Its inauguration is taken to coincide with 18 February, 3102 BC. [...] Since Kali Yuga years are normally counted as expired, they can be converted to AD years by subtracting 3101 or 3100, depending on the month.[87]

Immediately after Modi's victory, ABISY announced in August 2014 that it had completed four research projects into: a) tracing the route of Saraswati river and, thereby, establishing the historicity of the *Vedas* wherein the river—now lost and believed to be dead—is mentioned; b) countering the old theory that Aryans migrated to India and claiming that they originated among Adivasis or *janjatis*;[88] c) dating the *Mahabharata* epic, Shankaracharya and Buddha; and d) finalising research on the uprising of 1857 which Savarkar had called the first war of independence. In the next ten years, it would compile a Puranic encyclopedia, reinterpret their original meaning, and establish them as 'India's real history'.

A lot of effort is expended in overwriting an old Hindutva historiography that subscribed to a foreign Indo-Aryan origin for caste Hindus who then colonised and civilised India. The new revisionism strenuously asserts, instead, that a common origin unites Savarna/Aryans and tribal/Adivasis who actually belong to the same stock. Only later did a more advanced part separate itself and migrate outwards to civilise the rest of the world. Remaining Adivasis, quite clearly, were left behind because they failed to advance. This, though not said openly, clearly explains why some became marginalised, dispossessed, often pauperised. In a brilliant move, then, affinity is proclaimed, only to cover over and perpetuate age-old discriminatory and oppressive practices. Instead of structural transformation in Adivasi conditions, real immiseration is compensated for by imagined and symbolic incorporation into the Aryan fold. Such incorporation is politically crucial, given the success of Christian missionary education, conversion and social mobility projects, Maoist influence in Adivasi areas, and secessionist politics among these deprived sections in the Northeast.[89] Interestingly, the new origin story cancels the older historical narrative of Aryan conquests which Savarkar had described. That has become an embarrassing reminder of the 'foreignness' of caste/*savarna* Hindus.

How exactly is the incorporation attempted? We circle back to another aspect of their historical project: the significant process of writing and disseminating the new histories. They constitute a historiographical movement which starts at the grassroots and moves upwards into research publications. ABISY collects oral myths at Kulu in Himachal Pradesh from Adivasis, locates analogues in Brahmanical myths, and claims mutual affinity and common origin.[90] It draws local subalterns and elites into the process of writing new histories.

Daniela Berti found in 1996 that Kulu tribal deities are believed to speak directly to institutionalised mediums about their lives. ABISY appropriates these 'secret and inspired stories' to fold local legends into Hindu 'histories' and cultural traditions. Initially gods told their lives to a low caste/tribal, illiterate—but divinely-inspired—medium who then recited those words to the king. Devender Singh, ex-king and staunch RSS, now transcribes them and hands them over to ABISY to interpret their meaning. A local tribal legend about eighteen snakes, for instance, has been arbitrarily pulled into the Brahmanical Ganesh myth: its authenticity, apparently, borne out by 'geological' research. Western science—as always—provides imagined accreditation.

Little attention has been paid so far to RSS work on local histories, national textbook controversies having obscured them altogether.[91] Local lore is more permeable to RSS history writing since they do not require evidential scaffolding, apart from divine inspiration. ABISY works on a heroic scale. RSS *pracharak* Ram Singh Thakur gave up a pre-partition faculty position at Lahore University to dedicate himself to it fulltime. He now lives in a single room at the Keshuv Kunj RSS hostel, and travels untiringly despite his old age, to supervise the *Itihas Darpan* publications. He ensures that they inculcate 'national consciousness of India's glorious past' and 'denunciation of the damage caused by Muslim and Christian invaders'.[92] The president of Kulu's ABISY is a lawyer who organises seminars to prove that tribes are a part of Hindu culture. He draws in 'local intellectuals'—school teachers and priests— as historians who interpret '*bharta*', or lives of local gods, and annex them to the Brahmanical cosmogony. Since the entire mountainous region is supposedly the abode of sages, contemporary ascetics are also drawn into the project in the role of historians. Berti cites a letter by Devender Singh who wrote to many villages to join this 'good work', merge local tribal mediums with Hindu sages and 'local discourse mostly from local elites' (royals, and priests) with Sanskrit texts and gods. He opposes 'Communist' histories of subaltern lives and resistance.[93] Ex-royals, however oppressive their past record, still enjoy considerable local veneration. Singh's presence in the project therefore carries much weight.

We see the same endeavour in Nagaland, which is heavily Christianised.[94] Traditional Nagas worshipped gods associated with rocks, hills and rivers. Nineteenth-century Christian missionaries and earlier Vaisnava proselytisers had already made considerable dents into their belief systems. Now a wholesale Hinduisation is being carried out under anti-Christian and anti-insurrectionary auspices: fuelled, initially, by the Niyogi Commission findings of 1959 on supposed links between the two. RSS outfits worked closely from the 1960s with the Ramakrishna Mission—a very prestigious religious institution, famed for its educational projects—to absorb local cults and deities into a Hindu pantheon.[95] They organise local Hindu festivals and conferences with constructive employment-generating programmes for women and children. And that brings us to a crucial aspect of Hindutva's pedagogic package. Among deeply marginalised groups and places, history teaching is handed out along with charity. The stitching of minimal welfare together with Hindutva education vastly expands the scope for the RSS historical vision.

At Arunachal Pradesh, affordable *Shakti Peeths* or RSS schools expanded, hand in hand, with attacks against churches from 1977, under the RSS-affiliated Vivekananda Kendra (VK). By 2010, Arunachal had thirty RSS schools with 400 teachers and more than 10,000 students. All followed the residential *gurukul* model with non-stop monitoring of students and classes on the *Gita*, yoga, and 'topical issues'.

In 1993, it established the Vivekananda Institute of Culture at Guwahati, to make it 'the regional intellectual fountainhead'. The Institute developed a strong academic profile, frequently offering seminars, lectures, research projects: especially into histories of local communities, to involve them in exploring their own traditions while simultaneously absorbing them within Hindutva. There is great emphasis on denouncing 'alien' influences. Local beliefs are injected with Brahmanical analogues to traditional sun and moon worship.[96]

Inclusionary strategies are allied to exclusionary ones. If marginalised tribals are gathered into the folds of Brahmanical belief, conflict with non-Hindus is simultaneously produced to strengthen subaltern incorporation through shared violence.

Golwalkar had a brief 'spiritual' affiliation with the Ramakrishna *Math* in the 1930s. Later he founded the Vivekananda Rock Memorial at Kanyakumari, at the confluence of Bay of Bengal, Arabian Sea and Indian Ocean in 1963, to dedicate the RSS ideal of Hindu nationalism to Vivekananda. This was blessed by the Ramakrishna Mission, authorised custodians of Vivekananda's memory. But opposition came from local Christians who claimed the rock for St Xaviers. The Madras Government eventually upheld the Hindutva claim. The disputed site unleashed massive mobilisation of Hindu religious institutions on a national level. Even high-level Congressmen supported the RSS project.

The VK was launched in 1972 to combine Vivekananda's ideal of philanthropy and service with Hindu nation-building. Cadres are generally unmarried, women forming 50 per cent of them in 2010. In 2010, it ran 944 service projects across the country: informal schooling for pre-school children, health centres, yoga training, hostels, vocational training for women, water management, rural housing, agricultural renewable energy methods. The V.K Medical Research Foundation in Assam offers online medical help.[97]

A Hindutva sense of the cultural past, with its lethal mix of ethnic pride and ethnic hatred, pervades all projects. But it is so deftly woven into a strong fabric of much-needed charity that it often proves irresistible.

Sites of historical pedagogy: journal of history

Itihas Darpan is Hindutva's strongest academic face.[98] A bi-annual and bilingual journal, it has intermittently appeared from 1995. The ICHR has been sponsoring it from 2016.[99] The RSS office at Keshuv Kunj, Delhi, houses the headquarters, giving it a metropolitan cast. It has thirteen regional branches, linked to multiple universities. By 2014, 500 university professors were helping it. In July, ABISY head Y.S. Rao was appointed ICHR chairperson and regional ABISY functionaries filled up its posts, leaving no gap between the national/governmental and the RSS.

Savarnas, Sanskrit and Brahmanical texts clearly dominate the production: T.P Verma and Gunjam Aggarwal—neither a known historian—being editor and sub-editor. The front page proves the Hinduness and

Hindutvaness of its 'Indianised' history: a Ganesh logo at top, photos of RSS founder Hedgewar and of second supremo Golwalkar at bottom, and the *Om* symbol affixed to most essays.[100] The very first article is a homage to Golwalkar who represents '*Gyanajyoti*' or the radiance of knowledge, and who recovered Hindu splendour and unity: '*Vaibhav Prasad, ekatmabodhak tattvagyan*'. Next comes a homage to Vivekananda. History, it appears, is nothing but heritage, its writing an act of obeisance. Most articles cover prehistoric or ancient times and archaeology has pride of place: showing where Hindutva's academic strength lies.

They call themselves 'scientific' because the articles use footnotes and cite sources: knowing these basics is a source of pathetic pride. Citations remain vague, nonetheless, as the 'scientific' lesson is not yet fully learnt: one of them simply mentions 'a large number of articles available on various websites'.[101] Very few refer to any historical work that has been published in the last two decades. An exception is a reference to Dipesh Chakrabarty's *The Calling of History* on Jadunath Sarkar, for reasons that I have discussed above.[102] Few authors have academic and institutional affiliations. The April 2016 issue, for instance, names six without any at all, while four are research scholars, eleven have had some university connections and there are two whose academic status is not mentioned. Preeti Kumar, a contributor, is described as 'w/o Mr. Sanju Kumar'—whoever he may be. Those with university affiliations come from small North Indian towns: Gorakhpur, Faizabad, Dumka. Not all teach history. Many are associated with very different kinds of institutions that have little to do with historical research or teaching: Makhanlal Chaturvedi National Journalism and Communication University, Bhopal, or Gurukul Kangri.

English articles aim at an academic appearance, with glossy and profuse maps and illustrations. Most try to push back dates of various archaeological sites[103] and to establish India's influence on other ancient civilisations. They do not attack Islam or Christianity and they do try sometimes to discuss non-Hindu religious cultures, especially Buddhism: though not Indian Islam or Christianity. The non-combativeness is a sharp contrast to their other historical endeavours that we discussed earlier. Possibly, this has to do with hopes for an international readership where shrill diatribes may prove counterproductive. Most Hindi articles, on the other hand, depend on Puranic and Dharmashastric sources, are critical of western authorities to the point of not using them at all, and are bent on proving the incomparable excellence of Hindu sacred art, literature and laws. An article by Ratnesh Tripathi on Vedic education,[104] for example, extols Brahmanical discipline and celibacy norms for students. Another by Arun Kumar[105] unabashedly proclaims that modern science emanates from the Vedas. Harsh Vardhan Singh Tomar's article is an unsubstantiated, unreferenced eulogy for unique Hindu tolerance. *Manusmriti*—which upholds caste and gender discipline—is presented as a compilation of 'useful' social regulations to stem anarchy and disorder. It is supposedly a text that adapts itself wonderfully to changing times—though no examples are cited for this—and provides the perfect recipe for our disordered, '*bisrinkhal*' times. Vedic sages—confused with Manu—apparently desired that all *Varnas* must love one another. Complete silence reigns with regard to caste inequality. There is a strenuous attempt to establish continuity between an imagined Saraswati River-based culture and Vedic civilisation, in order to push back the antiquity of the Vedas.[106]

Whether in English or in Hindi, there is a striking absence of articles on medieval and modern times: except for stinging denunciations of Marxist historians, predictably branded as anti-national. It could be a failure of nerve about challenging the anti-RSS scholarship on colonial times as yet, given that it is one of the most advanced branches of Indian history-writing. Medieval history-writing, on the other hand, would inevitably involve the usual abuse of Muslim dynasties. That is postponed for the time being to retain and consolidate the image of sober academic propriety. Ethnic pride rather than communal hatred is the focus here.

Concluding reflections

Let me end with a few pointers to the areas of strength for Hindutva histories. The concrete content of Hindutva history is simple and thin. The simplicity, however, relieves its votaries of the burden of complex thinking. Yet another important source of strength lies in the fact that RSS historical assumptions are not made in a vacuum: some do plug into frameworks that are otherwise scholarly. A notion of history as combat between good and evil, heroes and demons, for instance, has become fairly standard over time, even in left-nationalist histories. The latter's heroes would be secular-nationalist leaders while the British would be the villains: entirely distant from the conventional RSS demonology, but the overarching binarised patterning of historical understanding still shares some structural similarities.

A post-colonial preference for the cultural rather than the political-material also inadvertently creates some space for their brand of cultural nationalism:

of course, with values entirely reversed or overturned in the Hindutva version. Yet, in both, to an extent, culture is a static construct, expressing the innate essence of a whole people, pitted against the foreign. Dalit histories from the early twentieth century came to offer a critical counter-narrative to cultural organicity, followed by Marxist class-based and feminist frameworks. These threw up serious challenges and alternatives. For all their ritual genuflections to Ambedkar, Hindutva cannot accommodate a serious critical engagement with problems of caste, nor, indeed, with any kind of internal power lines.[107]

RSS history is driven by political needs, popular beliefs and myths and construction of memory-work. These imperatives assert their privileges against investigative history: claiming that 'your history' comes in the way of 'my memory' and relativising all narratives so that the question of academic evaluation and cross checking, of ascertaining validity of narrative claims, methods and purposes, do not arise. History becomes a flat field where all kinds of memories have an equally interesting status. Inadvertently, again, some strands of post-modernist emphases on challenging truth claims of empirically-verified histories open up some space for this.

Given that Hindutva challenges academic historical methods and narratives, why should their accounts of the cultural past become more popular and successful that scholarly ones? Left-secular historians—making up the bulk of Indian historians—have a complex and nuanced understanding of history and, needless to say, also an immeasurably more scholarly one. But they have, with few exceptions, confined their work to the realm of the properly academic: as, indeed, they should do, since their legitimate brief is to write honest, well researched and interesting histories. That realm, however, inevitably belongs to metropolitan centres and to highly educated middle-class academic circles.[108]

Their failure to compete with RSS public histories has often been blamed on their 'scientific', secular approach. That, however, is not a correct nor a fair diagnosis. The flaw actually lies in their circumscribed view of educational dissemination, a focus on national level textbooks: written by the best minds, no doubt, but in isolation from local, organic social-cultural processes. Once again, we are beset with an impossible problem: for without the resources that come with a metropolitan location, well researched and sound histories cannot be written at all.

It is the sheer quantity, continuity and intensity of the RSS's historical work, the massive cadre base that generates and teaches history at grass-roots levels, that makes all the difference. Neither any alternative political formation, nor academic one, ever achieved, nor tried to acquire, that range and depth of dissemination. It is the medium that really accounts for the relative success, not really the message.

And all that work produces a history that kills.

PART IV

ECONOMIC POLICIES AND 'MODINOMICS'

9

MERCHANTS OF HYPE AND HATE

A POLITICAL-ECONOMIC EVALUATION OF THE MODI REGIME

Pranab Bardhan

He seemed to sniff the tainted air of social cruelty, to strain his ear for its atrocious sounds...he took the part of an insolent and venomous invoker of sinister impulses which lurk in the blind envy and exasperated vanity of ignorance

> Joseph Conrad (describing a character in one of his novels).

The Modi regime came to power with a great deal of promise, particularly in the matter of *vikas* or economic development. As an economist I shall, of course, primarily go over many of the policies and programmes adopted since then that affect the economy, even though personally I am actually much more concerned about the long-term impact of the regime on the fabric of our society and polity. Sectarian poison regularly spewed by this regime and its associates is highly corrosive.

Let me start with a classification of the various policies of this regime under a few imperfectly descriptive categories:

A. Those that may be described as successfully executed hoaxes;

B. Those that are excellent public relations (PR) coups;

C. Those that are continuities with reasonable policies of the earlier United Progressive Alliance (UPA) regime over the decade 2004–14;

D. Newer policies which are steps in the right direction, in relatively earlier stages of implementation to allow much assessment;

E. Those that are definitely regressive.

The Hoaxes

Among the successfully executed hoaxes, I would count the promise of job creation (a move away from the supposed 'dole' regime of the UPA) that was a winning slogan in the 2014 general election. The successful 'Gujarat model of development' was to be reproduced in the rest of India, with a promise of creating 100 million new jobs by 2022. This appealed to the 'aspirational' youth, particularly in north India, where there has been a youth bulge in the demographics. That the Gujarat model of high growth was not exemplary in job creation (a substantial part of Gujarat's manufacturing growth was in highly capital-intensive activities like petroleum refineries and petro-chemicals) did not deter that appeal.

By now, it is clear even to the fawning media and politicians that the pace of job creation has not been particularly impressive. Some data (for example, the annual Employment-Unemployment Survey data of the Labor Bureau of the Ministry of Labor and Employment) even show a job decline for certain years. In particular, regular formal sector jobs, which hold the most allure for the aspirational youth as they leave the low-productivity jobs in agriculture, have remained a tiny proportion of the total employment. (The Employee Provident Fund data that are being cited for new formal sector jobs in some quarters[1] refer to employees newly brought under provident fund schemes, but these may not pertain to new jobs created.) The backlog of 'surplus workers' that include the under-employed (as estimated in the *India Employment Report 2016* on the basis of National Sample Survey data)[2] exceeds fifty million workers. This does not include the women who are often discouraged drop-outs from the labour force. Over the last four decades non-agricultural job growth in India has remained sluggish (except for a very short spell in the first decade of twenty-first century, and that too mainly in the construction sector), and Modi has hardly made any dent in this persisting pattern, despite the rhetoric. The relaxation of labour laws in several BJP-ruled states does not seem to have made much of a difference yet (this needs a more detailed quantitative study), suggesting that it was possibly not the main constraint on labour absorption, contrary to the widely-held belief in ruling political and business circles.

Another big hoax has been in the regime's supposedly spectacular fight against corruption. After insignificant progress in getting back the black money stashed in foreign accounts or from repeated announcements of tax amnesty, came the sudden 'bold' launching of demonetisation in November 2016. This has turned out to be one of the grandest hoaxes ever in Indian political history.

The announced objective was to vaporise the corrupt cash hoarded by the rich, but other objectives were also mentioned—to eliminate counterfeit money and target terrorism-funding. After some time when some people began doubting the efficacy of the corruption objective, that of stimulating the use of digital money was thrown in. The Reserve Bank of India (RBI) in its Annual Report[3] released in August 2017 has now admitted what was obvious to most people by January 2017 that almost all of the canceled notes (and probably some of the counterfeit notes) are now in the banking system. Either the black money in the form of hoarded cash was puny or was deftly returned with impunity by the hoarders, with corrupt complicity of some bank officials and low-income bank account holders. Demonetisation may even have provided an opportunity for legalising some of the counterfeit money. The total amount of counterfeit notes seized in 2016–17, as reported by RBI, came to a trifling 0.0008 per cent of total notes in circulation. As for encouraging the use of digital money, many other countries have done that without anywhere near the enormous hardship of demonetisation.

On the hardship itself we now have plenty of evidence, and not just from the bank queues in front of ATM's that the urban middle classes experienced, and even apart from the consequences of the day-to-day arbitrary changes in the bank regulations. This was an incredibly botched execution of a policy ('maximum government, minimum governance'), that was thought up by ignorant but arrogant leaders in Delhi foisted on an unprepared and confused bank bureaucracy. Primary survey data from wholesale and retail traders around Bangalore suggest an average fall of 20 per cent sales in December–January (about one-fifth of the respondents reporting more than 40 per cent drop in sales).[4] A survey in December–January[5] shows that in Panipat, a textile hub of north India, there was a collapse of domestic business sales of 40 to 80 per cent—as a result about half of 350,000 workers employed there were laid off, and there was no cash to pay wages. They report a similar story from

Tiruppur, the textile hub of south India. A report by the All-India Manufacturers' Organisation on the basis of a large survey shows that in the quarter October–December 2016 trading organisations lost 45 per cent of jobs and small and medium companies lost 35 per cent of jobs, followed by similar losses in the micro, small and medium companies in the next quarter.[6] Even in cases where jobs were not lost, wage rates went down.

These are reports from data on traders, companies and enterprises; no one has as yet given us estimates of job and income losses for poorer people in the villages on a sufficiently large scale. The *Economic Survey* 2017 of the Ministry of Finance notes the substantial rise in demand for work in the rural employment guarantee program, even though the stories about long delays of wage payments usually discourage such demand.[7]

The prime minister had cited Gross Domestic Product (GDP) data to taunt 'Harvard' academics, and now, more recently, even GDP data are not being helpful. In any case, his economic advisers did not dare tell him that those short-term GDP calculations, based mainly on projections from formal sector data, are meaningless in capturing the real GDP changes in the vast informal sector in times of economic shocks like demonetisation. They also refrained from informing him regarding the impact of these on the informal sector and the section of population it employs, where it is likely to have been the harshest.

Yet, (and this is the political magic of the hoax) many people thought—and survey evidence reflects their thinking—that all this hardship was worth bearing for the 'greater cause' of fighting corruption and punishing the dishonest rich, even as the latter actually got away quite easily.

It has been pointed out that real estate prices have gone down in the aftermath of reduced black money that otherwise fueled them. But as the *Economic Survey* shows, in the volume II cited above, the decline in the rate of rise in housing prices observed in the post-demonetisation months was a continuation of a decline that started before demonetisation, and later housing prices started rising again. The new Benami Properties Act is intended to curb the influence of black money in real estate, but it may not make much of a dent if the majority of land and property transactions are not registered. Additionally, a proposed bill to make such registration mandatory has remained inactive since 2013.

It has also been pointed out that black money in the form of evaded taxes substantially going down has been evidenced in the recent rise in the number of people submitting income tax returns. Again, as the *Economic Survey* has pointed out, the average income level reported for the new taxpayers is ₹2.7

lakh, only slightly above the tax threshold of ₹2.5 lakh. Hence, the new people brought under the tax net are not the 'super-rich' who had been evading tax all these years; they are more likely to be relatively small earners who have felt the pressure from banks being now more active in pursuing their account-holders through Aadhaar identification and its linking with PAN cards, the Goods and Services Tax (GST) flushing out non-taxpaying small traders, etc., and not necessarily just an effect of demonetisation.

PR coups

In general the PR spin by hype-merchants from the prime minister downward has succeeded in creating the impression—and the media have gone along with it—that the current regime is much cleaner. The large Nirav Modi-Mehul Choksi fraud case is still being investigated, but there is enough evidence to suggest how crony capitalists continue to game and loot the system. Let us ignore the state-level cases of the gigantic *Vyapam* scam in Madhya Pradesh (involving so far nearly forty mysterious deaths of witnesses and accused), or some of the cricket-related scams in Rajasthan, Delhi, etc., or how in the 2018 assembly elections in Karnataka more corruption-tainted candidates were bra-zenly put up by the BJP than any other party. The auctions for natural resources are now much cleaner, people say. Actually, they started being cleaner, under Supreme Court orders, in the last years of the UPA regime. In any case, thanks to the international mining boom being over, there is now less money to be made in the mining sector (even so the Supreme Court recently canceled eighty-eight mining leases in Goa). Investigative journalists have also pointed to the continuing coal scam in which the Adani Group is allegedly involved.

Attempts are reportedly being made to obstruct any action to be taken on the findings of the Directorate of Revenue Intelligence on the cases of large over-invoicing of power equipment and coal imports by some of the big corporate houses. Many stories about continuing corruption in government procurement, building and real estate deals, and land grabs abound, but Central Bureau of Investigation (CBI) and Enforcement Directorate (ED) are not overly active in pursuing them if they involve ruling party politicians and connected businesses. The intimidated non-government organisations (NGOs) and media largely keep quiet. This leads to very little coverage about them.

Then there is the elephant in the room, that is, the issue of the large-scale election funding, particularly for the ruling party (which, even from the reported corporate donations, are several times the donations to the other parties combined). Of course, most of the donations are unreported and undocumented. Political parties have been exempted from the Right to Information Act (RTI) and now from the Foreign Contribution Regulation Act (FCRA)—a blunt instrument regularly used to harass NGOs; this has been made retrospective back to 2010 (and now in the 2018 Finance Bill, made retrospective all the way to 1976). The attempts at reform in the form of 'election bonds'—allowing for corporate donations without limits or public disclosure and for largely anonymous donations from non-corporate entities—have made matters even less transparent, making a mockery of election funding reform.

The Lokpal Act of 2014—remember the hue and cry BJP made for its passing under UPA regime—remains unimplemented, and no *Lokpal* or ombudsman has been appointed in more than four years. (This is not surprising. The Prime Minister Narendra Modi, when he was the chief minister of Gujarat neglected to appoint a *Lokayukta* at the state-level throughout his term.) The government, however, had time to make an amendment to the Lokpal Act so that public servants no longer have to disclose the assets of their family members. Meanwhile, the Whistle-Blowers Act and RTI are being diluted (or enfeebled by large numbers of unfilled vacancies in the Information Commission offices). There is also an attempt to amend the Prevention of Corruption Act of 1988 to make initiating the investigation of a corruption charge against an official without the permission of a senior official impossible. Giving junior officials the authority for tax raids has also multiplied opportunities for extortion and arbitrary intimidation.

Yet, the rhetoric of slaying of the demon of corruption perpetuates in full force, and many people unquestioningly accept it. Modi refuses to face public questions in press conferences or in the parliament; one-way twitters and radio talks tend to be enough for the gullible.

Similarly, the Goods and Services Tax (GST) was introduced with great fanfare at a midnight session of the parliament and has been hailed as one of the biggest economic reforms in Indian history. (We are not supposed to remember that for quite some time one of the main opponents of this reform was a certain chief minister of Gujarat. With his fascination for acronyms he now calls GST a 'good and simple tax'. This, despite the fact that since then in the process of countering such opposition and complexities of negotiations, the proposed tax has now become less good and less simple compared to the version he had earlier opposed.) It has been proposed under the slogan of 'one nation, one tax', in spite of there being more than six tax rates. Furthermore, petroleum products, alcoholic beverages, etc. which account for a large part of existing state revenue have been taken out of the purview of the tax. Of course, it cannot be denied that like the UPA government before, the current government has contributed positively and energetically to the final enactment. But the GST in its hasty and haphazard implementation is causing a great deal of hardship, particularly to small businesses.

The official rhetoric also claims the Aadhaar identification of nearly a billion people as one of the great achievements of the current government. It is interesting to recall that during the UPA regime when Aadhaar was first introduced the BJP had strenuously opposed it. But the hasty manner in which the bill was passed by the ruling party as a 'finance bill' in the Lok Sabha precluded a serious discussion of many important issues like data security and threat to privacy. This is particularly problematic when the government is rather cavalier and ominous in applying its powers of surveillance. It can only be hoped that the government will not bypass the verdict of the Supreme Court on privacy as a fundamental right by continuing to allow government and private agencies the power to mine personal information. Meanwhile, large numbers of poor people are being coercively (and often illegally) denied welfare benefits for lack of proper Aadhaar identification.

Another PR success has been in the political arena. The ruling party has succeeded in creating the impression that it is a pan-Indian party rising above the narrow sectarian interests (of caste, community or language) that fragment Indian society or the 'vote bank' politics of other parties. In reality, its assiduous forgings of selected caste groups in different parts of India—like non-Yadav, non-Jatav groups in the Uttar Pradesh (UP) election—speak to the contrary. The vote bank it nurses is that of upper castes and other Hindu supremacists (along with the cult groups around the numerous Hindu godmen) and some upwardly mobile lower-caste groups that try to use Hindu symbols for announcing their arrival; and its linguistic practice even in official transactions is that of Hindi dominance. Its so-called nationalistic ideology is not pan-Indian at all; it is highly exclusionary, based on a narrow sectarian concept of 'Hindi-Hindu-Hindustan', while preemptively branding any dissent from this narrowness as 'anti-national'.

Continuities with UPA government policies

Apart from Aadhaar and GST, some other policies of the current regime are a continuation (hardly acknowledged) of earlier UPA government policies:

(a) The sanitation campaign, *Swachh Bharat*, is in many ways a continuation of the earlier *Nirmal Bharat* campaign, though it is arguable that the present policy has been much more energetic (and sometime even coercive) in implementation. But, contrary to claims made in administrative data which many find suspect, the publicised goal of making India free of open defecation by 2019 seems unattainable.[8] This is not just because the goal is simply too ambitious. It is mainly because both in concept and design the campaign, like the earlier UPA campaign, is highly defective, narrow and seemingly oblivious of why the earlier campaign did not quite succeed and why many of the toilets built with government help were not used for the purpose they were built. Apart from water supply problems and insufficient door-to-door social campaigns of public health information and awareness for which a bureaucratic approach is singularly unqualified, it has been noted that in villages and small towns pit latrine cleaning is the main issue as yet largely unresolved particularly with prevailing Hindu taboos.[9]

In a related but also much-hyped area of public sanitation, that of cleaning the highly contaminated Ganga (or Ganges) river, the National Green Tribunal in a recent judgment essentially declared its progress as a dismal failure so far.

(b) The decline in fuel subsidies accompanied by some direct cash transfer to customers, which started under the UPA regime, have now been pursued more vigorously for Liquefied Petroleum Gas (LPG) and diesel. With relatively low petroleum prices in the international markets for some time (a phase that now seems to be ending), this was an opportune time to carry out these subsidy reductions and streamlining, without hurting the consumer too much.

(c) The much-hyped Make in India program, like its UPA predecessor, the National Manufacturing Policy of 2011, has so far been a failure in increasing the manufacturing percentage of GDP. The basic macro-economic impasse that the current regime inherited, with private investment deceleration (particularly in the informal sector), stalled projects and the associated mountain of bad loans in the public banks have continued for too long (the latter growing to five times what it was at the beginning of the current regime). The Gross Fixed Capital Formation as percentage of GDP has generally been on the decline (from about 34 per cent in 2011 to about 30 per cent in 2014 to about 27 per cent in 2017). Attempts to compensate for the decline in private investment with an increase in public investment have been much too timid so far. In 2018, after years of delay, an announcement has been made to recapitalise the public banks by about 2.1 lakh crores of rupees (even though most estimates of the total amount of stressed assets exceed 10 lakh crores). It is not at all clear if this will be followed by any restructuring of public banks or reorientation in the regulation of bank lending. It has also been widely noted that the government is more hesitant in disciplining the large corporate borrowers and other cronies than it has been in dealing with the presumptive malfeasance of small borrowers.

(d) Just as Make in India has not succeeded in creating many manufacturing jobs, Skill India policy adopted in 2015 (a continuation of the earlier National Policy on Skill Development started in 2009) has largely missed skill training targets, has been badly implemented, and has seen poor employment outcomes. The Ministry of Skill Development has now abandoned the earlier much-hyped but unattainable target of training at least 300 million workers in new skills by 2022. Currently less than 5 per cent of the work force has formal vocational skills. Of the total of about 3 million people who have received some training by July 2017 under the current government scheme, less than 10 per cent of them have reportedly received any job offers.

(e) The highly publicised small and medium irrigation project, *Pradhan Mantri Krishi Sinchayee Yojana*, is largely a combination of three preexisting schemes. If one takes the average expenditure incurred earlier on the latter, there has hardly been any increase in government expenditure under the new scheme, and with not much of an impact. Even for major and medium irrigation projects, of the ninety-nine identified for completion by 2019 with the Long Term Irrigation Fund, so far only around ten have been partially done.

(f) There has been some moderate success in correcting some of the long-standing problems of under-investment in railways and in the continued program of construction of highways and particularly of rural roads (under the old and continuing *Pradhan Mantri Gram Sadak Yojana*). In general, however, the success of the Gujarat government under Modi in electricity, roads and water ('*bijli, sadak, pani*') is yet to be reproduced in the rest of India and remains quite far from it. In September 2017, Modi announced the so-called *Saubhagya* scheme for electricity connections for 40 million households. This seems to be a rehash of the *Gram Jyoti*

Yojana launched in July 2015 (which itself was a revised version of the *Grameen Vidyutikaran Yojana* launched by the UPA government in 2005).

(g) Like the previous prime minister, the current prime minister had promised thorough administrative reforms quite early on in his tenure, without delivering on them. Intense centralisation of power in the Prime Minister's Office (PMO) has actually made bottlenecks in administration worse and decision-making more arbitrary than before. More transfers of divisible funds to the state governments, mandated by the 14th Finance Commission, have increased the responsibility of the state governments. Neither NITI Aayog nor the pre-existing but dormant Inter-state Council have been successful in coordinating the execution of those state responsibilities particularly in the delivery of crucial public services or in guiding and disciplining the laggard states. The Modi government's many unilateral decisions, unwanted interventions in states with non-BJP governments, and arbitrary use of central agencies to harass non-BJP leaders in different states have often made a mockery of the rhetoric of 'cooperative federalism'.

(h) The campaign to get poor people to open bank accounts started under the UPA in connection with wage payments for the rural employment guarantee program, but it got a particular boost under the current regime with the *Jan Dhan* program. This is a significant step in financial inclusion, though many of the so-called new bank accounts are duplicates (for people who already have accounts) and often remain dormant, while the promised overdraft facility and insurance policy aspects are still largely non-functional, and effective banking agents are still rather scarce in remote areas where a bank branch is far away. The spread of mobile banking is still negligible, and when compared to Kenya, the picture is rather bleak

(i) In 2015, the new government started the Atal Pension Yojana (APY) for informal workers, which is a refined version of the contributory pension scheme National Pension System Lite that the previous government had introduced in 2010. Neither of these schemes has succeeded in enrolling more than a tiny fraction of the informal workers. While the APY scheme has more clarity and transparency compared to its predecessor, its rigidity in terms of default penalties and government co-contributions have made it unattractive for many poor informal workers.

New steps in the right direction

There are some new programmes, which are steps in the right direction, but it is as yet too early to have a proper evaluation of their progress for some of them, while for some others, independent assessments have been rare beyond the hyped data published on Ministry websites.

(a) The Insolvency and Bankruptcy Code of 2016 is expected to facilitate a faster resolution of stressed assets and loan defaults. Insolvency proceedings have already been initiated for about 400 companies, big and small, though some have complained about the lack of transparency in the process. The government has, justifiably, banned any defaulting promoters (i.e. founding shareholders) from bidding for their old assets in auctions. There is also a tribunal dedicated to the cause, which hopefully will cut down on delays in resolution. But in the numerous cases where land and built property are collaterals, the many structural distortions of the Indian land market make it difficult for the lender to appropriate the asset after default. Some legal loopholes in the Code have also been unearthed. Above all, the unrecovered loans of public banks are often less due to lack of procedures and codes for resolution, and more a result of political patronage and manipulation. Lack of transparency of accounting and poor quality of management and risk assessment, of course, continue to afflict Indian banking practices.

(b) The flagship programmes of crop insurance (*Pradhan Mantri Fasal Bima Yojana*) and e-marketing can over time become important policies in agriculture. While the coverage of crop insurance has improved, so far both the use of modern technology in assessing crop damage and the disbursement of claims and premium subsidy payments to farmers have been too tardy. For example, it is reported that even by mid-2018 six states have not paid the premium subsidy for 2016–17 crops. Lack of awareness among farmers and lack of information on the risk behavior of farmers also continue to afflict the scheme. It is widely believed that the scheme has so far mainly benefited the private insurance companies.

The government programme of e-Nam is conceptually plausible but creating an all-India spot market requires many time-consuming and organisationally difficult steps beyond just installing software. The programme has as yet delivered very little.

(c) UDAY is the programme for take-over of the massive debts of the power distribution companies by the state governments as a step toward their restructuring. However, without a substantial rationalisation of the power tariffs, there is no guarantee of not needing further bail-outs down the road. We also need an independent evaluation of the impact of UDAY on the reduction of transmission and distribution losses or of the demand for captive power plants, the extent of 'load-shedding', etc.

(d) *Ujjawala* is the programme for providing poor families with LPG connections. This is a bold, well-meaning programme (particularly in view of the massive indoor pollution problem in India arising from the use of other cooking fuels). But after the initial expansion, very few of the beneficiaries are reportedly returning for the refill of their cylinders. This is because they cannot avail of the LPG subsidy until they can repay the loan taken from the oil marketing companies toward the cost of the gas stove and the first cylinder. In general, the affordability and reliability of LPG supply are the main concerns for the use of the programme on a sustained basis. Currently, there is also very little data which are publicly available to assess the impact of the programme.

(e) The government has claimed tremendous progress in encouraging the inflow of foreign investment. However, much of the foreign investment is in the form of acquisitions and takeovers of existing ventures by foreign companies, and buying of distressed assets of existing companies, not greenfield investments. Some of it may not even be foreign, but more a form of recycling of money taken out of the country in the form, say, of over-invoicing of imports by domestic companies. One of the consequences of the foreign capital inflow has been to keep, until recently, the exchange value of the rupee artificially high which led to hurting exports.

(f) Much of the claimed controlling of inflation resulted from the movement of international prices (particularly oil and commodity prices). Since the end of 2017 some of those prices have been on the rise again. On the other hand, the economic misfortune for the country, in the form of two years of drought at the beginning of the Modi regime and continuing depressed world markets for Indian exports, are not under control of the current government. But the latter is responsible for the dearth of credit and infrastructure that afflicts small farmers as well as small and medium-sized exporters. With the world market perking up since 2017, the continued lack of marked success of Indian exports points to structural problems of competitiveness of Indian exports, even compared to some other developing countries.

(g) The government has inexcusably delayed its response to the long-simmering agrarian distress. The raising of Minimum Support Prices (MSP)

50 per cent above the cost proposed in the 2018 budget is unlikely to be very effective. This is partly because the cost basis used in the calculation is too low, and in any case for many crops MSP is already 50 per cent above that cost basis. More importantly, MSP mainly helps large farmers and traders (to whom the numerous small farmers sell at low post-harvest prices), and that too for a small number of main crops. For many other crops the infrastructure for government procurement, storage and distribution is simply not there. The long-term problems of Indian agriculture—inadequate rural infrastructure, water management and extension services, continuing monopoly grip of traders in marketing around *mandis*, inexorably declining land size often beyond economic viability with paltry relief from labor absorption in non-farm jobs, apart from the looming effects of climate change—have been neglected for too long by all governments. In the absence of a substantial dent in these problems the much-repeated goal of doubling farmers' income by 2022 will remain just hype.

Some large steps backward

Unfortunately, there have been quite a few steps 'backward' that have been taken under the current regime: some in the economic sphere, but others, more disastrously, in the socio-political sphere.

(a) In the environmental area, while the government's energetic investment in renewable energy should be lauded, a number of backward steps have been taken. In the name of easing business procedures many environmental clearances have been made, relaxing earlier forest, coastal and mining rules (sometimes secretively). Attempts have been made to dilute the Forest Rights Act for the Adivasis (tribal communities). This is illustrated by the giving of permissions to forest officials to bypass mandatory consent of *gram sabhas* (or village assemblies) in starting commercial operations on their traditional forest lands. In any case, the actual coverage of the Forest Rights Act over the last ten years has so far involved only a tiny percentage of the total forest lands originally meant to be covered. The Central Environment Ministry has also delegated some of its power for reviewing projects to state governments which have far lower capacity for such reviews.

(b) There has been a retreat from commitments made by the UPA regime (and also those by the current government in its early stages) on universal health coverage. The announcement of the National Health Policy

(2017) opens the door for more privatisation through its plans for 'strategic purchasing' of secondary and tertiary healthcare services, which is likely to hurt the availability or affordability of these services for the poor. Also, the use of primary health care increasingly for just screening and referral, with insurance-financed coverage assuring only secondary and tertiary services, will move the healthcare system away from the much-needed centrality of the local-level medical worker.

From time to time the current government has talked about a substantial rise in health expenditure, but so far it has remained mainly talk, and public health expenditure as a percentage of GDP remains abysmally low, even lower than in many developing countries.

In the budget of 2018, a new National Health Protection Scheme has been announced,[10] of providing insurance for the hospital cost (not outpatient services) of half a million rupees for hundred million poor families. Without much of a fund allocation in the budget it may be as much of an empty gesture as the announcement (as yet unimplemented) in the 2017 budget of extending the hospital insurance limit of the pre-existing RSBY (*Rashtriya Syasthya Bima Yojana*), operating in any case mostly in the less poor southern states (there too, often underutilised), to one lakh (one hundred thousand) rupees. In any case it does not make sense to talk about expanding the scale of a RSBY-like scheme all over India without carefully looking into why it has been a non-starter in the large poor northern states in the past.

On a deeper level, if it means following the American-style private insurance model, it will hardly solve India's massive health problems, and may end up mainly benefiting insurance companies and for-profit private hospitals. While risk-pooling of a large number of poor patients can lower costs, a multi-payer system (for at least 60 per cent of the population for inpatient services and for everyone for outpatent services) without adequate regulatory oversight and information campaigns and data infrastructure, and no emphasis on preventive public health and sanitation services, can still be highly expensive and ineffective, and atrociously burdensome on the poor for their out-of-pocket expenses for uncovered services (like the American system is, compared to those in most OECD countries). The proposal in the budget for a network of rural wellness centers for primary care has better potential, but it is as yet largely unfunded.

(c) The cow vigilantism and lynchings by self-styled vigilantes belonging to (or encouraged by) the ruling party affiliates have been wreaking havoc in livestock trade and transport, which may have serious consequences for the large livestock economy of the country and its largest agricultural export (buffalo meat).

(d) In general, the increased incidence of hate crimes and social violence, and the atmosphere of fear and intimidation for the minorities and dissenters are causing damage to the social and political fabric of the country, which in some sense is much more serious than any economic harm the other backward steps may cause. The so-called Gujarat model of development has not yet worked in large parts of the country, but the Gujarat model of hate and intolerance is very much evident everywhere, fostered by members of the Sangh Parivar and its associates, aided and abetted by a complicit police and bureaucracy and the selective silence (or wink-wink platitudes) of a prime minister with his occasional spewing of communal poison at election rallies. The government has failed to provide basic security for minorities and the minimum rule of law.

While the government (and media) are obsessively proud of India's improvement in the still low rank by the (highly flawed) Ease of Business index of the World Bank, the same Bank's extremeley low ranking of India in its Human Capital index was summarily rejected by the government officials. Very few people are aware that in the world ranking of 198 countries by the Pew Research Center on religious violence India is now in the 4th place from the bottom. In the World Press Freedom Index for 180 countries published by the media watchdog *Reporters without Borders* India is in 138th position. The Rule of Law Index of the World Justice Project ranks India 62nd out of 113 countries (worse than Ghana, Jamaica, Senegal or Mongolia).[11] The current regime is presiding over the creeping degeneration of Indian democracy into a kind of thugocracy: the leaders are mostly unconcerned, even shameless, about this.

(e) The obscurantism and intolerance regularly imposed on cultural institutions, packing of the administrative bodies of educational institutions with bigots and charlatans, and the gross distortion of history textbooks and curricula will also be part of the long-term social damage.

(f) The erosion of fundamental institutions, which began under earlier regimes, has continued at an accelerated pace—abuse of police, bureaucracy and public investigative and tax machinery for narrow short-sighted purposes of the political leaders, trampling of basic human rights of individuals in the name of sectarian communities taking offence or of public order or national unity, and the general violation of the letter and spirit of constitutional values. Systematic violation of these values and of the kind of civic nationalism that is based on these values make the ruling party and its affiliated organisations in some sense deeply anti-national.

Therefore, in my overall evaluation, the current regime has been mediocre at best in economic policy, while in socio-political matters it has been far worse.

10

CONTOURS OF CRONY CAPITALISM
IN THE MODI RAJ

A.K. Bhattacharya and *Paranjoy Guha Thakurta*

Crony capitalism is defined by the *Cambridge Dictionary* as 'an economic system in which family members and friends of government officials and business leaders are given unfair advantages in the form of jobs, loans, etc.' The *English Oxford Living Dictionaries* make the definition of crony capitalism a little simpler, describing it as 'an economic system characterised by close, mutually advantageous relationship(s) between business leaders and government officials.' Both definitions point to a nexus between government and businesses, who mutually benefit from this relationship. For businesses, this benefit results in contracts, orders, sweetheart deals and loans under special considerations. In India and elsewhere, political leaders and government officials gain overtly or covertly through this corrupt nexus by way of financial contributions or funds from those who own and control businesses, and those who benefit from favourable treatment by those in power and authority. Such an economic system has one set of clear losers—those who are not part of this nexus network, which includes the common person, ordinary businesses, other economic agents and, of course, the system which is meant to ensure transparent, responsive and good governance. Not only does a corrupt system disadvantage those outside the charmed circle of crony capitalists, it also deprives them of an opportunity to get a fair deal in whatever enterprise they undertake.

In practice, crony capitalism is in certain respects worse than nepotism. In nepotism, only some powerful people in authority grant favours to those related to, or associated with, them and these favours are showered mostly on the sly, often without necessarily tweaking the system to benefit the favoured ones. Instances of nepotism get exposed more easily as they mostly involve influential and well-placed bureaucrats or politicians working in the administration. Thus, once it is revealed that some undue favours have been showered in violation of rules, the government can, and often does, use anti-corruption provisions in the law to punish those who may have committed such acts of nepotism. In crony capitalism, on the other hand, the government apparatus becomes a key player, instead of individual officers or ruling party politicians. It creates an unfair and discriminatory system to benefit favourites and then tries to perpetuate that system so that the advantages to the favoured businesses can be sustained. It creates an unfair system. It undermines competition. It results in inefficiencies. And it thrives in a discretionary and opaque economic environment where physical controls are often preferred to transparently determined fiscal instruments. In short, crony capitalism grows roots in an economy, which has not seen genuine reforms and where licensing or regulatory controls rest with the government or its representatives without much oversight. Unsurprisingly, crony capitalism sees its worst manifestation in countries where the lack of reforms is aggravated by the absence of oversight bodies or an independent judicial system to address concerns of inequity, unfairness and favouritism.

In this essay, we examine crony capitalism in India during the first four years of the tenure of the Narendra Modi government in India which came to power in May 2014. We try to find out if crony capitalism has increased under Modi, whether it has taken new and different dimensions and if so, how it has impacted India's business environment at present and what its medium- and long-term consequences would be for the country's political economy. Our assessment reveals that the conventional indices to measure the prevalence of crony capitalism during the tenure of the Modi government are a little misleading. One set of indices apparently shows a decline in Indian crony capitalists' wealth as a percentage of the country's gross domestic product (GDP), but this decline is part of a trend that began well before Modi became the prime minister. If the crony capitalists' wealth has declined further in the first few years of the Modi government, there are many other reasons that are responsible for what is admittedly a healthy trend. Our analysis also shows that the nature of crony capitalism seen during the tenure of the Modi regime is an outcome of the way Indian industry has engaged with different governments in the decades after independence in 1947. Equally important in our assessment is how crony capitalism has evolved into a potent political issue with which the Modi government has engaged itself to apparently steer clear of its adverse fallout while trying out new instruments of engagement with big business, which in turn have given a fresh qualitative dimension to the politics-business nexus.

Looking back at crony capitalism in India

An evaluation of crony capitalism during the tenure of the Modi government will be incomplete unless it is placed in a contemporary historical context. It will be instructive to understand and analyse the roots and evolution of crony capitalism soon after India's independence in August 1947. Indeed, these roots can be traced a few years before India eventually gained political freedom after almost two centuries of British colonial rule.

The 'father' of the Indian nation, Mohandas Karamchand Gandhi, who led the freedom movement, believed that there should be trusteeship between capital and labour. His views on economic policies differed in many respects from Jawaharlal Nehru who went on to become India's first prime minister. Gandhi actively wooed 'nationalist' business leaders not only for financial support for his party but also played a role in making them treasurers of the Indian National Congress. Such individuals included Kasturbhai Lalbhai and Jamnalal Bajaj. Gandhi was assassinated on 30 January 1948 in the compound of Birla House, a spacious bungalow in New Delhi that was owned by the family of businesspersons led then by the prominent wealthy industrialist Ghanshyam Das Birla.

A few years before India gained freedom, it became clear to top Indian business leaders like Birla, J.R.D. Tata, Purshotamdas Thakurdas and Walchand Hirachand that massive investments would be needed after independence to build the infrastructure in the economy.[1] That the state would have to play a dominant role in both economic policy-making and in driving public investments in infrastructure and other basic industries was an almost foregone conclusion. They conceded that the few private enterprises that existed then would not have access to requisite resources to build roads, bridges, power plants, steel-making furnaces or cement factories. These businessmen were also acutely conscious of the commercial reality that investments in infrastructure and 'basic' or 'mother' industries would not yield adequate and remunerative returns in the short-run. Hence, they preferred the government of the newly independent nation-state to lead and fund initiatives on investments in infrastructure and basic industries.

Such thoughts provided the nucleus to the Bombay Plan that some of these industrialists announced in January 1944. It may seem ironical to many today but the fact is that the leaders of private enterprise in India put out an economic development plan for their newly independent country which provided prime importance to the state in investing and creating industrial and infrastructural capacities. Yes, the Bombay Plan did talk about doubling India's per capita income within fifteen years of independence (India's net per capita national income in 1950 was Rs 274 only), improving the general standard of living of the common man and earmarking an investment of Rs 10,000 crore over the next fifteen years in industry, agriculture, communications, health and education, among other things.[2] But the most important message of the Bombay Plan was that Indian business leaders believed in the idea that the government or the state would play a central role in economic development, presumably through controls, ownership and management. In many ways, the Bombay Plan was a precursor to the Industrial Policy Resolution of 1956 that mandated primacy to the public sector, which was expected to attain the 'commanding heights' of the economy.

It can be argued that both the Bombay Plan and the Industrial Policy Resolution had sown the seeds of crony capitalism in India. If the private sector wanted the state to use its resources to set up government enterprises in infrastructure and basic industries, it also logically followed that the same state would use its licensing controls to decide which private enterprise will be allowed to operate and set up an industrial unit in which sectors as long as they were not reserved for the state-owned enterprises. It was only a matter of time before this equation laid the foundation of an engagement between private businesses and the government that was a mutually advantageous relationship, one which also envisaged *quid pro quo* or an arrangement of give and take between the government and big business.

Not surprisingly, the Congress party used the favours done to Indian big business houses to great effect during its 1957 election campaign. The top Congress leadership was of the view that fighting the elections would require funds and help from big business. In 1955, Birla, the doyen of Indian industry, was escorted by T.T. Krishnamachari (who a year later would become the Nehru-led Congress government's finance minister) to meet Morarji Desai, who was at that time the party's treasurer and would later also become the country's finance minister. At that meeting, Birla was informed that none else than the then prime minister, Nehru, desired that India's business leaders should help the party collect funds for the forthcoming general elections.[3]

The nexus between the government of the day and big business was clear. And it was only to be expected that the government at some point in time would have to return the favours to the big businesses that helped the government in its hour of need. Some industrialists raised objections to their making financial contributions to the Congress. J.R.D. Tata was one of them.[4] They pointed out that they needed their companies' articles of association to be amended to allow them to make political donations. Birla played a leading role in organising political donations for the party. But there was no doubt that crony capitalism had begun to grow deep roots by then. Perhaps not entirely connected, but a couple of years earlier, Tata had lost the management and ownership of the airline Air India to the government. In 1953, Nehru had unceremoniously nationalised Air India, a Tata firm at that time. The decision to nationalise the airline was taken without any consultation and Tata was simply informed of the government's action. He was asked to continue as chairman of Air India, but even that post was snatched away from him in 1978 when Morarji Desai headed the Janata Party-led government. It could be argued that Tata was treated in that fashion perhaps because of his reservations about funding the election campaign of the political parties in a manner outlined by the ruling party politicians at that time.

The Birlas, on the other hand, never succeeded in setting up a steel plant, even though their proposal had met with all approvals until it reached the cabinet, where Nehru reportedly shot it down on the ground that it violated the basic principles of the policy that wanted all such basic heavy industries to be set up in the state sector. It is widely believed, without any documentary corroboration though, that the Birlas were denied the opportunity to set up a steel plant as they already had a car manufacturing plant. The Tatas on the other hand had a steel plant but could not get a car plant (until a long time later in the wake of economic policy liberalisation in the early 1990s), even though the group desired one. The Indian government it seemed was trying to be even-handed to both the two biggest industrial groups at that time. But the whiff of crony capitalism could not be missed in the atmosphere. Nor could its adverse impact on the pattern and pace of economic growth in India be overestimated.

The winds of change blowing in India from 1966 showed another aspect of crony capitalism. One after another, almost all basic industries were largely nationalised in the space of seven years—banking, insurance, coal, steel and petroleum. Simultaneously, the government introduced a series of economic laws that were ostensibly aimed at preventing the concentration of economic wealth in the hands of a few industrialists and set a foreign investment limit on all companies beyond which all permissions for expansion and growth would be subject to detailed scrutiny. Licensing controls were tightened and even credit flows to industry were brought under stricter regulation. One such law was the Monopolies and Restrictive Trade Practices (MRTP) Act which, however, did not really check the concentration of wealth with a few large business houses, which were able to 'game' the system of elaborate, complex rules and regulations that were often riddled with loopholes. The Bombay Plan that advocated state control of infrastructure and basic industries had helped sow the seeds of crony capitalism in India. The governments from 1947 to 1990 did not hesitate to use the existing laws of the land and licensing rules to decide which company or which big business group would get the right to set up which industrial plant or grow by how much. In return, big business was expected to take care of the interests of the ruling party.

The promoters of major private enterprises would invest relatively small proportions of their own funds in the form of equity or risk capital (often in the range between 8 and 12 per cent of the total capital) in the companies they set up, the bulk of the funds for capital investments as well as revenue expenditure coming from nationalised banks and government-controlled financial institutions. It used to be remarked that at one stage the rival Birlas held a higher stake in the Tata group's steel company than members of the Tata family! Be that as it may, just as there was arguably little that was 'private' about India's private enterprises, similarly there was little that was 'public' about the country's public sector corporations that were often run as if they were 'private' fiefdoms of powerful politicians, technocrats and bureaucrats. In other words, the promoters of private companies were dependent on government bodies to exercise managerial control over these corporate entities. This issue came to a head in the mid-1980s when London-based businessman Swraj Paul mounted hostile takeover bids to control companies in the Escorts group (promoted by the Nanda family) and the Shri Ram group. Paul was unsuccessful because the then Prime Minister Rajiv Gandhi intervened in favour of the original promoters and prevailed on government companies like the Life Insurance Corporation not to support the takeover attempts. The absence of reforms was telling as during those days there was no corporate takeover code, which offered one company or group transparent and market-based opportunities to acquire another company listed on a stock exchange.

The rise of the first-generation industrialist Dhirubhai Ambani who founded the Reliance group of companies marked a new dimension in the nexus between business and politics in India. In the days of the licence raj, Dhirubhai, more than most of his fellow industrialists, understood the importance of 'managing the environment', a euphemism for keeping politicians and bureaucrats happy. He made no secret of the fact that he did not have an ego when it came to paying obeisance to government officials, whether secretaries to the government of India or lowly office attendants or peons.[5] Dhirubhai did not subvert the process; he just made the best use of it. By the time the Reliance group's fortunes were on the rise in the 1980s, the Indian economy had become more competitive. It was now insufficient for those in power to merely promote the interests of a particular business group; competitors too had to be shown their place. That is precisely what happened to rivals of the Ambanis, and this was the important new dimension in the prevailing business-politics nexus in the country.

All these distortions and aberrations were expected to change with the economic reforms of 1991. With delicensing of industries, easier foreign investment norms, entry of the private sector in areas hitherto reserved for the public sector and removal of curbs on industrial expansion and trade, big business was to be freed from the obligation of enjoying favours doled out by the government. Crony capitalism was to end, or so it was claimed. But the next couple of decades saw a different avatar of crony capitalism growing fresh roots and expanding its influence over the relationship between businesses and the government. The policies of economic liberalisation failed to move beyond particular sectors such as foreign trade, fiscal policies and policies relating to financial intermediaries. Reforms of different sectors like civil aviation, telecommunications, roads, ports and airports were slow and halting in their pace. Infrastructure investments from the private sector were not forthcoming. In the early years after reforms, the government waited for private sector companies to come forward and made some controversial decisions to award contracts like the one to the American conglomerate Enron for setting up a power project in Dabhol, Maharashtra. In the subsequent years, a few privatisation deals were concluded without creating much of a controversy, but charges of crony capitalism resurfaced when land for establishing special economic zones was given to the then government's favourite big business groups, which grabbed them because of their real estate potential. The allotment of spectrum to telecom companies and coal mining contracts without following transparent methods of auctions led to charges of corruption and crony capitalism, creating a political environment that influenced the BJP's election campaign strategy in 2013–14 and helped shape public opinion that contributed to the party's victory in May 2014.

The political context of Modi's crony capitalism

The political context out of which the Modi government emerged is vital to understanding how the forces of crony capitalism have unleashed themselves during the last three and half years of its tenure. The BJP relentlessly attacked the Manmohan Singh government over the last three years of its term not only for its inability to check inflation and for a paralysis of decision-making, but also for the many scandals involving the way rights to use natural resources were awarded by the government to a few private sector players on terms that resulted in substantial losses to the exchequer, even though they were arguably notional. The revelation of these losses was made in reports of the Comptroller and Auditor General (CAG) on allocation of electro-magnetic spectrum used for mobile communications and the awarding of rights to mine coal to private sector companies.

The Manmohan Singh government showed little concern for the findings of the CAG reports. The response was akin to the way many governments react to a crisis. First, it refused to recognise that something wrong had happened. After the crises manifested themselves, the government went into denial mode, declining to recognise and accept the writing on the wall. The spectrum scam caused by the misuse of the norms devised specifically to benefit particular telecom companies meant only a notional revenue loss for the government. But more importantly, this flawed method of allocating a finite natural resource on a first-come-first-come basis and then tweaking even these norms, showed how government functionaries had used the system to favour a few business groups.[6] Similarly, the awarding of coal mining blocks to a certain industrial houses and business groups with influential political connections took place on the basis of a discretionary and opaque decision-making process, ignoring recommended methods of public auction.[7] Here also, the revenue loss for the exchequer was notional, but more important was the way it perpetuated an impression that business groups with connections with the government would receive special treatment, presumably in return for some favours.

Later, in December 2017, a special court examining charges of criminality in the allotment of the licences acquitted all the accused on the ground that the prosecution could not establish its case beyond doubt. The Modi government and its investigating agency has appealed against the court's verdict, but their failure to ensure conviction of the key accused is going to have serious implications on how the narrative on crony capitalism plays out in the months leading up to the 2019 general election, when the Modi government will seek to retain power.

The so-called 2G—or second generation telecom spectrum—scam was exploited to the hilt during the 2014 general election campaign, masterminded by Narendra Modi, who was then the prime ministerial candidate of the Bharatiya Janata Party (BJP). His campaign focused on speeding up development, creating jobs and eliminating black money. The third promise, which was linked to the environment that charges of crony capitalism against the Manmohan Singh government had created, and the promise of better days (*acche din*), reverberated well with voters along with his promise of an attack against corruption and black money. He famously remarked: *Na khaaonga, na khaane doonga* (Neither will I take illicit money, nor will I allow anyone else to do so).

As it turned out, international commodity prices began falling after the Modi government was formed. India has always been a net importer of commodities, primarily crude oil, gold, coal (despite India possessing one of the largest reserves of coal in the world), and even edible oils and pulses. Thus, the softening of commodity prices brought the inflation rate down to benign levels. From highs of 8–9 per cent in the last three years of the Manmohan Singh government, the annual inflation rate, based on the consumer price index, began declining steadily to reach a benign level of 3 per cent at the end of the third year of the Modi government. No special credit needed to be given to the Modi government for such 'exemplary' inflation management. The deceleration in the inflation rate was largely a function of declining international prices of commodities, including crude oil and gold, though the Modi government did some smart supply management of essential products and used the instrument of taxation to mop up much-needed revenue from petroleum products to stay on the path of steady fiscal consolidation.

But lower commodity prices had another positive impact on the Modi government. Softening commodity prices usually have an adverse impact on the fortunes of companies that rely on such commodities or natural resources producing them. Their turnover by value comes down and their profit margins also take a hit as a result. Their valuations in the marketplace suffer. It is widely acknowledged that companies relying on commodities and natural resources depend a lot on the government because of the latter's retention of controls in these sectors. Thus, these companies make it a point to become friendly with the government in power. Some of them even go to the extent of using means fair or foul to cultivate governments of the day, irrespective of their political leanings. Businesses that fail to strike a decent rapport with the new dispensation after a change in government lose out, just as those who can develop such links benefit. An example would be the manner in which particular corporate groups with close links to multinational corporations imported certain kinds of pulses (*tur* and *urad dal* in particular) that led to sudden spike in their prices in 2015. Investigations by the Income Tax Department indicate that the unnatural rise in the prices of pulses was a consequence of the formation of international and Indian cartels of traders. These allegations are denied by the players concerned. Reports prepared by tax officials also alleged there was money laundering in *dal* trading.[8]

It bears repetition here that crony capitalism is a direct outcome of the business-politics equation. The more unreformed the commodities and natural resources sector, the greater are the chances of crony capitalism prospering. However, during a downturn in the commodities cycle, all businesses in this space, whether they are in the good books of the government or not, suffer by way of a decline in their top line and a corresponding contraction in their bottom line. During the first few years of the Modi government, commodity prices remained soft and the companies that would have benefitted from their close connections with the government could not make any substantial gains. Thus, most indices that track the growth and spread of crony capitalism show a positive picture of a reduced footprint for such enterprises.

The puzzle over the crony capitalism index and India

Not surprisingly, the crony capitalism index maintained by *The Economist* showed an improvement in the first few years of the Modi government.[9] For instance, India's crony wealth in 2008 had reached a level of 18 per cent of its GDP, which placed it at the same level as that of Russia. Six years later, in 2014 coinciding with the start of the Modi government's tenure, India's crony capitalists accounted for a sharply lower 3.6 per cent of GDP. And by 2016, it declined to 3.4 per cent, which is the same level as that which prevailed in a developed and less crony economy like that of Australia. For purposes of compiling the index, *The Economist* chose to include those companies that operated in areas such as casinos, coal, palm oil, timber, defence, deposit-taking institutions, investment banking, infrastructure, oil, gas, chemicals, ports, airports, real estate, construction, steel, other metals, commodities, mining, utilities and telecommunication services.

It is important to note the trajectory of the improvement in India's crony capitalism index. Indian crony capitalists had begun losing their wealth from 2008 onwards in the wake of the global financial meltdown that hit the commodities and stock markets in India as well. What also led to the relative decline in the wealth of crony capitalists was the rapid rise in the wealth and prosperity of the non-crony sectors as the Indian economy had shown robust growth rates of 8–9 per cent in the first two years after the global financial downturn, before deceleration set in the last three years of the Manmohan Singh regime. But since deceleration affected the crony sectors (chiefly companies in infrastructure and telecommunication services) more than the non-crony sectors, the crony capitalism index continued to look better for India.

The fall in commodity prices after 2014 further enhanced the improvement in India's crony capitalism index. But what also helped the improvement in the index were a series of steps the Modi government took soon within months of its formation by enforcing auctions of coal mining blocks, fixing a more transparent and market-linked price for natural gas produced by private sector companies and by pushing for a more transparent and forward-looking tariff policy for the telecommunications sector, even though that spelt financial trouble for a large number of incumbent service providers and favoured the challengers entering that market. The Modi government also modified the double-tax avoidance treaties with Mauritius, Cyprus and Singapore, which were controversial and were seen as encouraging round-tripping of investments through these tax jurisdictions to gain pecuniary advantages. Simultaneously, the government displayed some resolve and firmness in tackling black money and cracked down on errant borrowers with the promulgation of an insolvency and bankruptcy code, through its central bank, the Reserve Bank of India. The net result of a combination of these steps was a continued improvement in the crony capitalism index during the tenure of the Modi government.

A shift in the pattern of business growth during this period also was helpful in ensuring a steady improvement in the index of crony capitalism, a trend that continued during the tenure of the Modi government helping no doubt its image as far as crony capitalism was concerned. A large number of new companies prospered in areas that did not operate under the kind of strict controls of the government and therefore did not earn the notoriety of crony capitalists. Sectors like pharmaceuticals, automobiles and consumer goods prospered and so did their new generation entrepreneurs. They represented the new face of India Inc. The composition of the sensex or sensitive index, India's benchmark stock market index of the Bombay Stock Exchange, changed with many of these new generation companies figuring there. Several new private sector banks, software service companies and pharmaceutical players became as prominent as the crony capitalists of past years. Of the eight companies that lost their place in the sensex between 2007 and 2017, six belonged to the infrastructure sector (cement, power, metals, commodities, etc.). The remaining two lost their valuation and therefore a place in the sensex, as they were hit by controversies and scandals. By 2017, the eight companies that replaced them in the sensex included those operating in the sectors of automobiles, healthcare, banking and consumer goods. Only two companies that made their entry were from the infrastructure sector—one of them being a state-owned company. That shine indeed rubbed off on to the Modi government, although the change was largely an outcome of a natural evolutionary process of India's corporate sector that had begun much earlier.

Another way of assessing how the crony sectors fared in this period is to look at their ability to access the primary capital markets to raise resources. From 2007 to 2010, the largest share in initial public offers (IPOs) of capital was accounted for by companies in the crony sectors like real estate, power and mining. Barring 2011, when financial companies had a 55 per cent share in total resources raised through IPOs, all other areas until 2014 saw companies in sectors such as telecommunications, power and infrastructure accounting for a share in IPOs ranging from 27 per cent to 61 per cent. In the first three years of the Modi regime—from 2015 to 2017, the sectors that had the largest share in IPOs were aviation and financial services. A shift away from crony sectors indicates how the Modi regime saw a reduced role by companies that are usually associated with crony capitalism.

The looming financial crisis, caused by the 'twin balance sheet problem' of the Indian economy, was no less responsible for the changing contours of crony capitalism during the tenure of the Modi government. The twin balance sheet problem refers to the high levels of loans taken by private companies from banks (mainly in the public sector) that have not been repaid and become what are called non-performing assets (NPAs) of banks. Several corporate entities operating in sectors such as telecommunications, steel, roads, power, ports, airports and real estate reported an unsustainably high and unhealthy level of indebtedness. That rendered them incapable of either executing the existing projects or planning new ones. This posed a major investment challenge in the economy, as this also began to pull down overall economic growth.

As a consequence, the banks, most of which were owned by the Union government, were saddled with huge amounts of sticky loans, or NPAs that gave no return to the lenders. This situation raised another problem for the government. Since many of these state-owned banks saw an alarmingly high level of their loans turning sticky or becoming 'stressed assets', there was an urgent need to recapitalise them. And as they were owned by the government, the recapitalisation money had to come from the central exchequer. With the challenges of reducing the government's fiscal deficit continuing to remain high on its agenda, the Modi government faced a dilemma. If it had to provide more capital for stressed banks, it should not be seen as bailing out banks which had lost money lent to companies that were part of the crony sectors. It did not want the opposition political parties to charge the government with having bailed out banks for lending indiscreetly to big businesses. Thus, it announced in late-2017 a bank recapitalisation package of Rs 2,11,000 crore, of which a large chunk of about Rs 1,35,000 crore would come by way of fresh government equity into state-owned banks. To ward off allegations of favouring banks that had helped big business by advancing them loans in an excessively risky and often irresponsible manner, the Modi government quickly announced its intention to introduce merit-based norms that would privilege those banks which act firmly to address their poor finances. Perhaps for the same reason, the government has not raised eyebrows over many BJP-ruled state governments promising debt waivers for farmers, so that critics cannot accuse the government of taking care of the interests of only big businesses or big banks and not poor farmers.

Similarly, even as the Modi government responded to this challenge by legislating an Insolvency and Bankruptcy Code that would resolve the stressed assets within a specified time frame, it was acutely conscious that its initiatives should not be interpreted as the government helping the crony-sector companies with a bail-out from their financial woes. When a few insolvency cases were resolved with the promoters of the stressed companies reclaiming their ownership after an open bidding process, the Modi government quickly realised the political backlash it would create giving the opposition political parties an opportunity to level charges of crony capitalism against it. It therefore lost little time in promulgating an ordinance to place stiff conditions that made it almost impossible for a delinquent promoter of a bankrupt company to be eligible for taking part in its auction. In short, the manner in which the government went about resolving the twin balance sheet problem showed its sensitivity to charges of crony capitalism by its opponents. Remember that most of the companies hobbled by indebtedness belonged to the traditional crony sectors—coal, infrastructure, oil, ports, airports, roads, real estate, steel, telecommunication services, etc.

This was certainly one of the main reasons why the Modi government took an inordinately long time in tackling the stressed assets problem of banks and the indebtedness of several Indian companies operating in infrastructure sectors. Delayed action on insolvency was perhaps because it was acutely conscious of the adverse political impact any government approval of a plan to restructure private sector debts would have on its image. Crony capitalism was certainly one of the charges that it did not wish to be accused of. The question remains as to whether the Modi government has stayed completely clear of charges of crony capitalism, since the resolution process began only at the start of the fourth year of the government's tenure and popular perception on such resolution efforts will be influenced by actions against promoters of highly indebted companies—whether they are forced to take a 'hair cut' through dilution in their shareholding and capital base or they are being given a bailout by allowing them to retain the companies.

Funding of elections and crony capitalism

Corporate funding of elections is another instrument which indicates the extent of crony capitalism in a country. For many decades in India, political funding has remained a clandestine operation. In the first few decades after independence, companies were disallowed to provide funds to political parties. Subsequently, laws such as the Representation of the People Act, the Companies Act and the Income Tax Act were amended to allow and even incentivise political donations by individuals, partnership firms, Hindu undivided families (a unique legal entity in India) and even companies. The incentives included tax exemptions for both the donor and political party that receives the donation, provided the accounts are maintained transparently and the political parties concerned filed their returns regularly in compliance with the prevailing laws. Another step was taken by the Income Tax Department in January 2018 to make such political funding more transparent and accountable. All cash donations to political parties above Rs 2,000 were to be recorded and these details were subject to scrutiny.

However, corporate funding of political parties continues to be largely a cloak-and-dagger affair. Given the nature of the governments, corporate entities and even high net-worth individuals are wary of declaring their donations to a political party, particularly when it is in the opposition for fear of incurring the wrath of the ruling party. Leading political parties have begun filing their returns to the Election Commission of India, but the amounts declared as donations received from corporate entities or individuals are negligible compared to the vast amounts that each of them spends during an election or even for running their party affairs in non-election time. For instance, the total income reported by the ruling BJP during 2015–16 was only Rs 571 crore, a 41 per cent drop over its income of Rs 970 crore in 2014–15. The Congress was no better, as it reported an income of only Rs 262 crore in 2015–16, representing a higher decline of 56 per cent from Rs 593 crore in the previous year. Worse, only about 12 per cent of the total donations received by the two national parties came from known sources in 2015–16. In other words, 88 per cent of their income came from donations whose sources were not declared or known. Clearly, neither are companies making proper disclosures of their donations to political parties, nor are political parties making a clean breast of the money they receive from companies. For the past many years, therefore, this situation has provided a ready-made recipe for flourishing crony capitalism. Companies often make donations to the political party in power in return for favours through government concessions by way of favourable policies or preferential treatment for them.

An amendment to the Reserve Bank of India Act enabled the issuance of electoral bonds by the State Bank of India, the country's biggest bank in the public sector. A donor could thus purchase these bonds from authorised banks against cheque or digital payments and transfer them to a political party of their choice. The political party in question could encash them within a prescribed time limit. This way the identity of the donor would remain undisclosed for all records kept by the political party in question.

However, these steps are yet to make a dent on the nexus between the corporate sector and political parties that gives rise to crony capitalism. It is not clear why cash donations are allowed even up to Rs 2,000. This rule can obviously be misused by securing the donation of a large amount in smaller instalments of less than Rs 2,000 each in cash, thus defeating the very purpose of the change in the rule. Similarly, the identity of the purchaser of electoral bonds under the proposed scheme may not enter the records of the political party in question, but the information on who purchased the bonds from the State Bank of India would be available to the banking system and nothing would stop the government of the day from seeking access to such information. Thus, political funding by corporate bodies is likely to remain opaque in spite of these moves that are aimed at making the entire operation transparent.

So, has crony capitalism grown under the Modi regime? The crony capitalism index shows it has been reined in and its growth has decelerated. But the manner in which it has responded to the challenges of resolving stressed assets of banks or tackling corporate indebtedness in many sectors of the economy suggests that it is extremely wary of crony capitalism. Consider the manner in which the Modi government responded to the controversy that erupted over a suit that the prime minister wore for the Republic Day celebrations in 2015 when the chief guest on the occasion was the then US President Barack Obama. It was reported that the cost of the suit was over Rs 10,00,000, a price tag that, however, was denied by Rameshkumar Bhikabhai Virani, a non-resident Indian businessman, who had gifted it to the prime minister. It became controversial because of its reported price and also because the name of Narendra Modi was monogrammed on the black suit. Soon after the suit controversy erupted, the opposition leaders launched a tirade against Modi charging his government as a *suit-boot ki sarkar* (a government for the rich, or those who wear suits and boots). The Modi government reacted swiftly to control the damage and in less than a month, on 20 February 2015, the suit was auctioned. Significantly the reserve price was kept at Rs 11 lakh, but the final price at which the suit was auctioned was Rs 4,31,31,311 or nearly 400 times higher, and the proceeds were donated to a fund meant for cleaning the River Ganga/Ganges. The quick auction helped Modi heave a sigh of relief. It was subsequently alleged that the Surat-based trader Laljibhai Patel who bought the suit had been 'favoured' by being allotted government land for building a private sports club.[10]

The Modi government's sensitivity to charges of crony capitalism was evident when in 2017 a website, *thewire.in*, reported that the business of Jai Amit Shah, son of BJP President Amit Shah, had grown rapidly after the Modi government was formed and that it had received some loans from a government agency under a scheme.[11] The website report mentioned no specific wrongdoings, but the government's response was swift and aggressive. Not only were the contentions in the report denied, senior BJP leaders, including a cabinet minister, told the media that the report had factual inaccuracies, that no favours were shown to Jai Shah and that a Rs 100-crore civil suit along with a criminal case was being filed against the website including the writer and its editors. Such a reaction only goes to show how wary the Modi government has been of being accused of crony capitalism. It is another matter that Jai Shah failed to appear in court for two consecutive hearings leading many to believe that this was an instance of a strategic lawsuit against public participation (SLAPP) aimed at intimidating and harassing those who put out unpleasant truths in the public domain. In another earlier instance of a 'sweetheart deal', the controversial former functionary of the Indian Premier Leage (IPL) cricket tournament, Lalit Modi (who is absconding in London) reportedly purchased shares at a hefty premium (9,618 times the face value of the shares) in a company controlled by Dushyant Raje, son of the BJP Chief Minister of the state of Rajasthan Vasundhara Raje.[12] These allegations were similar to the charges that had been levelled by Modi and the BJP against Robert Vadra, son-in-law of the then president of the Indian National Congress Sonia Gandhi. A major real estate group, DLF, had purchased land purchased by a company controlled by Vadra in 2008, also at a huge premium, enabling the firm to earn large windfall profit of Rs 50 crore.[13]

A three-year wait before the Modi government swung into action to force insolvency proceedings against indebted companies is also proof of its apprehensions on this front. And when action was indeed taken, it was done by riding on the shoulders of the Reserve Bank of India, the country's central bank and apex monetary authority. With the help of an amendment to the RBI Act, the government leaned on the central bank to put pressure on banks to take quick action on resolving their stressed assets, which in many cases could rescue companies in a financial logjam. In the process, the political establishment distanced itself from any steps that might be construed to be helping big business. The government's mindset also revealed itself in the way it had demonetised 86 per cent of the total currency in circulation on 8 November 2016. The highly disruptive move was justified on many occasions as a step against the rich who had black money. Demonetisation was thus packaged as an anti-rich and pro-poor move, but highly destabilising for the economy as it hurt the interests of some of the weakest sections of the population, including daily-wage workers, small traders and shopkeepers, farmers, women and senior citizens. Politically, it did not impact the fortunes of the BJP which won by a handsome margin the state assembly elections in the country's most populous state, Uttar Pradesh, that were held within months of demonetisation. In Gujarat, where assembly elections were held in December 2017, the BJP retained its majority though it lost as many as sixteen seats compared to what it had won in 2012. The crackdown on over 200,000 shell companies, for not complying with the basic rules of filing returns and for laundering money, was also a Modi government step that certainly helped the regime counter any impression that it was encouraging crony capitalism.

Early in the tenure of the Modi government, an attempt was made to dilute the provisions in the land acquisition law to make it easy and hassle-free for private companies to acquire lands for setting up projects in the infrastructure sector. This was the first instance when Modi sensed that opposition political parties could get together and use the dilution in the land acquisition law to label him as pro-business and, by implication, supportive of crony capitalism. After all, it was a question of amending the law to allow private companies to acquire land on easier terms and improve the 'ease of doing business'. Soon, the Modi government dropped the proposal of amending the land acquisition law and instead asked the states to embrace land leasing as an alternative. However, even as the government entered the fourth year of its tenure, no state government has tried to introduce land leasing, confirming the earlier apprehensions over a political backlash arising out of any steps that are seen as pro-business.

However, to argue that crony capitalism under the Modi regime either disappeared or was kept under check would be incorrect and misleading. Conscious of steering clear of accusations of crony capitalism, the Modi government has put in place new terms of engagement with industry that ironically may sow new seeds of crony capitalism. The revival of the public-private partnership (PPP) model in implementing infrastructure sector projects in building roads, metro railway projects and airports, in particular, should help the country reduce its widening infrastructure gap, but as in many PPP projects the awarding of contracts without following transparent norms can result in sweet-heart deals. The pressure on the Modi government to award such projects is huge as private sector firms are either incapable of taking up such projects on their own or are not interested in entering a sector that is decidedly difficult with limited likely financial gains. At the same time, the Modi government also has felt the need to expedite the awarding of these contracts and the implementation of these projects.

The principle of PPPs has now been extended to the defence sector as well in the form of a strategic partnership scheme. A few private sector companies have been roped in to partner with multinational defence giants. For instance, the Anil Ambani-led Reliance Dhirubhai Ambani Group and the Gautam Adani-led Adani Group are among those who have joined hands with foreign companies to set up defence equipment projects in India. There have also been reports suggesting that state governments ruled by the BJP facilitated the operation of mines in collaboration with an Adani Group company just years after the supreme court had cancelled the allotment of 214 coal blocks for captive mining.[14] Whereas no apparent impropriety in the award of these contracts has so far come to light, questions have been raised as to why and under what circumstances these partnerships were decided and, most importantly, whether there was a transparent bidding method adopted before a decision to opt for them was taken. Gautam Adani is an industrialist who is known to be close to the prime minister—Modi used aircraft owned by the Adani Group in March, April and May 2014 for campaigning across the country in the run-up the general elections that year. Adani had lobbied hard in favour of Modi when was chief minister of Gujarat when certain businesspersons had spoken against him for his inability to control the anti-Muslim communal riots in the state in 2002. Adani has also participated actively in wooing foreign investors during successive 'Vibrant Gujarat' meetings held in Gujarat's capital, Gandhinagar and its contiguous city, Ahmedabad.

Questions relating to alleged favours granted to particular business groups have also been raised about the awarding of contracts to build the much-hyped 'Smart Cities' projects, although what are supposed to be transparent bidding processes are meant to be in place. The systems and processes followed for the allocation of land and the award of contracts to various big business houses for building 'special economic zones' meant to promote exports had become controversial earlier during the Manmohan Singh regime when the UPA government was periodically accused by the BJP, then the principal opposition party, of promoting crony capitalism. A similar fate could well await the award of projects to build so-called Smart Cities under the Modi regime.

In the first few years of its tenure, the Modi government has come under close scrutiny because of the manner in which Baba Ramdev and his Patanjali Ayurved Limited have seen phenomenal growth. Both Ramdev (who is supposed to be a spiritual guru of sorts) and Modi belong to the Hindu Right and have benefitted from the propagation of a narrowly-defined ideology of nationalism defined by the Rashtriya Swayamsevak Sangh (RSS), the ideological parent of the Sangh Parivar or the 'family' of organisations whose political arm is the BJP. The two even campaigned together from the same platform during the general elections in 2014. While Modi catapulted himself to prime ministership of a BJP government with a single-party majority, which was last witnessed three decades earlier, Ramdev, a co-founder of Patanjali Ayurved, has grown his healthcare business to Rs 10,000 crore and has targeted to expand his business by 100 per cent in a year or so entering new areas of businesses. A Reuters review of state government documents revealed recently that Patanjali had received an estimated Rs 65 crore of discounts for the land parcels it acquired from various state government, which, significantly, were ruled by the BJP.[15] All the state governments that granted those discounts— Maharashtra, Uttar Pradesh, Haryana and Assam—have denied that any special favours were shown to Patanjali. But what is incontrovertible is the close ties that Ramdev enjoys with the ruling BJP party in New Delhi and in many states.

Another area of concern has been the way sector regulators have been allowed to use discretion under the Modi regime, raising questions over whether a new form of crony capitalism is taking shape not with the help of the government's direct action, but through regulatory interventions. If the government were to be seen openly pushing for debt restructuring of indebted companies, it could attract charges of favouritism and eventually of crony capitalism. But the Modi government has carefully chosen the RBI to do the heavy lifting in preparing the list of indebted companies that need to be picked up for early resolution of their debts. Thus, the RBI prepares the list of such companies, thereby distancing the government from the exercise. Indeed, the Essar Group, one of whose companies was listed for a time-bound debt resolution plan, moved the court alleging discrimination. It was alleged that some other companies, equally indebted by using another yardstick, were left out and not subjected to an expeditious time-bound insolvency and debt resolution plan. The court ticked off the central bank for the manner in which it dealt with the indebted company, but it finally ruled in favour of the regulator. But nowhere was the government in the picture. Nor was it accused of any favouritism, even though the government's tacit role in determining that list of stressed companies could not be ruled out. Similarly, the telecom sector regulator (the Telecom Regulatory Authority of India or TRIA) has issued orders that were seen as favouring one player, Reliance Industries Limited, and disadvantaging its incumbent rivals. Experts and former telecom regulators have even questioned the logic of how the regulator decided on tariffs to force the choice of a certain technology. If at any point in time, anybody levels charges of favouritism, they would be against the regulator, not the government.

In early 2018, a series of financial scandals attracted considerable public attention. A group of firms led by diamond merchants from Modi's home state, Gujarat—Nirav Modi and Mehul Choksi—were accused of defrauding India's second-largest public sector bank, Punjab National Bank to the sum of over $1.8 billion—making it one of the biggest, if not the biggest, bank frauds of its kind in the country.[16] They were thereafter declared absconders after they left the country. Belatedly realising that apart from Nirav Modi and Mehul Choksi, other economic offenders in the past had also left the country to remain largely outside the jurisdiction of Indian laws, the Modi government quickly introduced a bill in parliament to take possession of the Indian assets of such offenders. The Fugitive Economic Offenders Bill was introduced in parliament in March 2018, within days of the cabinet approving such a law. It was yet another indication of the Modi government's sensitivity to charges of crony capitalism.

But financial scandals and reports about sweetheart deals continued unabated. The chief executive officer and managing director of the country's largest bank in the private sector, ICICI Bank (formerly Industrial Credit and Investment Corporation of India) Chanda Kochhar was apparently aware of loans that had been disbursed by the bank she headed to the Videocon group of companies whose promoter, Venugopal Dhoot, in turn, struck sweetheart deals with her husband and relatives through a company called NuPower.[17] While the bank denied any corruption or conflict of interest, investigating agencies are reportedly examining the transactions.[18]

In conclusion, the data on crony capitalism as well as anecdotal evidence do present a picture of its declining incidence during the Modi government's tenure, but the credit for this should not go only to the ruling dispensation, but also to the evolutionary process of India Incorporated that has thrown up new leaders in new areas like technology, software services and retail—all of which have relatively less dependence on government patronage. But it would not be correct to suggest that fault lines of crony capitalism during the Modi government regime have diminished, let alone disappeared. A government keen on speeding up investments with the help of public-private partnerships and strategic partnership between foreign and Indian private companies has to be wary of accusations of crony capitalism. Many scandals during the Manmohan Singh period took time before entering the public domain. The same story may be repeated once again.

PART V

THE OTHERED 40 PER CENT: THE HINDU NATION AND ITS MARGINS

11

DALITS IN POST-2014 INDIA

BETWEEN PROMISE AND ACTION

Sukhadeo Thorat

It will not be an exaggeration to say that the Bharatiya Janata Party (BJP) tried to appropriate Dr B.R. Ambedkar, knowing completely that Ambedkar's views on many issues deviated considerably from the party's ideological position. This was particularly the case with Prime Minister Narendra Modi who, allegedly, felt 'indebted' to Dr Ambedkar for inspiring him to push forward the cause of depressed castes. This appropriation of Dr Ambedkar was brought into play by making open commitments to Dalit upliftment. These commitments were reflected in the BJP's 2014 poll manifesto which promised to do many things for the Dalits: a section titled 'SCs, STs and other Weaker Sections: Social Justice and Empowerment' spelt out a new approach towards the development of Scheduled Castes (SC) and Scheduled Tribes (ST). It read:

> The BJP is committed to bridge the gap, following the principle of *Samajik Nyaya* (social justice) and *Samajik Samrasata* (social harmony). The social justice must be further complemented with economic justice and political empow-

erment—we will focus upon empowering the deprived sections of society. Steps will be taken to create an enabling ecosystem of equal opportunity—for education, health and livelihood. We will accord highest priority to ensuring their security especially the prevention of atrocities against SCs and STs.[1]

The manifesto further identified the following specific areas for action:

- A high priority for SC would be to create an ecosystem for education and entrepreneurship.
- BJP is committed to eradication of untouchability at all levels.
- BJP is committed to eliminate manual scavenging.
- BJP will follow more effective ways to pull these people out of the poverty line.
- BJP will ensure that the funds allocated for schemes and programmes for SC—are utilised properly.
- A mission mode project would be made for housing, education, health, and skill development.
- Special focus would be [placed] on children, especially the girl child, with regard to health, education, and skill development.[2]

In economic empowerment, the focus was on livelihood so as to reduce poverty, with priority given to education, entrepreneurship, skill development, and housing. In social empowerment, it promised to provide security by assigning priority to the prevention of atrocities against SCs and the eradication of untouchability.

In the following pages, we will assess the policies and the outcomes of the initiatives proposed by the BJP in its manifesto by using the data which have been made available by the government so far.

Financial Allocation under Special Component Plan from 2014/15 to 2018/19

The allocation of funds to the Special Component Plan (SCP) for the Scheduled Castes is the main instrument for uplifting of the Scheduled Castes. Therefore, the priorities of the government are generally reflected in the financial allocation under this SCP for the Scheduled Castes in the annual budget of the Union government. Now, the financial allocation under the Special Component for Scheduled Castes (SCSC) in the last five years does not reflect the priorities spelt out in the BJP 2014 manifesto for their economic and social empowerment. The Union government is required to allocate funds to the SCP for development of SCs across central (federal) ministries in proportion to their population share, that is 16.6 per cent. However, the old problem of low allocation continued under this government during the five years of its duration. The ratio of Plan allocation (on central and centrally-sponsored schemes) for SCs to total plan allocation was 8.79 per cent in 2014/15, 6.63 per cent in 2015/16, 7.06 per cent in 2016/17, 8.91 per cent in 2017/18, and 6.55 per cent in 2018/19 (Graph 1). The average allocation to the SCP for five years between 2014 and 2018 comes to a mere 7 per cent which is about ten percentage points short of the 16.6 per cent SC population in the country. According to the National Campaign on Dalit Human Rights (NCDHR), *Dalit Arthik Adhikar Andolan* (Dalit economic rights movement), these ten percentage points represent Rs 2752.72 billion.[3] This low allocation has naturally affected several schemes.

Besides, the reporting on the SCP in the Union Budget 2017/18 marks a significant departure from the earlier budgets. The name, that is, 'Scheduled

Graph 1: Proportion of SCSP/SCC allocation to total plan outlay (CS+CSS) schemes

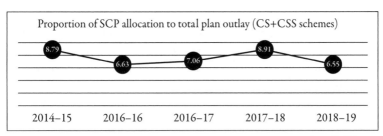

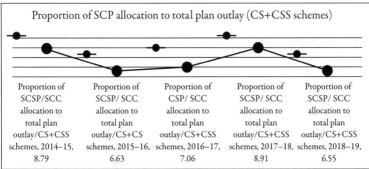

Note: CS: Central schemes, CSS: Centrally sponsored schemes.
Source: National Campaign on Dalit Human Rights, *Dalit Adivasi Budget Analysis 2018–19*, Delhi: Dalit Arthik Adhikar Andolan, 2018.

Caste Component Plan', has been replaced by a new term: 'Allocation for Welfare of Scheduled Castes'. The new terminology has taken away the focus from the 'Special allocation' under the Special Component Plan for SCs. We may recall that earlier, the Ministry of Social Welfare was renamed as Ministry of Social Justice and Empowerment in 1998 with a purpose to bring a clear focus on social justice and empowerment, rather than on the mere notion of social welfare, with its condescending overtones. Whatever the purpose behind the change in nomenclature, it certainly takes away the clear focus that the SCP had accorded to the empowerment of and social justice for Dalits. Besides, in the absence of the specific mention of 'special' allocation under the SCP and the norms for allocation, there is now no clarity on the parameters for assessing the allocations reported by different ministries or departments under the heading of 'Welfare of Scheduled Castes'.[4]

Another matter of concern is the indirect consequences of combining the plan and non-plan expenditure into one. In the Union Budget 2017–18, the government merged the plan and non-plan components of the budget. We know that the allocation under the SCP is for development of SCs under plan expenditure. The likely consequences of the merging of developmental (plan) and non-developmental (non-plan) expenditure, is that some of the non-plan expenditure, such as salaries, and administrative expenditure, may be shown as part of the total. This may reduce the actual expenditure on schemes related to the economic development of SC, which has, in fact, happened in the budget for 2018/19.

Impact on Educational Financial Schemes

The low allocation to the SCP has affected some flagship schemes financed by the Union Ministry of Social Justice and Empowerment. The scholarship schemes are cases in point. The post-matriculation scholarships for SCs, which were started by Dr B.R. Ambedkar in 1945, is one such scheme whose allocation has been badly affected due to low allocation under the SCP. The post-matriculation scholarship scheme with all its limitations has been the main source of development of higher education of Dalits. It is meant for the day to day maintenance of the poor SC students including fees. About 5.1 million SC students across the country have faced immense difficulties due to delayed or pending release of funds of more than Rs 80 billion by the Union government to the state governments for the last three consecutive years. Further, the 2018/19 budget has allocated only Rs 30 billion towards scholarship for SCs.

Non-payment of scholarship money to SC students resulted in increasing dropouts from colleges and universities. The former Secretary of the Ministry of Social Justice and Empowerment, P.S. Krishnan, had written a letter to the Finance Minister on 9 November 2016 seeking payment of arrears of post-matriculation scholarships to the tune of Rs 110 billion, pleading that the amount would not raise the fiscal deficit much.[5] But the government seems to be more concerned about the fiscal deficit than the fate of the 5.1 million poor SC students. Similarly, the delay in the release of funds to the University Grants Commission (UGC) for the National Fellowship for Scheduled Castes and Scheduled Tribes (earlier called Rajiv Gandhi Fellowship) for Ph.D. students across the country has also put many SC research students in extreme hardship, at a time when the enrolment rate of SCs in higher education remains quite low compared to 'others', that is non-SC/ST groups. For instance, in 2014 the enrolment rate in higher education was 22 per cent for SCs, compared with 29 per cent of Other Backward Classes (OBCs) and 41 per cent of others.[6] In this context, since the goal of the policy under the BJP 2014 manifesto was to reduce the gap between the SCs and others in education attainment, the government should have increased the allocation for the fellowship schemes rather than reducing the amount.

More recently, the Allahabad high court had given a verdict against the present practice in central universities of implementing reservation at the university level and suggested replacement by reservation at the departmental level, a change that would result in under-representation. The central government instead of going to the supreme court, lent support to the Allahabad high court decision through an order by the University Grants Commission and thus remained insensitive to the likely fall in the posts under reservation for faculty in the universities, where the representation of SCs/STs is already low.

A tale of two suicides

The problem of discrimination against Dalits in institutions of higher education such as state universities is an old one. It was recognised by the previous government. The Ministry of Human Resource Development (MHRD), under Kapil Sibal asked the UGC to pass a regulation against caste discrimination against Dalit students and other marginalised students in higher education institutions. Today, these regulations are not effectively enforced. In fact, the continuing problem of caste discrimination grabbed the attention of the entire nation after the suicide of a Dalit student named Rohith Vemula, in the University of Hyderabad in January 2016, and of another Dalit research scholar, Muthukrishnan Jeevanantham, in Jawaharlal Nehru University in Delhi, in March 2017. Rohith Vemula's controversial suicide, in the light of casteist discrimination in the university space, triggered nationwide outrage among Dalits and other sections of society. A case was filed under the Atrocity Act against the university's vice chancellor and the Union labour minister. While the students sought his removal, the vice chancellor was sent on leave. The university finally reopened with an assurance from the Ministry of Human Resource Development that the guilty would be treated under the Atrocity Act, that the vice chancellor would not be brought back, and that the remedial assistance for Dalit and students from other weaker sections would be strengthened. Other assurances by the government to the agitating students included increased participation of Dalit students and faculty in decision making, and regularisation of the National Fellowship for Scheduled Castes and Scheduled Tribes. Also, a special education programme would be introduced to sensitise students about caste and gender discrimination in universities through courses in civic learning. The government however reneged on its assurances and did exactly the opposite on some of them, while maintaining silence on others. In a bid to save the minister and the vice chancellor from trial under the Atrocity Act, all-out efforts were made to prove that Rohith Vemula was an OBC and not a Dalit, so that the case could not be registered under the Atrocity Act. Also, the vice chancellor was brought back with honour. No initiative was taken on the rest of the demands. Yet another opportunity arose for the MHRD after the suicide of Dalit research scholar Muthukrishnan in Jawaharlal Nehru University. Similar promises were made, to no avail.

On the contrary, during this time, some decisions detrimental to the interests of SCs/STs/OBCs were taken: the UGC's admission rule of six MPhil/PhD students per faculty member was enforced in central universities, with a complete disregard to the interests of the SC/ST/OBC students. This rule led to a drastic fall in admissions in central universities. For example, in Jawaharlal Nehru University, the total net admissions fell from 502 students in 2016/17 to only 130 in 2017/18. Correspondingly, the intake of SC students declined from 141 in 2016/17 to 37 in 2017/18, while that of ST students fell from 75 to 16, and that of OBC students from 265 to 76 during the same period. The rule could have been changed by the UGC at any time to avoid these consequences. However, the question that begs an answer is how the faculty in Jawaharlal Nehru University and other central universities ended up with more than six PhD students—in some cases running to fifteen. The reason can be traced to a decision by the previous government. The earlier government provided 27 per cent reservation to OBCs, and to avoid a fall in the admission of general category students (non-SC/ST/OBC), it took a bold decision and the number of positions by 27 per cent, thus leading to a 54 per cent jump in the admission of students, which is rarely done. This landed the faculty with more than six MPhil/PhD students each. What the government should have done is to revise the decision of six students per faculty member till the situation became normal. That was not done. Instead, it reduced the admission by 70 per cent. What a contrast between two approaches of governance! While the previous government changed the rule to avoid the negative consequences of OBC reservation on non-SC/ST/OBC groups and to safeguard their interest, under the new dispensation, the rule is implemented in letter and spirit to the detriment of the SC/ST/OBC students. The option would have been to change the rule in the interest of all students, as rules have to be for the good of the people and not otherwise. We know that the enrolment rate of SC/ST/OBC students in higher education is much lower than for others.[7] Therefore, the need was to increase their admission—but in practice the opposite has happened.

Another decision that has caused pain to SC/ST students is the rule regarding the procedure of admission to MPhil/PhD. The rule framed in 2016 prescribed a minimum of 50 per cent marks in the written entrance examination to qualify for interview and then made the selection entirely on the basis of the interview, making the entrance test only qualifying in nature. The provision of relaxation of marks to SC/ST students was withdrawn. The SC/ST/OBC students were seeking reduction in the interview marks and selection mainly on written examination, because they had provided evidence of discrimination in the interviews. The government on the other hand did exactly the opposite: making selection solely on the basis of interview. What message did the Dalits receive from these policy decisions in higher education after 2014 which are detrimental to their interests?

Entrepreneurship promotion among the Scheduled Castes

Another area which received priority in the 2014 BJP manifesto was promotion of entrepreneurship among the Scheduled Castes. As a follow-up, the Union government has developed a special scheme called SC/ST Hub for improving the ownership of enterprises by these communities with a financial allocation of Rs 4.99 billion. The responsibility to implement the schemes has been given to the Ministry of Micro, Small and Medium Enterprises (MSME). The policy makers in MSME acted hastily and rushed to the US to draw lessons from policies related to Blacks (African-Americans), Latinos and women. Further, the Ministry also hired an international consultancy, for a hefty fee of about Rs 4.6 million per month, resulting in a cost of Rs 150 to 180 million for three years. The Ministry did not consider any Indian organisation suitable for providing advice. Thus, the fund was wasted by the MSME on conclaves and seminars to educate SCs/STs, and also by outsourcing the work to private parties. Under the procurement policy, the Ministry was required to make 4 per cent of its purchases from SC/ST enterprises, but the ratio has reached only 0.39 per cent.

The present policy under the SC/ST Hub should have been framed taking into account the specific situation of Dalit enterprises. According to the Sixth Economic Census 2013, there are about 52.3 million establishments categorised as 'Private: Proprietary' in the country, out of which 5.96 million are owned by Dalits, that is about 11.4 per cent of the total number of 'private proprietorship' establishments.[8] A whopping 83 per cent of the Dalit enterprises are small household enterprises run with family labour, while just about 16 per cent of them employ six or fewer workers and less than 1 (0.9) per cent of SC enterprises employ more than six workers. The Economic Census 2013 also indicates that a very high proportion of Dalit enterprises do not have a formal permanent place or set up outside of the household premises and a bank account. This high proportion of Dalit household enterprises operate with low capital, turnover and income. Due to low incomes, they remain steeped in poverty. In 2011/12, about 24 per cent of SC non-farm self-employed people were poor, which is higher than high-caste self-employed. The government should have planned for these 5.97 million SC household enterprises. The SC enterprises also face discrimination in various market and non-market institutions. A primary survey conducted in 2013 brings out the nature of discrimination faced by Dalit manufacturers and service providers in rural areas.[9] The survey covered 336 Dalit business households including grocery, eateries including restaurants, and transport (car, jeep, autorickshaw, and cycle-rickshaw). In case of Dalit grocer respondents, 37 per cent of them spoke of the unwillingness on the part of high-caste people to buy from their shop, except some specific packaged goods. About 28 per cent of the SC grocery owners attributed their caste background as a reason for refusal by high castes to buy from their shops. About 12 per cent of SC people reported being restricted from buying from grocery shops owned by high castes. Similarly, SC restaurant or eatery operators reported that the bulk of their customers belonged to their own caste. The proportion of high-caste customers was much smaller. About 44 per cent of SC restaurant/eatery owners reported caste background as the reason for refusal by high castes to eat from their restaurants/eateries. In case of transport, about 65 per cent of SC entrepreneurs mentioned that high-caste people avoid using their transport. According to the respondents, the discrimination has negative consequences such as being forced to close down business or operate at low profit margins often resulting in high loans.

The government should have based its policy on the empirical evidence. In fact, the government should have used this opportunity to learn from the experience of Malaysia and South Africa, instead of the US policy of entrepreneurship development.

Reservation under attack

From time to time some prominent persons from the BJP and the RSS have argued against caste-based reservation and in favour of positive discrimination policies relying on socio-economic criteria. Some have asked for the exclusion of economically better-off Dalits from reservations, although they have subsequently backtracked from this position. They apparently do not realise that quotas in jobs, education and elected assemblies are policy instruments developed to provide legal safeguards against caste discrimination that involved denial of equal economic and civil rights to Dalits due to their caste identity. Both economically better-off and worse-off face discrimination on the grounds of caste. Caste discrimination is neutral to economic standing, both poor and non-poor Dalits have suffered from caste discrimination, and therefore, both need reservation to ensure their fair share in jobs, education and in political governance. The non-poor SCs may be excluded from financial support, but they would need safeguards against discrimination in jobs, education, and political spheres in the form of reservation.[10]

Besides, the government has pursued an aggressive policy of privatisation of the economy, education, and the health sector without showing any concern about the impact of this policy on job reservations for Dalits. Privatisation means automatic de-reservation. Before Narendra Modi took over power, the proportion of permanent government employees in the non-farm regularised salaried worker category had diminished from 23 per cent in 2004/05 to

18 per cent in 2010/12, due to privatisation and recruitment for government jobs on contract. This percentage has further declined after 2011/12 but there is no data available yet. The previous government had taken an initiative, at least, to have voluntary and self-regulatory affirmative action policy of some sort for the private sector, which the private sector accepted and implemented. Under the present regime, the leadership in NITI Aayog (the erstwhile Planning Commission) has openly advised the government against any affirmative action policy, voluntary or otherwise, for the private sector.

Preventing atrocities against the Scheduled Castes

The prevention of atrocities against the SCs received prime consideration in the BJP manifesto 2014, which said, 'We will accord highest priority to ensuring their security, especially the prevention of atrocities against SCs and STs...'.[11] After the infamous Una incident in Gujarat in the summer of 2016, which involved criminal assault on four Dalit men for skinning cows by self-styled cow-protectors or *gau rakshaks* (despite the fact that they had not killed these cows but were skinning animals which were already dead) a five-hour special discussion on the status of atrocities on the Dalits in the country took place in the Lok Sabha (lower house of parliament). At the end of the discussion, the government promised to take steps to stop atrocities against SCs. However, in subsequent annual reports of the Ministry of Social Justice and Empowerment, we do not find any new initiatives or special measures to carry forward the mandate of the Lok Sabha. Table 1 provides data on the incidents of atrocities registered by the SCs from 2012 to 2016. We can see the sudden jump in cases under the Atrocities Act between 2012 and 2016—from 12,638 to 40,401. This is presumably due to the increasing trend to register cases of atrocities under the Atrocities Act, and less under the regular Indian Police crime act. The help by civil society organisations has also played a part. We will therefore avoid 2012 and 2013 and focus on the situation during the BJP regime between 2014 and 2016. In 2014, the total number of cases registered under Protection of Civil Rights Act and Prevention of Atrocities Act were 40,401. The number decreased to 38,670 in 2015, and further to 35,719 in 2016. The number of cases declined marginally but the number remained high with an annual average of 39,957 cases. The crime-wise data break-down shows that crimes against SC women such as rape, attempt to rape, sexual harassment, kidnapping and abduction of SC women to compel them to marry, assault or use of criminal force on women with intent to disrobe, and assaults on SC women to outrage their modesty have increased.[12]

Table 1: Total, PCR and PoA Crimes Committed against Scheduled Castes, 2012–16 (All India)

Year	Total Crime	Total PCR Crime	Total PoA Crime	PCR + PoA Crime
2012	33,655	62	12,576	12,638
2013	39,408	62	13,975	14,037
2014	47,064	101	40,300	40,401
2015	45,003	106	38,564	38,670
2016	40,801	27	35,692	35,719
Yearly Ave 2014–16	44,289	44	38,185	38,263

Source: National Bureau of Crime Report, *Crime in India Report, 2014–2017*. New Delhi: Ministry of Home Affairs, GoI, 2017.
Note: PCR, Protection of Civil Rights Act; PoA, Prevention of Atrocities Act.

Table 2: Crimes against SCs registered under PoA Act in major states, 2014–16

	States	2014	2015	2016
1	Andhra Pradesh	2104	2263	1889
2	Bihar	7874	6293	5448
3	Chhattisgarh	359	216	243
4	Gujarat	1075	1009	1156
5	Haryana	444	510	604
6	Himachal Pradesh	113	91	15
7	Jharkhand	903	736	18
8	Karnataka	1865	1841	429
9	Kerala	712	695	721
10	Madhya Pradesh	3294	3546	4918
11	Maharashtra	1763	1795	1518
12	Odisha	1657	1821	1796
13	Punjab	123	147	91
14	Rajasthan	6734	5911	5028
15	Tamil Nadu	1486	1735	1205
16	Telangana	1427	1292	1101
17	Uttar Pradesh	8066	8357	9361
18	Uttarkhand	60	80	36
19	W. Bengal	130	150	93
	All India	40300	38564	35692

Source: National Bureau of Crime Report, *Crime in India Report, 2014–2017*. New Delhi: Ministry of Home Affairs, GoI, 2017.
Note: PoA, Prevention of Atrocities Act.

The state-wise picture shows that about five states have shown an increase in registered cases under the Prevention of Atrocities Act between 2014 and 2016 (Table 2). Out of these five states, except Odisha, the rest are BJP-ruled states (Gujarat, Haryana, Madhya Pradesh (MP), Uttar Pradesh (UP)).

We also look at the crime rate against SCs in terms of number of cases registered per hundred thousand of population in various states (Table 3). At the all India level in 2016, about twenty cases were registered under the Atrocities Act per hundred thousand of population. In nine states, the rate was higher than the all India average of twenty cases per hundred thousand. It was particularly high in MP (43), Rajasthan (42), Bihar (34), Gujarat (32), Andhra Pradesh (AP) (27), Kerala (26), and Odisha and UP (25). So, in eight states where the atrocity rate is higher than the all India average, four are BJP-governed states and in Bihar it is a partner in the coalition state government. This shows that not only did majority of BJP-governed states show an increase in atrocity cases against SCs, but also that the rate of atrocity is high in these BJP-ruled states. Given the BJP's promise for more security to Dalits, we would have expected some special efforts on the part of BJP governments. But first four top states in terms of the atrocity rate against Dalits are BJP-administered ones.

Over the years, a change in the nature of atrocities against Dalits has also come to light. The new trend is the collective or mass involvement in atrocities against SCs, which indicates a rise in community-level animosity against Dalits. Correlatively, we observe multiple atrocities in a single incident or a series of linked events.

Table 3: Rate of Registered Total and POA Crimes against Scheduled Castes, 2014–16

	States	RATE of Registered TOTAL Crimes			RATE of Registered POA Crimes		
		2014	2015	2016	2014	2015	2016
1	Andhra Pradesh	48.7	52.3	27.6	24.9	26.8	22.4
2	Bihar	47.6	38.9	34.4	47.5	38.0	32.9
3	Chhattisgarh	32.6	31.4	7.4	11.0	6.6	7.4
4	Gujarat	27.7	25.7	32.4	26.4	24.8	28.4
5	Haryana	16.2	16.3	12.5	8.7	10.0	11.8
6	Himachal Pradesh	7.1	5.5	6.7	6.5	5.3	0.9
7	Jharkhand	22.7	18.5	13.2	22.7	18.5	0.5
8	Karnataka	20.4	19.0	17.8	17.8	17.6	4.1

9	Kerala	26.8	24.7	26.6	23.4	22.9	23.7
10	Madhya Pradesh	36.6	36.9	43.4	29.0	31.3	43.4
11	Maharashtra	13.3	13.7	13.2	13.3	13.5	11.4
12	Odisha	31.5	32.1	25.0	23.1	15.3	25.0
13	Punjab	1.4	1.7	1.5	1.4	1.7	1.0
14	Rajasthan	65.7	57.3	42.0	55.1	48.4	41.1
15	Tamil Nadu	10.7	12.3	8.9	10.3	12.0	8.3
16	Telangana	31.2	30.9	28.1	26.3	23.8	20.3
17	Uttar Pradesh	19.5	20.2	25.2	19.5	20.2	22.6
18	Uttaranchal	3.2	4.9	3.4	3.2	4.2	1.9
19	W. Bengal	0.7	0.9	0.6	0.6	0.7	0.4
	INDIA	23.4	22.3	20.3	20.0	19.2	17.7

Source: National Bureau of Crime Report, *Crime in India Report, 2014–2017*. New Delhi: Ministry of Home Affairs, GoI, 2017.
Note: The rate of crimes indicates incidence per hundred thousand SC population based on Actual Census, 2011; PoA, Prevention of Atrocities Act.

Yet there is another new trend which seems to have emerged more prominently after 2014. There are more punitive operations in the 'open' by members of the high castes, particularly by groups of young people. These are openly committed heinous crimes, which the supreme court described as 'shockingly cruel and inhumane.' The high castes act as a self-styled police force to punish Dalits for what they think are violations of rules, but most of the times these rules promote some illegal observations of the caste system or reflect the Hindu nationalist agenda. There are several of these cases, but the most heinous and ugly crime, which led to outcry, was that of Una, in Gujarat, where so-called *gau rakshaks* openly assaulting the Dalit youths, humiliating them, their half naked bodies in full view of public and police. The purpose was to psychologically hurt the Dalits where it hurts the most.

What explains this new trend of open punishment? We can get some idea by looking at the *Manusmriti*, a text that is still referred to by the high castes even today. The *Manusmriti* prescribed monitoring by the community and punishment for violation of caste codes, such as ex-communication, social and economic boycott of the *shudras* or Dalits and other violent forms. So, the community is supposed to act as police force. The *Manusmriti* also prescribes the nature of punishments such as flogging, slitting of the tongue, thrusting of an iron rod or hot oil into the mouth and ears, severing limbs, slit on buttocks, lips to be gashed, urinating on part of the body, cutting of hands, the death penalty, corporal punishment, cutting the offending part of body and destruction of property, burning on a fire, shave with urine and so on to the untouchables or Dalits for violation of the caste code.[13] The violent forms used by the high castes in present times include several of these methods. The verbal violence includes caste abuse, humiliation, intimidation, threatening, forcing to consume undesirable substance like urinating in mouth, parading naked in public view, shaving of moustache and head. Acts of physical violence include physical attack, abduction, murder, torture, lynching, burning to death, cutting part of the body and damaging property. Community-level physical violence includes social and economic boycott, arson, riot, setting fire to the houses and property of Dalits, group attack with sticks or stones and other instruments. Sexual violence takes the form of sexual assault, sexual harassment, molestation, rape, gang rape, rape in view of relatives, outraging modesty, stripping and parading women. From this list one is not surprised at the similarity between the punishments prescribed by the *Manusmriti* and the method of violence used by high castes in rural areas in present times.

In law and theory, the *Manusmriti* is now a thing of the past. If the *Manusmriti* is a thing of the past, how can high castes in rural areas deploy violent methods as prescribed in the book against Dalits for violation of traditional caste rules? This means the traditional caste code still continues to influence the behaviour of high castes in many spheres, if not all. The traditional methods of punishment continue to dominate the minds of people as the legacy of the past, and they use such actions to enforce a code that provides them religious sanction. Although the Indian constitution and the country's laws prohibit the use of traditional methods of punishment, the high castes subtly used these traditional methods in new and modified forms. In *Annihilation of Caste*, in 1935, Bhimrao R. Ambedkar observed that 'the acts of the people are merely the results of their belief inculcated up on their minds by the *shastras* and that people will not change their conduct until they cease to believe in the sanctity of the *shastras* on which their conduct is founded'.

Unfortunately, the *Manusmriti* is still very much alive in the habits, norms, and customs of high-caste people in a latent form and comes to the fore when committing atrocities. The atrocities against Dalits have been committed before the BJP came to power in 2014. But there was no ideological agenda then. After 2014, the official promotion of the old social system encourages youth to use the old means with impunity, through several militant outfits. The frequent pronouncement by senior leaders to reinvigorate the old Vedic social organisation illustrates this trend. After all a statue of Manu who is regarded as the father of the legal code of caste inequality was erected in front of the Rajasthan high court, as a symbol of justice during the BJP regime in the state. The government refused to remove the statue despite several protests by Dalits.

The relegitimisation of caste

The Dalits have also begun to feel extremely insecure over the growing tendency that directly or indirectly justifies the social order based on the old four-fold caste structure, although occasionally, views are expressed against the caste system and the institution of untouchability. From time to time some people justify the social order based on Vedic ideology and the teaching of the *Bhagavad Gita*. In making a case for this Vedic framework or the *Gita*, no distinction is drawn between the religious ideology and the social ideology contained in these Hindu religious texts, as in Hinduism the religious ideology and social ideology can be embedded in each other. By not drawing any distinction between the two, the supporters of the Vedic ideology or the *Gita*, indirectly lend support to a society based on the *Varna* system (which is a parent of the caste system).

After carefully scanning through Hindu religious literature, like the *Rig Veda, Gita, Manusmriti*, and other *smritis*, which form the storehouse of religious ideas and sources of Hindu Social order, Ambedkar provided ample evidence that the *Varna*/caste system was present in the Hindu religious texts. It is indisputable that the *Rig Veda* first laid down the theory of *Chaturvarna* in what is known as the *Purushasukta*. A lone stanza in the *Rig Veda* states: 'His mouth was the Brahman, His two arms were made the warriors, His two thighs that which was the Vaishya, from the His feet was born the shudra'.

The *Bhagavad Gita* upholds the *Varna* system; Lord Krishna states: 'I myself have created the arrangement known as Chaturvarna, assuming them different occupations in accordance with native capacities.' The *Manusmriti* converts the *Varna* into caste system by bringing endogamy—marriage within the caste—and social separation. Manu states: 'But for the sake of the prosperity of the worlds, he caused the Brahamans, the Kshatriyas, the Vaishya, and Shudras to proceed from his mouth, his arms, his thighs and his feet. But in order to protect this universe, he assigned separate (duties and rights) occupations to those that sprang from his mouth, arms, thighs and feet.' Similarly, in the *Mahabharata* Bhishma preaches: 'The highest duty of a crowned king is to worship brahmans, they should be protected—respected, bowed to and revered as if they were one's parents.' Valmiki, the author of the *Ramayana* tells us that Shambuka was sacrificed because his behaviour deviated from the caste codes. In the *Arthashastra*, Kautilya requires every *Varna* to perform its functions, and declared that a person who observes his duty attains heaven and infinite bliss.[14] From this Ambedkar concludes that there is not much difference between the teaching of the *Vedas*, the *Gita* and the *Manusmriti*. He observed:

> The only difference one finds is that Vedas and the Bhagwat Gita deal with general theory, while the *Smritis* are concerned in working out the particulars and details of that theory. But the essence of all of these texts is that they are woven on the same pattern, the same thread runs through each of them, and they are finally part of the same fabric. Nothing is to be gained in picking and choosing between them. The (social) philosophy of Hinduism will be the same whether one takes the *Manu Smriti*, the *Vedas* or the Bhagwat Gita.[15]

The consequences were that the Hindu social order produced injustices, provoked immense suffering and humiliations for untouchables.[16]

The point that I want to emphasise is this: the Indian constitution grants freedom to all to practice their own religion. It is the right of the Hindus to preach and practice the Hindu religion. However, as mentioned above, the *Vedas, Gita, Smritis, Ramayana* and *Mahabharata* also advocate a social order (as part of religious teachings), which is based on the *Varna* system, later converted into the caste system. While preaching religious morality based on these religious texts, which is the right of those Hindus who believe in it, they should also openly deny the social order propagated by Hindu religious texts. Many do not realise that by not denying this social system, they are being hugely insensitive to Dalits or ex-untouchables. This silence and denial indeed causes insecurity and immense concern among Dalits.

Besides, Dalits are equally concerned about the disturbing trend which attempts to restrict their freedom of expression often with the use of violence. After an article in *The Indian Express*, titled 'What upper castes owe' on the Una atrocity,[17] the present writer received an advisory and indirect warning as a Dalit writer—a portion of the same is reproduced below:

> Hinduism is a great and ever evolving faith and there are people of all the four varnas in every caste-according to their respective act. An evil practice like untouchability can never be Hindu. Responsible intellectuals from SCs, STs, and BCs must appreciate that blaming Hinduism for all miseries does them more harm than good, in the long run—They must realise that continuing to blame the religion as a whole or entire upper castes for the faults of few individuals will only be counterproductive in the longrun...

If they revere Hinduism—their ancestral faith, and can show devotion that rivals the commitment of devout adherents of Islam, it will surely earn them respect even from the upper castes despite the anger at the loss of opportunities due to the policy of reservation... The need for the intellectuals from the SCs/ STs/BCs to think constructively and to act responsibly for the sake of amity between castes is greater now than ever before... Intellectuals from SCs/STs/ BCs have a huge task in front of them, of uniting all the politicians from their communities and motivating them to work with a single-minded devotion, for a new constitution that will permanently secure the interests of their future generation, meanwhile, they must summon up all the resources at their command to study carefully, on a regular basis, the impact of any delay in replacing of the present constitution in their long term interest.

The wide gap between Dalits and others still persists

The BJP manifesto promised 'to develop policies and schemes in a manner such that it brings about tangible improvement,—outcome that could be seen as an indication of reduction in the gap between SC and others'. Unfortunately, there is no data to study the changes in the gap from 2014 to 2018, as none of the recent National Sample Survey reports have been published. The latest data are up to 2011/12 on poverty, employment, ownership of assets, and education, a year or two preceding the BJP's coming to power at the centre.

In 2012, about 22 per cent of the people were poor. The poverty rate was 30 per cent for SCs, 20 per cent for OBCs and nine percent for high castes. The poverty of SCs is three times more than that among high castes. Similarly in 2014, enrolment rates at the higher secondary level was 97 per cent for high castes, followed by 80 per cent for OBCs and 73 per cent for SCs; and the enrolment rate for higher education was 43 per cent for high castes, 29 per cent for OBCs and 20 per cent for SCs. Thus, in terms of human development indicators like poverty and education, the SCs lag far behind the higher castes. The reasons are obvious. The Dalits lack income earning assets. In 2013, almost 45 per cent of the country's wealth was owned by high castes, which exceeds their population share of 21 per cent—in fact, it almost twice their population share. The OBCs owned about 31 per cent, which is fairly close to their population share of 36 per cent. The SCs however owned only 7 per cent of the country's wealth, which is much less than their population share of 16.6 per cent.[18] Since Dalits lack income earning assets, they resort to wage employment in a much greater proportion than others. But in the labour market they suffer from discrimination and face high unemployment. In 2012, the unemployment rate was 5.86 per cent at the all-India level, but it was 7.3 per cent for SCs compared to 5.2 per cent for OBCs and 4.3 per cent for high castes.[19] This was the situation in the gap in human development between the SCs and others in 2012–14, when the BJP took over in 2014.[20] We have no reason to believe that the gap got reduced after 2014. Given an inadequate allocation under the SCP on various schemes, particularly the education, and deceleration in employment, the gap may have widened, rather than reduced.

Concluding observations

We have analysed the policies of the BJP government against the promises made in the 2014 party's election manifesto in selected spheres. The manifesto promised Dalits economic empowerment with a focus on education, and entrepreneurship. In social empowerment, it promised to provide security by assigning priority to the prevention of atrocities against SCs. It also promised to reduce the gap in human development between the SCs and others.

It emerged from our empirical study that the government priority for the economic empowerment of Dalits is not reflected in financial allocations under the SCP. The average allocation to the SCP during the five-year period of Modi's term remained around 7 per cent, much below the 16 per cent mark. Low allocation affected many sectors, particularly education. The post-matriculate scholarships for SCs were affected badly due to a backlog of Rs 80 billion owed to the states in 2018/19, which caused immense hardship to Dalit students resulting in drop outs. Besides, an attempt to bring changes in the admission procedure reduced the intake of SC/ST/OBC students as research scholars in central universities. The decision of the court to introduce reservation at the department level (which will reduce the quantum of reservation) has also generated immense discontent among Dalit students and faculty members. The story of the SC/ST Hub is not different from that of education. As against a target of 4 per cent purchases from SC/ST enterprises, the Ministry of Micro, Small and Medium Enterprises achieved a procurement rate of merely 0.39 per cent. Most importantly, the number of incidents of violence against Dalits remains high, particularly in important BJP-governed states. Despite the fact that the acquittal rate in atrocity cases is very high, mainly due to wilful negligence of the administration, the supreme court made changes in the Prevention of Atrocities Act, taking out the provision of non-anticipatory bail, and action against officials without departmental inquiry, which is likely to encourage wilful negligence in its implementation.

Above all, the Dalits feel insecure due to occasional pronouncements to bring back the old social order based on Vedic social ideology.

All these developments have left Dalits extremely insecure, concerned and anxious. They have begun to feel that they are losing ground in what they have achieved so far. This is reflected in growing discontentment among Dalits. The expression of the discontent is reflected in voluntary uprisings by Dalits, particularly the youth in protest against the changes in the Atrocities Act. There is also a disturbed feeling among the students due to reversals in some education programmes. The loss of confidence in electoral methods led some youth to resort to forming a non-political group like the UP-based Bhim Army. After the Una incident, some people affected by atrocities lost whatever little faith they had in the liberal elements in Hinduism, and therefore some converted to Buddhism. At the political level Dalit political parties and collective action groups are shifting towards the secular forces. The most significant example is Dalit leader Mayawati's Bahujan Samaj Party or BSP's understanding with Samajwadi Party in Uttar Pradesh. These are obvious reactions to the gradual ideological shift away from our past efforts to build a society based on justice, equality and individual freedom.

12

ROHITH VEMULA'S REVOLUTIONARY SUICIDE

Abdul R. JanMohamed

Upon reading Rohith Vemula's suicide note, I felt a strong need to understand the structural forces (as oposed to the mundane history of how often he had been victimised by the administration and students at Hyderabad University) that drove him to this act—an act that could be seen as the end result of depression and utter personal dejection or, alternately, as a political gesture of defiance, an illocutionary utterance that transformed him from being a victim to becoming a heroic symbol. Having been born in Kenya, having been removed for over three generations from the ideological forces and battles that form and consume Indian culture (including the Hindu-Muslim agonistic embrace), I felt I had no immediate stake in the matter; I felt my distant kin-ship could allow me an ideologically dispassionate appreciation of Vemula's suicide and its political valences, one not steeped in various, deeply ideological discourses that circulate around untouchability in India. I decided therefore to approach the matter from a Western perspective, from a viewpoint informed by phenomenology of the 'touch' as articulated in the works of philosophers from Edmund Husserl to Jacques Derrida.

However, my brief examination will also be informed by my ongoing work on the political economy of death in the formation of slavery. I have argued elsewhere that in principle slavery is only made possible by the deployment of the threat/fear of death, that a slave will only become a slave, in the end, if he is afraid to die and if in exchange for actual death he is willing to live a life of 'social death'.[1] I have argued that under slavery a dialectic of death articulates itself around the threat/fear of death and that a complex political economy forms around the 'exchange' of life and death. Articulated from perspective of the phenomenology of touch and the dialectics of death, this paper claims that Vemula's suicide constitutes a liberating embrace of his own political ontology: his suicide transforms his deeply aporetic formulation '[his] birth as a fatal accident' into 'a liberating necessity'; it transforms a life that was in effect a form of 'social death' into a 'symbolic death' that resonated throughout society and that in effect endowed him with a form of immortality, a status akin to 'star dust' that he seems to have valued highly.

It may be best to begin an appreciation of the enormously horrifying effects, intended or not, of 'untouchability' via an eidetic reduction of the concept of 'untouchability'. But before turning to Husserl and Derrida's reduction of the touch and its place in the production of human sociality, let us imagine the crucial role of touching in a mythical scene of 'anthropogenesis', that is, of the birth of the human as a self-conscious species, such as Hegel's master-slave dialectic, or the biblical Adam and Eve story, or any number such stories that exist in other cultures.

Imagine the fate of a child who is never touched from the moment of birth. We can safely posit in this scenario that the enveloping, nurturing, and protective warmth of the mother's womb is a matrix absolutely necessary for the production of the child and that in this matrix the child is 'touched' in every possible way by that nurturing matrix. What happens, then, if after the moment of birth, that child is never 'touched', literally but also metaphorically? That child will die in a matter of days without the intervention of physical human touch. In order to live, to 'survive', to abide in life, a child has to be touched often and perhaps almost continuously. Literally, she has to be touched in order to be fed, to be cleaned, to be soothed when she is upset, to be clothed, to have her wounds treated when appropriate, etc. On the symbolic register, the child also has to be 'touched' by way of being taught a language (and more generally educated into a human symbolic world), and, to emphasise the obvious, the incorporation into the symbolic world constitutes the core of anthropogenesis. In short, it is impossible to imagine the existence of human sociality without the predication of 'touchability'. To designate some individual child as literally untouchable is to condemn it to certain physical death; by the same logic, to condemn a child to a metaphorical or social 'untouchability' is to condemn it to a 'socio-political death'. If a child is touched minimally but sufficiently to prevent him from physically dying but forced to remain more or less 'untouchable' in a symbolic, cultural sense, then he is implicitly pushed into the realm that Giorgio Agamben defines as the space of 'homo sacer'.[2] According to Agamben, the act of killing a person placed in this zone by society is considered neither a homicide nor a form of sacrilege; in other words, a creature in this zone is viewed neither as human nor as divine, nor, one should add, as an animal, for in Hindu mythology animals are not considered 'untouchable'. However, paradoxically within Hindu culture humans who touch any part of dead animals, professionals like butchers, tanners, shoemakers, and, of course, the 'sweepers', are considered untouchable. This clearly links some, if not all, aspects of untouchability as being produced by proximity to or the 'touching' of death. This links the formation of untouchables as a caste to the function of death in slavery and, as we will see, in the Derridian theorisation of the touch.

In considering the anthropogenetic function of the touch it may be useful to deploy Frantz Fanon's often-ignored distinction between 'ontogenesis' and 'sociogenesis'.[3] While the act of touching is absolutely necessary on the onto-logical register for anthropogenesis, on the sociogenetic register the process of incorporating this ontological necessity into human sociality permits so many societies to 'politicise' the valences of touching. That is, by ethically, politically, economically, and aesthetically valorising various modalities of (un)touchabil-ity, a given society can designate varied zones of privilege as well as varied zones of exploitability. Some societies can and do thus create highly codified zones into which certain parts of the population can be herded and con-demned, in practice if not in principle, as homo sacer, as those who can be killed when necessary (and the threshold of 'necessity' can be lowered to cir-cumstantial whim in some cases). And such designations of untouchable humans are of course accompanied by drastic economic exploitation that allows those in charge to accumulate enormous wealth (especially given a scenario of generational accumulation). The ontogenetic necessity of the 'touch' is thus converted into a sociogenetic mechanism for the appropriation and accumulation of surplus value.

A specific contrast of sociogenetic machinery used for the purposes of exclusion can help clarify the matter. The act of excommunication within the

Catholic religion and culture is similar in some aspects to the creation of the untouchable caste. Both formations, it should be noted, are grounded in religious or faith traditions that shape and reflect larger cultural realities, and both have deeply penetrating effects on structures of political subjectivity. Each act of excommunication corresponds to the violation of specific and well-articulated religious and social doctrines and practices. And most, if perhaps not all, excommunications are reversible given appropriate penance. Baptism, via the ritual of 'communion', incorporates the individual into the Catholic community; violation of certain principles or social norms then can lead to an 'excommunication'. By contrast, within the Hindu caste system the designation of a large group of individuals as 'untouchable' amounts to a generic form of segregation that hovers indefinitely between ontological and socio-political registers. Untouchability, unlike excommunication, is hereditary and irreversible. The origins of 'untouchability' are thus buried in the murky depths of the intersection between ontogenesis and sociogenesis and seem adamantly non-negotiable.[4]

The role of touching within the mythic or metaphysical views of anthropogenesis can be supplemented by a technical analysis of the phenomenology of touching, ranging from Edmund Husserl to Jacques Derrida and the commentaries on the work of both philosophers. However, space permits only brief engagement with some points crucial to an appreciation of 'untouchability' as a socio-political form and of their role in Rohith Vemula's 'revolutionary suicide'. Husserl's mapping of the haptic experience, that is of the constituting capacity of the sense of touch and the act of touching, claims that such an act is a mode of 'double apprehension', that it links and hence constitutes that which does the touching and that which is touched.[5] In his commentary on distinctions between Husserl and Derrida's phenomenology of touching, Eftichis Pirovolakis claims that 'Husserl actually writes that the "same" tactile sensation, that is, a single sensation is apprehended doubly, both as a sensation of the touching hand or finger, and as a feature of the object by which the touching hand or finger is touched.'[6] For Husserl this double apprehension is a unique feature of the sense of touch, not replicated by other senses such as sight (which, however, becomes far more dominant in the constitution of human epistemology and sociality). For Husserl the haptic constitution of immediate experience of the lived body is founded on the sense of touch in contradistinction to all the other senses. But, as Pirovolakis points out, Derrida deconstructs the Husserlian principle of auto-affective immediacy and introduces between the touching and the touched the structural presence not only of other senses but also of absence as such:

The constitution of the body proper thus described would already presuppose a passage outside and through the other, as well as through absence, death, and mourning as well as through 'ecotechnics' and the techne of the bodies... We should then reintroduce the outside itself, the other, the inanimate, 'material nature', as well as death, the nonliving, the nonphysical in general, language, rhetoric, technics, and so forth...[7]

The most important difference, for present purposes, in Derrida's insistence on replacing Husserl's privileging of the auto-affection of the touch with the hetero-affection of sight and then eventually yoking them together in 'several types of auto-hetero-affection' is the introduction of 'absence, death, and mourning' (p. 180). Thus, where Husserl's privileging of the haptic experience is designed to provide apodictic presence to both the touching and the touched (hence privileging a form of immediate 'communion' and kinship), Derrida's introduction of mediation via various modes of absence has the effect of introducing distance and undermining absolute proximity and seamless contiguity (hence privileging the possibility of 'excommunication' and disjunction). However one adjudicates this debate on the onto-phenomenological register, I would argue that on the sociogenetic register a dialectical oscillation between the drive for seamless contiguity and the inevitable introduction of distance, particularly when mediated by the absent-presence of death, is more useful for mapping a political economy of the horrors produced by the deployment of 'untouchability' within Hindu notions of caste distinctions. To the extent that Husserl's phenomenological description is correct, the haptic sense can be seen, on the sociogenetic register, as absolutely essential for the constitution of a community, indeed of sociality as such—remember the child that can die very quickly if never touched. If on the other hand Derrida's description, including in particular his insistence on the eternal presence of 'absence', is viable, then death, as one of the most radical versions of absence, must be seen as always present in the process of anthropogenesis. Untouchability as a political categorisation thus speaks at once to a powerful desire for a cohesive community and to the apparently equally powerful need for exclusion, the exclusion being necessary to valorise cohesiveness of those included within the community. This tension within the processes of inclusion/exclusion should be conceived not so much as a 'binary opposition' but rather as a constant dialectical tension amenable in principle to socio-political adjudication.

However, the caste system strenuously militates against any possibility of dialectical movement or political adjustment, mainly because the distance between those who occupy the position of transcendental touching and those objectified as 'untouchable' is mediated by death, or perhaps more accurately by the threat of death and the designation of 'homo sacer'—those for whom murder lies outside the structures of homicide and sacrilege: the untouchable are neither quite human nor really divine. Nor, it would seem, can they be classified with animals, for after all an animal like the cow can and does possess some divinity within Hindu culture. Gandhi implicitly understood these forms of excommunication because he tried to re-categorise the untouchables as *harijans* in an attempt to include them within the realm of the divine.

As evinced by texts like *Aporia* and *The Gift of Death*,[8] Derrida profoundly maps the role of death in the processes of anthropogenesis and sociality. However, his work rarely descends to the function of death in defining and sustaining various political economies that are generated via the sociogenic deployment of death. An adequate appreciation of the latter depends radically on a necessary distinction between the role of death on the ontogenetic and sociogenetic registers. The theoretical contemplation of the role of death within (existentialist) ontological discussions from Martin Heidegger to Derrida almost always presume that death is a 'natural' event—a product either of old age and illness or a (natural) accident: that is to say as an eventuality not produced by deliberate human intentionality or action. In contrast, we must appreciate that all societies have been adapt at transforming the natural eventuality of death into a political instrument: the threat of death and the periodic infliction of death have always been used to coerce recalcitrant populations and appropriate the land, labour, and property of the people unable to resist the political deployment of death. It might even be possible to argue that the fear and threat of death are instrumentalised by first being yoked into a symbiotic unit and then by its systematic deployment in the structures not only of primitive accumulation but also of various kinds of market-based political economies. In fact, one can argue that the very designation of a group as 'untouchable' provides the basis for a mode of primitive accumulation: to designate a group as permanently belonging to the margins of sociality is akin to the process of setting up 'enclosures' that Marx uses as an example of primitive accumulation that preceeds exploitation of labour via structures of market exchange. Untouchability is, in effect, a form of enclosure, located at the intersection of ontogenetic and sociogenetic registers, that provides a permenant pool of highly exploitable labour.

While the political instrumentalisation of death is too vast for even a cursory exploration in the present context, I would like to touch on some salient aspects of the political economy that weaves itself around the 'exchange' of life and death within the context of New World slavery and Jim Crow society in the US. The political economy constructed by the caste structure of untouchability is, I think, in some ways akin to that produced by slavery, and the similarities, in turn, will facilitate a better understanding of the valences of Rohith Vemula's suicide as an act of resistance to the oppressive structure created by untouchability.[9]

The success of slavery ultimately relies on the threat of death. While the master may prefer to rely on lesser forms of coercion, when these fail the threat of death and the occasional lynching define the bottom line of this form of 'exchange'. As Orlando Patterson has argued, the slave 'lives' under a conditionally commuted death sentence, and while the conditional clause demands complete obedience, the commutation can be revoked at the master's whim.[10] The slave lives in what Patterson calls a zone of 'social death': the slave has no social (or civil) right or legal socio-political existence except as property within the legal structure of the master's society. Building on the work of Patterson and on my analysis of Richard Wright's depiction of the use of the threat of death in Jim Crow society in the US South, I have articulated the dialectical socio-political structure that characterises all slave societies as well as, I suspect, the structuration of untouchability. The precondition for the slave's social death is the possibility of his 'actual death': the slave acquiesces, even if temporarily and provisionally, to social death because he is afraid of being killed in refusal or resistance. However, actual death also functions as a potential negation of social death: if the slave is 'willing' to die instead of continuing to function as a socially dead being and as a person living constantly on the edge of his actual death, then he can no longer be enslaved—he can be killed, but he will no longer remain a slave. If he survives that confrontation with actual death, then he is reborn in a state of what I call 'symbolic death', which consists of a liberating combination of the slave's physical survival, the death of his slave mentality, and his rebirth in a different subject position. The most pristine and penetrating articulation of this dialectic can be found in the work of Frederick Douglass generally and in his account of his prolonged fight with the slave breaker, Covey.[11] As I have also argued elsewhere, the dialectics of death forces the slave to enter into an unconscious death contract with the master, and the moment of symbolic death in effect consists of a complex renegotiation of that contract.[12]

For the present purposes, I would like to emphasise that the unconscious death contract permeates all the capillary structures of the slave's psyche. The slave is not constrained as a 'whole, intact subject' by external socio-political apparatuses; rather, slavery persists by disarticulating the mind of the slave. The individual subject cannot function adequately when different psychic apparatuses that constitute her subjectivity are prevented from their 'normal' tasks. While the disaggregation of the slave psyche can take many forms, we can briefly explore the truncation of desire within the slave psyche by using Toni Morrison's exploration of the labyrinthine psycho-political effects of the slave's interpellation by death. Morrison depicts the vicissitudes of the slave's desire for 'life', while the slave lives under the imminent threat of death, by figuring life as a 'flirt', who constantly tortures the slave by forcing her to follow the master's desire rather than her own.[13] However, Morrison makes it perfectly clear that life, like an insatiable flirt, will persist in forever inviting the slave to succumb to her forbidden desire and to bind with the object of that desire. The irrepressibility of desire and its strict prohibition produce an aporia that succinctly defines the contradictory relation between life and death under slavery: the slave who wants to 'live', who wants to survive, has to ensure the success of that particular desire by beating to death the apparatus of her own desire in general as well as her capacity to bind with the objects of her desire because the pursuit of her desire can lead to a quick death. Such a slave cannot afford to see death only as an external threat, as an eventuality that is controlled by someone else. Instead, she must internalise the possibility of death and become the agent who will deploy it against herself, deploy it to police her desire for a 'full' life, a life that binds with all the things in life that give her pleasure, including wives, husbands, parents, children, etc. The slave's survival, her life, depends on her becoming a successful agent of death. And ironically, her success in this aporetic endeavour will ensure that she has effectively collaborated in her own formation as a death-bound-subject. Yet his production of the self as a death-bound-subject is never complete because life is always enticing, always urging erotic attachment. Thus, for the slave, life will always have to be beaten to death. The slave is bound by this deathly struggle as long as she lives; the valences that constitute her subjectivity are condemned to oscillate constantly between life and death within the contradictions produced by slavery.

It seems to me that Rohith Vemula's suicide note is far more revealing if read within the context of untouchability as akin to slavery.[14] By all accounts, he was an effective student leader of the Ambedkar Student Association at Hyderabad University. According to the *Indian Express*:

- From July [2015], the university stopped paying Rohith his monthly stipend of Rs 25,000 (excluding House Rent Allowance, HRA), with friends alleging that he was targeted for raising issues under the banner of Ambedkar Students Association (ASA). A university official denied the allegation, blaming the delay on 'paperwork'.

- On August 5, the university set up an inquiry against Rohith and four other ASA members, two days after they allegedly assaulted ABVP leader N Susheel Kumar.

- On August 17, [Union minister Bandaru] Dattatreya wrote to HRD Minister urging action and claiming that the 'Hyderabad University...has in the recent past, become a den of casteist, extremist and anti-national politics'.

- After a series of flip-flops, the five were suspended in September. On December 17, the decision was upheld.

- On January 3, after the sanction was confirmed, the five moved out of their hostel rooms to a tent they set up inside the campus and began a 'relay hunger protest'.

- On Sunday, police recovered a 'suicide note' in the room where Rohith hanged himself. It read: 'I feel a growing gap between my soul and my body. And I have become a monster.'[15]

In addition to this relatively straightforward description by Janyala, Indian newspapers and magazines are full of accounts testifying to the Hindutva movement's draconian oppression of various minorities. In Vemula's case there is little doubt that the university authorities, egged on by Hindu nationalist student groups, drove him to his suicide. To state the obvious, the university's decision, supported and indeed instigated by the Moditva/Hindutva movement, to expel a group of Dalit students who were protesting against caste discrimination is itself a form and an instance of caste discrimination. As under slavery in the US and under the Apartheid government in South Africa, to protest against one's disfranchisement becomes a criminal offence. Apartheid law makes this form of exclusion crystal clear: in response to the civil-rights campaigns against Apartheid, the South African government passed the Suppression of Communism Act in 1950 and the Criminal Law Amendment Act in 1953. The former outlawed any action that 'aims at bringing about political, industrial, social or economic change within the Republic by the promotion of disturbance or disorder, by unlawful acts or omissions'. The latter act prohibits the violation of any law 'by way of protest or in support of any campaign against any law or in support of any campaign for the repeal or modification of any law'.[16] This absolutist exclusion is an explicit version of a set of laws that produces the Homo Sacer; the laws and social practices that produce the 'untouchable' are implicit versions of the same.[17]

The overwhelming effect of reading Vemula's suicide note is an impression that social divisions caused by untouchability have been internalised by the psyche so that, as under slavery, the subject becomes disaggregated. Untouchability, it seems, permeates the very structure of intrapsychic relations. It is always with himself, Vemula says, that he has problems: he feels his mind and body becoming alienated from one another; the self, he feels, is 'empty' and 'unconcerned' about itself; and the suicide is attributed to this 'unconcern' for himself. All of these are signs of psychic apparatuses unable to connect with each other, unable to touch each other, so that the psyche is unable to function as a 'coherent' or even semi-coherent unit. (Husserl's privileging of apodictic presence (a figure of coherence?) via the unique sense of touch, the double apprehension that characterises touch, is figured through the relationship between two fingers of the same hand, wherein each figure is capable of simultaneously being the touching and the touched.)

One of the most damaging aspects of psychic disaggregation is that the slave's or untouchable's inability to follow his desire and therefore to control his future robs him of all future-oriented teleology. This blockage manifests itself in Vemula's note as an aporia: on the one hand he says that there 'was no urgency' in his life; on the other hand, he feels he 'always was rushing. Desperate to start a new life'. This contradiction robs the subject of any temporal control. To the extent that one's life, as what Sartre calls a 'project', consists of an aggregation, organisation, and prioritisation of various teleologically oriented acts, a dysfunctional temporality militates against any attempt to weave a coherent trajectory for the self. Put differently, it seems that Vemula's experience and internalisation of his 'social death' deprives him of the very capacity to start a life. Untouchability as a cancerous contamination easily moves from the intrapsychic back to the interpersonal realm: the ability to love, he feels, is hampered by pain of rejection. Untouchability seems to permeate all social relations and indeed the only realm that remains uncontaminated by a 'living death' is the ontological realm, that which ironically is 'untouched' by humans: his love for 'stars [and] nature' is contrasted with sociogenic bonds 'which have long since divorced from nature.' He sees human feelings as 'second hand', human love as 'constructed', human beliefs as 'coloured', human sociality as produced and 'valid[ated] through artificial art.' In short, Vemula's experience of untouchability leads to a radical rupture between the realms of ontogeny and sociogeny, the former remaining the repository of purity while the latter has been contaminated by the horrors permitted by the structure of untouchability. The deep structure of Vemula's view of 'life' consists of rejecting 'life' in its entirety: 'Know that I am happy dead than being alive.' Desire for positive attachment is relegated to the onto-genic realm: 'I believe that I can travel to the stars.' It would seem that he has totally internalised his death and embraced (touched) it mentally and emotionally before physically killing himself.

This, the most striking aspect of his note, is formulated via a complex aporia that he repeats several times: 'My birth is my fatal accident.' 'Fatal' (from Latin *fatale*, meaning both predestined and deadly) defines the life of an individual as untouchable, as a form of 'social death', as a life that is always already foreclosed, a life full of debt that can never be paid off, as the life of a person categorically barred by those who are privileged to live a full life. This sense of predestined social death, however, is contradicted within the term 'fatal accident'. While one's birth is indeed always an accident in the sense that it is a product of infinite chance and innumerable circumstances, the process that fixes one as a slave (or as a racialised being or as an untouchable) produces an experience of what we might call 'accidental necessity'. When I am the subject of a racist society, I experience my racialisation as a necessity in the sense that I am categorised by definition, i.e. by social necessity, as a generic, inferior being: within the values and rules of that society I cannot escape that categorisation. However, my birth within a given group that is ostracised is, on the ontological register, a matter of chance and accident. The production of a racialised, genderised, enslaved, or outcast subject creates an aporetic experience that yokes social necessity with ontic accident, and Vemula's formulation captures the core of that aporia.

Finally, and most importantly, I think the sentence 'My birth is my fatal accident' should be read as a profound illocutionary utterance, which, accompanied by his suicide, transforms Rohith Vemula into a figure of political resistance. It takes his given condition of a socially dead being and transforms it via his actual death into a symbolic death, which is in effect the death of the subject position occupied by the slave and, at the same time, his rebirth in a different, now liberated and empowered subject position. Frederick Douglass, in the passage cited earlier, calls this a moment of 'resurrection'.[18] 'My birth is my fatal accident', when accompanied by his suicide, transforms Vemula from being one of thousands of Dalit victims of untouchability into a man who reconfigures and rearticulates his death as a political necessity. While his illocutionary gesture rendered him physically dead, it also ensured his political immortality. His suicide must be seen in the light of what Huey P. Newton called 'revolutionary suicide'.[19] Vemula's suicide, which must be distinguished from the myriad forms of self-destructive behaviors to which victims so often succumb, is a form of political agency that transforms his latent condition (social death) into a manifest condition (symbolic death). Rohith Vemula is dead; long live Rohith Vemula! His suicide resonates throughout the world, and, in doing so, it provides me (a random, disconnected observer) with the occasion to touch him—to touch him not as a transcendental subject touching an outcaste, untouchable object, but as one finger implicitly apprehending its presence and functionality by touching another finger of the same hand.

13

HINDUTVA INCORPORATION AND SOCIOCONOMIC EXCLUSION

THE ADIVASI DILEMMA

Nandini Sundar

The fundamental question that William Reich raises in his book, *The Mass Psychology of Fascism*, seems uncannily as if it could have been written for India today: 'What was it in the masses that caused them to follow a party the aims of which were, objectively and subjectively, strictly at variance with their own interests?'[1] While this applies to the Indian public at large, for whom successive measures like demonetisation and the accompanying loss of jobs, at least initially, barely dented,[2] and in many cases increased, the popularity of Narendra Modi, perhaps nowhere is this question more central than when discussing the fatal attraction that the BJP holds for Adivasis and Dalits. Why do Adivasis vote in such large numbers for a party which is clearly aligned with the industrialists who want to displace them; why do Dalits align with a party whose ruling ideology is so clearly contemptuous of them?[3] Even more unthinkably, enabled by skilful political alliances, in 2018 the BJP is in power in almost all the states of the Northeast—despite warnings by the church of their anti-Christian agenda, and despite the clear divergence between cultural practices like beef eating and the Hindi-Hindu-centred nature of the BJP. While political preferences cannot be read off from social origins or conditions like a map, and a vulgar theory of interests is bound to fail, what these questions also point to is the need to investigate how preferences are being shaped, as well as the irreducibility of politics, spectacle, power and money that determines voter allegiance.

Of course, voting does not fully reflect ideological preferences, and people vote for a variety of reasons—to get incumbent parties out of power, for a particular candidate, for money and other instrumental reasons.[4] In the case of Adivasis, electoral victories have several structural underpinnings. Unlike the Dalits, the Scheduled Tribes (STs) do not have common cause across states or leaders like Ambedkar and Mayawati who can represent them nationally. Even in areas where they are dominant, especially in the reserved seats, they do not vote uniformly.[5] In terms of political representatives too, most of them are beholden to their parties and to traders and corporate houses for election expenses, which means that they take pro-business stands as against the core interests of their tribal constituencies. In fact, some of the worst looting of natural resources has been witnessed under tribal leaders like Arjun Munda in Jharkhand. Moreover, as immigrants increasingly change the demographics of scheduled areas, candidates necessarily have to straddle the immigrant and ST vote. Finally, the aspirations of the scheduled tribes are themselves changing under the impact of the media, schooling and the market, and the slogan of 'jal, jangal, zameen' (water, forest/jungle, land) does not encapsulate all their political ambitions.

Votes are often produced by sheer efficiency and electoral machines, such as that increasingly perfected by the BJP under Amit Shah, whose sole mission in life other than getting himself and his accomplices out of difficult criminal cases appears to be to win elections.[6] But the BJP's electoral fortunes in 2018 and previously, were strongly scripted by RSS cadres, and fronts like the Vanvasi Kalyan Ashram, whose apparently disinterested but in practice deeply political 'social work' in areas of state lack are an important factor in getting the BJP votes.[7] The rise in RSS *shakhas* or cells in Tripura from 60 in 2014 to 265 in 2018 suggests that ideological indoctrination is both a reason and outcome of elections, in an ever-deepening spiral.[8]

Apart from its efficient electoral machinery, the BJP's enormous control over both mainstream media and social media ensures that what is simply doublespeak—being silent on beef bans in the Northeast but lynching Muslims over the same issue in mainland India—is pitched as clever 'ideological flexibility'. Much of the BJP's success in Nagaland and Tripura is also an outcome of clever silences and tantalising promises—holding out the promise of a 'framework agreement for Nagaland', and flirting with the Indigenous People's Front of Tripura's (IPFT) demand for a separate state without making any concrete guarantees.

On the other hand, there are several countervailing factors—such as the fundamental need to defend Adivasi land and resources, food preferences, and the long historical background of oscillation between Hindutva attempts at incorporation and Adivasi resistance—that suggest that the spread of Hindutva among Adivasi groups today will continue to be a fraught process, even if Adivasi assertion is nowhere yet as marked as Dalit pride. In understanding how Hindu nationalism is changing tribal India, both in the Northeast and in mainland India, one has to look back to see its historical roots and understand the present as a deepening of an old process. At the same time, there is something qualitatively new in the sheer weight of its dominance and aggression, which suggests that the Adivasis of India, like the country itself, are poised on the cusp of a major change.

Old and new forms of 'Sanskritisation': Changes in the Hindu mode of tribal absorption

The relations between Hindu incorporation and Adivasi politics go back centuries, in the mutual appropriation and antagonism of religious practices and cults. For instance, several scholars have noted the relationship between local Adivasi practices of animal spirit or tree worship, developing into the worship of Mother Goddesses and their further appropriation into Hinduism, through association with one of the Goddesses of the Hindu pantheon, generally Durga/Kali/Sakti, in order to form regional cults.[9]

At one level the old process of what N.K. Bose (1941) called the 'Hindu mode of Tribal absorption' continues, in which Adivasi cultures and beliefs were left intact for the most part except when they went against the grain of Brahmanical belief. As Manish Kunjam, an Adivasi leader in Bastar put it to me in an interview in 2016, there is a qualitative difference in the way that Hinduism and Christianity convert:

> The RSS enters Adivasi rituals and changes them from within, while Christian missionaries say point blank that Adivasis should not worship their traditional

gods. The RSS goes around telling people they are also Hindus. In the name of worshipping the village Devi, they introduce the worship of Hindu goddesses such as Sita and Durga, thus bringing in new elements into the Adivasis' traditional religion. Through songs and stories about Hindu gods like Ram and Sita, they influence people into thinking these gods are more powerful. Since there is no organised propaganda about our own gods, people think they are not as important.[10]

It is important to note that this kind of long term absorption has taken place not just under the aegis of the RSS but also a variety of Hindu sects, particularly Bhagat or temperance movements of different sorts. These do not necessarily have any direct political affiliations, and may even represent a form of assertion against the state,[11] but in today's context when the Hindu Right has been trying to consolidate several small sects under its umbrella, they often end up as force multipliers to RSS conversions.

The conversation practices of the state and 'modernisation'

'Modernisation' performs the same kind of role of changing identities and religious beliefs, albeit more insidiously. Old-fashioned Hinduisation is more total today because the reach of the post-colonial state, media and market is so much greater. State practices like censuses which record Adivasis as Hindus are major enablers in the conversion of Adivasis and others to Hinduism, and indeed, the decennial census has long been a battlefield for identity assertion.[12] However, state practice is contradictory, in that judicial pronouncements on Adivasi personal law have distinguished them from Hindus.[13]

Schools are a major purveyor of Hindu identity because most of the teachers in central India tend to be non-Adivasi outsiders, or even if they are Adivasis, are taught that 'culture' and 'modernity' require a certain kind of lifestyle. The reach of cell phones, Whatsapp forwards and television means that images celebrating Hindu festivals like Diwali or Holi are now common in Adivasi areas as well. I once got a Whatsapp forward showing a cow being brutally butchered by Muslims (Afghans judging by their attire) from an Adivasi friend in Bastar, with a line about how terrible this was. When I pointed out that his own community ate beef, he accepted the point, but the ease with which phones allow you to transmit views with only superficial absorption is worrying.

In addition to their own traditional festivals linked to the cycle of agriculture and forest flowerings, people have now started celebrating what they are repeatedly taught in schools are 'national' festivals. The huge amount of immigration into hitherto Adivasi-dominated regions also means that the sheer weight of immigrant rituals and festivals drowns out indigenous practices. At the entrance to Jagdalpur, the former capital of Bastar state, there is a huge statue to Maharana Pratap, the Rajput hero, while their own rebel hero Gunda Dhur who fought the British in 1910 is consigned to a small park on the side. However, in the last twenty years, thanks to Adivasi assertion at least a few local colleges, roads etc. have been named after Gund Dhur.

Unlike the process which Srinivas (1952, 1962) called Sanskritisation, when lower castes and Adivasi groups attempted to elevate themselves in the caste hierarchy through emulation of upper caste or dominant caste cultural practices, the emphasis in the current RSS regime is not on changes in caste position but belonging to a politically charged religion. The mode of Hinduisation promoted by the VHP and RSS is a profoundly aggressive and targetted phenomenon, as manifested in the campaigns over *ghar wapasi* or 'returning home' (suggesting that adivasis were always Hindu) which were conducted in the first NDA regime of 1999–2004, and which periodically resurface under BJP rule. RSS conversion is about identifying as a Hindu *vis-à-vis* other religious groups, and in many cases involves denying caste within Hinduism.

The long debate over 'conversion'

The accusation of forced and fraudulent conversion as a stick with which to beat Christian organisations is an old one that dates back to the pre-independence period, and one which had signifcant support within the Congress too. There was perhaps some truth in the charge—even Verrier Elwin, the well known proponent of Adivasi isolationism, reneged on his earlier positions and launched a broadside against Christian missionary activity in Mandla in the 1940s, allying with organisations like the Gond Seva Mandal and the Arya Dharam Seva Sangh, to shut down mission schools in Mandla.[14] However, Elwin seems to have played too easily into the hands of the Hindu Mahasabha whose contempt for him was in no way reduced by his new willingness to work with them.[15]

The setting up of the Vanvasi Kalyan Ashram (VKA), the main front of the RSS which deals with Adivasis, in 1949 is inextricably linked to their animus against Christian missionaries, as against any genuine desire for Adivasi welfare. Ironically, the founder of the VKA was sent to Jashpur on the advice of the Gandhian A.V. Thakkar with the support of then Congress Chief Minister of Madhya Pradesh Ravi Shankar Shukla. The VKA now has branches across the country. They run hostels for Adivasi children, conduct games, carry out health work in villages etc. In the process, they slowly indoctrinate the children and their parents to hate people from other religions.[16] Even in government schools, children are taken off to attend RSS *shakhas*.[17]

The Niyogi Commission, or the Christian Missionaries Enquiry Commission as it is officially known, was another moment when the interests of the RSS and the Congress government of Madhya Pradesh meshed rather well. Set up by the Shukla government in 1954 under the chairmanship of Dr. Bhawani Shankar Niyogi, retired justice of the Nagpur high court, the Commission's mandate was to enquire into complaints that Christian missionaries used force or monetary incentives to convert people. Given its composition and methods, the Commission's findings were a foregone conclusion, with all the blame falling on missionaries.

The first NDA regime under Atal Bihari Vajpayee saw a huge resurgency of anti-missionary ideology, with the gruesome burning alive of Graham Staines in Odisha, attacks on churches in the Dangs, mass 'reconversion programmes' in Jashpur and so on. Massive programmes were organised to bring Adivasis into the Hindu fold, and leaders like Swami Aseemanand, Asaram Bapu, Swami Lakshmananda and others became prominent. As one citizen's enquiry committee noted in 2006:

> But the real design is to convert adivasis into the Hindutva version of Hinduism, in the name of ghar-vapasi (homecoming) and shudhikaran (purification). This process in the region received a great boost on 18 January, 2002 when almost 2.5 lakh adivasis were mobilised to join a Vishal Hindu Mahasangam (grand Hindu gathering) at Jhabua in neighbouring Madhya Pradesh. For over 100 days, 300 full timers of Vanvasi Kalyan Parishad and Vishwa Hindu Parishad fanned out to the remotest villages of the Jhabua district, distributed photographs and statues of Hindu gods and goddesses, particularly Hanuman, and adivasis were taught Hindu pooja (worship), rituals and bhajans. In the last seven days of the preparations of Vishal Hindu Mahasangam, more than 4000 Sangh workers lived with tribal leaders in their family homes. Firebrand Hindutva speakers like Praveen Togadia and Sadhvi Ritambhara addressed the Mahasangam, and their speeches were characteristically laced with provocation, hate and venom. Next at Alirajpur (again in Madhya Pradesh) in February 2004, a Hindu Sangam was organised, in which about 40,000 adivasis participated.[18]

Service work

One of the ways in which the BJP has ensured that its service organisations are the only game in town is by cutting off funds to all possible competitors, both secular NGOs and Christian organisations. For instance in 2017, the *Guardian* reported that 'India's largest international donor, the Christian charity Compassion International, was forced to cease its Indian operations in March after the government cut off its foreign funding over concerns it was using the money for proselytisation.'[19]

The RSS fronts have also been able to operate with almost complete impunity, even when they engage in patently illegal acts. For instance, in 2016, journalist Neha Dixit reported how thirty-one girls (mostly tribal) from five border districts of Assam, including very small ones, were trafficked by Sangh organisations—Sewa Bharati, Rashitriya Sevika Samiti—to Punjab and Gujarat and placed in Saraswati Shishu Mandirs in order to 'Hinduise them'. Despite directions to return them by the Assam State Commission for the Protection of Child Rights and other semi-government organisations, the Sangh organisations managed to evade the orders thanks to their BJP-controlled parent governments.[20] Rather than anything happening to the abductors, the magazine which reported the story suffered a major pushback by the government, leading to an overhaul of its editorial staff.

In Bastar too in 2015, a father told me of four children from his village being taken away by an organisation to Haridwar. He had not seen his child for two years. In any case, the 'children of Naxal victims' are often taken away by Sangh organisations and trained in their schools.

Violence—mass violence and small scale incidents

Perhaps the most large-scale incident of anti-Christian violence in the recent past took place in 2008 in Kandhamal, Odisha, when the killing of Swami Lakshmananda by the Maoists was used as a pretext to unleash a pogrom against Dalit and Adivasi Christians. According to one report: 93 people were killed, over 350 churches and worship places which belonged to the Adivasi Christians and Dalit Christians were destroyed, around 6,500 houses were burnt or demolished, over forty women were subjected to rape, molestation and humiliation, and several educational, social service and health institutions were destroyed and looted. More than 56,000 people were displaced.[21]

Since the BJP came to power in 2014, the frequent lynching of Muslims and attacks by cow vigilantes has dominated the news, but the attacks on Christians have also been a recurring theme,[22] especially in the tribal and Dalit pockets of Chhattisgarh, Maharashtra, Madhya Pradesh and Odisha. Unlike Kandhamal, or Gujarat in 2002, most of these have been sporadic and small scale to escape widespread outrage. Churches have been destroyed, pastors attacked, a nun sexually assaulted etc. Apart from the national government choosing to celebrate good governance day on Christmas in 2014, forcing children and teachers to come to school, several BJP states have made their anti-conversion laws more draconian.

It is true that evangelisation, especially driven by American funds, and under the influence of the Joshua Project and such like, is vastly increasing, and the tribal areas of Telangana and Andhra Pradesh are dotted with small churches. Church services can take several hours with people giving testimonies and extended sermons by the pastors. But while this introduces all sorts of tensions within villages as the converts stop contributing to collective village events, the tension is exacerbated and turned into local level violence by the VHP.[23]

The enabling power of hate: The pride of the newly recruited footsoldier

Since at least 2002, Adivasis have been deployed as footsoldiers in the RSS's pogroms: in 2002, Adivasis were used to attack Bohra Muslims in Godhra, Tejgadh etc.;[24] and from 2005 onwards young Adivasi boys have been conscripted as Special Police Officers in Chhattisgarh, Maharashtra and elsewhere ostensibly to fight against Maoists but in reality to divide and defeat formerly united villages. Under the aegis of the Central Reserve Police Force (CRPF) and local police, a slow conversion under the garb of modernisation is also visible.

In the last couple of decades, the RSS has even more aggressively mobilised among Dalits by appealing to local heroes like Raja Suhel Dev.[25] Among Adivasis too, RSS texts and practices involve some degree of acknowledgement of local traditions, even as the overall thrust is on Hinduising and 'civilising' them.

Finally, one way in which Adivasi religion is being systematically destroyed is through mining on their sacred hills such as Niyamgiri in Odisha, Raoghat in Chhattisgarh, and Surjagarh in Maharashtra. These are sites where festivals are celebrated with people coming from distant places. However, there is little acknowledgement of this on the part of the state; no facilities are provided, and instead the sites are cordoned off with heavy paramilitary presence.

Resistance

While the Hindutva onslaught is overpowering there are also a few signs of resistance, both on the cultural and political fronts. The assertion is particularly marked among some communities like the Santhal and Bodos, who have developed their own script and are publishing extensively in these languages, but is slowly spreading elsewhere too.[26] Here I present just one example of what form this assertion can take.

Of late, Mahisasur/Mahishasura has become something of an icon of resistance against Hindutva. In 2016, Hindutva forces (as well as sections of the Congress) accused JNU students, Adivasi leaders and others attempting to celebrate Mahisasur with upsetting Hindu sentiments. In 2016 an FIR was registered against Adivasi leader Manish Kunjam under Section 295 (intentionally insulting the religion of a particular class) of the IPC for forwarding a Whatsapp message about Durga and Mahisasur. The FIR against Manish Kunjam led to local anger among Adivasi leaders.

The message started by asking rhetorically who Durga was (answer: a *veshya* or sex worker) and who Mahisasur was (answer: a *moolnivasi* raja, or indigenous king), and asked the reader to ponder over why in Bengal, Durga idols are considered incomplete till earth is brought from the house of a sex worker. It is another matter that sex workers are beginning to resent this.[27] The Whatsapp goes on to explain the origins of this practice saying that the Brahmins, being unable to fairly defeat in arms the brave Santhal raja, Mahisasur, sent a beautiful sex worker, Durga. She plied him with alcohol and other amusements for eight days till on the ninth day, seeing her chance, she killed him. The message goes on to say that the Brahmins not only defeated the *moolnivasi* raja, but actually made the Adivasis worship his killer, Durga (Shakti being seen as an appropriation of an Adivasi mother goddess). It also asks readers whether deities/demons with several arms and half animal bodies can actually exist as humans, and to think rationally about these depictions. Finally, it addresses the *moolnivasi samaj*—who had been prevented by Brahmanical ideology from reading for themselves—to awake and recognise their ideological subjection. The message ends with '*Namo Buddhai, Jai Bharat, Jai Moolnivasi*' (Greetings to Buddha, Victory to India, Victory to the Indigenous).

Durga's position is ambivalent—indicative of the long history of appropriation and exclusion and symbolising perhaps the ultimate fate of the Adivasi under Hindutva. The dark skinned Durga can be seen as both originally an Adivasi goddess as well as (once appropriated by the gods) the slayer of an Adivasi king, Mahisasur, in some primal form of counterinsurgency where Adivasis are pitted against Adivasis. Even as Hindutva is appropriating and denying Adivasi gods, it is also facing resistance from a wide variety of Adivasi groups. The battle remains joined.

14

KASHMIRIS IN THE HINDU *RASHTRA*

Mridu Rai

If general elections in May 2014 had brought the Bharatiya Janata Party (BJP) to national power—and Narendra Modi to the office of prime minister—with an unexpectedly commanding majority, the year ended with another record-making victory in state elections. The party had, for the first time in its history, made an inroad into the elected power structure of Jammu and Kashmir (J&K) and formed a coalition government with the Kashmir-based People's Democratic Party (PDP). Since 2014, then, Kashmir is at perihelion with the Hindu *rashtra* (Hindu nation) or at least the ambition of bringing one into being. It has been feeling more directly than before the heat of the rhetoric and agendas the BJP and its affiliated organisations the Rashtriya Swayamsevak Sangh (RSS) and the Vishwa Hindu Parishad (VHP) deploy through their ideology of Hindutva (Hindu-ness). In this project Kashmiri Muslims are made to serve as contrapuntal symbols—of terrorist violence, illegitimate religious impulses, sedition—for contriving a mythical Hindu nation. As is argued here, this evocatory purpose Kashmiris serve is so essential to Hindutva's discursive politics that it renders any 'resolution' of the

Kashmir 'problem' an unlikely prospect under the Modi-led BJP. This essay discusses the place of Kashmiris in this re-imagination of the Hindu nation.

Dominance through impunity

Since 1989, when Kashmiris began a popularly backed armed rebellion against Indian rule, the Valley's civil society has experienced the highest level of militarisation anywhere in the world. There are about 700,000 members of the Indian armed forces in the Valley, producing an astonishing average of one soldier for every eleven civilians. As a result, the death toll is in calamitous figures at perhaps 70,000 killed. Equally disquieting is the number of those forcibly 'disappeared'—some 8000—many of them probably dead. War waged through the rape of women, children and incarcerated men, torture, the declining health of civil liberties, and of the mental worlds of individuals, has many worried. Deaths here are not all the outcome of conflict between armed opponents; many of those killed in Kashmir have been bystanders caught in crossfire, victims of extra-judicial executions or of custodial torture. In a disturbing revelation in 2009, the investigations of the International People's Tribunal on Human Rights and Justice in Indian-administered Kashmir (IPTK) uncovered 2,700 unmarked graves and over 2,943 unidentified bodies from fifty-five villages across the Valley. Contrary to the state's routine claims that those buried were unnamed foreign militants, the IPTK concluded that many (in those cases where the remains could be exhumed and identified) were local Kashmiris, some militant and others not, either killed through extra-judicial means or 'disappeared' by Indian security forces.[1]

In Kashmir after 1990, then, there has been less governance—as most people would understand the term—than control of its population through the daily infliction of terror and violence. As the IPTK's report puts it, the 'diverse techniques of rule used by the military and paramilitary in Kashmir generate and circulate death and the fear of death'.[2] This unacknowledged psychological strategy supplements the overt use of force to crush civilian resistance and its support for the insurgency. Projecting Kashmir as an intractable security threat has authorised the operation of a variety of laws and practices (discussed below) that sanction impunity in the agents—civilian, military or paramilitary—of Indian occupation. The preference for militarisation and militaristic modes of dominance has allowed the Indian state to eschew its responsibility both of administering Kashmir through democratic engagement with its people and of seeking negotiated settlement with all segments of the political public. Modi's government has shifted this security state's apparatus into high gear and infused it with a new symbolism to design the dominance of a Hindu *rashtra*.

The new BJP

The BJP has been in national office before. However, its current structure and political tenor is significantly different from the last time it had held power under Prime Minister Atal Bihari Vajpayee (1996, and 1998–2004). First, under Vajpayee the BJP may have been the largest single party at the centre but it had depended on a coalition of several political groups together forming the National Democratic Alliance (NDA). In 2014 Modi's BJP was still part of the NDA but having established a majority in the lower house of parliament on its own it was relatively unshackled from (and un-moderated by) its earlier dependence on coalition partners.[3] The BJP can bulldoze its preferred policies through parliament by the sheer heft of its numbers in the Lok Sabha (the lower house).[4]

Second, in its earlier presentation in power—except for a brief period during and following the Kargil 'war' (May–July 1999) and the attack on the Indian parliament (13 October 2001)—the BJP had cultivated détente with Pakistan. With the loosening of tensions with the rival national claimant to Kashmir, many saw in Vajpayee's administration a unique period of willingness to engage with the concerns of all Kashmiris. Poetically inclined, he composed a catchy slogan to capture the spirit of conciliation he intended for his government, undertaking to explore paths to peace within the framework of '*Insaaniyat, Jamhooriyat aur Kashmiriyat*' (humanity, democracy and Kashmiri-ness).[5] In the end, these remained imaginative but empty words. However, when his government invited the separatist All Parties Hurriyat Conference[6] leaders to talks in early 2004—ultimately fruitless—he had gone further than Modi has done despite appropriating Vajpayee's famous catchphrase. Under Modi, Delhi's stance towards Pakistan has displayed heightened bellicosity, celebrating 'surgical strikes' on Pakistani territory as acts of vengeance, and warning of ever more drastic action.[7] This raising of the walls is matched by aggressive measures in Kashmir, as discussed below, in the name of securing the nation from alleged terrorism exported by Pakistan.

Third, while the BJP under Vajpayee was a centralised organisation, it was nothing like the monolithic entity under the absolutist direction of a single leader—Narendra Modi—it has become since 2014.[8] The erasure of contending voices in the party's national leadership is matched by subservience imposed on regional satraps.[9] Indeed, the functioning of the BJP's state units—including in J&K—is calibrated to duplicate on the ground the party's priorities at the centre. Its parts have been assembled into a centrally operated machine modulated to the single-minded pursuit of electoral victory. To the latter end, the ideology of Hindutva—if it ever had any moral depth—has been compacted into easily digestible essentialisations for both mobilising and manufacturing animosity towards different groups moulded into undeserving, pampered/appeased citizens. These include *inter alia* Dalits, Muslims, Christians and women, against whom violence in different forms has been unleashed with extraordinary flagrancy since 2014.

More dangerously still, Modi's BJP has gone beyond the party structure itself to unleash a populist Hindutva through a number of freewheeling individuals and groups. These stormtroopers—whose actions the party can disavow when necessary since they have no formal affiliation with it—have *carte blanche* to engage in hate-speech and to perpetrate a range of atrocities against groups such as those mentioned above. Such acts have gone unchecked, drawing at most ambiguous verbal reprimand from the party's highest rank-holders long after their effect of terrorising non-compliant members of civil society has been achieved. Therefore, even while the party leadership can conceal its Hindu supremacist agenda under the guise of '*vikas*' (development), its foot soldiers advance Hindutva's murkier work in full public view. These new attributes of the BJP have had deleterious effects in Kashmir.

The BJP-PDP coalition in J&K

In state elections held in November and December 2014, the BJP had won twenty-five of the eighty-seven seats in J&K and the PDP twenty-eight. The Jammu and Kashmir National Conference (NC) and the Congress party had won fifteen and twelve seats respectively, with the seven remaining going to other parties and independents. Ahead of the polls, however, the BJP had declared its goal was to win forty-four or more seats; this would have required bagging most in Jammu and some in Kashmir and Ladakh. It struck out everywhere but in Jammu (where it secured twenty-five of the thirty-seven seats in contention). As the party with the second largest tally of seats, however, it earned its ticket to govern through power sharing. On 1 March 2015, the PDP and the BJP assumed the reins of government jointly. The chief minister was a Kashmiri: that was the PDP's Mufti Mohammad Sayeed, succeeded, after his death on 7 January 2016, by his daughter Mehbooba Mufti.

As Mufti Sayeed had stated at the outset, the coming together of two parties with such dissimilar ideologies was as the merging of the north and south poles. The Common Minimum Programme (CMP) they negotiated contained, to the chagrin of the BJP's Jammu cadres, elements indicating the Modi government's determination outwardly to conciliate the Kashmiri half of the alliance. The coalition partners undertook to follow Vajpayee's principles mentioned earlier. They pledged to 'initiate a sustained and meaningful dialogue with all internal stakeholders' and 'all political groups irrespective of their ideological views and predilections.' The Hurriyat Conference was presumably included. The CMP committed also to re-examining the situation in so-called 'disturbed areas' with a view to advising the union government on whether the Armed Forces Special Powers Act (AFSPA) should continue to apply there.[10] The greatest blow for the more hard-nosed BJP politicians in J&K was the declaration that the *status quo* on Article 370 was to remain.

These concessions represented a significant climb-down for the BJP's state politicians. They were being asked to set aside an older troika of ideas popularised by Shyama Prasad Mookerjee, the founder in 1951 of the Bharatiya Jan Sangh (BJS), the precursor of the BJP. The slogan of '*Ek Vidhan, Ek Pradhan aur Ek Nishan*' (One constitution, one sovereign head and one flag) had demanded the full integration of J&K with India through the abrogation of article 370. This was a cause for which many Hindus in Jammu had agitated under the leadership of the Praja Parishad party with the support of the RSS and BJS between 1949 and 1953; it had remained a live wire since. And Modi had re-energised it when he had paid homage to the movement during his election campaign in the state in 2014.

However, for the central BJP leadership, claiming some manner of victory in Muslim-majority J&K—no matter how superficial—was worth appearing to be sensitive to Kashmiri concerns. The cost of paying lip service to Kashmiri demands was cheap while yielding rich dividends by enabling the party to float the lotus over one more province. As of June 2018, the party controls—either independently or in a coalition—twenty of the twenty-nine states of the union. India tinted saffron is the BJP's aim, no matter how weak the wash.[11] The rescindment of article 370 and the complete subsumption of all parts and aspects of India in a monolithic, centralised 'Hindu' sovereignty may be Hindutva's final ambition but until that shore is reached, every pragmatic compromise must provide a stepping-stone in its direction. State cadres would have to bend before this priority. In November 2015, Hari Om Mahajan, a senior leader from Jammu, was suspended (for six years) from the BJP for publicly criticising his party's policies including its alliance with the PDP.

While the state unit of the BJP is not permitted to disrupt the grander designs of the central leadership, it is not discouraged from pandering to its local Hindu constituency in conjunction with non-party saffron organisations. There are several causes that have been exploited by them such as agitating for the rights of mostly Hindu and Sikh refugees settled in the state following Partition and, on the other hand, mobilising for the expulsion of the less than 6,000 Muslim Rohingya refugees who, also escaping violence and persecution, live in Jammu. But an effort at Hindu mustering that provoked particular outrage—in Kashmir, India and internationally—related to the abduction, rape and murder in January 2018 of Asifa, an eight-year-old girl of the Muslim Bakerwal community, in the Kathua district of Jammu. Following investigations, eight Hindu men, including four policemen and a former government-functionary-turned-priest, were accused of the crime. Hindu opinion in Jammu was rapidly rallied in defence of the accused. On 9 April Hindu lawyers attempted to physically prevent the police from filing charges in court. At the same time, Hindu Right-wing groups in Jammu organised demonstrations in support of the eight suspects with two BJP ministers of the J&K government attending one such rally. Finally, Narendra Modi made contact with the Indian public via two tweets on 13 April, condemning in conspicuously generic language such 'incidents'[12] regardless of 'which state or area they occurred in'. The latter statement served to minimise the particular vexation the Hindu Right-wingers' actions represented in the context of J&K. Modi's tweets equally noticeably omitted any condemnation of the BJP legislators who had supported the Hindu Right-wing defenders of the rapists and murderers.[13] There could be no more telling illustration of the roles the party's state cadres and populist Hindutva-infused groups were encouraged to play in keeping the political temperature up.

But, as mentioned earlier, resolving the 'Kashmir problem' has not been a priority for the national BJP. A Kashmir in turmoil allows the state to fortify itself endlessly. Instantiating strategic disingenuousness, the party has avoided frontal assaults on long-standing Kashmiri demands, working instead through proxies—its state unit, the RSS, Kashmiri Pandit organisations, and even the armed forces—to keep the political climate volatile. This is not to suggest that the BJP has created the troubles in Kashmir *ex nihilo*; no Indian party is innocent of political malfeasance in the Valley. But there has been a new intensity not only in the smothering of rebellion but also in provoking it. No less significantly, an ever-restive Muslim Kashmir has provided a valuable foil against which both dissent and difference in India itself has been sought to be erased to support the construction of a monolithic upper-caste-dominated Hindu *rashtra*.

Territorialising identity: religion and race

Kashmir is isolated through various discursive strategies to make it serve both as a dangerous exception threatening the Indian/Hindu body politic but also as a containable menace. A speciality of the Hindu Right—shared in different degrees by other parties—has been the construct of religious differences mapped onto the three sub-regional segments of the state. This becomes the basis for a three-way perspectival division of the state. In this view, Jammu is Hindu, Ladakh Buddhist and Kashmir Muslim. The BJP has reinterpreted the outcome of the 2014 elections to confirm this understanding. Its majority win there made Hindu Jammu a reality—and 'the backbone of the nation in the state'[14]—and its routing in the Valley reinforced the paradigm that Kashmir is Muslim and anti-national. But the BJP won no seats in Ladakh either: the Congress won three out of four, an independent Shia candidate taking the last. Yet a supposedly Buddhist Ladakh—Hindutva claims Buddhists as 'their own' on the erroneous premise that their religion is merely an offshoot of Hinduism—is automatically assimilable in the *rashtra*. On demographic grounds alone, this classification is an oversimplification.[15] While the largest proportion of Kashmir's population is undoubtedly Muslim, significant parts of Hindu-majority Jammu are overwhelmingly Muslim, too. And Muslims are in a majority in one of the two districts of supposedly Buddhist Ladakh.[16] But the more significant question is whether numbers alone permit the essentialising of any territory along lines of religion. The answer of Hindu Right-wingers is resoundingly in the affirmative since their majoritarian politics of claiming India as a Hindu *rashtra* functions precisely through such logic. Kashmiri Muslims, though a majority in the Valley, are successfully outnumbered in a sea of Hindu Indians.

Hindutva's aim of crafting internal religious 'others' is also reinforced through racialising discourses tacked onto territorially nationalist rigidities. As Mona Bhan shows, Hindu supremacist groups—particularly the RSS—have worked systematically to claim Buddhists even in Muslim-majority Kargil as 'pure Aryans' and therefore essentially Hindus. This is part of a broader project that aims 'to Hinduise Kashmir's border regions within the context of the ongoing Kashmiri struggle for *azadi* [freedom]'.[17] The latter is reconfigured not as a political struggle for long overdue rights but as an illicit

Islamic jihad. This works in tandem with support for the native Hindus of Kashmir—the Pandits—and their contention that they are the 'aboriginal' inhabitants of the Valley banished by violent Muslims engaged in sedition against the nation since 1989. A British colonial, Indian nationalist, and their own versions of history and sociology had already construed Pandits not just as the 'first peoples' of Kashmir but also, since they all claim to be Brahmans steeped in chaste Sanskrit learning, as among the highest Aryans. The default position ascribed to Kashmiri Muslims is that of the non-Aryan alien excrescent element in the organic Hindu/Aryan national body. Needless to say the racialising rhetoric to seclude or exclude Kashmiri Muslims is forced against the grain of both historical and ethnological evidence. Only a minority of Kashmir's Muslims are descendants of 'outsiders'; the vast majority were converted over centuries after the fourteenth from the same 'stock', so to speak, as the Pandits. Such inconsistencies notwithstanding, Hindutva's rhetoric constructs all Muslims in India as racially foreign and—when placed on a scale that privileges 'Aryans' as the genetically 'pure' master race—as inferior peoples (the *mleccha* or unclean barbarian of classical Brahmanical Sanskrit). Such thinking has seeped into the minds of India's agents administering occupation in Kashmir, slipping out as justification when applying the crudest force. Angana P. Chatterji's conversations in 2011 with illegally detained Muslim pro-freedom protestors in Kashmir are revealing. Police officers attempting to extort confessions of guilt compounded physical violence with verbal denigration. One particular detainee was told: 'Your "race" is deranged. You are criminals.... Your mother is a whore'. His reply could only be uttered privately as he fainted from pain: that Kashmiris 'are a people, not a race' whose struggles are 'against India's brutalities'.[18]

Chatterji's interview dates to 2011 when a Congress-led alliance held power at the centre. However, such racialised differentiation of Muslims has been the stock-in-trade of Hindu Right-wing constituencies at least since the foundation of the Hindu Mahasabha (1915) and the RSS (1925); it is only more recently that this perspective has acquired state power. In any case, as Chatterji writes elsewhere, there has been a longer history of alignment of the Indian military and paramilitary forces 'with Hindu majoritarian ideological interests vis-à-vis Jammu and Kashmir'. This is seen, for instance, in the armed forces' cooperation 'with Hindu nationalist/militant groups' in campaigns such as Operation *Sadbhavana* (Goodwill) launched in 1998 ostensibly to promote development and empowerment activities among civilians in J&K but in fact extending the military's capacity to both 'control and appease civil society'.[19]

Of course, the Congress party is no stranger to religious majoritarian politics. Indira Gandhi had introduced it in J&K most demonstrably during her electoral campaign in 1983 when, confronted with the NC's reluctance to form an alliance in Kashmir, she cynically invoked the danger that Kashmiris (Muslims) posed to national integrity in order to cultivate Hindu voters in Jammu.[20] And there is no denying that the Congress has also indulged in what is termed 'soft-Hindutva' to steal the thunder from the BJP's 'hard-Hindutva'. However, the Congress variety of majoritarian politics eschews defining India as the nation of a racially pure homogenous Aryan/Hindu people. No matter how tattered the Congress' secular principles in actuality, even the formal adherence to them has salvaged some room for at least the idea of a composite Indian nation. Actuated by political opportunism, over the decades the Congress has sought to cultivate so many different social, cultural and economic constituencies—upper-caste, lower-caste, rural, urban, tribal, religious minorities—that it cannot afford the reduction of the national essence to a single religio-cultural group. The Congress, however, is responsible for opening the door to Hindutva forces and giving them the opportunity to usurp with greater brazenness (and arguably more efficiently) its own more improvisatory politics of religion. The greater danger posed by the BJP's majoritarian discourse under Modi is that its invocation of a racially homogenous nation hinges on what Carl Schmitt had called 'the friend/enemy' distinction in public life allowing the political leader to decide whom one could live with and with whom not.[21] Such a perspective leaves groups marked as different, open even to extermination with the assurance that any violence against them will be met with either approbation or acquiescence-through-silence from large numbers of upper-caste Hindus in India—the tacit core of the nation.

The violent Kashmiri Muslim

On 13 December 2014, while addressing a rally in Jammu, Modi commended all the people of J&K for sending 'a clear message to the world that the EVM [electronic voting machine] is more powerful than the AK-47' especially in elections so 'important for [the] integrity and sovereignty of India'.[22] The high voter turnout even among Kashmiris (65 per cent) was cause for jubilation. Modi was assuming—like many Indians have always simplistically done—that Kashmiris in the polling booth were endorsing India's sovereignty and integrity. Another unfounded supposition in his statement was that the 'bullet'—a preference for violent means of expressing the popular will—has been the norm in Kashmir (the EVMs were the nationalist Hindu's weapon). What is forgotten is the long history of rigged elections, climaxing in 1987, which had been one among a series of provocations that turned most Kashmiris away from the ballot and some towards armed insurgency. But that connection is routinely ignored and 'terrorism' is made to emerge fully formed from unexplored shadows. This has also provided the state with an alibi for the use of extreme force against even non-combatants and to impose draconian laws— such as the AFSPA and the Public Safety Act (1978, amended in 1990)[23]— that bear down heavily on civilians. The constructed symbol of the violent Kashmiri Muslim—for whom a 'state of exception' is declared, putting them beyond the pale of ordinary laws and the entitlement to human rights—has been useful for instituting a social contract among some citizens that creates India as an orderly, secular, non-violent democratic nation.

Not only must Kashmiris be Muslims but also of a virulent kind in the order of Islamists and jihadis. The assumption is that the struggle for *azadi* or freedom is no more than a cover for founding a violent theocracy. The call by some Kashmiris for a '*Nizam-e-Mustafa*'—by which is meant a rightful social and political order—is wildly misinterpreted to connote a desire for 'rule by mullahs'. The involvement of Pakistani outfits such as the Lashkar-e-Taiyyaba (LeT) or the Jaish-e-Muhammad (JM) in strikes against Indian security forces, their small numbers notwithstanding, corroborates such thinking. Equally incriminating is the presence, among the separatist leaders, of the Jamat-e-Islami (JI) led by Syed Ali Shah Geelani; the JI's goal since its foundation has been the breaking away of Kashmir from India and its merger with Pakistan. What is obfuscated, however, is that while Geelani himself may be held in high regard among many Kashmiris, his vision of Kashmir's future in Pakistan is not shared by most. Several admittedly impressionistic surveys have suggested that the ideology of independence—abjuring both India and Pakistan—based on a secular and democratic polity remains the most widely supported in Kashmir (and opposed in Jammu and Ladakh). It is only through determined distortion that Kashmiris opposed to Delhi's rule can be made into Islamist terrorists working to establish an ISIS-style Caliphate. Similarly, it is only through deliberately mangling reality that the BJP proclaimed that a 'Hindu can never be a terrorist'.[24]

The branding of Kashmiri Muslims as irredeemably violent underlies also the BJP's plan announced in 2015 of setting up protected settlements in the Valley for repatriated Pandit refugees, effectively quarantining their Muslim neighbours from them. And then, following Burhan Wani's killing (discussed below) on 8 July 2016, the anger of some Kashmiri Muslims allegedly spilled into incidents of stone throwing on Pandit 'transit camps'. Kashmiri Pandits reacted with anxiety and anger. Relying on such reports, the novelist Siddhartha Gigoo wrote of 'raging mobs of Muslim youth pelt[ing] stones' at these camps and such 'persecution' forcing Pandits already once displaced 'to leave Kashmir...again and return to the camps' in Jammu.[25]

However, Gigoo's ire may have been misdirected. While all major segments of Kashmiri Muslim opinion have openly welcomed the return of the Pandits, they have also opposed all proposals for setting up segregated colonies for Pandits. They may have good reason to be suspicious of the BJP government's motives, seeing such measures as cynical attempts to pit one religious group against the other. The history of displaced Pandits since 1990 has shown that not all of them have been immune to having their suffering hijacked by the Hindu Right. Gigoo's characterisation of the stone-pelting on Pandit transit camps as 'persecution'—a repetition of alleged religiously-based 'persecution' in 1990—perhaps unwittingly illustrates the alignment of his community's thinking with that of Hindu supremacists.

While Pandits view the reassurances by 'separatist' groups of a safe return to their homeland with cynicism, perhaps the Hindu Right's motivations merit some scepticism too. It is telling that the Modi government's proposal for separate Pandit settlements was twinned with a plan to establish '*sainik* (soldiers') colonies' for retired members of the armed forces. Presumably the Pandits and soldiers are to serve as the pillars of Hindutva's annexation of the Valley. Indeed, Tarun Vijay of the BJP, purportedly the scheme's mastermind, said India's soldiers had earned 'a piece of [the] land' for which 'they have been shedding their blood'. The colonising aim was also explicit in Vijay's suggestion that settling former soldiers would 'bring the fragrance of Indianness and the principal mainstream of patriotic India' to Kashmir thereby overpowering 'the smell of stone-pelting and guns'.[26]

Beyond exploiting its rhetorical value, the BJP's actual investment in a Pandit return 'with honour' has been cosmetic. A news report from February 2018 describes the shoddy arrangements at the Hawl transit camp in Pulwama district (Kashmir) where the state has only provided derelict pre-fabricated huts devoid of electricity or water. Interestingly, Pandits located at Hawl accuse the state of having purposefully located them to in an area where 'militant attacks were on the rise'.[27] Pandits repatriated through protected segregation function as the vanguard of an irredentist Hindu *rashtra*. They serve as constant reminders of the incompatibility of the violent Kashmiri Muslim's

traditions with those of a peaceable Hindu nation. The state's security apparatus, while ostensibly intended to protect Pandits, functions also as guardians
of the boundaries separating the two radically differentiated 'cultures'—one a
'friend', the other an 'enemy'.

Kashmiri Pandits and Kashmir's special status

On 1 October 2017, just over two and a half years after the BJP-PDP coalition
took office, the deputy chief minister of the state, Nirmal Singh (BJP), reiterated that 'Article 370 had caused more harm than anything'. A day earlier the
RSS chief, Mohan Bhagwat, had demanded an amendment of India's constitution 'for the people of Jammu and Kashmir to be completely assimilated with
the rest of the country'.[28] The BJP at the Centre, while allowing its state cadres
and the RSS to keep stoking the issue, has made no move to abrogate the
offending article. That symbol is worth more barely alive than absolutely dead.

The most significant aspects of autonomy embodied in Article 370 had
been whittled decades ago; by 1964–65 there were only a few contentious
issues remaining. Among them is the reservation of certain entitlements
within the state to 'permanent residents', namely the rights to acquire immov-
able property, to vote in elections and eligibility for certain government positions and scholarships. Article 35A of the Indian constitution, added under
article 370 through a Presidential Order in 1954, not only allows the state's
legislature to define who permanent residents are but also guarantees these
special provisions for them.

Ironically, these were (except voting rights), beneficences the Dogra *maharaja* Hari Singh had granted in 1927 following agitations spearheaded by his
more privileged Hindu subjects especially Pandits; their concern had been to
stem the steady accumulation of wealth (including land) by and recruitment
to the administration's higher rungs of growing numbers of 'outsiders'. But until
recently, it was non-Pandit Hindu supremacists who had demanded the withdrawal of such reservations for permanent residents. National integration being
the highest goal, the only way to achieve it, in their view, was by allowing patriotic (Hindu) Indians to make the state—especially the Valley—their home.

On 27 August 2017, at its annual national convention held in Jammu,
Panun Kashmir (Our Own Kashmir)—a reactionary organisation of migrant
Pandits founded in 1991—also demanded, besides its long-standing plea to
rescind article 370, the revocation of article 35A. This was an unexpected
move since Pandits had campaigned so vigorously for the special provisions

enshrined in it. Another demand made at the same meeting was an old one—mooted since 1991—for a centrally administered union territory to be carved out in the Valley as their separate homeland.[29] One would have thought that such a homeland would have been best guaranteed precisely by article 35A. An explanation for this turn-around may lie in the altered outlook of Pandit refugees. Many have come to view their community's return to Kashmir an unrealistic prospect so long as the insurgency continues. Therefore, the protections article 35A provided have become irrelevant to them. Allowing large numbers of Hindus to acquire land, employment and other incentives to settle in the state may be the next best thing. Being seen as willingly sacrificing their privileges as permanent residents in the interests of full national integration would be a worthwhile bargain in return for the saffron brotherhood's help in realising their dream of a homeland in the Valley—their *Panun Kashmir*—and the Hindu *rashtra* protecting it. That the experiment with the transit camps has not been a resounding success has certainly angered Pandits who have excoriated the government. However, Pandits must hope that their display of patriotism will bear fruit eventually. This relationship with the Hindu Right echoes remarkably the partnership that had evolved under the Dogra rulers of the state (1846–1947) when the latter, outsiders in Kashmir but seeking legitimacy to govern it from the all-India domain of Hindu ritual and tradition delineated by British colonialism, forged a power-sharing pact with Pandits at the expense of the larger Muslim subject population.[30]

The symbolic importance of Burhan Wani

On 8 July 2016, Indian soldiers killed Burhan Wani, a twenty-two year old commander of the Hizb-ul Mujahideen (HM), the armed auxiliary of JI. About 200,000 Kashmiris attended his funeral on the following day. Burhan Wani was a Kashmiri who, like many others, experienced first-hand the peremptory brutality of the Indian armed forces. Deployed through different gestures—from unnecessary beatings, to needlessly humiliating demands for identity proofs, to lewdness towards women in public—the coarse affronts (leave alone killings, rapes, disappearances, torture) by those exercising Indian dominance have been an everyday occurrence intended to choke all sense of dignity and honour out of Kashmiris. Such injuries to civilians have alienated Kashmiris as much as has the thwarting of their political demands. It is said that Wani had turned to armed militancy after witnessing the gratuitous thrashing of his elder brother (later killed by the security forces). Burhan Wani fought to end India's stranglehold over his homeland; he, like so many of his compatriots, understood well that the physical assaults and insults meted out to them were only the symptoms of a deeper colonisation. So far as is known, Wani was not directly involved in killing any Indian though he may have 'masterminded' hits. What made him particularly dangerous was that he spurned anonymity and offered up his identity on social networks on the internet—the most widely spread medium of the age—while advocating violent retaliation against Indian security forces. One does not defy the Indian armed forces so publicly and hope to survive to old age.

As has often been said, the generation that has come of age in the second decade of the twenty-first century in Kashmir comprises individuals who have only ever experienced militarised Indian occupation. Experience has taught them that armed resistance certainly means torture, imprisonment, death or being 'disappeared'. Therefore, since 2008 the most characteristic feature of Kashmiri agitation has been formidable, massive, but non-violent street protests. Burhan Wani's chosen method of armed war is not that of most Kashmiris. Yet many honour his struggle. The thousands-strong funeral processions for Wani's successors and other militants have become a potent and non-violent challenge to the Indian state. The collective mourning for Wani and others demonstrates a long-standing sympathetic symbiosis between armed militancy and non-violent opposition. Except in instances of the most egregious violence,[31] the two strands inform, push, and create legitimation and political spaces for each other. Following Wani's killing, some eighty-eight Kashmiris—taking only the official figures—took up weapons in 2016.[32] However, many more took to unarmed or stone-armed resistance as the Valley erupted again into months of protests, drawing heavy repression from the Indian state. By the end of 2016, over a hundred Kashmiri civilians had been killed—comparable in goriness to the summer of 2010—and of the approximately 6,000 injured over 1,100 had been blinded by pellet guns.[33]

Contrary to suggestions that resurfaced, Kashmiri protests in 2016, especially after Wani's killing, were neither the handiwork of Pakistan nor emanations of some innate terrorist instinct. Many who joined the armed movement (and the unarmed protests that followed) had canvassed for the PDP during the 2014 assembly elections especially in south Kashmir where the party has a strong base in three districts (including Wani's home district of Tral). Kashmiris here voted to ward off the BJP's announced electoral conquest of Kashmir. That those polls still produced an alliance with the BJP refuelled disillusionment with the democratic process especially in south Kashmir. But disaffection with Indian dominance—and solidarity with 'martyrs' like Burhan—extends across Kashmir. State-speak musters facts differently. In May 2017, Venkaiah Naidu, the then BJP president, dismissed the reports of a spike in militancy as a media-fed canard. 'Except for south Kashmir' he asserted, 'the state is in peace'. The BJP's schizophrenic stance—projecting violence as ever roiling in Kashmir on the one hand and minimising it on the other—only appears inconsistent. In the same interview, Naidu rejected any possibility of holding talks with Hurriyat leaders, breaking yet another pledge made in 2015.[34] There must be violence somewhere in Kashmir to blame for shifts in policy including countermanding commitments made in the CMP (which it should be clear by now was a fig-leaf, not an abiding covenant); and yet it must not be on such a scale as to suggest the BJP had lost control. At the end of 2016, bypassing the convention of seniority determining succession, the BJP appointed General Bipin Rawat as the new army chief. He would buttress the party's rhetorical claim of having a firm hold on Kashmir.

Mission helter-skelter

On 15 February 2017, an incensed Bipin Rawat breathed fire at Kashmiris. On the preceding day four soldiers (and four militants) had been killed in two counter-terrorist operations in northern Kashmir. 'Those who obstruct our operations during encounters and are not supportive', he warned, 'will be treated as overground workers of terrorists'.[35] Rawat was referring to a new form of protest visible since 2017: unarmed Kashmiri civilians hurling stones (and sometimes abuse) at security forces while they were engaged in deadly gun-battles with militants. Another unprecedented dimension of the agitations has been the participation in them of uniformed schoolgirls and college women. Paradoxically, the more Rawat has threatened against interfering with army manoeuvres the more widespread the phenomenon has become. The frustration of not knowing how to deal with this form of rebellion has clearly pushed the army chief into ever more brash stances.

In the speech mentioned above, Rawat went on to place the onus on 'the local population' to ensure their 'local boys' desisted from 'acts of terrorism'. Failing this, he said, the army would 'treat them as anti-national elements and go helter-skelter for them'. Whereas the Indian army has taken pride in being a disciplined force, the threat of going 'helter-skelter' suggests instead the mind-set of a rogue militia. Coming from the chief of one of the world's largest armies, they become not just words of war but also portents of a reign of terror in which no distinction will be made between civilian protestors and armed combatants.[36] The degree of permissiveness in its rules of engagement the army had seized soon became clear.

On 9 April 2017, during a by-election in Budgam, an officer of the 53 Rashtriya Rifles, Major Leetul Gogoi, received news of disturbances at a polling station where some election officials were reportedly besieged by an 'angry stone-pelting mob'. According to the major, when he arrived on site he had 'a fraction of a moment' in which to defuse a dangerous situation without inflicting loss of life. He shanghaied a Kashmiri shawl-weaver called Farooq Ahmad Dar, alleging he was instigating stone-pelters, tied him to his jeep's bonnet and used him as a deterrent against the 'violent' crowd. Dar was driven around for five hours, through seventeen villages, covering a distance of twenty-eight kilometres, with a placard tied to his chest identifying him as a stone pelter—hardly signs of a spur-of-the-moment decision taken under unusual pressure. Dar denied repeatedly that he was either a stone-pelter or had anything to do with them; he had come from voting earlier and was on his way to a condolence meeting in a nearby village. In fact, he was something of a rarity on that day as only 7 per cent of the constituency's voters had turned up. As a video recording of the incident flew from phone to phone and through social media networks, Kashmiris erupted in anger while the Indian political and military establishments broke out in plaudits.[37] Prompted by the unrest, the police registered a case against the major and the army ordered a Court of Inquiry. On 22 May 2017, even before the investigation was concluded, the army awarded Gogoi a commendation card for his 'sustained efforts during counter-insurgency operations'. Some days after, high-ranking army sources revealed that the Court of Inquiry had acquitted Major Gogoi of wrongdoing.[38]

The J&K State Human Rights Commission sought to palliate, to the limited extent its powers allowed, the effects of what many Kashmiris viewed as human rights abuse compounded by insensitivity in rewarding the culprit. On 10 July 2017, it directed the state government to pay Rs 10 lakhs to Farooq Dar as compensation. Aware of its limited jurisdiction, the commission clarified it was not expressing 'any opinion regarding the alleged involvement of officers of the Indian Army'.[39] And yet its instruction to make reparation was in itself a reprimand of the army's conduct. But on 6 November 2017, the state government refused to comply despite the interim report of a police investigation's confirming that Dar had indeed voted on that fateful morning.[40] The government's justification for not compensating Dar was that it had fulfilled its responsibility by filing a complaint at the appropriate police station and, therefore, paying Dar when the investigation was ongoing would be 'tantamount to establish[ing] the guilt of the accused [Gogoi] without affording him an opportunity of being heard' (sic).[41] Such solicitude semaphored the PDP's incapacity to challenge the army-central government combine in defence of a Kashmiri's human and civil rights.

Meanwhile Rawat defended Gogoi's actions as a display of 'innovation' in the 'dirty war' that confronted the Indian army in Kashmir. 'We are a friendly Army', he said, 'but when we are called to restore law and order, people have to be afraid of us.' He even regretted Kashmiris did not give him the excuse to deal with them more decisively: 'In fact, I wish these people, instead of throwing stones at us, were firing weapons at us. Then I would have been happy. I could do what I [want to do]'.[42] Such blatant admissions of the desire to exterminate a people engaged in civil disobedience would be expected to draw condemnation in any democracy.

But the prime minister did not check Rawat's aggressiveness at any time. As mentioned earlier, Modi's contrived silences are a strategy. Other party members, however, stepped up to commend the army. On 24 May 2017, the then defence minister, Arun Jaitley, on a visit to the state seemed to provide absolution for Gogoi's 'innovation' and the army's defence of it. 'Military solutions are to be provided by military officers', he said. In a 'war-like zone' they should not 'have to consult Members of Parliament' added the civilian head of the war ministry.[43] Both institutions seemed to act through a manoeuvred division of labour. So Bipin Rawat returned to Caesar what was his when he maintained 'it was for the government to decide' about political initiatives 'to reach out to the people'.[44] But this separation of the functions of war and politics is a smokescreen: the BJP's militaristic confessional nationalism and an interventionist army—both being antithetical to Indian democracy—are mutually dependent and therefore support each other.

Silencing dissent

The suspension of the constitutionally guaranteed right to freedom of expression in Kashmir is by now a well-established practice. Whether it is through clamping down on academic and political freedoms in educational institutions, monitoring phone conversations, placing civil rights activists under aggressive surveillance, suspending the internet or even arresting individuals for airing their views on social media platforms, the silencing of even non-violently expressed dissent in the Valley is routine.

But in February 2016, in an occurrence rarely witnessed since the Emergency of 1975–77, the BJP government openly assailed the civil liberties of Indians for displaying solidarity with Kashmiris. On 9 February, a cultural programme was organised on the campus of the traditionally anti-establishment Jawaharlal Nehru University in New Delhi. Its purpose was to protest through commemoration the 'extra-judicial' killing of Afzal Guru (on the same day three years earlier),[45] the hanging in 1984 of the pro-freedom Kashmiri rebel Maqbool Butt, and to express solidarity with the Kashmiri struggle for the right to self-determination. The event was disrupted by the student's wing of the BJP, the Akhil Bharatiya Vidyarthi Parishad (ABVP), provoking a group of unidentified outsiders attending the event to shout slogans calling for India's destruction and Kashmir's freedom. The central government reacted sharply by jailing Kanhaiya Kumar, the president of the JNU students' union, on charges of sedition. The court where he was produced, and by extension the Indian judicial apparatus, dissolved into chaos as lawyers assaulted not only the prisoner but also his supporters present in the room. The judge was transparently biased and quoted a Hindu film song to deliver an *ad hominem* sermon on patriotism. Later, two other students—Umar Khalid and Anirban Bhattacharya—were similarly charged and jailed. As of mid-2018, although all three are out on bail, the cases of sedition against them are still open.

With this incident Modi's BJP opened a new chapter in the state's infringement of constitutional liberties. Not content with muzzling freedom of expression in the Valley, it would brook no support for Kashmiris in India either. The BJP's continuously growing domination of state power was being extended into all spaces in mainstream Indian civil society and the ABVP has been its instrument for controlling every unconquered academic space. Hindutva's project requires extirpating dissenting voices within India. Indeed, if suppressing Kashmiri aspirations helps consolidate a Hindu *rashtra* in India, keeping a regime of impunity in place in Kashmir is contingent on a quiescent or a silenced Indian public.

Concluding remarks

While it is not the task of the historian either to be prescriptive or to predict the future, it is within her remit to draw attention to lessons the past teaches. These concluding paragraphs attempt to point to some of them.

The most potent aspect of the Kashmiri struggle has been the resolute commitment of most Kashmiris to remain non-violent in the face of the gravest provocations. This has given the movement its highest legitimacy and stripped the Indian government of its own as it has felt pressed to adopt increasingly ruthless measures to suppress it. There is historical precedent for the Indian state to keep in mind: the genius of Mohandas Karamchand Gandhi's brand of anti-colonial resistance lay precisely in drawing the ferocious retaliation of colonialism against a non-violent movement to show that the British ruled India through brute force, not the consent of Indians. Steadfast Kashmiri adherence to civil disobedience has not only belied the Indian state's branding of them as an inherently violent 'race' but also lent truth to the Kashmiri insistence that it is the Indian government that is a terrorist. Kashmiris have paid a high price for restraint but the cost would undoubtedly be greater if they should resort to violence. After all, India's top-man in uniform has already indicated he would like nothing better so that the army—already showing little respect for the laws of legitimate war or human rights—might deploy its superior violence without curbs or qualms.

Among the many unfounded stereotypes of Kashmiri Muslims is the contention that they represent the forces of Islamic fundamentalism. This aids the self-legitimation of the BJP and its allies in consolidating a mythic Hindu nation. But to be a Muslim and to be an Islamist are different things. Here the onus of correction lies not on Kashmiri Muslims—who cannot be expected to prove a negative—but on those who have invented that label. An important constituency the Hindu Right has annexed to perform that service ever since 1989 (and even further back in the past) comprises Kashmiri Pandit refugees. Alliance with the BJP, however, has not brought the anticipated rewards. Indeed, nearly three decades after their 'migration' this is a realisation that is long overdue. Instead Pandits, such as those represented by Panun Kashmir, have continued to write themselves out of their homeland and, at the same time, assist in its unravelling.

And Indian civil society cannot remain indifferent to what happens in Kashmir. Hindutva's project has shown that Kashmiri Muslims are not the only 'others' it seeks to suppress but, turning its strategies in the Valley onto the heartland, it finds many 'internal others' that it must silence. As the deputy home minister, Kiren Rijiju, vocalised it most explicitly: 'If you support Afzal Guru, if you support separatists, you are anti-national'. As the BJP has designed it, a stand on the Kashmiris' struggle is an important test of an Indian's patriotism. However, four years of Modi's BJP seems to have instilled forgetfulness of a cardinal principle: as it was envisioned, India's democracy neither compels its citizens' adherence to any particular political ideology nor is it founded on any religio-cultural identity.

Postscript

Since writing the above there have been several dramatic developments relating to J&K but there is one with immediate relevance for this essay that warrants discussing even if briefly. This was the BJP's decision, on 19 June 2018, to pull out of the coalition in the state, bringing down its elected government. Making the announcement the party's general secretary, Ram Madhav, claimed that remaining in the alliance had become 'untenable'. The BJP, he maintained, had joined the coalition in J&K solely with the aim of 'restoring peace' and 'encouraging fast development' in the province. Despite the central government's providing every assistance in the implementation of these goals—including the appointment of an interlocutor to consult all 'stakeholders' on behalf of Delhi—the state government had not only failed to 'achieve the intended objectives' but 'terrorism and radicalisation [wa]s on the rise in the state'. Illustrating the latter, Madhav pointed to the murder on 14 June of the Kashmiri journalist Shujaat Bukhari.[46] This act further demonstrated, according to him, that 'even press freedom is in danger'; this sudden solicitude for their freedom of expression may have surprised many Kashmiris. With such a thorough breakdown in the state's governance, 'keeping [the] national interest in mind and that Kashmir is an integral part of India', the BJP felt it was 'time that the reins of power in the state be handed over to the governor'.[47] While ostensibly inculpating the state government collectively, by withdrawing the BJP from the alliance Madhav was manifestly blaming its Kashmiri half constituted by the PDP for misgovernment and escalating violence in J&K.

Although it is still too early for reliably determining the BJP's strategy underlying this turn-about, there are some intriguing aspects of the story that might be highlighted. The BJP's J&K leaders had been summoned on short notice to Delhi for a meeting with the party high command, specifically Amit Shah—the BJP president and leader with the greatest clout after Modi—early on the morning of 19 June. They had been told that 'the party leadership wanted to discuss strategy ahead of the 2019 Lok Sabha elections'. Reports have also suggested that it was only after meeting Ajit Doval, the National Security Adviser, that Shah informed the gathered J&K BJP politicians about the decision to withdraw from the alliance. And tellingly, the home minister

Rajnath Singh had not been consulted—some quarters of Indian public opinion suggesting that he was seen as too accommodating of the PDP's pleadings for a 'softer' approach in Kashmir.[48] The consultation of Doval and the sidelining of Rajnath Singh—if true—would support suggestions that the PDP's ouster had become necessary to enable an all-out offensive in the Valley in the name of thwarting security threats. Indeed, it would appear that even the Director-General of Police of the state, S.P. Vaid, had 'hinted that the PDP was getting in the way of carrying out counterinsurgency operations in the Kashmir Valley'.[49] Governor's rule—under which J&K has been placed since 20 June—gives central governments direct access, by-passing distracting interventions by democratically elected leaders, to a state's administration.[50]

This may indeed be the BJP high command's gameplan for the national elections slated for 2019. Indeed, on the day after the BJP's withdrawal from the coalition, Ram Madhav seemed to be scripting the party's new campaign narrative. Speaking on 20 June, he stated: 'We have not abandoned Kashmir, we have sacrificed the government for the betterment of people and larger national interest' (sic).[51] The party's giving up a pawn to save the king should come as no surprise: as has been argued, the BJP's game is now set on a national board. It would appear to have lost the state of Jammu and Kashmir but has it in fact? Jammu has been and remains its citadel and Kashmir was never won. Furthermore, the party has recoded its actions as self-denial for the greater national good. In any case, Kashmiris have always been meant to serve other purposes, which it should be obvious they will continue to do. In national elections, J&K counts for very little: it sends up only six members to the Indian parliament. However, by providing the powerful symbols of Islamic terror within the nation that the BJP alone can defeat, Kashmiris will continue to be useful in corralling many of the other 540-odd members of the Lok Sabha. But as it is perilous for historians to turn soothsayers, time should be allowed to tell.

15

PLAYING THE WAITING GAME

THE BJP, HINDUTVA, AND THE NORTHEAST[1]

Arkotong Longkumer

The Bharatiya Janata Party (BJP), a prominent member of the Sangh Parivar (family of organisations), emerged as the single largest political party in India, winning the general election in 2014. One of the first things they did was to appoint a Sangh Parivar worker, Padmanabha Balakrishna Acharya, as the eighteenth governor of Nagaland. The symbolic association of Acharya with Nagaland signalled an unambigious message: the BJP are here to stay. When the governor of Nagaland celebrated his first Republic Day in office, he published a pamphlet that was interpreted by the Christian audience as having a distinctively religious message. In the programme pamphlet, there was a poster of *Bharat Mata*—'Mother India'—standing on a lotus and holding the tricolour with the country's map as the background. That this could be issued by the governor of a majority Baptist Christian state with a strong regional culture of its own, obviously raised many eyebrows, with the Nagaland Pradesh Congress Committee (NPCC) leading the charge: '...at a time when the country was faced with onslaught of the RSS-led communal forces, the "needless action" of the Governor was "perhaps an ominous sign of a greater agenda espoused by the BJP-RSS combine, being unfolded to change the secular fabric of the nation".[2]

In this chapter, I offer a preliminary ethnographic and media examination of the ways, and the extent to which, the BJP has been (and still is) negotiating its status in the region. I want to suggest that this status has been accomplished by honing a self-sufficient and dynamically structured political machine and by the adoption of an agenda that transcends religious, social and cultural boundaries.[3] But an analysis of their momentary success must be tempered by realities on the ground that highlight complexities with regard to the national-regional dynamic. In order to understand these developments, I present an analysis of two aspects of the BJP's approach: its utilisation of key alliances that have emerged in reaction to the failures of regional and central governments, and its projection of itself as a secular party that encompasses but also moves beyond exclusively 'Hindu' sentiments. The challenges to present itself as a 'secular' party highlights the fascinating ironies of how the BJP seeks to remove the term 'secular' from the constitution, while in the Northeast it has maintained success precisely through its self-presentation as a secular party. This chapter highlights this double-think—the situational/regional differences in political self-presentation that demonstrate the malleability of their ideology while at the same time managing the BJP's complex relationship with the RSS.

The BJP model of nationalism and the Northeast

Despite wielding power at the centre, it remains a challenge for the BJP to persuade the whole of India that this is an attractive proposition, and nowhere is this more the case than in the Northeast of India. This region has long resisted the central government-driven nation-building project, with feelings of alienation fostered by various government policies and programmes since Indian independence in 1947. Until now, the BJP, with its projection of a largely Sanskritic culture and language, and strong desire for territorial homogeneity in the form of *Bharat Mata* (Mother India), has generally remained ineffective and without influence in the region. However, in recent years, and to the surprise of many, the BJP has formed governments in Manipur, Assam, and Arunachal Pradesh, and developed strong alliances in Christian states such as Nagaland and Meghalaya. In just three years it has grown from a negligible presence to having over eighty Members of the Legislative Assembly

(MLA). It has managed to capture, it seems, the local imagination. How did this dramatic transformation in the party's fortunes occur and what are its implications? In order to answer this question, first, however, it is important to understand something of the context and the ideology of the BJP.

With its traditional base in the north and northwest of the country and an ideology (inherited from its predecessor the Jana Sangh) premised upon 'Hindi, Hindu, Hindustan', the BJP's poor performance in the 1996 Lok Sabha elections exposed its inability to project itself as a 'national party'.[4] According to Michael Gillan's post-1996 prognosis, the BJP needed to radically refashion its ideology if it wanted to be viable in the east and the south of the country, where its presence remained limited. First it had to position itself as '*the* ascendant, pre-eminent *national* party political force'.[5] In order to accomplish this it needed to articulate a strategically viable ideology of accommodating regional voices, without disowning their main Hindu nationalist base. Whether it was issues related to territory, identity, or national security, the BJP had to be ready to engage groups within a broader ambit than their previous ideological positions had allowed. Consequently, they had to think seriously about implementing a national strategy that sought to make alliances with regional parties.[6] This was seen as a way to harness their collective image as a 'national party' and also to make inroads into regions, such as the Northeast, where their cultural and political capital was comparatively limited.

A tempestuous borderland region sharing borders with China, Burma, Bhutan and Bangladesh, and marked by armed conflict since 1947 with various indigenous movements, not to mention the disastrous Sino-Indian war in 1962 which exposed the weakness of the outlying flanks of the nation-state, making inroads in the Northeast is not easy for any new party, let alone for one largely seen to represent dominant 'Hindu' interests. These complexities, particularly in protecting the boundaries of India and fashioning loyal subjects first and foremost, also make it vital for the BJP to gain support within the region, if they are to succeed in their national agenda of integrating cultures, languages, and nation into one coherent entity.

The Northeast states with the strongest current BJP presence—Manipur, Assam, and Arunachal Pradesh—each harbour vociferous 'separatist' movements and sensitive border issues, which in the words of the political scientist Sanjib Baruah, together take the form of a 'durable disorder'.[7] In the case of the first two states, armed conflict has been widespread since around Indian independence. Arunachal Pradesh, similarly, has seen Naga nationalist groups such as the National Socialist Council of Nagalim-Isak Muivah (NSCN-IM) and the National Socialist Council of Nagaland-Khaplang (NSCN-K) play an active role in its southern, Naga, districts, while at the same time sharing its religious and cultural orbit with Tibet and China. The BJP has been astute in recognising that the region requires long-term and focused attention as a matter of urgency to improve not only the BJP's fortunes but to assert the national outlook of one nation. Even Nagaland, a bastion of Baptist Christianity with a history of vibrant national movements, long suspicious of any Hinduising force, has seen the entry of the BJP into the state political machine, where it has formed an alliance with the current ruling regional party, the Naga People's Front (NPF).

BJP/RSS activity in the region is a consequence of the Hindutva's ideological vision of *Akhand Bharat* (greater India, or undivided India). According to a political advisor to the BJP chief minister in Manipur, writing for NDTV, 'For the nation to be culturally and nationally integrated in spirit and not just geography, the Northeast is important. For the BJP, the Northeast is not a peripheral state but the heart of India'.[8] Used initially in Hindu nationalist discourse expressing discontent about the partition of the sub-continent (i.e. Pakistan and India), and advocating its restoration as one country,[9] this use of *Akhand Bharat* in the context of the Northeast is novel in the way they visualise a region that has historically been marginal in the 'Hindu' imagination. *Akhand Bharat* encompasses regions that are culturally linked or influenced by a Sanskritic culture that forms the Indian subcontinent and extends to Southeast Asia and Central Asia. The Indologist Sheldon Pollock has described this as the 'Sanskrit Cosmopolis'.[10] If the Northeast is seen as the connecting tissue that links parts of the Indian subcontinent with their south-eastern counterparts, then, the Northeast has to be 'reconstructed' to establish the region as the centre of this 'Sanskrit Cosmopolis'.[11] This cultural map of India, beyond the 1947 borders, must be re-established to bring about salient political influence eastward—towards China and Southeast Asia.[12]

Building key alliances

In 2016, the BJP formed its first government in Assam, which was headed by a tribal leader from the Sonowal Kachari community, Sarbananda Sonowal. The BJP General Secretary, Ram Madhav, who played a crucial role in stitching together a 'dream alliance' between the Asom Gana Parishad (AGP) and the Bodo People's Front (BPF), said that victory in Assam was an important ideological win.[13] Some commentators have suggested that the Assam victory opened the doors to the Northeast.[14] The key idea that secured the party's win was their focus on Assamese identity. This was seen as coming under threat by the Congress-led government who were closely associated with the All India United Democratic Front (AIUDF) in protecting 'illegal Bangladeshi' immigrants. To save Assamese culture, language and land, 'The BJP has promised a *khilonjia Sarkar* [indigenous government]', according to the political scientist Sanjib Baruah. 'Khilonjia—a non-Sanskritic word that means original inhabitant, indigenous or autochthonous'—was used as a keyword to anchor the election battle very much within the ideological landscape of Assam.[15] Here the 'foreigner' was clearly the face of the Muslim, headed by the AIUDF leader, Badruddin Ajmal, in juxtaposition to Sonowal's, an indigenous Kachari. The facial phenotype, or facescape,[16] that defines national citizenship, said it all.

Although projected as a recent indigenous concern by the media, it is important to note that the BJP/RSS have been formulating this position for a while. Their earliest presence was in Assam when the RSS established a base in the state in 1946. Since then, the RSS have been involved in establishing schools, aiding in relief work (like the 1950 Assam earthquake), and organising important events like the Vishwa Hindu Parishad (VHP) conference in Guwahati in 1967 to highlight their presence and to disseminate their message of Hindu nationalism. This message was directly to counter Christian proselytisation, especially in tribal areas, and to stop Muslim 'illegal' immigration—or 'infiltration'—from Bangladesh into Assam and the Northeast.[17]

Grassroots organisation and mobilisation with the help of various RSS affiliated workers already present in the region was skilfully deployed to bring the BJP to power in Assam. It took careful tactical planning for nearly two years for the BJP to be able to poach a crucial competitor from the Congress, Himanta Biswa Sarma, thereby unsettling the Congress leadership in Assam.[18] These tactical games were also evident in Arunachal Pradesh in 2016 that saw Pema Khandu form the government when thirty-three out of forty-three of the People's Party of Arunachal (PPA) MLAs merged with the BJP, effectively bringing about a BJP government. Similarly in Manipur, N. Biren Singh, a former Congressman is now heading the BJP alliance; in Nagaland too, with only one BJP MLA, three joined from the National Congress Party (NCP) taking its numbers to four in 2014.

Switching political parties in this way could suggest a simple political strategy on the part of regional MLAs—to side with the party in power at the centre. It also supports the BJP who are effectively promulgating what they might call regional alliances with a national outlook. In other words, they use the symbols and language of the states that they are in, without abandoning the idea of the centralised model and the ideology of a homogenous nation. An example of this is the way the BJP has represented the image of *Bharat Mata* in the state of Tripura. Using tribal women with customised attires in elections posters to stand in for *Bharat Mata*, the BJP argue that 'The idea is to make the "alienated tribes" of the North East feel part of Bharat and claim Bharat Mata'.[19] This centralised model is further evident in the appointment of a leader to manage the affairs of the BJP (in Assam Ram Madhav effectively played this role), as well as their close nexus with the RSS and affiliates who provide ideological and organisational support that is very much aligned with the key aim of the BJP/RSS message in the Northeast: that of national unity and cooperation with regard to development as well as protecting the interests of the states.

While the BJP present these alliances, and themselves, as something new, there is also a sense in which it is politics as usual in these areas. I want to draw on two particular examples from Assam, where the BJP has been particularly successful. These two districts—Karbi Anglong and Dima Hasao—border the state of Nagaland, and demonstrate the complexities of the region that the BJP must negotiate. Both districts come under the Sixth Schedule and therefore are Autonomous Councils. The Sixth Schedule[20] is a special provision under the Constitution of India in the administration of tribal dominated areas. In Assam, there are three such Autonomous Councils, demarcating 'tribal areas': Bodoland Territorial Council; Karbi Anglong Autonomous Council; and Dima Hasao Autonomous District Council. Each council has wide-ranging legislative powers from managing land, agriculture, roads and bridges, to revenue, public health, education, and so on. The governor is technically the overseer of the council and has the power to appoint four unelected members to the council from unrepresented, minority groups; though in practice, it is usually the political parties who choose, and the governor simply ratifies their choices.

It is also these two districts which border the state of Nagaland and therefore are crucial areas within the Naga 'Framework Agreement', an agreement recently signed by the government of India (GOI) and the NSCN-IM outlining the basis on which the talks between the two parties are happening, leading to a workable agreement concerning the Indo-Naga conflict. The Sixth Schedule in theory protects regional powers, but issues of territory, though in an important sense a regional concern, can be overruled by the national authority. These dynamics however have ramifications in an area where there are several actors contesting territorial boundaries. In one way, it is these complexities that have contributed to the BJP rise, turning acute difficulties to their advantage.

Politics as usual?

In the Dima Hasao district of Assam, a senior BJP worker told me that when the local party was formed in 1997, they only had one member. Since then, the numbers have grown gradually and in 2012 they had fifty-two members. When the then Congress Chief Minister, Tarun Gogoi, visited Dima Hasao, the majority of them left to join the Congress party, leaving only six in the BJP. Since the BJP government formed in Dima Hasao, they have roughly 1,000 members on all levels. Although the BJP has won seats in the Dima Hasao Autonomous Council (DHAC) in previous elections, since 2013 they have not secured any seats, due to the popularity of the Congress. In 2015, oddly, the BJP formed the DHAC government, without winning any seats— but by attracting sixteen members through defection in the thirty-member council and thus forming the DHAC government. It now has a stable majority of twenty-four members, none of whom were BJP candidates when elected. So why are these members switching allegiances?

The main reason is the alignment of region-state-centre—staying with the party in power. A BJP worker in Karbi Anglong told me that this alignment is crucial. For these two small Autonomous Councils this balance is vital because they need development money, largely dependent on the state exchequer, and without the right regional-state synergy, life becomes difficult for the smaller regions. Because of the pressure of development, the constituents look at the political structures in the state and centre before voting. The confluence between the three levels is important, said a BJP worker in Dima Hasao, because 'without power, one can't do anything'. She even said that, 'if the Congress comes to power in the centre and the state, the constituency will vote Congress'. I asked if she would change parties if Congress came to power. She replied that 'if I'm elected in the BJP party, and if Congress comes to power, then I will join Congress because I need to bring development to my villages'. A parallel process is also happening in Karbi Anglong. A first-time BJP member said to me that he joined the BJP to represent his community due to the fact that they have no representative in the KAAC. Being a Christian, he does not fully agree with the BJP, nor does he know much about

BJP ideology. For him, it is important that his community's voice is heard and the dominant party, for now the BJP, is the ideal platform. The BJP is then largely an instrument through which to protect community development and interests, and to voice concerns. Regardless of party affiliations—whether Congress, BJP, or the regional Autonomous State Demand Committee (ASDC)—these defections are bound to happen, he said.

In both Dima Hasao and Karbi Anglong, the situation appears similar. There are no deep ideological anchors for the BJP. This suggests the BJP's rise may be transient. While their counterparts, the RSS, are highly inventive and effective in certain regions of the Northeast, the BJP is still a nascent force in terms of accruing political capital.[21] Moreover, for many local people, there are far more important issues at play such as development, territorial politics, and power. On the surface it may seem as if the BJP is on the ascendency due to the diligent mapping of their activities and pathways created by a few *karyakatas* (workers) to imprint the ideology of the BJP onto the landscape, but local priorities offer a different explanation. This is the challenge for the BJP, as it seeks to collaborate with regional players who are characterised by intense competition and rivalry over ideologies. It may mean that the BJP will have to sacrifice maximum leverage in order to maintain regional allies. Conversely, it might push the BJP's one-party rule, which is necessary to maintain its core ideological platform of 'one language, one culture, one nation', to rethink its structure and organisation to build a strong regional base, at the expense of forging partnerships with local alliances.[22]

Local politics: territoriality

In these regions of Assam, there are two issues that are central to any understanding of local politics. They are subject to the Sixth Schedule but the dominant concern is the territorial politics of 'Greater Nagaland' that is in play at the moment between the GOI and the NSCN-IM through the 'Framework Agreement'. In an interview with a local BJP activist, from the Rengma Naga tribe in Karbi Anglong, it was clear that understanding territorial politics is important because it will show how the BJP understands the history of the region, and that it is not simply riding a wave of popular support. NSCN-IM has always maintained that any future solution or settlement to the Indo-Naga issue would encompass all regions that are inhabited by the Naga people, including parts of Dima Hasao and Karbi Anglong districts, forming 'Greater Nagaland'.

The Assam Government, however, has clearly stated that they will not make any compromise on the territorial restructuring of state boundaries. The Assam BJP Chief Minister, Sarbananda Sonowal, in the *Economic Times*, stated that 'not an inch of [the] state's land will be parted with and the territorial integrity of [the] state will be protected'.[23] There is considerable uncertainty over the 'Framework Agreement', with only the occasional speeches by the NSCN-IM leadership hinting at the creation of 'Greater Nagaland'. However, the Assam Government's position has been reiterated by the GOI's interlocutor for Naga talks, RN Ravi, as recently as October 2017.[24] This presents a complex problem for the BJP. In Dima Hasao district of Assam, with a sizeable Zeme Naga population, who want to be included in 'Greater Nagaland', many are of the view that it is the BJP that will bring this settlement. A Zeme Naga woman activist, a senior figure in the BJP organisation in Dima Hasao, told me that the people in her constituency have been discussing the news seen on TV in August 2015 when Modi hinted that a solution to the Indo-Naga issue might materialise in eighteen months. For those in the village, they see this as good news primarily because the Nagas will have their own government 'ruled by our own people' and the Zeme Nagas will not be under the majority Dimasa people in Dima Hasao district, but under 'Greater Nagaland', and it will be 'like independence'. Jobs, greater access to local government, less red tape are all expected because the 'people in government will be our people', an exciting and attractive proposition to many Naga people in villages.

In Karbi Anglong, the minority Rengma Naga tribe are unable to publicly voice their support for 'Greater Nagaland', due to the dominance of the Karbi tribe in local politics. The Karbi anxiety over 'Greater Nagaland', if it comes to fruition, is that large swathes of land within Karbi Anglong will form part of the Naga homeland and the hard won 'autonomous status' in 1951 with the formation of the KAAC will mean nothing, and will be folded within it. So how does the BJP's grand design for political power fit this precarious arrangement in terms of the territorial politics of 'Greater Nagaland'?

The BJP's greatest strength is also their greatest weakness. Known for their strong party discipline, following protocols, and taking their commands from the central authority, their political model seems unassailable. There appears to be little empowering of local authorities to approach issues intuitively. For example, a BJP worker in Dima Hasao told me that the BJP/RSS workers are often silent about issues such as the Framework Agreement, to a certain degree to maintain party discipline in order to minimise unfounded rumours, but also to maintain a spectre of neutrality in dealing with each community. So the question is, will the BJP with its strong hierarchical setup, command enough respect in maintaining party order in the face of obvious contestation over the restructuring of state boundaries if the issue of 'Greater Nagaland' becomes a reality? The party's Assam unit chief Ranjit Das indicated that 'the state might have to part with its land'. Furthermore, 'There is a possibility that some disputed areas along the Assam-Nagaland border will enter Greater Nagaland'.[25]

In other words, there seems to be a division over the issue of 'Greater Nagaland' with the Assam BJP chief minister denouncing it, while his counterpart Ranjit Das is hinting towards an alternative possibility. This is where the BJP appears contradictory and its future uncertain: the BJP is centralised and yet regional; promoting national unity, yet willing to divide territory.

Appeasing the Nagas and accommodating their request will show a real commitment to solving the longstanding conflict and instability in the region. At the same time, will the BJP side-line the hard-earned respect in Assam as shown recently by their electoral success by re-negotiating Assam territory? Not grasping this complexity could be another challenge for the BJP. Though slowly making inroads into regional politics, they are still driven by an ideology that might not fully materialise into local variations and dynamics. In Karbi Anglong, a student activist told me that the BJP are not popular due to their close relationship with the RSS. The growing RSS presence has meant that they are supporting their BJP candidates for the local elections. I have been told that out of the twenty-six elected members in the KAAC, around six of the candidates have backing from the RSS.[26] The pressure exerted by the RSS is creating an obstacle for the BJP.

A local BJP party worker, who is a Christian, said to me that in the KAAC, aside from the twenty-six elected members, there is room for four nominated candidates decided by the KAAC, and ratified by the governor of Assam. He is one of the candidates being considered for nomination by the KAAC, but his nomination has been blocked by vested interests both in the district and in the state capital. The chief minister has his own candidates, so too does the RSS *pracharak* in Karbi Anglong, who is lobbying for his '*Khasi* Hindu' (an ethnic group belonging primarily to the state of Meghalaya) candidate. The Christian BJP candidate even met the RSS head of Assam in Guwahati, who said that protocol has to be maintained as there is a clear line of authority—centre/state/region—and that his hands were tied with regard to intervening. In other words, the say of the regional *pracharak* carries more weight and the centre might do his bidding and override other local equations.

The BJP want to highlight their 'secular credentials' which are said to be a key driver in their success in the Northeast. But this is being challenged on the ground, as the BJP Christian candidate, he informed me, was denied the nomination purely on 'communal' (religious) grounds. Furthermore, for the first time since the formation of the autonomous council of Karbi Anglong in 1951, three tickets have been issued by the BJP, with RSS backing, to non-tribals. Previous Congress governments also issued single tickets to non-tribals, but as one tribal BJP activist recounted, issuing several was unprecedented. The Sixth Schedule, which led to the formation of the autonomous councils in the Northeast, empowered the tribal bodies to form governments and to take control of development within their regional bodies. However, due to the structure of the BJP as a political party, the Sixth Schedule safeguards are being challenged.

As a BJP worker put it to me, crudely: 'It is openly acknowledged that those who have benefited from the refashioning of the Sixth Schedule are the Bengalis and the Biharis'. Even though they are of the same party, the tribals feel uncertain of how to approach this issue because, he said, 'India has a democratic and secular constitution which does not help us as, if we object to the Bengali/Bihari members on tribal/non-tribal divide, then we in the BJP will be branded as communal'. The communal idea in the two instances—the candidate's perception of being judged through a religious lens, and his inability to voice his concern publicly due to the safeguards of the constitution—is an interesting example of how there are divisions between on the ground politics, and the tactical discourse of BJP's secular presentation, which they are keen to maintain in order to demonstrate their 'neutrality'. I suspect these instances are not a one off but will multiply. This has not only brought about the revitalisation of the regional party, ASDC, to fight for the Sixth Schedule to protect tribal interests (in itself an ethno-national project) but again demonstrates the contradiction within the BJP approach. And the backlash could have consequences for the future of the BJP in the region.

Secular politics and its malcontents

Some attribute the effectiveness of the BJP's work in the Northeast to their avowedly 'secular' credentials. This is something that is persistently maintained by the BJP leaders, despite close and continuing links with the RSS and its affiliates. After the Assam election victory in 2016 and the anxiety of Muslims in Assam over the rise of the BJP/RSS nexus, the BJP general secretary told *The Hindu* that 'Assam's secular identity will be safe'.[27] While this slogan has been maintained by the BJP, on the ground at least things are slightly different.

The idea of the secular provokes an ideological battle over what is religious and secular. In safeguarding their secular credentials, the BJP are able to assert that theirs is solely a political party, dealing with live issues that affect ordinary people. Demonstrating the separation of the BJP and the RSS, Ram Madhav said to the *Indian Express*, 'The RSS has been actively working in the Northeast for many decades, but in social and service areas. They don't do politics. But the RSS's association with every section of society helped us. There were many social organisations and groups that helped us and some of these were RSS-backed'.[28] The RSS has indeed worked for many years establishing schools and social centres in the Northeast,[29] but the mobilisation of RSS workers, and organisations, during elections indicates more fuzzy, and arbitrary, boundaries between 'politics' and the 'social', despite the claims of being untainted by each other.

Indeed, there was further debate when it was rumoured that the BJP national government was planning to remove 'Socialist Secular' from the Indian constitution which describes India as a 'Sovereign Socialist Secular Democratic Republic'. Whatever the intention of the BJP was, at least in Nagaland, this stirred debate on the nature of secularism and the safeguarding of Christians in India, generally. Seasoned Naga activists like Dr Wati Aier argue that this could demonstrate a tacit support by those in power for hardliners and fringe elements (read RSS) within the BJP. Such elements, argues another scholar turned activist Professor Temsula Ao, are dangerous. She points to the fact that the omission of 'Socialist Secular' indicates a larger plan because 'such an important document in such a momentous occasion...sees the fringe elements coming to the forefront [and] disrupting the harmony of the nation'. Indeed, Niketu Iralu, another advocate for social justice in Nagaland, suggests that there has always been an undercurrent of Hindu national identity simmering under the surface of this 'secularism', and this climate only contributes to a sense of anxiety for minority religious groups. Even though the BJP's language talks of development for everyone, many suspect it is motivated largely by the BJP's idea of assimilating national identity.[30]

At the time of the arrival of the BJP in Nagaland in 2012, people openly questioned its religious allegiances to Hinduism, arguing that they clashed with those of Nagaland as a Christian state. Reflecting on some of these issues a few years later, Asangba Tzüdir, in an opinion column, published in the local

Morung Express in June 2017, writes that the 'BJP is being seen as a possible threat to the very foundation of Christianity if it comes to power in the next Nagaland General Assembly elections'. This fear is rooted, very much, Tzüdir suggests, through their use of 'imagery'—through glorifying a non-Christian Naga leader, Rani Gaidinliu—and by using 'Hindu rituals' in BJP functions and events. The counter-narrative of Hindutva, now formally established through the BJP, will dismantle the dominant image of Nagaland as a Christian state, argues Tzüdir.[31]

These claims are being countered by the face of K.J. Alphons, the Christian BJP Union Minister of Tourism from Kerala, in charge of the election battle in Meghalaya. Demonstrating a careful reading of the political situation by the BJP, Alphons's appointment addresses two issues. First, appointing someone opposed to the beef ban in Kerala is an attempt to alleviate the BJP's image in Meghalaya as the party that imposed a nationwide beef ban in 2015. This ban was opposed by considerable numbers in the state, even organising a 'beef party' during the visit of the President of the BJP, Amit Shah, and leading to the resignation of BJP workers over 'this imposition' as recently as 2017.[32] Second, Alphons's position as a Christian in charge of a Christian-dominated state is significant. Appealing to Christians in the region he has argued that his Christian background has had no impact on joining the BJP, nor on his ascendency to the rank of union minister. In his recent visit to Shillong (Meghalaya; another majority Christian state) in October 2017, he said:

> A lot of people asked me that being a Christian why am I joining this party? People were angry with me. They said if Modi comes to power, churches will be burnt and destroyed and Christians will be beaten up. In the three-and-a-half years since Modi became Prime Minister, has any church anywhere in India been burnt or destroyed? The answer is no. Not one church in India has been touched by the BJP government. Has any Christian anywhere in India been beaten up? The answer is no.[33]

Such a move highlights the BJP's inventive and malleable character, and willingness to pay attention to the acute political sensitivities in the region. A senior BJP party worker in Nagaland offered a different biblical refrain. He told me that for him joining the BJP is not an issue because he can separate his 'religious' identity as a Christian from his 'political' identity as a BJP worker. Using the story of Daniel, in the Old Testament, he noted how, like Daniel who served Nebuchadnezzar in Babylon to the best of his ability even though he was a Jew and rose through the ranks to become an important administrator, he too is serving the BJP although he is a Christian. His hope is to bring about a new kind of politics that is not based on clan, village, or tribal identity, but one that is issue-based politics. And he hopes that the BJP will provide that platform.[34]

In fact, with the arrival of the BJP in the Northeast, one could argue now that the emotional baggage of Hindutva, with its ideological drive to make India 'Hindu' is being carefully managed, with the BJP/RSS combination interested in asking people to invest in the nation, not solely as a set of ideological categories, but as functional and practical sets of action that can tackle corruption, immigration, political and military conflict, and peacebuilding. This is what the prime minister's visit to Nagaland in 2014 illustrated. Speaking in English and using the Naga nationalist phrase *Kuknalim* (literally victory to Nagaland), and not the usual '*Bharat Mata ki Jai*' (victory to Mother India), Narendra Modi offered developmental packages around the idea of making the Northeast the capital of 'organic agriculture' labelling this as Natural Economic Zones (NEZs) contrasting it with Special Economic Zones (SEZs) that are largely man-made.[35] Borrowing the economic language of *Swalambhan* (self-reliance), and combining it with the 'Integral Humanism' of Deendayal Upadhyaya, Modi's speech appeared to evoke the connection between humanity, nature, and life, overseen by a 'spirit' regulating the culture and nation. In other words, Modi's vision, in line with Integral Humanism, is to create an indigenous economic model, using natural resources.[36] (Modi often talks about the Naga chilli, the hottest in the world, and the Jalukie pineapple as examples of what he means by NEZ.)

Similarly, the RSS chief Mohan Bhagwat, during his recent visit in October 2017 to Tripura—a state currently ruled by the Communist Party of India (Marxist)—ahead of the 2018 elections, made the statement that 'Anybody living in India is a Hindu.'[37] He was asserting that the meaning of Hindutva is to unite all communities, regardless of religious background. Including Muslims and Christians in this fold, he noted that 'We have no enmity with anyone. We want welfare of all. To unite all is the meaning of Hindutva.'[38] Indeed, the malleability of this kind of 'new Hindutva,'[39] in contrast to the historically openly chauvinistic one, is what is making the BJP's entry into the Northeast of such significance.

Conclusion

The entry of the BJP into the Northeast in the last decade and their electoral wins in Assam and Manipur have greatly enhanced their political capital in a region that has resisted the dominant model of the Indian state since independence. Many governments have tried to appease the indigenous governments through big development packages, while at the same time launching a military conflict against those not wanting to accede to this model of democracy and governance. The Congress, as a national party, has largely lost its force in the Northeast in the last elections, but it remains to be seen if they will be able to reinvent themselves amidst the shift towards the more regional power blocks. The BJP's entrance is interesting and significant for three reasons.

First, the BJP is offering to solve the long protracted Indo-Naga issue; the Naga movement is often known as the 'mother of all insurgencies' (termed so by the Indian military establishment) in the Indian Union. The prime minister has benefitted from the work his predecessors have done since a cease-fire was signed between the GOI and the NSCN-IM in 1997 (with political talks between the two entities starting in 2001). The 2015 'Framework Agreement' is the fruit of that process. Promises and grandstanding aside, the future of the region, in terms of BJP electoral strategy, is very much dependent on this agreement. If the BJP are simply interested in short-term goals, particularly travelling the dusty road to get to where they are in Assam, Manipur and Arunachal Pradesh, then they may honour their alliances in these states and keep the territorial boundaries intact. If however they decide to honour the Nagas' demand for Greater Nagaland, then their long-term interest in the region will be established—securing the borders of the nation, using these areas to influence the larger Southeast Asia region (the idea of *Akhand Bharat*, Greater India), and building a strategic presence that counters the threat of China, their main regional competitor. Compromises would have to be made of course on both counts.

Second, the relationship between the BJP and the RSS is interesting for the future of the BJP as a 'secular' political party in the Northeast. The RSS and their affiliates have had a far longer presence in the Northeast than the BJP, and provide foot soldiers to the BJP cause. Finding a compromise over ideological factors, and also over on the ground tactics is important to prevent the BJP from being seen simply as a 'Hindu nationalist' party.[40]

Finally, there is a sense that the focus on development and the anti-corruption stance of the BJP will bring about real change. Bringing their ideas to fruition is difficult, particularly, as I have shown, if party discipline is not maintained and if the BJP makes alliances that justify the ends rather than the means. With roughly a year in government for the BJP in the region, they still have to negotiate the different alliances and tribal politics that have been rooted in clan, village, and customary practices over the *longue durée*. Emerging victorious with an electoral mandate is not the only way to gauge success; the imprint of the party has to go deep into the psyche of a region long marginalised.

PART VI

DIPLOMACY AND GLOBAL ASPIRATION

16

FOREIGN POLICY UNDER MODI

BETWEEN ASPIRATION AND ACHIEVEMENT

C. Raja Mohan

Foreign policy has been an unexpected area of vitality for India under Prime Minister Narendra Modi. When he took charge as prime minister in 2014, few had expected Modi to be enthusiastic about international affairs. As a provincial leader, it was widely believed that Modi might be none too comfortable with the world of diplomacy. However, he seemed so drawn to the world of global politics that he invited criticism at home for spending too much time abroad.[1] While that perception might not be accurate, it reflected the new energy and dynamism that he brought to India's international relations. Nor can anyone contest the fact that there has been a general advance in the consolidation of many key relationships. However, for many critics, disappointments abound—especially on the bilateral ties with Pakistan and China. Others are frustrated that Modi's India did not take full advantage of the opportunities that came its way with the United States and the West.

One needs to be careful though in judging the foreign policy outcomes of any government in India or abroad. No leader, even of the most powerful nation, can control the external environment that has so many sovereign actors. There are also moments when significant changes in the structure of regional and international relations introduce great uncertainty in the conduct of diplomacy. At home, there are always significant constraints on a leader to pursue any kind of foreign policy strategy—especially the one of aligning multiple domestic constituencies in favour of declared foreign policy goals. Equally important is the enduring inertia of the intellectual, political and bureaucratic establishments that resist any significant innovation in external relations. Assessment of the success or failure of a leader's diplomacy cannot be made without considering the larger external context and internal pressures.

India's external environment had presented Modi multiple advantages and also imposed new constraints on him. For example, the growing assertion of a rising China along with the new geopolitical uncertainties generated by US President Donald Trump was not something anyone in Delhi or the world was fully prepared for. In the terribly polarised domestic environment under the Modi government, few of the many critics of his domestic policies are willing to give him credit for diplomatic advances. His blind supporters, meanwhile, have little time for the complexities of India's foreign policy under Modi. The truth, as ever, lies somewhere in between. Modi had indeed set some ambitious goals for India's international relations, but the achievements do fall short of the goals set. These limitations do not in any way reduce the long-term salience of the structural shift in India's worldview that Modi might have engineered.

This chapter does not purport to be a comprehensive assessment of Modi's foreign policy during the first four years of his tenure.[2] It focuses on the broad movement of Indian diplomacy under Modi and the kind of challenges it has had to confront. The appreciation of Modi's foreign policy here seeks to avoid both of the traps mentioned above. This chapter begins with a brief review of Modi's inheritance and principal contribution in terms of the big ideas guiding India's international engagement. Two subsequent sections analyse the new elements in India's engagement with the great powers under PM Modi and his gains and setbacks in the neighbourhood. The chapter concludes with a brief analysis of Modi's enthusiasm for promoting India's soft power and its negation by the country's deepening internal fault lines. A number of other issues have not been taken up for consideration, not because they are not important, but because the focus here is on giving substantive treatment to a few critical issues.

Inheritance and innovation

The structural reorientation of India's foreign policy dates back to 1991, when India was compelled to change the nature of its economy—from a closed to open one—and adapt to the end of the Cold War. Successive prime ministers—P.V. Narasimha Rao, Atal Bihari Vajpayee, Manmohan Singh and Modi—worked to advance India's globalisation and move away from a doctrinaire foreign policy that went by the name of non-alignment and was the flip side of the emphasis on economic isolationism. The changes in India's international engagement involved mobilising external capital and technology for India's development, upgrading India's underdeveloped relations with the US, Europe, China and Japan, holding onto the partnership with post-Soviet Russia, reconnecting to the extended neighbourhood, seeking reconciliation with Pakistan, and integrating the subcontinent. All these objectives were pursued while fending off some of the new challenges from the unipolar moment in international affairs—especially protecting the nuclear weapons programme and preventing third-party intervention in Jammu and Kashmir.[3]

Modi had no reason to depart from this agenda. What he brought to this was a majority electoral mandate, strong political will and much personal energy to the pursuit of the broad set of interests that were laid out in 1991. As the first party leader with a majority in the Lok Sabha since Rajiv Gandhi, Modi did not have to constantly look over his shoulder like his predecessors. At sixty-four in 2014, Modi was relatively young in comparison to his immediate predecessors and brought a vigour and energy not seen since the days of Rajiv Gandhi. If on one hand Modi was liberated from the pressures of coalition politics and the need to defer to the state governments in the conduct of foreign policy, his political will and decisiveness put an end to the constant handwringing and ambivalence that guided India's international engagements after the Cold War on the other. Prime Minister Manmohan Singh, for example, was unable to follow through on many of his bold foreign policy initiatives, thanks to the political hesitations in the Congress party and the pressures from coalition partners. While he did manage to win the parliamentary approval of the civil nuclear initiative, many issues were left unresolved, including those relating to nuclear liability. Modi, however, was determined to wrap up the residual issues from the historic civil nuclear initiative with the US launched by Singh and President George W. Bush. Modi also pushed through the parliamentary ratification of the land boundary agreement with Bangladesh that Singh had negotiated, but could not mobilise political support for. Modi also did what Singh could not in relation to climate change—to move away from rigid defensive position.[4]

However, Modi was not just about getting over the last mile problems that the UPA government faced during its decade-long rule. His biggest contribution to Indian foreign policy was to nudge the Indian establishment to get past the fixation with non-alignment. Although the principal ideological makeover of Indian foreign policy after 1991 was about moving beyond non-alignment, neither the government nor the so-called strategic community could really shake off the demons from the past. Modi built his foreign policy on the recognition that India's position in the international system had gone through a fundamental transformation. High growth rates since 1991 had seen a steady improvement in India's relative position in the international system. While the idea of India's prospects for becoming a great power began to emerge in India's strategic discourse at the turn of the century, the Congress leadership, especially Sonia Gandhi, seemed uncomfortable with the proposition. Addressing a major national convention in Delhi in 2006, Gandhi stated: 'I am somewhat uneasy with the very word "superpower". For too many of us, it evokes images of hegemony, of aggression, of power politics, of military might, of division and conflict.' Cautioning against a new triumphalism in the national elite, Gandhi reminded the audience of 'large sections of our society that have yet to enjoy even the basics of a decent quality of life and standard of living'. She added: 'The successes we record must not lead to false illusions of grandeur and power. They should not wrap us in a cocoon of self-satisfaction which cuts us off from the day-to-day lives of the vast majority.'[5]

While her caution was sensible, it also underlined an enduring reluctance within the left of centre political spectrum to think about the global power shift and reassess India's international role and position. Unsurprisingly, in its second term, the UPA government (2009–14) resurrected the idea of non-alignment.[6] Modi, however, chose to look beyond the idea of non-alignment. References to 'non-alignment' tended to disappear from his speeches.[7] While the term 'strategic autonomy' often slipped into his articulation, it was never defined as resistance to embarking on productive ventures with the West. Instead, he articulated the idea of India as a 'leading power'.[8]

While the notion of a leading power has not been fully fleshed out either, Modi was shifting away from the idea of a vulnerable India rowing the treacherous waters of great power competition to one where India could become a pole in her own right in the multipolar world. This was complemented by the recognition that in the current international flux, India should not treat any one power as untouchable. In the past, there was hesitation in drawing too close to any power, especially the United States and the West. This was justified in the name of non-alignment and strategic autonomy. Modi suggested that close relations with the US will improve India's overall position among the major powers. Modi also insisted that all major powers are engaging with others and Delhi's emphasis must be on 'India First' rather than constrained by any pretence of *moralpolitik* or ideological predilections. The conviction that India can and should actively shape its external environment has also been a dominant theme in Modi's foreign policy. That core belief has been matched with a deep sense of pragmatism. It certainly remains to be seen whether the notion of India as a 'leading power' will survive Modi or whether Delhi will revert to the comforting world of a reactive diplomacy. But there is no question that if there is a single idea that captures Modi's conduct of international relations, it is the notion of *realpolitik*.[9]

Great power relations

After the Cold War, India focused on improving its relations with all the major powers, including the US, Europe, Russia, China and Japan. Thanks to the harmony among the great powers, it was relatively easy for Delhi to simultaneously advance with all of them.[10] This situation, however, began to change towards the end of the first decade of the new millennium. As tensions began to re-emerge among the great powers, India had to cope with an increasingly complex dynamic. How far should India go with the United States without provoking China? Can it sustain the campaign on 'global multipolarity' in partnership with Russia and China while deepening the 'natural alliance' with the United States? And above all, how should it assess and respond to the dramatic rise in China's power? India's historic civil nuclear cooperation agreement with the United States and a deepening defence engagement with Washington during the UPA years was met with considerable concern at home as well as in Beijing and Moscow. For many, it marked a structural shift in India's international orientation away from non-alignment and strategic autonomy and closer to the United States and the West.[11]

As China sought strategic primacy in Asia, Beijing expressed apprehensions that India's strategic partnership with the United States would lead to the formation of a countervailing coalition.[12] Russia, whose relations with the United States and the West steadily deteriorated, had to deal with the potential loss of dominance over the lucrative Indian arms market as well as the potential defection of India from the coalition for a multipolar world that it had constructed after the collapse of the Soviet Union. The potential difficulties with China and Russia, however, were arguably compensated by the new openings with the US allies in Europe and Asia. If Manmohan Singh seemed too hesitant in dealing with the new possibilities and challenges for India, Modi was more than eager to seize the former and address the latter with self-assurance. He seemed confident enough to simultaneously intensify the strategic engagement with the United States and reassure Russia and China that India will not act against their interests.

Modi indeed shared Singh's political instinct that the partnership with the US must be the pillar around which its great power relations must be built. But unlike the Congress leadership, Modi was ready to shed the 'historic hesitations' in engaging with the United States.[13] These hesitations were not just on the left of the Indian political spectrum. The fear and suspicion of the West was equally strong within the BJP and its nativist mass base. Like Atal Bihari Vajpayee before him, Modi seemed unencumbered by that tradition. Modi moved quickly to impart fresh energy to the defence engagement, embraced American ideas on constructing the Indo-Pacific as a geopolitical entity and re-joined the quadrilateral political partnership with Washington, Japan and Australia.[14] In retrospect, it would seem all these moves were part of a logical evolution of the framework of engagement with the United States that Modi had inherited. Yet, on each of these issues, there was strong resistance within and outside the government to move forward with the United States. Modi's decisiveness and the recognition of the importance of building strong ties with the US were critical factors behind the decision. However, Modi's enthusiasm for the United States was not an unconditional one that many of his 'new-liberal' supporters would have liked to see. His strategy was to match the US partnership with stronger relationships with Japan and the European powers, hold on to the traditional partnership with Russia, and demonstrate the political will to confront and cooperate with China. At the core of his strategy was a belief that India must make the best of all relationships while managing the contradictions that emerge.[15]

When he came to power, Modi sought to build a special personal relationship with the Japanese premier Shinzo Abe.[16] Japan was among the first countries that he visited after he became the PM. The framework of annual summitry provided the basis for significant advances in the strategic partnership with Japan.[17] He also chose to end Delhi's neglect of the European powers, especially France.[18] The significant forward movement in both the relationships during Modi's tenure provided a very different basis for imagining India's quest for a multipolar world. In the 1990s, India's emphasis on a multipolar world was largely about limiting the dangers from American hyperpower. It was a hedge against the potential American unilateralism that could hurt India's core national interests—such as securing territorial integrity (Kashmir) and strategic assets (nuclear weapons programme). Even as these threats from the unipolar moment ebbed, the anti-Western tinge of the 'multipolar' frame endured. Even more important, as China's power rapidly rises, the main threats to India's core interests on Kashmir (where India's sovereign claims are challenged by the China-Pakistan Economic Corridor) and nuclear issues (Beijing is the only major power opposing India's entry into the Nuclear Supply Group) are now seen as coming from Beijing.

It was no surprise then that India's emphasis has shifted from the construction of a 'multipolar world' to the promotion of a 'multipolar Asia'. Amidst China's growing comprehensive national power and the political will to assert it, balancing Beijing in Asia has become the central challenge to India's strategic policies. That Russia has drawn ever closer to China and may not be of much use in limiting Beijing's power, making India's partnership with the West that much more important. The prospect of a US retrenchment from Asia or an appeasement of China, however, demands that India devote special attention to the middle powers like France and Japan. Under Modi, the quest for a multipolar world is now seen as resting on stronger alignment with middle powers in Eurasia and the Indo-Pacific.

Meanwhile, Delhi's own growing material capabilities are making it possible to imagine India as a power in its right that can contribute to the construction of a stable regional and international system. In practice this has meant advancing ties with the US as far as possible while recognising the new constraints on American power imposed by its volatile domestic politics and the shrinking options in retaining its Asian primacy. Even as India's comprehensive national power has grown, its strategic gap with China has become wider than ever before. China's GDP at US$ 12 trillion is nearly five times larger than that of India, and Beijing's defence budget is more than three times as big. Even as this asymmetry begins to reflect in the growing tensions on the disputed border and China's power radiates all across India's neighbourhood, Modi's Delhi has chosen to stand up to Beijing's pressures at the Doklam Plateau[19] in the Bhutan sector of the border during the summer of 2017, to publicly criticise President Xi Jinping's Belt and Road Initiative,[20] and to purposefully contest China's geopolitical thrust in India's neighbourhood.

Modi, however, appreciated the need to avoid a premature confrontation with China and manage the bilateral relationship prudently, and preserve a measure of common ground wherever possible. Modi's patience with Xi Jinping appears to have paid off to a degree, as China began to modulate its policy towards India after Doklam. The uncertainty in the international arena, marked by the growing trade and other tensions between Trump's America and China, may have provided an opportunity for the two sides to take a fresh look at bilateral relations after the deterioration of bilateral relations during 2016 and 2017.[21]

If the Wuhan 'informal summit' between Xi and Modi in April 2018 provided a breather for Delhi and Beijing, the Sochi summit between Modi and Putin in May 2018 provided for a recalibration of India-Russia ties that seemed to have headed south under Modi. If Russia was concerned about the new warmth between India and America, Delhi had its concerns about Russia's deepening embrace of China and its flirtations with Pakistan and the outreach to the Taliban. Meanwhile, there is no denying that the regional and global trajectories of India and Russia are diverging. Delhi is also conscious that India's GDP at around US $ 2.6 trillion is nearly double that of Russia and can deal with Moscow on the basis of mutual benefit rather than sentimentalism or nostalgia. Nevertheless, Modi was quite clear, that he would not let go of the partnership with Russia in a hurry despite the new wrinkles.[22]

The neighbourhood

Delhi's great power relations were not conducted on an abstract plane. They were in a dynamic two-way interaction with the developments within India's neighbourhood—immediate and extended. The changing dynamic of great power relations opened up new opportunities for Modi and presented new challenges. Modi's tenure began with the decision to invite all leaders of the subcontinent and the prime minister of Mauritius to attend his swearing-in ceremony as PM. The surprising invitation to Mauritius probably represented Modi's interest in the diaspora links as well as the maritime dimension of India's national policy. Modi's tenure began with a strong commitment to visit all neighbouring countries on a priority basis and travel to the extended neighbourhood—Southeast Asia, Indian Ocean islands, Central Asia and the Middle East. The ideas that India must pay greater attention to its own neighbourhood and reach out to the extended region was not Modi's inventions. They had been integral to India's foreign policy since the end of the Cold War.

Even as Delhi's engagement with the neighbourhood acquired greater intensity under Modi, there was no escaping the structural challenges to India's neighbourhood policy.

The idea that Delhi must look beyond the immediate neighbourhood and integrate regions abutting the subcontinent into India's foreign policy priorities was first articulated by Prime Minister Inder Kumar Gujral in the mid-1990s. In some ways, this marked a return to the more integrated perspective of India's strategic geography that came to the fore during the years of the British Raj. Prime Minister Narasimha Rao's launch of the Look East Policy at the beginning of the 1990s, his outreach to post-Soviet republics in Central Asia, and the growing weight of the Gulf region in India's political economy helped define the new importance of the 'extended neighbourhood' in India's foreign policy. Gujral's successors, Atal Bihari Vajpayee and Manmohan Singh signalled a strong bipartisan commitment to promoting good neighbourly relations with the South Asian states as well as increased India's reach and influence in the extended neighbourhood.

Even as the extended neighbourhood began to demand considerable energy and attention in Delhi, India was under some compulsion to redefine her mental maps. Two new geopolitical categories—Eurasia and the Indo-Pacific—began to loom large over India's worldview.[23] India's inclusion as a full member of the Shanghai Cooperation Organisation in 2018, after a prolonged wait, began to strengthen Delhi's sensitivity to the unfolding geopolitics of Eurasia. Modi also ended India's ambiguity towards the idea of 'Indo-Pacific'—which began to intrude into India's geopolitical lexicon during the Manmohan Singh years. He embraced it with some enthusiasm while defining it in India's own terms rather than those of the United States.[24] For Delhi, the ideas of Eurasia and Indo-Pacific were not merely new geopolitical categories. They were also about competing ideas about India's geopolitical orientation. Will India be drawn closer to the continental coalition against the West led by Russia and China? Or is getting deeper into a maritime coalition led by the United States in the Indo-Pacific? The tension mirrored the post-Cold War divide in the Indian mind between idea of a natural alliance with America and the quest for multipolarity in partnership with Russia and China. The resolution of this tension was not going to come through an abstract doctrinal discussion on foreign policy, but the effectiveness of its engagement with the extended neighbourhood. Modi made significant efforts at strengthening this engagement with different regions of the extended neighbourhood. But many challenges remain.

One area of new focus under Modi was on the Indian Ocean. In early 2015, Modi travelled to three Indian Ocean island states—Seychelles, Mauritius and Sri Lanka—and articulated a strategy that was called SAGAR (security and growth for all; the acronym means 'ocean').[25] This was the first articulation of Indian interests and the means to achieve them since the issue came to fore in the 1960s when the UK announced the withdrawal of its forces from the east of Suez and America stepped in to fill the vacuum in the Indian Ocean. If Indira Gandhi's response was focused on collective security and opposition to external presence, Modi was claiming a larger national responsibility of India in securing the Indian Ocean, a willingness to work with outside powers and a renewed focus on maritime multilateralism.

During 2015, Modi's also made a trip all the five Central Asian states and emphasised India's continuing interest in regional connectivity, joint efforts to counter terrorism, greater security cooperation, and a promise to enhance India's economic performance. With the lack of direct physical access constraining India's ambitions, Modi put new stress on institutional integration with Central Asia as well as bilateral security cooperation[26] The signing of the Ashgabat Agreement on connectivity, the full membership of the SCO, and partnership with Russia and Iran to develop access seemed to provide a more substantial and institutional basis for long-term engagement with the region.

One of the surprising diplomatic advances under Modi has been in the Middle East. Given Modi's publicly proclaimed enthusiasm for the partnership with Israel and the Hindu nationalism championed by his party, the last thing one would have expected was progress in the relationship with key Muslim nations of the Middle East. Modi traveled twice to the United Arab Emirates and once to Saudi Arabia. His strong personal ties with the rulers of the two kingdoms produced unprecedented depth in the engagement with the two countries. Modi also became the first Indian prime minister to visit Israel and Palestine. Even as the conflict between Iran and the Sunni Arab states and Israel sharpened, India did seem to have the room to engage key players in the region.[27]

Modi renamed the 'Look East Policy' as 'Act East Policy' to signal a new energy to Indian diplomacy with the region. With an institutional framework centered around the ASEAN already in place for India's engagement with the East Asian region for nearly two decades, Modi had to simply build on that foundation. The deepening relationship with the ASEAN was celebrated by hosting all the ten leaders of the ASEAN at the annual Republic Day celebrations in Delhi during January 2018. While changing the name of the Look East policy into Act East policy under Modi raised the expectations in

Southeast Asia, there was disappointment in the region that Delhi could not really follow through, especially on trade liberalisation. From the region's perspective, India remained a major part of the problem in finalising the Regional Comprehensive Economic Partnership. The connectivity agenda too was defined by India's slow pace. On maritime-security cooperation, there was a sense that India did not fully seize the opportunities that came its way.[28] As we will see below, some of these problems were integral to India's regional policy and not just limited to Southeast Asia. Many of these problems also afflicted India's engagement with its immediate neighbours in South Asia.

The first of these is the China factor. If India's traditional ties with China were defined by the boundary problem at the bilateral level and the prospects for international cooperation, the regional dimension has become an increasingly important element of bilateral relations in the Modi era. The idea of regional rivalry has long been part of the Sino-Indian mix—India was quite clearly unprepared to cope with China's growing economic and strategic profile in the subcontinent and the Indian Ocean. If the UPA government was hesitant to confront China's regional push, Modi's NDA government demonstrated greater political will and initiative in resisting Beijing in the region. Delhi, however, is conscious of the prospect that this will be a prolonged contestation, over a couple of generations at least, and there might be multiple setbacks in the near term. Although Modi was committed to greater efforts in preserving India's primacy in the subcontinent and natural advantages in the Indian Ocean, there was no way India could match either the Chinese resources or the speed of translating policy declarations into tangible outcomes.[29]

A second important trend has been Delhi's decision to overcome its past hesitations to working with other powers in the subcontinent and the Indian Ocean in the security domain. As pressure from China mounted, Delhi discarded some of its past inhibitions. Under Modi, India has been more willing to team up with the US—whether it is embracing the concept of the Indo-Pacific or re-joining the quad to balance China's growing regional assertiveness. India's balancing strategy in the region, however, is not tied to the apron strings of the United States. It has involved working with other powers like France to strengthen India's position for example in the western Indian Ocean, where Paris has long had a pivotal role.[30]

Third, the emphasis on partnerships did not mean India was going to reduce its own independent security activism in the region. Under Modi, there has been a distinct uptick in developing security cooperation in the region. Some important moves included the supply of helicopters to

Afghanistan, offering substantive amounts of assistance for military procurement[31] ($500 million each to Vietnam[32] and Bangladesh),[33] agreements to develop military facilities in Seychelles, Mauritius, negotiating new access arrangements (Oman), and deepening military cooperation with Singapore.[34] The fact, however, has been that the inability to reorganise India's higher defence organisation and the absence of a developed defence industrial base prevented Delhi from addressing the growing demand for security cooperation with it across the Indian Ocean region.

Fourth, on the economic front, commerce, connectivity, and regional integration were the declared objectives of Modi's foreign policy. On trade liberalisation, Delhi moved to a distinctly negative position deeply disappointing many of its main partners, including the ASEAN and others in the east.[35] On connectivity, India decided to work with Japan to boost regional connectivity between India and her neighbours and jointly pursue strategic economic projects in South Asia and the Indian Ocean.[36] The fruits of this policy are visible in Japan's deep involvement in the modernisation of transport infrastructure in India's Northeast. India also revived the long-stalled project on trilateral highway to connect the Northeast with Burma and Thailand. Delhi also overcame the internal bureaucratic hurdles to gain a contract to develop Iran's Chabahar port project. Under Modi, India has also stepped up the development projects in the immediate neighbourhood including in Afghanistan, Bangladesh, Bhutan, Nepal and Sri Lanka. But India is some distance away from bringing speed and efficiency to the conception and implementation of projects in the neighbourhood. These internal weaknesses and external challenges continue to hobble India's ambitions to deepen regionalism through commerce and connectivity.

In the immediate neighbourhood of the subcontinent, the gap between PM Modi's ambitions to reclaim India's leadership in the subcontinent and the results from his policy initiative remains large. Many of the problems listed above acquire a much sharper dimension in the neighbourhood. To be sure, Modi set himself a high tempo, but soon discovered how hard it is to overcome the structural obstacles to recasting the international relations of the subcontinent. Yet towards the end of the period under review, India's difficulties in dealing with the neighbourhood seemed as intractable as ever. For critics, India's regional policy under Modi was marked by unprecedented floundering.[37] Before we examine the merits of that argument, let us look at the broader dynamic in the subcontinent and locate the advances and setbacks in various bilateral relations within that context.

Not all of this was due to Delhi's handling of the region under Modi as some of his critics allege. Nor has the policy been bereft of important successes. In Afghanistan, the era of relative stability is over. The rise of the Taliban with the support of Pakistan has raised questions about the stability of the regime in Kabul. While this could limit India's future role in the region, the demands from Washington to take greater responsibilities in Afghanistan and the Trump administration's new pressures on Pakistan are opening up new possibilities for Delhi.[38] Yet, there should be no doubt, India's role can't be the principal external shaper of Afghanistan's future. That position certainly belongs to Pakistan, thanks to the geography of the Northwest.

India's ties with Bangladesh have seen considerable advance under Modi, thanks to the partnership with Sheikh Hasina, a long-standing votary of improved relations with India. Together, the two leaders moved forward the relationship on a range of issues—from trade transit to counter-terror cooperation. Modi helped push the parliamentary ratification of the boundary settlement but could not persuade the Chief Minister of West Bengal, Mamata Banerjee to sign off on a pact sharing Teesta waters with Dhaka that was negotiated during the UPA years. If Mamata was (not?) more interested in the agenda of regionalism and reconciliation, Delhi-Dhaka ties might have made far more sweeping transformation. Mamata's obstructionism revealed once again the limits of Delhi's power in engineering major foreign policy challenges in the neighbourhood.[39]

Unlike Hasina in Bangladesh, there has been no real partner in Pakistan who could facilitate even minimal progress in bilateral relations. This has been a structural problem that confronted not just Modi but all of his recent predecessors.[40] Modi, however, created a perception that as a strong leader he could force a basic change in the paradigm. But neither his bold moves—such as landing in Lahore at short notice at the end of 2015 nor his prolonged confrontation with Pakistan since then—could alter the calculus of the Pakistan army towards India. Premier Nawaz Sharif, who seemed eager to explore a *modus vivendi* with India, did not have the freedom to run an India policy of his own. If India's ability to engage the powerful Pakistan army was limited by continuing cross-border terrorism, Delhi's attempt to deter Rawalpindi resulted in turning the Line of Control in Jammu and Kashmir into a line of permanent confrontation. Unlike his predecessors, Modi faced a more benign international environment on India-Pak relations. The economic gap between India and Pakistan has steadily grown wider and in favour of the former. The West, with a view to step up economic and strategic cooperation, gave up any pretence of public pressure on India to negotiate on Kashmir. The Trump administration stepped up the pressure on the Pakistan army to stop supporting cross-border terrorism. Modi's successors therefore might have to come terms with the fact that India's leverage with the Pakistan army remains quite limited.[41]

The Doklam confrontation with China on Bhutanese territory during 2017 has revealed the growing complexity of India's relationship with Bhutan amidst China's rise and its ingress south of the Himalayan slopes. Although it was Bhutan's border with China that India was defending, questions arose as to whether Bhutan was fully on board with Delhi's confrontation with Beijing. China's willingness to cut a separate boundary deal with Bhutan has reinforced the growing sense in Thimphu that they need to conduct their relations with Beijing on an independent basis rather than as an adjunct to India's relations with China. As Bhutan's sense of sovereignty grows along with domestic political pluralism, India's relations with Bhutan have acquired new levels of complexity. This again is a structural problem that will endure long after Modi leaves office.[42]

The developments in Maldives and Nepal[43] showed the perennial problems associated with India's involvement in the domestic politics of the neighbouring countries. If Modi was accused of intervening in Nepal on the question of Madhesi rights in the new constitution, he has been roundly criticised for not doing so in Maldives to protect the opposition from the government. In Sri Lanka, Delhi got much credit, rightly or wrongly, for 'regime change' in the 2015 elections that saw the defeat of strongman Mahinda Rajapaksa. The crisis in Maldives has been persistent through the 2010s and the question of Indian decision-making in relation to its domestic dynamic has been a matter of intense public discourse. Many in Delhi believe India could have intervened more forcefully to ensure the regime in Malé remains friendly. But Delhi, under both UPA and NDA, appears to have avoided hard options despite the desire of some factions in Malé seeking intervention in their favour.[44]

The contrast with Delhi's approach to Nepal could not have been more different. The Modi government did not appear to see the dangers of pushing for minority rights for Madhesis in Nepal beyond a point. Delhi had got accustomed to playing arbiter in Nepal's domestic disputes and picking winners. But India's unofficial blockade of supplies to Nepal during 2015–16, inflamed Nepali nationalism and encouraged its then Prime Minister, K.P. Oli to play the China card and return to power with a much stronger majority in parliament in the general elections of 2017. Although India and Oli began to mend fences, India appears to have done much damage to itself. Its half-hearted coercion did not compel the Nepali nationalists to change course on the constitution. Disappointed, the Madhesis who were banking on Delhi to gain their rights created a solid space for China to entrench itself in the Himalayan Republic.[45]

In debating the Nepal policy, official Delhi often talked of the dangers of ethnic conflict in Nepal turning it into another Sri Lanka. But the argument got turned upside down. Much in the manner that India's support for the Tamil cause in Sri Lanka resulted in the loss of political support among the majority Sinhala community, its focus on the Madhesis lost it the affection of the Nepali majority. Fortunately, the crisis did not turn into a prolonged violent conflict in Nepal and has given some space for Delhi to limit the huge damage. In Sri Lanka itself, the Modi government differentiated itself from the previous government by seeking a more balanced approach to the internal conflict in Sri Lanka and embarking on an intensive outreach to the majority community. India also took some important steps towards resolving the fisheries dispute with Sri Lanka and pitched for the infrastructure projects in the island nation. Even as the overall optics of the relationship improved significantly, Delhi has not been able to persuade the friendly government either into taking big steps to resolve the ethnic question or win any major infrastructure contracts.[46]

What comes across so clearly during the first four years of Modi's tenure as PM, is the difficulty of nudging countries, however small they might be, into bending to external pressures on domestic political issues that cut to the bone. The presumed 'loss of influence' for Delhi in the neighbourhood reflects more of India's internal political contentions rather than an accurate assessment of India's possibilities and limits. While India did inherit the role of a hegemon in the subcontinent from the Raj, it was never in a position to sustain it in the same form. Thanks to the partition and its bitter legacies, Pakistan quickly moved to a strategy of balancing against India. Within a decade of independence, most of India's other neighbours too did not hesitate to pursue similar strategies. The outreach from Islamabad, Colombo, and Kathmandu towards China began by the early 1960s. While the West was the preferred balancer in the second half of the twentieth century, the rise of China has presented them with unprecedented opportunities for acquiring greater 'strategic autonomy' in relation to India. On its part, Delhi had failed to 'modernise' the forms of hegemony, if you will, in the subcontinent. India's prolonged inward economic orientation tended to fray the natural geographic interdependence in the region. Its continuous insertion of itself into the internal politics of the neighbouring countries does create leverages, but it also creates a systemic resentment against Delhi and reinforces the compulsions for balancing. India's challenges in the neighbourhood have been accumulating over the decades. Modi has not created them nor has he transcended them.

Soft power

The emphasis on promoting India's soft power has been a very distinctive feature of Modi's foreign policy.[47] Although 'soft power' as a term gained currency only in the early years of the twenty-first century, the idea that cultural strengths can attract and persuade others has long been very much a part of modern statecraft. Independent India was quick to establish the Indian Council of Cultural Relations to promote Indian culture abroad. Bollywood did even more to raise India's international profile. The religious connect with large parts of Asia played an important role. India's godmen and spiritual gurus acquired huge influence across the world. India's expansive global footprint—through a growing diaspora—also helped spread Indian cuisine and arts around the world. India's successful maintenance of a democratic form of governance in a multi-cultural setting lent Delhi a huge credibility across the world. Its scientific and technological strengths reinforced the growing international perception of India's inevitable rise to the ranks of great powers.[48]

For his part, Modi highlighted some of these multiple natural strengths with greater gusto than any of his recent predecessors. The important gains from India's soft power promotion were somewhat negated by India's new and intense culture wars at home. On the positive side, Delhi's success in getting the United Nations to declare an International Yoga Day reinforced the growing popularity of yoga around the world. The PM's public demonstration of his personal skills at yoga underlined his deep commitment to sustaining one of India's great inheritances. His persistent outreach to the diaspora in all his visits abroad helped the Indian communities abroad gain a new sense of pride in their Indian heritage and inject a sense of commitment to India's success.[49] It also made the Indian government and its diplomatic missions more sensitive to the concerns and interests of growing number of Indians travelling abroad for work, study or leisure.[50] The PM sought to make India more accessible through a long overdue liberalisation of the visa regime.[51]

But there is no escaping the negative side of the ledger. Modi's focus on promoting Hindu-Buddhist culture abroad inevitably raised questions about the government's interest in promoting only parts of Indian tradition and the promotion of the darker side of Hindu nationalism internally.[52] Its obsessive emphasis on promoting Hindi in India's international communication generated concern among the non-Hindi-speaking Indian communities abroad. Modi's outreach to the diaspora was criticised for the PM's temptation to take domestic arguments beyond the water's edge. Even more important, the fresh divisions in the diaspora began to reflect the growing societal conflict at home. Worse still, it did not take long for it to emerge that the diaspora could be a double-edged sword. The disastrous visit of the Canadian prime minister to India in early 2017[53] revealed the negative influence of Sikh extremists on Ottawa and the consequences for India's engagement with a very important country. Not all countries were enthusiastic about Modi reaching out to their citizens and residents over the heads of the government.

More troubling was the inevitable external impact of the deepening internal tensions over caste and religion. The declining Western interest in promoting human rights meant that few major countries were willing to criticise Modi. Even key Muslim nations like Saudi Arabia stayed away from the issues despite the mounting pressure at home on the Muslim minority from a newly empowered Hindu nationalism. But beyond the state to state diplomacy, India's image as a tolerant society and a model for multi-religious and multi-cultural coexistence has taken a big beating in the Modi years. Delhi's image as a rising S&T power was blunted by the new focus on cow-worship and silly Hindu nationalist claims about India's past technological achievement. Although India liberalised the visa regime, it remains a relatively difficult place to enter.[54] It is even harder to visit India for conferences or short-term studies. Visas for internships and work permits remain as difficult as ever.

That India has trouble opening up to the outside world and coming to terms with modernity remains a deeply disappointing development after a quarter century of economic reform and three centuries of encounter with modernity. There is no doubt that divisive, conservative and feudal forces have gained much ground, and this spells serious trouble for India's advance at home and abroad. Although Modi has set a new aspirational international identity for India as 'a leading power', demonstrated India's self-assurance in dealing with great powers and lent a new energy to India's engagement with the neighbourhood, the inertia against economic and political modernisation and the resurgence of nativism are likely to hobble India's near term prospects on the global stage.

17

SCULPTING THE SAFFRON BODY

YOGA, HINDUTVA, AND THE
INTERNATIONAL MARKETPLACE

Jyoti Puri

By successfully lobbying the United Nations (UN) to adopt an international yoga day, Prime Minister Narendra Modi recuperated yoga as India's invaluable gift to the world.[1] Coming at the end of his maiden statement to the UN in September 2014, Modi's proposal must have had a sizeable impact, for within months and with widespread support, the General Assembly passed the resolution, paving the way for June 21, summer solstice in the northern hemisphere, to be observed as International Yoga Day (IYD). Endorsing the view that yoga is an ancient Indian practice, the UN, too, stressed its holistic benefits for health and wellbeing.

Since then, the day has been marked with fanfare around the world and perhaps nowhere more so than in India, where yoga has been elevated to the national stage in an unprecedented way. IYD is celebrated widely as a matter of great national pride, garnering widespread participation from ordinary citizens, public figures, and Hindu nationalist leaders. Under Modi's stewardship, state institutions have taken the lead in orchestrating annual large-scale impact-generating celebrations. The first IYD was successfully aimed at entering the Guinness Book of World Records for the biggest yoga class ever held. All state employees were initially mandated to practice yoga and though it was later made optional, pressure remained to participate in the day's programme. Keeping up the momentum in 2017, Modi personally guided as many as 50,000 people in performing yoga in the city of Lucknow, an event timed to coincide with his party's, the Bharatiya Janata Party (BJP), win in that state.

But, yoga's widening popularity in India and its embrace by Modi, the BJP and other proponents of Hindu nationalism is historically contingent. As a child growing up in Mumbai in the 1970s, I recall well yoga's first national exposure precisely because it was not widely practiced at the time. It came via Dhirendra Brahmachari, mentor and yoga teacher to Indira Gandhi, who was at the helm of the Congress Party, which profited from sectarianism but, unlike the BJP, did not traffic in religious nationalism. Every Sunday morning, Dhirendra Brahmachari would introduce principles and postures of yoga on Doordarshan, the sole state-run television channel. Clad in ascetic robes (the colour wasn't obvious then since we had a black and white TV set), he executed various postures via a bare-chested young man and a young woman wearing a fitted t-shirt and leggings. It was a first for Indian television. It was also the first time I heard the English-language word 'menses', a synonym for menstruation, even though the discussion between Dhirendra Brahmachari and the host was in Hindi. While the show gave a glimpse into yoga's gendered aspects, it would be longer before yoga's Hindu nationalist genealogy came to the forefront.

My awareness as a middle-class and -caste young woman of the resurgence of Hindu nationalism was also through television. From 1987–88, Doordarshan broadcast, also on Sunday mornings, the standardised version of the epic *Ramayana*. As students of media at the time, my friends and I mocked its hyper-dramatised and poorly crafted quality. It was not difficult to be dismissive because of the record-breaking audiences who watched the serial and even installed the leading actors as gods in temples. But, my father's caution that this was the first national populist dissemination of a Hindu epic was eye opening in ways that he didn't intend. This awareness accounted for why the *Ramayana* swiftly gave way to the other epic *Mahabharata* and then the even more blatantly Hindu nationalist series, *Chanakya*, and it explained why communal riots in cities like Mumbai ought to be understood as Hindu nationalist violence on Muslims.

Yoga began gaining traction among the urban privileged around the same time. During trips from the US to India in the 1990s, the years when the economy was being liberalised and opened to foreign capital in new ways, I was struck by yoga's gradual expansion alongside aerobics, jogging and other fitness forms. Still, it would be a while before yoga instructors became widely available for home visits and in studios, and the Aastha channel was established to fill needs exposed by middle-class upward mobility and consumerism. As a technology focused on the self, modern yoga was perfectly suited to the intensifying neoliberal ethics of self-improvement and self-care in that milieu.[2] In the interim, I saw English-language books on yoga and 'how-to' videos lying around the homes of people I knew. In many ways, yoga's acceptance in the West and packaging as a vehicle to offset the ills of modernity and consumerism cleared the path for its widening purchase in India. Its adaptation in the West shaped yoga as a wellness form that was exported back to India. Not surprisingly, Hindu nationalists and Hindu ascetics such as Baba Ramdev sought to reclaim yoga from the sway of the West (while taking advantage of lucrative global markets), and deploy it in the service of the nation.[3] Although the Hindu Right is not the only constituency championing yoga, and indeed their bids at appropriating yoga have been contested by others, yoga is increasingly being used to advance questionable forms of nationalism geared toward internal and external audiences.[4] While this exclusionary and elitist nationalism, whereby India is rendered a Hindu nation and Hinduism itself is reduced to an upper-caste variety, has been long in the making, what is troublingly apparent is how yoga is being mobilised in its service.

Explicably, then, IYD celebrations have drawn concerns and criticisms from minority groups for whom yoga is freighted with religious and upper-caste impositions, not least because yoga's protagonist-in-chief, Modi, is also the envoi of ideologies of Hindu supremacy, abbreviated as Hindutva. Even though yoga has multiple histories in the subcontinent—for instance, Buddhist, Sufi, Jain, Tantra, Nath—and postural yoga has complex transnational trajectories, chanting *om*, doing sun salutations, and embracing yoga's Sanskrit terminology are associated with upper-caste Hinduism. At a moment when Hindutva's emissaries are bent on washing India of its Muslim cultural roots (and Muslims) and promoting Brahmanical Hinduism—for instance, banning beef, rewriting textbooks, enabling cow protection movements that have murdered Muslim and Dalit Bahujan farmers, and unleashing sexual and gendered violence particularly against minority communities—it is particularly difficult to disentangle Hindutva from yoga.[5] The insistence that yoga is about health and wellbeing or about peace and harmony (per the newly refurbished ministry devoted to yoga and indigenous health systems) is insupportable when, in fact, any criticisms of yoga have precipitated crude allegations of antinationalism and sedition, the targets of which are typically Muslim communities.

This essay takes up the historical contingency of Hindu nationalism and its traffic in a popular strand of yoga, involving postures, controlled breathing and other ancillary practices aimed at enhancing individual health and wellbeing. Although yoga has included—and continues to include—a varied set of histories, practices, and meanings, I am interested in exploring why this iteration of yoga, which has gained wide purchase in India as well as in the US, Europe and elsewhere, is now being given such pride of place by the Hindu Right wing. Hindutva is neither a static nor a unitary ideological and political project, but exploring the convergence of support around yoga raises the question of its political and cultural significance to pro-Hindu forces. Why does yoga assume such prominence at this historical moment? Why was it highlighted by Modi in his first speech as head of state to the UN, a statement that had the attention of the international community of nations but also constituencies at home, where it was being closely monitored? How do we understand the symbolism of this gesture, and its material implications? What does the text of Modi's statement tell us about the place of yoga in Hindu majoritarian itineraries and what does this reveal about Hindutva's culturally supremacist visions and desires? Why establish proprietorship over yoga just so that it can be given away as a gift, notwithstanding the problems of giving something that is already in use?

As I interpret the text of Modi's UN statement, what stands out is an insistence on India's Hindu roots, its stability and strength, and its spirituality. These themes are historically consistent with Hindu nationalist platforms and they echo laterally with other initiatives, such as the Make in India programme that Modi inaugurated only two days before his 2014 appearance at the UN General assembly. However, yoga makes these themes uniquely visible and allows a glimpse into the ways that it becomes a means for branding the nation in Hindutva's idioms and ideologies. Developing a national brand has been underway formally and informally since the 1990s, a process to which various governments have contributed. But, looking at nation branding through the lens of yoga especially at a moment of high visibility provides an opportunity to consider the image-making that is currently underway, advancing Hindutva's exclusionary programmes at home while also navigating the imperatives of international politics, the needs of business and foreign invest-ment, and other musts of neoliberal capital.

Branding the nation

Modi's approximately 35-minute-long speech to the UN General Assembly on 27 September 2014 was delivered in Hindi. It began with the idea of India's ancient civilisation and its unique view of the world as one family. This, he said, predisposes India toward multilateralism and to working alongside other nations in advancing the UN's mission. These opening notes set the scene for the rest of the remarks which catalogued the UN's achievements and the role that it still needs to play in the world, and weaved in issues of democracy, South Asian regional politics, and terrorism. Calling for creating peace in the world, inclusive forms of development, and a sustainable world, Modi worked his way to yoga, before issuing a final call to arms. Therefore, what began as a narrative about India's singularity came full circle with yoga. It substantiated the chronicle of an ancient spiritually-oriented civilisation with resonance for the present, thereby rendering both yoga and India as simultaneously timeless and ahead of their time.

Yoga, however, is not the only site for producing and disseminating such narratives of the nation.[6] During and since the 2014 elections, the BJP and Modi blitzed slogans such as 'India First', 'acche din' (good days, or good times), 'Make in India' (MII), and 'minimum government, maximum govern-ance'. MII was introduced as a programme two days before Modi's address at the UN, providing further glimpses into the larger story of which IYD is a piece. A flagship programme of the Modi government, MII was designed to align the nation with the priorities of Foreign Direct Investment (FDI) and to boost business internally. Targeted internationally, toward Non-Resident Indian and local business leaders, the programme represented India as an investment-friendly destination, one that was identified with 'red carpet' rather than 'red tape'. Resonating with the account delivered to the UN shortly thereafter, Modi's speech introducing MII also folded the past and the future to suggest that despite India's developmental lag, it is already ahead of its time—through an educated workforce, technological savvy, a sizeable con-sumer market, and reduced governance.

Further, Modi and the BJP are not the only ones to condense the nation in these pithy, easily communicable ways for international and national con-sumption, for these messages are the outcome of branding India, a process that began in the post-liberalisation era. Although branding is a mode of address typically associated with corporations and organisations seeking to define themselves as they compete for clients and consumers, it has become increasingly ubiquitous. Corporations, educational institutions, non-governmental organisations or not-for-profits and other entities strive to make their unique qualities, the attributes of their products and services, legible and persuasive to consumers. Sometimes this entails a visible blurring of the market, culture, and politics and one notable trend in the Indian context has been the Hinduisation of some brands.[7] Individuals, too, position themselves in this terrain through branding, with Modi becoming a pioneer in this respect by developing what is called 'Brand Modi'.[8]

Nations are no less immune to the interplay of culture, economy and politics, and are being trademarked in order to increase leverage in the context of global capitalism and international governance. Nation branding is fundamentally about shaping political, economic, and cultural opinions on the international and global stages. To be sure, representing national identity for internal and external influence has long been around, but what is historically specific are the ways that nations are being branded akin to corporations, ever since the success of destination branding strategies in tourism.[9] Nation branding is largely understood to be apolitical, externally oriented messaging about national identity aimed at increasing exports, tourism, investment, improving a nation's image, and such.[10] In India, state-led efforts to brand the nation formally date to the creation of the India Brand Equity Foundation (IBEF) in 1996 and the project was revived in 2002 by the BJP government with the intention, as Ravinder Kaur notes, to transform India into a corporate brand.[11]

But, scholarly critics such as Somogy Varga are clear-eyed that nation branding is also an internally directed and conservative process that transforms national identity, and lets it be shaped outside of the democratic arena, a point that Kaur's discussion of IBEF also confirms.[12] In this neoliberal order, states become handmaidens to the logics of foreign investment and global capital, a task which the BJP has prioritised by producing the Incredible India and India Shining campaigns over the years. As Kaur notes, these efforts mark a shift from nation building to nation branding where image is of foremost importance. Social media, websites, and such are well suited to this kind of brand messaging and the BJP has been particularly effective at harnessing their potential during the 2014 elections, while Modi routinely uses them as platforms for communication.[13]

The point that I am leading up to, however, is not just that Modi and the BJP have played an important part in this machinery to transform the nation, or that nation branding has only occurred under their watch. Rather the point is to consider how they have advanced this project, the kinds of brand identities and images that they have produced, and the ways in which they have imprinted their visions on Brand India. The very premise of nation branding—which means collapsing the differences between citizens and consumers and letting market rationalities dictate national vision—is deeply flawed regardless of political affiliation, but when brands code nations in majoritarian, even supremacist, and exclusionary idioms, it makes coming to grips with them all the more urgent. Brand identities are inimical to nation building and the interests of many citizens, residents, and immigrants, and they can last well beyond their political immediacy. The BJP's current political sway will diminish at some point, nonetheless what is likely to persist are the religious, casteist, and gendered beliefs that inform Brand India and risk becoming further sedimented in populist narratives about the nation.

Yoga is apposite for Hindutva's ongoing project of branding the nation. It provides a pathway for historicising the nation, while simultaneously reaching into individual's hearts, minds, and bodies. Yoga functions both symbolically and materially, as the nation's metaphor and its literal embodiment. In what follows, I show how a particular historically situated understanding of yoga, what has come to be known as postural yoga, facilitates the project of Hindu majoritarianism and call attention to its elemental themes—of this majoritarianism and its itineraries.

Saffron nation

When Modi began his statement with reference to ancient India, which he consistently referred to as *Bharat*, and its unique intelligence, majoritarian audiences at home were predisposed to interpreting as fact the myth that national history begins with Hinduism. Nowhere in his remarks did Modi use the word Hindu, but precisely because of the settled associations between antiquity, epistemology and upper-caste Hinduism even outside of India, he didn't have to. Numerous scholars have shown that romanticist orientalisms and anti-colonial nationalisms converged to bring India into history as Hindu and upper-caste to boot. What is pertinent here is that yoga was instrumental to this process of historicisation as well as to the inception of anti-colonial Hindu nationalisms, which have persisted in India.

Swami Vivekananda (1863–1902) is the pivotal figure in modern genealogies of yoga and Hindu chauvinism. Vivekananda's singular contribution was to develop an anti-colonial stance by transforming Hinduism into a nationalist ideology.[14] Motivated by the need to counter colonial rule and especially the racism endemic to it, Vivekananda paradoxically drew on European romanticist orientalists' reconstructions of Indian history. Pivoting around selective Brahmanical scriptures, these European orientalist discourses provided him and others with the groundwork on which to construct anti-colonial but explicitly Hindu notions of the past. Embedded in these reconstructions were ideas of Hindu civilisational greatness, a golden period so to speak, that needed to be rejuvenated in order to combat colonial rule and Western hegemony.

To this end, Vivekananda revived what he called *Raja Yoga*, a modern-day blend of Patanjalian Yoga, Samkhya philosophy, and neo-Vedanta spirituality.[15] As Peter van der Veer usefully summarises:

> The typical strategy of Vivekananda was to systematise a disparate set of traditions, make it intellectually available for a Westernised audience and defensible against Western critique, and incorporate it in the notion of 'Hindu spirituality', carried by the Hindu nation that was superior to 'Western materialism' brought to India by an aggressive and arrogant 'British nation'.[16]

Vivekananda's rendition of yoga was no different in this respect and quite pliable to the needs of anti-colonial Hindu supremacy.

The idea of yoga was particularly fertile to this incipient Hindu nationalism because it could be revived as a sign of ancient Indian civilisation and its spiritual wealth, while also sidelining other religious and cultural legacies. As a reinvented and systematised discipline, it also aligned with Vivekananda's bent toward making asceticism, spirituality, and such more practical, especially in service of what he describes as man-making as well as nation-building at a moment when both were in question—native masculinity was in crisis and nationalism was inchoate. He recuperated yoga toward, as Joseph Alter succinctly describes, 'a kind of no-nonsense, self-confident, muscular—and, therefore, masculinised—spiritualism'.[17] Vivekananda's legacy lies in discursively tying together yoga, Indian antiquity, Eastern spiritualism, and an embodied masculinist Hindu nationalism.[18] Even though he was dismissive of postural yoga and had little influence on the iterations that abound today, Vivekananda helped clear the path for Hindu nationalist pre-occupation with building strong, virile male bodies through physical regimens that continue to this day. At the same time, as Alter cautions, militant strands of Hindu nationalism, the Rashtriya Swayamsevak Sangh (RSS) being a case in point, incorporated yoga but did not prioritise it in their programmes for building Hindu corps. By itself, postural yoga was seen as not muscular, masculine or militant enough for RSS programmes, which have favoured training with *laathis* (staves), wrestling, and such.

Therefore Modi, the BJP, and other Hindu nationalist groups rallying around yoga, with the RSS insisting that it be mandatory for students, represents something of a departure. In fact, the proposal for establishing an international yoga day was borrowed from a Lisbon-based guru, Amrtya Suryananda Maha Raja, né Jorge Veiga e Castro. Suryananda had been campaigning for an international yoga day for fourteen years until the cause was taken by H.R. Nagendra, founder of the Swami Vivekananda Yoga Anusandhana Samsthan (aka Yoga University) in Bengaluru, the nephew of a high-ranking official in the RSS, and the guru who initiated the young Modi into yoga while he was still a foot soldier in this organisation.[19]

At a moment of yoga's high popularity in India and especially the West, Modi and others draw upon earlier histories of anti-colonial but exclusionary and elitist nationalism. While the post-liberalisation context is quite different from the conditions under which Vivekananda crafted *Raja Yoga* as a response to colonial rule and especially colonial racism, what is consistent is using yoga to saffronise India—defining India as Hindu (thereby reducing the nation's religious and cultural pluralism) and promoting ideologies of a glorious and superior Hinduism (the violent brunt of which is borne by religious and cultural minorities).

Stable nation

Upon introducing the theme of ancient intelligence, Modi shifted seamlessly to India's commitment to multilateralism, the historic role of the UN, briefly pausing to catalogue its achievements, before going to mention democracy and increasing stability in parts of the world. It was a series of quick changes, raising the question of what connects India's firm belief in multilateralism to the UN's list of collective institutional work toward peace and security, human rights, and economic development to democratic surges in South Asia, West Asia, and North Africa and increasing stability in Latin America.

At first glance, the underlying thread is India's explicit and subtle imaging. By referencing India's ancient and unique worldview (rather than India's status as a UN founding member) that predisposes it toward multilateralism, Modi positioned the nation as an important UN member-state. In this rendering, India is a steady co-partner in advancing the UN's mission, helping end wars, preventing conflict, maintaining peace, providing for the hungry and the children, and protecting the planet. It remained at the heart of the ensuing narrative as the speech wound forward, but in less explicit ways. Modi made mention of democracy's swells in Afghanistan, Nepal and Bhutan, its inroads in West Asia and North Africa and Asia, and emphasised increasing stability in Latin America, while absenting India from this list. In this projection, India is the standard-bearer, suggesting that its democratic journey is already complete and its stability is not in question.

In fact, stability is an important underlying theme of this speech and, I would suggest, of the Hindu nationalist brand. The leitmotif framed the entire statement, allowing Modi to introduce India as a nation undergoing rapid social and economic transformation (read: modernisation) but also representing it as constant through reference to ancient culture and a bent toward multilateralism. Implying strength and steadiness, stability, as I see it, is fundamentally about how the Hindu Right has been seeking to distinguish the nation on the global and international stage. To be sure, the idea that India is a strong, stable democracy cuts across party and ideological lines, but what requires underscoring is how this representation issues directly from the Hindu Right's nationalist aspirations.

Analysing Hindutva's surge in India since the 1980s, Thomas Blom Hansen cogently notes 'that its practices are centrally concerned with notions of national honour and how a vibrant sense of national community can stabilise social identities, governances, and the larger social order, and ultimately extract a much-desired global recognition of India's place among the leading nations in the world'.[20] The difficulties with such desires, however, are that the national community is understood through overt religious, casteist, gendered and sexual refusals (Muslims, Dalit Bahujan, women, gay and lesbian subjects, and other such categories of personhood and being). Further, making the argument that India, a state confronting the urgencies of widespread poverty, illiteracy, routine caste, gender, and sexual violence, and brutal state repression in several parts of the country, is a premier nation is challenging to say the least. Nonetheless, this need has driven BJP governments' national policy from conducting nuclear tests and launching unmanned spacecraft to promoting India as a destination for foreign investment. Thus, when yoga is mobilised as sign and symbol of India's illustriousness, it asks to be read in light of such desires and aspirations—to understand the speech's progression—from Indian antiquity and its defining beliefs to yoga as India's unique gift to the world—as allegories of national strength and stability. Postural yoga, in all its connotations of physical and emotional potency, steadiness, and constancy, works well for this brand image.

At the same time, yoga represents a material resource in line with the metaphors of stability and strength by alluding to a nation of healthy and fit citizens, suitable for the needs of serving the global economy. Various governments, including the BJP, have delivered Indian labour to foreign investors, ranging from operating call centres, providing commercialised surrogacy, 'donating' organs, populating clinical trials to manufacturing goods of all kinds. As a promissory note of health and wellbeing, yoga supports these economic programmes. In fact, what distinguishes the Hindu Right's appropriation of yoga is the objective of producing physically fit citizens in service of the Hindu nation.[21] As Chandrima Chakraborty argues, yoga in this context is about 'technologies of the self', or what she calls somaticized religio-nationalism, that advances Hindutva's ideological projects.[22]

Spiritual nation

The remarks about stability took Modi directly to the topic of Pakistan, leading him to establish terrorism as a crucial problem facing the world, to call for inclusive development globally and a sustainable world, and then finish with a flourish—yoga. Prefacing that his government has prioritised advancing friendship and cooperation with India's neighbours since day one, Modi reaffirmed this intention toward Pakistan. He expressed his desire to engage in serious nonpartisan dialogue in a peaceful environment, without the shadow of terrorism, in order to increase peace and cooperation. But, Pakistan, too, is liable for coming forward to seriously engage in this nonpartisan dialogue, according to him. Nonetheless, expressing doubt about the success of resolving issues through this forum in the next breath, Modi shifted attention to flood-affected people in Kashmir, describing how his government served people in (Indian-occupied) Kashmir and offered to help Kashmiri people in Pakistan. Then, with yet another abrupt shift and a gesture to a time of flux and change around the world, he went on to focus on the threat of terrorism that is affecting Asia as well as the rest of the globe. Asking UN member nations to adopt the Comprehensive Convention on International Terrorism, he noted the importance of inclusive development, eradication of poverty worldwide, and living in a sustainable world as a lead up to yoga.

This is where the earlier themes of saffronisation and stability meet spirituality. Suggesting that respect for nature is integral to Indian spirituality, Modi went on to call special attention to yoga amidst discussions about climate change and holistic healthcare, unity with nature, or what he called 'back to basics' in English in a speech that was in Hindi. (Notwithstanding the fact that India's rivers and cities are among the most polluted in the world.) Modi's remarks derived from established discourses of Hindu spiritualism that were produced in opposition to and as a remedy for Western materialism. Therefore, extolling yoga as the invaluable gift of ancient Indian tradition, he described it as a modality that unites mind and body, thought and action, restraint and attainment, harmonises man (sic) and nature, and represents an overall vision for health and wellbeing and a means to fight climate change. Here again, Modi's remarks repeated the ways that Vivekananda and others insisted upon yoga's Hindu genealogies while also disentangling yoga from Hindu ritual practices to promote it in the West. The desacralisation of yoga has been another reason why militant Hindu nationalists had stopped short of wholeheartedly embracing yoga, but Modi was adhering to common understandings of yoga as a secular spiritualised practice, emphasising one's health and wellbeing. This Hindu nationalist stance on yoga and Indian spirituality is a historical anomaly, raising questions about how India is being re-branded and to what effect.

Seen from this angle, spirituality emerges as the third theme shaping Modi's statement, linking his remarks on Pakistan, terrorism, but also on inclusive development and eradication of poverty, to yoga. Spirituality here is shorthand for innate tendencies toward dialogue, peace, self-control, and service in ways that are loosely associated with yoga. According to this perspective, India's inherent orientation toward spirituality positions it as a model of restraint and control in implicit contrast with Pakistan's inclinations toward terrorism and its failures to work toward resolving political tensions. In this context, control and restraint are masculinist idioms, deriving from ascetic traditions that were the forerunners of modern yoga and which also influenced discourses and practices of Hindu nationalism. India, in this account, is open to dialogue, even friendship and co-operation. The reference to the ravages of flooding in Indian-occupied Kashmir and the charity and generosity toward Pakistan further confirm India's spiritual bent, even as the brutal state repression in Indian-occupied Kashmir is sidestepped. While spiritual India as brand identity may be less than convincing to India's neighbours, it is part of the political strategy designed to appeal to select internal and external audiences.

Modi's gesture toward Pakistani terrorism and his subsequent discussion of terrorism in West Asia and around the world are also legible in contrast with spirituality. For Vivekananda and others, notions of Hindu spirituality were developed in opposition to projections of Western materialism but also Islam, a stance that continues to define Hindu nationalism.[23] Further, for the Hindu Right and leaders of the likes of Modi, terrorism and extremism are coded Muslim, which explains why the Indian-sponsored convention aimed at combatting terrorism that Modi asked to be adopted is opposed by the Organisation of Islamic Cooperation at the UN, among others. Thus repeated references to India's distinct philosophical and cultural traditions culminating in yoga are Modi and his government's attempts to distance India from Islam while 'linking West', a phrase and policy that he spelled out two days before his UN speech in his MII address. Marking a rupture with India's twenty-five year old 'look East' policy of partnering with Southeast Asia, it also departs from Hindutva's anti-West stance.

Closing thoughts

Modern postural yoga—as a secular spiritualised set of practices, emphasising poses, stretching, and breathing toward health and wellbeing—begins its journey as a response to colonial rule and European racism. Although there is little similarity between Vivekananda's *Raja Yoga* and the postural yoga that has subsequently come to dominate widely, and despite considerable difference between colonial and postcolonial contexts, yoga is still being used to advance majoritarian itineraries. Vivekananda's crafting and popularisation of yoga was troubled even then, what with the efforts to deny India's religious, cultural, and caste pluralism, but the Hindu Right's recent appropriation of yoga is more starkly advancing culturally supremacist ideologies. In a nutshell, it is being used to extend and amplify the project of saffronising India, while erasing sidelined Hindu traditions, making invisible those who remain at its margins, and rendering religious minority groups, particularly Muslims and Christians, outside the fold of the nation. While the principles of diversity and secularism remained aspirational in the postcolonial India that I knew as a young person, what has been especially painful to witness is their steady erasure under the rise of Hindutva and the role that postural yoga is playing in it.

Despite the emphasis on yoga as a tool for health and wellbeing, it would be a mistake to see Hindutva's promotion of yoga separately from the politics of cow protection and lynching, the ongoing saffronisation of textbooks, attempts to terrorise Muslim and Dalit communities, and erase especially Islamic and Christian cultural traditions and legacies. Is it any wonder, then, that for Muslims, Christians, and others who have been on the outside of elitist Hinduism the mandate to participate in the 2015 IYD in India represents a form of religious assimilationism and a fresh assault on religious and cultural practices? Chanting *om* and performing sun salutations, which were originally part of the first IYD programme, are unambiguously tied to upper-caste Hinduism. Paying obeisance to the sun through *surya namaskaar* derives from a Vedic tradition, and Sanskrit, the primary language of postural yoga, is also decidedly associated with Brahmanical Hinduism.

If yoga is furthering Hindutva's culturally supremacist ideologies internally, then it is also serving external branding needs through citations of Hindu cultural superiority. For leaders such as Modi, who by all accounts has a limited repertoire of yoga postures, promoting yoga has meant redefining its relationship to Hindutva as a means of securing India's place among the leading (read: Western) nations of the world. But in contrast to the nuclear testing and launching of rockets and satellites that are intended as evidence of India's global ascendancy, yoga signals India's unique relevance to a world in need of spiritual but secular truth in ways that resonates with but also rewrites earlier Asian values discourses. Invoking ancient wisdom through yoga is an attempt to place India on a par with other national brands—freedom and democracy as a US brand identity, or civilisation as a European trope. Yoga has come to be recognised by the Hindu Right as 'soft power',[24] implying that it allows India to exert influence externally without the use of force or coercion. Taking this position, one such commentator on IYD in *Hinduism Today* echoes Vivekananda's stance from a century before, suggesting that 'Spreading increasingly, powerfully, globally are India's national ideas of nonviolence, religious tolerance, devotion and soul-stirring philosophy'.[25] Notwithstanding the urgencies of staggering state, religious, gendered, caste-based and sexualised violence in the Indian context, appropriating yoga fuels the Hindu Right wing's global aspirations and is related to the overall vision that has driven militarisation, regional imperialism, and neoliberal development particularly, although not solely, under the reign of the BJP.

Contending for the global recognition of India's superiority, these efforts to promote yoga also reverse earlier anti-Western stances motivated by colonial rule and imperialism. In this altered context, yoga represents a means of 'linking West', allying with it politically and economically, while making common cause with the West's Islamophobic 'war on terrorism'. Distancing India from Islam and its neighbours is part of this strategy. In a context where it also appears necessary to deliver the nation, its labour and its consumers to the interests of foreign capital, yoga is mobilised to trademark India as Hindu, stable, strong, and spiritual, aligning with other neoliberal projects such as Make in India and Incredible India. Promoting yoga, it turns out, is about the convergence of nationalist, supremacist, neo-imperial, and neoliberal imperatives.

While it is difficult and perhaps too early to assess the impact of this saffronised Indian brand, the associations between yoga and high Hinduism outside of India seem to be gaining strength. For instance, a recent article on yoga's uptake in Pakistan assumes yoga's Hindu heritage, ignoring yoga's many histories in South Asia, including those closer to Islam.[26] The Hindu-identified diaspora in countries such as the US has wholeheartedly welcomed yoga's elevation and its routine dissemination though Indian TV channels, yoga camps, etc. Community spokespersons are engaged in seeking to wrest yoga from its desacralised, culturally appropriated, and commodified forms abounding in North America. While there is compelling reason to be critical of what some have identified as the yoga industrial complex, dominated as it is by white women and men, reproducing Hindu nationalist renditions of yoga is not the solution either. Rather the challenge, as I see it, is to come to grips with the convergences of Western cultural appropriation and commodification and casteist and gendered Hindu nationalism that are activated by performing forms of yoga, which are about saying *namaste*, lighting incense, chanting Sanskrit hymns, citing Patanjali, bowing to statues of Ganesh, and other such practices masquerading as authenticity.

PART VII

WHAT RULE OF LAW?

18

AGGRESSIVE HINDU NATIONALISM

CONTEXTUALISING THE TRIPLE *TALAQ* CONTROVERSY

Flavia Agnes

Within a polarised environment, where 'neutral, secular, liberal and progressive' voices demanding justice for Muslim women are placed in opposition to the 'bearded, misogynist and patriarchal' Muslim clerics, it closes the space for Muslim women to express a nuanced view regarding the present controversy over triple *talaq* and enforces upon them an artificial identity question. B.S. Sherin, a research scholar of comparative literature in Hyderabad, articulates her concern:

> It is truly unfortunate that Muslim women's identity is highlighted only in terms of personal laws, especially after the Shah Bano case. This overarching focus on personal law presents any improvement of Muslim women's lives as contingent only on the reform of personal laws. By raising the question of personal laws and of community-binding, the larger implications of culture, class and region on the lives of Indian Muslim women are deferred. Muslim women themselves have come out in large numbers against the present campaign on Triple Talaq to say what is much more urgently needed is empowerment and education. But their

voices do not receive larger audience. The recent appearance of articulate, practicing Muslim women challenging 'progressive voices' has been written off as 'motivated by patriarchal forces' or 'indoctrinated'.[1]

Campaigns for the enactment of rights and laws have been an important plank for the Indian women's movement. But unless the rights are located within the everyday lived realities of women's lives, they remain hollow words in a statute book and do not empower women. These rights have to be linked to local, subaltern struggles for effective implementation and to change the ground reality of women within these communities.[2]

When and how did the issue of lack of rights of Muslim women under their personal laws come to the fore? Why did the media not publicise the gains secured by Muslim women through the process of litigation during the last three decades? Why is there an overemphasis on triple *talaq* today to the exclusion of all other gender concerns? Is gender being construed as a neutral terrain, disjunct from the contemporary political reality? Within a sharply polarised environment where gender is pitted against community rights, and there are no easy solutions, what would be the most viable strategy to ensure dignity and offer protection to Muslim women and secure their economic rights? These are some critical issues which I will untangle in this chapter as I explore the contentious issue of triple *talaq*. The aim is to provide an intersectional and historical context which will help to clear some misconceptions surrounding the rights of Muslim women under the Muslim personal law regime.[3]

The tightrope walk

The *suo motu* (on its own) reference to constitute a special bench to examine discriminatory practices of Muslim law such as polygamy and triple *talaq*, was made by a two-judge bench comprising of Justices Anil Dave[4] and Arun Kumar Goel, in *Prakash v. Phulawati*[5] on 16 October 2015 while deciding an appeal concerning the rights of a Hindu woman to ancestral property. In an unprecedented manner, responding to stray comments by an advocate present in court and relying upon some articles in the press, the judges made a reference to the Chief Justice to constitute a special bench to examine discriminatory practices which violate the fundamental rights of Muslim women. This came to be titled as 'Re: Muslim Women's Quest for Equality'.[6]

The Constitutional Bench headed by Chief Justice Jagdish Singh Khehar heard the arguments in this matter along with four other judges—Justices Kurian Joseph, Rohinton F. Nariman, Uday U. Lalit and S. Abdul Nazeer

(Muslim), during the summer vacation, 11–18 May 2017. Appreciating the strategy of placing four minority-community judges on a five-judge bench, Professor Tahir Mahmood, an authority on Islamic law, commented that such a move was needed since the unruly media debates had given the issue the colour of a majority-minority tussle.[7] In the same spirit, to keep a tight rein over the proceedings and to narrow down the scope of the arguments, the constitutional bench also declined to examine the issue of Muslim polygamy and confined the arguments strictly to the question—whether instant triple *talaq* constitutes a core belief among Sunni Hanafi followers of Islam in India.[8]

Tagged along with the original reference were several subsequent writ petitions/intervener applications by individual Muslim women, Muslim women's organisations including the RSS-affiliated Rashtrawadi Muslim Mahila Sangh, the All India Muslim Personal Law Board (hereafter AIMPLB)[9] and other affiliate organisations such as the Jamiat Ulama-i-Hind, etc.

The hearing aroused a great deal of public interest, as the packed court room, even while the court was on summer vacation, and the extensive reporting of the case each day indicate. This is not surprising considering that the issue had received wide media publicity since August 2015, when an NGO working with Muslim women, the Bharatiya Muslim Mahila Andholan (BMMA) had released a report, 'Seeking Justice Within Family', based on interviews with 4,710 women from the lower economic strata. Though the report examined many aspects of Muslim women's lives, the press statement which was issued flagged triple *talaq* and polygamy as the primary concerns of Muslim women in India, overriding concerns of poverty, illiteracy and marginalisation.[10]

According to Abusaleh Shariff and Syed Khalid, the publicity that the issue received is next only to demonetisation which affected the majority of Indians while the issue of triple *talaq* affected a miniscule minority of Muslims.[11] Commenting upon the manner in which this issue was used by the prime minister during the election campaign in Uttar Pradesh, the authors, relying upon the 2011 Census data, brought out the fact that the number of deserted Hindu women who live in deplorable conditions far exceeds the number of Muslim divorcees and deserted women. The numbers are staggering—out of 2.3 million separated and abandoned women, around 2 million are Hindus, as against 280,000 Muslims. And yet no attention is paid to them, even while the prime minister was lamenting over the plight of Muslim divorcees. They also pointed out that despite the hype, divorce among Muslims is much lower than in the majority community. However, they conceded that divorcees and deserted women face destitution, loss of rights and social stigma, but it is not a unique problem confronting the Muslim community but a more pervasive social problem located within patriarchy.

It needs to be emphasised here, as those who have campaigned for abolition of arbitrary triple *talaq* have repeatedly urged, numbers are insignificant. Even if a few women are divorced in an arbitrary manner, it still constitutes violation of their fundamental rights. The campaigners were objecting to the right of a Muslim husband to use his power of divorce in an arbitrary manner against a defenceless woman and the lack of a corresponding right for the woman which amounts to gender discrimination.[12]

However, giving the issue communal flavour, the then newly appointed Chief Minister of Uttar Pradesh, Yogi Adityanath (a member of an extreme Hindu Right-wing organisation, the Hindu Mahasabha, and founder of its militant youth wing, the Hindu Yuva Vahini)[13] compared triple *talaq* to the disrobing of Draupadi.[14] Another of his cabinet colleagues, Swami Prasad Maurya (also a member of RSS), commented that Muslims resort to *talaq* to keep 'changing wives' to 'satisfy their lust' and leave their wives to beg on the street which aroused the wrath of members of the Muslim Women's Personal Law Board who demanded his resignation.[15]

These statements from Sangh Parivar leaders illustrate the Hindu nationalist strategy of disseminating the discriminatory stereotype of the Muslim man as a sexual threat, which fuels the cultivation of masculinist heteronormativity among Hindu men. The RSS provides us with the best example of this trend. It has branches known as '*shakhas*' which are training grounds to prepare the young to be foot soldiers to defend the 'motherland'. They inculcate hatred towards Muslims who are viewed as the 'other' both of the nation and of Hindus, at a very young age. Their rigorous and disciplined training prepares them both emotionally and physically to attack Muslims who are viewed as stronger than them (because they consume non-vegetarian food). The fear of an imminent Muslim attack makes young boys trained into the RSS ideology to be always battle-ready. In this ideology Muslims are projected not only stronger and more masculine but also sexually more virile. The battles are fought in the name of protecting the Hindu sisters and the Hindu motherland, and this discourse is enhanced by oversignified stories of Muslim womens' mistreatment by Muslim men. Today there are many more fringe outfits which project the same ideology and hence the rot has seeped into the composite social fabric and torn it asunder. This ideology works against Hindu women as the RSS projects Hindu women as passive objects to be 'protected'.

Moreover, the issues of Muslim divorce and polygamy have been projected as an appeasement to Muslim men and an injury to Hindu men as the latter are denied the right to have unlimited number of wives which the custom and Hindu scriptures had sanctioned. A petition filed by an 'aggrieved' Hindu before the Bombay high court in 1952 (Narasu Appa Mali) challenging the provision of monogamy for Hindus on the ground that it discriminates against Hindus since Muslims are granted this privilege is reflective of this sentiment.[16] This judgement occupies a centre space in the debate on whether personal laws are subject to fundamental rights as the judgement in its anxiety to uphold the constitutional validity of Hindu monogamy held that personal laws are not subject to fundamental rights. The supreme court has skirted this issue and never addressed it frontally, nor has it struck down this ruling as unconstitutional.

However, the demand to abolish polygamy among Muslims was projected as a concern for Muslim women to camouflage its communal undertone. In the recent controversy over triple *talaq*, the right-wing political parties projected it purely as a concern for Muslim women, though the demand was used as a stick to beat the Muslim community and to project them as backward and anti-women.

The fact that the RSS has also been campaigning for abolition of triple *talaq* and had intervened in the supreme court case reflects the tightrope walk Muslim women who are demanding a change in their personal laws are faced with, when a right-wing anti-Muslim government is in power. In this situation, the ideal solution would be adopting the policy of 'reform from within', for the Muslim Personal Law Board to issue a clear statement that arbitrary and instant triple *talaq* is un-Quranic and hence invalid and mandate that all divorces must essentially be through the prescribed Quranic mode of *talaq-e-hasan* or *talaq-e-ahasan*.[17] This would send a clear signal to the Muslim community. The Board's refusal to come out with such a statement led to a stalemate where the supreme court was compelled to intervene and declare the law.

The tightrope walk of Muslim women is also located within a context in which abstract notions of rights inherited from Euro-American liberal political traditions are present in some form in the constitution of India under Article 14, which is premised on all are equal and have to be treated equally. However, an exception has been carved out under Article 15 (3) to provide a space for special protection to the marginalised—scheduled castes, scheduled tribes, women and children. But Muslims do not figure in this; rather, a special protection for minorities is provided under Articles 25–26 which is also a fundamental right. In essence, there is a tension between individual rights and group rights within the constitution itself, which is being exploited by Hindu Right-wing groups to exacerbate relations within Muslim communities and families.

The rising wave of Hindu fundamentalism

Since the BJP-led NDA coalition government came to power in 2014, dislodging the earlier UPA coalition led by the Indian National Congress (perceived by minorities as a more secular and inclusive party), Hindu fundamentalism has escalated to a new height. The extreme right-wing outfit, the RSS, provides the present regime its ideological mooring of building a Hindu *rashtra* (nation). Within this political framing, the projection of Muslim as anti-national, terrorist and enemy of the Hindu nation, has gained credence and the secular fabric of the country has been ruptured. The forces of communalism have spread far and wide and taken roots even among the middle and lower classes. The Uttar Pradesh (UP) state elections in 2017 have given a boost to the party as it gained power with a thumping majority, dislodging the Samajwadi Party which gave Muslims a voice. The choice of Yogi Adityanath, a prominent member of the RSS and an avowed Muslim hater, as chief minister, has served to highlight the extent to which the Hindu majority vote could be mobilised around an anti-Muslim agenda. It is interesting to note that the BJP did not field a single Muslim candidate and the number of Muslims in the state legislature reduced from seventy-four in 2012 to a mere twenty-four in 2017.[18]

Though the BJP, as part of the NDA, was in power between 1998–2004, Congress was ruling in several states. Even at the centre, Congress had sufficient seats to play an important role as the opposition. There was always the hope that Congress will soon return to power. Prime Minister Atal Bihari Vajpayee, though belonging to the BJP, was considered to be a moderate. For this reason, he was chosen as the prime minister rather than L.K. Advani, who was considered to be more extremist. The secular fabric of the country was intact though there were occasional disruptions to communal harmony by way of riots. But apart from the Gujarat carnage when Modi was the Chief Minister of Gujarat, the others were contained locally.

In 2018, the situation is different. The BJP is ruling in most states (sometimes along with other local political parties) and the RSS is playing a visible role in governance and in influencing public policies. All state institutions have been taken over by the right-wing extremist ideology. Educational institutions have turned saffron. Independence of the judiciary is at stake. Lynchings of Muslims are going on every day on the pretext that they are cattle thieves. Muslim livelihoods are vanishing, and there is a total neglect of Muslim-dominated areas, which are termed as 'Muslim ghettos' and breeding grounds of terrorists—Biwandi and Malegaon are some examples.

In this context, the triple *talaq* controversy divided secular groups further in the name of protecting the Muslim woman and led to further demonising the Muslim male. Pushed to the wall, the Muslim Personal Law Board played a negative role, which earned them the label of archaic, patriarchal, and anti-women. This served to complicate matters further. In 2018, even Congress, the traditional supporter of Muslims, wished to distance themselves from them in order not to alienate the Hindu vote bank.

It appears that under the present regime, Muslim as a political identity has ceased to matter. The huge Muslim population of about 200 million is passing through a most difficult phase. A deluge of anti-Muslim tirades, in the form of love jihad,[19] *ghar wapasi*[20] and cow vigilantism, have been unleashed upon the largely poor, uneducated and deeply religious community. The beef ban and the more recent ban against cattle slaughter has led to the loss of trade and livelihood of large sections of Muslims. The ascendance of the holy cow into the political arena has given rise to cow vigilantism with (self-designated "cow protector") squads roaming the countryside posing a grave risk to the lives of ordinary Muslims. The lynching of fifty-year-old Mohammed Akhlaq at Dadri in Uttar Pradesh, by a mob of 100 *gaurakshaks* just a few kilometres away from the capital city in September 2015, and the prime minister's refusal to make a public statement condemning the action of such unruly mobs, came in for sharp criticism from secular sections of society.[21] Since then there have been several other such mob killings in different north Indian states.[22] The most poignant of these is the stabbing of a young sixteen year old, Junaid, on the Delhi–Mathura local train on 22 June 2017 during the holy month of Ramzan in a totally unprovoked manner, while fellow travellers looked on.[23]

These brutal killings of Muslims by violent mobs have failed to interrupt the routine business of our legislatures. They have not stirred the collective social and political conscience of a society meant to be governed by the rule of law. According to Apoorvanand, a human rights activist and scholar, the harsh truth is that India's legislators and parliamentarians seem to have deserted the country's Muslims.[24] However, the spontaneous protests organised by secular and human rights groups in most major cities of India, under the slogan 'not in my name', finally led the prime minister to issue a statement against these lynchings.[25]

It is against this political backdrop of Muslims being pushed to the status of second class citizens[26] that we must examine the exaggerated interest in the issue of triple *talaq* by the mainstream media and the government's eagerness to reform the Muslim Personal Law ostensibly to secure the rights of Muslim women. While the lynching of Muslims did not arouse public conscience, triple *talaq*, which hit the headlines around the same time, witnessed unprecedented media publicity. This makes one wonder whether non-reporting of lynchings and heightened publicity given to triple *talaq* form two sides of the same coin, of treating Muslims as the 'other', which then feeds into the global phenomenon of Islamophobia.[27]

Islamophobia

This term is borrowed from the US and other western countries where there is a calculated move to instil fear of Muslims among the citizens. A similar situation is taking place in India, which seems to have the sanction from the West, even when basic human rights of Muslims are violated. The view that every Muslim is a terrorist and a suspect prevails. When there are terrorist attacks in any part of the country, every Muslim, even a Muslim child, is made to pay a price and has to vouch for his or her patriotism.

A popular slogan coined by Hindu extremist organisations in the late 1990s is '*Hum do, hamare do, woh panch, unke pachees*' (We are two and we have two children whereas they are five [husband and four wives] and they have 25 children). This slogan was used to raise the demand for enacting a Uniform Civil Code by creating a fear psychosis among Hindus that if a Uniform Civil Code (UCC) is not enacted, Muslims will multiply and become a majority, which will change the demographic profile of India. This is an absurd proposition, but it went down well with the Hindu masses to create hatred against Muslims and votes for the BJP in the 1998 elections.

In 2018, Islamophobia plays out in many different ways in India: the frequent arrests of Muslims under draconian laws, long periods of incarceration without bail, denial of basic human rights in many spheres of civilian life, denial of jobs to Muslims, preventing Muslims from renting flats in Hindu-dominated areas.... Muslim children are unable to attend schools, and garbage cleaning trucks of the local municipality do not visit Muslim-dominated areas due to lack of regular bus routes. The situation continues to deteriorate.

The making of *Shayara Bano*

Soon after the Re: Muslim Women's Quest for Equality to the chief justice was made, a BJP activist Ashwini Upadhyay filed a petition pleading for the enactment of a UCC. When the petition came up before the bench presided over by the then Chief Justice T.S. Thakur, it was dismissed on the ground that the issue falls squarely within the domain of the legislature.[28] However, the bench assured that if a victim of triple *talaq* approaches the court, it would examine whether instant and arbitrary triple *talaq* violated the fundamental rights of a Muslim wife. So, by the time Shayara Bano received the *talaqnama* sent by her husband by post, the ground for filing the writ petition was firmly laid and the mantle of being a crusader for the cause of Muslim women's rights fell upon her shoulders. It is interesting to examine the background of this case.

Initially, Bano's brother had contacted a supreme court lawyer for transferring the case filed by her husband in the family court at Allahabad, for restitution of conjugal rights (in effect, to ask her to return to the matrimonial home—a far cry from 'instant triple *talaq*'), to her native place in Kashipur, in Uttaranchal.[29] Since Bano did not want to return to her husband and instead, wanted to contest the case after it was transferred to Kashipur, to bring to an end the long drawn litigation, the husband's lawyer resorted to the frequently used device of sending a *talaqnama* by post to Bano.[30]

When the talaqnama was brought to the notice of her lawyer in the supreme court, he advised his client to file a PIL on the ground that the *talaqnama* violated her dignity, though Shayara Bano has consistently maintained that she does not wish to return to her abusive husband. While the case brought a great deal of publicity, Bano's core concerns—access to her children, regular monthly maintenance, and a fair and reasonable settlement for the future, issues which had to be litigated in the local magistrate's court, under relevant statutes, the Domestic Violence Act (DVA) and the Muslim Women (Protection of Rights upon Divorce) Act (MWA for short)—remained unaddressed.

It was rather tragic that during the entire period while the triple talaq controversy was raging, the media continued to project that Muslim women are devoid of rights rather than dwell upon the entire judicial discourse which had held instant and arbitrary triple *talaq* invalid. The conspiracy of silence regarding landmark rulings such as *Danial Latifi* in 2001[31] (which upheld the right of a divorced Muslim woman to a lump sum amount as fair and reasonable settlement for the future) and *Shamim Ara* ruling in 2002, has caused Muslim women great injustice.

Legal precedent in *Shamim Ara*

In 2002, in the landmark ruling *Shamim Ara v. State of Uttar Pradesh*,[32] the supreme court invalidated arbitrary triple *talaq* and held that a mere plea of *talaq* in reply to the proceedings filed by the wife for maintenance cannot be treated as a pronouncement of *talaq* and the liability of the husband to pay maintenance to his wife does not come to an end through such communication. In order for a divorce to be valid, *talaq* has to be pronounced as per the Quranic injunction.

In the same year, a full bench in the Bombay high court in *Dagdu Chotu Pathan v. Rahimbi*[33] had held that a Muslim husband cannot repudiate the marriage at will. The court relied upon the Quranic stipulation: 'To divorce the wife without reason, only to harm her or to avenge her for resisting the husband's unlawful demands and to divorce her in violation of the procedure prescribed by the Shariat is haram'. All stages stipulated in the Quran—conveying the reasons for divorce, appointment of arbitrators, and conciliation proceedings between the parties—are required to be proved when the wife disputes the fact of *talaq* before a competent court. A mere statement in writing or oral deposition before the court about a *talaq* given in the past is not sufficient to prove the fact of a valid *talaq*.

These judgments in turn relied upon two earlier judgments of Justice Baharul Islam pronounced in 1981 while presiding over the Gauhati high court. In the first case, *Sri Jiauddin v. Anwara Begum*,[34] the court had held that though the Muslim marriage is a civil contract, a high degree of sanctity is attached to it. While the law recognised the necessity of dissolution of marriage, it could be effected only under exceptional circumstances and for a reasonable cause. An attempt at reconciliation by two relatives—one from each of the parties, is an essential condition precedent to *talaq*.

Later in the same year, a division bench of the Gauhati high court presided over by Justice Baharul Islam in *Rukia Khatun v. Abdul Khalique Laskar*[35] affirmed the earlier legal position as follows:

> The correct law of *talaq* as ordained by Holy Quran is: (i) *talaq* must be for a reasonable cause; and (ii) it must be preceded by an attempt at reconciliation between the husband and wife by two arbiters, one chosen by the wife from her family and the other by the husband from his. If their attempts fail, *talaq* may be effected.

Following *Shamim Ara*, there were a plethora of verdicts which declared instant triple *talaq* invalid and safeguarded the rights of women approaching the courts for maintenance.[36] The settled position in law can be summarised as below:

i. *Talaq* must be for a reasonable cause.

ii. *Talaq* should be pronounced only after reconciliation attempts have failed. Appoint an arbitrator, one from each side to help in the reconciliation as stipulated in Verse 4:35 of the Quran.

iii. *Talaq* may then be pronounced once (even if three *talaqs* are pronounced at one time they are to be treated as a single utterance).

iv. *Talaq* must be followed by a waiting period (*iddat*) of three months. For pregnant women, *iddah* is till the termination of pregnancy.

v. *Talaq* can be revoked mutually at any time during the *iddat* period and the parties can start living together.

vi. If differences cannot be resolved during the *iddat* period, the husband must fulfil all his contractual obligations towards his wife: return of *mehr*, valuables, belongings, payment of maintenance for the *iddat* period and a full and final settlement for her and her children for the rest of their life (as per the provisions of the Muslim Women (Protection of Rights Upon Divorce) Act, 1986).

vii. If the husband and wife resolve their differences after the *iddat* period, a fresh marriage contract, with a fresh *mehr*, would have to be entered into before resuming their marital life.

Despite this, the mainstream media continued to project a biased view that once the husband pronounces *talaq*, the wife is stripped of all her rights. This bolstered the misconception that a husband who pronounces instant triple *talaq* is absolved of his legal obligation of providing maintenance to the wife. Ironically, even women's rights groups working with Muslim women to empower them became co-conspirators in this conspiracy of silence as they too endorsed the view projected by the media that Muslim women have no rights. So they did not help Muslim women to approach the court to enforce their rights in local courts which the superior courts had secured for them.

It is due to the selective amnesia regarding the struggles of Muslim women over several decades[37] and the heightened Islamophobia prevailing within a majoritarian Hindu nationalism that the hype around the issue of triple *talaq* was created and sustained. Within this political scenario, the petition filed on behalf of Shayara Bano came to be hailed as the first instance where a helpless Muslim woman, who is devoid of rights, had challenged the validity of triple *talaq*.

A brief summary of the triple *talaq* verdict

The full bench of the supreme court pronounced the much awaited verdict on 22 August 2017, amidst much media speculations, three months after the arguments had concluded, just a week prior to the retirement of the then chief justice.[38] It was not anyone's case that arbitrary and instant triple *talaq* is a desirable mode of dissolving a Muslim marriage. Even the AIMPLB had brought out a circular listing the eight stages which the couple must go through before the *talaq* becomes final and irrevocable. What was under contest was the most appropriate manner for reforming the Muslim personal law—through the intervention of the courts, the legislature or through the Muslim clerics.

Though the hype created by the media in the preceding two years had made it out as a clear open and shut case, on this critical issue, the verdict split. It may surprise many that the operative part of the elaborate and complex ruling comprising of three different and diverse judicial opinions captured in 395 pages is just one line: 'By a majority of 3:2 verdict the practice of talaq-e-biddat—triple talaq is set aside.'

The opinion of the Christian minority judge on the bench, Justice Kurian Joseph, expressed in just twenty-seven pages, helped to clinch the issue. He concurred with Justices Nariman and Lalit that the practice of triple *talaq* does not form the core of the Sunni Muslim religion. But at the same time, he also concurred with Chief Justice Khehar and Justice Nazeer that the personal laws of minorities are protected by the constitution as a fundamental right, a clear statement against the enactment of a Uniform Civil Code, contained in article 44 of the constitution, which is merely a directive principle of state policy (and not an enforceable fundamental right).

Though three judges gave a verdict that triple *talaq* is invalid, they differed in their reasoning for declaring it so. Justice Nariman (for himself and Justice Lalit) held that since the word '*talaq*' is mentioned in the Sharia Application Act 1937, it forms part of a statute and becomes 'law in force'. Hence, it is amenable for being tested against the fundamental rights and declared it unconstitutional.

The Sharia Application Act does not mention the word 'triple *talaq*' or '*talaq-e-biddat*'. The views expressed by Islamic legal scholars is that a mere recognition of Muslim personal law by the Sharia Application Act does not give it a statutory status.[39] Justice Joseph concurred with this view and held that triple *talaq* could not be tested against the touchstone of fundamental rights. He preferred to stay within the realm of Islamic law and examined whether instant triple *talaq* forms an essential and core religious practice. Since the supreme court in *Shamim Ara* (2002)[40] had already declared instant triple *talaq* invalid, and had laid down the valid procedure for pronouncing *talaq*, he had no hesitation in concluding that triple *talaq* is not an essential core of Islamic law in India and hence held the same invalid. The judgement was hailed by the media and by all contesting factions as 'historic', though it merely followed the dictum of *Shamim Ara* and did not lay down any new law.[41]

Individual Muslim women and Muslim women's groups were jubilant since they viewed the judgement as a clear victory to the position espoused by them that the supreme court must declare the practice of instant and arbitrary triple *talaq* invalid. The opposing faction, i.e. the AIMPLB, who argued that the government should not interfere with the right of minorities to their tradition, culture, belief, and faith were overjoyed since the majority view held that personal laws are an integral part of the freedom of religion guaranteed under articles 25–26 of the Indian constitution, which courts are duty-bound to protect.

The Hindu Right-wing groups projected the carefully crafted and delicately poised judgement as an anti-Muslim verdict. The challenge to patriarchal monopoly was transformed into a minority-bashing exercise by BJP supporters. They projected that the supreme court had the courage to strike down triple *talaq* due to the support extended by the Prime Minister, Narendra Modi, to the cause of Muslim women's rights and claimed the entire credit for the same.

Criminalising triple *talaq*

As per article 141 of the constitution, the supreme court verdict is the law of the land. Since the supreme court had declared the law on the subject, initially the government issued a statement that it does not find it necessary to legislate on this issue.[42]

However, barely four months later, the government, in great haste, introduced a bill in the Lok Sabha (lower house) on 28 December 2017 to criminalise triple *talaq* on the ground that despite the historic ruling, triple *talaq* has continued unabated and hence there was an urgent need to enact a law with penal provisions as a deterrent.[43] Despite opposition from the Congress and other opposition parties, the bill was passed on the same day. However, when it reached the Rajya Sabha (the upper house), it met with several obstacles and hence it is still pending at the time of writing. The demand of the opposition is that it should be referred to a parliamentary expert committee for further scrutiny has not been conceded and hence the bill is still pending.

There is no doubt that parliament has the legislative competency to enact a law regulating marriages and divorces of minority communities. The Narendra Modi government, which has an overwhelming majority in the Lok Sabha, has the required numbers to pass the legislation. However, the ethical issue involved here is whether this parliament—which has the least representation of Muslims—has the moral authority to enact a law without a public debate and without arriving at a consensus from the representatives of the community. The government is intending to override a well-established norm that laws for minority communities must be enacted after holding discussions with community leaders/representatives, legal experts, and other stakeholders, and after striving to reach a consensus.

Several studies have shown that rather than approaching the formal structures of law, women from marginalised sections use informal community-based mechanisms to negotiate for their rights. Women find the religion-based dispute resolution forums such as *darul qazas*[44] more accessible than courts and police stations as there is a general fear among the poor of accessing these formal structures. At times women move in and out of formal and informal forums as well as between secular and religious spaces of dispute resolution. The research of Gopika Solanki and Sylvia Vatuk provides us with valuable insights on the multiple ways in which women negotiate for their rights.[45] Anindita Chakrabarti and Suchandra Ghosh, drawing upon two years of fieldwork at a sharia court situated in a large Muslim ghetto in Khanpur, argue that, while addressing issues arising out of family disputes, the key concerns for women are enmeshed within kinship rules, household economies, and family intrigues.[46]

Against this ground reality, how will a law penalising triple *talaq* help empower Muslim women? While mere utterance of the word '*talaq*' thrice may not dissolve the marriage, incarcerating the husband certainly will, as the enraged husband may resort to the approved Quranic form to pronounce triple *talaq* over a three-month period, thus leaving the wife high and dry.

Against severe criticism that criminalising oral pronouncement of triple *talaq* will render the situation of Muslim women even more precarious, the government included certain clauses regarding maintenance and child custody, which are totally meaningless, as there are already adequate legal provisions to safeguard the rights of Muslim women in this regard under DVA and

MWA. If the wife, her family and the larger community around her accept oral *talaq* as valid, and prefer to move on, there is no space for anyone else to interfere.

A parallel can be drawn here with the situation of thousands of deserted Hindu wives who prefer to retain the marriage tag rather than claim their rights under any prevailing statutes. There are many who argue that if desertion of the wife is not a criminal offence how can triple *talaq* be rendered so, when the impact of these two actions upon the aggrieved woman is similar.

While these are general concerns, the more pressing concern for secular and human rights groups is that the statute has the possibility of fuelling a fear psychosis within the Muslim community. There are concerns already around incarceration of Muslim youth over false charges of terrorism and by raising the 'love jihad' bogey, which is used to tarnish all interfaith marriages between Muslim men and Hindu women as politically motivated. This law will provide additional armour to the police to enter Muslim homes and arrest Muslim men.

The title of the bill—Muslim Women (Protection of Rights on Marriage) Bill, 2017—is meant as a throwback to the statute enacted in 1986, the Muslim Women (Protection of Rights on Divorce) Act. Through a creative interpretation, this statute has ensured that a divorced Muslim wife is entitled to a lump sum maintenance as fair and reasonable settlement, a right which has far more advantages for a divorced wife than the earlier provision and has better protected the rights of divorced Muslim women than their counterparts from other religions.

Despite this, there is a deliberate attempt to portray the MWA as a statute that deprived Muslim women of their crucial right of maintenance. Not just communal media, but even women's groups and secular organisations endorse this view. The enactment has been viewed as a backward move of 'Muslim appeasement' by the Rajiv Gandhi-led Congress government and a glaring example of the failure of the state's commitment to secularism at the behest of Muslim religious fundamentalists.

According to Saptarshi Mandal,[47] it is this narrative of a Congress government buckling under the pressure of conservative Muslim organisations and compromising women's rights in 1986 that the Modi government is trying to capitalise on through the title of the new bill. The title is worded to contrast the illusory protection given to Muslim women's rights 'on divorce' by the 1986 Act, with its own supposedly radical protection offered to them 'on marriage'.

Conclusion

The comments of the prime minister, the UP chief minister and other ministers clearly show how effectively the BJP used the issue of triple *talaq* as part of a political agenda, but they could do it with a clear conscience. They were not doing it *suo motu* (at their own initiative)—the demand had come from Muslim women themselves. Their only interest was to secure the rights of Muslim women who are burdened under the yoke of gender unjust practices of Muslim law.

I am reminded of Zakia Pathak and Rajeswari Sunder Rajan's famous essay, 'Shahbano'. To justify the bizarre and sinister formulation—'Hindu men are saving Muslim women from Muslim men'—the Muslim woman must invariably be projected as devoid of rights and lacking agency, and the Muslim male as premodern, lustful, polygamous, and barbaric.[48] This formulation alone provides the moral high ground for the government to adorn itself with the mantle of saving 'Muslim sisters'.

It is this scary formulation that compelled Shah Bano Begum[49] to relinquish her claim to maintenance in 1985 and assert her Muslim identity as opposed to her claims of gender justice. Faced with a similar dilemma, it is anyone's guess as to how the ordinary burka-clad Muslim woman of faith will respond to this intervention that is being hoisted in her name by a right-wing government.

The spontaneous outbreak of protests by concerned citizens in almost every major city against the wanton killing of Muslims has dented the government's image as a champion of liberating Muslim women from barbaric and premodern Muslim men. What appears far more barbaric and pre-modern is the public lynching of Muslim men by the extreme right-wing Hindutva groups, a practice supported by the criminalisation of Muslim men.

Sherin sums up the current dilemma:

> A viable feminist approach cannot de-historicize Muslim woman as a transcendental subject of gender negating her immediate religious and political realities. Gender is always contingent; located historically, materially and socially. Under the current realities of Muslim existence in India, clamour for gender justice for Muslim women cannot exclude Muslim men as part of their community identity and as equal participants in their political destiny. The faith Muslims attempt to protect is not an ahistorical spirituality, but the spirituality whose symbolic markers are constantly wiped out and demolished from the face of the modern nation state.[50]

As a lawyer defending women's rights, it is not my argument that Muslim women must continue to suffer gender unjust practices till broader community concerns are resolved. But the current political reality demands a more nuanced and pragmatic approach to address these injustices through multiple mechanisms available to Muslim women, both judicial- and community-based, rather than flaunting the violations, totally out of context, as a whip to beat the community with, as though gender injustice is the exclusive prerogative of Muslim men.

19

'BELIEF' IN THE RULE OF LAW AND THE HINDU NATION AND THE RULE OF LAW

Ratna Kapur

From how we dress to what we eat, how we worship and where we worship, to how we love and who we love, the Hindu Right has been dictating its idea of the Hindu nation in the management, surveillance, regulation and disciplining of the everyday lives of its citizenry. In the process, they have partly been aided and abetted by the Indian judiciary. This article focuses on the politics of 'belief' or faith and how the Indian judiciary has significantly endorsed the identity of the Indian state as a Hindu nation through the discourse of rights. I trace the work that 'belief' does in the context of legal contests over the meaning of secularism, that includes the meaning of equality and gender equality, as well as the freedom of religion. I illustrate how the higher judiciary in India is shaping the identity of the nation in the image of Hindu majoritarianism, primarily through its interpretation of these rights.[1]

This article focuses on how the politics of 'belief' is the central thread that stitches together the relationship between secularism, equality and religion in law and pivotal to crafting the Hindu Right's project of constructing the

Indian nation as a Hindu *rashtra* (nation).[2] The analysis of Indian secularism has been subject to rigorous scrutiny. However, there remains an underlying conviction that secularism is an inherently neutral liberal concept that has been threatened and manipulated primarily by the rise and politics of the Bharatiya Janata Party (BJP) since the early 1990s.[3] I argue that religion is integral to the understanding of secularism in India (and offers insights relevant to other liberal democratic states). I illustrate this point by analysing how religion (of the minority community) is invariably set up in opposition to gender equality in both legal advocacy as well as the advocacy of the Hindu Right. This oppositional framing obscures the majoritarian underpinnings and normative scaffolding of the right to gender equality as well as how the Hindu Right is using gender equality to position itself as a saviour of Muslim women from what it claims is the discriminatory and subordinating treatment by Muslim men. I present this argument in relation to the debate over the Uniform Civil Code (UCC), which is intended to supersede the separate personal religious laws of each community that govern matters of marriage, divorced, succession and other family matters. I specifically discuss the majoritarian underpinnings of gender equality in relation to the supreme court's 2017 decision on triple *talaq* as well as its interventions on what has been described as the 'love jihad' (love revolution) cases, involving the conversion of Hindu women to Islam and their subsequent marriage to Muslim men. I further illustrate my argument by analysing the role of religion in the constitutional discourse of secularism in India and how this has been used as a technique to establish and reinforce Hindu majoritarianism and transform the very identity of the Indian nation-state. I discuss a series of decisions by the Indian supreme court to illustrate how the higher judiciary has endorsed the Hindu Right's majoritarian and homogenising understanding of religion that serves this primary objective of establishing the nation's identity as Hindu.

The role of progressive groups, including feminist and human rights advocates, who are opposed to the Hindu Right's makeover of the Indian nation, are ironically deeply implicated in the type of politics of faith being advanced in and through the discourse of secularism, gender equality rights and freedom of religion. I argue that that there remains a critical need on the part of progressive groups, who may also belong to the Hindu majority, to reflect on the deeper epistemological challenges being presented by the injection of belief and faith into legal contests over the meaning and content of these concepts and rights.

'Belief' in secularism in Indian constitutional law

Globally, the concept of secularism has been a contested one, although there is a predominant assumption that it is based on neutrality—that is, the separation of religion and state. As Talal Asad has persuasively argued, the 'secular' is a problematic term even in the liberal democratic 'West', being based on a flawed assumption that it is a neutral epistemology and non-religious.[4] Asad demonstrates how secularism depends on and is circumscribed by the conceptual boundaries of religion in the West as well as the post-colony. In postcolonial India, secularism is not based on the separation of religion and state or state neutrality, but on the equal treatment of all religions, that includes the right to worship and tolerance.[5] This model thus acknowledges the presence of religion in secularism and the role of the state in ensuring the equal treatment of religion.

Orthodox or conservative forces in the Hindu Right, a nationalist ideology that seeks to establish India as a Hindu state, are increasingly defining the meaning and parameters of the constitutive elements of secularism, in particular equality and religion, in pursuit of their nationalist agenda. Central to the ideology of the Hindu Right—that is Hindutva—is the installation of religion and culture as primary attributes of nationalism and citizenship identity.[6] In the area of constitutional law the struggle over the meaning of secularism and the place of religion in politics remains highly contested.[7] Paradoxically, the Hindu Right has sought to redefine the meaning and parameters of the various components of secularism to suit their majoritarian political agenda and increasingly come to cast itself as the true inheritor of Indian secularism by influencing the meaning of equality and freedom of religion. In the following sections I examine specifically how the Hindu Right has deployed the rights to equality and freedom of religion to advance its Hindu majoritarian agenda. This project has been more aggressively pursued ever since the Hindu Right's political wing, the BJP, won an overwhelming majority in the 2014 national parliamentary elections.

Equality in the hands of the Hindu Right

The Hindu Right's struggle for ideological hegemony stretches across a broad range of discursive fields—history, politics, religion, economics, as well as law. I consider the way in which law and legal discourse are being deployed by the Hindu Right to advance its current political and ideological agenda. The legal

355

and political concept of secularism and its key ingredients—equality and religious freedom—have come to play an increasingly central role in this discursive struggle for the hearts and minds of Hindu subjects. The Hindu Right has made considerable advances in its efforts to infuse these concepts with new meaning, consistent with the discourse of Hindutva, the right's guiding ideology that seeks to establish India as a Hindu state partly through an attack on minority rights.

The discursive strategies of the Hindu Right have been based partly on bringing a very particular understanding of equality to the popular understanding of secularism, with powerful results that play out in the context of the rights of Muslim women as well as in the treatment of the Muslim community as a whole. This tension is most clearly illustrated in the debate over the Uniform Civil Code (UCC). There has, however, been surprisingly little attention paid to the question of the meaning of equality within the discourse of secularism. This neglect has become a dangerous silence that the Hindu Right has been only too willing to exploit in its quest to claim the terrain of secularism as its own.

The concept of equality has become a foundational discourse in Hindutva's attack on minority rights and in its agenda for women. The Hindu Right's approach to equality provides the basis for their understanding of secularism through which they seek to redefine the relationship between religion and politics in Indian society. The concept of equality is, at the same time, a central discursive element in the communalist efforts to rearticulate the role and identity for women in India. The precise meaning of the concept within the Hindu Right depends on the context in which it is being deployed. In much of its contemporary political rhetoric, the Hindu Right deploys a formal understanding of equality. In the context of the attack on minority communities and the discourse of secularism, 'equality' refers to the requirement of formal equal treatment—that is sameness in treatment. And any special protections of the rights of religious minorities is cast as 'appeasement', and a violation of the true spirit of 'secularism.' In the context of women, however, equality is used to argue in favour of sameness of treatment between women of different religious communities but is also used to affirm the difference between (Hindu) men and women and justify the difference in treatment between them.

At the same time, this logic also presumes a set of differences between Hindu men and Muslim men. The nationalist resistance to colonial rule, and the freedom struggle gave rise to a hegemonic masculinity—namely the Hindu male protector—constructed from mythological warrior figures as well as a reworked asceticism that projected his manliness and single-minded focus on the nation and its salvation.[8] The assertion of a muscular nationalism aligned with the emergence of a virile, heteronormative, powerful Hindu masculinity that protects the nation and its women is articulated not only in relation to the predations of the colonial ruler but also of the 'Other', namely the Muslim.[9] This embrace of muscularity is in part a response to the legacy of colonial rule, where the native male subject was cast as effeminate, emasculated and subordinated. This dominant Hindu masculinity is also an expression of Hindutva's 'racial' project that posits Hindus as a race indigenous to India, while simultaneously casting the Muslim as an outsider, whose fealties lie elsewhere and hence are a threat to the very identity and existence of the Indian (read Hindu) nation. Based on this logic, the Muslim is not entitled to equality unless he demonstrates his loyalty by relinquishing any claims to 'special treatment', surrendering his cultural difference, and assimilating into the norms of the Hindu nation.

The Hindu Right's discursive strategy in relation to equality becomes most evident in the struggle over the adoption of a UCC. One of the issues long advocated by the Hindu Right has been the demand for a UCC, the object of which is to unify all personal laws that currently govern issues of marriage, divorce, guardianship, property, and other familial matters. In the 1980s, the Shah Bano case became the focus of their campaign for the reform of personal laws and the enactment of a UCC in accordance with article 44 of the directive principles of the constitution.[10] The demand for a UCC is articulated within the discourse of formal equality. The Hindu Right deploys this discourse to claim the sameness of all women, and that all women must be equal. This move presents Hindu men as the legitimate protectors of all women, including Muslim women. At the same time, when the Hindu Right argues that all women must be treated equally, they mean that Muslim women should be treated the same as Hindu women, despite the continuing legal discrimination faced by Hindu women on several fronts including maintenance and inheritance.[11] Thus, any recognition of difference as between the women in different religious communities is seen to violate the constitutional guarantees of equality, which in their view, requires the formal equal treatment of all those who are the same. Muslim women, as women, should be the same as Hindu women—and therefore they should be treated the same in law. At the same time, there is no argument in favour of treating all women the same as privileged and entitled Hindu men. Both in relation to women as well as to Muslims, Hindutva seeks to protect and expand the dominance of majoritarian males.

The majoritarianism that underscores this position was on display in 2017 involving a constitutional challenge to the practice of triple *talaq*—that is, the pronouncement of divorce by a Muslim man to legally separate from his wife by thrice uttering the word '*talaq*' that immediately brings an end to their marriage.[12] The issue before the supreme court was whether this practice was 'fundamental to religion' and part of an enforceable fundamental right to freedom of religion. The practice has been opposed not only by women's organisations, but more importantly by Muslim women who are not allowed a similar right and suffer disadvantage resulting from this unilateral and abrupt pronouncement.[13] The practice continues to be backed by the All India Muslim Personal Law Board (AIMPLB), which argues that triple *talaq* is a legitimate way to end a marriage and any interference with the practice would constitute an interference in the right to religious freedom and expression guaranteed under article 25 of the Indian constitution.[14] The court case became politicised with the BJP supporting a ban of the practice, a position that serves its interests in denigrating the Muslim community, specifically Muslim men, and remains consistent with its own political and ideological position. At the same time, in supporting the rights of Muslim women, in particular the right to equality, it seeks to brandish its liberal credentials and also set up the issue in opposition to the right to freedom of religion (for Muslims). The Muslim woman is placed in the awkward and risky position of choosing either between her right to formal equality (backed by the Hindu Right) or religious freedom (attached to conservative Muslim and male control of religious institutions). This tension is contrary to the central objective of the petitioners who, as Muslim women, painstakingly sought to steer the case in the direction of the right to gender equality while at the same time preserve their right to religious identity and expression.

In August 2017, the supreme court set aside the practice of triple *talaq*. There was euphoria on the streets, with Muslim women also celebrating the decision. At one level the intervention by Muslim women becomes as an example of resistance to the dominance and consolidation efforts of both Hindu and Muslim men. It simultaneously marks a successful bid to be included within the terms of gender equality, while at the same time affirming cultural difference. At another level, a closer reading of the case puts into question the hailing of this decision as a major victory for gender justice and women's equality. The Muslim man not only retains the right to pronounce *talaq* against his wife over a period of a few months, but the 395-page rambling and unwieldy decision offers little sound jurisprudential grounds to advance women's rights to equality. Nor does the judgment disrupt the Hindu majoritarianism that is sought to be advanced in and through the discourse of equality by the Hindu Right. Instead, throughout the judgment, the Muslim woman is repeatedly reduced to a suffering victim, mute and/or without agency. In casting her as a victim, the judges simply affirmed the prevailing position that Muslim women require to be rescued from Muslim men, a position that coincides with that of the Hindu Right and its attempts to further demonise and stigmatise Muslim men. In the process, the historical, cultural and political causes of the Muslim woman's exclusion and discrimination remain unaddressed. Abu-Lughod discusses a similar concern in relation to women in the Arab world, arguing that the focus on rescuing women from the veil is informed by a savior mentality that obscures the political and historical explanations for Muslim women's oppression and discrimination.[15] At the same time, the court's logic reiterates the subordinate position of all women *vis-à-vis* men, by casting them as vulnerable, weak and in need of assistance. There is a particularly egregious moment in the dissent where the then Chief Justice J.S. Khehar offers his interpretation of a line in the Quran that compares the relationship between a husband and wife to a man's tilth or fertile soil. According to the judge this verse refers to the solemnity of sex between a husband and wife. He interprets with approval several verses from the Quran that analogise marital sex with a man sowing his fields 'in order to reap a harvest, by choosing his own time and mode of cultivation, by ensuring that he does not sow out of season, or cultivate in a manner which will injure or exhaust the soil.'[16] Such judicial pronouncements are not only woefully inadequate in providing any sensible or useful guidance on gender discrimination, they also reflect the court's continued inability to comprehend women, Muslim and non-Muslim, as bearers of rights entitled to full equality as Indian citizens.[17] By confining its reasoning to the terrain of faith and religion, the court's analysis remains blunted and myopic. Not only does faith emerge as rigid, fossilised and static, gender continues to be understood within a protectionist framework. While the framing of gender within a protectionist discourse in judicial decisions is not anomalous, it is acutely evident in the context of the Muslim woman. The implicit approval and interpretation of the chief justice that the Quran declares 'men as protectors, and casts a duty on them to maintain their women,'[18] coincides neatly with the position of the Hindu Right on women more generally as in need of protection, but also how that saviour in the context of Muslim women, can only be a Hindu man.

The court's decision in the triple *talaq* case encouraged the BJP government to immediately propose a bill outlawing the practice and treating it as a criminal act that carries a punitive sentence. While the court issued no direction to parliament to enact legislation, the decision afforded an opportunity to the Hindu Right to further its agenda of demonising and incarcerating Muslim men as intolerant, discriminatory and dangerous. The government hurriedly drafted a bill prescribing a fine and imprisonment of a husband for up to three years if he pronounced a triple *talaq*.[19] As the bill stalled in Parliament, the executive subsequently issued an ordinance criminalising triple *talaq*. The celebration by Muslim women of the supreme court case is not misplaced, but the very fact that the case has encouraged the criminalising of the Muslim man is cause for concern. The issue is no longer about the contest between equality rights and the right to freedom of religion, but the (Hindu) state's use of criminal law to advance its agenda and further persecute Muslim men.

The protectionist approach and saviour mentality adopted in relation to Muslim women by the Hindu Right was evident in the case of Hadiya, a twenty-four-year-old medical student from Kerala, who in 2014 converted to Islam of her own volition. Her parents were unsuccessful in their efforts to challenge her conversion in the high court of Kerala. Two years after her conversion, Hadiya married Shefin Jahan, a Muslim man. Her parents once again brought a legal challenge reasserting that Hadiya had been forced to convert, the marriage was a sham and alleging she was being recruited by the Islamic State in Syria and about to be taken out of India. In May 2017, the Kerala high court ruled that a 'girl aged 24 years is weak and vulnerable' and easily exploited. Given her vulnerability and the court's conclusion that Shafin Jahan was associated with persons having extremist links, it held the marriage to be a sham.[20] The court annulled the marriage and handed custody of Hadiya to her parents. Even though there was a finding that Hadiya (who the court referred to by her Hindu name, 'Akhila', throughout the judgement) had converted to Islam of her own free will, the court held that there was a serious apprehension of Hadiya crossing over to Syria and joining the Islamic State. The court directed that Hadiya be placed in the protective custody of her parents. Her husband Shafin promptly moved the supreme court of India against the lower court's order primarily because it violated the autonomy of an adult woman and was 'an insult to the independence of women in India'.[21]

Through a series of subsequent orders, the supreme court directed the National Investigation Agency (NIA), the main mechanism established by the central government in 2008 to combat terror in India, to launch an investigation into the Hadiya case. The agency was to assess if Hadiya had been brainwashed, and whether her marriage was an isolated case or part of a larger operation to force Hindu women to convert and marry Muslim men with the intention of recruiting them for terror operations. Hadiya remained confined to her parent's home. Civil rights groups, including the state human rights commission as well as the women's human rights commission, expressed their alarm at the supreme court's order for a NIA probe into the case, arguing that the court had gone beyond its jurisdiction and expanded the proceedings by ordering such a probe.

Hadiya was eventually produced before the supreme court where she declared that her marriage was consensual and asserted that she wanted her freedom.[22] The court permitted Hadiya to continue her medical studies, but directed her to reside in the university hostel as opposed to with her husband or even on her own. The court ordered that the NIA probe continue, though it was barred from inquiring into the legitimacy of the marriage. Ultimately, in its final ruling, the court set aside the lower court judgement and upheld the validity of the marriage. Not only did it hold that Hadiya had the right to choose whom she wished to marry, and that such a choice could not be affected by matters of faith, but also that the right to choose what to wear, what to eat, what to believe, and whom to marry was essential to an individual's autonomy as well as right to life.[23] Justice Chandrachud, in a concurring though separate decision, specifically held that Hadiya had absolute autonomy over her person and that the strength of the constitution lay in the plurality and diversity of culture that the court was duty-bound to uphold. While the broader implications of this judgement have the potential to push back Hindutva's homogenising efforts in the area of marriage, family, faith, equality and secularism, the question remains why, throughout the legal proceedings, the supreme court continuously treated Hadiya either as a victim, acting under false consciousness, or infantilised her, depicting her as incapable of making informed decisions about her marriage, faith and future? There is a troubling paradox in this result, where the supreme court came to its conclusion only after dragging Hadiya through endless legal detours and subjecting her to state surveillance as well as incarceration in her parental home that continuously undermined the very autonomy that they ultimately upheld. Shortly after the decision upholding her marriage, Hadiya was clearly of the view that she was subjected to intense legal and social scrutiny simply because she embraced Islam.[24]

The final judgment in the Hadiya case introduced a counter-hegemonic wobble that has the potential to push back the tides of Hindu majoritarianism in the legal arena. At the same time, the language of paternalism evident in the triple *talaq* judgment and throughout the Hadiya proceedings circumscribes the judicial respect for women's personal and sexual autonomy more generally, and the capacity of a Muslim woman to exercise her right to choose more specifically. The very fact the supreme court ordered the intelligence probe by the NIA in the Hadiya case to continue to determine if there was any criminality involved, even after declaring she had full freedom to marry the person of her choice, is indicative of the greater scrutiny to which a Muslim woman's choices are subjected. The saviour mentality that seeks to save Muslim women from the injustices of Muslim men persists. Thus, the court's interventions and intense scrutiny of the choices of a Muslim woman, especially of a Hindu woman turned Muslim, through the intelligence and surveillance apparatus of the state, ultimately serves to reinforce the myth of 'love jihad.' The term manufactured and propagated by the extreme elements of the Hindu Right wing has been deployed in the hope of generating fear over an unsubstantiated claim that hordes of Hindu women are converting to Islam and being duped into marriage to Muslim men by feigned declarations of love.[25]

With Muslim women at the helm of both the cases discussed, an important opportunity was lost by the court to develop a robust jurisprudence on gender equality based on the intersectionality of gender and religious (as well as class, ethnic or racial) identity and to push back against the tides of Hindu majoritarianism in the area of secularism and equality. Not only do these decisions remain tentative in their commitment to women's agency and their claims as rights-bearing subjects, in both cases the court reinforces the position advanced by the Hindu Right on faith and gender. In the triple *talaq* case, the subordination of Muslim women by Muslim men remains pervasive, while in Hadiya's case, the capacity of a Hindu woman to convert to Islam and marry a Muslim man, remains suspect and subject to heightened scrutiny.

These cases cast a spotlight on how secularism is the site on which secular judges are determining the legitimate content and parameters of a religion and where the Hindu Right is advancing their majoritarian agenda in and through the discourse of equality, as well as criminal law. Such a move continues to advance the identity of India as a Hindu nation, and Muslims as outsiders or primitive as claimed to be demonstrated in their treatment of women. They are called upon to either assimilate into the normative nationalised subject imagined by Hindutva or be demonised as backward, anti-national and insufficiently modern in gender relations. Hindutva purports to be the true secularists in this strategy, presenting progressive forces as pseudo-secular and anti-national.

These cases continue to have contemporary relevance for the way in which the politics of faith operates in and through equality in general, and gender equality specifically. In the triple *talaq* case, gender equality is advocated in and through the discourse of secularism, where the BJP argues that triple *talaq* violates both secularism and equality. Secularism is violated because the Muslim community is being treated differently. And equality is violated because Muslim women are treated differently from Hindu women. Secularism and equality are both used to reinforce the image of the Muslim community as 'Other' while simultaneously advancing an assimilationist agenda under the dictates of Hindu majoritarianism and Hindu male supremacy. And in so doing, the discourse of equality is being used to undermine substantive equality—that is, real equality between women and men that addresses historic and systemic disadvantage on the grounds of gender, and substantive secularism—that is, equal respect and accommodation for minority communities. In the case of a Hindu woman who chooses to convert to Islam, her decision is read as an act of false consciousness and brainwashing, given the pervasive view that Muslim women are indeed subordinated in Islam and hence there can be no active, fully informed choice to become a Muslim. The rush to criminalise Muslim men after the supreme court's holding on triple *talaq* is indicative of how the Hindu Right intends to pursue an assimilationist agenda through coercive means and, simultaneously, to further stigmatise and criminalise Muslim men. The unstated norm of the Hindu majority remains the reference point against which others are judged and into which these others are expected to assimilate or be expelled as legible and legitimate subjects of the Indian (read Hindu) nation.

Coming back to the Hindu Right's campaign to adopt a uniform civil code, it is important to understand that such a code is not seen as a threat to Hindu norms and practices since the Hindu Rights' version of the UCC would be one that would be based most closely on existing Hindu norms and practices. The Hindu Right's position on the UCC highlights the majoritarianism implicit in a formal model of equality. The Hindu Right's demand for a UCC is intended to unify all personal laws that currently govern issues of marriage, divorce, guardianship, property, and other familial matters. And, as discussed above, its demand is articulated within the discourse of formal equality. This move is nothing short of a bid to consolidate the supremacy of Hindu majoritarian values behind claims of formal equality and sameness. The UCC has come to be cast in highly dichotomous and polarised terms and this dichotomised discourse has inadvertently allied one segment of the women's movement with the Hindu Right, and its vicious attack on minority rights, despite their efforts to distinguish their position.[26]

One of the issues that remains invisible or unaddressed is that the entire debate on equality and the UCC is taking place within the confines of religion and religious difference. There is little attention paid to how the personal laws as well as any proposed UCC both continue to function within a very narrow definition of family—heteronormative, marital, built upon gender and sexual stereotypes and exclusive of subversive sexual arrangements, or diverse sexual orientations and gender identities. Progressive groups, queer community activists and other sexual subalterns need to recognise the extraordinary political opportunity provided by the UCC to disrupt the current framing of this issue as exclusively one between dominant and minority religious communities. By reconsidering their interventions on the UCC and treating the matter as a queer or subaltern issue they can take advantage of the unique opportunity presented by the UCC for reshaping the identity of the nation in terms that push back the tides of religious majoritarianism and the increasing traction being secured in favour of a Hindu *rashtra*. The issue presents a new avenue for progressive actors that are currently despairing over the destructive capacities of the Hindu Right and remain in search of a political ground from which to launch an effective riposte.

The right to freedom of religion

In this segment, I discuss how the right to freedom of religion, much like equality, has been used to establish and reinforce Hindu majoritarianism through secular law in India in recent history. The construction of religion and religious identity have been integral to the formation of secularism. The struggle over the meaning of the right to freedom of religion has also involved a struggle over the contours and content of religion. This struggle has been partly provoked by the framework of secularism. A key site for this struggle involves the dispute over the legal title to the property at Ayodhya. The Hindu Right claims that Ayodhya was the birthplace of the Hindu god Ram, and that a commemorative Hindu temple was destroyed to build a mosque.[27] This claim became the justification for the destruction of a sixteenth-century mosque, the Babri Masjid, on 6 December 1992 that Hindu parties claim stood on the exact spot of Ram's birthplace. They have persistently argued that worship at this spot is a core ingredient of Hinduism and thus a part of their right to religious liberty. Although several millions of gods and goddesses live with Indians on the sidewalks, streets, in taxicabs and in their homes, Ram has been accorded the status of the über-god in the discourse of the Hindu Right.

As several historians and writers have argued, the claim that Ram is the central Hindu deity runs counter to the polytheist character of Hinduism, transforming its pluralist character into one that accords well with a modernist and monotheist construction of religion.[28]

The supreme court has weighed in at several points to give increasing validity to the Hindu Right's interpretation of the right to freedom of religion, that is also a key component of Indian secularism. Initially the court's position on secularism differed substantially from that promoted by the Hindu Right, demonstrating a commitment to pluralism, and to holding back the tides of intolerance and Hindu majoritarianism in the name of secularism.[29] However, since the mid-90s there has been a shift, with the court endorsing an understanding of secularism where its rationale has been derived primarily from Hindu scriptures, in the name of secularism.

In *Ismail Faruqui*, the supreme court heard a challenge to the constitutional validity of the central government's acquisition of the disputed site in Ayodhya, after the destruction of the Babri Masjid.[30] The land acquired included the place where the mosque once stood as well as the surrounding area with the purpose of establishing two trusts for the construction of a Ram temple, a mosque, a library, and a museum, as well as providing amenities for pilgrims. The petitioner, a Muslim, claimed that the acquisition was anti-secular and slanted in favour of the Hindu community since it sought to simply accept the demolition as a *fait accompli*, instead of rebuilding the mosque that had been destroyed by a criminal act. The petitioner further argued that the acquisition of the land including the disputed area interfered with the right to worship of Muslims and was thus a violation of their right to freedom of religion. The majority of the judges rejected the argument that the acquisition violated the constitutional principle of secularism.[31] In the name of secularism, the majority opinion praised the principle of religious toleration found in Hindu scriptures and also concluded that a mosque was not an essential part of the practice of the religion of Islam, and that prayer (*namaz*) by Muslims could be offered anywhere.[32] The court held that the land acquisition did not violate the religious freedom of Muslims. In this case, the court endorsed an understanding of secularism where the rationale was derived primarily from Hindu scriptures and accepted the claim that secularism existed in India largely because of the religious toleration found in the Hindu scriptures. The court also remarked that those responsible for the demolition of the Babri Masjid were miscreants and their acts of vandalism could not be treated as representing the Hindu community.[33]

Another set of crucial cases, popularly described as the Hindutva decisions, involved a challenge to speeches appealing to the Hindutva ideology of the Hindu Right during an election campaign. The supreme court held that the appeal to Hindutva simply represented an appeal to Indianness and 'a way of life of people of the subcontinent rather than an attitude hostile to persons practicing other religions or an appeal to religion,' and that it was difficult to appreciate how 'the right wing's position could be assumed to be equated with narrow fundamentalist Hindu religious bigotry.'[34] The court's position not only elides the meaning of Hinduism with what the right wing says it means, it also assumes that Hinduism stands for Indianness, thereby leaving no room for other non-Hindu ways of being Indian. 'Indianisation' is assumed to represent the political and cultural aspirations of all Indians through the construction of a uniform national culture that is Hindu in its essence.[35] It thus held that the speeches were used to 'promote secularism or emphasise the way of life of the Indian people and the Indian culture' and to challenge religious discrimination rather than facilitate it.[36] The speeches were thus in conformity with the right to freedom of religion and did not constitute incitement to hatred against non-Hindus.

The court's conclusion that Hindutva constitutes a way of life of the people of the subcontinent was erroneous on several grounds. In eliding the meaning of Hinduism with that of Hindutva, the court failed to recognise that the term has historically had a specific meaning associated with the political philosophy of the Hindu Right. Furthermore, in characterising the speeches as secular it failed to appreciate the broader discursive and legal struggle over the meaning of secularism in which the Hindu Right has been the main protagonist.

Increasingly, the Hindu Right has advanced its agenda more aggressively in and through the right to freedom of religion. A key example of this approach is found in the decision of the Allahabad high court on the Ayodhya dispute. In 2010, deciding a long pending suit dealing with the partition of the disputed site in Ayodhya, the court held in favour largely of the Hindu parties, in allocating to them the land on which they claimed Ram was born, and in the process partly recognising the right to worship at the site as an essential ingredient of the Hindu faith. While this case was based on suits filed by varies claimants, including religious groups, the decision had important constitutional ramifications. It set aside the plurality and diversity of arguments within Hinduism over the status of various deities, where many Hindus do not worship Ram, instead privileging one interpretation over others and essentially upholding a particular conception of Hinduism. While all parties have filed appeals in this case, the BJP has been quick to declare that the law upheld faith. The decision indicates how the majoritarian claims and the Hindu Right's narrow interpretation of Hinduism or what Thapar has called a 'syndicated Hinduism' now constitutes the most significant challenge to the model of secularism extant in Indian politics and law as well as the achievement of their central goal—establishing a Hindu State.[37]

In February 2017, a seven-judge bench of the supreme court termed religion as a private relationship between the individual and their god. Hearing a cluster of challenges to the interpretation of a provision of the Representation of Peoples Act, 1953 (RPA 1953) dealing with appeals to religion during election campaigns, the majority held that elections were a secular exercise and that an appeal for votes during elections on the basis of religion, caste, race, community or language, even that of the electorate, would amount to a 'corrupt practice' and result in the disqualification of the candidate.[38] The provision mandates that it would amount to a 'corrupt practice' if a candidate or his agent or any other person, with his consent, appeals for votes on religious or such grounds. The majority held that the relevant provision imposed a blanket ban on any reference or appeal to religion, race, community, caste and language during elections and that such an appeal to religion would amount to 'mixing religion with State power'. The dissenting opinion authored by Justice D.Y. Chandrachud pointed to the historic discriminations and deprivations suffered by the masses on the ground of religion, caste and language and how these continued to be a part of the social realities of Indians. He stated:

> How can this be barred from being discussed in an election? Religion, caste and language are as much a symbol of social discrimination imposed on large segments of our society. They are part of the central theme of the Constitution to produce a just social order. Electoral politics in a democratic polity is about social mobilisation.[39]

One interpretation of this case is that it amounts to barring the speech of Muslim candidates or candidates from other religious minorities, given that the court has already ruled that an appeal to Hindutva was not an appeal to religion but a way of life of the people of the subcontinent.[40]

The implications of these majoritarian norms in the court's rulings in the Hindutva cases as well as the more recent decisions on the RPA 1953, have bolstered the position of the Hindu Right. Not surprisingly, these decisions have been hailed as victories by the right, who have repeatedly cited these holdings as endorsements of the true meaning and definition of secularism.

The rights to freedom of religion and equality become co-joined in the Hindu Right's effort to claim secularism as their own. The pursuit of religious liberty is taking place by using the concept of equal respect for all religions as a method for attacking the rights of religious minorities and ultimately subordinating their identities and erasing the differences of their cultural heritages. Secularism in the Hindu Right's vision requires that all religious communities be treated the same, and the role of religion is crucial to pursuing this vision. Any laws that are intended to protect the rights of religious minorities are vilified as appeasement measures or special treatment and as a violation of the constitutional mandate of equal treatment. The vision of secularism within the discourse of the Hindu Right comes to equate secularism with a Hindu state. Religious minorities are to be treated the same as the (Hindu) majority. Within this formal approach to equality, the majority becomes the norm against which all others are judged. Secularism, then, is no longer about the protection of rights of religious minorities, but rather becomes about the assimilation of minorities. This vision requires that religious minorities must be treated the same as the Hindu majority, where religious minorities are effectively assimilated into the Hindu majority. By emphasising the model of formal equality—that is, the formal equal treatment of all religions—the Hindu Right's vision of secularism operates as an unmodified majoritarianism whereby the majority Hindu community becomes the norm against which all others are to be judged and treated. Secularism ends up as a powerful tool in the Hindu Right's quest for discursive political power. The principle of protecting minorities virtually disappears. Hinduism, reframed through the political ideology of Hindutva as homogenous, monotheistic and institutionalised, comes to occupy the space of universal truth and is therefore the legitimate framework for adjudicating competing truth claims.

As in the case of the right to equality cases, interventions on the part of progressive groups in cases that involve the issue of secularism remain uninterrogated. There is simply an implicit assumption that the Hindu Right is anti-secular and that secularism can be restored through an assertion of the secular credentials of feminists, the left and other progressive forces. However, this assumption fails to account for the dextrous ways in which the Hindu Right has engaged with secularism that remain consistent with a dominant liberal interpretation of secularism based on the separation of religion and the state. It further obscures the faith credentials of progressive players under the guise of neutrality, agnosticism or atheism.

The failure of progressive players, including a strand of feminist politics, to engage with the politics of faith has been one reason that the terrain has been left open to be defined almost entirely by the Hindu Right. Part of the explanation for this lies in the almost exclusive focus on gender violence and women's victimisation by feminists that fails to address alterity and the politics of difference, in particular religious difference. In drawing attention to religion and religious difference, some segments of the feminist movement as well as the left have responded defensively, resisting any questioning of their secular and atheistic credentials and refusing to relinquish their monopolistic hold on gender as a universal category. However, in the course of the past three decades, the destruction of the Babri Masjid in 1992, the Hindu-Muslim riots in Bombay in 1993, the victory of the Hindu Right in national elections in 1999 and more significantly in 2014, the slaughter of over 1,000 Muslims in Gujarat in 2002, and more recently, the increasing targeting of Muslim men through gender equality in the courts, highlights the need to reflect on the majoritarianism that is also present in feminist and leftist politics. This reflection is critical to understanding the different ways in which secularism, gender equality and the right to freedom of religion have played out in the lives of minority religious groups, in particular women within these communities. While feminists and other progressive actors have more recently struggled to address the issue of religious difference, they have done so primarily to the extent that the universalised category of gender remains intact. In the process, they have aggravated their distance, and produced an estrangement from Muslim women. Given the ways in which secularism, gender equality and religious freedom continue to be informed by the politics of majoritarianism, this fuels a deep suspicion within Muslim minority communities, which aggravates their marginalisation and, at times, even encourages a deeper embrace of faith-based practices as a form of resistance to assimilation. The fact that the Hindu Right has been able to easily align with feminist agendas on the UCC, gender equality and even sexual violence, is cause for concern and calls for more mindful and thoughtful interventions in this fraught terrain. The Hindu Right has been able to successfully appropriate the gender agenda and re-tune the campaign to align with its own ideological campaign—where it is not just any man who is to blame for the inequalities, discrimination and violence experienced by women, it is the Muslim man.

In light of this analysis, charges of the Hindu Right being anti-secular are blunt and ineffective tools in countering the ways in which the Hindu Right is colonising liberal rights discourse that is not only consistent with Hindutva ideology, but has conferred on them the appearance of reasonableness that has proved enormously persuasive.

Conclusion

In this chapter I have demonstrated how, contrary to popular perceptions, Hindutva is holding itself out to be a truly secular project by equating Hindutva with 'Indianness' and presenting 'Indianness' as the normative foundation of subcontinental culture and the way of life of its people. Hindutva becomes the lynchpin for determining who is a legitimate subject of the nation and who is not. The 'Other' is tolerated but only to the extent that she is willing to surrender claims to special rights or 'special treatment'. The 'Other' becomes a rights-deserving subject to the degree that she surrenders her difference and embraces the assimilationist project of majoritarianism. The judiciary has played a central role in legitimising the Hindutva project and its understanding and meaning of secularism, equality and religion. The project has acquired traction in the legal arena to the extent that the very meaning and content of equality, gender equality, and religious freedom, key components of secularism, are being reshaped and redefined in the image of the Hindu Right's ideological pursuit of Hindutva. The validation of Hindutva through law has been accompanied by the violence of exclusion, in particular, the production and reification of the Muslim as 'Other' and inferior; the subservience of Islam to Hindutva, of the minority to the fictive majority, that is deemed essential to the prosperity and modernisation of India; and the reduction of women's equality to the status of Hindu women, subjugated to Hindutva's male/heteronormative dominance.

For those committed to the countering the politics of belief that have been aggressively pursued by the Hindu Right and found validation in law and the decision of the higher judiciary, at least two critical moves are required. The first is to understand the challenge being posed to those who belong to the Hindu majority, even those who are committed to progressive politics, including feminists, who need to address how their interventions may be implicated in advancing the politics of faith in law. Whether one is a 'practicing' Hindu or not, at a political level it is not an identity that is easily relinquished nor disguised under the masks of atheism, agnosticism, nor indeed claims to being secular. By not addressing issues of faith in law as well as at the intimate, subjective level, being either indifferent or inattentive to it, can implicate progressive politics in the growth of the intolerance and violence being directed at minority groups by the Hindutva brigade. The distancing from religion, for fear that secular politics may be a casualty of such recognition, neglects to consider how faith is integral to secularism in law. Second, setting up religion in opposition to equality, in particular gender equality, does not move in a direction that is liberating but forces women in minorities to choose between freedom of religion and equality when they want both. Such a choice not only intensifies the increasing estrangement between minority and majority communities, (Hindu) feminists and women in religious minority communities, it also obscures how the Hindu Right has also pursued its Hindu male majoritarianism in and through the discourse of equality, and continues to successfully co-opt feminist politics into its pursuit of faith in law.

A conscious shift in how progressive groups engage with the politics of belief is imperative. What is at stake in Hindutva's success in defining itself as a supra-cultural force and the only force that is truly secular is the very identity of the Indian nation. And this project is being forged partly on the anvil of law branded with a judicial seal of approval. In rendering Muslims and other religious minorities as well as women as subservient to Hindu (male) greatness, the country is entering into a dangerous alignment where exclusion, hatred and bigotry establish the foundation for instantiating and expanding this alleged greatness.

PART VIII

GENDER AND NATION

20

QUEER PRESENCE IN/AND HINDU NATIONALISM

Paola Bacchetta

In this chapter, I attempt to open up a space for a discussion of the place of specifically queer gender, sexualities and relationalities, in a postcolonial nationalist formation: right-wing Hindu nationalism in India. However, throughout, it will be helpful to keep this in mind: instead of particularising Hindu nationalism or any other form of Indian nationalism, or even postcolonial nationalisms more widely, we might consider how this analysis, or perhaps parts thereof, resonates well beyond this immediate national, regional and specific geo-political context.

At present, a number of insightful feminist and queer analytics address the place of gender and sexuality in nationalisms, empire, colonialism and (post) coloniality. Many explain how dominant (internal elite and/or colonial) sectors of society impose heteronormativity in colonial and colonised sites. To date, most analytics of nationalism either explicitly state or carry the underlying presupposition that heterosexuality is integral to nation formation. In general, the nation is understood as an oppressive family writ large.[1] For some scholars, the nation-family is primarily characterised by sexism;[2] and for others mainly by heterosexism.[3] In turn, Lisa Duggan, writing about the US., highlights the construction of new models for homonormativity in which some LGBT subjects can be incorporated into the US nation as citizen-subjects on condition that they emulate models of heteronormativity.[4] She gives as examples the homonormative reduction of queer relationalities to gay marriage, and gay enlistment in the US military. Following that, Jasbir Puar, in research based in the US, posited that we are living in homonationalist times, which she defined as a new period in which the state constructs a model for acceptable national homosexuality, and deploys the status of homosexuals as a standard by which to judge the level of civilisation of countries in the global south. These are not just discourses, but rather homosexual status is deployed in foreign policy in much the same way as the status of women. To arrive at this operation, newly assimilate-able LGBT subjects are divided from racialised subjects, especially Muslims, and from hyper-queer subjects who do not conform to the national homosexuality model; these latter are farther demonised and excluded from the nation.[5] Drawing on these insights to consider contemporary Europe, Jin Haritaworn and I proposed the notion of homotransnationalisms to account for how multiple States affiliate (a phenomenon we called homotransnationalism1), and/or a plurality of civil societies align (or homotransnationalism2), in order to mobilise their now common notion of homonormativity against one or several global southern states.[6] While studies of homonationalism and the collective efforts Haritaworn and I refer to as homotransnationalism currently abound, paradoxically, to date there is not one study of the place of queer sexualities specifically in postcolonial nationalisms. This chapter hopes to contribute to opening that area of inquiry through a focus on Hindu nationalism.

Hindu nationalism is perhaps most renowned in India and transnationally for its high profile, extremist anti-Other practices. That is, in contrast to Indian nationalism (India's official nationalism) which self-identifies as pluralist and inclusive of Indians of all faiths as citizens, Hindu nationalism seeks to eliminate all who do not conform to the Hindu nationalist notion of Hinduism from the Indian citizen-body: nearly all Indian Muslims, Sikhs, Buddhists, Parsis, Jains, Christians, Jews, etc. But, Hindu nationalists also reject all Hindus who are not in line with Hindu nationalist definitions of Hinduism. How they represent their Others has shifted in time, often according to which Hindu nationalist organisation most monopolises the public discursive space, and additionally, in relation to (and not always in conformity with) changes in normative values in India and various parts of the world.

Thus, today the voice that is most heard in India is that of the Bharatiya Janata Party in power, while the norms that dominate are those entwined with neo-liberal capitalism that dominates in India and in the world.

Briefly, in what follows I will present five inter-related arguments. First, queerphobia (the de-valorisation of queer[s]), and queerphilia (the exalted love of queer[s]), and specifically not queerphobia alone as might be expected, are integral to the formation, maintenance, everyday life and mobilisations of Hindu nationalism. Second, in Hindu nationalist discourse and practice, queer gender and sexualities (and specifically not queer subjects and affective relationalities) have historically not been positioned exclusively on the 'Them' side of Hindu nationalism's 'Us vs. Them' binary as might be expected, but rather they have always been placed on the 'Us' side as well. Importantly, how and where queer genders and sexualities manifest has shifted in time. In an earlier period bigender, and not binary gender, based on models of sainthood, was integral to the embodied authority of leaders while rank and file members were to be virulently masculine along colonial cisgender, heterosexual lines. In the present period Hindu nationalist leaders are newly developing selective models for rank and file Hindu nationalist queer national-normative subjects and relationalities that are deemed to varying degrees assimilate-able into the Hindu nation (albeit assigned different statuses therein). In other words, at present Hindu queer subjects have an increasingly more ambiguous status in Hindu nationalism that includes some dimensions of acceptance and invitation into the Hindu nationalist fold. Fourth, both historically and at present, in conformity with and by extension of an early colonial queerphobic model, Hindu nationalists assign de-valorised queer gender and sexuality, in terms of either lack or excess, to all Others of the Hindu nation, that is, to mainly Muslim Others. Fifth, each set of Hindu nationalist queer constructions draws on different kinds of referents for support. Hindu nationalist queerphobic representations are mainly effects of Hindu nationalist re-workings of colonial misogynist notions of gender and sexual normativity. In contrast, the queer-philic figurations draw largely on re-productions and reworkings of genders and sexualities as they appear in (a range of) Hindu religious symbolics. In turn, the queer national-normative constructions are generally legitimised via Hindu religious symbolics in which queer genders and sexualities abound, as might be expected, but instead are most often presented as primarily tied up with (unavowed) neoliberal and (explicit) western modernity desires.

Integral to my arguments are these four operations: xenophobic queerpho-bia; queerphobic xenophobia; queerphilic idealisation; and selective queer national-normativisation. By xenophobic queerphobia, I mean a particular form of queerphobia that justifies itself by constructing some models of queer as originating outside the nation (xenophobia). An example is the historic Hindu nationalist representation of the self-identified Indian queer. In an early period Hindu nationalists rather uniformly claimed that queer is 'not Indian' and that the British brought homosexuality to India. This claim reverberates with yet another xenophobic queerphobic operation, in which the colonial British designated British homosexuality as the oriental vice, as not British but rather as the result of excessive British immersion in India.

In turn, queerphobic xenophobia signifies a particular type of xenophobia in which queer is assigned (often metaphorically) to all the designated Others of the nation regardless of their sexual conduct or identity. The primary objects of Hindu nationalist queerphobic xenophobic operations have been Muslim men. The self-identified queer Muslim (or other Other) stands at the intersection of xenophobic queerphobia and queerphobic xenophobia.

By queerphilic idealisation I mean to signal a certain attitude towards some idealised leaders-as-symbols, who are always in and above the masses and who can be represented as incorporating both hetero-genders (masculinity and femininity) into his/her persona.

Finally, the notion of selective queer national-normativisation is a way to discuss the new Hindu nationalist gesture towards inclusion of some homosexual and transgender subjects into Hindu nationalism.

Some additional points of precision, again in the form of definitions, are in order, perhaps beginning with terms I elect not to employ (much): homosexual, lesbian, gay. Foucault,[7] followed by others, has demonstrated that the identitary term homosexual (and by extension lesbian and gay in current usage) are recent inventions in western languages, with their genealogy in nineteenth-century Europe. Foucault identifies a shift from the notion of same-sex sexuality as a genital act requiring repression, to the construction of a homosexual identity and personality type. In the Indian context there are myriad historical ways to present representations of homosexual and other queer relationalities. They abound in Hindu religious texts, Urdu poetry, temple carvings, songs, and oral knowledges. They exist across castes, religions, and economic statuses. Some examples are representations of divinities such as *ardhanarishwara* or the half-female half-male figure of the god Shiva, the sex change of Sikandin in Vyasa's classical *Mahabharata*, or various figures of pregnant kings and transgender and intersex subjects in Sanskrit texts.[8]

There are old and newer homosexual identitary terms as well. At least from the 1980s onward, Indian activists and academics have forged, recuperated or revived a plethora of these. They include: *khush* (happy, gay); *bhagini* (vaginal sister); *sakhi* (woman friend of a woman); *samlingkami* (desirous of the same sex); *dost* (male friend of a male); *jankha* (effeminate gay man, man to woman transvestite); *gandhu* (insulting term: one who is done up the ass); *zenana* (effeminate gay man); *chay number* (number six: outrageous flaming gay man).[9] Moreover, as Siddharth Gautam Gupta pointed out long ago, with or without such terminology, the organisation of erotic desire and its expression may vary not only from the construction of desire and its expression in other parts of the world, including the global north, but also within India across disparate classes, castes and other social divisions born of relations of power (personal communications; see also the film *Khush* by Pratibha Parmar). There are also in some of the very oldest to recent sources a range of terms for transgender subjects in different Indian languages including *Hijira, Aravani, Aruvani, Jagappa*, and more.

However, as yet, no non-English Indian language term has surfaced or been invented under which could be united the whole range of dissident gendered and sexed subjects, practices, lifestyles and identities. Thus, as a transient measure in this essay I deploy the term queer insofar as, among other things, it can be made to signal inclusivity in the language in which I am writing, English. At the same time, I want to flag that the term queer is deeply inadequate in the South Asian context. It does not necessarily consider the complexities of Indian gender, sexual, subject and relational formations historically, contextually. Here, I want to 'out' my adoption of queer so as to help avoid what Patel insightfully calls 'dichotomised fluency' wherein the reality of a discourse formed in a smaller scale context is translated or reframed in the terms of a dominant universalised discourse without acknowledgement of the process, resulting in two very different representations, with the dominant effacing the smaller-scale context.[10] Perhaps one way to attempt to circumvent such effacement will be to be mindful of contextualisation, and fractionalise and reunify the term queer itself in the text where relevant.

My sources include the internal publications of primarily two Hindu nationalist organisations: the Rashtriya Swayamsevak Sangh (RSS, 'National Self-Volunteer Organisation'), India's most extensive Hindu nationalist formation, founded in 1925, which now has about 2.5 million members and has an additional 200 affiliated organisations; and the Bharatiya Janata Party ('Indian People's Party', or BJP), the RSS's electoral wing founded in 1980. I also engage with the publications of the separate but related Hindu Shiv Sena ('Hindu Shiv Corps', or HSS). And, finally, I take account of statements by

BJP, RSS and HSS leaders that appear in a variety of kinds of media. Elsewhere I demonstrate that there are gendered differences, and even incompatibilities, between Hindu nationalist men's and women's discourse and practice.[11] So I will specify that this present chapter concerns exclusively Hindu nationalist men's discourse and practice, not women's. The RSS provides the bulk of my data for earlier periods because in the times concerned it was the central organ for the production of Hindu nationalist men's ideology, with its publishing companies, bookstores, and massive distribution networks. In contrast, today, as the BJP holds national and often local political power in India, it appears more extensively in the media scape in our times.

In what follows, I will begin with a first section that contextualises the traffic (from Britain to India) in various forms of queerphobia that later surface in Hindu nationalism. In the second section, I will discuss queerphobia and queer-ambiguity in Hindu nationalist discourse. In the third, I address the paradoxical queerphilic and queer-ambiguous reinsertion of queerness in Hindu nationalism, before arriving at some concluding remarks.

The traffic in queerphobia: genealogies

Indian repression of dissident gender and sexuality certainly pre-dates colonialism, as should become evident below. But, precolonial repression differs from current forms in extent and in content. Precolonial queer repression occurred only rarely and only in localised, limited time/spaces that co-existed with queer acceptance elsewhere within the borders of the territory currently delineated as India. Colonialism introduced queer repression across the subcontinent. The British inscribed prohibitions against homosexuality in Indian national law (see below) that have only recently been overturned. In the postcolonial period, across the political spectrum, the discourses, practices and policies that denigrate queers carry the weight of colonialism's discursive and institutionalised baggage.

The colonial genealogy of current forms of Hindu nationalist queerphobic xenophobia is vast and multi-dimensional. However, here I will point to two areas: orientalist discourse and colonial law.[12] As Prakash has remarked, Indian orientalism was a European enterprise, formed in colonial relations of power, from its inception.[13] Beginning in 1757, it operated to reconstruct knowledge of India. This process was multifaceted. But what concerns us here is that orientalism, as it constituted, reconstituted, and redefined the Hindu symbolic, worked to condemn or marginalise what now are designated as dissident Indian genders and sexualities.

It is interesting to consider how this process operated. To make sense of the multitude of Hindu sacred texts, oral traditions and practices, orientalists divided them into two categories which are still reproduced today in some circles: a 'Great Tradition' (comprised of texts of the Brahmin elite, or 3 per cent of the Hindu population); and a 'Little Tradition' (Hinduisms of the masses). Orientalists selectively translated 'Great Tradition' works and left 'Little Tradition' works by the wayside. As Chakravarty and Nandy have argued,[14] orientalists' selectivity centred texts in which male subjectivities could be understood in conformity with British notions of proper masculinity, and wherein femininity and women could be marginalised. In doing so they put in place forms of misogyny that would underlie both colonial and postcolonial queerphobia. Some examples are the colonial use of the epics the *Mahabharata* and the *Ramayana*, wherein wars provide a backdrop for colonial interpretive procedures regarding colonial-normative masculinity.

However, the same 'Great Tradition' texts that circumscribe 'proper' colonial gender, also marginalise, condemn or propose punishment for queer conduct and figurations. This, for instance, is the case of the two epics, and some of the *dharmashastras* (law books) such as the *Manusmirti*. Orientalists ignored the vast array of sources that accept or even celebrate queer within their own categories of 'Great Tradition' and 'Little Tradition'. Some examples are: the *Kamasutra* which includes a chapter entitled '*Auparishtaka*' (oral congress) valorising same sex relations; lesbian folk tales from Himachal Pradesh;[15] practices such as *maitri karar* (friendship agreement, a form of marriage between women); and iconography such as in the Tara-Taratini temple of Orissa.

Orientalists selectivity proceeded, yet coincided with, administrative efforts to maintain colonial rule; they were based in a common field of intelligibility. As Nandy demonstrates, to sustain their rule the British discredited Brahmins (who held symbolic power), co-opted *rajas* of princely states (who held material power), and formed a class of Indian collaborators for the army and civil service.[16] To this effect, the British constructed Brahmin men as effeminate, and created a category of Indian 'martial races' as the ideal of Hindu masculinity based on *kshatriya* (warrior and princely caste) manhood.[17] To justify colonialism to their own people in England, the British framed their colonial presence in terms of a civilising mission, a notion that rested in part on the construction of upper-caste Hindu men as oppressive to women and Dalit Bahujan men as sexually promiscuous and out-of-control. This British invention was part of a wider British colonial field of intelligibility, with its own set

of categories, logics, presuppositions and conclusions. Through it the colonis-
ers conceptualised the colonies, and here colonial India, along lines that
McClintock describes as the porno-tropics, wherein colonised space and
subjects serve as 'a fantastic magic lantern of the mind onto which Europe
projected its forbidden sexual desires and fears'.[18]

Colonial administrative policy towards queer sexuality was an exemplary
Foucaldian operation involving surveillance, deterrence, repression and punishment of men's queer conduct, albeit in a reworked order. Women, considered passionless and sexually passive in the British colonial field of
intelligibility, and thus without sexual subjectivity, were not encompassed in
these operations. The first targets of what we could today call 'queerphobic
queer cleansing' were the British themselves, beginning with the Imperial
Army. For instance, as Ballhatchet notes, British administrators officially
organised an Indian female prostitution apparatus to prevent same-sex acts
between British soldiers.[19] They preferred that British men engage in inter-
racial extra-marital heterosex instead of intra-racial homosex. When the prostitution solution proved ineffective to deter their peers' queer practices,
British administrators passed the Army Act of 1850 which punished British
homosex with imprisonment of up to seven years.

It was not until 1861, with the imposition of the British legal system in
India (again, IPC) that sodomy and thus same sex acts (again, among men)
were outlawed among Indians across the whole of British-held subcontinental
territory (via IPC article 377). Soon thereafter the colonial administration
organised surveillance of upper=class Indian men with whom the British were
in frequent contact. As Ballhatchet remarks, Lord Curzon, Viceroy from 1899
to 1905, 'had grimly drawn up a list of princes with homosexual tastes' to
survey and attempt to dissuade them.[20]

Subjects of queerphobia and queer-ambiguities

Against that backdrop, here, I will discuss two large zones of queerphobia and
queer-ambiguities: collective and individual internal and external subjects of
the Hindu nation as Hindu nationalists conceptualise them.

The Hindu nationalist-citizen-body

Historically, the RSS describes its citizen-body, the Hindu people, in masculine terms: 'the men born in the land of Bharat' and 'sons of the soil'.[21] Where

RSS ideologues insert neutral terms, they too signify the masculine.[22] Thus, the citizen-body is a male homosocial entity, to the exclusion of women. It is, in the sense of McClintock's[23] gendered interpretation of Anderson's[24] formulation: 'a fraternity of men' characterised by 'deep horizontal comradeship.' In the words of M.S. Golwalkar,[25] major RSS ideologue and second *sarsanghchalak* (RSS supreme leader) from 1940 to 1973:

> Let us approach every son of this soil with the message of one united nationhood and forge them all into a mighty, organised whole bound with ties of mutual love and discipline. Such an alert, organised and invincibly powerful national life alone can hope to stand with its head erect in the present turmoils of the war-torn world.

The category 'Hindu nationalist men' was historically a subgroup, an avant-garde, within the Hindu citizen-body. Read at the connotative level, the united Hindu nationalist men were a metaphor for the Hindu nationalist phallus: mighty, alert, invincibly powerful, and of course, 'erect'. The RSS' ideal bond of 'love' rests on Hindu male repression of homosexuality. But, as Lane argues in another context,[26] drawing on Derrida's[27] notion of friendship as *philia* and its distinction from *eros*, heterosexuality is also a threat because it risks disrupting male-to-male homosocial intimacy. Thus, for the RSS, the operative sexuality binary for Hindu nationalist men was not so much hetero versus homo; rather, it is a-sexuality verses both hetero- and homosexuality. In this logic, the most committed of Hindu nationalist men were supposed to avoid all sexual contact in order to remain faithful to the collectivity of Hindu men. Accordingly, the self-proclaimed celibate *sarsanghchalak*, *pracharaks* (full-time RSS workers), and *swayamsevaks* (RSS members) who permanently renounced *grihasthya* (the life of the married householder) were (and remain) the most ideal of all Hindu men. The BJP's highest level leaders were also self-proclaimed celibates, including both Atal Bihari Vajpayee, India's former BJP prime minister, who was also India's first unmarried prime minister, and the BJP incumbent since 2014, Narendra Modi.

Hindu nationalist man

For the RSS the central individual unit of the Hindu people and of the RSS always was and remains the ideal rank-and-file Hindu nationalist man. In earlier days the RSS described him as: a hypermasculine, chivalrous warrior along *kshatriya* lines; celibate along Brahmanical *sannyasin* (wanderer detached from material world) lines; and 'respectful of women'.[28] This model actually disrupted colonial-induced heteronormativity because it posited a-sexual hypermasculinity as ideal, but reinserted heteronormativity at the level of gendered identity, insofar as hypermasculinity itself rests on a hetero gender-sex-sexuality binary. Several operations underlie this construction: 1. RSS resistance to colonial representations of the Brahmin as effete through positing Hindu male hypermasculinity; which coincides with 2. the RSS reproduction of the colonial *kshatriya* model; and finally 3. RSS resistance to the colonial notion of Indian hypersexuality through its opposite, a-sexuality; which intersects with 4. RSS selectivity of the *sannyasin* model of a-sexuality in the dominant 'Great Tradition' Hindu symbolic.

The RSS has always assigned the unacceptable Hindu male the negative characteristics it split off and rejected from itself. Thus, the unacceptable Hindu man is anti-national, sexually promiscuous, materialistic, westernised, and worse: he embodies physical and mental characteristics readable as feminine in contemporary bi-lingual elite discourse informed by western notions of gender and sexuality.[29]

For the RSS, all Hindu men could be ideal if they would peel away the layers of *maya* (illusion) which blind them to their essential Hindu nationalist selves. This processual concept of achieving the ideal identity reproduces Brahmanical Hindu discourse on spiritual realisation as a process of unknowing the material world. It also re-inscribes, albeit in reverse, the western liberal notion of 'Progress' as it operates in Enlightenment and current development narratives of third world 'progress'.[30] That is, for the RSS, the ideal is to be achieved through a linear movement back to a point in time prior to colonialism.

M.S. Golwalkar presents this processual transformation in his major text, *Bunch of Thoughts* through the use of a gendered analogy in a story entitled 'How "Woman" Became a Soldier!'[31] It takes place in World War I when the English recalled retired Indian soldiers back to the army. One such soldier does not wish to return, so the police search for him. Golwalkar writes:

> When the soldier came to know of this he put on a woman's clothes and hid himself in the house. When the police came, his wife told them that he was not in the house [...] But the police suspected deception. They called out that 'sister,' found out the truth and took him away. The soldier was sent to his old platoon. He was then given the army dress and made to join the ranks. When he stood there with the soldier's dress on, he was asked whether he would like to return home. He replied with a new resolve in his voice that he was now a soldier [...]; he would now only go to a battlefield. Indeed the dress had made all the difference!

In this almost Althusserian passage Golwalkar presents the figure in progression: soldier to husband, to a man in feminine drag and back to soldier again. The gender and sex trajectory is made to be dependent upon clothing as an interpellative element. The attainment of the ideal via shedding feminine clothing parallels the (Hindu) notion of peeling away *maya* for self-realisation. But, in addition, the achievement of masculinity requires an inverted movement of re-clothing (as the before and after soldier) through self effort. Thus both femininity and masculinity are associated with *maya*. The RSS puts the principle of gender as costume and performance into practice with the uniform that is obligatory for *swayamsevaks*. Also in the passage, Golwalkar associates *grihasthya* with failed masculinity: the truly masculine Hindu man leaves his wife and home to become (again) a soldier. Here a certain dichotomy is reproduced: on the one hand, there is ideal a-sexuality (soldier); and on the other, an unacceptable hetero and queer combine (the man's relation to his wife requires being in feminine drag). In the present era, especially of digital media, the ideal *swayamsevak* is less an a-sexual figure, less modelled upon the celibate *pracharak*, possibly as a mode to ensure more massive recruitment among the overwhelming heteronormative majority.

These RSS notions of ideal masculinity and transformation have long been translated into practice in the BJP's 'promotion of a robust sports and physical culture' for youth.[32] This includes making 'physical education and sports coaching compulsory' in schools, organising sports meets, allocating state funds for Olympic Games preparation, and requiring one year of rigorous service from all Indian youth.[33]

In an earlier phase, the gendered binary of RSS discourse was officially extended in a new twist that included direct queerphobic pronouncements against lesbian and gay subjects, as sexual subjects, and their explicit exclusion from the Hindu nation. More recently, the Hindu nationalist position on queer subjects is much more complex and contradictory. None of the organisations has a uniform view on homosexuality.

Internally, one current Hindu nationalist position is that homosexuality is immoral but is not a crime; instead, it can be 'fixed'. The RSS suggests that homosexuals can be transformed into proper citizens of the Hindu nation after successful de-homo-ing therapy. Thus, in March 2016 the RSS leader Dattatreya Hosabale tweeted that 'homosexuality is not a crime, but socially immoral act in our society. No need to punish, but to be treated as a psychological case'.[34] The proposal of de-homo-ing re-conversion therapy circumvents the issue of enforcing and thereby reinforcing colonial queerphobic law (IPC

377). De-homo-ing re-conversion is coherent with other RSS re-conversion schemes such as the 'Sanskritisation' (Hindu nationalisation) of Dalit Bahujan, Muslim, Christian and other non-Hindu and non-Hindu-nationalised subjects. Religious re-conversation presumes Hindu nationalism's Others as culturally and religiously deficient subjects, a section of which can be properly re-trained. De-homo-ing therapy, like re-conversion, is based on the idea of possible re-education. Just as cultural and religious re-conversion reinforces the notion of Hinduism as the sole religion-culture of the nation, so does de-homo-ing therapy clearly establish both heterosexuality and asexuality as the exclusive sexualities of the nation.

A second position on homosexual subjects is that there are now too many of them in the public space, and so they need to be accepted. This idea arose after the annual gay pride marches across India made it impossible to ignore the numbers. However, it also came about in the present age of homonationalism at a time when India is massively inserted into capitalism and needs to prove its good treatment of queers if it is to avoid boycotts and compete in today's world. Thus, in late 2015, the BJP Minister of Finance Arun Jaitley referred to 'the jurisprudential development on gay rights the world over' and maintained that 'when millions of people the world over are having alternative sexual preferences, it is too late in the day to propound a view that they should be jailed'.[35] For Jaitley criminalisation is 'archaic' 'in the present era when there is a universal movement towards their acceptability'.[36]

Yet another Hindu nationalist position is to continue to reject homosexuality as not Indian. Thus in 2016 the International Secretary General of the RSS' cultural-religious wing, Champat Rai, said the 'practise (homosexual acts) was influenced by western culture and it is against Indian culture. [...] Bharat will not accept this as it is a country with a glorious past and a thousand-year-old tradition'.[37] Having equated homo subjects with the West, the Rajya Sabha MP from the BJP, Subramanian Swamy, also expressed disdain over gays who 'flaunt' their queerness, and warned against the proliferation of 'gay bars'.[38]

Finally, there is a great difference across all these positions between attitudes towards homosexual and transgender subjects. Across the board, there is transgender recognition and transgender tolerance-to-acceptance. A BJP-led parliamentary panel affirmed transgender rights in 2017.[39] Under the BJP Government, following both Nepal and Pakistan, third gender became a recognised national legal status. In contrast, there are no such rights in the US, a country that imagines itself as more humane and more democratic than thou.[40]

Muslim men

The ideal Hindu nationalist citizen-body rests upon the exclusion of a series of Others who embody, albeit differentially, 'improper' (also 'impure'?) gendering, sexuality, and nationalisation. Thus, in an operation based on auto-referentiality, in the sense of Guillaumin,[41] the RSS has long projected the gender of Indian Muslims as masculine, parallel to the Hindu nationalist homosocial citizen-body. Historically, the RSS has divided Indian Muslim men into three categories:[42] 1. Muslims-as-foreign-invaders, which designates upper class and political leadership; 2. Muslims-as-ex-Hindu-converts, as lower caste; and 3. Hindu-Muslims, a more recent invention, designating hypothetical Muslims who, insofar as their conduct would be consistent with Hindu nationalism's religious, nationalist, gender and sexual normativity, could be re-assimilated back into the Hindu nation. Underlying the first two categories are three common characteristics: hypermasculinity, hypersexuality and anti-(Hindu)nationalism. The RSS has long maintained that Muslim men engage in 'riots, rapes, looting, raping and all sorts of orgies' as they seek to undermine the Hindu nation.[43]

The RSS has produced its notion of Muslim men as excessively masculine and excessively sexual by re-assigning orientalist and British administrative discourse about Hindus to Muslims. Here, the RSS reiterates the colonial idea that Hindu and Muslim 'communities' are incompatible, an idea that, as historians Chandra, Pandey, and others have amply demonstrated, served Britain's official divide and rule policy.[44] The RSS also projects onto Muslims the promiscuity and aggression that the British had earlier assigned to lower-caste Hindus, and diverts its anger towards them. The RSS states about Muslims: 'Times without number we had to gulp down insult and humiliation at their hands'.[45] Here, the RSS portrays active-hypermasculine Muslim men rendering Hindu men passive-effeminate in a not-so-disguised homo-sexualised relation. To elaborate, Golwalkar states:

> The more our leaders tried to appease the Muslims, the more their separatist and aggressive appetite was whetted. The British too, set about to sharpen their separatist teeth and claws in a bid to set them against nationalist forces. The Muslims were placed in a position in which they were wanted by both the British and the nationalists and their price was rising higher and higher.[46]

In some versions, the RSS presents Muslims as hypermasculine ('aggressive') to the point of animality (with sharp 'teeth and claws') and as subjects of both British and Congress Party men's attraction. Yet, the terms of the homoerotic relationship are displaced. In this new threesome, Muslim men feature as male prostitutes whose price rises as the British and Congress men bid for their favour, while RSS men are positioned as voyeurs.

Today, the earlier construction of Muslims-as-foreign-invaders remains constant. We see, however, with the BJP's electoral desire to obtain Muslim votes, a major shift in the models for Muslims-as-ex-Hindu-converts and Hindu-Muslims. For example, in a demonstration of Hindu-Muslim figuration and Hindu-national-incorporation, the RSS decided to publicly honour the poet-laureate of Bangladesh, Kazi Nazrul Islam, in Bengal in India on his birthday (25 May) and more, to translate his works into all Indian languages. The RSS gave as its rationale that Kazi Nazrul Islam opposed British rule, united Hindus and Muslims, and even wrote about Durga Puja and the goddess Kali.[47] This sudden glorification of Kazi Nazrul Islam directly followed public conflict between the BJP and the state government of Bengal over what Hindu nationalists deem a vote bank policy that disadvantages Hindus. It also appeared in the wake of some Muslim clerics' call to ban the RSS.[48] Again, the redrawing of boundaries of 'Us' vs. 'Them' to enlarge the 'Us' and reposition Hindu nationalism as inclusive both serves BJP electoral designs, and aligns modern India more fully with discourses of dominant neo-liberal democracies (good and bad Muslims, good and bad queers).

Western men and westernised Hindu elites

Historically and into the present the RSS has constructed the nations and citizen-bodies of the West in hypermasculine and hypersexual terms:[49] 'The insatiable hunger for physical enjoyment does not allow one to stop within one's own national boundaries. On the strength of its state power, the stronger nation tries to subdue and exploit the other in order to swell its own coffers. [...] Moral bonds are all snapped.' Here, in an inversion of the coloniser's construction of India as the porno-tropics, the RSS and other Hindu nationalist organisations represent the West as the porno-west. In Hindu nationalist logic, the unleashed sexuality of the western world threatens to feminise and engulf the Hindu nation in a scenario that reads like rape.

The Hindu nationalist construction of a porno-west also serves as a backdrop for representing and denouncing so-called 'westernised Hindu men' as sexually out-of-control. Let us hear, for example, the Hindu nationalist response to Deepa Mehta's film *Fire*, in which two sisters-in-law in a joint family develop a lesbian relationship. The film was released in India in

December 1998. It was condemned by all Hindu nationalists. After it had circulated for a few weeks, Hindu Shiv Sena activists protested by trashing the cinemas in which it was shown. The RSS declared:

> The Shiv Sena chief Bal Thakeray may be accused of using force and 'lumpen methodology' to suppress the voices that do not suit his cultural worldview. But the attack on the indigenous value-system by the ultra-westernised elite, who regard the nation as not more than a piece of land with a bundle of cultural and political rights, is more appalling than the action of the Shiv sainiks.[50]

Further, the RSS stated that Indian 'ultra-westernised elite' leftists had resorted:[51]

> to explicit lesbianism and other perversities to challenge the traditional set up. That way one day all the pornographic flings of Mona [sic] Lewinsky-Clinton duo may become the role model, if the aim is to disintegrate the family *a la* western society. The method may not appeal to the female fraternity in general but Deepa Mehtas and Shabana Azmis of the day must have their fling even when western feminist prophets like Germaine Greer, the writer of *The Female Eunuch*, are returning to sober, civilised, domesticated ways, accepting even male superiority as a natural course of things.[52]

Here the RSS proposed some interesting equations: the dangers of anormative heterosexuality (Lewinski and Clinton) and lesbianism; 'civilisation' (Western and Hindu nationalist) and 'male superiority'; but also domestication as the desirable 'sober' reincarnation of feminism (through the figure of Greer).

This earlier position on lesbianism is interesting to consider alongside the current complexities of Hindu nationalist positions on homosexuality as mentioned above, including acceptance motivated by neo-liberal and capitalism desires.

Congress party men and their queer nation

The RSS has historically constructed its Indian political opponents, especially those of the Indian National Congress Party, as internal Others who are queer because they are improperly (Hindu) nationalised. Congress men 'woo and appease the anti-Hindu communities thus encouraging them in their aggressive designs'.[53] If in an above quoted passage the RSS feels that 'Muslims were placed in a position where they were wanted' by Congress secular nationalists, here the RSS figures Congress men in turn as seductive effeminates who actually encourage their own rape by Muslim men. In an operation that links queer gender, sexuality and secular nationalism, the RSS locates Congress male femininity in Congress politics: 'The concept of territorial nationalism has verily emasculated our nation and what more can we expect of a body deprived of its vital energy'?[54] Here, the 'body deprived' is the citizen-body as a collective (now potentially missing) phallus.

For the RSS, the Congress' secular territorial nationalism signifies national-miscegenation because it promotes queer fusion between Muslim and Hindu men. Golwalkar describes territorial nationalism as an 'unnatural', 'hybrid nationalism' thus:

> It is like attempting to create a novel animal by joining the head of a monkey and the legs of a bullock to the main body of the elephant! It can only result in a hideous corpse. [...] If at all some activity is seen in that body it is only of the germs and bacteria breeding in that decomposing corpse. And so it is that we see today the germs of corruption, disintegration and dissipation eating into the vitals of our nation for having given up the natural living nationalism in the pursuit of an unnatural, unscientific and lifeless hybrid-concept of territorial nationalism.[55]

In the above passage, Hinduism and Islam are racialised into biological categories in line with eighteenth- through twentieth-century 'scientific' biological racism. The Hindu nationalist citizen-body (elephant) is surgically decapitated and its lower limbs are severed; the (Hindu) head and legs are discarded and replaced with a Muslim (monkey) head and Muslim (bullock) legs. For the RSS, the cohabitation of 'incompatible' religions in the same nation-space implies a racialised-religious reassignment to the citizen-body that signals castration. The 'un-natural' and 'unscientific' cutting operation is reinforced by the figure of Muslims as disease eating into the RSS' 'vitals'. Thus, territorial nationalism spells the simultaneous end of Hindu masculinity and of the Hindu collective phallus; it signals death itself ('the decomposing corpse'). The sexualised metaphors of hybridity as castration and death, inter-nationality and inter-religiosity, are located specifically at the intersection of nineteenth-century scientific constructions of race and the homosexual, wherein, as Somerville has remarked, via the term 'intermediate sex' homosexuals became the 'half breeds' of sexology.[56] For the RSS, Congress' territorial nationalism forces the citizen-body to become the (castrated) 'intermediate sex' of nationalism. (Are there intersections with Brahmanisation and notions of purity?)

Hindu queers

Historically, the metaphoric queerness that Hindu nationalists assign to all their Others relies on the queerness of Hindu queer subjects as the ultimate sign of the degraded Hindu nation. In the RSS' early biography of Dr (Doctorji) Hedgevar, the RSS founder, we find that:

> Doctorji had bought from an exhibition a couple of fans made of palm-leaves and bamboo. One of them carried a picture of Chatrapati Shivaji, and on the other was a picture of the famous actor Balgandharva in a female role. Doctorji explained, 'I intentionally brought these two just to show the contrast between the condition of Maharashtra some 300 years ago, and our present times'.[57]

Shivaji Bhonsla (1627–80), a multi-semic historical figure, is for the RSS an exemplary Hindu nationalist man who defeated the ruling Mughal Empire and built a 'Hindu Empire'. The RSS constructs Balgandharva (1888–1967), a celebrated male actor renown for playing romantic female roles, as a Hindu queer signifying the Hindu nation's downfall.

Also, historically, the Hindu queer subject was transformed into a sign of western secularism, the disease that provokes the end of the Hindu nation. For example, in the RSS newspaper, *Organiser*, following the release of the film *Fire* mentioned above, we find the following sarcastic humorous rendition:

> Secularism can not be served, supported and sustained unless the Hindu mind-set is maligned and the Hindu tradition traduced. Funnily enough, if secularism means debunking ancient Bharat, lesbianism means upholding ancient Greece. For it was in the ancient Greek city of Lesbos that for the first time the ladies teaching at a school for girls taught homosexuality to their pupils. [...] It proves that modern India wants to become as modern as ancient Greece. [...] West is best, and nothing coming from the best, ancient or modern, can ever go out of fashion for us. [...] ...if secularism is to spread like a plague, lesbianism must spread like an epidemic, no?[58]

This RSS correlation of queer with the West proceeds by forgetting what the RSS has already effaced: the long genealogy and ample present of queer gender and sexual presence in India in Hindu (and other) contexts, as mentioned above.

Queerphilia and queer-ambiguity: reinscriptions

Above we have seen a tremendous amount of Hindu nationalist queerphobia, and more recently some Hindu nationalist queer-ambiguity. Paradoxically, at certain points, the RSS reinserts into its own discourse forms of what the RSS itself identifies elsewhere as anormative gender and sexuality. Perhaps gender and sexuality are objects of continual negotiation because of their centrality to, and variation within, the differential discourses upon which Hindu nationalist ideologues draw. Here, I will point to two sites of RSS queerphilic and queer-ambiguous re-inscription.

Hindu nationalist leaders

We could begin with Dr Hedgevar, the deceased RSS founder, whom M.S. Golwalkar describes as 'the Hindu ideal of man in flesh and blood'.[59] For Golwalkar Dr Hedgevar is 'irresistible', 'childlike', full of 'sweet words which appeal to the heart' such that 'the more one came near him the more one would love and adore him'.[60] Golwalkar elaborates:

> what an ocean of love he was to us! [...] The boundless affection of the mother's heart, the sleepless care and diligence of the father and the inspiring guidance of the guru found their culmination in that single bosom. [...] The worship of such a soul transcends the worship of an individual and becomes the worship of the ideal itself. He is verily my chosen deity.[61]

Here, we find a bi-gendered Hedgevar ('mother's love' and father's 'diligence') who is guru and finally a divinity ('my chosen deity'). This figuration is possible in Hindu nationalism insofar as it relies on the highly valorised image of bi-gendered Hindu divinities. In fact it is consistent with representations of other highly respected human bi-gendered figures, including those whom the RSS despises: Mahatma Gandhi, whom Hindu nationalists assassinated, is a case in point.

Similarly, the public image Hindu nationalists have constructed for India's former prime minister from the BJP, Atal Bihari Vajpayee, is bi-gendered. His 1998 official biography by a BJP member C.P. Sharma, entitled *Poet Politician: Atal Bihari Vajpayee*, insists on his sensitivity; he learned as a child that he had 'the right to cry' and that lesson was 'permanently etched on his mind'.[62] He loves children and 'becomes a child amongst them'.[63]

More importantly, in the title of Sharma's book, the terms poet and politician are thickly semiotic. I will point to only two most pertinent associations for each. First, poet is aligned in colonial discourse with feminine flakiness and dreaminess in contrast to prized hard male rationality, and in dominant Hindu discourses with the esteemed Brahmin as opposed to illiterate masses. Politician in India often retains an off-putting association with British rule or by extension corrupt postcolonial governments, and yet in Hindu nationalist discourse politician is joined to the respected *kshatriya*. While Vajpayee's biography is primarily about his political exploits, Sharma positions a poem at the beginning of every chapter and weaves the Vajpayee-the-poet thematic throughout. For Hindu nationalists the production of Vajpayee as both poet (Brahmin) and politician (*kshatriya*) correlates him as a *rishi* (seer, sage) endowed with divine (political) inspiration, thus capable of predicting the renaissance of the Hindu nation.

Finally, in biographies of Narendra Modi, he, too, is described in both Brahmanical terms as a writer and in line with the *Kshatriya* model as 'having all the qualities of an army Commander'.[64] Modi is overwhelmingly presented in neoliberal terms as a self-made man who arose from the poor to become the national leader. He is also presented, however, as a saintly person with a 'delicate heart' in his attachment to the poor, a quality that in the global north today is associated with effeminacy.[65]

In Vajpayee, Hedgevar and Modi's representations, qualities which could be read as queer gender in a colonial grid are instead read through the Hindu symbolic as attributes of bi-gendered divinities. But this is only possible because all three men are always already powerful political symbols, un-connected to weakness, ideal Hindu nationalists, and most importantly their queer gender is totally a-sexual. In contrast, Balgandharva is unacceptable to Hindu nationalists because he is perceived to be apolitical and highly sexual.

While Hedgevar and Vajpayee are specifically read through a Hindu nationalist lens, the principle of bi-gendered political leaders might be wider. For example, we can find analogies with other extremist right-wing representations of 'visionaries': Hitler as a sensitive artist who wished to make the world vegetarian;[66] Mussolini as an 'artist' moulding the people;[67] Maurras as creative writer; and George Bush who combines fumbling effeminacy (as pampered son) with cowboy machismo ('hunt 'em down and smoke 'em out'). Thus, while Hindu nationalism draws on particular traditions of bi-gendered beings, there is a general trope of attaching normative notions of male and female to strong male political leaders.

Materialised enactments

But what of queer sexuality? Hindu nationalist leaders and rank-and-file perform it in violent anti-other events. Queerphobic xenophobia supplies the motivating energy for Hindu nationalist enactments of queer-ambiguity. The riot situation as a liminal space of panic that stretches the present seemingly onward forever is an exemplary locus for this acting-out operation.[68]

A plethora of studies have documented what I would call the Hindu nationalist reordering of Muslim gender, sex and sexuality under the surgical knife as weapon in such conditions. To evoke two examples: in the 1947 Partition violence and in the 2002 Gujarat pogroms, Hindu nationalists cut off Muslim women's breasts and then gang raped them.[69] In the 2002 turmoil they cut Muslim women's foetuses from their wombs before murdering them. By laying the Hindu nationalist mark onto a Muslim woman's flesh and removing breasts, they transform her into a eunuch. They then used the eunuch as a conduit for their own male sexual bonding through gang rape. The ripping out of foetuses ensures the dis-continuation of Muslim genealogies in future time. But more, in both instances, 1947 and 2002, Hindu nationalist men castrated Muslim men before murdering them, thereby producing the cathartic reversal of the fantasmic Muslim-as-hypermasculine-hypersexual. Dismemberment frees up the now sexless Muslim ex-male body for a deferred religious-reassignment and gender and sexual reordering that cannot take place (for he is dead). But it also separates and annihilates the body parts that, in a passage above, were fantasised as fused in a deadly hybrid Congress-inspired citizen-body. In these *passages à l'acte* Hindu nationalists move from the metaphorical-discursive queering of Muslims to their material queering. Paradoxically, far from guaranteeing Hindu nationalist male a-sexual normativity, these crimes queer the perpetrators as makers and rapists of eunuchs and other bodies generally considered ambiguously anormative.

Some concluding remarks

To conclude I would like to make two points. First, I want to signal that in India, critical peoples of many political persuasions, faiths, genders and sexualities have consistently and skilfully resisted Hindu nationalist anti-Muslim and anti-Queer discourses, across all scales, including the village, city, region, nation, and transnationally in the diaspora. Such work is done daily but also at specific conjunctures. To cite just one historical high-profile example, while Hindu nationalists were protesting against Deepa Mehta's 'lesbian' film *Fire*, mentioned above, activists formed a counter force, an immense alliance, to defend the rights of Indian queers. This counter-mobilisation converged as part of the larger struggle against (Hindu nationalist or other) repression, censorship and exclusion.[70] In recent years, Dalit movements and LGBTIQ movements have become increasingly more visible in India. In fact they are also intersecting at certain points. Gay Pride marches now include Dalit constituencies. If earlier some lesbian activists carried signs in the *Fire* defence demonstrations stating 'Hindu and lesbian', today one can observe signs in

Gay Pride marches reading 'Dalit and queer.' Insofar as Hindu nationalism is an upper caste based and oriented movement, the radical wings of current queer movements and Dalit movements, and their new intersections, function as inoculations against Hindu nationalism and also invoke the idea of a totally different kind of present and future society.

Second, throughout, I have alluded sporadically to practices of queerphobic xenophobia, xenophobic queerphobia, queerphilic idealisation, selective queer national-normativisation, and to the presence of queer-ambiguity, that exist in some right-wing nationalisms beyond India. Hopefully, further research will bring to visibility their extent and forms across the globe. In this way, perhaps, we can configure local to transnational political strategies expansive enough to undo queerphobia, xenophobia and all anti-Other discourses and practices in their many identifiable forms and dimensions, from multiple fronts, for all. But, also, perhaps we will be able to complicate the current binary in which queer acceptance is imagined as always already a good thing and is systematically associated with the left, while queer repression is assigned to the right. In fact, in many places across the globe queer acceptance to date has been conditional upon the violence of queer-normativisation, in which queer-normativity is upheld to construct ever more unacceptable others. Thus, instead of hoping for queer-inclusion in any context of ongoing inequalities, in the global north or south, across the left or right, perhaps we can create and converge in radical struggles that enrich and support practices of freedom for all.

21

REMAKING THE HINDU/NATION

TERROR AND IMPUNITY IN UTTAR PRADESH

Angana P. Chatterji

We heard about Babri Masjid, about Gujarat...about other places.
Then, we saw Muzaffarnagar. The flames of hatred surrounded us.
We are being engulfed. There is fear everywhere.
Can we ever be ourselves again?
Muslim woman, Uttar Pradesh (2014)[1]

The next moment

Muzaffarnagar 2013 marked Uttar Pradesh as the next frontier in Hindu nationalism's incursion into the body politic. Between 27 August and 17 September of that year,[2] massified violence targeted the Muslim community in Muzaffarnagar. At the onset, two Hindus accused and killed a Muslim youth for allegedly sexually harassing a Hindu woman and relative. In the violence that ensued, sixty-two people died,[3] ninety-three suffered injuries,[4] women were gang raped,[5] and approximately 40–50,000 people were displaced.[6] Three months after the violence, relief centres were shut down.

The All India Democratic Women's Association (AIDWA) specified in their report that the 'attacks were pre-planned', and that the 'Bharatiya Janata Party (BJP)/Rashtriya Swayamsevak Sangh (RSS)[7]... made communal speeches, and orchestrated communal conflagration'.[8] The AIDWA report further stated that there were at least five reported cases of rape[9] (all gang-rape) of Muslim women during the Muzaffarnagar mass violence. Survivors named the perpetrators in First Information Reports (FIRs).[10] AIDWA also reported that Muzaffarnagar had 'the highest number of "[honour]" killings' in Uttar Pradesh, one–two per month.[11]

Concentrating on the contemporaneous, evolving Hindu nationalist imperative to create a majoritarian nation in India,[12] this article is a provisional historiographic and genealogical exploration of the discursive practices, infrastructure, and events of majoritarian and gendered impunity, surrounding and following the 2014 elections in Uttar Pradesh.[13] The article marks the emergent and deepening relations between Hindu cultural dominance and nationalist Hinduism, and examines their imprint on minority/Othered subjects.

Majoritarian contours

Ideologically adherent to Hindutva ('Hindu-ness'),[14] and premised on Brahmanical dominance, Hindu nationalists are amplifying their seemingly irreversible crusade to render India into a Hindu state. Uttar Pradesh, foundational to this experiment, has been witness to the aggressive infiltration of Hindu nationalists into its vital institutions in recent years, including the election commission, bureaucracy, media, and academic establishments, together with efforts to curtail the judiciary into compliance with majoritarian mandates.

Two recent ballots in the state—the parliamentary elections of 2014, led by the BJP and supported by the Sangh Parivar family of Hindu nationalist organisations,[15] as well as the state assembly elections of 2017—delivered a decisive victory for Hindu nationalists. At the state level, the parliamentary wing of Hindu nationalism in India, the BJP, had previously governed Uttar Pradesh from June 1991–December 1992 and again from November 1999–March 2002, before ascending to power in March 2017.[16] The electoral victories of 2014 and 2017 shifted the framework of democratic and republican governance, and especially impacted people's fundamental rights; the right to life and livelihood, to equality before the law, to non-discrimination, and to freedom of religion.[17] Expressly, 2017 spiralled the negation of the rights of religion, caste, and tribe-based minorities,[18] as highlighted in this article.

The state assembly elections of 2017 in Uttar Pradesh were crucial to the future aspirations of the BJP, both regionally and at the centre in Delhi. The installation of Yogi Adityanath, reportedly a far-right ideologue,[19] as chief minister, underscored the tensions and strategies prevalent in-between far-right Hindu nationalist organisations (currently unconstrained by political and constitutional obligations) and the BJP. Ideological differences between the BJP and Adityanath encoded the latter's instatement as chief minister. His ascendance was meant to appease the militant wing of Hindu nationalism and constrain vigilante action. Simultaneously this served to signal the further legitimation of hyper-authoritarian imperatives within the state government and sanction and normalise extremist movements within civil society and what Partha Chatterjee terms 'political society'.[20]

In Uttar Pradesh, economic development is a compelling force in *realpolitik*. At the majoritarian front lines, developmental agendas are enmeshed with political governance, crony capitalism, and electoral politics. In this, the state has been aided by the strident support of the central government led by Narendra Modi for the creation of a Hinduised state, and the assimilation, segregation, and marginalisation of religious minorities and other vulnerable groups. The primary focus of the 2014 elections, the promise to deliver large-scale development, failed to produce adequate results. In attempting to mask the above, the BJP and allied Hindu nationalist civil society organisations have been prioritising a divisive strategy that pits minority groups and their concerns in adversarial relation to one another.[21] Obscuring intrinsic, inequitable relations of power, Hindu nationalists represent minorities and their allies as collectively oppositional and menacing to majority lives. In doing so, the BJP and Hindu nationalist organisations effect greater estrangements between majority and minority in the furtherance of a majoritarian state. In discourse/practice, such intent is focused on positing the BJP and the Sangh Parivar as proven allies of Hindus within a conflictual polity, and in securing national re-election in 2019.

Issues relevant to Uttar Pradesh that are foremost in the BJP's national agenda include: a populist government, the Ayodhya campaign and Babri Masjid, forcible conversions to Hinduism (routinely expatiated by Hindutva affiliates as 'reconversion'),[22] hampering consent-based conversion to non-Hindu faiths, framing 'love jihad',[23] opposing reservations and cattle slaughter, promoting hate speech, and advocating for the flying of the tricolour (national flag) on *madrassas*.

While the Freedom of Religion Act is not in force in Uttar Pradesh, some of its protocols appear to be practiced in the state. One such custom is the submission of an affidavit, a form that is filled out by the person seeking to convert, and attested by the priest/clergy performing the conversion, who verifies that the conversion is non-coercive.[24] Freedom of Religion Acts have been interpreted and implemented by Hindu nationalists and the courts in ways that criminalise and infantilise those who emigrate to non-Hindu faiths, calling for their 'reconversion'. Further, while freedom of religion laws do not prohibit conversion, the tenets and principles of these laws are operationalised to bolster Hindu majoritarianism, and to target religious minority communities and impede their right to conversion and freedom of religion, all of which are in force in Uttar Pradesh.[25]

In focusing on the above agenda, Hindu nationalist groups have increased their cadre and grassroots base and command the support of a sizeable segment of Hindu civil society. Their role in orchestrating vigilante, racialised[26] and aggression/violence-based activism is reportedly expanding. Given their relationship to the current Uttar Pradesh government and the national government, resistance from minority and vulnerable groups toward Hindu nationalist groups and activities is routinely met with or used to incite violence against non-Hindus. These acts and events function to effectuate a majoritarian security state.[27] The everyday and large-scale, episodic targeting of vulnerable communities is supported by the deeply rooted structural inequalities of caste, class, and hetero/normative gender, strengthening cultures of violence and facilitating governance through fear.[28]

Subtext[29]

The BJP- and Sangh Parivar-led arrival (2014 onward) is borne of a multitude of convergences. Contingent to this is perhaps the long- and deeply-held commitment that extends well beyond the Hindu Right, that Hindus are privileged to India. Hindu cultural dominance is the historical and political precursor to Hindu majoritarianism.[30] It has both an uncensored and submerged/suppressed legacy elemental to the very construction of modern[31] and post/colonial India.[32] Hindu cultural dominance permeates the national ethos and *volk* in ways that are simultaneously un-proclaimed and loud. It has shaped dominant culture (in representations and celebrations of what is India and in the pervasiveness of caste, for example), politics and ideology (among the Congress Party, socialists, communists, Maoists, in varying degrees, as well as the BJP), and law enforcement (police, paramilitary, and armed forces).[33]

Castefication and Hindutva-isation[34] have been integral to the amalgamation of nationalist politics in India.[35] The unrelenting prevalence of the Hindu male in society and culture rendered Hindutva as India's manifest destiny.[36] The Othering of subalterns, mediated by issues of caste, ethnicity/race, religion, gender, sexuality, ability, and class in the constitution, laws, policies, political economy, and public imaginary, has been formative of national governance. Patriotic Hinduism deepened because of such prejudice. The significance and scope of the 'Hindu' as majoritarian, the nationalist Hindu, is not merely prefatory to the BJP's or the Sangh Parivar's current ascendance, rather it has been fundamental to India's body politic. The translation of the above premise into political strategy[37] has been used to varying degrees by the dynastic Congress government in configuring India as an emergent regional power.[38] The discontinuity between the Congress and the BJP lies perhaps in the degree to which Hindu ascendancy was prioritised or kept in check by previous governments, including the BJP central government of 1998–2004, and the current BJP/Modi government's actions in fascizing majoritarian politics.[39]

Veena Das writes that we have been unable 'to name that which died when autonomous citizens...[of India]...were simultaneously born as monsters'.[40] The post-1947 moment prioritised territorial sovereignty, national unification, and subject-formation. At the intersections of history, geographicity,[41] and residual conflict, the dominance of Hindus, fraught relations to Othered-subjects, and a multi-party system shaped India's 'conflicted democracy'.[42]

Post-1947, religion-based altercations have been emblematic of relations between majority and minority. Across the nation, sites of epical violence correspond to experiments in dispossession. Public history is witness to the rearrangement of rights, entitlements, and governance of minority/Othered subjects: Delhi (1947, 1984), Calcutta/Kolkata since 2001 (1946), Kota (1953), Rourkela (1964), Ranchi (1967), Ahmedabad (1969), Bhiwandi (1970), Aligarh (1978), Jamshedpur (1979), Moradabad (1980), Meerut (1982), Hyderabad (1983), Assam (1983, 2008), Bhagalpur (1989), Bhadrak (1991), Ayodhya (1992), Bombay/Mumbai since 1995 (1992–93), Gujarat (1969, 2002), Marad (2003), Mau (2005), Goa (2006), Bhinga (2007), Jammu (2008), Orissa/Odisha since 2011 (1991, 2007, 2008), and Muzaffarnagar (2013).[43]

The borderlands are witness to decades-long political violence and the violation of self-determination: Punjab (1984–95), Kashmir (since 1990),[44] and Manipur (since 1958).[45] Further, the ongoing nationalisation of forest and public lands has led to the severe erosion of the traditional and customary rights of local communities, further augmented by projects of careless globalisation and large-scale maldevelopment. This has devalued and disfigured the cultures and livelihoods of Adivasis (tribal, indigenous communities)[46] and Dalits (formerly 'untouchable' groups),[47] endangering their well-being, creating the fault lines via which to promulgate their violent induction into 'civilisational' processes. The Hindutva-isation and securitisation of Adivasis and Dalits through their violent incorporation into Hinduism helped construct the hegemon of the Hindu majority in India, as exemplified in the Narmada Valley, Jharkhand, and Chhattisgarh, fortifying elite claims for the Hindu-isation of the polity.[48]

The arbitrariness, challenges, and failures of ad hoc commissions and central and state human rights bodies to respond to episodic mass violence have been endemic. The successive institutionalisation of impunity laws in 'disturbed'/conflict areas, such as the Armed Forces Special Powers Act, and the negation of criminal command responsibility have created extraordinary situations in which the human rights[49] of peoples and communities cannot be upheld. The failure and absence of justice frameworks and processes, and the lack of transitional and transformative justice, psychosocial restitution, and historical dialogue for long-standing and new conflicts and episodes of mass violence have significantly and accumulatively contributed to the disillusionment and un-belonging of minority/subaltern communities and to the creation of an aspirational/collaborator nationalist class.

The communal politics of the 1950–60s gave way to the racialisation and mass killing of Muslims and Sikhs in the 1980s.[50] In-between, in 1975–77, Indira Gandhi imposed a national emergency.[51] Post-Emergency, the spaces/ practices of Hindu cultural dominance mutated into and contoured Hindu majoritarianism. With it, the reach and impact of the Sangh Parivar across India's heartland intensified, galvanising the onset of the movement that led to Ayodhya 1992, Bombay 1992–93, the BJP in power in central government in 1998–2004, Gujarat 2002, Orissa 2007–8, Muzaffarnagar 2013, and to the Modi/BJP victory of 2014.

Through the above, Hindu/nationalist organisations and leaders sought to progressively control and encode the symbolic, idiomatic, and functional aspects of statehood to varying degrees. These aspects of statehood include: security, territory, and population (drawing on Michel Foucault).[52] Security: weaponisation, militarisation, trade, control over and production of information, biopolitical regulation of the population, mainstreaming practices from conflict zones that enforce and routinise states of exception (Giorgio Agamben), and regional dominance; Territory: rendering India as synonymous with Hindu-ness, the hyper-sacralisation of the flag as an homage to a racialised identity, Kashmir as integral to India, projecting a strong nationalist image abroad, and tense India-Pakistan relations; and Population: the ascendance of the majority population and its forms of knowledge, and the marginalisation of minorities and local/disqualified knowledges and ways of being, as a strategy of governance.

The expanse of power captured and inhabited by the BJP and the Sangh Parivar incrementally authorised the co-production and conjoining of Hindu nationalism (wherein nationalism is modified by Hinduism) with nationalist Hinduism (wherein Hinduism is modified by nationalism, majoritarianism, and statehood), a nonpareil characteristic of the post-2014 present.

Ideology, race, and gender

'Hinduism is a religion, Hindutva is an ideology for political mobilization', Romila Thapar contends.[53] She writes: 'Hinduism is a mosaic of belief systems, some linked, others not. Hindutva has the characteristics of a sect that reformulates selected beliefs to create in this case a socio-political organisation with an attempt at ideological coherence'.[54] Gurharpal Singh has noted that India is an 'ethnic democracy',[55] structured around sharp divides 'between the core and peripheral regions'.[56] 'Ethnic democracy' has been explained as a political and discursive system distinguished by majoritarian dominance,[57] and, in the South Asia context, by communalism.[58] Communalism is habitually used to describe the long-standing tensions that govern relations between Hindus and Muslims, Hindus and Christians, and Hindus and Sikhs, and 'while the framework of "communalism" presents relevant insights, it is inadequate in explicating majoritarianism, whose evolving dynamics are intimately linked to the racialisation of the Other in contemporary India'.[59]

The racialisation of difference has manifested in the latticework of social hierarchy and victimisation. The ordering of social discrimination has been formative of the institutionalisation of social, political, economic and legal inequalities in India, and to rendering them defensible. The Othering of minorities/marginal subalterns is actuated through their simultaneous homogenisation and assimilation into national culture.[60] The minority subject, both an outsider and an insider, is always vulnerable, and seen as an impediment to 'Indian-ness' by majoritarian groups.[61] Majoritarian manoeuvres in defining marginal subalterns as second-class subjects, the 'enemy within', are integral to the Hinduisation of the political economy and its globalisation. Hinduism functions as a 'meta-ethnicity', and although 'minorities have been granted individual and, in some cases, collective rights, the recognition of these rights has been based on a tactical accommodation' of dominant Hinduism.[62] In the context of India, the process of minoritisation[63] is akin to that of racialisation in the global north, whereby 'racial', 'inferior',[64] and 'anti-national' connotations have been ascribed to minorities, and manipulated to victimise them.[65]

Post-9/11 and post-2008 Mumbai,[66] representations of the minority/Othered as dangerous anti-nationals abound,[67] while majoritarian (religion and gender-based) violence against minorities continues unimpeded.[68] The racialisation of the minority/Othered (already present, now escalated) erroneously identifies them with a predisposition to violence, in turn prompting violence against them. The demands and hostilities that organise conflict and upheaval between minority and majority are depicted as provocations inherent to history and culture, or as responses to minority reassertions.[69] The immoderations of such hostility are understood to be thwarted by the secular nature of the state,[70] even as the secularisation of the post/colony corresponds to projects that nationalise the secular, circumscribing the secular within majoritarian discourses and practices.[71] Hindutva casts suspicion upon and vigorously contests any form of secularism that resists dominant renderings. Oppositional secularisms are deemed pseudo-secular and as such are defined as anti-national, seditious.[72] Secularism, ethics, and freedoms protective of minority rights are singled out and in conjunction, discourses, practices, individuals, and communities are targeted.[73]

While religionised violence (via the politicisation of religion, rendering it an object of violence) has been determinative of the post/colonial Indian state,[74] hyper-nationalist experiments to transition from a conflicted democracy to a majoritarian state have been accelerated and reimagined since the onset of the twenty-first century.

Gendered and sexualised violence inevitably accompanies majoritarian mobilisations.[75] Gendered and sexualised violence are instruments of cultural, economic, and psychosocial control and oppression used by both state functionaries and nationalist cadres at the grassroots in India to provoke, subjugate, threaten, violate, silence, enforce assimilation, and to elicit submission and assertion. Women from the majority community are manipulated, controlled, and deployed to submit to majoritarian principles, as typified by the words and actions of numerous male-identified Hindutva leaders. Minority women's bodies have been the battlegrounds of majoritarian assertation, and violence against minority women, as an objective and aspect of minoritisation, has persisted in the historical present.[76] Violence against minority women functions as a warning to majority women and minority men. Subaltern womxn's bodies are both targets and collateral damage, and aggression on them functions as a reward (for the perpetrator). In situations of massified violence and political conflict, sexualised violence is widespread. Yet, sexualised violence is routinely disregarded and often not adjudicated upon as a crime that is systemic of the very structure of conflict and violence.[77] Victimised-survivors are constrained to find spaces in which they may safely speak out and judicial systems that guarantee their right to acknowledgement, non-repetition, remedy, and reparation.

Men from minority communities are racialised as hyper-sexual. Muslim male violence is understood as representative of the culture and displayed as coequal with Muslim sexuality. Military and political discourse posits Muslims as 'dangerous', and the majoritarian agenda is signified as protective of Hindu and minority women against the ever-present aggressive threat of ravaging Muslim men. Violence against minority men is perpetrated to silence and to domesticate them, and to simultaneously constitute them as dangerous and in need of continual subordination and emasculation.

The perpetration of sexual violence against minority women by vigilante groups is an example, as in Gujarat 2002 during the organized massified violence against Muslims. There, the severing of breasts and tearing open of wombs and vaginas were gestural of the grotesque objectification of Othered/ Muslim women and their dis-gendering and sexualisation, and 'signal[ed] complex levels of deterrence against Muslim reproduction'.[78] Gujarat 2002 was a turning point in the reconstitution of Hindu majoritarian nationalism in India today.[79] The advances made in and through Gujarat 2002 enabled Hindu nationalists to make inroads in Orissa.[80] In Orissa, the violent events of 2007–8 saw the enactment of a promise made in 1949 by Madhav Sadashiv Golwalkar, an early RSS ideologue and unrepentant admirer of Nazi ideologies, through advancing an assault on the economic and physical sanctity of Christians, along with Adivasis, Dalits, and Muslims, seeking to turn them against each other.

Both these events (Gujarat 2002 and Orissa 2007–8) in India's recent history, and the sparsity of social and legal justice for those victimised, have significantly enabled the majoritarianisation of the polity from below. They helped effect a successful upheaval of the social and economic ethos, and further the demonisation and social isolation of minority communities. The events in Gujarat and Orissa widened the acceptability of public, performative, and sexualised violences in Hindutva's arsenal. Prior to and following the events of 2002 and 2007–8, both Gujarat and Orissa witnessed a massive growth in the ranks of the Hindu nationalist cadre at the village level and across semi-urban spaces, and the incorporation of Adivasis and Dalits as majoritarian collaborators.[81] In Orissa, in 2008, for example, the Hindu nationalist cadre engaged in Sangh Parivar organisations numbered approximately 10 per cent of the state's population of approximately 36 million people.[82]

The reverberations of the above shifts, discourses, actions, and events are palpable in the consolidation of the Hindu Right's authority in Uttar Pradesh, and in their current capture of state power.

Context

Uttar Pradesh is a powerful state and the most populous one in the union,[83] with 204.2 million people.[84] Hindus constitute 79.7 per cent of the state's population and Muslims 19.3 per cent, while various communities make up the remaining 1 per cent; including Buddhists (0.1), Christians (0.2), Jains (0.1), and Sikhs (0.3). The Muslim community in Uttar Pradesh numbers 38,483,967,[85] the largest among India's states, and segments of them are politically powerful.

Uttar Pradesh's economy, the second largest in India after Maharashtra, is pivotal to the country's economic growth and forcefulness. The Gross Domestic Product for the state was Rs 862,746 crore[86] in 2013–14,[87] over 8 per cent of India's Gross Domestic Product.[88] In 2012–13, Uttar Pradesh was the largest food grain-producing state in India.[89] Uttar Pradesh contributes between 12–15 per cent to India's total pool of manufacturing employment.[90] The state is home to prominent sites of spiritual and social significance, including Ayodhya, Varanasi, Kushinagara, and the Taj Mahal in Agra, and is a major tourist destination. In 2014–15, approximately 182.8 million domestic tourists and 2.9 million foreign tourists visited Uttar Pradesh.[91]

In contradistinction, the United Nations has noted that the 'poverty head count ratio for Muslims is highest in the states of Assam, Uttar Pradesh, and Gujarat'.[92] Records from 2011–12 evidence that 30.4 per cent of the rural population and 26.1 per cent of the urban population in the state live below the poverty line.[93] Those socially and economically marginalised are disproportionately religious minorities, and Adivasis and Dalits. Uttar Pradesh, a key national pulse point, is being positioned as an economic powerhouse. The Uttar Pradesh government launched a Non-Resident Indian Corporation in 2014, with a dozen offices across the state. The state is making concerted efforts to engage persons of Uttar Pradesh origin residing in the United States

(US) in planning for its future development. The state has accumulated size-able investments from US businesses.

Religio-cultural and legal contestations and religiously motivated targeting of faith-based national minorities and other vulnerable groups by majoritarian forces have impacted and compromised freedom of religion in Uttar Pradesh.[94] The indications of such compromise function on a continuum, at times heightened, then low, each reportedly serving to influence the other, leading to eventual escalations of violence and marginalisation. Minority groups, in particular Muslims, together with Christians, Buddhists and other vulnerable communities such as non-Hinduised Adivasis and Dalits, and Queer, LGBTIQ communities,[95] often live in precarious social and political conditions.[96] There are serious breaches in the rule of law. The urgency of the situation is acutely felt among the targeted, even as their experiences are underreported, and the crises experienced by them are neglected and remain unaddressed, intensifying impact. Further, the targeting of journalists, civil rights, human rights activists, and progressive civil society has had a damaging effect on vulnerable groups.

Recent history[97]

Is Uttar Pradesh the exemplar of majoritarian futures? Religious and ethnic minority communities in Uttar Pradesh are vulnerable and have been sub-jected to organised targeting, and periodically, to massified violence. In 2014, the State Minorities Commission of Uttar Pradesh stated that it had received 18,445 complaints between 2009 and 2014.[98] However, during that five-year period, records indicate that the commission published no annual reports, issued no adjudications, served no punishments, made no recommendations for compensation, undertook no investigations of particular complaints, and undertook no general study on the social and economic status of minorities.[99] Following Muzaffarnagar 2013, Hindu nationalist leaders from the Vishwa Hindu Parishad (VHP)[100] and the parliamentarian BJP were indicted for inciting violence, among other charges.[101] A compensation package offered by the government stipulated that Muslim victimised-survivors must leave their villages in exchange for monetary relief.[102]

Forcible conversion to Hinduism by Sangh Parivar organisations continues apace. Survival linked to non-Hindu conversions to Hinduism persists akin to indigenous conversions to Catholicism under colonialism and settler colo-nialism.[103] In early December 2014, hundreds of Muslims were reportedly 'reconverted' to Hinduism under duress at a public event in Agra. The Press Trust of India reported that: 'Members of the RSS allegedly tricked dozens of Muslims families into attending a meeting by telling them they would be provided financial help, but instead a Hindu religious leader performed a Hindu conversion ceremony; an investigation is underway'.[104] In September 2014, Christian Dalit members of the Seventh-day Adventist Church reported from Uttar Pradesh that they had been converted to Hinduism against their will. Further, the church was forcibly refashioned into a Hindu temple.[105] There are no available records of a police investigation into the matter. Dharam Jagran Samiti, an affiliate of the VHP, proposed to hold a large event to implement conversion in Aligarh on 24 December 2014, on the eve of Christmas celebrations,[106] to bring '4,000 Christians and 1,000 Muslims back into the folds of Hinduism'.[107] Following sustained criticism, the event was postponed, as per an RSS leader. Prior to the scheduled event, Hindu nationalist organisations reportedly 'sought to raise money for their campaign, noting that it cost nearly Rs 200,000 (approximately US$ 2,722)[108] for each Christian conversion and Rs 500,000 (approximately US$ 6,805) for each Muslim conversion'.[109] Hindu nationalist groups reportedly engage in providing 'monetary incentives to Hindus to convert Christians and Muslims to Hinduism'[110] while accusing the Christian clergy of incentivising Adivasis and Dalits into converting to Christianity.

Between 2011 and 2014, the number of cases filed drawing on the provisions of the Uttar Pradesh Prevention of Cow Slaughter Act, 1955, recorded a sharp increase. In 2011, 2,456 cases of cattle slaughter were registered. In 2012, 3,655 cases of cattle slaughter were registered. In 2014, 5,012 cases of cattle slaughter were registered. Between January and June 2015, 4,400 cases of cattle slaughter had been registered.[111] In September 2015, in Dadri, Uttar Pradesh, after a rumour circulated, Mohammad Ikhlaq was reportedly accused of cattle slaughter. A Hindu nationalist mob attacked Ikhlaq and his family;[112] Iklaq's son survived, albeit with critical injuries, even as Iklaq did not.[113]

Events indicate that in the past few years tensions have been on the rise between Muslims and Dalits in a number of areas in Uttar Pradesh. Both communities, deeply affected by social and economic marginalisation, require gainful employment, development assistance, and resources for agricultural sustainability. Social tensions percolate against the backdrop of Dalit conversions to Islam dating back to 1981, in response to caste oppression, and the subsequent and aggressive attempts at the Hindu-isation of Dalits and the targeting of Muslims in the past decade and a half.[114]

On 2 December 2015, *Ultra News RTN* posted a chart with information made available by the Home Ministry of India, demonstrating an increase in religiously-motivated violence in India and identifying Uttar Pradesh as the state with the largest incidences of violence.[115] Between 2010–16, 1,020 religionised conflicts were reported in Uttar Pradesh.[116] According to information tabled before the Lok Sabha (lower/people's house of parliament),[117] Uttar Pradesh had the largest incidence of state-wide annual counts of religionised violence from 2010–16,[118] with the exception for 2011 when it placed second after Maharashtra.[119]

Accompanying Adityanath's take-over as chief minister, Uttar Pradesh recorded sixty incidents of religionised violence in 2017, the highest in the nation.[120] Between March 2015 and March 2016, RSS *shakhas* (branches, centres or cells) in the nation witnessed 'the highest growth since 1925',[121] with 56,859[122] RSS *shakhas* reportedly operational across India in 2016,[123] and 8,000 RSS *shakhas*[124] functioning in Uttar Pradesh in 2017.[125] Further, in January 2018, the VHP-affiliated Adivasi education group, Ekal Vidyalaya Foundation, claimed on its website that the organisation operates 11,400 schools in Uttar Pradesh.[126] A swarm of Sangh Parivar workers inhabit the nationalist circulatory system, arising from the grassroots and extending across states. In February 2018, in Muzaffarnagar, RSS leader Mohan Bhagat stated that, if called upon, the organisation was positioned to mobilise an army within three days.[127]

Reinscribing gender

In an article authored by Adityanath in 2014, entitled *Matrushakti Bharatiya Sanskriti ke Sandharbh Mein* (Power of the Mother Figure in the Context of Indian Culture), he reportedly writes:[128] '*Shastras* [scriptures] have talked about giving protection to women. Just like *urja* [energy] left free and unchecked causes destruction, women also don't need independence, they need protection. Their energy should be channelized to be used productively', adding that, '*stree shakti* [women power] is protected by the father when a child, by the husband when an adult, and by the son in old age'. Further, Adityanath reportedly proclaimed that: 'If a man was to ever get the same attributes as women—that of humility, love and compassion—then he is equivalent to god. But if a woman adopts the qualities of men—that of bravery (*shaurya*) or masculinity (*purush-arth*)—then she becomes a devil (*rakshasa*)'.

Gendered and sexualised control and violence are used by Hindu nationalists to assert social control and to exact fear and obedience from subjugated populations in Uttar Pradesh. Women are considered to be the embodiment of the 'honour' of a community, and their rape is perpetrated to dishonour the community. Minority and lower caste women are perceived as symbols of their ethnic, religious, and racial community, and are targeted with gendered and sexualised violence to devastate and fracture the community.[129]

The governments formulated by Prime Minister Modi and Chief Minister Adityanath have increasingly raised the issue of Muslim women's rights in connection and conflation with the issue of the triple *talaq* (a form of instant divorce).[130] This is a complex situation, as the patriarchy within the Muslim community—as exemplified in the attitudes of the All India Muslim Personal Law Board—have curtailed constructive conversations on the issue within the Muslim community.[131] The new bill on triple *talaq* which cleared the lower house of parliament in late December 2017 and was tabled in the upper house of parliament in January 2018,[132] is symptomatic of this dilemma: through the criminalisation of an essentially civil matter.[133]

In September 2018, an executive body headed by Prime Minister Modi decreed the practice of *talaq* to be a criminal offense.[134] The decree will remain in force for a six-month period, during which the parliament must endorse the ordinance to ensure its continuance. It bears mentioning that several studies documenting the predicament of Muslim women and their rights under personal laws within the family, and their rights as citizens,[135] show that unreported cases of desertion and triple *talaq* are ten times more than those that reach the police stations. The issue of desertion and a social and financial safety net for a deserted spouse are rarely part of the public discourse.[136]

A country-wide study undertaken by the All-India Democratic Women's Association in 2011 estimated that 900 persons are subjected to honour killings annually.[137] Violence against inter-faith couples and their murder were also reported as 'honour killings' in the news, even as religion and caste may be relevant factors. The National Crime Records Bureau reported that 168 homicides were categorised as 'honour killings' in Uttar Pradesh in 2015. This makes up approximately 67 per cent of the all-India total of 251 honour killings for 2015. India started using honour killing as a category for data collection in 2014.[138] Women's rights activists state that such figures are greatly under-reported.[139] Activists pointed to the promotion of gendered sexual policing by caste councils, who predominate village life, as a factor in the rise of honour killings.[140]

In Uttar Pradesh, police records do not differentiate between religionised violence targeting elopement versus allegations of sexual assault. The police appear to be concerned with these cases relating to 'their potential to spark larger communal disturbances'.[141] The latest statistics available on inter-caste marriage in Uttar Pradesh comes from the National Family Health Survey of 2005–06, which estimated that only about 8.6 per cent of Uttar Pradesh marriages are inter-caste.[142] The 2015–16 National Family Health Survey does not record data from Uttar Pradesh. It is noteworthy that a National Council of Applied Economic Research study (2016) reported that 95 per cent of marriages in India take place within the same caste.[143]

Terror and violence

The Sangh Parivar's campaigns target minority women and men with multiple effects.[144] Gendered and sexualised aggression provides opportunities for Hindu nationalist groups and their cadre to assert themselves as socially dominant and as the cultural and moral police; to reinforce religious conversion from Hinduism as heinous, inciting violent responses from Hindu communities; and to widen electoral divisions between historically allied communities. In one illustrative case from the locality of Alipur Khera in Uttar Pradesh in 2016, the love jihad campaign contributed to the segregation of groups based on religious identity, eliciting violent responses to a single inter-faith marriage.[145]

Below, I cite select examples from actions either directly undertaken by Sangh Parivar organisations or affiliates to discipline and terrorise minority/ subaltern communities, or those resultant from the undercurrent of hate and estrangement fostered by the Sangh Parivar and majoritarian culture at large, with respect to religious minorities, Adivasis, Dalits, LGBTIQ persons, and women. These events reportedly transpired in Uttar Pradesh between January 2014 and September 2018. Each of these events require acknowledgement, justice (to humanitarian, criminal, and human rights violations), reparation and the right of victimised-survivors to participate in reparative processes, and our attentiveness.

January 2014: Concerned by the incapacity of the state government to pursue justice in the Muzaffarnagar anti-Muslim violence of 2013, counsel Kamini Jaiswal filed a petition before the supreme court. The petition requested that a special investigation team from outside of the state,[146] headed by a woman officer, be appointed to lead the investigation into the violence, including reported instances of gang-rape.[147] March 2014: In mass ceremonies, 550 marriages took place in the relief centres that were set up after the Muzaffarnagar violence. It was reported that the first fifty-five marriages were incentivised by the Uttar Pradesh state government's offer of Rs 100,000 (approximately US$ 1,361)[148] and household goods.[149]

May 2014: Two sisters from the Dalit community in Budaun district, aged fourteen and fifteen, who had gone to the open fields as there was no toilet in their home, were found hanged from a mango tree the following day. Hundreds of villagers staged a silent protest against police inaction in the case, refusing to allow the police to take the bodies down until arrests were made. Autopsies confirmed the gang-rape of the two girls and their death by strangulation before being hanged.[150] The Central Bureau of Investigation of India (CBI) disclaimed that rape and murder had taken place, and alleged that the victims had committed suicide.[151] Various progressive civil society groups protested the CBI's narrative.[152]

August 2014: A non-governmental Hindu nationalist organisation, Jayati Bharatam, filed a petition before the supreme court to mobilise a Special Investigation Team probe into forced conversions of women to Islam, alleging that forty–fifty Hindu girls had been abducted and may be gang raped and converted to Islam. The supreme court declined to entertain the claim, stating that the group had not provided evidence to support their allegations, such as complaints from the parents of the girls, or any complaints registered with the police or with the National Commission for Women. The supreme court then warned the group against actions that may 'disturb the secular fabric'.[153] August 2014: A woman, identified as a Hindu, reported that she had been kidnapped, gang-raped, and forcibly converted to Islam. However, on 12 October, the same woman registered a complaint with the police against her own parents, declaring that her parents had forced her to make false charges against a Muslim man.[154]

August 2014: While the Uttar Pradesh BJP chapter removed love jihad as an electoral issue, many other Sangh-affiliated groups coordinated to mobilise Sangh Parivar supporters at the district level and to organise debates.[155] August 2014: RSS launched a new public campaign called a '*rakhi* drive',[156] where RSS volunteers in western Uttar Pradesh tied *rakhis* on the wrists of local Hindus, encouraging them to 'protect their religion' and to protect Hindu young women from love jihad.[157] September 2014: To promote the circulation of the narrative of love jihad, Sangh Parivar organisations implemented a public campaign denouncing Muslims for undertaking love jihad.[158]

September 2014: Two days before the parliamentary by-elections, on September 13, Islamophobic pamphlets on love jihad with discriminatory language against Muslims were distributed in Vadodara and Manipur by hand

and via messaging apps. Though the pamphlets have the addresses and phone numbers of the VHP offices in Rajkot and Mainpur, respectively, printed on them, the VHP in both areas disavowed them.[159] The pamphlets connect the concept of love jihad with 'the rule of Muslim Mughals in India centuries ago—a popular thesis with Hindu nationalists who postulate that Hinduism was weakened by foreign/Muslim rule'.[160] It has been observed that the love jihad campaign further weakened Jat and Muslim alliances that had historically formed the electoral 'backbone' of the Rashtriya Lok Dal political party, thereby weakening Muslim electoral power.[161]

November 2014: The head of the Government of India's National Commission for Women, Lalitha Kumaramangalam, called love jihad a 'media hype', and stated that if the media stopped writing about it, 'people will stop speaking [about it]'. She did not address the issues at play in the filing of false charges against Muslims. November 2014: Meerut District witnessed at least five 'honour killing' incidents in one week involving interfaith couples.[162] In Meerut, Danista (Muslim) and Sonu (Hindu) were killed by Danista's family;[163] in Siwaya village, when a Muslim woman married a Dalit man, the woman's brothers shot her.[164]

January 2015: The Uttar Pradesh government resolved to award each inter-caste marriage in the state with a commendation, medal, and a cash award of INR 50,000 (approximately US\$ 680).[165] This action highlighted the precarity of inter-community relations. May 2015: A fourteen year old Dalit girl was abducted from her home in Sankror village and gang raped by four men.[166] July 2015: A village council (*khap*) in Bhagpat ordered the rape of two Dalit sisters as punishment for their brother's elopement with a higher-caste woman.[167] The *khaps*, generally composed of men from more powerful castes, have been known to issue commands that restrict the sexual freedoms and social autonomy of women. Further, these injunctions may enforce the segregation of communities by issuing condemnations of inter-caste and inter-religious marriages.[168]

October 2015: Two investigative portals—*Cobrapost* and *Gulail* (2015)—reported that Hindutva groups used 'violence, intimidation, and emotional blackmail to break up Hindu-Muslim married couples'. The sting operation entitled, 'Operation Juliet: Busting the Bogey of Love Jihad', found Hindutva groups 'forcibly [rescuing] girls', and terming them 'victims of love jihad'. The sting operation based its claims on recordings obtained from Delhi, Muzaffarnagar and Meerut in Uttar Pradesh, Mangaluru in Karnataka, and Ernakulam and Kasaragod in Kerala.

Cobrapost and *Gulail* (2015) purportedly documented the involvement of VHP functionaries in multiple cases of love jihad. Once such functionary from Mangaluru reportedly admitted to his role in the arrest of a Muslim man on kidnapping charges and in convincing the woman to reverse her decision to be with a Muslim. The functionary reportedly stated that, if the girls 'don't understand, we use force'. According to a BJP member of the legislative council for Karnataka, the Sangh Parivar has also infiltrated the ranks of the police at the district level. Reportedly, the Hindu Helpline in Kerala had administered drugs to 'rescued' girls, purportedly causing 'temporary amnesia', to 'bring the girl under control'.[169]

February 2016: The Bajrang Dal launched the *'Bahu Lao, Beti Bachao'* ('Bring a Daughter-in-Law, Save a Daughter') campaign to motivate Hindu men to marry non-Hindu women to convert them Hinduism.[170] May 2016: The Uttar Pradesh government proposed dismissing certain stipulations for the registration of marriages, such as the prerequisite for two witnesses and the certification by a local representative, actions that may capacitate forced marriages.[171]

May 2016: The Bajrang Dal conducted a training exercise with arms in Ayodhya where some participants were disguised as Muslims.[172] September 2016: Bijnor violence:[173] Approximately 100 [Hindu] Jats gathered at Pedda with weapons and attacked the Muslim community. Pedda is a hamlet on the outskirts of Bijnor city, approximately 150 kilometres from Delhi, in Bijnor district in Uttar Pradesh. Reportedly, one individual or multiple persons from the Jat community gathered on that day in Pedda shot at Muslim community members, killing three people and wounding twelve others.[174]

A first-hand account of a Muslim woman survivor-witness in Pedda noted that: 50–60 persons raided her one-story house with revolvers, iron rods and swords, killing her spouse, brother-in-law, and niece, and injuring eight. Context: Hindu boys allegedly harassed a Muslim girl from the eighth grade, who was on her way to school with a cousin, following which an altercation ensued that later turned into a Hindu-Muslim confrontation. It is of note that Pedda has a population of 3,000 people, with a near equal number of Muslims and Jats. Many Muslims work as daily wage labourers in the fields that are owned by Jats. Others from the Muslim community find employment in Bijnor city, cutting hair, and as stone and wood workers.[175] The violence in Pedda was believed to be a 'deliberate act to drive a wedge between the two communities', before the state assembly elections.

October 2016: It has been reported that of the approximately 12,000 'low-key' communal incidents recorded between 2010–16 in Uttar Pradesh, almost

15 per cent involved women. These events involved 'alleged sexual violence to elopement'.[176] In one instance in 2016, in the locality of Alipur Khera in Uttar Pradesh, a love jihad campaign was a factor in the segregation of Muslims and Hindus from each other based and in the call for Hindus to boycott Muslims.[177] November 2016: The Hindu Mahasabha conducted a *ghar wapasi* campaign in Aligarh for a nineteen year old woman who stated on the same day that she had been coerced to convert to Islam and that she had been raped by an in-law.[178]

January–March 2017: In Uttar Pradesh, the BJP's election manifesto vowed to establish 'anti-Romeo' squads (read: anti-Muslim) to 'protect' women attending college.[179] February 2017: The Hindu Jagran Manch protested Valentine's Day celebrations in Agra.[180] This protest did not have explicit links to the elections. On the same day, Bajrang Dal members harassed and assaulted couples who were seen in public in Odisha and Bihar, reinforcing the role and position of Hindu nationalist groups as sexual and moral police, and in administering public punishment.[181]

February 2017: Amnesty International released a report on the status of seven cases of gang-rape from the 2013 Muzaffarnagar violence; one which ended in acquittal, two of which had not recorded evidence from the survivor, and four that were unresolved.[182] March 2017: Shortly after the BJP's electoral win in Uttar Pradesh, the police launched the anti-Romeo campaign. While, ostensibly, this initiative intended to stop sexual harassment of women in public places, it's practice was similar to the love jihad campaign targeting Muslim communities.[183] April 2017: The Uttar Pradesh Anti-Terror Squad launched its own *ghar wapasi* campaign to 'deradicalize[e]... misguided youth'. This campaign shared its name with the Sangh Parivar's *ghar wapasi* campaign seeking to convert persons of non-Hindu faiths to Hinduism, including through force and duplicity.[184] April 2017: Members of the Hindu Yuva Vahini forcibly entered a house in Meerut to confront a Muslim man from Muzaffarnagar and a woman of another faith. The woman and man were taken to a police station under duress, where the woman was released with a warning, and the man was charged with obscenity.[185]

April 2017: Across five locations in western Uttar Pradesh, the Uttar Pradesh Navnirmaan Sena (Reconstruction Army), a far-right political organisation, put up large hoardings/billboards with the missive: '*Bharatiya sena par pathar maarne waale Kashmiriyon ka bahishkar...Kashmiriyon UP chhodo varna*' ('Social boycott of Kashmir youth who pelt stones at the Indian Army. Leave UP or else'). The Hindu Yuva Vahini (Hindu Youth Army) endorsed the stance of the Navnirmaan Sena. The president of the Meerut wing of the Yuva Vahini stated that: 'They [Kashmiri youth] are criminals and they can disturb the harmony of any place in India. It is better that they remain in Kashmir and the army should be given a free hand to deal with them'.[186]

May 2017: In Saharanpur, approximately twenty-five Dalit homes were torched, in which one person was killed, as a result of upper-caste violence.[187] May 2017: In Bulandshahr district, members of the Hindu Yuva Vahini beat Gulam Ahmad to death. They accused Ahmad, sixty years of age, of aiding the elopement of a younger Muslim man with a Hindu woman.[188] November 2017: In Balia, the police asked a Muslim woman BJP worker to remove her *burqa* while she was attending a rally in support of Chief Minister Adityanath.[189] December 2017: The Hindu Jagran Manch announced a 'reverse' love jihad, stating that it planned to 'marry 2,100 Muslim women to Hindu men'.[190]

January 2018: The *Times of India* reported that Sangh Parivar groups were using a network of informers who reported on interfaith couples, to assist Hindutva groups in targeting couples with love jihad-related apparatus of attack,[191] terror, and incarceration.[192] In March 2018: Local BJP leaders met with Chief Minister Adityanath, following which the state government of Uttar Pradesh ensued a process to seek the withdrawal of the 131 cases connected with Muzaffarnagar 2013. Persons of Hindu descent were the accused in all of these cases.[193] June 2018: In Sardhana in Meerut district, a Pentecostal pastor was released on bail, following his arrest on charges of forcibly converting people to Christianity. He was handcuffed by the police for allegedly attacking Bajrang Dal activists.[194]

August 2018: In its strategy session for Uttar Pradesh, gearing up to the 2019 national elections, the BJP concentrated on the ways and means via which to manipulate the sentiments of Dalits and marginalised caste groups. The BJP determined to continue to appropriate the legacies of subaltern leaders, such as that of Bhimrao R. Ambedkar, the iconic anti- and de-colonial leader of Dalit descent, through the strategic insertion of present-Hindutva (Modi) within historic nationalism (Ambedkar).[195] Hindutva seeks to become the rallying cry that unites a fragmented nation, offering the pathway to Indian-ness. Outreach to Dalits and marginalised castes allows the BJP to lay claim to inclusivity and multiculturalism, even as Hindu nationalists promote anti-Dalit and anti-subaltern caste discourses in cementing connections with the traditional and Brahmanical foundations of Hindu nationalism.[196]

September 2018: In Bareilly, activists of the Bajrang Dal, Bharatiya Hindu Sena, and the VHP confronted and assaulted two Christian priests, and forcibly took them to the local police station. The Hindutva activists accused the two priests of conducting forcible conversions. The two priests were released by the police and the Hindutva activists only after they gave a written statement declaring that they had not organised, and would never organise, conversions to Christianity.[197] September 2018: In Meerut, a woman student and her Muslim friend were studying in a room when VHP activists forcibly entered their room and physically attacked the both of them, following which they summoned the police. A video posted on social media that went viral documented two police officers verbally and physically abusing the twenty year old Hindu student. She was asked to report a false complaint against her Muslim friend for rape, and she refused. Following which, the police asked the parents of the Hindu student to file false charges against the Muslim friend, and the parents also refused.[198]

Repressive authorisations

More than twenty-six years have elapsed since Ayodhya, December 1992. In January 2019, India is governed by a powerful far-right central government. As India mutates into a repressive-majoritarian polity in discourse and practice, the terror-producing state disregards and violates the rights of minorities, privileging the rights of Hindus over the rights of all. The imperative of this majoritarian agenda is to render supreme the mythos of the Hindu in India, and to have it frame what is 'Indian'. This mission is amplified at present in Uttar Pradesh. The oppressive effects of this discriminatory agenda resound in local governance across Uttar Pradesh, its economic development and corporatism, and its regional and international relations.

The tentacles of majoritarian governance stretch and expand from state (Uttar Pradesh) to country (India) and like-minded diasporic enclaves in mobilising a massive infrastructure encompassing an ultra-sophisticated technological and military arsenal, and an aggressive regional presence.[199] The cumulatively partisan state, while underway for decades and inherent to the inception of the republic, unfolds in different registers as led by the parliamentary BJP and the proliferating Sangh Parivar. The hyper-majoritarian core is intimate with and derives its power from a bourgeoning and devoted rank-and-file cadre that seek to police city streets and villages, making ever-permeable the delimits of domestic and public life. This structural and embedded impunity is bolstered by an increasingly sectarian police, paramilitary, and army. It is constitutive of a conflicted, authoritarian, crisis democracy, of states of exception without-end.[200]

Its fervour is uncompromising, intolerant, and subsuming of difference, proscriptive of dissent. Millions of ordinary citizens of Hindu India watch, and participate to various extents through action and silence, legitimating this new moment.

The consolidation of Uttar Pradesh as a majoritarian frontier is contingent on the discipline and subjugation of a heterogeneous body politic. Hetero/ normative[201] gender and ethnic relations, xenophobia and misogyny, cultural and economic anxiety, aspirations of the underclasses, minoritisation, and hate and violence are critical components of the majoritarian apparatus. Majoritarian anti-bodies to difference imprint minority lives, permeating counter-memory,[202] social and material relations, domestic and public realms, haunting every day and future life. Performative and portentous, the threat, event, and effect of fear and violence condition power relations between majority and minority, formative of culture and identity.

Will civil and political society-organised movements and resistance effectively diminish the hold of majoritarian dominance on future India? Offering optimism, in May 2018, the incumbent BJP lost the two Lok Sabha seats[203] from Gorakhpur and Phulpur in the Uttar Pradesh by-elections, and a state assembly seat from Noorpur constituency.[204]

Will the BJP and Sangh Parivar's power endure in the upcoming 2019 national elections in Uttar Pradesh and at the centre?[205] If so, will it signal a twenty-first-century, post/colonial turned neo-imperial rendition of despotism, the reign of majoritarian fascists and micro-fascism in India?[206] Will the future evince the normalisation of militarised nationalism, of India as an ethno-racialised security state evolving within the precarious continuum between biopower and necrogovernance?[207]

In a video which surfaced in 2014, Adityanath reportedly stated that: 'If [Muslims] take one Hindu girl, we'll take 100 Muslim girls. If they kill one Hindu, we'll kill 100 Muslims'.[208]

'We are submerged in pools of fear', a Muslim woman from Uttar Pradesh tells me.[209] 'The pools are deep. Unending. Suffocating. Like a well. I cannot get out. We cannot hear each other'.

'What connects the pools to each other?' I ask.
She says: 'Shreds of skin. Lost memory. Forgetting'.

NOTES

INTRODUCTION

1. Cited in Chehabi, Houchang E. and Juan Linz, *Sultanistic Regimes*, Baltimore and London: The Johns Hopkins University Press, 1998, p. 4.
2. Linz, Juan and Alfred Stepan, *Modern Nondemocratic Regimes in Problems of Democratic Transition & Consolidation*, Baltimore: Johns Hopkins University Press, 1996.
3. Gellner, Ernest and Ghita Ionescu (eds), *Populism—Its Meanings and National Characteristics*, London: Weidenfeld and Nicholson, 1969, p. 1.
4. On Modi's populism, see Jaffrelot, Christophe and Louise Tillin, 'Populism in India', in Cristobal Rovira Kaltwasser, Paul Taggart, Paulina Ochoa Espejo and Pierre Ostiguy (eds), *The Oxford Handbook of Populism*, Oxford: Oxford University Press, 2017, pp. 179–94.
5. Jaffrelot, Christophe, 'Narendra Modi and the power of television in Gujarat', *Television & New Media*, 16, 4 (May 2015), pp. 346–53.
6. Laclau, Ernesto, *On Populist Reason*, London: Verso, 2005. Laclau derives the term 'empty signifier' from the idea of 'floating signifiers' in semiotics, which are pluriform and open signifiers that can be filled by many kinds of content. Referring to the classical example of Juan Peron in Argentina, Laclau argues that the populist leader makes himself into an 'empty signifier', the element that can complete and heal a broken and crisis-ridden nation. Trump's assertion that only he can make America great again fits this description, as does Modi's boastful references to his physical strength that supposedly can protect the nation.
7. Germani, G., *Authoritarianism, Fascism and National Populism*, New Brunswick (NJ): Transaction Books, 1978.
8. See, Anderson, Perry, 'After Nehru', *London Review of Books*, 34, 15 (2012), pp. 21–36.
9. Jaffrelot, Christophe, 'The Modi-centric BJP 2014 election campaign: New techniques and old tactics', *Contemporary South Asia*, 23, 2 (June 2015) pp. 151–66.
10. Jaffrelot, Christophe, 'Narendra Modi between Hindutva and subnationalism: The Gujarati asmita of a Hindu Hriday Samrat', *India Review*, 15, 2 (2016), pp. 196–217.
11. Chatterji, Angana P., *Violent Gods: Hindu Nationalism in India's Present; Narratives from Orissa*, Gurgaon: Three Essays Collective, 2009. See also: British Broadcasting

Corporation, 25 Sep. 2013, 'Muzaffarnagar: Tales of death and despair in India's riot-hit town', British Broadcasting Corporation, https://www.bbc.com/news/world-asia-india-24172537, last accessed 10 Aug. 2018.

12. Müller, Jan-Werner, *What Is Populism?*, Philadelphia: University of Pennsylvania Press, 2016.

13. For a comparative perspective, see Jaffrelot, Christophe, 26 Dec. 2016, 'An era of Caesars', *The Indian Express*, https://indianexpress.com/article/opinion/columns/an-era-of-caesars-trump-putin-erdogan-nationalism-populism-authoritarianism-4444811/, and Jaffrelot, Christophe, 26 Feb. 2018, 'The lure of the populists', *The Indian Express*, http://carnegieendowment.org/2018/02/26/lure-of-populists-pub-75647.

14. Shils, Edward, *The Torment of Secrecy*, Melbourne: Heinemann, 1956, p. 98.

15. See Chatterji, Angana P., Shashi Buluswar, Mallika Kaur, *Conflicted Democracies and Gendered Violence: The Right to Heal: Internal Conflict and Social Upheaval in India*, New Delhi: Zubaan, 2016.

16. Smooha, Sammy, 'The model of ethnic democracy: Israel as a Jewish and democratic state', *Nations and Nationalism*, 8, 4 (2002), p. 479.

17. Ibid.

18. In a conversation with Thomas Blom Hansen in Bombay on 21 Oct. 1992, Vinay Saharasbuddhe, then Executive Director of the RSS think tank Rambhau Mhalgi Prabodhini, and currently member of the Rajya Sabha for the BJP, said: 'Like many in the Sangh, I am full of admiration for Israel [...] Jews from across the world created a safe and strong national home for the Jewish people who suffered for so many centuries. They give their people unity and a strong army to protect them. [...] in a similar way you can say that Hindus also suffered for centuries but never found unity. Savarkar was the first to point out that India must be a homeland for the Hindu, first and foremost, his national home [...] our movement is simply saying to the ordinary Hindu: this country is ours and we should be proud of it. What is wrong with that?'

19. Baru, Sanjaya, *The Accidental Prime Minister: The Making and Unmaking of Manmohan Singh*, New Delhi: Penguin, 2014.

20. Anna Hazare campaign, see Subrahmaniam, Vidya, 'Deconstructing the Anna Hazare campaign', *The Hindu*, 16 Apr. 2011, https://www.thehindu.com/opinion/lead/Deconstructing-the-Anna-Hazare-campaign/article14687083.ece

21. See an insiders' explanations for this mobilisation in Andersen, W. and S. Damle, *The RSS: A view from inside*, Delhi, Penguin, 2018.

22. The Land Acquisition, Rehabilitation and Resettlement Act 2013 (LARRA) is a case in point. Jenkins, R. 'Business interests, the state, and the politics of land policy in India', in Jaffrelot, C., A. Kohli, and K. Murali (eds), *Business and Politics in India*, New York: Oxford University Press, 2019, pp. 124–50.

23. Aarefa Johari, 'Controversial MP Sakshi Maharaj has a trail of rape and murder charges behind him', *Scroll.in*, 10 Jan. 2015, https://scroll.in/article/699597/controversial-mp-sakshi-maharaj-has-a-trail-of-rape-and-murder-charges-behind-him, last accessed 12 Feb. 2018, and Chaturvedi, R.M., 'A look at BJP MP Sakshi Maharaj's long list of crimes', *The Economic Times*, 21 Oct. 2015, http://m.economictimes.com/news/pol-

itics-and-nation/a-look-at-bjp...-sakshi-maharajs-long-list-of-crimes/amp_article-show/49474193.cms.

24. Alt News, 'What do these Nathuram Godse fans have in common? They are all followed by PM Modi on Twitter', Alt News, 2 Oct. 2017, https://www.altnews.in/godsefans-common-followed-pm-modi/.

25. Jaffrelot, C., 'Ramdev, Swami without sampradaya', The Caravan, 1 July 2011, http://www.caravanmagazine.in/perspectives/ramdev-swami-without-sampraday and Priyanka Pathak-Narain, Godman to tycoon: The untold story of Baba Ramdev, New Delhi, Juggernaut, 2017.

26. Jha, Dhirendra K., Shadow armies: Fringe organizations and foot soldiers of Hindutva, New Delhi: Juggernaut, 2017.

27. Stokes, Bruce, Dorothy Manevich and Hanyu Chwe, 'The state of Indian Democracy', in Pew Research Center, Global attitudes and trends, 15 Nov. 2017, http://www.pewglobal.org/2017/11/15/the-state-of-indian-democracy/, last accessed 26 June 2018. For comparing India to other countries, use this link: http://www.pewglobal.org/2017/10/16/globally-broad-support-for-representative-and-direct-democracy/.

28. Stokes, Bruce, Dorothy Manevich and Hanyu Chwe, 'Indians satisfied with country's direction but worry about crime, terrorism', in Pew Research Center, Global attitudes and trends, 15 Nov. 2017 http://www.pewglobal.org/2017/11/15/indians-satisfied-with-countrys-direction-but-worry-about-crime-terrorism/, last accessed 26 June 2018.

29. Stokes, Bruce, Dorothy Manevich and Hanyu Chwe, 'India and the world', in Pew Research Center, Global attitudes and trends, 15 Nov. 2017, http://www.pewglobal.org/2017/11/15/india-and-the-world/, last accessed 26 June 2018.

30. Ibid.

31. The present conflict in Kashmir has been sustained with impunity since 1990, characterised by draconian laws, and enforced disappearances, extrajudicial killings, sexualised violence, and unknown and mass graves, see Chatterji, Angana P., Parvez Imroz, Gautam Navlakha, Zahir-Ud-Din, Mihir Desai and Khurram Parvez, Buried Evidence: Unknown, Unmarked and Mass Graves in Indian-administered Kashmir, Srinagar: International People's Tribunal on Human Rights and Justice in Indian-administered Kashmir, 2009, http://www.kashmirprocess.org/reports/graves/BuriedEvidence Kashmir.pdf; also Chatterji, Angana P., 'The militarized zone', in Tariq Ali, Hilal Bhatt, Angana P. Chatterji, Pankaj Mishra and Arundhati Roy, Kashmir: The Case for Freedom, London: Verso, 2011; Chatterji, Angana P. 'Witnessing as feminist intervention in India-Administered Kashmir', in Ania Loomba and Ritty Lukose (eds), South Asian Feminisms, Durham: Duke University Press, 2012, pp. 181–201. Article 35A of the Constitution of India authorises the state legislature of Jammu & Kashmir to determine the permanent residents of the state and grant them particular rights and privileges.

32. Sangh Parivar: family of Hindu nationalist and militant organisations. See also the online discussion board at Quora on this topic, https://www.quora.com/Why-do-Indian-Hindus-find-it-uncomfortable-if-their-neighbours-are-muslims-or-their-neighbourhood-has-large-muslim-population.

33. Pai, S. and S. Kumar, Everyday communalism, Delhi, Oxford University Press, 2018.

34. For an analysis of this sense of anger in a comparative perspective, see see Mishra, Pankaj, *Age of Anger: A History of the Present*, Delhi: Penguin Books, 2018. For an Indian vignette, see chapter 4 of Poonam, Snigdha, *Dreamers: How Young Indians are Changing the World*, London: Hurst, 2018.

35. Centre for the Study of Developing Societies (CSDS), *State of Democracy in South Asia*, New Delhi: Oxford University Press, 2008, p. 236.

36. Heller, Patrick and Leela Fernandes, 'Hegemonic aspirations: New middle-class politics and India's democracy in comparative perspective', *Critical Asian Studies*, 38, 4 (2006), pp. 495–522.

37. Palshikar, Suhas, 'Politics of India's middle class', in Imtiaz Ahmad and Helmut Reifeld (eds), *Middle Class Values in India and Western Europe*, New York: Routledge, 2018, p. 178.

38. See the section of S. Poonam's book titled 'Angry young men': Poonam, S., *Dreamers: How Young Indians are Changing the World*, London: Hurst, 2018, p. 118.

39. See the portrait of Chatterjee, M. 'The ordinary life of Hindu supremacy: In conversation with a Bajrang Dal activist', *Economic and Political Weekly*, 53, 4 (27 Jan. 2018), https://www.epw.in/engage/article/ordinary-life-hindu-supremacy.

40. Pande, M., 'Angry Hanuman: This viral image that won Modi's praise symbolises today's aggressive, macho India', *Scroll.in*, 26 May 2018, https://scroll.in/article/879108/angry-hanuman-this-viral-image-that-won-modis-praise-symbolises-todays-aggressive-macho-india and Bhowmick, N., 'Militant Hinduism and the reincarnation of Hanuman', *The Wire*, 4 Apr. 2018, https://thewire.in/communalism/noidas-thriving-militant-hinduism-and-the-resurrection-of-hanuman.

41. Kapur, A., 'Deity to crusader: the changing iconography of Ram', in G. Pandey (ed.), *Hindus and others: The question of identity in India today*, New Delhi: Viking, 1993, pp. 74–109.

42. We draw on elaborations by Giorgio Agamben and Michel Foucault: Agamben, Giorgio, *Homo Sacer: Sovereign Power and Bare Life*, Daniel Heller-Roazen (trans.), Stanford: Stanford University Press, 1998.; Agamben, Giorgio. *State of Exception*, Kevin Attell (trans.), Chicago: University of Chicago Press, 2005; Foucault, Michel, *Security, Territory, Population: Lectures at the Collège de France, 1977–1978*, Graham Burchell (trans.), New York: Palgrave Macmillan, 2009; also, Schuilenburg, Marc, *The Securitization of Society: Crime, Risk, and Social Order*, George Hall (trans.), New York: New York University Press, 2015.

43. Chatterji et al., *Conflicted Democracies*, op. cit., p. 25.

44. Chatterjee, Partha, *The Politics of the Governed: Reflections on Popular Politics in Most of the World*, New York: Columbia University Press, 2004.

45. See Jaffrelot, C., A. Kohli and K. Murali (eds), *Business and Politics in India*, New York: Oxford University Press 2019.

46. For example, 'Village Defense Committees have been constituted in Jammu as civilian "self-defense" militias... VDC members are predominantly men, of Hindu and Sikh descent, and some "trustworthy" Muslims, who are recruited by Hindu nationalist groups', making 'militarization a necessity to securing the rights of local non-Muslim minorities, obscuring the relations of the Indian state to militarized Hindu national-

ism', Chatterji, Angana P., 'Witnessing as feminist intervention in India-administered Kashmir', in Ania Loomba and Ritty Lukose (eds), *Feminisms in South Asia: Contemporary Interventions*, Durham: Duke University Press, 2012, p. 236.
47. See, Chatterji et al., *Conflicted Democracies*, op. cit.; Hansen, Thomas Blom, *The Saffron Wave: Democracy and Hindu Nationalism in Modern India*, Princeton: Princeton University Press, 1999; Hansen, Thomas Blom, *Wages of Violence: Naming and Identity in Postcolonial Bombay*, Princeton: Princeton University Press, 2001; Jaffrelot Christophe, *Religion, Caste and Politics in India*, New York: Columbia University Press, 2011.

1. DEMOCRACY AGAINST THE LAW: REFLECTIONS ON INDIA'S ILLIBERAL DEMOCRACY

1. Bajpai, Rochana, *Debating Difference, Group Rights and Democracy in India*, Delhi: Oxford University Press, 2011.
2. Jayal, Niraja Gopal, *Citizenship and Its Discontents: An Indian History*, Cambridge and London: Harvard University Press, and New Delhi: Orient Blackswan, 2013.
3. De, Rohit, *A People's Constitution. The Everyday Life of Law in the Indian Republic*, Princeton: Princeton University Press, 2018.
4. See statements by Union Minister Anant Kumar Hegde at a meeting in December 2017 organised by Brahman Yuva Parishad. 'I feel happy because he (the person) knows about his blood, but I don't know what to call those who claim themselves secular' (Press Trust of India, 26 Dec. 2017, 'Union minister Hegde hints at removing "secular" from Constitution', *The Economic Times*, https://economictimes.indiatimes.com/articleshow/62241135.cms).
5. I owe this point to Niraja Gopal Jayal who provided incisive comments on an earlier draft of this paper.
6. This was the first time in the history of independent India that the government turned its full force against members of the upper middle class and the political elite. After Indira Gandhi's return to power in 1980, civil rights concerns receded from center stage to a more marginal if vocal activist community. Both of India's most prominent civil rights organisations were founded during these years—the People's Union for Civil Liberties (founded in 1976 by J.P. Narayan, among other people), and the People's Union for Democratic rights (founded in 1977).
7. Habermas, Jurgen, *A Berlin Republic. Writings on Germany*, Lincoln: University of Nebraska Press, 1997; Mueller, Jan-Werner, *Constitutional Patriotism*, Princeton (NJ): Princeton University Press, 2007.
8. Wike, Richard et al., 16 Oct. 2017, 'Democracy widely supported, little backing for rule by strong leader or military', Pew Research Centre, http://www.pewglobal.org/2017/10/16/democracy-widely-supported-little-backing-for-rule-by-strong-leader-or-military/.
9. Bayly, C.J., *Recovering Liberties. Indian Thought in the Age of Liberalism and Empire*, Cambridge: Cambridge University Press, 2011.
10. See, Mantena, Karuna, *Alibis of Empire: Henry Maine and the Ends of Liberal*

Imperialism, Princeton: Princeton University Press, 2010; Mehta, Uday Singh, *Liberalism and Empire: A study in Nineteenth Century Liberal British Thought*, Chicago: University of Chicago Press, 1999; Pitts, Jennifer, *A Turn to Empire: The Rise of Liberal Imperialism in Britain and France*, Princeton: Princeton University Press, 2005.

11. Singha, Radhika, *A Despotism of Law: Crime and Justice in Early Colonial India*, Delhi: Oxford University Press, 1998.

12. Chandavarkar, R, *Imperial Power and Popular Politics: Class, Resistance and the State in India, 1850–1950*, Cambridge: Cambridge University Press, 1998.

13. Beverley, Eric, *Hyderabad, British India and the World: Muslim Networks and Minor Sovereignty, c. 1850–1950*, Cambridge: Cambridge University Press, 2015.

14. Baruah, Sanjib, *Durable Disorder: Understanding the Politics of Northeast India*, Delhi: Oxford University Press, 2007.

15. Many of these central forces were formed in the 1960s. The biggest are: the Central Reserve Police Force (formed in 1939), with a strength of 313,000; the Border Security Force (formed in 1965), strength 257,000; the Assam Rifles (1835), strength 63,000; Central Industrial Security Force (1965), strength 144,000; Indo-Tibetan Border Police (1962), strength 89,000; National Security Guard (1985), strength 7,500; Sashasta Seema Bal (Bhutan Border and Election service) (1963), strength 76,000. In addition, each state has military police but numbers are not publicly available. The expansion of security forces has steadily increased since the 1960s, regardless of which party dominated the Union government.

16. https://en.wikipedia.org/wiki/Armed_Forces_(Special_Powers)_Act. See also the report by the committee headed by Justice Jeevan Reddy, *Report of the Committee to Review the Armed Forces Special Powers Act, 1958*. Government of India, Ministry of Home Affairs, New Delhi 2005.

17. https://en.wikipedia.org/wiki/Unlawful_Activities_(Prevention)_Act. See also, http://www.satp.org/satporgtp/countries/india/document/actandordinances/the_unlawful_activities_act1967.htm. For a critical assessment see https://thewire.in/115353/uapa-anti-terrorism-laws/

18. TADA was widely criticised after its draconian application through mass arrests after the bomb blasts in Bombay in March 1993. It lapsed in 1995. It was replaced by Prevention of Terrorist Activities Act (POTA) in 2002, but this act was also deemed unconstitutional and was repealed in 2004.

19. The support for a strong state came from many quarters, including Communist Party of India (CPI) and Shiv Sena. Both parties also supported the Emergency in 1975–76 (see Lockwood, David, *The Communist Party of India and the Indian Emergency*, Delhi: SAGE India, 2016). For an account that comes close to a defence of the Emergency by one of India's prominent historians, see Chandra, Bipan, *In the Name of Democracy. JP Movement and Emergency*, Delhi: Penguin Random House, 2017.

20. It was the excesses during Emergency rule that triggered the first systematic enquiry into policing practices in the country. The National Police Commission (1977–81) produced eight substantial volumes with many recommendations for reform. Twenty years later the Ribeiro Report (1999) echoed many of these recommendations and so did the Padmanabhaiah Report (2000), the Malimath Report (2003) and the Soli

Sorabjee Report (2005). In 2006, the supreme court intervened directly and ordered a number of police reforms to be undertaken. Six years later, the Court again ordered both the Union government and the state governments to implement a series of reforms. Very little has changed for more than 40 years. There is extensive press reporting on the excesses of the police throughout the country, see for instance reporting on the now routinised practice of extra-legal encounter killings that was pioneered by the Bombay Police. 'Mumbai Police Detection Unit', Wikipedia, https://en.wikipedia.org/wiki/Mumbai_Police_Detection_Unit; Varma, Subodh, '1,654 shot dead in encounters between 2004–2014', *The Times of India*, 3 Nov. 2016, https://timesofindia.indiatimes.com/india/1654-shot-dead-in-encounters-between-2004-2014/articleshow/55216190.cms. This policy has been embraced since 2017 by the BJP government in Uttar Pradesh, resulting in more than 1,000 deaths in less than two years. Shalabh, 'Over 900 encounters in Yogi Adityanath regime, 31 goons gunned down', *Times of India*, 10 Jan. 2018, https://timesofindia.indiatimes.com/city/lucknow/over-900-encounters-in-yogi-adityanath-regime-31-goons-gunned-down/articleshow/62444444.cms. There are also multiple reports on the extensive use of custodial torture, see for instance: Manubarwala, Aditya, 'Revisiting India's obligations against custodial torture', LSE Human Rights, 19 May 2017, http://blogs.lse.ac.uk/humanrights/2017/05/19/revisiting-indias-obligations-against-custodial-torture; Human Rights Watch, *Bound by Brotherhood*, https://www.hrw.org/report/2016/12/19/bound-brotherhood/indias-failure-end-killings-police-custody.

21. Jigeesh, Am, 'Why does CBI have a conviction rate of just 3%?', *The Hindu Business Line*, 31 Oct. 2017, http://www.thehindubusinessline.com/news/national/why-does-cbi-have-a-conviction-rate-of-just-3/article9935407.ece

22. Chakrabarty, Dipesh, 'In the Name of Politics. Democracy and the Power of the Multitude in India', *Public Culture*, 19, 2007, pp. 35–57.

23. Naregal, Veena, *Language, Political Elites and the Public Sphere. Western India under Colonialism*, London: Anthem Press, 2001; Mitchell, Lisa, *Language, Emotion and Politics in South India. The Making of a Mother Tongue*, Bloomington: Indiana University Press, 2009; Mantena, Rama, S., 'Vernacular Publics and Political Modernity: Language and Progress in Colonial South India', *Modern Asian Studies*, 47, 5 (2013), pp. 1678–1705.

24. Rajagopal, Arvind, *Politics after Television. Hindu Nationalism and the Reshaping of the Public in India*, Cambridge: Cambridge University Press, 2001; Ghassem Fachandi, *Pogrom in Gujarat. Hindu nationalism and Anti-Muslim Violence in India*, Princeton: Princeton University Press, 2012; Hansen, Thomas Blom, 'Recuperating Masculinity: Hindu nationalism, Violence and the Exorcising of the Muslim Other', *Critique of Anthropology*, 16(2), 1996, pp. 137–72.

25. Bate, Bernard, *Tamil Oratory and the Dravidian Aesthetics, Democratic Practice in South India*, New York: Columbia University Press, 2009.

26. Talwalker, Clare, 'Kindred Public: the modernity of kin fetishism on western India', *Postcolonial Studies*, 12, 1 (2009), pp. 69–88.

27. Ibid., p. 86.

28. The large crowds attending Ambedkar's death anniversary at the Chaityabhoomi located

in the upscale neighborhood of Dadar in Mumbai, has for decades provoked much anger and resentment among local caste Hindus.

29. Warner, Michael, *Publics and Counter Publics*, New York: Zone Books, 2005; Pandian, M.S.S., 'One Step Outside Modernity. Caste, Identity Politics and Public Sphere', *Economic and Political Weekly*, 37, 18 (2002), pp. 1735–41.

30. See *Crime in India, Statistics*, National Crime Records Bureau, Ministry of Home Affairs, Government of India, http://ncrb.gov.in/, 2016. Space does not permit a deeper analysis here of regional distribution of such public order disturbances but it seems clear that the now easily accessible crime statistics should provide an interesting, if far from reliable, source for social scientists interested in public protests in India. For an analysis of the possible correlation between riots and other public disturbances, and the rate and scale of public service delivery, see Justino, Patricia, *Civil Unrest and Government Transfers in India*, IDS Evidence Reports (108), Sussex: IDS, 2015. However, the problem in Justino's analysis is that she does not account for the differentiation of different kinds of 'unrest' and their possible differential causes. In her analysis the variable is public service delivery alone, again a category that she only applies in a highly aggregated manner that cannot account for, or possibly explain, regional differences.

31. Other ways of measuring this could be the incidences of police shooting or *lathi* charge, for instance. Here the Crime Bureau tells us, almost unbelievably, that in 2016 there were 184 instances of firing wherein 92 civilians were killed and 352 injured. In the same incidents we are told that as many as 727 policemen were injured. There were 2,184 cases of *lathi* charge where 35 civilians died, and 759 were injured. Again one is surprised to read that the police claims as many as 4,713 injured policemen in the same incidents (Crime Statistics, 2016, op. cit., Table 16B.1).

32. Cook, Ian M., 'Immoral Times: Vigilantism in a South Indian City', 2019 (in this volume).

33. Blom, Amelie and Nicholas Jaoul, 'Introduction: The Moral and Affectual Dimension of Collective Action in South Asia', *SAMAJ, South Asia Interdisciplinary Journal*, 2 (2008), https://samaj.revues.org/1912.

34. Eckert, Julia, *The Charisma of Direct Action. Power, Politics and the Shiv Sena*, Delhi: Oxford University Press, 2003; Hansen, Thomas Blom, *Wages of Violence. Naming and Identity in postcolonial Bombay*, Princeton: Princeton University Press, 2001; Sen, Atreyee, *Shiv Sena Women. Violence and Communalism in a Bombay Slum*, Bloomington: Indiana University Press, 2007; Bedi, Tarini, *The Dashing Ladies of Shiv Sena. Political Matronage in Urban India*, Albany (NY): State University of New York Press, 2016.

35. The theme of hurt collective emotions has now become the predominant motif in Hindu nationalist mobilisation, all structured closely by IPC 295A: the movement claims that scholars (such as Wendy Doniger), filmmakers, films, books or even the presence of beef and non-vegetarian food offend 'Hindu feelings'; or that journalists or critics of the Modi government, disregard the true feelings of Hindus, a claim that can only be 'proved' by displays of passion and the willingness and felt 'need' to perpetrate violence.

36. Wilkinson, Steven, *Votes and Violence. Electoral Competition and Ethnic Riots in India*, Cambridge: Cambridge University Press, 2006.

37. Basu, Amrita, *Violent Conjunctures in Democratic India*, Cambridge: Cambridge University Press, 2015.

38. Cody, Francis, 'Populist Publics. Print Capitalism and Crowd Violence beyond Liberal Frameworks', *Comparative Studies of South Asia, Africa and the Middle East*, 35, 1 (2015), pp. 50–65.

39. Pandey, Gyanendra, *The Construction of Communalism in Colonial North India*, Delhi: Oxford University Press, 1990.

40. 'The Maharashtra Prevention of Dangerous Activities of Slumlords, Bootleggers, Drug-Offenders and Dangerous Persons Act, 1981', PRS, http://www.lawsofindia.org/pdf/maharashtra/1981/1981MH55.pdf.

41. Most police actions before and after riots have conventionally targeted individual 'charge sheeters' or what in police parlance is known as 'notorious characters'. Thanks to the dogged work of activists such as Teesta Setalvad and others, the judicial aftermath of the pogrom in Gujarat in 2002 was the first high-profile instance of individuals being named, prosecuted and convicted of crimes committed in the context of crowd violence. However, in most cases, suspects were acquitted, or cases dismissed on the grounds of insufficient evidence. For an overview of the judicial aftermath of the Gujarat pogrom, see *When Justice becomes the Victim. The Quest for Justice after the 2002 violence in Gujarat*, Stanford Law School, 2014, http://humanrightsclinic.law.stanford.edu/wp-content/uploads/2016/05/When-Justice-Becomes-the-Victim-secure.pdf.

42. *Crime in India 2016*, op. cit., Statistics. http://ncrb.gov.in/ Table 18A.1

43. Ibid.

44. The categories and tables rendered by the National Bureau of Crime Statistics changes and varies from year to year making robust multi-year comparisons very difficult. In the 2014 figures, we are told that 308,544 persons were arrested in connection with rioting. Of those 90 per cent were charged (284,733). Only 64,922 (Table 12.3) got out on bail which means that most others were released while a few would have been kept in custody. We are also told that the total number of persons charged in a pending trial is 2,575,243 in 2014. Out of those as many as 1,462,757 (both figures are from Table 12.4) are on bail while the status of the remaining one million individuals is unclear.

45. *The Srikrishna Commission report into the Bombay Riots in 1992–93*, Mumbai, https://www.sabrang.com/srikrish/vol1.htm, 1998.

46. Local residents showed me extensive footage of these raids, filmed on smart phones from street corners and roof tops during the time the operation was unfolding.

47. Schmitt, Carl, *The Concept of the Political*, Chicago: University of Chicago Press, 1920/2007;

48. Hansen, Thomas Blom, *The Saffron Wave: Democracy and Hindu Nationalism in Modern India*, Princeton: Princeton University Press, 1999.

49. See Ghassem-Fachandi, 2012 for a particularly fine and disturbing study of the eros and disgust of collective violence.

50. Jaffrelot, Christophe, *India's Silent Revolution: The Rise of the Lower Castes in North India*, London: Hurst & Co./New York: Columbia University Press, 2003; Witsoe, Jeffrey, *Democracy against Development. Lower Caste Politics and Political Modernity in India*, Chicago: University of Chicago Press, 2013.

51. On divine kinship, see, Michelutti, Lucia and Forbess, Alice, 'From the Mouth of God. Divine kinship and popular democratic politics', *Focaal. Journal of Global and Historical Anthropology*, 67 (2013), pp. 1–18.

2. A *DE FACTO* ETHNIC DEMOCRACY? OBLITERATING AND TARGETING THE OTHER, HINDU VIGILANTES, AND THE ETHNO-STATE

1. Huntington, Samuel, *The Third Wave: Democratization in the Late Twentieth Century*, Norman: University of Oklahoma Press, 1991.

2. See, for instance, Diamond, Larry, 'Thinking About Hybrid Regimes', *Journal of Democracy*, 13, 2 (2002), pp. 21–35 and Gilbert, Leah and Payam Mohseni, 'Beyond Authoritarianism: The Conceptualization of Hybrid Regimes', *Studies in Comparative International Development*, 46, (2011), pp. 270–97.

3. Collier, David, and Steve Levistky, 'Democracy with adjectives: conceptual innovation in comparative research', *World Politics*, 49,3, (1997), p. 430–51, Zakaria, Fareed, 'The rise of Illiberal Democracy', *Foreign Affairs*, 76, 6, (1997), pp. 22–43; Schedler, Andreas, (ed.), *Electoral Authoritarianism. The Dynamics of Unfree Competition*, Boulder: Lynne Rienner, 2006; Peter Smith and Melissa Ziegler, 'Liberal and illiberal democracy in Latin America', *Latin American Politics and Society*, 50, 1 (2008), pp. 31–57; Levitsky, Steven and Lucan A. Way, *Competitive Authoritarianism. Hybrid Regimes after the Cold War*, Cambridge: Cambridge University Press, 2010, and Morlino, Leonardo, 'Are there hybrid regimes? Or are they just an optical illusion?', *European Political Science Review*, 1, 2 (2009), pp. 273–96.

4. Smooha, S., 'The model of ethnic democracy: Israel as a Jewish and democratic state', *Nations and Nationalism*, 8, 4 (2002), p. 479.

5. Ibid., p. 486.

6. Smooha, S., 'Ethnic democracy: Israel as an archetype', *Israel Studies*, 2, 2 (1997), p. 217.

7. Smooha, S., 'The model of ethnic democracy', p. 489.

8. Smooha, S., 'Ethnic democracy', p. 217

9. Cited in Peled, Y. and Navot, D., 'Ethnic democracy revisited. On the state of democracy in the Jewish state', *Israel Studies Forum*, 20, 1 (2005), p. 17.

10. Singh, Gurharpal, 'India as an ethnic democracy', Sciences Po Archives, 23 Mar. 2004, https://hal-sciencespo.archives-ouvertes.fr/medihal-01411920v1.

11. Jaffrelot, C. and S. Bhutada, 'The uniform code', *The Indian Express*, 13 July 2018, https://indianexpress.com/article/opinion/columns/indian-police-service-muslim-police-officials-5257238/, last accessed 16 July 2018.

12. Shaikh, Z., 'Ten years since Sachar report, Muslims still 3 percent in IAS, IPS', *The Indian Express*, 18 Aug. 2016, http://indianexpress.com/article/india/india-news-india/ten-years-since-sachar-report-muslims-still-3-in-ias-ips-2982199/, last accessed 11 May 2018.

13. In 2015, the Modi government decided no longer to make public the percentage of Muslims in the Indian police, which amounted to rescinding an innovation introduced by the Vajpayee government in 1999 (Sheikh, Z., 'Data on Muslims in police will no longer be public', *The Indian Express*, 30 Nov. 2015, http://indianexpress.com/article/

india/india-news-india/data-on-muslims-in-police-will-no-longer-be-public/, last accessed 11 May 2018.)

14. The official sources used here, which are difficult to access and incomplete, are the annual reports by the National Crime Records Bureau, called *Crime in India*, in the chapter 'Police strength, Expenditure & Infrastructure'. See these links: http://scrbwb. gov.in/CII/CD-CII2004/cii-2004/CHAP17.pdf, http://ncrb.gov.in/StatPublica-tions/CII/CII2005/cii-2005/CHAP17.pdf, http://ncrb.gov.in/StatPublications/ CII/CII2008/cii-2008/Chapter%2017.pdf, http://home.up.nic.in/CII-ADSI%20 2011/Data/CD-CII2011/cii-2011/Chapter%2017.pdf

15. Common Cause and CSDS, *Status of Policing in India Report 2018*, Delhi: Lokniti-CSDS and Common Cause, 2018, p. 193.

16. Ibid., p. 93.

17. Ibid., p. 97.

18. Tiwary, Deeptiman, 'Over 55 per cent of undertrials Muslim, Dalit or Tribal: NCRB,' *Indian Express*, 1 Nov. 2016, http://indianexpress.com/article/india/india-news-india/ over-55-per-cent-of-undertrials-muslim-dalit-or-tribal-ncrb-3731633.

19. Tiwary, Deeptiman, 'Share of Muslims in jail bigger than in the population, show NCRB data,' *The Indian Express*, 3 Nov. 2016, http://indianexpress.com/article/ explained/muslims-daliots-undertrials-in-prison-ncrb-3734362.

20. Cohen, S. *The Pakistan Army*, Karachi: Oxford University Press, 2006, pp. 59–60.

21. Cited in Khalidi, O., *Khaki and the Ethnic Violence in India. Army, Police and Paramilitary Forces During Communal Riots*, New Delhi: Three Essays, 2003, p. 11.

22. Wilkinson, S. I., *Army and Nation. The Military and Indian Democracy since Independence*, Cambridge: Harvard University Press, 2015, p. 139.

23. Khalidi, O., *Khaki and the Ethnic Violence in India*, op. cit., p. 24.

24. Cited in ibid., p. 23.

25. Cited in ibid., p. 23.

26. Wilkinson, S. I., *Army and Nation*, op. cit., p. 188.

27. Ibid., p. 184.

28. Ahmed, Ali, 'The missing Muslim army officers', *Economic and Political Weekly*, 53, 4 (27 Jan. 2018), p. 12.

29. Khalidi, O., *Khaki and the Ethnic Violence in India*, op. cit., pp. 62–3.

30. Reserve Bank of India, 'Employment in Public and Organised Private Sectors' in Handbook of Statistics on Indian Economy, New Delhi: Directorate General of Employment and Training, Ministry of Labour & Employment, Government of India, 2014, https://www.rbi.org.in/scripts/PublicationsView.aspx?id=15804, last accessed 15 July 2018.

31. For more details see Jaffrelot, C.,'The Muslims of India' in Jaffrelot, C. (ed.), *India since 1950: Society, Politics, Economy and Culture*, New Delhi: Yatra Books, 2011, pp. 564–80.

32. Shaikh, Z., 'Ten years since Sachar report, Muslims still 3 percent in IAS, IPS', *The Indian Express*, 18 Aug. 2016, http://indianexpress.com/article/india/india-news-india/ten-years-since-sachar-report-muslims-still-3-in-ias-ips-2982199/, last accessed 11 May 2018.

33. See *Kulhaiya*, 2018, 'Muslim IAS Officers List 2018', http://www.kulhaiya.com/education/upsc-ias-hindi/muslim-ias-toppers, last accessed 14 May 2018.
34. Shaikh, Z., op.cit.
35. Ummid, 'Maharashtra Civil Services (sic): Only 05 Muslims in list of 435 successful candidates', Ummid, 7 Apr. 2015, http://www.ummid.com/news/2015/April/07.04.2015/maharashtra-mpsc-results-2015.html, last accessed, 14 May 2018.
36. Press Trust of India, 'Maharashtra government does away with 5% job quota for Muslims', *Business Standard*, 4 Mar. 2015, http://www.business-standard.com/article/pti-stories/maharashtra-government-does-away-with-5-job-quota-for-muslims-115030401498_1.html, last accessed, 14 May 2018.
37. Jaffrelot, C., *India's Silent Revolution: The Rise of the Lower Castes in North India*, New York: Columbia University Press; London: Hurst; New Delhi: Permanent Black, 2003, p. 242.
38. Jaffrelot C., and Kalaiyasaran A., 'The Myth of Appeasement', *The Indian Express*, 20 Apr. 2018 https://indianexpress.com/article/opinion/columns/muslims-socio-economic-development-5144318/, last accessed, 15 June 2018.
39. *The Indian Express*, 'Telangana assembly passes bill to increase Muslim quota despite BJP protest', *The Indian Express*, 16 Apr. 2017, https://indianexpress.com/article/india/muslim-quota-reservation-telangana-assembly-passes-bill-to-increase-muslim-quota-despite-bjp-protest-4615466/, last accessed, 14 May 2018. The only state in which total quotas exceed 49 per cent is Tamil Nadu.
40. Vishnoi, A. and S. Chishti, 'BJP's Muslim score: 7 of 428 fielded, no winners', *The Indian Express*, 19 May 2014, http://indianexpress.com/article/india/politics/bjps-muslim-score-7-of-482-fielded-no-winners/, last accessed 14 May 2018.
41. On the notion of 'Muslim vote' and its limits, especially regarding the idea that Muslims vote for Muslim candidates, see Heath, Oliver, Gilles Verniers and Sanjay Kumar, 'Do Muslim voters prefer Muslim candidates? Co-religiosity and voting behaviour in India', *Electoral Studies*, 38, (2015), pp. 10–18.
42. Cited in Jha, Prashant, *How the BJP Wins: Inside India's Greatest Election Machine*, Delhi: Juggernaut Press, 2017, p. 174.
43. Jaffrelot, C., and Kalaiyasaran A., op. cit.
44. For further detail, see Jaffrelot, C., Virginie Dutoya, Radhika Kanchana and Gayatri Rathore, 'Understanding Muslim voting behaviour', *Seminar*, 602, (2009), pp. 43–8.
45. Jaffrelot, C., and G. Verniers, 'Invisible in the House', *The Indian Express*, 28 May 2014, http://indianexpress.com/article/opinion/columns/invisible-in-the-house/, last accessed 14 May 2018.
46. The fact that this minister was a Shia may not be just by chance, given the affinities between this community and the BJP in Uttar Pradesh, see Jaffrelot, C. and Haider Abbas Rizvi, 'A curious friendship', *The Indian Express*, 9 May 2018, http://indianexpress.com/article/opinion/columns/a-curious-friendship-uttar-pradesh-shia-leaders-yogi-adityanath-5168745/, last accessed 14 May 2018.
47. Gupta, S., 'Do minorities matter?', *The Print*, 11 Aug. 2017, https://theprint.in/2017/08/11/do-minorities-matter/amp/, last accessed 14 May 2018.

48. The first one was Yunus Khan in Rajasthan (S., Rukmini, 'Just one Muslim among 151 ministers in BJP-ruled states', *The Hindu*, 5 Nov. 2014, http://www.thehindu.com/news/national/just-one-muslim-among-151-ministers-in-bjpruled-states/article6564 908.ece, last accessed 31 May 2018). The second one was Mohsin Raza Naqvi, a Shia who was appointed in the UP government in 2017. On the co-option of Shias by BJP, see Jaffrelot and Rizvi, 'A curious friendship', op. cit.

49. See Jaffrelot, C., 'The Muslims of Gujarat during Narendra Modi's chief ministership', in Hasan, Riaz (ed.), *Indian Muslims. Struggling for Equality and Citizenship*, Melbourne: Melbourne University Publishing, 2016, pp. 235–58; Jaffrelot, C. 'The meaning of Modi's victory', *Economic and Political Weekly*, 43, 15 (12 April 2008), pp. 12–17 and 'Gujarat Elections: The Sub-text of Modi's "Hattrick"—High Tech Populism and the "Neo-middle Class"', *Studies in Indian Politics*, 1,1 (2013), pp. 79–96.

50. Mannathukkaren, N., 'The fast disappearing Muslim in the Indian republic', *The Indian Express*, 22 Jan. 2018, http://indianexpress.com/article/opinion/the-fast-disappearing-muslim-in-the-indian-republic-bjp-mla-hindu-saffron-religion-5034205/, last accessed 14 May 2018.

51. Verniers, G., 'The rising representation of Muslims in Uttar Pradesh', *The Hindu Centre for Politics and Public Policy*, 8 Apr. 2014, https://www.thehinducentre.com/verdict/commentary/article5886847.ece, last accessed 30 May 2018, and Verniers, G., 'Upper hand for upper castes in House', *The Indian Express*, 20 Mar. 2017, https://indianexpress.com/article/explained/bjp-narendra-modi-rajnath-singh-adityanath-devendra-fadnavis-upper-hand-for-upper-castes-in-house-4576599/, last accessed, 16 July 2018.

52. Saldanha, A., 'Muslim representation in UP assembly plummets with 2017 elections', *The Wire*, 14 Mar. 2017, https://thewire.in/culture/muslim-representation-up-plummets, last accessed 30 May 2018.

53. Favarel-Garrigues, Gilles and Laurent Gayer, 'Violer la loi pour maintenir l'ordre. Le vigilantisme en débat', *Politix*, 115, 29 (2016), p. 9.

54. A Virginian planter turned politician, Charles Lynch presided over people's courts to try anti-revolutionary elements who remained loyal to the British.

55. Pratten, David and Atryee Sen (eds), *Global Vigilantes: Anthropological Perspectives on Justice and Violence*, London: Hurst, 2006.

56. Cited in Deshpande B.V. and S.R. Ramaswamy, *Dr. Hedgewar, the epoch maker*, Bangalore: Sahitya Sindhu, 1981, p. 188.

57. Golwalkar, M.S., *We, or Our Nationhood Defined*, Nagpur: Bharat Prakashan, 1939, p. 50.

58. For a more detailed analysis, see chapter 1 of Jaffrelot, C., *The Hindu Nationalist Movement and Indian Politics*, London: Hurst, 1996.

59. Upadhyaya, D., *Integral Humanism*, New Delhi: Bharatiya Jana Sangh, 1965, p. 43.

60. On this ambivalent status, see Jaffrelot, C. 'The Militias of Hindutva: Communal Violence, Terrorism and Cultural Policing' in L. Gayer, and C. Jaffrelot (eds), *Armed Militias of South Asia. Fundamentalist, Maoists and Separatists*, London: Hurst, 2009, pp. 199–235.

61. This speech, taken from reports of the Delhi Police Criminal Investigation Department (CID) on file at the Nehru Memorial Museum and Library, was cited by Guha,

Ramchandra, 'They too wrote our history', *Outlook*, 22 Aug. 2005, https://www.out-lookindia.com/magazine/story/they-too-wrote-our-history/228341https://www.out-lookindia.com/magazine/story/they-too-wrote-our-history/228341. It is accessible at: https://ia601501.us.archive.org/26/items/IndiaDelhiPoliceFilesOnTheRSSDP Records5thInstalmentHome47File138/India%20Delhi-police-files-on-the-RSS-%28DP-Records-5th%20Instalment-Home-47%20File138%5D.pdf.

62. For more details, see Jaffrelot, C., *The Hindu Nationalist Movement*, op. cit., pp. 87–90 and pp. 273–4.

63. Jaffrelot, C., 'The Militias of Hindutva: Communal Violence, Terrorism and Cultural Policing', op. cit., pp. 199–236.

64. The terms of the debate are clearly presented in Favarel-Garrigues, Gilles and Laurent Gayer, op. cit., pp. 15ff.

65. Johnston, Les, 'What is vigilantism?', *The British Journal of Criminology*, 36, 2 (1 March 1996), pp. 220–36, https://doi.org/10.1093/oxfordjournals.bjc.a014083

66. Brown, R. M., *Strain of Violence: Historical Studies of American Violence and Vigilantism*, New York: Oxford University Press, 1975.

67. Abrahams, Ray, *Vigilant Citizens: Vigilantism and the State*, Cambridge: Polity Press, 1998.

68. Such a division of labour had operated before at the state level, mostly on the occasion of riots. See Jaffrelot, C., 'The 2002 Pogrom in Gujarat: The Post-9/11 Face of Hindu nationalist Anti-Muslim Violence', in J. Hinnels and R. King (eds), *Religion and violence in South Asia*, London and New York: Routledge, 2006, pp. 173–92.

69. On 'Love Jihad', see Gupta, C., 'Allegories of "love *jihad*" and *ghar wapsi*: interlocking the socio-religious with the political' in Mujibur Rehman (ed.), *Rise of Saffron Power. Reflection on Indian Politics*, New Delhi: Routledge, 2018, pp. 84–110.

70. Verma, L., 'As 12 seats in UP prepare to vote, 2 RSS magazines discuss "love jihad"', *The Indian Express*, 6 Sep. 2014, http://indianexpress.com/article/india/india-others/as-12-seats-in-up-prepare-to-vote-2-rss-magazines-discuss-love-jihad/, last accessed 5 Apr. 2018.

71. Cited in ibid.

72. Cobrapost and Gulail, 'Operation Juliet: Busting the bogey of "Love Jihad"', 4 Oct. 2015, http://cobrapost.com/blog/operation-juliet-busting-the-bogey-of-love-jihad-2/900, last accessed 30 June 2018.

73. Ibid.

74. Ibid.

75. Ibid.

76. A. Vatsa and Apurva, 'BJP leader's son among 15 named in Dadri lynching chargesheet', *The Indian Express*, 24 Dec. 2015, http://indianexpress.com/article/india/india-news-india/bjp-leaders-son-among-15-named-in-dadri-lynching-chargesheet/99/print/, last accessed 26 Mar. 2018.

77. Mander, Harsh, 'A country for the cow: The chronicle of a visit to cow vigilante victim Pehlu Khan's village', *Scroll.in*, 25 Apr. 2017, https://scroll.in/article/print/835315, last accessed 26 Mar. 2018; Mander, Harsh, 'Pehlu Khan, one year later', *The Indian Express*, 21 Apr. 2018, http://indianexpress.com/article/opinion/columns/pehlu-khan-rajasthan-cow-lynching-5145631/, last accessed 1 June 2018.

78. Khan, Hamza, 'Rajasthan: Muslim man ferrying cows dead in Alwar, police probe vigilantes', *The Indian Express*, 13 November 2017, http://indianexpress.com/article/india/rajasthan-muslim-man-allegedly-killed-by-cow-vigilantes-in-alwar-investigation-on-4934166/, last accessed, 26 Mar. 2018.

79. The Wire, 'Muslim men lynched in West Bengal over cow theft suspicions', *The Wire*, 28 Aug. 2017, https://thewire.in/171413/west-bengal-cow-lynching/, last accessed 26 Mar. 2018.

80. Huffington Post India, 'Two Muslim men, suspected of stealing cows, lynched in Assam', *Huffington Post India*, 18 Apr. 2017, https://www.huffingtonpost.in/2017/04/17/two-muslim-men-suspected-of-stealing-cows-lynched-in-assam_a_22062982/, last accessed, 26 Mar. 2018.

81. Shukla, Saurabh and Aloke Tikku, '3 arrested for beating up men near Delhi for allegedly carrying beef', NDTV, 15 Oct. 2017, https://www.ndtv.com/cities/would-have-burnt-me-alive-disabled-man-attacked-on-beef-charges-recalls-horror-1763077, last accessed 26 Mar. 2018.

82. The website 'Lynchings Across India' inventories most of these lynchings: https://uploads.knightlab.com/storymapjs/3880ebf0c4ae695337dae06e048988a9/lynchings-acres-india/draft.html, last accessed, 26 March 2018.

83. On this process of 'normalisation', see S. Halarnkar, 10 Sep. 2017, 'This photograph of two murdered teens should disturb an India that has normalised hate', Scroll.in, https://scroll.in/article/print/849804, last accessed 26 Mar. 2018.

84. 'Database on bovine-related violence (from January 2010 to September 2, 2017)', Indiaspend.org, https://docs.google.com/spreadsheets/d/13REUhD4fW6olOy_SjobWQRA1qQg3VY1pp87XMRJwJW4/pubhtml, last accessed, 26 Mar. 2018. See also http://data.indiaspend.com/hate-crime (Last access, 30 June 2018).

85. Abraham, D., and O. Rao, 16 July 2017, '86% killed in cow-related violence since 2010 are Muslim, 97% attacks after Modi govt came to power', Hindustan Times, https://www.hindustantimes.com/india-news/86-killed-in-cow-relat...after-modi-govt-came-to-power/story-w9CYOksvgk9joGSSaXgpLO.html, last accessed 26 Mar. 2018.

86. S. Dayal and S. Siwach, 15 Oct. 2017, 'Mob assaults two for 'carrying beef' in Faridabad, three who came to their aid', The Indian Express, http://indianexpress.com/article/india/mob-assaults-two-for-carrying-beef-in-faridabad-three-who-came-to-their-aid-4890872/, last accessed, 26 Mar. 2018.

87. Mander, Harsh, 'A country for the cow', op. cit.

88. Its predecessor, the Gau Raksha Samiti (cow protection committee) was founded in 1998.

89. A person convicted of cow slaughter and for selling beef can be sentenced up to ten and five years in jail respectively.

90. Marvel, Ishan, 'In the name of the mother. How the states nurtures the gau rakshaks of Haryana', *The Caravan*, 1 Sep. 2016, http://www.caravanmagazine.in/reportage/in-the-name-of-the-mother, last accessed 2 May 2018.

91. Ibid.

92. Ibid.

93. Ibid.

94. Cited in Ibid.

95. The kind of osmosis observed in Haryana prevailed also in Punjab to a lesser extent before Congress won the state elections in 2017 (Singh, Pragya, 'Four stomachs to fill', *Outlook*, 15 Aug. 2016, https://www.outlookindia.com/magazine/story/four-stomachs-to-fill/297662, last accessed 2 May 2018.

96. Marvel, Ishan, op.cit.

97. Biswas, P.S., 'Maharashtra govt appoints officers to implement beef ban', *The Indian Express*, 3 June 2016, http://indianexpress.com/article/cities/mumbai/maharashtra-state-govt-appoints-officers-to-implement-beef-ban-2831536/99/print/, last accessed 2 May 2018.

98. Nair, Smita, 'Refrain in Sangh turf: Cards will give us power', *The Indian Express*, 23 Aug. 2016, https://indianexpress.com/article/india/india-news-india/maharashtra-government-beef-ban-gau-rakshak-id-cards-animal-husbandry-modi-sangh-turf-2991489/, last accessed 2 May 2018.

99. Singh, Pragya, op.cit.

100. Singh, Pragya, op.cit. In many cases, the police were once again complicit when they did not actually take part in the same sort of extortion. They, for instance, demanded bribes to turn a blind eye on cow smuggling, or on the sale of dishes prepared with cow meat by Muslim restaurants and shops. (Rai, S., 'Mewat: Police taking bribes from vendors to allow sale of beef biryani', *India Today*, 10 Sep. 2016, https://www.indiatoday.in/mail-today/story/beef-biryani-mewat-sample-testing-police-bribe-34 0263–2016–09–10, last accessed 2 May 2018. *Gau rakshaks* and the police are thus involved in activities that are not only illicit but that also qualify as organised crime.

101. Panda, A., 'Speaking out: Modi condemns cow vigilantism in India', *The Diplomat*, 8 Aug. 2016, https://thediplomat.com/2016/08/speaking-out-modi-condemns-cow-vigilantism-in-india/, last accessed 2 May 2018. Soon before, he had tweeted: 'The sacred practice of cow worship & the compassion of Gau Seva can't be misused by some miscreants posing as Gau Rakshaks.' (Ibid.)

102. Press Trust of India, 'Punjab: Gau Raksha Dal chief Satish Kumar arrested', *The Indian Express*, 21 Oct. 2016, http://indianexpress.com/article/india/india-news-india/punjab-gau-raksha-dal-chief-satish-kumar-arrested-2988508/, last accessed, 2 May 2018.

103. Deshpande, A., 'PM Narendra Modi's remark that 80 per cent gau rakshaks are fake should have been avoided: RSS', *The Indian Express*, 9 Aug. 2016, http://indianexpress.com/article/india/india-news-india/narendra-modi-fake-gau-rakshak-rss-beef-ban-cow-slaughter-gujarat-dalit-thrashing-2962750/, last accessed 2 May 2018.

104. Cited in Ishan Marvel, op. cit.

105. Deshpande, V., 'PM Narendra Modi's remark that 80 per cent gau rakshaks are fake should have been avoided: RSS', *The Indian Express*, 9 Aug. 2016, http://indianexpress.com/article/india/india-news-india/narendra-modi-fake-gau-rakshak-rss-beef-ban-cow-slaughter-gujarat-dalit-thrashing-2962750/, last accessed 2 May 2018.

106. Dahat, P., 'RSS chief backs gau rakshaks, lauds Army', *The Hindu*, 11 Oct. 2016, http://www.thehindu.com/news/national/RSS-chief-backs-gau-rakshaks-lauds-Army/article15479013.ece, last accessed 2 May 2018.

107. Berman, Bruce and John Lonsdale, *Unhappy Valley. Conflict in Kenya and Africa*, 1, *State and Class*, 2, *Violence and Ethnicity*, London: James Currey, 1992.
108. Berman, Bruce and John Lonsdale, *Unhappy Valley*, 1, op. cit., pp. 36–8.
109. Even if parallels to anti-miscegenationists and lynchings in the US does spring to mind.
110. Cobrapost and Gulail, 'Operation Juliet: Busting the bogey of "Love Jihad"', op. cit.
111. Ibid.
112. As early as the 1930s, Hindu nationalists have promoted democracy for this reason (Jaffrelot, C., 'Hindu nationalism and democracy' in: Frankel, F., Z. Hasan, R. Bhargava and B. Arora (eds), *Transforming India. Social and Political Dynamics of Democracy*, Delhi: Oxford University Press, 2000, pp. 353–78.
113. Cited in Smooha, S., 'Ethnic democracy', op. cit., pp. 206–7.
114. Cited in ibid.
115. Ibid., p. 216
116. Ibid., pp. 219–20
117. Ibid., p. 220
118. Ibid., p. 233.
119. Smooha, S., 'The model of ethnic democracy: Israel as a Jewish and democratic state', op. cit., p. 481.

3. IMMORAL TIMES: VIGILANTISM IN A SOUTH INDIAN CITY

1. Forum Against Atrocities on Women, *Fact Finding Report*, Mangalore, 2012.
2. Ibid, p. 2.
3. Ibid, p. 10.
4. The journalist was arrested along with the attackers because it was alleged he did not inform the police once he heard about the plan. In his defence, he claimed he waited until he was sure the attack would take place (he was tipped off and arrived at the scene before the attackers) and then tried to call the police but could not get connected. The journalist later gave a statement to the above-mentioned report stating that he heard the city's Commissioner of Police saying, 'Why should ... [he] report the incident? Doesn't he have sisters? Does he not hit them? Does anyone show that on TV. I will teach him a lesson. He [the journalist] has said that there is Taliban culture in Mangalore.... This time I will not leave him. We will fix him. He may have any number of influential friends. But I will definitely fix him.' Ibid, p. 11.
5. Of course there is no way of knowing exactly who sent this. The errors in the original are preserved here.
6. There are no reliable figures on India-wide numbers of moral policing incidents. The most common form of analysis has been to use newspaper reports. This not only suffers from under reporting (victims are often scared of being 'shamed'), but also English language and online media bias. Mangaluru-based activists have compiled incidents based on newspaper reports that also include Kannada-language and print-only publications.
7. 'Home Stay Attack', YouTube, https://www.youtube.com/watch?v=ngCaju1TCtc, last accessed 18 Aug. 2017.

8. 'Pub Attack' YouTube, https://www.youtube.com/watch?v=lEbD2aXs-XU, last accessed 18 Aug. 2017.

9. NDTV, 'Muslim man Stripped, tied to pole and beaten by mob in Mangalore, 13 arrested', NDTV, 25 Aug. 2015, http://www.ndtv.com/india-news/man-stripped-and-beaten-by-moral-police-inmangalore-1210717, last accessed 15 Sep. 2015.

10. Analysis of newspapers reveals that from 1 Aug. 2008 to 15 Feb. 2009 there were forty-five instances, see: PUCL-K, *Cultural Policing in Dakshina Kannada*, Mangalore: People's Union for Civil Liberties, 2009.

11. Pinton, Stanley and Chethan Misquith, 'Moral cops run riot, split communities, genders', *The Times of India*, 5 Jan. 2018, https://timesofindia.indiatimes.com/city/mangaluru/moral-cops-run-riot-split-communities-genders/articleshow/62377172.cms, last accessed 15 May 2018.

12. This is also suggested by journalistic coverage about communalism and vigilantism. See, Siddiqui, Zeba, Krishna N. Das, Tommy Wilkes and Tom Lasseter, 'Emboldened by Modi's ascent, India's cow vigilantes deny Muslims their livelihood', Reuters, 6 Nov. 2017, https://www.reuters.com/investigates/special-report/india-politics-religion-cows/, last accessed 15 May 2018; Mahaprashasta, A.A., 'With Modi's Blessing, BJP's Communal Agenda Gets a Boost in Coastal Karnataka', *The Wire*, 10 May 2018, https://thewire.in/communalism/with-modis-blessing-bjps-communal-agenda-gets-a-boost-in-coastal-karnataka, last accessed 15 May 2018.

13. Hansen, Thomas Blom, 'Sovereigns beyond the State: On legality and authority in urban India' in T.B. Hansen, and F. Stepputat (eds), *Sovereign Bodies: Citizens, Migrants, and States in the Postcolonial World*, Princeton: Princeton University Press, 2005, pp. 169–91.

14. Blom, Amélie and Jaoul, Nicolas, 'Introduction. The moral and affectual dimension of collective action in South Asia', in A. Blom, and N. Jaoul (eds), *South Asia Multidisciplinary Academic Journal*, 2 (2008), https://doi.org/10.4000/samaj.1912.

15. Deshpande, Satish, 'Hegemonic spatial strategies: The nation-space and Hindu communalism in twentieth-century India', *Public Culture*, 10, 2 (1998), https://doi.org/10.1215/08992363-10-2-249, 1998, pp. 249–83.

16. Das, Gurcharan, *India Unbound: A Personal Account of a Social and Economic Revolution*, New York: Knopf, 2000.

17. Brosius, Christiane, *India's Middle Class: New Forms of Urban Leisure, Consumption and Prosperity, Cities and the Urban Imperative*, London and New York: Routledge, 2010.

18. Kaur, Ravinder and Thomas Blom Hansen 'Aesthetics of arrival: Spectacle, capital, novelty in post-reform India', *Identities*, 23, (2016), pp. 1–11, https://doi.org/10.1080/1070289X.2015.1034135.

19. Rajagopal, Arvind, 'Indian democracy and Hindu populism: The Modi regime', *Social Text*, 27 Feb. 2015, https://socialtextjournal.org/periscope_article/indian-democracy-and-hindu-populism-the-modi-regime/, last accessed 19 July 2018.

20. Hansen, Thomas Blom, *The Saffron Wave: Democracy and Hindu Nationalism in Modern India*, Princeton: Princeton University Press, 1999, p. 8.

21. Ibid.

22. Fernandes, Leela, 'India's middle classes in contemporary India', in K.A. Jacobsen (ed.), *Routledge Handbook of Contemporary India*, London: Routledge, 2016.

23. Gopalakrishnan, Shankar, 'Defining, constructing and policing a "new India": Relationship between neoliberalism and Hindutva', *Economic and Political Weekly*, 41, 26 (2006), pp. 2803–13.

24. Ibid.

25. Oza, Rupal, *The Making of Neoliberal India: Nationalism, Gender, and the Paradoxes of Globalization*, New York: Taylor and Francis, 2006.

26. Both research periods included interviews with members of Hindu nationalist organisations, cross-community couples, and left-wing/progressive social activists, group discussions with college students, and participant observation with various groups in the city as part of a wider project examining urban change.

27. Directorate of Census Operations, 'Census of India 2011', Bengaluru: Government of India, 2011, http://www.census2011.co.in/census/city/451-mangalore.html.

28. Cook, Ian M., 'Sizing the City', *City*, (2018) DOI: 10.1080/13604813.2018.1549836.

29. For instance the district does indeed have a lot of colleges. Mangaluru has eight and Udupi, north of Mangaluru, 8.9 engineering colleges per 100,000 of the 18–24 age group, more than the state capital Bangalore's seven. See, Paul, Samuel, et al., *The State of Our Cities: Evidence from Karnataka*, New Delhi: Oxford University Press, 2012, p. 29.

30. This was expressed to me either in conversation or could be the comments section on news reports that appear about moral policing, e.g. 'Can these jobless goons/rowdies, be sent to our country's borders and fight our enemies and help our soldiers'. See, Dsouza, Eulalia, Comment, Daijiworld.com, http://www.daijiworld.com/news/newsDisplay. aspx?newsID=488942, last accessed 17 May 2018.

31. Tambe, Ashwini and Shruti Tambe, 'Sexual incitement, spectatorship and economic liberalisation in contemporary India', *Interventions*, 15, 4 (2013), p. 506.

32. Robbins, Joel, 'Between reproduction and freedom: Morality, value, and radical cultural change', *Ethnos*, 72, 3 (2007), pp. 293–314, https://doi.org/10.1080/00141 840701576919.

33. Kapur, Jyotsna, *The Politics of Time and Youth in Brand India: Bargaining with Capital*, London: Anthem Press, 2013.

34. Laidlaw, James, *The Subject of Virtue: An Anthropology of Ethics and Freedom*, Cambridge: Cambridge University Press, 2014.

35. Chatterjee, Moyukh, 'Bandh Politics: Crowds, Spectacular Violence, and Sovereignty in India', *Distinktion: Journal of Social Theory*, 17, 3 (2016), pp. 294–307, https://doi. org/10.1080/1600910X.2016.1258586.

36. Rajagopal, Arvind, 'The Rise of Hindu Populism in India's Public Sphere', *Current History*, 115, 780 (2016), p. 123.

37. Hansen, Thomas Blom, 'Democracy against the law: Reflections on India's illiberal democracy', (in this volume).

38. Often, if police are called to incidents, then their first inclination is to diffuse the situation rather than act in a way that might bring about unwanted attention or future responses. Meanwhile those who are attacked often cover their faces from cameras. It

is usually the moral policemen who want as many people to know about the attacks as possible.

4. REFLECTIONS IN THE CROWD: DELEGATION, VERISIMILITUDE, AND THE MODI MASK

1. Bourdieu, Pierre, 'La délégation et le fétichisme politique', *Actes de la recherche en science sociale*, 52–53 (1984), pp. 49–55.
2. Bourdieu, Pierre, *Language and Symbolic Power*, Cambridge: Polity Press, 1991, p. 204; emphasis in the original.
3. Shah, Ghanshyam, *Caste association and political process in Gujarat: A study of the Gujarat Kshatriyas Sabha*. Bombay: Popular Prakashan, 1975
4. In the political history of Gujarat one can see an alignment of the Patel community with Jain and Hindu Vaishnavas (Vania), i.e. traditional elites, whereas Kshatriya leadership usually implies a conglomeration of lower-caste groups (mainly OBCs).
5. While Modi hailed from a low-caste background, few commented explicitly about that fact at the time. This was to change more than a decade later when he began his national campaign for prime ministership. In 2001, I remember more prosaic discussions: A particular group of academic interlocutors in Ahmedabad, for example, obsessed for weeks over the question whether the new chief minister might be an occasional chicken eater or whether he was a *brahmachari* (celibate). These two attributes did not align together well in local logic. Eating chicken can indicate a low social status, but could also signify the lifestyle of the Gujarati middle class that might indulge more or less clandestinely in alcohol and meat consumption. Celibacy, by contrast, could indicate a certain measure of religious piety, but could also express the austerity of the secular national volunteer (*svayamsevak*), whose office is considered a selfless gift (*seva*): a sacrifice to the nation.
6. For an overview of major violent clashes in Ahmedabad since the 1960s see, Kumar, Megha, *Communal and Sexual Violence in India. The Politics of Gender, Ethnicity, and Conflict*. London: IB Tauris, 2016. Kumar seems to be unaware of my own work on the Gujarat pogrom.
7. 'There is no doubt in my mind that in the majority of quarrels the Hindus come out second best. My own experience but confirms the opinion that the Mussalman as a rule is a bully, and the Hindu as a rule is a coward.' (Gandhi, M.K., 'Hindu-Muslim Conflict, its Causes and Cure', *Young India*, 29 May, 1924.) Gandhi wrote this statement in 1924, a month after his release from prison and while north India was engulfed in serious communal violence. Expressing his deep frustration at the time, it remains puzzling how stable the stereotype remains even today despite all evidence to the contrary. This stability points to what is often occluded from analyses of violence, namely, the inner life of protagonists and the question of how external acts relate to an internal world. Gandhi's frustration in 1924 remains generative for a violent Hindu nationalist script today that ignores historical context (anti-colonial agitation in the pre-Independence period) and appropriates Gandhi's words by making them fit their own needs.
8. Ghassem-Fachandi, Parvis, *Pogrom in Gujarat. Hindu Nationalism and anti-Muslim Violence in India*, Princeton, NJ: Princeton University Press, 2012, p. 135
9. Borneman, John and Ghassem-Fachandi, Parvis, 'The concept of Stimmung: From

indifference to xenophobia in Germany's refugee crisis', *Hau: Journal of Ethnographic Theory*, 7(3) 2017, pp. 105–35.

10. Mink, Louis O., 'Narrative Form as Cognitive Instrument', in Canary, R.H. and Kozicki, H. eds. *The Writing of History. Literary Form and Historical Understanding*. Madison: University of Wisconsin Press, 1978, p. 147.

11. Ghassem-Fachandi, op.cit., p. 32–37

12. See, Setalvad, Teesta, *Foot Soldier of the Constitution: A Memoir*, Delhi: LeftWord Books, 2014, pp. 40–42. Note that Setalvad does mention instances of violence already in the afternoon of Wednesday 27 Feb.

13. Mitta, Manoj, *The Fiction of Fact-Finding: Modi and Godhra*, Noida: Harper Collins, 2014, p. 103; Kumar, Megha, *Communal and Sexual Violence in India*, p. 195.

14. This tale included rumours that Hindu girls had been abducted by Muslims attackers from Sabarmati Express at the Godhra railway station for the purposes of 'enjoy' (*enjoi levaa maate*), i.e. raped and killed (Ghassem-Fachandi, 2012, pp. 66–76; Kumar, 2016, p. 196–7).

15. It should not escape notice that the reduction of Mahatma Gandhi's understanding of Hindu-Muslim relationships to a one-liner itself suggests a form of cruelty against the symbolic father of the nation.

16. The invocation of spontaneity or of a wider popular acceptance of violence is not unique to the Gujarat context or limited to recent historical periods. Quite the contrary, it forms part of a larger Hindu nationalist strategy of collective violent mobilisation and identification. For a case in point, compare Bal Thackeray's detailed enunciations accompanying Shiv Sena violence in Bombay in the 1960s (see Hansen, Thomas Blom, *Wages of Violence: Naming and Identity in Postcolonial Bombay*. Princeton: Princeton University Press, 2001). The same holds true for the systematic sexualisation of communal violence, which preceded Gujarat 2002 and has a longer history (see Kumar, Megha, *Communalism and Sexual Violence. Ahmedabad since 1969*, Delhi: Tulika Books, 2017, pp. 32–7).

17. Freud, Sigmund, 'Die Verneinung', *Theoretische Schriften, 1911–1925*, Wien: Internationaler Psychoanalytischer Verlag, 1925, pp. 399–404.

18. Ghassem-Fachandi, op. cit., pp. 191–187 and 211–12

19. Ibid., p. 156

20. The practice can be dramatised: in 1990, L.K. Advani received a *tilak* of blood by a supporter, a member from the Bajrang Dal, during his ethno-religious *Rath Yatra* procession (see Jaffrelot, Christophe, *The Hindu Nationalist Movement in India*. London: Hurst, 1996).

21. Ghassem-Fachandi, op.cit.

22. The Muslims who visited this *Sadhavna* event to honour Modi were critiqued from within their own respective constituencies for their willingness to appear on stage and embrace the chief minister. His refusal to wear the *topi* obviously only confirmed these suspicions.

5. TOWARD HEGEMONY: THE BJP BEYOND ELECTORAL DOMINANCE

1. This is a slightly revised version of the article published in *Economic and Political Weekly*,

53 (33), 18 Aug. 2018, 36–42. Emerging from a paper originally presented at the seminar held at King's India Institute, I have benefitted from comments by the participants, particularly by Katherine Adeney and Louise Tillin. The present version has also benefitted from the comments of an anonymous referee who carefully read the draft and nudged me to think of a couple of complicated issues. I am thankful to the reviewer and to the participants at the seminar. Usual disclaimers apply.

2. The United Progressive Alliance was a coalition government that constituted the ruling majority in the Indian Parliament for two consecutive terms preceding the 2014 BJP government.

3. The present chapter thus looks at the political aspect of hegemony implying the ability of key political players to construct narratives and get large sections of the society to subscribe to those narratives. Needless to say, this ability and the construction of convincing narratives are both dependent on and supported by configurations obtaining in the field of political economy. For a discussion of this aspect of hegemony, see Achin Vanaik, 'India's Two Hegemonies', *New Left Review*, 112, July–Aug. 2018, 29–59. I thank James Manor for drawing my attention to this. Vanaik's argument implicitly endorses the view that the BJP is indeed engaged in the larger politics of crafting hegemony.

4. Yadav, Yogendra, 'Reconfiguration in Indian Politics: State Assembly Elections, 1993–95', *Economic and Political Weekly*, 13–20 Aug, vol. 31, no. 2–3, (1996), pp. 95–104.

5. Palshikar, Suhas, 'Congress in the Times of Post-Congress Era: Surviving sans Politics', *Economic and Political Weekly*, 9 May, vol. 50, no. 19, (2015), pp. 39–46.

6. For a discussion of many of these features, see Palshikar, S. and Suri, K.C., 'Critical Shifts in the Long Term, Caution in the Short Term. India's 2014 Lok Sabha Elections', *Economic and Political Weekly*, 49 (39), 27 Sept. 2014.

7. This was reminiscent of Modi's speech after he won the 2012 Gujarat assembly elections. Then too, he spoke more about the all-India than the Gujarat-specific context.

8. Palshikar, Suhas, 'India's Second Dominant Party system', *Economic & Political Weekly*, 52 (12), 18 Mar. 2017, pp. 12–15.

9. State parties wold either get defeated—something that has already happened in UP—or be forced to join hands with the BJP—as in Bihar and Tamil Nadu. While the BJP poses a challenge to the BJD in Odisha, it may push JDS in Karnataka to a weaker position. One can also look carefully at the BJP's efforts to neutralise the Shiv Sena in Maharashtra. Yet, a few key state level players would still remain: TMC, Shiv Sena, DMK, TRS and TDP etc.

10. The caveat about Muslims applies—and that makes the BJP a Hindu party in any case.

11. It is this political economy aspect, attractive to the middle classes and profitable to the corporate interests that sustains the efforts to build a hegemonic project, see below. Palshikar, Suhas, 'Half of Achche?', *Outlook*, 9 Jan. 2017 https://www.outlookindia.com/magazine/story/half-of-achhe/298307; accessed 14 Sept. 2017.

12. Vora, Rajendra and Suhas Palshikar, 'Neo-Hinduism: Case of Distorted Consciousness', in Jayant Lele and Rajendra Vora (eds), *State and Society in India*, Delhi: Chanakya, 1990, pp. 213–43.

13. Hansen, Thomas Blom, 'The Vernacularization of *Hindutva*: BJP and Shiv Sena in

Rural Maharashtra', *Contributions to Indian Sociology*, vol. 30, no. 2, (1996), pp. 177–214.

14. The three public speeches given by the RSS chief, Mohan Bhagwat in Delhi in September 2018 exemplify the flexibility in the usage of the terms Hindu and Hindutva almost producing an effect that there is nothing exclusionary in the idea of Hindutva. The speeches and interaction with audience, titled 'Bharat of the Future', are *par excellence* instances of the new hegemony this chapter talks about. They are available at the official website of the RSS: http://rss.org//Encyc/2018/9/18/Bharat-of-Future-An-RSS-perspective.html; http://rss.org//Encyc/2018/9/19/Bharat-of-Future-An-RSS-Perspective-day-2-mohanji-bhagwaat.html; and http://rss.org//Encyc/2018/9/20/Bharat-of-Future-An-RSS-Perspective-Day-3.html.

15. For a discussion of different phases of evolution of ideology of Hindutva, see Palshikar, Suhas, 'The BJP and Hindu Nationalism: Centrist Politics and Majoritarian Impulses', *South Asia: Journal of South Asian Studies*, December 2015, Vol. 38, No. 4, pp. 719–35.

16. On 30 November 2016, the supreme court of India ruled that playing the national anthem of India before the screening of films will be mandatory for all cinema halls and standing up in its respect will be mandatory for everyone present. See Rajagopal, K., 'National Anthem must be played before screening of films: Supreme Court', *The Hindu*, 30 Nov. 2016 https://www.thehindu.com/news/national/National-anthem-must-be-played-before-screening-of-films-Supreme-Court/article16729264.ece, last accessed 8 July 2018.

17. General Secretary of the party who sought to aggressively popularize the slogan 'Shining India' during campaign for the 2004 elections—a slogan that failed to attract voters then.

18. The three were some of the most popular campaigns launched by the ruling BJP government.

19. On 8 November 2016, Prime Minister Narendra Modi announced that currency bills of 500 and 1000 rupee will cease to be legal tender. See 'Demonetisation of Rs. 500 and Rs. 1000 notes: RBI explains', *The Hindu*, 9 Dec. 2016 https://www.thehindu.com/news/national/Demonetisation-of-Rs.-500-and-Rs.-1000-notes-RBI-explains/article16440296.ece, last accessed 8 July 2018.

20. In 2011, there was widespread agitation in India against corruption in public offices. For a timeline on the movement and its key figures, see Kurian, 'A Timeline of the Anti Corruption Movement in India Under Team Anna,' *Youth ki Awaaz*, 17 June 2012, https://www.youthkiawaaz.com/2012/06/a-timeline-of-the-anti-corruption-movement-in-india-under-team-anna/, last accessed 8 July 2018.

21. In August 2017 a parliamentary committee chaired by a Congress MP circulated a detailed questionnaire on the question of the First Past The Post system and the feasibility of shifting to alternatives.

22. Vaishnav, Milan, 'Finance Bill Makes Funding for Political Parties More Opaque Than Ever', Op-ed, *Hindustan Times*, 29 Mar. 2017, http://carnegieendowment.org/2017/03/29/finance-bill-makes-funding-for-political-parties-more-opaque-than-ever-pub-68445, last accessed 14 Sep. 2017.

23. Arvind Kejriwal is the leader of the Aam Aadmi Party, which came to power as the government of the Delhi National Capital Territory in 2015.

24. Dasgupta, Swapan, 'Congress vs. BJP? No, it's the establishment vs the outsider', *Times of India*, 25 Aug. 2013, https://blogs.timesofindia.indiatimes.com/right-and-wrong/congress-vs-bjp-no-it-s-the-establishment-vs-the-outsider/; last accessed 14 Sep. 2017.

25. As one pro-Modi commentator puts it, Modi is doing both: managing India and changing it; Dasgupta, 2017, op. cit.

26. The idea of doing away with VIP culture, however, did not gain much political traction and therefore the BJP quickly set it aside. It no more constituted the core if its rhetoric. This again suggests a certain amount of flexibility to adapt to popular sentiment while at the same time trying to shape the popular sentiment.

27. The term 'sickular' popularised by the social media spokespersons of the present regime also indicates the success in steering the discourse.

28. This is what Modi reportedly said: '*Gaon mein agar kabristan banta hai, to gaon mein shamshaan bhi banana chahiye. Agar Ramzan me bijli milti hai, to Diwali me bhi milni chahiye. Agar Holi me bijli milti hai, to Eid par bhi bijli milni chahiye. Bhedbhav nahin hona chahiye* (If a village gets a graveyard, it should get a cremation ground too. If there is electricity during Ramzan, there should be electricity during Diwali too. If there is electricity during Holi, there should be electricity during Eid too. There should not be any discrimination).' See 'Has PM Modi's Diwali, Ramzan bhed-bhav remark given more fodder to Opposition?', *Indian Express*, 20 Feb. 2017, https://indianexpress.com/elections/uttar-pradesh-assembly-elections-2017/narendra-modi-diwali-ramzan-bhed-bhav-remark-given-more-fodder-to-opposition-fatehpur-up-uttar-pradesh-elections/, last accessed 8 July 2018.

29. Reform of Muslim personal law has been for long a contentious issue. While it was an article of faith for the socialists and progressives at one stage, since the late 1980s the BJP has taken it up as a core issue. The practice of oral and instant divorce (triple *talaq*) was challenged in the supreme court by private parties, and the court ruled this practice to be constitutionally untenable: https://www.sci.gov.in/supremecourt/2016/6716/6716_2016_Judgement_22-Aug-2017.pdf. The BJP government claimed this to be its major victory and, following the court ruling, the government sought to criminalize the practice by first trying to legislate and failing that issued an ordinance to that effect; https://timesofindia.indiatimes.com/india/cabinet-clears-ordinance-to-criminalise-triple-talaq/articleshow/65878986.cms.

30. Palshikar, Suhas, 'What Makes BJP Really Different?', *Economic & Political Weekly*, vol. 52, no. 19, (2017), pp. 12–13.

31. See http://rashtriyasewa.org/.

32. Thachil, Tariq, *Elite Parties, Poor Voters: How Social Services win Votes in India*, Cambridge: Cambridge University Press, 2014.

33. Many Hindutva organisations in fact do not even have a direct formal link with the RSS, see Jha, Dhirendra, *Shadow Armies of Hindutva*, New Delhi: Juggernaut, 2017.

34. For the full speech in Hindi: https://www.youtube.com/watch?v=xes7EHvvf_0; for detailed report, http://www.oneindia.com/india/i-see-new-india-modi-victory-speech-after-big-up-win-2372645.html; both accessed 25 May 2017.

35. 'Mann ki baat Full Text,' *India Today*, (2017), http://indiatoday.intoday.in/story/mann-ki-baat-pm-narendra-modi-gst-full-text/1/1014472.html, last accessed 14 Sep. 2017.

36. Verma, L., 'Harvard vs hard work: with GDP data, PM Narendra Modi snubs note ban critics,' *Indian Express*, 2 Mar. 2017, http://indianexpress.com/elections/uttar-pradesh-assembly-elections-2017/harvard-vs-hard-work-with-gdp-data-pm-modi-snubs-note-ban-critics-4550000/, last accessed 14 Sep. 2017.

37. Palshikar, Suhas, *Indian Democracy, Oxford India Short Introductions*, New Delhi: OUP, 2017.

6. CAN MODI AND THE BJP ACHIEVE AND SUSTAIN HEGEMONY?

1. My use of this term differs somewhat from the familiar usage by Antonio Gramsci. Along with Suhas Palshikar and Ashutosh Varshney, I take it to mean 'overwhelming supremacy' over alternative power centres within and beyond government. For a sophisticated discussion of the concept, see P. Anderson, *The H-Word: The Peripeteia of Hegemony*, London: Verso, 2017. Yogendra Yadav's use of the term is closer to that of Gramsci: 'What is to be Done?', *Seminar*, no. 699, Nov. 2017.

2. Amit Shah, 'BJP president and Modi's right-hand man', *Times of India*, 20 Aug. 2017.

3. See for example, Krishnan, Kailash K., 'India at 70: Culture of One-Party Dominance', *The Wire*, 28 Aug. 2017, https://thewire.in/government/india-one-party-dominance-democracy-bjp. Shergill, J., 'BJP's Repeated Attempts...Threatening Parliament's Authority', *The Wire*, 27 Nov. 2017; and Achary, P.D.T., 'The Creeping Threat to the Autonomy of Parliament', *The Wire*, 28 Nov. 2017, https://thewire.in/government/india-one-party-dominance-democracy-bjp, last accessed on 19 June 2018.

4. The Wire Analysis, 'Justice Jayant Patel's Resignation Marks a Moment of Crisis for the Judiciary', *The Wire*, https://thewire.in/law/justice-jayant-patels-resignation-marks-moment-crisis-judiciary, last accessed on 19 June 2018.

5. Bhatnagar, Gaurav Vivek, 'Key projects for marginalised suffer after NGOs lose FCRA licences', *The Wire*, 27 Jan. 2017, https://thewire.in/government/key-projects-for-marginalised-suffer-after-ngos-lose-fcra-licence.

6. Gupta, Shekar, 'Modi is by far India's most powerful, domineering, instinctive-and very popular-political figure. Why then is his government floundering?' *India Today*, 20 Aug. 2015, https://www.indiatoday.in/magazine/national-interest/story/20150831-speaking-truth-to-the-great-orator-820310-2015-08-20. See also Guha, Keshava, 'The BJP's head of information technology just issued a warning to every journalist in the country', *Scroll.in*, 30 Nov. 2016, https://scroll.in/article/822940/the-bjps-head-of-information-technology-just-issued-a-warning-to-every-journalist-in-the-country, last accessed on 20 July 2018; Johari, Aarefa, 'Attacks, bans, censorship: On World Press Freedom Day, a report on India's 'shrinking liberty', *Scroll.in*, 3 May 2017, https://scroll.in/article/836394/attacks-bans-censorship-on-world-press-freedom-day-a-report-on-indias-shrinking-liberty; The Wire Staff, 'Stories on Amit Shah's assets, Smirti Irani's "degree" vanish from TOI, DNA', *The Wire*, 30 July 2017, https://thewire.in/media/amit-shah-assets-smriti-irani-degrees-toi-et-outlook/amp/, last accessed on 19 July 2018;

Venkataramakrishnan, Rohan, 'BJP leaders condemn Gauri Lankesh murder and blame Congress—but many right-wingers are gleeful', *Scroll.in*, 6 Sep. 2017, https://scroll. in/article/849757/bjp-leaders-condemn-gauri-lankesh-murder-and-blame-congress-but-many-right-wingers-are-gleeful, last accessed on 20 July 2017; Srivas, Anuj, 'Hindustan Times editor's exit preceded by meeting between Modi, newspaper owner', *The Wire*, 25 Sep. 2017, https://thewire.in/media/hindustan-times-bobby-ghosh-narendra-modi-shobhana-bhartia, last accessed on 19 July 2018; Kohli, Karnika, 'Times of India takes down a story the BJP finds embarassing, again', *The Wire*, 26 Sep. 2017, https://thewire.in/media/times-of-india-vasundhara-raje-bjp-narendra-modi-press-censorship, last accessed on 19 July 2018. The Wire Staff, 'Anonymous threat to NDTV's Ravish traced to exporter followed by Prime Minister Modi', *The Wire*, 27 Sep. 2017, https://thewire.in/media/anonymous-threat-ndtvs-ravish-traced-exporter-followed-prime-minister-modi, last accessed on 19 July 2018; The Wire Staff, '"Is my life in danger?" Ravish Kumar writes open letter to PM Narenda Modi', *The Wire*, 29 Sep. 2017, https://thewire.in/culture/ravish-kumar-narendra-modi-social-media-trolls-twitter-death-threat, last accessed on 19 July 2018; Pisharoty, Sangeeta Barooah, 'Rajasthan government moves to gag media from reporting on official wrongdoing', *The Wire*, 21 Oct. 2017, https://thewire.in/government/rajasthan-government-moves-gag-media-reporting-official-wrongdoing, last accessed on 19 July 2019; and Gupta, Monobina, 'India's freedoms now rest in the hands of comprador media', *The Wire*, 4 Dec. 2017, https://thewire.in/government/indias-freedoms-now-rest-hands-comprador-media, last accessed on 20 July 2018.

7. The Wire Staff, 'Documentary on Modi's Banaras election as all too real for Censor Board', *The Wire*, 30 Aug. 2015, https://thewire.in/film/documentary-on-modi-kejriwal-electoral-battle-doesnt-pass-muster-with-censors; and Sahu, Manish, 'Right-wing group vandalises home of 'Game of Ayodhya' director Sunil Singh', *Indian Express*, 5 Dec. 2017, https://indianexpress.com/article/india/right-wing-group-vandalises-home-of-game-of-ayodhya-director-sunil-singh-4968313/, last accessed on 19 July 2017.

8. See for example, *Indian Express*, 16 Feb. 2016; *Times of India*, 19 July 2017; *Hindustan Times*, 24 July 2017; and *The Wire*, 24 Aug. 2017. For an article on the undermining of universities, parliament and the federal system, see Krishnan, Kailash K., 'India at 70: Culture of one-party dominance menacing democracy', *The Wire*, 28 Aug. 2017, https://thewire.in/government/india-one-party-dominance-democracy-bjp, last accessed 19 July 2018.

9. See for example, *Scroll.in*, 3 January 2017.

10. See for example, *Indian Express*, 16 Feb., 15 Mar. and 5 Sep. 2016; *The Wire*, 2 May 2016 and 23 and 26 Aug. 2016; and *Economic Times*, 3 Mar. and 25 Aug. 2016.

11. *Business Standard*, 11 April 2016.

12. Peri, Maheshwer, 'One question Prime Minister Narendra Modi needs to focus on: How many jobs have we added?', *Scroll.in*, 26 Apr. 2017, https://scroll.in/article/835704/one-question-prime-minister-narendra-modi-needs-to-focus-onhow-many-jobs-have-we-added.

13. Waghmare, Abhishek, 'Six indicators of India's looming demographic disaster', *Scroll.*

in, 3 May 2016, https://scroll.in/article/807490/six-indicators-of-indias-looming-demographic-disaster. See also Jaffrelot, Christophe, 'India's jobless growth is undermining its ability to reap the demographic dividend', *Indian Express*, 29 Apr. 2016, https://indianexpress.com/article/opinion/columns/economic-survey-india-unemployment-2775236/, last accessed on 19 July 2018.

14. M.K. Venu, 'Reality Check: Is Modi Turning Into a Caricature of Himself?' *The Wire*, 15 Aug. 2016, https://thewire.in/politics/modi-independence-day-speech, last accessed on 20 July 2018.

15. A. Singh, '"Make In India" logo designed by foreign firm, says RTI', *The Times of India*, 14 Jan. 2016, https://timesofindia.indiatimes.com/india/Make-In-India-logo-designed-by-foreign-firm-says-RTI/articleshow/50573386.cms, last accessed on 19 July 2018.

16. D. Mohan, 'Modi's Economics in 2016: More Facade, Less Development', *The Wire*, 5 Jan. 2017, https://thewire.in/economy/india-economy-modi-2016, last accessed on 20 July 2018.

17. '"Make In India" yet to spur manufacturing, says panel', *The Hindu*, 3 Aug. 2017, https://www.thehindu.com/business/make-in-india-yet-to-spur-manufacturing-says-panel/article19420928.ece. See also P. Bardhan, 'The illusion, the reality check', *Indian Express*, 5 Aug. 2017, https://indianexpress.com/article/opinion/columns/narendra-modi-government-corruption-illegal-cash-demonetisation-4782852/, last accessed on 19 July 2018.

18. Punj, Shweta and M.G. Arun, 'No jobs and rising prices behind gloom in economy: Mood of the Nation poll', *India Today*, 18 Aug. 2017, https://www.indiatoday.in/magazine/cover-story/story/20170828-narendra-modi-government-economic-crisis-102 9959-2017-08-18.

19. Confidential communication, 3 Sep. 2017. See also S. Kumar and P. Gupta, 'Public anger over unemployment a big challenge for Modi govt', *Livemint*, 29 June 2017, http://www.im4change.org/latest-news-updates/public-anger-over-unemployment-a-big-challenge-for-modi-govt-sanjay-kumar-and-pranav-gupta-4682196.html, last accessed on 20 July 2018. See also the BJP's Subramanian Swami's argument that the government sought to cook statistics on demonetisation, Express News Service, 'Modi govt pressurised CSO to give out good data on demonetisation, claims Subramanian Swamy', *Indian Express*, 24 Dec. 2017, https://indianexpress.com/article/india/narendra-modi-govt-put-pressure-on-cso-to-give-out-good-data-claims-subramanian-swamy-4996553/; and T. Singh, 'Fifth Column: Not a good week for Modi', *Indian Express*, 24 Dec. 2017, https://indianexpress.com/article/opinion/columns/fifth-column-not-a-good-week-for-narendra-modi-4996393/, last accessed on 20 July 2018.

20. Singh, P., 'PM Modi, The Buck Stops with You', Outlook, 4 September 2017, https://www.outlookindia.com/website/story/pm-modi-the-buck-stops-with-you/301231, last accessed on 19 June 2019.

21. Mehta, P.S. and A. Kulkarni, 'It Is Time to Address India's Abysmal Job Creation Record', The Wire, 25 Nov. 2016, https://thewire.in/economy/india-abysmal-job-creation-record, last accessed on 19 June 2018.

22. Maiorano, D., and J. Manor, 'Poverty Reduction, Inequalities and Human Development

in the BRICS: Policies and Outcomes', *Commonwealth and Comparative Politics*, 55, 3, pp. 278–302.

23. Mohan, Rakesh and Anu Madgavkar, 21 July 2017, 'Labour in India: Quality of quantity counts', *Economic Times* (blog), https://blogs.economictimes.indiatimes.com/et-commentary/labour-in-india-quality-of-quantity-counts/

24. Talukar, Sreemoy, 'Three years of Narendra Modi govt: Opposition is scattered, but unemployment remains biggest headache', *First Post*, 16 May 2017, https://www.firstpost.com/india/three-years-of-narendra-modi-govt-opposition-is-scattered-but-unemployment-remains-biggest-headache-3449582.html.

25. Punj and Arun, op. cit.

26. Kumar, S. and P. Gupta, 'Public Anger over Unemployment a big challenge for Modi govt', *Livemint*, 29 June 2017, https://www.livemint.com/Politics/a55gq3d3Rv R2AXTSV0853I/Public-anger-over-growing-unemployment-a-big-challenge-for-M. html, last accessed on 20 July 2018.

27. Punj and Arun, op. cit.

28. P. Bardhan, Indian Express, 15 Aug. 2017.

29. Lokniti-CSDS-ABP News Gujarat Pre-Election Tracker, Round 3, p. 6. http://www.lokniti.org/pdf/Gujarat-Tracker-3-Report.pdf, last accessed on 19 June 2018.

30. K. Vissa, 'For India's Farmers, Budget 2018 Is Nothing but a Hoax', *The Wire*, 3 Feb. 2017, https://thewire.in/agriculture/indias-farmers-budget-2018-nothing-hoax, last accessed on 19 June 2018.

31. Gulati, A. and S. Saini, 'From Plate to Plough: Raising farmers' income by 2022', *Indian Express*, 28 Mar. 2016, https://indianexpress.com/article/opinion/columns/from-plate-to-plough-raising-farmers-income-by-2022-agriculture-narendra-modi-pradhan-mantri-fasal-bima-yojana/.

32. Dash, Jatindra, Rajesh Kumar Singh, Mayank Bhardwaj, 'PM Modi's promise to double rural income leaves farmers, experts cold', *Reuters*, 8 Apr. 2016, https://in.reuters.com/article/india-farmers-income-modi-economic-growt-idINKCN0X50D4.

33. Vissa, Kirankumar, 'Why the budget is deceptively "pro-farmer"', *The Wire*, 3 Feb. 2017, https://thewire.in/agriculture/why-the-budget-is-deceptively-pro-farmer; Sharma, Devinder, 'Does the banking system really want to help farmers?', *The Wire*, 30 Mar. 2017, https://thewire.in/agriculture/banking-system-farmers-loans

34. Mohan, D., 'Modi's Economics in 2016', *The Wire*, 5 Jan. 2017, https://thewire.in/economy/india-economy-modi-2016, last accessed on 19 June 2018.

35. Gulati and Saini, op. cit.

36. Interview, Sobin George, Bangalore, 23 Aug. 2017. See also *Indian Express*, 2 Sep. 2017, https://missionias.com/current-affairs/the-indian-express-2nd-september-2017/101 92/, last accessed 19 June 2018.

37. Interview with N.C. Saxena, New Delhi, 18 July 2017.

38. Interview with Aruna Roy, Bangalore, 23 July 2017.

39. Gupta, Shekar, 'Modi is by far India's most powerful, domineering, instinctive-and very popular-political figure. Why then is his government floundering?' *India Today*, 20 Aug. 2015, https://www.indiatoday.in/magazine/national-interest/story/20150831-speaking-truth-to-the-great-orator-820310–2015–08–20.

40. *Indian Express*, 12 July 2017.
41. *India Today*, 28 August 2017.
42. Manor, J., 'Currency Crisis', *Nikkei Asian Review*, 13 Jan. 2017. On how a mocking, satirical social media campaign against the BJP went viral: R. Khanna, *Catchnews*, 13 September 2017. See also, S. Sharma, 'No Matter Who Wins Modi is no longer larger than life in Gujarat', *Scroll.in*, 12 Dec. 2017, https://scroll.in/article/861033/no-matter-who-wins-modi-is-no-longer-larger-than-life-in-gujarat, last accessed on 20 July 2018.
43. Mukhopadhyay, N., 'Narendra Modi after Bihar: For whom the polls toll', *Economic Times*, 10 Nov. 2015, https://blogs.economictimes.indiatimes.com/et-commentary/narendra-modi-after-bihar-for-whom-the-polls-toll/, last accessed on 20 July 2018.
44. Such attacks continued during the Gujarat state election campaign in late 2017.
45. This tactic was adeptly used by P.V. Narasimha Rao. See Manor, James, 'The Political Sustainability of Economic Liberalization in India', in R. Cassen and V. Joshi (eds) *India: The Future of Economic Reform*, Delhi: Oxford University Press, 1995, pp. 339–63.
46. Reliable Lokniti surveys charted a marked decline between 2016 and 2017 in the belief that *achhe din* would come, from roughly 60 per cent to 40 per cent. See also *India Today*, 28 Aug. 2017.
47. Chaturvedi, S., 'Demonetisation's Failure Won't Hurt Modi, He's already changed the narrative', *The Wire*, 31 Aug. 2017, https://thewire.in/economy/narendra-modi-demonetisation-failure, last accessed on 20 July 2018.
48. Kohli, K., 'Remplates Tweets', *The Wire*, 2 Sep. 2017: *Economic Times* enquiries revealed 'that ministries have been paying agencies as much as Rs 2 crore [20 million] a year to manage social media...to counter bad publicity', https://thewire.in/politics/narendra-modi-demonetisation-failure-paid-social-media-campaign.
49. Interview with Kaushik Basu, former World Bank Chief Economist, *Indian Express*, 2 Sep. 2017. In the same issue, see also Kumar, D., 'Impact of Demonetisation Lingers On': 'growth is on a secular declining path from October–December 2015' from 9.1 per cent to 5.7 per cent, lower than China's. The Asian Development Bank echoed this view (PTI report, *The Hindu*, 13 Dec. 2017).
50. Singh, P., 'PM Modi, The Buck...'.
51. In a mid-2017 poll, 24 per cent found Modi 'not afraid of taking risks', but ominously for him, 23 per cent said that 'he is all talk and no action'. *India Today*, 28 Aug. 2017.
52. Polling shows this to be his most popular action. Ibid.
53. Manor, J., 'India's States: The Struggle to Govern', *Studies in Indian Politics*, 4, 1, (2016) pp. 8–21. Last accessed on 19 June 2018. http://journals.sagepub.com/doi/abs/10.1177/2321023016634909; and Singh, T., 'Fifth Column: The past is still with us', *Indian Express*, 11 Mar. 2018, https://indianexpress.com/article/opinion/columns/rewriting-history-tavleen-singh-indian-civilisation-nehru-rss-hindutva-secular-fifth-column-the-past-is-still-with-us-5093411/, last accessed on 19 June 2018.
54. Manor, J., 'Modi Stuck between Two Promises', *Nikkei Asian Review*, 27 June 2015, https://asia.nikkei.com/NAR/Articles/James-Manor-Modi-stuck-between-two-promises, last accessed on 19 June 2018.

55. *The Hindu*, 25 and 26 Aug. 2017.

56. ENS, *Indian Express*, 8 Oct. 2014.

57. Editorial, *The Hindu*, 6 Jan. 2015.

58. Shaikh, Z., *Indian Express*, 6 Jan. 2015.

59. ENS, *Indian Express*, 6 Jan. 2015.

60. PTI, 'Dadri Lynching', *PTI*, 2 Oct. 2015; and BBC, 1 October 2015.

61. Varadarajan, S., *The Wire*, 8 Aug. 2016. See also *The Wire*, 21 Mar. 2017; and *Indian Express*, 1 Aug. 2017.

62. Mehta, P.B., 'May the Silent be damned', *Indian Express*, 27 June 2017, https://indianexpress.com/article/opinion/columns/junaid-pehlu-khan-mob-lynching-religion-minorities-hindu-muslim-politics-4723451/, last accessed on 20 July 2018. At that time, the BJP did not rule that state. For other examples of blaming victims, see *The Wire*, 3 Aug. 2016; Apoorvanand, 'The BJP's communal strategy failed in Bihar. So why are Modi and Shah repeating it in Uttar Pradesh?', *Scroll.in*, 22 Feb. 2017, https://scroll.in/article/829964/the-bjps-communal-strategy-failed-in-bihar-so-why-are-modi-and-shah-repeating-it-in-uttar-pradesh, last accessed on 20 July 2018; Rathi, N., 'Mob, political complicity provide convenient cover to gau rakshaks to operate', *Indian Express*, 28 Apr. 2017, https://indianexpress.com/article/opinion/web-edits/mob-provides-a-convenient-cover-to-gau-rakshaks-operate-political-complicity-4630599/, last accessed on 20 July 2018; Hindustan Times, 'Why have cops filed case against dead Mumbai biker for negligent driving? Experts break it down', *Hindustan Times*, 24 July 2017, ProQuest (1922442140); *Frontline*, 21 July 2017; Bhattacharjee, M. F., 'The Lynching of a Nation', *The Wire*, 25 June 2017, https://thewire.in/communalism/the-lynching-of-a-nation, last accessed on 20 July 2018. That last article (drawing on an initial report in *The Telegraph*) lists numerous cases in which victims were blamed and sometimes charged with crimes.

63. Wire Staff, 'Dalit Family Stripped, Beaten As 'Gau Raksha' Vigilantism Continues', *The Wire*, 13 July 2016, https://thewire.in/politics/dalit-family-stripped-beaten-as-gau-raksha-vigilantism-continues, last accessed on 20 July 2018.

64. Hindustan Times, 'Video: Couple assaulted over suspicion of carrying beef speak out', *Hindustan Times*, 15 Jan. 2016, https://www.hindustantimes.com/india/mp-muslim-couple-assaulted-on-a-train-for-carrying-beef/story-No6DGrWDiXzpKk2W-psL5KM.html.

65. Sharma, Vishal, 'Cow activist, 4 others held after 2 Muslim cowherds hanged to death', *Hindustan Times*, 25 Apr. 2018, https://www.hindustantimes.com/india/five-arrested-after-two-muslim-cowherds-hanged-to-death-in-jharkhand/story-KcHi7nNS22Y-6CXAych5eBJ.html

66. Sikdar, Shubhomoy, 'Three students beaten up in Begampur' *The Hindu*, 31 Mar. 2016, https://www.thehindu.com/news/cities/Delhi/three-students-beaten-up-in-begampur/article8411359.ece.

67. Press Trust of India 'Those who don't say "Bharat Mata Ki Jai" have no right to stay in India: Fadnavis', *The Hindu*, 1 Apr. 2016, https://www.thehindu.com/news/national/other-states/those-who-dont-say-bharat-mata-ki-jai-have-no-right-to-stay-in-india-fadnavis/article8429147.ece

68. Palshikar, S., 'Where Freedom Has Gone', *Indian Express*, 21 Aug. 2017. https://indianexpress.com/profile/columnist/suhas-palshikar/ Last accessed on 19 June 2018.

69. *The Hindu*, 6 March 2016. Last accessed on 19 June 2018.

70. Wire Staff, *The Wire*, 3 August 2016. https://thewire.in/ Last accessed on 19 June 2018.

71. Wire Staff, *The Wire*, 3 August 2016. https://thewire.in/ Last accessed on 19 June 2018.

72. Santosh Kumar, R.B. 'Cow Vigilantes', *Indian Express*, 24 July 2016, https://indianexpress.com/article/india/india-news-india/cow-vigilantes-in-chikmagalur-seven-from-bajrang-dal-booked-for-attacking-dalits-2932283/, last accessed on 19 June 2018.

73. Modi's constant public statements on a vast array of topics are carefully calculated. So are his silences on this one.

74. Jha, P.S., 'Cow Vigilantism Is Tearing Apart India's Social Fabric', *The Wire*, 24 Oct. 2016, https://thewire.in/communalism/cow-vigilantism-tearing-apart-indias-social-fabric, last accessed on 19 June 2018.

75. Ghatwai, M., 'Cops on Run after RSS Man's Arrest...', *Indian Express*, 17 Oct. 2016, https://indianexpress.com/article/india/india-news-india/cops-on-run-after-rss-mans-arrest-families-say-hounded-for-doing-job-3085276/, last accessed on 19 June 2018.

76. *Hindustan Times*, 24 July 2017. https://www.hindustantimes.com/, last accessed on 19 June 2018.

77. Bhattacharjee, Manash Firaq, 'The Lynching of a Nation', *The Wire*, 25 June 2017, https://thewire.in/communalism/the-lynching-of-a-nation, last accessed on 19 June 2018.

78. Bhalla, S., 'Cow vigilantism—or minority hunting?', *Indian Express*, 12 April 2017, https://indianexpress.com/article/opinion/columns/cow-vigilantism-or-minority-hunting-ajmer-lynching-gau-rakshaks-bjp-rajasthan-hindu-muslim-4609449/, last accessed on 25 June 2018.

79. *Scroll.in*, 21 Apr. 2017.

80. *The Wire*, 28 Apr. 2017.

81. Trivedi, D., 'Hatred unleashed', *Frontline*, 21 July 2017, https://www.frontline.in/cover-story/hatred-unleashed/article9748029.ece, last accessed on 25 June 2018.

82. Singh, T., *Indian Express*, 7 May 2017.

83. Venu, M.K., *The Wire*, 23 Apr. 2017. See also Sahu, M., *Indian Express*, 23 Apr. 2017.

84. *The Hindu*, 16 Apr. 2017, https://netajiias.com/the-hindu-newspaper-16-april-2017-free-pdf-download/?nocache=1, last accessed on 20 June 2018.

85. Singh, T., *Indian Express*, 7 May 2017.

86. Iqbal, M., *The Hindu*, 24 Apr. 2017.

87. Bhattacharjee, M.F., 'The Lynching of a Nation'.

88. *The Hindu*, 18 June 2017.

89. *Scroll.in*, 22 May and 1 July 2017. See also *The Hindu*, 18 June, and 16 and 17 Aug. 2017.

90. *New York Times*, 6 June 2017.

91. *Indian Express*, 20 Mar. 2017. Adityanath's own pre-election affidavit in 2017 listed the following criminal charges standing against him: two counts of 'injuring of

defiling a place of worship with intent to insult the religion of any class', two of 'Promoting enmity between different groups on grounds of religion...', two of 'rioting armed with a deadly weapon', one of 'Mischief by fire or explosive substance...', one of criminal intimidation, and one of attempted murder (Scroll Staff, 'Hindutva Unleashed', *Scroll.in*, 18 Mar. 2017). In 2015, he had remained silent from the chair as a supporter 'gave a call to dig up the graves of Muslim women and rape them' (PTI report, *The Wire*, 18 Mar. 2017). In January 2018, the government that he headed announced that it would not permit prosecutions on the charges that he faced. Adityanath had given amnesty to Adityanath.

92. Indian Express, 27 June 2017. See also in Frontline's cover story, 21 July 2017, the ominous comments by Mahant Nritya Gopal Das, and retired high court Justice Rajinder Sachar's reference to "an oppressive regime that literally wants to do away with minorities".

93. See for example 2017 reports from an array of states in *Hindustan Times*, 19 and 24 July and 4 Sep.; *The Hindu*, 8, 10, 11 and 21 July; *Scroll.in*, 6, 12 and 25 July; *The Wire*, 29 July, 3, 21 Aug., 23 Sep. and 14 Oct.; *Indian Express*, 11–14 July, 5 Aug. and 13 Nov.; *Deccan Chronicle*, 16 and 28 Aug. In Uttar Pradesh in July, 5,000 Hindu 'religious soldiers' were being trained to 'fight like commandos' to control cow smuggling (*Hindustan Times*, 20 July 2017). In August, the BJP chief minister of Chhattisgarh said that he would 'hang' cow killers. *The Wire*, 21 August 2017 deals with multiple incidents. For a spate of attacks on Christians as Christmas approached, see *Scroll.in*, 17, 19, 20 and 22 December 2017.

94. Gopalakrishnan, S., 'Are Saffron Groups Bringing Mob rule to one of India's Last Peaceful States?', *The Wire*, 23 Sep. 2017, https://thewire.in/politics/uttarakhand-bjp-saffron-groups, last accessed on 25 June 2018.

95. *Hindustan Times*, 6 Sep. 2017.

96. *The Hindu*, 17 Dec. 2014.

97. 'Radical Shift', *The Caravan*, 1 Nov. 2015 http://www.caravanmagazine.in/perspectives/radical-shift-sangh-loosening-grip-fringe-elements, last accessed 19 June 2018.

98. For example, after describing that murder as 'unfortunate', he then expressed distaste for 'pseudo-secularism' which in the BJP's formulation entails the appeasement of minorities. Ibid. and Bhattacharjee, M.F., *The Wire*, 25 June 2017.

99. In late August, Modi deplored violence in the name of religion, but he spoke immediately after anti-government riots by devotees of a guru who had been convicted of serious crimes. On that occasion, his reference to violence in 'one part of the country' focused on that episode rather than on attacks against Muslims. *Deccan Herald*, 28 Aug. 2017.

100. Apoorvanand, 'The BJP's Communal Strategy Failed in Bihar, So Why are Modi and Shah Repeating it in Uttar Pradesh?', *Scroll.in*, 22 Feb. 2017, https://scroll.in/article/829964/the-bjps-communal-strategy-failed-in-bihar-so-why-are-modi-and-shah-repeating-it-in-uttar-pradesh, last accessed 25 June 2018.

101. Mehta, P.B., 'Power and Insecurity', *Indian Express*, 13 Dec. 2017. Similarly, during the 2015 Bihar election campaign, he had spoken, implausibly, of a 'devious plan', a 'conspiracy' to take reservations from Dalits and 'backward' castes and to give them

to Muslims. These claims failed to convince. See Manor, J., 'Undone by Their Own Mistakes: How the BJP Lost Bihar', *Economic and Political Weekly*, 5 March 2016, p. 65. On the Gujarat campaign, see Achom, D., 'Congress Clapped...', *NDTV Convergence*, 27 Nov. 2017.

102. Bal, H.S., 'Radical Shift', *The Caravan*, 1 Nov. 2015, http://www.caravanmagazine. in/perspectives/radical-shift-sangh-loosening-grip-fringe-elements, last accessed on 21 June 2018.

103. *Economic Times*, 16 Dec. 2014.

104. Singh, S. in the *Indian Express*, 5 Aug. 2017.

105. Apoorvanand, 'Gau Rakshaks Rejoice', *The Wire*, 21 Aug. 2017, https://thewire.in/ communalism/bihar-nitish-kumar-cow-vigilantism, last accessed on 21 June 2018.

106. Bal, H.S., 'The Sangh's Loosening Grip on Its Fringe Elements', *The Caravan*, 1 Nov. 2015, http://www.caravanmagazine.in/perspectives/radical-shift-sangh-loosening-grip-fringe-elements, last accessed on 21 June 2018.

107. Gopal, N., Bengaluru: *Deccan Chronicle*, 2017.

108. Manor, 'Undone by their own Mistakes: How the BJP Lost Bihar', *Economic and Political Weekly*, 51, 10 (2016). https://www.epw.in/journal/2016/10/special-articles/undone-its-own-mistakes.html, last accessed on 21 June 2018.

109. Manor, J., 'In Part a Myth: The BJP's Organisational Strength', in K. Adeney and L. Saez (eds), *Coalition Politics and Hindu Nationalism*, New Delhi and London: Routledge, 2005, pp. 55–74.

110. I am grateful to Sanjay Kumar for this information.

111. Manor, J., 'An Odisha Landslide Buries Both National Parties: Assessing the State and Parliamentary Elections of 2014', *Contemporary South Asia* 23, 2, (2015) pp. 198–210. https://doi.org/10.1080/09584935.2015.1019426. Last accessed on 21 June 2018.

112. Farmers' discontents with unfulfilled promises are already emerging. Parth, M.N., 'In the Quest for Promised Relief, Farmers in Maharashta Are facing Further Losses', *The Wire*, 4 Sep. 2017, https://thewire.in/agriculture/farmers-maharashtra-interim-relief, last accessed on 21 June 2018.

113. This was a Lokniti survey in Gujarat, Karnataka, Odisha and Uttar Pradesh. I am grateful to Sanjay Kumar and Siddharth Swaminathan for this information. The final version of this study will be published soon.

114. Interview with a meticulous analyst of UP election statistics, New Delhi, 13 July 2017.

115. Manor, 'Undone by Its Own Mistakes: How the BJP Lost Bihar', *Economic and Political Weekly*, 51, 10 (2016). https://www.epw.in/journal/2016/10/special-articles/undone-its-own-mistakes.html, last accessed 21 June 2018.

116. Chapter four of Jha, D.K., *Shadow Armies: Fringe Organizations and Footsoldiers of Hindutva*, New Delhi: Juggernaut, 2017, pp. 96–7 and 100.

117. Manor, J., 'Lucky in Its Adversaries: A Slipshod Congress Gains a Majority in the Karnataka Election', *Economic and Political Weekly*, 48, 47 (2013) p. 53, https://www. epw.in/journal/2013/47/special-articles/lucky-its-adversaries.html, last accessed on 21 June 2018. Polarisation also backfired in September 2014 UP by-elections. The BJP got Yogi Adityanath 'to deliver a string of hate speeches' but then lost. Roy, S., *Business Standard*, 23 Sep. 2014.

118. BJP chief ministers who gained re-election in this way include Shekhawat (Rajasthan), Chouhan (Madhya Pradesh) and Raman Singh (Chhattisgarh).

119. Manor, James, '"Ethnicity" and politics in India', *International Affairs*, 72, 3 (May 1996), pp. 459–75, http://www.jstor.org/stable/2625551, last accessed on 20 Jun. 2018.

120. *Hindustan Times*, 16 July 2017.

121. Manor, James, 'The Trouble with Yeddyurappa', *Economic and Political Weekly*, 44, 13 (26 Mar. 2011), pp. 16–19. http://www.jstor.org/stable/41152276, last accessed on 20 Jun. 2018.

7. SANGH AND SARKAR: THE RSS POWER CENTRE SHIFTS FROM NAGPUR TO NEW DELHI

1. FP Staff, 'Mohan Bhagwat's Vijaya Dashmi speech: Key takeaways from the RSS chief's annual address', *FirstPost*, 1 Oct 2017, https://www.firstpost.com/india/mohan-bhag-wats-vijaya-dashmi-speech-key-takeaways-from-the-rss-chiefs-annual-address-4096745.html, last accessed on 28 June 2018. In 1925, Dr K.B. Hedgewar founded the RSS on the Vijaya Dashmi day at Nagpur. Since then, every year, on this day, the RSS chief (*Sarsanghchalak*) delivers his Vijaya Dashmi Speech at Nagpur. After the Modi government came to power in New Delhi, this speech has been broadcasted on the state-run Doordarshan and All India Radio, thus demonstrating the Indian state's awe and respect for the RSS.

2. Sharma, Hemender, 'Dattatreya Hosable of RSS: Probe Jay Shah only if prima facie charges true", *India Today*, 12 Oct. 2017, https://www.indiatoday.in/india/story/dat-tatreya-hosabale-rss-general-secretary-jay-shah-yashwant-sinha-amit-shah-1062996-2017-10-12, last accessed on 28 June 2018. 'The annual Dussehra speech of the sarsanghchalak in Nagpur is sort of a policy document for us. This year we decided to take this policy document to opinion makers of the country. A healthy democracy requires a healthy discussion and we have got positive feedback on our policy document.' RSS joint general secretary Dattatreya Hosabole's interview, 12 Oct. 2017.

3. Bhagwat appeared to have more political clout than his former counterpart Rajendra Singh, who only addressed to the top UP bureaucrats and police officers during the Vajpayee government. See Pralay Kanungo, *RSS's Tryst with Politics: From Hedgewar to Sudarshan*, New Delhi: Manohar, 2002, p. 259.

4. Ramachandran, Smriti Kak, 'RSS does not support trolling, says its chief Mohan Bhagwat', *The Hindustan Times*, 13 Sep. 2017, https://www.hindustantimes.com/india-news/rss-does-not-support-trolling-says-its-chief-mohan-bhagwat/story-5KlOgpfCB-mAMGXiSzZguBK.html, last accessed on 28 June 2018. This oft-repeated defence looks hollow as the RSS has been out in the open to control the party and influence governance.

5. While this once looked like a rhetoric, it now looks closer to reality as the BJP has already brought twenty-two out of thirty states under its control, systematically wiping out the Congress, state after state, which included its strong bastion, the northeast of India.

6. Deshpande, Vivek, 'Bhagwat pats Modi govt, pushes Swadeshi model of development',

The Indian Express. 4 Oct. 2014, https://indianexpress.com/article/india/india-others/rss-chief-praises-modi-govt-for-good-governance/, last accessed on 28 June 2014.

7. 'Full text of Speech by RSS Sarasanghchalak Mohan Bhagwat on Vijaya Dashmi—2014, Nagpur', *Samvada*, http://samvada.org/2014/news/full-text-of-speech-by-rss-sarasanghchalak-mohan-bhagwat-on-vijaya-dashmi-2014-nagpur/, last accessed on 28 June 2018.

8. Satyapal Singh, a former police commissioner, who became minister of state in the Ministry of Human Resources Development, claimed that Darwin's theory was 'scientifically wrong' and should be removed from the curriculum; though he later retracted this statement.

9. Kanungo, Pralay, 'A Yogi for New India', *Outlook*, 3 Apr. 2017, https://www.outlookindia.com/magazine/story/a-yogi-for-new-india/298651, last accessed on 27 June 2018.

10. Raza, Danish, 'Saffronising textbooks: Where myth and dogma replace history', *Hindustan Times*, 8 Dec 2014, https://www.hindustantimes.com/india/saffronising-textbooks-where-myth-and-dogma-replace-history/story-CauM4dmmsPGrjZ3A-PAvNxO.html, last accessed on 27 June 2018.

11. The Telegraph, 'Sangh chief addresses 50 varsity heads', *The Telegraph*, 27 Mar. 2017, https://www.telegraphindia.com/1170327/jsp/nation/story_142942.jsp, last accessed on 27 June 2018.

12. Press Trust of India, 'India is a Hindu nation and Hindutva is its identity, says RSS chief Mohan Bhagwat', *The Indian Express*, 18 Aug. 2014, https://indianexpress.com/article/india/india-others/india-is-a-hindu-nation-and-hindutva-is-its-identity-says-rss-chief-mohan-bhagwat/, last accessed on 27 June 2018.

13. Majumdar, Arkamoy Dutta, 'Indian Muslims must realise their forefathers were Hindus: RSS chief Mohan Bhagwat', *Livemint.com*, 3 Oct. 2017, https://www.livemint.com/Politics/Aw7CTiZsBdXqsmCKvwmyHO/Indian-Muslims-must-realise-their-forefathers-were-Hindus-R.html, last accessed on 27 June 2018.

14. 'RSS Akhil Bharatiya Karyakari Mandal (ABKM) baitak from 12th Oct to 14th Oct', *Samvada.org*, 12 Oct. 2017. http://samvada.org/2017/news/rss-akhil-bharatiya-karyakari-mandalabkm-baitak-12–14-oct-2017/, last accessed on 28 June 2018.

15. PTI, 'RSS can prepare an army within 3 days: Mohan Bhagwat', *The Times of India*, 12 Feb. 2018, https://timesofindia.indiatimes.com/india/rss-can-prepare-an-army-within-3-days-mohan-bhagwat/articleshow/62877231.cms, last accessed on 28 June 2018.

16. The RSS gracefully purges unwanted top *pracharaks* by sending them on 'sabbatical'; for instance, the erudite K.N. Govindacharya went to oblivion after his sabbatical. But Soni is still holds the position of the *sah-karyavah* and has been back in the ring.

17. Kumar, Santosh, 'Parivar-party-government synergy is the new buzzword', *India Today*, 11 June 2015, https://www.indiatoday.in/magazine/special-report/story/20150622-rss-modi-opposition-saffron-parivar-mohan-bhagwat-819861–2015–06–11, last accessed on 28 June 2018.

18. Press Trust of India, 'Govt moving in the right direction, we are not reviewing it: RSS', *The Tribune*, 4 Sep. 2015, http://www.tribuneindia.com/news/nation/govt-moving-

in-right-direction-we-are-not-reviewing-it-rss/128670.html, last accessed on 28 June 2018.

8. HOW THE SANGH PARIVAR WRITES AND TEACHES HISTORY

1. All India Press Trust of India, 2 July 2017 reported Junaid's killing. Afrazul's death was reported in Mander, Harsh, John Dayal, and Kavita Shrivastava, 'Rajasthan hate murder: The other tragedy in Afrazul's killing is a famine of compassion, outrage', *Scroll.in*, 18 Dec. 2017, https://scroll.in/article/861826/rajasthan-hate-murder-the-other-tragedy-in-afrazul-khans-murder-is-a-famine-of-compassion-outrage.

2. Hindutva is different from Hinduism as the faith of Hindus. It is the self designation of an organisational combine. The term was coined by V.D Savarkar in 1923, who claimed that it referred to the cultural essence of Indian nationhood. We will discuss this later (see Savarkar, Vinayak Damodar, *Hindutva: Who Is A Hindu*, 1923; reprint Delhi: Bharatiya Sadan, 1989.

3. The RSS, which calibrates the entire Hindutva combine, was founded in 1925.

4. Akhil Bharatiya Itihas Sankalan Yojana, *Visions and Perspectives*. Delhi: ABISY, 1973; Akhil Bharatiya Itihas Sankalan Yojana, *Itihas Darpan*, Apr. Delhi: ABISY, 2016; Akhil Bharatiya Itihas Sankalan Yojana, *Itihas Darpan*, Oct. Delhi: ABISY, 2016.

5. Sarkar, Tanika, 'Educating the Children of Hindu Rashtra: RSS Schools in Delhi', in C. Jaffrelot (ed.), *The Sangh Parivar: A Reader*, Delhi: Oxford University Press, 2005; Scroll, 'India: RSS Schools in the Hindu Nationalist Education Project', 2009 *Scroll. in.*; Bakaya, Akshay, 'Indianise, nationalise, spiritualise: The RSS education project is in expansion mode', *Scroll.in*, 30 Aug. 2016, https://scroll.in/article/815049/indianise-nationalise-spiritualise-the-rss-education-project-is-in-for-the-long-haul.

6. For the BJP, see Basu, Amrita, *Violent Conjunctures in Democratic India*. UK: Cambridge University Press, 2014.

7. On this, see Sarkar, 'Educating the Children of Hindu Rashtra: RSS Schools in Delhi', op. cit.; Scroll, 2016, op. cit.

8. *Ancient India* (Textbook for Class XI), Delhi: NCERT, 2002; *Contemporary India* (Textbook for Class IX), Delhi: NCERT, 2002.

9. CPDHE, *Orientation Course 90*, Delhi University, Winter School, unpublished, 2017; *Orientation Course 91*, Delhi University, Winter School, unpublished, 2017; *Refresher Course on Indian Thought, Culture and Thinking (Bharatiya Bodh)*, Delhi University, Winter School, unpublished, 2017. Some teachers attending the lectures handed their notes to me. A report on the course was also published (see The Wire, 'Hindutva Politics in Command at Delhi University: Complaint of Teacher (Dis)orientation', *The Wire*, 19 Feb. 2018, https://thewire.in/education/hindutva-politics-command-du-complaints-mount-disorientation-teachers.

10. Akhil Bharatiya Itihas Sankalan Yojana, *Visions and Perspectives*, op. cit.; *Itihas Darpan*, Apr. Delhi: ABISY, 2013; *Itihas Darpan*, Oct. Delhi: ABISY, 2013; *Itihas Darpan*, Oct. Delhi: ABISY, 2013; *Itihas Darpan*, Apr. Delhi: ABISY, 2016; *Itihas Darpan*, Oct. Delhi: ABISY, 2016.

11. On the restructuring of the Indian Council of Historical Research, see Chopra, Ritika,

'Office-bearer of RSS history wing set to join ICHR', *The Indian Express*, 21 Jan. 2017, https://indianexpress.com/article/india/office-bearer-of-rss-history-wing-set-to-join-indian-council-of-historical-research-4484453/.

12. Sarkar, Tanika, 'Hindutva's Hinduism', in Zavos, J., P. Kanungo, D.S. Reddy, M. Warrier, E. Williams (eds), *Public Hinduisms*, Delhi: Sage, 2012.

13. See chapter 2 of Basu, T. et al., *Khaki Shorts and Saffron Flags: A Critique of the Hindu Right*. Delhi: Orient Longman, 1993; Katju, Manjari, 'The Bajrang Dal and Durga Vahini', in C. Jaffrelot (ed.), *The Sangh Parivar: A Reader*, Delhi: Oxford University Press, 2005; Mathur, Shubh, *The Everyday Life of Hindu Nationalism: An Ethnographic Account*. Delhi: The Three Essays Collective, 2008

14. On the 'historical' arguments used in the *Ramjanambhhomi* campaign, see, Bhattacharya, Neeladri, 'Myth, history and the politics of Ramjanambhhomi', in Sarvepalli Gopal (ed.), *Anatomy of A Confrontation*, New Delhi: Viking, 1991. See also 'The Many Worlds of Indian History' for the larger historical agenda in Sarkar, Sumit, *Writing Social History*. Delhi: Oxford University Press, 1997.

15. Firstpost, 'History according to puranas: RSS's next big project', *Firstpost*, 18 Aug. 2014, https://www.firstpost.com/politics/history-according-to-puranas-rsss-next-big-project-1669673.html.

16. For the different wings under the Sangh, see, Jaffrelot, C. (ed.), *The Sangh Parivar: A Reader*, Delhi: Oxford University Press, 2005; Basu, et al., op. cit.

17. Hansen, Thomas Blom, *Wages of Violence: Naming and Identity in Postcolonial Bombay*, Princeton: Princeton University Press, 2001, pp. 37–101.

18. Savarkar, V.D., *Six Glorious Epochs of Indian History*, S.T Godbole (trans. and ed.), second edition, Bombay: Veer Savarkar Prakashan, 1985.

19. Ibid., pp. 1–2.

20. Ibid., pp. 411–17.

21. Ibid., p. 4.

22. Savarkar (1923), as quoted in Jaffrelot, Christophe (ed), *Hindu Nationalism: A Reader*, Princeton: Princeton University Press, 2007. pp. 94–5.

23. Though the constitution designates it as official language, the BJP has recently asked the UN to make it our national language (Mathew, Liz, 'Making Hindi Official Language', *The Indian Express*, 6 Jan. 2017).

24. Jaffrelot, Christophe, *Hindu Nationalism: A Reader*. Delhi: Permanent Black, 2009, p. 2.

25. Savarkar, *Six Glorious Epochs*, p. 143.

26. Ibid., pp. 157–9.

27. Savarkar, V.D., *The Six Glorious Epochs of Indian History*, Delhi: Rajdhani Granthagar, 1971, pp. 85, 131.

28. Interview granted to T. Basu, Sumit and Tanika Sarkar, P.K. Datta and Sambudha Sen, Feb. 1991.

29. Hegde, Anantkumar. 'If not for #Buddhism, we would have had an #AkhandBharath & #Islam would have met a more stiff resistance in the desert itself!' Twitter, 4 Apr. 2017, https://twitter.com/AnantkumarH/status/851648443512520704; Sinha, Pratik, 'Newly sworn Minister Anantkumar Hegde's Twitter account gives a peek into

his mindset', Alt News, 4 Sep. 2017, https://www.altnews.in/newly-sworn-minister-anantkumar-hegdes-twitter-account-gives-peek-mindset/.

30. Savarkar, *The Six Glorious Epochs of Indian History*, op. cit. pp. 129–30.
31. Savarkar, *Hindutva*, op. cit.
32. Ibid.
33. Savarkar, *The Six Glorious Epochs of Indian History*, op. cit., pp. 129–30.
34. Ibid., p. 130
35. On actual imperial practices of Muslim rulers, see Raziuddin Aquil's excellent and balanced historical account: Aquil, Raziuddin, *In the Name of Allah: Understanding Islam and Indian History*, Delhi: Penguin, 2009.
36. Sarkar, *Writing Social History*, op. cit.
37. Ibid.
38. On the recent violence under the Hindu Right-wing Karni Sena on the representation of the legend in the film, *Padmavati*, later renamed *Padmaavat* (2018, dir. Sanjay Leela Bhansali), see *Indian Express*, 17 and 21 Nov 2017.
39. Basu, et al.,1993, op. cit., chapter 2.
40. Ibid., p. 172
41. Against Junaid Khan and against Afrazul Mohammad, in June and December 2017, respectively, for instance, who were killed brutally just because they are Muslims: see Times of India, 'Accused in Junaid Khan's murder case has confessed: Haryana police', *Times of India*, 10 July 2017, https://timesofindia.indiatimes.com/city/delhi/accused-in-junaid-case-has-confessed-police/articleshow/59518467.cms: Afrazul was killed in revenge for so called 'Love Jihad' or abduction of Hindu women by Muslim men, though he was not personally involved in any cross community romance. His murder was filmed and triumphantly circulated on the social media. See Menon, Shruti, 'Behind Rajasthan killing, mistaken identity, "love jihad" lie, hate clips', NDTV, 6 Dec. 2017, https://www.ndtv.com/india-news/behind-rajasthan-killing-mistaken-identity-love-jihad-lie-hate-videos-1792369.
42. Taken from Agha Shahid Ali, 'Your history gets in the way of my memory'; see https://fingerprintsonglass.wordpress.com/2015/02/10/my-memory-keeps-getting-in-the-way-of-your-history-four-poems-by-agha-shahid-ali/.
43. Ibid., p. 169.
44. Basu, et al., 1993, op. cit., p. 461.
45. Keer, Dhananjay, *Veer Savarkar*. Bombay: Popular Prakashan, 1966; Longkumer, Arkotong, *Reform, Identity and Narratives of Belonging: The Heraka Movement in North East India*. London: Continuum International, 2010, p. 539.
46. Lecture on 25 Nov. 2017 by Aseervathan Achary, retired Railways Department official and now BJP *karyakarta* or officeholder, lecturing to college teachers at Delhi University (CPDHE *Orientation Course 90, 91*, 2017 op. cit.).
47. Savarkar, 2003, op. cit. pp. 146–8.
48. See Jaffrelot, 2009, op. cit. p. 91–2; Basu, et al., op. cit. 1993, chapter 1.
49. Sarkar, Sumit and Sarkar, Tanika, *Caste in Modern India: A Reader*, Delhi: Orient Black Swan, 2013.
50. 'Hindutva' cited in Jaffrelot, 2009, op. cit. p. 92

51. Bhatt, Chetan, *Hindu Nationalism: Origins, Ideologies and Modern Myths*, London: Berg Publishers, 2001.

52. Golwalkar, M.S., *We, or Our Nationhood Defined*, Nagpur: Bharat Prakashan, 1938.

53. Rao, Shrenik, 'Hitler's Hindus: The rise and rise of India's Nazi-loving nationalists', *Haaretz*, 14 Dec. 2017, https://www.haaretz.com/opinion/hitlers-hindus-indias-nazi-loving-nationalists-on-the-rise-1.5628532.

54. Hameed, Syeda, 'No country for Afrazul', *The Indian Express*, 12 Dec. 2017, https://indianexpress.com/article/opinion/columns/no-country-for-afrazul-khan-rajasthan-hacking-hate-crime-4978472/.

55. Mohan, 'Indianise, nationalise, spiritualise', op. cit.

56. Bhattacharya, Nandgopal, *Moulabader Khama Nei*, Calcutta: Nabapatra Prakashan, 1994, p. 45.

57. Roy, Esha, 'Dateline Naxalbari', *The Indian Express*, 25 June 2018, https://indianexpress.com/article/india/dateline-naxalbari-bjp-left-naxals-in-north-bengal-land-grabbing-cases-4665880/.

58. Jafrelot, Christophe. 'Hindu Nationalism and the Social Welfare Strategy: Seva Bharati as an Educational Agency', in Jaffrelot, C. ed. *Sangh Parivar: A Reader*. Delhi: Oxford University Press, 2005. [0]

59. Scroll, 2016 op. cit.; Sarkar, Tanika, 2005, op.cit.

60. Bharati, op.cit.

61. Ibid.

62. Sarkar 2005 op.cit.

63. Scroll 2016 op.cit.

64. NCERT, *Ancient India* (Textbook for Class XII), Delhi: NCERT 2002, pp. 1–2,

65. Ibid., p. 3.

66. Ibid., p. 14.

67. Ibid., p. 20.

68. NCERT, *Contemporary History* (Textbook for Class XI), Delhi: NCERT, 2002, p. 4.

69. Ibid., p. 7.

70. Ibid., p. 5.

71. Ibid., p. 6.

72. Ibid.

73. Chopra, Ritika, 'More Space in School textbooks for ancient Indian Knowledge Systems and Tradition', *The Indian Express*, 29 May 2018; Chopra, Ritika, 'A New Set of Nationalist Icons', *The Indian Express*, 30 May 2018.

74. Scroll, 2009, 'India: RSS Schools in the Hindu Nationalist Education Project', *Scroll. in.*

75. Agarwal, Ranjana, *Orientation Course*, Kurukshetra University, unpublished, 2017.

76. Dr Nirmal Jain, Lecturer, Satyavati College, 25 Nov. 2017.

77. Pathetically, Sudarshan Ramabhadran, Deputy Director, India Foundation, mentions a list of such scholars, including 'Harvard educated' Diana Eck, 5 Dec. 2017.

78. Jha, Anurag, 24 Nov. 2017.

79. Achary, Asservathan, 25 Nov. 2017. Also Ganguly, Anirban, 27 Nov. 2017.

80. Kumar, Kapil, 28 Nov. 2017.

81. See Chakrabarty, Dipesh, *The Calling of History: Sir Jadunath Sarkar and his Empire of Truth*, Chicago: University of Chicago Press, 2015.

82. Kumar, Kapil, 28 Nov. 2017.

83. Chopra, 'Office-bearer of RSS history wing set to join ICHR', op. cit.

84. Firstpost, op. cit.

85. Journal published by ABISY, literally translating to 'Mirror of History'.

86. *Itihas Darpan*, Apr. Delhi: ABISY, 2013.

87. Solomon, Richard, *Indian Epigraphy: A Guide to the Study of Inscriptions in Sanskrit, Prakrit and Other Indo-European Languages*, Delhi: Munshiram Manoharlal, 1998, pp. 180–81.

88. *Adivasis, Janjatis* are common words to refer to tribal groups.

89. The Hindustan Times, 21 Aug. 2014, Delhi: *Hindustan Times*; The Indian Express. 18 Aug. 2014, Delhi: *Indian Express*.

90. Berti, Daniela, 'The memory of Gods: From a secret autobiography to a nationalist project', *Indian Folklife*, 24 (Oct. 2006), pp. 15–18.

91. Berti, Daniela, 'Hindu nationalists and local history: From ideology to local lore. *Rivista Di Studi Sudasiatici*, 2, 1 (2008), pp. 7–38.

92. Ibid., pp. 6–9.

93. Ibid., pp. 19–26.

94. Thomas, John, 'From sacred rocks to temple: Recasting religion as identity in north eastern India' in N. Bhattacharya and J. Pachuau (eds), *Landscape, Culture and Belonging: Writing the History of Northeast India*. New Delhi: Cambridge University Press, forthcoming.

95. Longkumer, Arkotong, *Reform, Identity and Narratives of Belonging: The Heraka Movement in North East India*, London: Continuum International, 2010, pp. 134–9.

96. Kanungo, Pralay, 'Fusing the ideals of the math with the ideology of the Sangh? Ecumenical Hinduism and Hindu nationalism, Vivekananda Kendra', in J. Zavos, P. Kanungo, D. Reddy, M. Warrier, R.B.William (eds), *Public Hinduisms*, Delhi: SAGE Publications, 2012.

97. Ibid., pp. 126–33

98. I could only locate three issues with the help of Akash Bhattacharya: October, 2013 and April and October, 2016.

99. The April 2016 issue puts that in a big black box on the front cover.

100. ABISY, 2013 op. cit.

101. Jain, Mahavir Prasad, 'A Brief Survey of the Politics of Indian Historiography', Apr. 2016, p. 57,

102. Ibid.

103. Verma, T.P., 'Saraswati: The River and the Civilization', Oct. 2016

104. Vaidic Shiksha Paddhati. October, 2016.

105. 'Param Shiv Ka Shrishti: Vigyan Aur Ved Vidya Bharati', *Akhil Bharatiya Shiksha Sammelan, Alternative Model of National Education*, Dec. 1990–Mar. 1991.

106. Akhil Bharatiya Itihas Sankalan Yojana, *Visions and Perspectives*. Delhi: ABISY, 1973; Akhil Bharatiya Itihas Sankalan Yojana, *Itihas Darpan*, Apr. Delhi: ABISY, 2016; Akhil Bharatiya Itihas Sankalan Yojana, *Itihas Darpan*, Oct. Delhi: ABISY, 2016.

107. Sarkar, Sumit, *Writing Social History*, Delhi: Oxford University Press, 1997, pp. 30–32.
108. Ibid., pp. 1–49.

9. MERCHANTS OF HYPE AND HATE: A POLITICAL-ECONOMIC EVALUATION OF THE MODI REGIME

1. Including in a claim made by Modi in a television interview aired on 22 Jan. 2018.
2. Ghose, Ajit K., *India Employment Report 2016*, Delhi: Oxford University Press, 2016. [0]
3. 'Annual Report 2017', Reserve Bank of India, https://rbidocs.rbi.org.in/rdocs/AnnualReport/PDFs/RBIAR201617_FE1DA2F97D61249B1B21C4EA66250841F. PDF, last accessed 8 July 2018.
4. Banerjee, A. and Kala, N., 'The economic and political consequences of India's demonet', *VoxDev*, https://voxdev.org/topic/institutions-political-economy/economic-and-political-consequences-india-s-demonet, last accessed 8 July 2018.
5. Mankar, R. and Shekhar, S., 'Demonetisation and the Delusion of GDP Growth', *Economic and Political Weekly*, https://www.epw.in/journal/2017/18/commentary/demonet-and-delusion-gdp-growth.html, last accessed 8 July 2018.
6. See the account of Janardhanan, Arun, 'Demonetisation: 35 per cent job losses, 50 per cent revenue dip, says study by largest organisaiton of manufacturers', *Indian Express*, 9 Jan. 2017, https://indianexpress.com/article/india/demonetisation-35-per-cent-job-losses-50-per-cent-revenue-dip-says-study-by-largest-organisation-of-manufacturers-4465524/.
7. See Chapter 10 ('Social Infrastructure, Employment and Human Development') of Ministry of Finance, *Economic Survey[0]. Vol. II*, Government of India, 2017, p. 168 ff. (http://mofapp.nic.in:8080/economicsurvey/pdf/167–185_Chapter_10_Economic_Survey_2017–18.pdf).
8. The state of Gujarat has been administratively declared as completely open-defecation-free for some time, but a 2018 CAG report finds that this is not the case. 29 per cent of households do not even have access to toilets, not to speak about the use of toilets.
9. Yadavar, Swagata, 'Casteism Will Not Allow Swacch Bharat Abhiyan To Succeed', *IndiaSpend*, 13 Aug. 2017, http://archive.indiaspend.com/cover-story/casteism-will-not-allow-swacch-bharat-abhiyan-to-succeed-24444, reproduced at https://scroll.in/article/847117/interview-the-surprising-links-between-casteism-open-defecation-and-high-infant-mortality-in-india.
10. 'Budget 2018: Jaitley announces "world's largest healthcare Programme"', *The Hindu*, 1 Feb. 2018, https://www.thehindu.com/business/budget/budget-2018-jaitley-announces-worlds-largest-healthcare-programme/article22618631.ece, last accessed 19 July 2018.
11. These rankings are available online at: https://qz.com/959802/india-is-the-fourth-worst-country-in-the-world-for-religious-violence/; https://rsf.org/en/ranking; https://worldjusticeproject.org/our-work/wjp-rule-law-index/wjp-rule-law-index-2017%E2%80%932018

10. CONTOURS OF CRONY CAPITALISM IN THE MODI RAJ

1. Kudaisya, Medha M., *The Life And Times of G.D. Birla*, Delhi: Oxford University Press, 2003, pp. 235–6.
2. Ibid.
3. Ibid.
4. Ibid
5. Thakurta, Paranjoy Guha, 'The Two Faces of Dhirubhai Ambani', *Seminar*, No. 521, http://www.india-seminar.com/2003/521/521%20paranjoy%20guha%20thakurta. htm.
6. Comptroller and Auditor General of India, 2010: http://www.cag.gov.in/sites/default/ files/audit_report_files/Union_Performance_Civil_Allocation_2G_Spectrum_ 19_2010.pdf.
7. Comptroller and Auditor General of India, 2012: http://www.cag.gov.in/sites/default/ files/audit_report_files/Union_Performance_Commercial_Allocation_Coal_Blocks_ and_Production_Ministry_Coal_7_2012.pdf.
8. Ghosh, Subir, 'When the Nation Could Not Feel the Pulse: The Spike in Prices of Tur and Urad Dal Was a Fallout of Cartel', *Economic and Political Weekly*, June 2017, http:// www.epw.in/journal/2017/25–26/web-exclusives/when-nation-could-not-feel-pulse. html.
9. 'Comparing Crony Capitalism Around the World', *The Economist*, May 2016, https:// www.economist.com/blogs/graphicdetail/2016/05/daily-chart-2.
10. Dasgupta, Manas, 'BJP returns "favour", Modi suit buyer to get back land', *The Tribune*, April 2018, http://www.tribuneindia.com/news/nation/bjp-returns-favour—modi-suit-buyer-to-get-back-land/96506.html.
11. Singh, Rohini, 'The Golden Touch of Jay Amit Shah', *The Wire*, October 2017, https:// thewire.in/business/amit-shah-narendra-modi-jay-shah-bjp.
12. Sharan, Abhisek, 'Transactions between Raje's son Dushyant and Lalit Modi under scanner', *Hindustan Times*, June 2015, https://www.hindustantimes.com/india/trans-actions-between-raje-s-son-dushyant-and-lalit-modi-under-scanner/story-IrFapmI-vMbBo1AGRpgmPiK.html.
13. Ohri, Raghav, 'Robert Vadra made gains of Rs 50 crore from a land deal in Haryana in 2008: Dhingra Panel', *Economic Times*, 28 Apr. 2017, https://economictimes.india-times.com/news/politics-and-nation/robert-vadra-made-gains-of-rs-50-crore-from-a-land-deal-in-haryana-in-2008-dhingra-panel/articleshow/58407295.cms.
14. MS, Nileena, 'Coalgate 2.0', *The Caravan*, 1 Mar. 2018, http://www.caravanmagazine. in/reportage/coalgate-2–0.
15. Bhatia, Rahul & Lasseter, Tom, 'As Modi and his right wing Hindu base rise, so too does a celebrity yoga tycoon', *Reuters*, 23 May 2017, https://www.reuters.com/inves-tigates/special-report/india-modi-ramdev/.
16. Guha Thakurta, Paranjoy, 'PNB scandal poses difficult questions for PM Modi', Al Jazeera, 23 Feb. 2018. https://www.aljazeera.com/indepth/features/india-pnb-scan-dal-poses-difficult-questions-pm-modi-180223095412160.html.
17. Express Web Desk, 'Videcon gets Rs 3250 cr loan from ICICI Bank, bank CEO's hus-

band gets sweet deal from Venugopal Dhoot', *Indian Express*, 29 Mar. 2018, http://indianexpress.com/article/business/banking-and-finance/videocon-gets-rs-3250-crloan-from-icici-bank-chanda-kochhars-husband-gets-sweet-deal-from-venugopaldhoot-5115267/.

18. Pandey, Munish Chandra, 'CBI to question ICICI Bank CEO', *Business Today*, 1 Apr. 2018, https://www.businesstoday.in/sectors/banks/cbi-icici-bank-ceo-chanda-kochhar-deepak-kochhar-videocon/story/273823.html.

11. DALITS IN POST-2014 INDIA: BETWEEN PROMISE AND ACTION

1. Bharatiya Janata Party, *Election Manifesto 2014; Ek Bharat: Shreshtha Bharat, Sabka Saath Sabka Vikas*, New Delhi: BJP, 2014.
2. Ibid.
3. National Campaign on Dalit Human Rights, *Dalit Adivasi Budget Analysis 2018–19*, Delhi: Dalit Arthik Adhikar Andolan, 2018.
4. Centre for Budget and Governance Accountability (CBGA), *What do the Numbers Tell: An Analysis of Union Budget 2017/18*, CBGA, February 2017.
5. Krishnan, P.S., 'Budget 2018/19 from the view point of Scheduled Caste and Scheduled Tribes', 3 Feb. 2018, Letter to Union Finance Minister.
6. Thorat, Sukhadeo and Khalid Khan, 'Private sector and equity in higher education: Challenges of growing unequal access and equity', in Varghese, N.V., Sabharwal N. and Malish, C.M. (eds) *India Higher Education Report*, Delhi: Sage, 2016.
7. Thorat, Sukhadeo and Khalid Khan op. cit.
8. Central Statistics Office, *All India Report of Sixth Economic Census, 2013*. New Delhi, Ministry of Statistics and Programme Implementation [Government of India], 2013, pp. 28, 56, http://mail.mospi.gov.in/index.php/catalog/167/download/2124.
9. Indian Institute of Dalit Studies, *Caste, markets, and economic outcomes: A study of caste-based market discrimination, and its consequences on income and poverty, and policy implications*, Delhi: 2013.
10. Thorat, S.K., Tagade N. & Naik, A. K., 'Prejudice against reservation policies', *Economic and Political Weekly*, 51(8), 20 Feb. 2016, pp. 61–9.
11. Bharatiya Janata Party, op.cit., p. 16.
12. National Bureau of Crime Report, *Crime in India Report, 2014–2017*. New Delhi, Ministry of Home Affairs, GoI, New Delhi, 2017
13. Ambedkar, B.R., 'Philosophy of Hinduism', in *Dr Babasaheb Ambedkar Writings and Speeches*, Vol. 3, Bombay: Education Department, Government of Maharashtra, 1987, and Buhler, G., *The sacred books of the past, The laws of Manu*, Vol. 25, Delhi: Motilal Banarsidas, 2006.
14. Mani, Braj Ranjan, *De-brahmanising History: Dominance and Resistance in Indian Society*, Delhi: Manohar, 2011.
15. Ambedkar, B.R., 'Philosophy of Hinduism'.
16. Ambedkar, B.R., 'The Hindu social order: Its essential features', in *Dr Babasaheb Ambedkar Writings and Speeches*. Vol. 3, and Tola, Fernando and Dragonetti, Carmen. *Brahmanism and Buddhism*, Buenos Aires, Argentina: Institute of Buddhist Studies Foundation, FIEB-COCEPT, 2013.

17. Thorat, Sukhdeo, 'What upper castes owe', *Indian Express*, 16 Sep. 2016, https://indianexpress.com/article/opinion/columns/dalit-reservation-discrimination-upper-caste-una-flogging-3033276/.

18. National Sample Survey, *Debt and Investment Survey, 2013*, Delhi: National Sample Survey Organisation, Ministry of Statistics and Programme Implementation, 2016.

19. National Sample Survey, *Employment and Unemployment Situation in India, 68th round, (July 2011–June 2012), Report No. 554 (68/10/1)*, New Delhi: National Sample Survey Organisation, 2014.

20. Thorat, Sukhadeo, 'Graded Inequality: Relative Role of Endowment factors and Discrimination', paper presented in Conference on Caste and Race, SOAS University of London, May 2017.

12. ROHITH VEMULA'S REVOLUTIONARY SUICIDE

1. JanMohamed, Abdul R., *The Death-Bound-Subject: Richard Wright's Archaeology of Death*, Durham: Duke University Press, 2005.

2. Agamben, Giorgio, *Homo Sacer: Sovereign Power and Bare Life*, Stanford: Stanford University Press, 1998.

3. Fanon, Frantz, *Black Skin, White Masks*, New York: Grove Press, 2008.

4. A fascinating question that cannot be pursued here: what are the valences, differences, and implications of exclusion based, on the one hand, on structures of 'communication' and, on the other hand, on structures of the 'touch'? The former is more ensconced in the 'symbolic' realm, whereas the latter seems grounded in the biological, physical register.

5. Husserl, Edmund, *Ideas Pertaining to a Pure Phenomenology and to a Phenomenological Philosophy: Second Book, Studies in the Phenomenology of Constitutions*, London: Kluwer Academic Publishers, 1989. See Chapter 3.

6. Pirovolakis, Eftichis, 'Derrida and Husserl's phenomenology of touch: "Inter" as the uncanny condition of the lived body', *Word and Text*, 3, 2 (2013), pp. 99–118.

7. Derrida, Jacques, *On Touching–Jean-Luc Nancy*, Stanford: Stanford University Press, 2005, p. 180.

8. Derrida, Jacques, *Aporia*, Stanford: Stanford University Press, 1993, and *The Gift of Death*, Chicago: The University of Chicago Press, 1996.

9. B.R. Ambedkar's comparison of slavery and untouchability is somewhat disappointing. In order to stress the cruelty and abuses perpetrated by the structures of untouchability, he compares it to unusually liberal and benign examples of Roman and New World slavery in chapter 3 of his *Writings and Speeches*, Vol 5, New Delhi: Ambedkar Foundation, Ministry of Social Justice and Empowerment, Govt of India, 1989. His description of New World slavery in Chapter 8, however, more accurately recapitulates the atrocities practised in the US. But it contradicts his assertions in chapter 3. In one respect, though, his comparison is very accurate. Slavery, he implies, relies more on what Gramsci calls 'dominance' (i.e. coercion's reliance on the use of force) than on hegemony (that is, coercion via the acceptance and internalisation by the oppressed of the rules, regulations, values, etc., of the oppressor). As Ambedkar says, untouchability is a form of

'enslavement without making the Untouchables conscious of their enslavement. It is slavery though it is untouchability. It is real though it is indirect. It is enduring because it is unconscious. Of the two orders, untouchability is beyond doubt the worse.' *Writings and Speeches*, Vol 5, p. 15.

10. Patterson, Orlando, *Slavery and Social Death*, Cambridge (Mass.): Harvard University Press, 1982.

11. This battle with Mr. Covey was the turning-point in my career as a slave. It rekindled the few expiring embers of freedom, and revived within me a sense of my own manhood. It recalled the departed self-confidence, and inspired me again with a determination to be free. The gratification afforded by the triumph was a full compensation for whatever else might follow, even death itself. He can only understand the deep satisfaction that I experienced, who has himself repelled by force the bloody arm of slavery. I felt as I never felt before. It was a glorious resurrection, from the tomb of slavery, to the heaven of freedom. My long-crushed spirit rose, cowardice departed, bold defiance took its place; and I now resolved that, however long I might remain a slave in form, the day had passed forever when I might be a slave in fact. I did not hesitate to let it be known of me, that the white man who expected to succeed in whipping me, must also succeed in killing me. From this time I was never again what might be called fairly whipped, though I remained a slave four years afterwards. I had several fights, but was never whipped. Douglass, Frederick, *The Narrative of the Life of Frederick Douglass*, New York: Library of the America, 1994, p. 65. What Douglass calls 'resurrection' is what I classify as 'symbolic death'. For an analysis of this see JanMohamed, Abdul, 'Between speaking and dying: Some imperatives in the emergence of the subaltern in the context of U.S. slavery', in Rosalind Morris (ed.), *Can the Subaltern Speak? Reflections on the History of an Idea*, pp. 139–55, New York: Columbia University Press, 2010. Within the US context this understanding of the dialectics of death also underlies the attitude of resistance articulated by people like Malcolm X, Martin Luther King, Jr., and Huey P. Newton in his *Revolutionary Suicide*. The same knowledge permeates the political positions as well as the actions of Steve Biko and Nelson Mandela in the South African context. Mahatma Gandhi further articulates this by using the possibility of his own death, his potential suicide, as an instrument of political resistance.

12. See Chapter 8, 'Renegotiating the death contract' in JanMohamed, *Death-Bound-Subject*.

13. Morrison, Toni, *Beloved*, New York: Random House, 2004, pp. 128–9.

14. It is unfortunate that Vemula's diary is not yet available to the public. Judging from his suicide note, I suspect that the diary would more fully reveal the aporetic capture of his sensibility than the suicide note by itself does.

15. Janyala, Sreenivas, 'Behind Rohit Vemula's suicide: How Hyderabad Central University showed him the door', *Indian Express*, 20 Jan. 2016, http://indianexpress.com/article/india/india-news-india/behind-dalit-student-suicide-how-his-university-campus-showed-him-the-door/.

16. Dugard, John, 'The legal framework of Apartheid' in N. J. Rhodie (ed.), *South African Dialogue*, Philadelphia: The Westminster Press, 1972, p. 96.

17. The similarities in the Apartheid and current Indian legal/social systems raise the possibility of comparing Vemula's suicide with Steve Biko's 'suicidal' decision to face his own death. See Biko's essay 'On Death' in his *I Write What I Like*, London: Heinemman, 1987.

18. Rohith Vemula's poem, 'One Day', evokes a similar notion of resurrection. See Vemula, Rohith, 'One day', *The Quint*, 16 Jan. 2018, https://www.thequint.com/videos/rohith-vemula-poem-tribute-death-anniversary-i-will-resurrect.

19. 'Revolutionary suicide does not mean that I and my comrades have a death wish; it means just the opposite. We have such a strong desire to live with hope and human dignity that existence without them is impossible. When reactionary forces crush us, we must move against these forces, even at the risk of death.' Newton, Huey P., *Revolutionary Suicide*, New York: Penguin, 2009, p. 3.

13. HINDUTVA INCORPORATION AND SOCIOCONOMIC EXCLUSION: THE ADIVASI DILEMMA

1. Reich, Wilhelm, *The Mass Psychology of Fascism*, New York: Farrar, Straus, Giroux, 1970.

2. On 8 Nov. 2016, all 500 and 1,000 rupee notes were banned, amounting to some 87 per cent of India's currency. Apart from being directly responsible for the deaths of some 150 people, demonetisation also led to several small businesses being shut down, and some 1.5 lakh jobs being lost.

3. In the 2014 Lok Sabha elections, the BJP won 66 out of 131 reserved seats, and while one could argue that this reflects the general pattern, these are constituencies which have traditionally voted for the Congress.

4. Guha, Ramachandra, 'Adivasis, Naxalites and Indian democracy', *Economic and Political Weekly*, 42, 32 (11 Aug. 2007), p. 3308.

5. Thachil, Tariq and Ron Herring, 'Poor choices: de-alignment, development and Dalit/Adivasi voting patterns in Indian states', *Contemporary South Asia*, 16, 4 (2008), pp. 441–64; Vaid, Divya, 'Electoral participation among the Adivasi community', *Economic and Political Weekly*, 44, 39 (26 Sep. 2009), pp. 102–5.

6. Jha, Prashant, *How the BJP Wins: Inside India's Greatest Electoral Machine*. New Delhi: Juggernaut Press, 2017.

7. Thachil, Tariq, *Elite Parties, Poor Voters: How Social Services Win Votes in India*, Cambridge: Cambridge University Press, 2014.

8. Roy, Esha, 'How Tripura was won', *The Indian Express*, 4 Mar. 2018, https://indianexpress.com/article/india/tripura-assembly-elections-2018-results-bjp-manik-sarkar-amit-shah-narendra-modi-5085186/.

9. Nandi, Ramendra Nath, *Religious Institutions and Cults in the Deccan, C. A.D. 600–A.D. 1000*, Delhi: Motilal Banarsidass, 1973, pp. 114–23; Eschmann, Anncharlott (ed.), *The Cult of Jagannath and the Regional Tradition of Orissa*, New Delhi: Manohar, 1986, pp. 79–97.

10. Sundar, Nandini, 'Yes, eating beef is part of many Adivasi cultures', *The Wire*, 7 Nov. 2015, https://thewire.in/politics/yes-eating-beef-is-part-of-many-adivasi-cultures.

11. See, for instance, Hardiman, David, *The Coming of the Devi: Adivasi Assertion in Western India*, Delhi: Oxford University Press, 1987.

12. Sundar, Nandini, 'The Indian census, identity and inequality', in Ramachandra Guha & Jonathan P. Parry (eds), *Institutions and Inequalities: Essays in Honour of André Béteille*, New Delhi: Oxford University Press, 1999.

13. Saldanha, Julian, *Conversion and Indian Civil Law*, Bangalore: Theological Publications in India, 1981, pp. 47–56; see also Sangari, Kumkum, 'Gender lines: personal laws, uniform laws, conversion', *Social Scientist*, 27, 5–6 (1999), pp. 17–61.

14. Undated typescript titled, 'Bhumijan Seva Mandal', in Elwin correspondence, Bhulabhai Desai papers, Nehru Memorial Museum and Library (henceforth NMML).

15. Sundar, Nandini, 'Verrier Elwin and the 1940s missionary debate in central India', in Tanka Bahadur Subba and Sujit Som, (eds), *Between Ethnography and Fiction: Verrier Elwin and the Tribal Question in India*, Himayatnagar: Orient Longman, 2005, pp. 86–127.

16. Sundar, Nandini, 'Adivasi vs. Vanvasi: The politics of conversion and re-conversion in Central India', in Satish Saberwal and Mushirul Hasan (eds), *Assertive Religious Identities*, New Delhi, Manohar, 2006, pp. 357–90; Chatterji, Angana P., *Violent Gods; Hindu Nationalism in India's Present; Narratives from Orissa*. Gurgaon: Three Essays Collective, 2009; Froerer, Peggy, *Religious Division and Social Conflict*, New Delhi: Social Science Press, 2010.

17. Information from an Adivasi resident of Narainpur, Chhattisgarh, January 2018.

18. Citizen's Inquiry Committee, *Untold Story of Hindukaran (Proselytisation) of Adivasi (Tribal) in Dang: A Report*, 2006, http://indianculturalforum.in/2016/10/14/untold-story-of-hindukaran-proselytisation-of-adivasi-tribal-in-dang-a-report/.

19. Safi, Michael, 'Christmas violence and arrests shake Indian Christians', *The Guardian*, 24 Dec. 2017, https://www.theguardian.com/world/2017/dec/24/christmas-violence-and-arrests-shake-indian-christians.

20. Dixit, Neha, 'Operation #BetiUthao', *Outlook Magazine*, 8 Aug. 2016, https://www.outlookindia.com/magazine/story/operation-betiuthao/297626.

21. Mathew, Binu, '"Voices from the ruins of Kandhamal" and why I cried after watching the film', Countercurrents, 21 July 2016, https://countercurrents.org/2016/07/21/voices-from-the-ruins-of-kandhamal-and-why-i-cried-after-watching-the-film/.

22. World Watch Monitor, 'Indian Christians faced almost as many attacks in first half of 2017 as all of 2016', 8 Aug. 2017, https://www.worldwatchmonitor.org/2017/08/hinduisation-of-india-leads-to-more-anti-christian-violence/.

23. Sundar, Nandini, 'A journey through the shifting battlefronts of land and human souls', *The Wire*, 30 May 2015, https://thewire.in/2780/a-journey-through-the-shifting-battlefronts-of-land-and-human-souls/.

24. Devy, Ganesh Narayandas, 'Adivasis and Dalits: Tribal voice and violence', in Siddharth Varadarajan (ed.), *Gujarat: The making of a tragedy*, New Delhi: Penguin Books, 2002, pp. 246–70.

25. Narayan, Badri, *Fascinating Hindutva: Saffron Politics and Dalit Mobilisation*. New Delhi: Sage Publications, 2009.

26. Xaxa, Virginius, 'Politics of language, religion and identity: Tribes in India', *Economic and Political Weekly*, 40, 13 (26 Mar. 2005), pp 1363–70.

27. Mitra, Dola, 'Annals of earth', *Outlook Magazine*, 12 Oct. 2009, https://www.outlookindia.com/magazine/story/annals-of-earth/262075.

14. KASHMIRIS IN THE HINDU *RASHTRA*

1. Chatterji, Angana P., Parvez Imroz, Gautam Navlakha, Zahir-Ud-Din, Mihir Desai and Khurram Parvez, *Buried Evidence: Unknown, Unmarked and Mass Graves in Indian-administered Kashmir*, Srinagar: International People's Tribunal on Human Rights and Justice in Indian-administered Kashmir, 2009, http://www.kashmirprocess.org/reports/graves/BuriedEvidenceKashmir.pdf.

2. Ibid., p. 17.

3. The picture changed by end-May 2018 when losses in several by-elections reduced the number of BJP members in the Lok Sabha from 282 to 272; it retains its majority by a sliver at 50.46 per cent.

4. For instance, on 28 Dec. 2017 the Lok Sabha passed, without debate or reference to committee, a bill that criminalises the practice of *talaq-e-biddat* (instant divorce by repeating the word *talaq* three times) among Muslims.

5. The specific aspect of Kashmiriyat invoked was a much-mythicised tradition of cross-religious harmony deemed peculiar to Kashmiris.

6. In 1993, some twenty-six Kashmiri separatist parties came together as the umbrella All Parties Hurriyat Conference.

7. In anticipation of general elections due in 2019 and as part of an exercise in show-casing its achievements, the BJP commemorated 29 September 2018 as 'surgical strike day', marking the two-year anniversary of the covert cross-border action the army had undertaken two years earlier to liquidate alleged 'terror camps' in Pakistani territory. This strike in 2016 had been in retaliation for 'terrorist' hits on army camps inside the Indian border. The celebration in 2018 was of the 'strong answer' Modi had given Pakistan in 2016.

8. Indicating the co-existence of different sites of authority in the older version of the party is the oft-repeated cliché of Vajpayee and Lal Krishna Advani representing its moderate and hard-line facets respectively.

9. The kind of power Modi had asserted within the BJP as the chief minister of Gujarat (2001–14) now appears unimaginable in any of the party's regional leaders.

10. The AFSPA was applied to J&K in 1990 to contain the insurgency. The act permits the armed forces to shoot-to-kill, search and arrest, all without a warrant, ensuring for them immunity from prosecution.

11. The drama surrounding state elections in Karnataka in May 2018 illustrated the degree of the BJP's determination to win every state (unsuccessfully this time).

12. Coinciding with developments in Kathua, charges of raping a minor had also been levelled against a BJP legislator in Uttar Pradesh.

13. The Wire, 'Narendra Modi breaks silence on Kathua, Unnao rapes, promises justice', *The Wire*, 13 Apr. 2018, https://thewire.in/women/kathua-unnao-rape-narendra-modi, last accessed 25 May 2018. The two ministers were eventually made to resign. It is remarkable, however, that the BJP-PDP government did not fall until June 2018.

14. Press Trust of India, 'Kashmiri Pandits demand homeland, revocation of Article 370', *The Indian Express*, 27 Aug. 2017, http://indianexpress.com/article/india/kashmiri-pandits-demand-homeland-revocation-of-article-370–4816348/, last accessed 20 Feb. 2018.

15. Government of India, *Census of India 2011: Jammu and Kashmir Religion Census*, https://www.census2011.co.in/data/religion/state/1-jammu-and-kashmir.html, last accessed 7 Jan. 2018.

16. In fact the census of 2011 and the one preceding it reveal that Ladakh, taken as a whole, has a Muslim majority.

17. Bhan, Mona, '"In search of the Aryan seed": Race, religion, and sexuality in Indian-Occupied Kashmir', in Haley Duschinski et. al. (eds), *Resisting Occupation in Kashmir*, Philadelphia: University of Pennsylvania Press, 2018, pp. 74–102.

18. Chatterji, Angana P., 'The militarized zone', in Tariq Ali, Hilal Bhatt, Angana P. Chatterji, Pankaj Mishra and Arundhati Roy, *Kashmir: The Case for Freedom*, London: Verso, 2011, p. 94.

19. Chatterji, Angana P., 'Witnessing as feminist intervention in India-administered Kashmir', in Ania Loomba and Ritty Lukose (eds), *Feminisms in South Asia: Contemporary Interventions*, Durham: Duke University Press, 2012, p. 236.

20. She did the same with the Sikhs to win over Hindus in Punjab, Haryana and other parts of India.

21. Schmitt, Carl, *The Concept of the Political*, Expanded Edition (1932), trans. by G. Schwab, Chicago: University of Chicago Press, 2007, pp. 26–9.

22. Pargal, Sanjeev, 'Cong, NC, PDP offenders; oust them from power: Modi', *Daily Excelsior*, 14 Dec. 2014. http://www.dailyexcelsior.com/cong-nc-pdp-offenders-oust-power-modi/, last accessed 25 Dec. 2017.

23. The PSA allows the state to detain any person without charge or trial for up to two years on the mere suspicion that they may in the future engage in activities harmful to the state.

24. Express Web Desk, 'Hindu cannot be terrorist, there is nothing called Hindu terror: Haryana minister Anil Vij', *The Indian Express*, 22 June 2017, http://indianexpress.com/article/india/hindu-cannot-be-terrorist-there-is-nothing-called-hindu-terror-haryana-minister-anil-vij-4715414/, last accessed 24 Dec. 2017.

25. Gigoo, Siddhartha, 'Like threads suspended', *Outlook*, 7 Nov. 2016, https://www.outlookindia.com/magazine/story/like-threads-suspended/298041, last accessed 15 Feb. 2018.

26. Motta, Showkat A., 'Sainik colony, don't we live there already?', *Outlook*, 27 June 2016, https://www.outlookindia.com/magazine/story/sainik-colony-dont-we-live-there-already/297329, last accessed 7 June 2018.

27. Bhat, Suhail, 'KPs in Hawl transit camp demand relocation due to security threats', *Daily Excelsior*, 15 Feb. 2018, http://www.dailyexcelsior.com/kps-hawl-transit-camp-demand-relocation-due-security-threats/, last Accessed 8 June 2018.

28. Asian News International, 'Article 370 has only caused harm to Jammu-Kashmir: Deputy Chief Minister Nirmal Singh', *The New Indian Express*, 1 Oct. 2017, http://www.newindianexpress.com/nation/2017/oct/01/article-370-has-only-caused-harm-

to-jammu-kashmir-deputy-chief-minister-nirmal-singh-1665281.html, last accessed 7 Dec. 2017.

29. Press Trust of India, 'Kashmiri Pandits demand homeland, revocation of Article 370'.

30. For a fuller discussion see Rai, Mridu, *Hindu Rulers, Muslim Subjects: Islam, Rights and the History of Kashmir*, Princeton: Princeton University Press, 2004.

31. For instance, the kidnapping and killing of six Western tourists in 1995 by a shadowy group called Al Faran was widely condemned in Kashmiri civil society as indefensible. More recently, in 2017 and 2018, the killing of several Kashmiris employed in the Indian army and the J&K police has also been deplored albeit less unequivocally since some view them as 'collaborators'.

32. One must treat with caution accounts claiming the Valley is awash again with terrorists. Police records suggest that as of mid-2017 there were 282 active militants in Kashmir, a figure that includes 'foreign' fighters. Rashid, Toufiq, 'Let's talk about Kashmir: Number of homegrown militants swells after Burhan Wani's death', *Hindustan Times*, 3 July 2017, http://www.hindustantimes.com/india-news/let-s-talk-about-kashmir-number-of-locals-taking-up-arms-swells-after-burhan-wani-s-death/story-26x PfrqLgAwlyflh2lCtgP.html, last accessed 15 Dec. 2017.

33. Pandey, Neelam, 'Losing sight in Kashmir: Pellet guns shatter many dreams', *Hindustan Times*, 3 Oct. 2017, http://www.hindustantimes.com/india-news/losing-sight-in-kashmir-pellet-guns-shatter-many-dreams/story-BGbMhAFEfxlm8eEaMNHN1N.html, last accessed 27 Nov. 2017.

34. Anonymous, 'Kashmir problem confined to 5 districts of south Kashmir: Naidu', *Kashmir Reader*, 31 May 2017, https://kashmirreader.com/2017/05/31/kashmir-problem-confined-5-districts-south-kashmir-naidu/, last accessed 12 Dec. 2017.

35. Express Web Desk, 'Army Chief Bipin Rawat: Those displaying Pak, ISIS flags in Kashmir to face harsh action', *The Indian Express*, 17 Feb. 2017, http://indianexpress.com/article/india/army-chief-bipin-rawat-those-not-supporting-our-operations-will-be-treated-as-workers-of-terrorists/, last accessed 14 Dec. 2017.

36. It should be noted the term 'OGW' (over-ground worker) has gained extraordinary currency in state-security parlance ever since its coining by Bipin Rawat. That an unofficial category such as this, one moreover that is attributed arbitrarily by those controlling state-power, is routinely used to legitimise violence to the point of eliminating life is one more disturbing legacy of Indian state-action in Kashmir. It is yet another assault on civil liberties with dangerous portents not just for Kashmir—where it is already deployed routinely—but for all Indians dissenting with the party in power. A recent parallel, in August 2018, was the arrest for engaging in 'urban naxalism'—in other words, functioning as OGWs of the naxalites—of a number of Indian civil rights activists; the only thread unifying these otherwise disparate voices appears to be that they have each openly criticised the BJP government's functioning.

37. Press Trust of India, '2 Army officers back award to Major Leetul Gogoi, ex-general condemns act', *Live Mint*, 24 May 2017, http://www.livemint.com/Politics/22y0kE QmJyNM0ubjEmtF2O/2-Army-officers-back-award-to-Major-Leetul-Gogoi-exgeneral.html, last accessed 17 Dec. 2017.

38. Negi, Manjeet Singh, 'Nothing found against Major Leetul Gogoi in court of inquiry,

say Army sources', *India Today*, 25 May 2017, http://indiatoday.intoday.in/story/army-sources-mejor-leetul-gogoi-stone-pelter-keep-srinagar-by-poll-human-shield/1/962366.html, last accessed 17 Dec. 2017.

39. Press Trust of India, '"Human shield": Rs. 10 lakh compensation for Farooq Dar, directs rights body', NDTV (online ed.), 10 July 2017, https://www.ndtv.com/india-news/human-shield-10-lakh-compensation-for-farooq-dar-says-rights-body-1722950, last accessed 16 Dec. 2017.

40. Rashid, Toufiq, 'Cops confirm Kashmir "human shield" had voted before being tied to army vehicle', *Hindustan Times*, 25 Sep. 2017, http://www.hindustantimes.com/india-news/cops-confirm-kashmir-human-shield-had-voted-before-being-tied-to-army-vehicle/story-a7jAMA8JiJv4RVj8SIvJVK.html, last accessed 17 Dec. 2017.

41. Press Trust of India, 'J&K government refuses compensation to Farooq Ahmed Dar, civilian used as a human shield', *The Wire*, 7 Nov 2017, https://thewire.in/194954/jk-government-refuses-compensation-farooq-ahmed-dar-civilian-used-human-shield/, last accessed 16 Dec. 2017.

42. Unnithan, Sandeep, 'The gloves are off: Hardliner Gen Bipin Rawat fights Kashmir insurgency, with government's backing', *India Today*, 1 June 2017, http://indiatoday.intoday.in/story/general-bipin-rawat-jammu-kashmir-stone-pelters-major-leetul-gogoi/1/968000.html, last accessed 14 Dec. 2017.

43. Press Trust of India, 'Army Chief Bipin Rawat meets Arun Jaitley, briefs on Kashmir situation', *News Nation*, 26 May 2017, http://www.newsnation.in/india-news/army-chief-bipin-rawat-meets-arun-jaitley-briefs-on-kashmir-situation-article-172302.html, last accessed 14 Dec. 2017.

44. Press Trust of India, 'Kashmir "human shield" row: Dirty war has to be fought with innovative ways, Army Chief Bipin Rawat says', *Times of India*, 28 May 2017, https://timesofindia.indiatimes.com/india/Kashmir-human-shield-row-Dirty-war-has-to-be-fought-with-innovative-ways-Army-Chief-Bipin-Rawat-says/articleshow/58880274.cms, last accessed 14 Dec. 2017.

45. Guru had been accused of conspiring in the 13 Dec. 2001 attack on the Indian parliament on very little evidence and was sentenced to death by hanging on 9 Feb. 2013.

46. Shujaat Bukhari was the editor of the Kashmiri newspaper *Rising Kashmir*. Four gunmen killed him and two bodyguards right outside the newspaper's office in central Srinagar. Although no group has claimed responsibility for Bukhari's murder, Indian state sources hold Pakistan-based armed groups responsible. There is, so far, no conclusive evidence either way.

47. The Wire, 'BJP pulls out of alliance in Jammu and Kashmir, calls for Governor's rule', *The Wire*, 19 June 2018, https://thewire.in/politics/bjp-pdp-alliance-jammu-and-kashmir, last accessed 4 July 2018.

48. Yasir, Sameer, 'Jammu and Kashmir govt falls apart: Rajnath Singh, PDP's most-trusted BJP leader, left out of alliance-ending talks', *Firstpost*, 20 June 2018, https://www.firstpost.com/politics/jammu-and-kashmir-govt-falls-apart-rajnath-singh-the-pdps-most-trusted-bjp-leader-left-out-of-alliance-breaking-talks-4549171.html, last accessed 4 July 2018.

49. Ibid.

50. In India, governors are not elected officials but effectively appointees of the political party in power in New Delhi.

51. Sharma, Vibha, 'No "muscular" approach to Kashmir, says Ram Madhav', *The Tribune*, 20 June 2018, http://www.tribuneindia.com/news/nation/no-muscular-approach-to-kashmir-says-ram-madhav/608168.html, last accessed 4 July 2018.

15. PLAYING THE WAITING GAME: THE BJP, HINDUTVA, AND THE NORTHEAST

1. This chapter was written before the regional elections in February 2018 which saw the rise of the BJP in Tripura (forming the government), and forging alliances with regional parties that went on to form the state governments in Nagaland and Meghalaya. This paper does not take into account the post-February 2018 situation.

2. 'NPCC irked by Governor's programme pamphlet', *Nagaland Post*, 30 Jan. 2015.

3. Fieldwork for this chapter was conducted between 2014–16 for a larger project on Hindu nationalism in the region. Follow up interviews were conducted with the different BJP interlocuters in 2017. I do not use personal names, nor pseudynms, due to the sensitivity of their views, nor do I use specific designations. Instead I use the general term 'BJP worker'.

4. Gillan, Michael, 'Assessing the "national" expansion of Hindu nationalism: The BJP in southern and eastern India, 1996–2001', *South Asia: Journal of South Asian Studies*, 25, 3 (2002): 17–39; Hansen, Thomas Blom and Jaffrelot, Christophe (eds), *The BJP and the Compulsions of Politics in India*, OUP, 2001 [1998], p. 31.

5. Gillan, 'Assessing the "national" expansion', p. 18 (original emphasis).

6. Ibid., pp. 31–2.

7. Baruah, Sanjib, *Durable Disorder: Understanding the Politics of Northeast India*, New Delhi: OUP, 2005.

8. 'Yes, BJP wants all of Northeast, will go for the kill'. *NDTV*, 24 July 2017.

9. Jaffrelot, Christophe, *The Hindu Nationalist Movement in India*, New York: Columbia University Press, 1996, p. 108.

10. Pollock, Sheldon, 'The cosmopolitan vernacular', *Journal of Asian Studies* 57,1 (1998), 6–37.

11. Longkumer, Arkotong, 'The power of persuasion: Hindutva, Christianity, and the discourse of religion and culture in Northeast India', *Religions* 47, 2 (2017), 203–27.

12. It must be noted that the formation of the VHP by S.S. Apte in 1964 was partly to strengthen the boundaries of the Indian state, due first to the Indo-China war in 1962, that threatened the flanks of the Indian state, particularly Arunachal Pradesh, and then, subsequently the foundation of the state of Nagaland, an openly Christian state, in 1963, and the Pope's visit to Bombay in 1964. The threat of China and the activities of Christian missions in 'denationalising' its citizens was seen as an obvious threat to the 'Hindu' family, and it was encumbent on 'Hindu society' to protect themselves against the Christian, Islamic and Communist forces (Jaffrelot, op. cit., p. 197–8).

13. Baruah, Sanjib, 'BJP's win in Assam resulted from a consolidation, across faultlines, on the issue of citizenship', *Indian Express*, http://indianexpress.com/article/opinion/col-

umns/assam-assembly-elections-2016-results-bjp-sarbananda-sonowal-2829474/, last accessed 31 Dec. 2017.

14. In terms of size and electoral representation Assam is the largest state in northeast India, having fourteen Members of Parliament in the Lok Sabha, compared to the average of two in other states.

15. Ibid.

16. Wouters, Jelle J.P., and Tanka B. Subba, 'The "Indian Face," India's Northeast, and "The Idea of India"', *Asian Anthropology* 12, 2 (2013), 126–40.

17. Bhattacharjee, Malini, 'Tracing the emergence and consolidation of Hindutva in Assam', *Economic and Political Weekly*, 51, 16 (2016), 80–87.

18. 'Assam's secular identity will be safe: Ram Madhav', *The Hindu*, http://www.thehindu. com/elections/assam2016/assams-secular-identity-will-be-safe-ram-madhav/article86 22488.ece, last accessed 31 Dec. 2017.

19. 'What BJP posters of Bharat Mata in Tripura tribal gear say about its North East strategy', *Scroll.in*, https://scroll.in/article/859755/what-posters-in-tripura-of-bharat-mata-in-tribal-gear-say-about-the-bjps-north-east-strategy, last accessed 15 Jan. 2018.

20. This is article 244 of the Indian Constitution for the administration of tribal dominated areas in four states in the Northeast—Assam, Meghalaya, Tripura and Mizoram.

21. I do not intend to downplay the importance of grassroots Hindutva ideological work here. On the contrary, much of the BJP's success has happened because of the presence of the RSS and affiliates like the VHP and the Kalyan Ashram.

22. Gillan, 'Assessing the "national" expansion', pp. 55–6.

23. 'Won't part with even an inch of Assam: Sarbananda Sonowal', *Economic Times*, http://economictimes.indiatimes.com/articleshow/61343558.cms, last accessed 31 Dec. 2017.

24. 'No change in territorial boundary of States: Ravi', *Assam Tribune*, http://www.assamtribune.com/scripts/detailsnew.asp?id=oct1617/at056, last accessed 31 Dec. 2017.

25. 'Nagaland talks tempo worries neighbours Assam, Manipur and Arunachal Pradesh', *Indian Express*, http://www.newindianexpress.com/nation/2017/oct/29/nagaland-talks-tempo-worries-neighbours-assam-manipur-and-arunachal-pradesh-1686436. html, last accessed 31 Dec. 2017.

26. A local journalist in Nagaland writing about the elections in Assam relayed to me that in her presence some new BJP workers were told by senior members to 'fall at the feet' of RSS bigwigs if they want a party ticket to contest elections.

27. 'Assam's secular identity will be safe: Ram Madhav', *The Hindu*, 12 Sep. 2016.

28. 'We started working on Assam even before 2014 polls', *Indian Express*, http://indian-express.com/article/india/india-news-india/ram-madhav-bjp-national-secretary-assam-elections-2016-results-2812864/, last accessed 1 Jan. 2018.

29. See Bhattacharjee, op. cit.; Kanungo, Pralay, 'Casting community, culture and faith: Hindutva's entrenchment in Arunachal Pradesh', in Berti, Daniela, Nicholas Jaoul, and Pralay Kanungo (eds), *Cultural Entrenchment of Hindutva: Local Mediations and Forms of Convergence*, Abingdon: Routledge, 2011; Longkumer op. cit.

30. 'Can Secularism Survive India's right-wing'?, *Morung Express*, 6 Feb. 2015.

31. 'A Counter-narrative Politiking', *Morung Express*, 6 June 2017.

32. 'Meghalaya BJP leader quits over beef party; another may be asked to resign', *Hindustan Times*, http://www.hindustantimes.com/india-news/meghalaya-bjp-leader-quits-over-beef-party-another-may-be-asked-to-resign/story-b0Q5zfRQECSlH88AhNIVbK. html, last accessed 1 Jan. 2018.

33. 'Minister: BJP is Secular', *Telegraph*, https://www.telegraphindia.com/states/northeast/minister-bjp-is-secular-181216, last accessed 30 Dec. 2017.

34. I was told that the BJP does not get into customary, clan, village, and tribal politics, which shows a particular national outlook, but circumventing this is difficult particularly in the regional politics of tribal states. More research is required to substantiate this point.

35. Longkumer, Arkotong, '"As our ancestors once lived": Representation, Performance and Constructing a National Culture amongst the Nagas of India', *Himalaya* 35, 1 (2015), 51–64.

36. Hansen, Thomas Blom, *Wages of Violence: Naming and Identity in Postcolonial Bombay*, Princeton University Press, 2001, p. 294.

37. 'Anybody living in India is Hindu, says RSS chief Mohan Bhagwat in Tripura', *Hindustan Times*, http://www.hindustantimes.com/india-news/rss-chief-mohan-bhagwat-visits-tripura-says-anybody-living-in-india-is-hindu/story-HiyoiUsDGwCMyV99DFHNfL. html, last accessed 1 Jan. 2018.

38. Ibid.

39. Berti, Jaoul, and Kanungo (eds), op. cit.

40. Hansen and Jaffrelot (eds), op. cit.; McGuire, John and Ian Copland (eds), *Hindu Nationalism and Governance*, New Delhi: OUP, 2007.

16. FOREIGN POLICY UNDER MODI: BETWEEN ASPIRATION AND ACHIEVEMENT

1. PTI, 'I am being criticised for working more', *The Hindu*, April 2016, https://www.thehindu.com/news/international/narendra-modi-in-shanghai-i-am-being-criticised-for-working-more/article7214086.ece, last accessed 6 July 2018.

2. Thanks to the excitement about the new energy in Indian diplomacy, a number of volumes that sought to take stock of the changes have been published. See for example, Raja Mohan, C., *Modi's World: Expanding India's Sphere of Influence*, New Delhi: Harper Collins, 2015; Ganguly Anirban, Chauthaiwale, Vijay and Sinha, Uttam, *The Modi Doctrine: New Paradigms in Indian Foreign Policy*, New Delhi: Dr. Syama Prasad Mookarjee Research Foundation, 2016; Singh Sinderpal, ed., *Modi and the World: (Re) Constructing India's Foreign Policy*, Singapore: World Scientific, 2017.

3. For a review of India's post Cold War foreign policy, see Malone David, *Does the Elephant Dance? Contemporary Indian Foreign Policy*, Oxford: OUP, 2011; and Raja Mohan, C., *Crossing the Rubicon: The Shaping of India's New Foreign Policy*, London: Penguin Books, 2005 [2003].

4. Sitaram, Varun and Shivani, Anushka, 'India warms up to climate action', *Expert Brief*, Council on Foreign Relations, November 2015, https://www.cfr.org/expert-brief/india-warms-climate-action, last accessed 6 July 2018.

5. Cited in Amelia Gentleman, 'Letter from India: India can't wait to put the "super" before "power"', *New York Times*, 23 Nov. 2006, https://www.nytimes.com/2006/11/23/world/asia/23iht-letter.3642086.html, last accessed 6 July 2018.

6. 'Nonalignment 2.0: A Foreign and Strategic Policy for India in the 21st Century', Centre for Policy Research, February 2012, http://www.cprindia.org/research/reports/non-alignment-20-foreign-and-strategic-policy-india-twenty-first-century, last accessed 6 July 2018.

7. Pant, Harsh, 'How India is bidding adieu to non-alignment', *Outlook*, March 2015, https://www.outlookindia.com/website/story/how-india-is-bidding-adieu-to-non-alignment/293705.

8. For a discussion, see Tellis, Ashley J., 'India as a Leading Power', Carnegie Endowment, April 2016. http://carnegieendowment.org/2016/04/04/india-as-leading-power-pub-63185, last accessed 4 July 2018.

9. To be sure, the idea of realpolitik has been associated with the foreign policy of Indira Gandhi; but it was in her era that the foreign policy had assumed radical tones and became ideological on international issues. It was only towards the end of her tenure that she began to correct these distortions.

10. For a set of insightful essays, see Rajagopalan, Rajesh and Sahni Varun, 'India and the great powers', *South Asian Survey*, Vol. 15, No1, January 2008, https://doi.org/10.1177%2F097152310801500102, last accessed 5 July 2018.

11. For a discussion of the changing India-US relationship in the UPA years and its impact on the domestic politics and foreign policy, see Raja Mohan, C., *Impossible Allies: India and the US in a Changing Global Order*, Delhi: India Research Press, 2006.

12. Madan, Tanvi, 'The US-India Relationship and China', *Brookings Report*, September 2014. https://www.brookings.edu/research/the-u-s-india-relationship-and-china/, last accessed 6 July 2018.

13. The signal on discarding historic hesitations was a definitive signal that PM Modi is not bound by the past. See his address to the US Congress, Washington DC during June 2016, http://www.mea.gov.in/Speeches-Statements.htm?dtl/26886/prime+ministers+remarks+at+the+us+congress, last accessed 6 July 2018.

14. Madan, Tanvi, 'The Rise, Fall, and Rebirth of the Quad', *War On the Rocks*, November 2017, https://warontherocks.com/2017/11/rise-fall-rebirth-quad/, last accessed 6 July 2018.

15. The most succinct articulation of this approach can be found in Modi's Townhall address on the second anniversary of the launch of the MyGov portal in New Delhi, August 2016, https://www.youtube.com/watch?v=mNnxHY5o6v0, last accessed 5 July 2018.

16. 'India-Japan relations strengthened under PM Narendra Modi's leadership: Sushma Swaraj', *The Free Press Journal*, March 2018, http://www.freepressjournal.in/india/india-japan-relations-strengthened-under-pm-narendra-modis-leadership-sushma-swaraj/1246631, last accessed 6 July 2018.

17. Chotani, Vindu Mai, *India-Japan Ties: Getting a Boost Under Modi and Abe*, New Delhi: Observer Research Foundation, November 2017, https://www.orfonline.org/research/india-japan-ties-under-modi-abe-personal-friendships-and-strategic-cooperation/, last accessed 2 July 2018

18. Pant, Harsh V., 'Macron and Modi: What France Can Do For India and What India Can Do For France', *The Diplomat*, March 2018, https://thediplomat.com/2018/03/macron-and-modi-what-france-can-do-for-india-and-what-india-can-do-for-france/, last accessed 6 July 2018.

19. Chaudhary, Dipanjan Roy, 'India's geopolitical status goes up after Doklam', *The Economic Times*, August 2018, https://economictimes.indiatimes.com/news/defence/indias-geopolitical-status-goes-up-after-doklam-standoff-ends/articleshow/60282585.cms, last accessed 6 July 2018.

20. For the official Indian criticism, see the statement from the Ministry of External Affairs in May 2017. http://www.mea.gov.in/media-briefings.htm?dtl/28463/official+spokespersons+response+to+a+query+on+participation+of+india+in+oborbri+forum, last accessed 2 July 2018.

21. Saran, Shyam, 'India-China relations in the age of Xi Jinping', *Yale Global Online*, 15 May 2018, https://yaleglobal.yale.edu/content/india-china-relations-age-xi-jinping, last accessed 2 July 2018.

22. Godbole, Shruti, *Future of the India-Russia Relationship post Sochi Summit*, Brookings India, July 2018, https://www.brookings.edu/blog/up-front/2018/07/02/future-of-the-india-russia-relationship-post-sochi-summit/, last accessed 2 July 2018.

23. Raja Mohan, C., *Remapping India's Geopolitics*, Carnegie India, January 2018, https://carnegieindia.org/2018/01/01/remapping-india-s-geopolitics-pub-75404, last accessed 2 July 2018.

24. See the speech by Modi at the Shangri La Dialogue in Singapore, June 2018, http://www.mea.gov.in/Speeches-Statements.htm?dtl/29943/prime+ministers+keynote+address+at+shangri+la+dialogue+june+01+2018, last accessed 5 July 2018.

25. See PM Modi's speech in Mauritius, March 2015, http://www.mea.gov.in/Speeches-Statements.htm?dtl/24908/address+by+prime+minister+to+the+national+assembly+of+mauritius+march+12+2015, last accessed 5 July 2018.

26. See Modi's speech to the national parliament of Kazakhstan, July 2015, http://www.mea.gov.in/Speeches-Statements.htm?dtl/25436/address+by+prime+minister+at+nazarbayev+university+astana+kazakhstan, last accessed 5 July 2018.

27. Pant, Harsh A., 'A new reality confronts India in the Middle East', *The Diplomat*, February 2018, https://thediplomat.com/2018/02/a-new-reality-confronts-india-in-the-middle-east/, last accessed 5 July 2018.

28. Mukherjee, Rohan, 'East by Southeast: Three challenges for India's Act East Policy', *Business Standard*, January 2018, https://www.business-standard.com/article/economy-policy/east-by-southeast-three-challenges-for-india-s-act-east-policy-118012300197_1.html, last accessed 2 July 2018.

29. For a discussion see, Pant, Harsh A., 'Sino-Indian Jostling in South Asia', *Yale Global Online*, January 2018, https://yaleglobal.yale.edu/content/sino-indian-jostling-south-asia, last accessed 5 July 2018. See also Brewster, David ed., *India and China at Sea*, Oxford: Oxford University Press, 2018.

30. Rehman, Iskander, 'India-France: Look to the Indian Ocean', *The Diplomat*, June 2015, https://thediplomat.com/2015/06/india-france-relations-look-to-the-indian-ocean/, last accessed 6 July 2018.

31. PTI, 'India gives four military helicopters to Afghanistan before key meet', *The Economic Times*, November 2016, https://economictimes.indiatimes.com/news/defence/india-gives-four-military-helicopters-to-afghanistan-before-key-meet/articleshow/556689 74.cms, last accessed 6 July 2018.

32. PTI, 'India signs 12 agreements with Vietnam, extends $500m for defence cooperation', *First Post*, January 2018, https://www.firstpost.com/world/india-signs-12-agreements-with-vietnam-extends-500m-for-defence-cooperation-2989334.html, last accessed 6 July 2018.

33. 'India commits $500 million credit for Bangladesh military', *The Indian Express*, April 2017, http://www.newindianexpress.com/world/2017/apr/08/india-commits-500-million-credit-for-bangladesh-military-1591435.html, last accessed 6 July 2018.

34. 'China and India compete over bases around Indian Ocean', *CNBC*, February 2018, https://www.cnbc.com/2018/02/28/military-china-and-india-compete-over-bases-around-indian-ocean.html, llast accessed 6 July 2018.

35. Bhattacharya, Pallab, 'ASEAN pushes for a liberalised trade pact with India', *The Daily Star*, January 2018, https://www.thedailystar.net/business/asean-pushes-liberalised-trade-pact-india-1526632., last accessed 6 July 2018.

36. 'India, Japan to work closely on connectivity', *The Straits Times*, September 2017, https://www.straitstimes.com/asia/south-asia/india-japan-to-work-closely-on-connectivity, last accessed 6 July 2018.

37. Mehta, Pratab Bhanu, 'India in a corner: Beneath the foreign policy bluster is a great floundering', *The Indian Express*, February 2018, https://indianexpress.com/article/opinion/columns/india-in-a-corner-defence-expenditures-military-modernisation-5064333/, last accessed 11 July 2018.

38. Raja Mohan, C., *America's Reset of Afghan Strategy: Potential Realignment of South Asian Geopolitics*, ISAS Insights, August 2017. https://www.isas.nus.edu.sg/wp-content/uploads/media/isas_papers/ISAS%20Insights%20No.%20456-%20Americas%20Reset%20of%20Afghan%20Strategy-%20Potential%20Realignment%20of%20South%20Asian%20Geopolitics.pdf, last accessed 11 July 2018.

39. Chatterjee, Garage, 'Sheikh Hasina Visit: To Improve India-Bangla Relations, Delhi must have Kolkata on Board', *Scroll.in*, April 2017, https://scroll.in/article/834083/sheikh-hasina-visit-to-improve-india-bangladesh-relations-delhi-must-have-kolkata-on-board, last accessed 7 July 2018.

40. Menon, Shivshankar, 'Hostile Relations: India's Pakistan Dilemma', *Harvard International Review*, Fall 2009, https://www.jstor.org/stable/42763315, last accessed 3 July 2018.

41. Grare, Frederic, 'India-Pakistan relations: Does Modi Matter?', *Washington Quarterly*, Vol. 37, No. 4, January 2015, https://doi.org/10.1080/0163660X.2014.1002158, last accessed 2 July 2018. See also Mazumdar, A., 'Narendra Modi's Pakistan Policy: A Case of Old Wine in New Bottles?', *The Round Table*, Vol. 106, No. 1, January 2017, https://doi.org/10.1080/00358533.2016.1272957, last accessed 4 July 2018.

42. Ahmad, Omair, 'Doklam standoff: Misunderestimating Bhutan's sovereignty', *The Wire*, July 2017, https://thewire.in/diplomacy/doklam-standoff-india-china-bhutan, last accessed 3 July 2018.

43. Bhadrakumar, M.K., 'Nepal, Maldives poised to move out of India's orbit', *Asia Times*, December 2017, http://www.atimes.com/nepal-maldives-poised-move-indian-orbit/, last accessed 6 July 2018.

44. For an explanation of the issues involved see, 'Maldives Crisis: India's stand, the China angle—all your questions answered', *Indian Express*, February 2018, https://indianexpress.com/article/world/maldives-crisis-india-china-mohamed-nasheed-abdulla-yameen-5057094/, last accessed 3 July 2018.

45. Chowdhury, Debashish Roy, 'Driven by India into China's arms, is Nepal the new Sri Lanka?', *South China Morning Post*, February 2018, https://www.scmp.com/week-asia/geopolitics/article/2134532/driven-india-chinas-arms-nepal-new-sri-lanka, last accessed 3 July 2018.

46. For a review of the relations, see Chahal, Husanjot, *India-Sri Lanka: Reorienting the Relationship*, New Delhi: Institute of Peace and Conflict Studies, June 2017, http://www.ipcs.org/comm_select.php?articleNo=5310, last accessed 5 July 2018.

47. For a comprehensive discussion see Kugiel, Patryk, *India's Soft Power: A New Foreign Policy Strategy*, New York: Routledge, 2017.

48. For a discussion of India's soft power and its limitations, see Mahapatra Debidatta, Aurobindo, 'From a latent to a "strong" soft power? The evolution of India's cultural diplomacy', *Palgrave Communications* 2, December 2016, https://www.nature.com/articles/palcomms201691, last accessed 2 July 2018.

49. Chaulia, Sreeram, 'How Modi mobilizes Indian Diaspora', *The Globalist*, December 2016, https://www.theglobalist.com/narendra-modi-indian-diaspora-politics-india/, last accessed 6 July 2018.

50. Vijay, Tarun, 'How Sushma Swaraj turned mother to distressed Indians abroad', *DailyO*, July 2016, https://www.dailyo.in/politics/sushma-swaraj-gurdip-singh-minister-of-foreign-affairs-diplomacy-indians-abroad/story/1/12098.html, last accessed 5 July 2018.

51. PTI, 'Govt approves new visa to attract foreigners, boost trade', *The Indian Express*, November 2016, https://indianexpress.com/article/india/india-news-india/govt-approves-new-visa-to-attract-foreigners-boost-trade-4403661/, last accessed 6 July 2018.

52. Hall, Ian, *Modi's new religious diplomacy*, International Studies Perspectives (forthcoming), 2018. https://www.academia.edu/36621723/Narendra_Modis_New_Religious_Diplomacy_International_Studies_Perspectives_forthcoming_2018_, Last accessed 10 July 2018.

53. Rabson, Mia, 'Sikh separatists in Canada drawing ire in Indian media before Trudeau visit', *The National Observer*, February 2018, https://www.nationalobserver.com/2018/02/07/news/sikh-separatists-canada-drawing-ire-indian-media-trudeau-visit, last accessed 11 July 2018.

54. Agarwal, Natasha, *Examining the limitations of India's Online Visa Regime*, ORF Issue Brief, 180, May 2017, https://www.orfonline.org/research/examining-the-limitations-of-indias-online-visa-regime/, last accessed 11 July 2018.

17. SCULPTING THE SAFFRON BODY: YOGA, HINDUTVA, AND THE INTERNATIONAL MARKETPLACE

1. This chapter has benefitted from feedback by a number of people. I would especially like to thank Angana Chatterji, Banu Subramaniam, Sarah Pinto, Ayesha Irani, Elora Chowdhury, Vrushali Patil, Evren Savci, Patrick Grzanka, Sinikka Elliott, and Emily Mann.

2. Godrej, Farah, 'The neoliberal yogi and the politics of yoga', *Political Theory*, 45, 6 (2017), pp. 772–800, https://doi.org/10.1177/0090591716643604; see also Markula, Pirkko, 'Reading yoga: Changing discourses of postural yoga on the yoga journal covers', *Communication & Sport*, 2, 2 (2014), pp. 143–71, https://doi.org/10.1177/21 67479513490673.

3. Chakraborty, Chandrima, 'The Hindu ascetic as fitness instructor: Reviving faith in yoga', *The International Journal of the History of Sport*, 24, 9 (2007), pp. 1172–86, https://doi.org/10.1080/09523360701448307.

4. It is important to note the difference between proponents of yoga who are pro-Hinduism but distance themselves from Hindu nationalism. For example, see Alter, Joseph S., *Yoga in Modern India: The Body Between Science and Philosophy*. Princeton: Princeton University Press, 2004.

5. For scholarship on the links between Hindutva and sexual and gendered violence, see Chatterji, Angana, P., *Violent Gods: Hindu Nationalism in India's Present; Narratives from Orissa Gurgaon:* Three Essays Collective, 2009; Chatterji, Angana, P., Shashi Buluswar, Mallika Kaur (eds), *Conflicted Democracies: The Right to Heal; Internal Conflict and Social Upheaval in India.* New Delhi: Zubaan Publishers Pvt. Ltd, 2016.

6. Bhabha, Homi K., 'DissemiNation: Time narrative and the margins of the modern nation', in *The Location of Culture*, London: Routledge, 1994.

7. Rajagopal, Arvind, 'Thinking through emerging markets: Brand logics and the cultural forms of political society in India', *Social Text*, 17, 3 (1999), pp. 131–49.

8. Kaur, Ravinder, 'Good times, brought to you by Brand Modi', *Television & New Media*, 16, 4 (2015), pp. 323–30, https://doi.org/10.1177/1527476415575492; see also Rajagopal, 'Thinking through emerging markets'.

9. Shamsi, Mohd Salman and Urooj Fatima, 'Making India through "Make in India" and destination branding', *Journal of Intellectual Studies & Theories* 4, (2016), pp. 938–51; see also Varga, Somogy, 'The politics of nation branding: Collective identity and public sphere in the neoliberal state', *Philosophy & Social Criticism*, 39, 8, (2013), pp. 825–45.

10. Iğsiz, Asli, 'From alliance of civilizations to branding the nation: Turkish studies, image wars and politics of comparison in an age of neoliberalism', *Turkish Studies*, 15, 4 (2014), pp. 689–704, https://doi.org/10.1080/14683849.2014.983689; Kaur, Ravinder, 'Nation's two bodies: Rethinking the idea of "new" India and its other', *Third World Quarterly*, 33, 4 (2012), pp. 603–21, https://doi.org/10.1080/01436597.2012.6574 20; Varga, 'The politics of nation branding'.

11. Kaur, 2012 op. cit.

12. Kaur, 2012 op. cit.; Varga, 2013 op.cit.

13. Chakravartty, Paula and Srirupa Roy, 'Mr. Modi goes to Delhi: Mediated populism

and the 2014 Indian elections', *Television & New Media*, 16, 4 (2015), pp. 311–22, https://doi.org/10.1177/1527476415573957; Kaur, 'Good times, brought to you by Brand Modi'; Pal, Joyojeet, 'Banalities turned viral: Narendra Modi and the political tweet', *Television & New Media*, 16, 4 (2015), pp. 378–87, https://doi.org/10.1177/1527476415573956.

14. Hansen, Thomas Blom, *The Saffron Wave: Democracy and Hindu Nationalism in Modern India*. Princeton: Princeton University Press, 1999.

15. Swami Vivekananda, *Raja Yoga*, Shardsofconsciousness.com, 2018 [1896], http://shardsofconsciousness.com/user/sites/shardsofconsciousness.com/files/ebooks/RajaYoga_Vivekananda.pdf, last accessed 6 Sep. 2017.

16. The notion of spirituality is itself a historical and discursive frame. For an informative discussion, see Peter van der Veer 2001, especially chapter three.

17. Alter, 2004 op. cit.

18. Alter, 2004 op. cit.; White, David Gordon, (ed.), *Yoga in Practice*. Princeton: Princeton University Press, 2011.

19. Barry, Ellen, 'Modi's Yoga Day grips India, and "om" meets "ouch!"', *New York Times*, 15 June 2015, https://www.nytimes.com/2015/06/16/world/asia/india-modi-yoga.htm; Mohan, Archis, 'The men behind International Day of Yoga', Rediff, 11 June 2015, http://www.rediff.com/news/report/the-men-behind-international-day-of-yoga/20150611.htm. This master also derives his influences from gurus who are most identified with concurrently propagating upper-caste Hindu nationalism and yoga—such as Swami Vivekananda and Swami Kuvalayananda: Jagat Guru Amrta Suryananda, 2017, Curriculum Vitae, http://www.jagatguruamrtasuryananda.org/en/jagat-guru-amrta-suryanand-maha-raja-curriculum-vitae, last accessed 3 Nov. 2017.

20. Hansen, 1999, op. cit., p. 11.

21. Chakraborty, 2007 op. cit.; Godrej, 2017 op. cit.

22. Chakraborty, 2007 op. cit.

23. For discussion on this point, see Joseph Alter, especially chapter one; also see Swami Vivekananda, *Raja Yoga*, Shardsofconsciousness.com, 2018 [1896], op. cit.

24. Nye, Joseph S., *Soft Power: The Means to Success in World Politics*, New York: Public Affairs, 2004.

25. *Hinduism Today*, Oct/Nov/Dec 2015, 'It's official: International Yoga Day', https://www.hinduismtoday.com/modules/smartsection/item.php?itemid=5635, p. 55.

26. Shah, Bina, 'In Pakistan, yoga rises above its Indian origins', *New York Times*, 8 Dec. 2017, https://www.nytimes.com/2017/12/08/opinion/yoga-pakistan-india.html, last accessed 8 Dec. 2017.

18. AGGRESSIVE HINDU NATIONALISM: CONTEXTUALISING THE TRIPLE *TALAQ* CONTROVERSY

1. Sherin, B.S., 'Shortcomings in the triple talaq debate', *Outlook*, 6 Nov. 2016, http://www.outlookindia.com/website/story/shortcomings-in-the-triple-talaq-debate/297366, last accessed 2 July 2017.

2. Mine has been an important voice articulating this concern on behalf of subaltern women

NOTES pp. [336–337]

across class, caste, and other marginalities. I have also written about concerns of Dalit women in the rape discourse and examined the way the courts view the rape of a Dalit, tribal or Muslim woman. These are important debates which help to bring nuances within mainstream feminism.

3. I belong to a tradition of legal pluralism where diverse rights co-exist under the constitution because of the protection given to religious and cultural minorities. Though I belong to the women's movements and have very strong feminist credentials, right from the time of the demolition of Babri Masjid in 1992, when there were riots in Mumbai, I changed my position as I met Muslim women whose sons had been shot at point blank range by the police. Muslim houses were burnt and looted, women and children were taking shelter in the durgahs and mosques while the men had fled. The article I wrote at that time which was published in *Economic and Political Weekly* was a turning point for me (Agnes, Flavia, 'Women's Movement aithin a Secular Framework—Redefining the Agenda', *Economic & Political Weekly* XXIX No. 19 (7 May 1994), p. 1123). My position challenged the established mainstream feminism, but it received a great deal of support by individuals within the feminist movement. Tanika Sarkar and Urvashi Butalia included this essay in an edited volume titled *Women and the Hindu Right*, New Delhi: Kali for Women, 1995. The Babri Masjid demolition and the riots that followed was the watershed moment for feminist politics in India.

4. Justice Dave was a judge of the Gujarat high court when Prime Minister Modi was the chief minister of the state. In August 2014, while speaking at a conference at Gujarat University he made the following comment, 'Had I been the dictator of India, I would have introduced Gita and Mahabharata in Class I', which was immediately picked up by the media. See The Indian Express, 'If I were dictator, would have made Gita compulsory in Class I: SC judge', *The Indian Express*, 3 Aug. 2014, http://indianexpress.com/article/india/india-others/if-i-were-dictator-would-have-made-gita-compulsory-in-class-i-sc-judge, last accessed 2 July 2017.

5. Prakash v. Phulawati, 16 Oct. 2015, 2 SCC 36.

6. Re: Muslim Women's Quest for Equality v. Jamiat Ulma-I-Hind, SMW(C) No. 2/2015.

7. Mahmood, Tahir, 15 May 2017, 'Ball in the Supreme Court', The Indian Express, http://indianexpress.com/article/opinion/columns/ball-in-the-supreme-court-triple-talaq-4655854/, last accessed 2 July 2017.

8. It needs to be clarified that several Shia sects such as Khojas, Bohra, Ismailis, Itna Asharis do not recognise instant triple *talaq* and have provided elaborate dispute resolution mechanisms for arbitration in family matters. Even among Sunnis there are sects such as Ahl-e-Hadith who do not recognise instant triple *talaq*. However, majority of north Indian Muslim are Hanafis who recognise instant triple *talaq*. Instant triple *talaq* is not the only form available to a Muslim couple to dissolve the marriage. The Muslim law recognises several other forms including the woman's right to dissolve the marriage, *khula*; divorce by mutual consent, *mubarra*; and a divorce pronounced by Qazi, *fasq*.

9. It is a representative body of Muslims of various denominations, however, it is dominated by clerics of Hanafi sect. Though a non-statutory body, it has great influence over matters of faith among followers of the Sunni sect of Islam in India.

10. Niaz, Noorjehan Safia and Zakia Soman, *Seeking Justice Within Family*, Bharatiya

Muslim Mahila Andolan, 2015. https://drive.google.com/file/d/0B620GpkWZ9-UQmx1T212WHpWelE/view.

11. Shariff, Abusaleh and Syed Khalid, 'Unimportance of triple talaq', *The Indian Express*, 29 May 2017, http://indianexpress.com/article/opinion/columns/unimportance-of-triple-talaq-supreme-court-muslim-law-4678304/, last accessed 2 July 2017.

12. Soman, Zakia and Noorjehan Niaz, 'Why triple talaq needs to be abolished', *The Wire*, 17 June 2016, http://thewire.in/43481/why-triple-talaq-needs-to-be-abolished/.

13. Adityanath is not a member of the Bharatiya Janata Party (BJP), and has had differences with the BJP. The BJP, in an attempt to contain Adityanath, appointed him the chief minister of Uttar Pradesh. He is even more fervent than Narendra Modi and the BJP.

14. Aiyar, Mani Shankar, 'What's at risk if triple *talaq* is declared unconstitutional', NDTV, 14 June 2017, http://www.ndtv.com/opinion/triple-talaq-vs-divorce-among-other-religions-1710918, last accessed 2 July 2017.

15. News 18, 'UP minister says Muslims use triple talaq to change wives, satisfy "lust"', 29 Apr. 2017, http://www.news18.com/news/politics/up-minister-says-muslims-use-triple-talaq-to-change-wives-satisfy-lust-1387283.html, last accessed 2 July 2017.

16. *State of Bombay v. Narasu Appa Mali*, All India Reporter 1952, Bombay, p. 84.

17. In the *talaq-e-ahasan* mode, a single pronouncement of *talaq* during the time of menstrual purity (*tuhr*) followed by *iddat* period of three lunar months (ninety days) and, if the wife is pregnant, until her delivery. In the *talaq-e-hasan* mode the husband pronounces *talaq* every month, during the three months of *iddat* period when the wife is in a state of menstrual purity. In both forms the husband must abstain from cohabitation. In the event of cohabitation, the *talaq* is automatically revoked. The husband must provide shelter and maintenance to the wife in the matrimonial home during the *iddat* period. Only if no cohabitation takes place during the period of *iddat*, the marriage is dissolved upon the expiry of the *iddat* period. The *iddat* period is supposed to be a cooling period, when the couple can reunite (Fyzee, A.A.A., *Outlines of Muhammadan Law*, New Delhi: Oxford University Press, 2002 [1964], pp. 152–4).).

18. Fareed, Faisal, 'Hundred days of Yogi Adityanath and Muslims: Challenging times ahead', *TwoCircles*, 21 June 2017, http://twocircles.net/2017jun21/411723.html, last accessed 2 July 2017.

19. The RSS has carried out a systematic propaganda campaign alleging the existence of a Muslim plot to seduce and convert Hindu girls. This term is used to foster a sense of insecurity amongst Hindus and to make ordinary Hindus suspicious against Muslims.

20. This term is used by the RSS and Vishwa Hindu Parishad (VHP) for religious conversions of non-Hindus to Hinduism.

21. British Broadcasting Corporation, 'Why India man was lynched over beef rumours', British Broadcasting Corporation, 1 Oct. 2015, http://www.bbc.com/news/world-asia-india-34409354, last accessed 2 July 2017.

22. Apoorvanand, 'Muslims must refuse to be killed', *The Wire*, 9 Apr. 2017, https://thewire.in/122420/muslims-must-refuse-killed-cow-beef/, last accessed 2 July 2017; see Philipose, Pamela, 'Our own Animal Farm', *The Indian Express*, 10 May 2017, http://indianexpress.com/article/opinion/columns/our-own-animal-farm-cow-protection-narendra-modi-yogi-adityanath-pehlu-khan-4648544/, last accessed 2 July 2017.

23. See Mander, Harsh, 'Junaid, my son', *The Indian Express*, 1 July 2017, http://indianexpress.com/article/opinion/columns/junaid-my-son-4729828.

24. Apoorvanand, 2017, op. cit.

25. Sharma, Manik, 'Not in my name: What have the protest marches across India been able to achieve?', *Firstpost*, 1 July 2017, http://www.firstpost.com/living/not-in-my-name-what-have-the-protest-marches-across-india-been-able-to-achieve-3764571.html.

26. See Mander Harsh, 'Sonia, sadly', *The Indian Express*, 18 Mar. 2018, http://indianexpress.com/article/opinion/columns/sonia-sadly-congress-muslims-party-sonia-gandhi-5100506/.

27. A term used for prejudice or negative feelings and attitudes towards Islam and Muslims. The term gained wide acceptablity in the Western world after the 9/11 attack on the twin towers of the World Trade Centre in New York in 2001.

28. Mahapatra, Dhananjay, 'Supreme Court leaves uniform civil code to Parliament, door ajar on triple talaq', *Times of India*, 8 Dec. 2015, http://timesofindia.indiatimes.com/india/Supreme-Court-leaves-uniform-civil-code-to-Parliament-door-ajar-on-triple-talaq/articleshow/50083462.cms, last accessed 2 July 2017. India is governed by a constitutional scheme of separation of powers between the three arms of the State: the legislature, the executive and the judiciary. The power of the judiciary is confined to examining the constitutional validity of an act or a rule but it does not have law-making power.

29. Nair, Shalini, 'Shayara Banu's fight against triple talaq', *The Indian Express*, 24 Apr. 2016, http://indianexpress.com/article/india/india-news-india/triple-talaq-supreme-court-ban-muslim-india-shayara-banu-2767412/, last accessed 2 July 2017.

30. Agnes, 2016, op. cit.

31. Danial Latifi v. Union of India, (2001) 7 SCC 740.

32. Shamim Ara v. State of Uttar Pradesh, AIR 2002 SC 3551.

33. Dagdu Chotu Pathan v. Rahimbi, 2003 (1) Bom CR 740.

34. Sri Jiauddin v. Anwara Begum, (1981) 1 GLR 358.

35. Rukia Khatun v. Abdul Khalique Laskar, (1981) 1 GLR 375.

36. Parveen Akhtar v. Union of India, 2003–1-LW(Crl)115; Najmunbee v. Sk. Sikander Sk. Rehman, I (2004) DMC 211; Mustari Begum v. Mirza Mustaque Baig, II (2005) DMC 94; Shahzad v. Anisa Bee, II (2006) DMC 229; Farida Bano v. Kamruddin, II (2006) DMC 698 MP; Dilshad Begum Pathan v. Ahmad Khan Hanif Khan Pathan, II (2007) DMC 738; Riaz Fatima v. Mohd. Sharif, I (2007) DMC 261; Masroor Ahmed v. State, 2008 (103) DRJ; Shakil Ahmad Jalaluddin Shaikh v. Vahida Shakil Shaikh, MANU/MH/0501/2016.

37. This selective amnesia of mainstream journalism is not limited to matters regarding to Muslims. There are many subaltern movements across different regions—the North East region, the tribal areas, within Dalit movements, etc. to regain their histories and reactivating local knowledge and knowledge of political struggles. The movements labeled as 'naxal movement' is one such attempt by marginalised communities within the backward tribal bests of Maharashtra, Madhya Pradesh, Chhatisgarh, Telegana, Jharkhand, etc. Similar movements are also going on within many North Eastern states

like Nagaland, Manipur, Tripura, etc. The recent incident that took place near Pune known as the *Bhima Koregaon incident* where Dalits were attacked by the Hindu nationalists for celebrating the 200th anniversary of the fall of the Peshwa (Brahmin) regime by fighting along with the British is yet another such attempt to claim their own history.

38. Shayara Bano v. Union of India, (2017) 9 SCC 1

39. (Mahmood 2017)

40. Shamim Ara v. State of Uttar Pradesh, AIR 2002 SC 3551

41. In an article written in a popular newspaper (cited above) the Islamic scholar Tahir Mahmood while commenting on the judgement lamented, 'How I wish the bench had just reiterated Shamim Ara, unanimously, approving this implication of the very sensible ruling given 15 years ago' (Mahmood, 2017).

42. Press Trust of India, 'No need for new law on triple talaq; SC verdict law of the land: Government', *Times of India*, 22 Aug. 2017, https://timesofindia.indiatimes.com/india/no-need-for-new-law-on-triple-talaq-sc-verdict-law-of-the-land-government/articleshow/60179929.cms.

43. Mustafa, Faizan, 'Why criminalising triple talaq is unnecessary overkill', *The Wire*, 15 Dec. 2017, https://thewire.in/gender/why-criminalising-triple-talaq-is-unnecessary-overkill.

44. *Darul qaza*: an alternative dispute resolution forum. Though termed a Sharia Court, *darul qaza* is a mediation centre and its decision is not binding on the parties.

45. Solanki, Gopika, *Adjudication in Religious Family Law: Cultural Accommodation, Legal Pluralism and Gender Equality in India*, New Delhi: Cambridge University Press, 2011; Vatuk, Sylvia, *Marriage and Its Discontents: Women, Islam and the Law in India*, New Delhi: Women Unlimited, 2017.

46. Chakrabarti, Anindita and Suchandra Ghosh, 'Judicial reform vs adjudication of personal law', *Economic & Political Weekly*, 52, 49 (9 Dec. 2017), pp. 12–14.

47. Mandal, Saptarshi, 'Instant Triple Talaq Bill: Tabling legislation in Parliament is political move, BJP's attempt to play protector of Muslims', *Firstpost*, 22 Dec. 2017m, http://www.firstpost.com/india/instant-triple-talaq-bill-tabling-legislation-in-parliament-is-political-move-bjps-attempt-to-play-protector-of-muslims-4270807.html.

48. Pathak, Zakia and Rajeswari Sunder Rajan, 'Shahbano', *Signs*, 14, 3 (1989), pp. 558–82.

49. This has reference to the controversial ruling, *Mohd Ahmed Khan v. Shahbano Begam* (1985) 2 SCC 556, where the supreme court upheld a Muslim woman's right to claim maintenance but certain comments against Islam and the Prophet led to a backlash within the community and the government enacted the MWA to undo the gains of this judgment. In the meantime, the woman who was central to the controversy, Shahbano Begam, retracted her claim to maintenance.

50. Sherin, B.S., 'Shortcomings in the triple talaq debate'.

19. 'BELIEF' IN THE RULE OF LAW AND THE HINDU NATION AND THE RULE OF LAW

1. The Indian judiciary consists of several layers of courts. Different courts have different

responsibilities, which depend on the functions and jurisdiction conferred on them through law. The supreme court is the highest court of appeal. This top layer is followed by high courts in each of India's respective states, followed a several tiers of lower courts, that include district courts and magistrate courts.

2. The Hindu Right consists of three primary actors, including the Bharatiya Janata Party (BJP) (Indian Peoples Party), which is responsible for formulating and pursuing the political agenda of the movement; the Rashtriya Swayamsevak Sangh (RSS) (National Volunteer Organisation), which was established in 1925 to build a strong Hindu community to counter British rule as well as Muslim separatism and responsible for developing and expounding the ideological doctrine of the Hindu Right; and the Vishwa Hindu Parishad (VHP) (World Hindu Council), founded in 1964 to popularise the Hindu Right's religious doctrine and consolidate its support at a grassroots level. The VHP also includes a militant youth wing, the Bajrang Dal (Hanuman gang) established in 1984. There are several other peripheral players associated with the Hindu Right parties, including the militant and virulently anti-Muslim Shiv Sena (Foot soldiers of Shiva). The movement collectively promotes the ideology of Hindutva—which posits Hinduism not simply as a religion but as a nation and a race that is indigenous to India (Jaffrelot, Christophe, *The Hindu Nationalist Movement in India*, New York: Columbia University Press, 1998; see also Sharma, Jyotimaya, *Hindutva: Exploring the Idea of Hindu Nationalism*, Delhi: Penguin Books, 2011). Jaffrelot discusses the understanding of Hindutva in the writings of V.D. Savarkar, the ideological leader of the Hindu nationalists during the struggle for freedom from colonial rule. Savarkar's definition of Hindutva includes 'an ethnic community possessing a territory and sharing the same racial and cultural characteristics' (Jaffrelot, op. cit., p. 27). Savarkar's writings on Hindutva continue to represent the ideological foundations of contemporary Hindu Right.

3. Dingwaney Needham, Anuradha and Rajeswari Sunder Rajan (eds), *The Crisis of Secularism in India*, Durham: Duke University Press, 2007, pp. 267–93. The contributions in Dingwaney and Sunder Rajan's book, while presenting an array of positions on secularism, remain largely committed to the view that the BJP is the central threat to secularism in India. There is little interrogation of the key assumption that secularism is based on the separation between religion and the state, which has in fact never been the governing model of secularism in India (Kapur, Ratna and Brenda Cossman, *Secularism's Last Sigh? Hindutva and the (Mis)-rule of Law*, Oxford: Oxford University Press, 2001; Smith, Donald, *India as a Secular State*, Princeton: Princeton University Press, [1963] 2015) and that the effort to restore liberal secularism cannot solve the problem of majoritarianism (Asad, Talal, *Formations of the Secular: Christianity, Islam, Modernity*, Stanford: Stanford University Press, 2005; Mahmood, Saba, *Religious Difference in a Secular Age: A Minority Report*, Princeton: Princeton University Press, 2016). See more generally Jakobsen, Janet R., and Ann Pellegrini, (eds), *Secularisms*, Durham, NC: Duke University Press, 2008.

4. Asad, Talal, *Formations of the Secular: Christianity, Islam, Modernity*, Stanford: Stanford University Press, 2005, pp. 21–66; see also Asad, Talal, *Genealogies of Religion: Discipline and Reasons of Power in Christianity and Islam*, Baltimore: John Hopkins University Press, 1993.

5. Cossman, Brenda and Ratna Kapur, 'Secularism's last sigh?: The Hindu Right, the courts, and India's struggle for democracy', *Harvard International Law Journal* 38, (1997), pp. 113–70; Kapur, Ratna and Brenda Cossman, *Secularism's Last Sigh? Hindutva and the (Mis)-rule of Law*, Oxford: Oxford University Press, 2001; Smith, Donald, *India as a Secular State*, Princeton: Princeton University Press, [1963] 2015.

6. Jaffrelot, Christophe, *The Hindu Nationalist Movement in India*, New York: Columbia University Press, 1998; see also Sharma, Jyotimaya, *Hindutva: Exploring the Idea of Hindu Nationalism*, Delhi: Penguin Books, 2011.

7. Jacobsohn, Gary J., *The Wheel of Law: India's Secularism in Comparative Constitutional Context*, Princeton: Princeton University Press, 2003, pp. 91–121; see also Baxi, Upendra, 'Siting secularism in the uniform civil code: "A Riddle Wrapped inside of an Enigma?"', in Anuradha Dingwaney Needham and Rajeswari Sunder Rajan (eds), *The Crisis of Secularism in India*, Durham: Duke University Press, 2007, pp. 267–93.

8. Chakraborty, Chandrima, *Masculinity, Asceticism, Hinduism: Past and Present Imaginings of India*, Delhi: Permanent Black, 2011.

9. Banerjee, Sikata, *Muscular Nationalism: Gender, Violence and Empire in India and Ireland 1914–2004*, New York: NYU Press, 2012.

10. Shah Bano, a seventy-three year old Muslim woman, who was divorced by her husband of forty years brought a petition for maintenance from her husband under section 125 of the *Code of Criminal Procedure*, 1973 (CrPC). According to Muslim personal law, she would only have been entitled to maintenance for the period of *iddat*—that is, three months after the divorce. In April 1985, the supreme court held that she was entitled to maintenance under section 125 and voiced the opinion that such maintenance would not be contrary to the Quran: *Mohammad Ahmed Khan v. Shah Bano Khan A 1985 SC 945*. The Hindu Right backed Shah Bano, invoking the right to equality and attempted in the process to demonise Muslim men. More orthodox and conservative elements of the Muslim community responded with outrage against the decision, and cries of 'religion in danger'. Many within the Muslim community suspected that the judgment was intended to undermine Islamic law in accordance with the agenda of the Hindu Right. The Congress government at the time, initially supportive of the supreme court decision, reversed its position, and responded by passing the *Muslim Women's (Protection of Rights on Divorce) Act*, 1986, (MWA, 1986), which provided that section 125 of the CrPC would not apply to divorced Muslim women. The women's movement, along with progressive Muslim organisations, campaigned against the bill. The Hindu Right also campaigned vigorously against the bill, which in its view was simply another example of the government 'pandering to minorities'. According to the act, which effectively codifies Muslim personal law of maintenance, a divorced woman's husband is obliged to return her *mehr* (dowery) and pay her maintenance during the period of *iddat*. If the divorced woman cannot support herself at the end of that period, her children, parents or relatives who would be entitled to inherit her property, are responsible for her support. If they cannot support her, the responsibility then falls to the state *Wakf* boards. See also Pathak & Sunder Rajan, 1989. For a discussion on the postcolonial politics of the 'universal' in relation to the UCC see Arya, 2006.

11. Agnes, Flavia, 'Liberating Hindu women', *Economic and Political Weekly*, 1, 10 (2015), pp. 14–17.

12. *Shayara Banu v. Union of India & Ors.*, 22 Aug. 2017, Supreme Court of India, available at https://indiankanoon.org/doc/115701246/.

13. Punwani, Jyoti, 'Muslim women: Historic demand for change', *Economic and Political Weekly* 51, 42 (15 Oct. 2016), http://www.epw.in/journal/2016/42/commentary/muslim-women.html.

14. The AIMPLB is a non-statutory, non-governmental organisation that was established in 1972. The board monitors the application of Muslim personal law, in particular, the Muslim Personal Law (Shariat) Application Act, 1937. It is a board that has been heavily criticised for presenting itself as the sole authority on Muslim personal law (Sunni law), for being a largely male, neo-conservative, and non-consultative body, whose views tend to fossilise Islamic religious practices, and for failing to address contemporary issues such as the rights of women, transgender persons and other minority members within the community in a progressive way: see for example Ahmed, 2007. The Board has been challenged in some of its edicts by the All India Muslim Women's Personal Law Board (AIMWPLB), established in 2005, and more recently by the Bharatiya Muslim Mahila Andolan (The Indian Muslim Women's Movement, BMMA), that spear-headed the challenge to triple *talaq* in the Indian supreme court. For an argument on how personal laws harm religious freedom see Ahmed, 2016.

15. Abu-Lughod, Lila, *Do Muslim Women Need Saving?*, Cambridge: Harvard University Press, 2013, p. 31.

16. *Shayara Banu v. Union of India & Ors.*, ibid., page 18, para 18(i).

17. For an analysis of the different positions of the judges see, Kapur, Ratna, 'Triple talaq verdict: Wherein lies the much hailed victory?' *The Wire*, 28 Aug. 2017, https://thewire.in/171234/triple-talaq-verdict-wherein-lies-the-much-hailed-victory/, last accessed 11 Dec. 2017.

18. *Shayara Banu v. Union of India & Ors.*, p. 28, para 19.

19. Section 4, Muslim Woman (Protection of Rights on Marriage) Bill 2017. The bill makes the practice of triple *talaq* a cognisable and non-bailable offence (section 7). The complaint can be made by anyone, not just the wife, and the husband is to provide a subsistence allowance for the wife and dependent children (presumably and somewhat incomprehensibly while he is in jail) (sections 5 and 6). The bill has been passed by the Lok Sabha (lower house) but has not cleared the Rajya Sabha (upper house) due to the demands by opposition parties to refer it to a select committee. At the time of writing, the BJP government has announced its intention to move an ordinance to implement the new legislation to by-pass the current deadlock.

20. *K.M. Ashokan v. Union of India and Ors.*, judgement dated 24 May 2017, available at http://www.livelaw.in/kerala-hc-nullifies-marriage-muslim-convert-fathers-habeas-corpus-petition-read-judgment/, last accessed 19 Dec. 2017, pp. 91–2, para. 50.

21. *Shafin Jahan v. Asokan K.M. and Others*, Special Leave Petition under article 136 of the Constitution of India arising out of the final judgement and order dated 24 May 2017 passed by the high court of Kerala, in WP (Crl) No. 297 of 2016, at 17. Available at http://www.livelaw.in/can-hc-nullify-marriage-two-adults-habeas-petition-girls-father-akhila-case-sc-read-petition/. See also Lata Singh's case, upholding the individual autonomy of an adult woman who had left home to marry a man of her choice: *Lata*

Singh v. State of Uttar Pradesh and Another, 7 July 2006, Supreme Court of India, available at https://indiankanoon.org/doc/1364215/.

22. Press Trust of India, 'I was not forced to marry or convert to Islam, want to be with husband, shouts Hadiya', *New Indian Express*, 25 Nov. 2017 http://www.newindianexpress.com/states/kerala/2017/.nov/25/i-was-not-forced-to-marry-or-convert-to-islam-want-to-be-with-husband-shouts-hadiya-1710813.html.

23. Mandhani, Apoorva, 'SC sets aside Kerala HC judgment annulling marriage between Hadiya and Shafin Jahan', *Livelaw*, 8 Mar. 2018, http://www.livelaw.in/breaking-sc-sets-aside-kerala-hc-judgment-annulling-marriage-hadiya-shafin-jahan/. See preliminary order upholding the marriage: *Shafin Jahan v. Asokan K.M. & Ors.*, Supreme Court of India, 8 March 2018, available at http://www.livelaw.in/breaking-sc-sets-aside-kerala-hc-judgment-annulling-marriage-hadiya-shafin-jahan/; G., Ananthakrishnan, 'Right to marry person of one's choice integral to right to life and liberty: SC on Hadiya case', *Indian Express*, 10 Apr. 2018, http://indianexpress.com/article/india/right-to-marry-supreme-court-hadiya-case-5131055/.

24. See quote from Hadiya after meeting PRI chief, Manorama Online, '"All this because I embraced Islam", says Hadiya after meeting PFI chief', *Manorama Online*, 10 Mar. 2018, https://english.manoramaonline.com/news/kerala/2018/03/10/hadiya-husband-visit-popular-front-chief-to-thank-him.html.

25. Khalid, Saif, 'The Hadiya case and the myth of "love jihad" in India', *Aljazeera*, 24 Aug. 2017, http://www.aljazeera.com/indepth/features/2017/08/hadiya-case-myth-love-jihad-india-170823181612279.html; see also Mahanta, Siddhartha, 'India's fake love jihad', *Foreign Policy*, 4 Sep. 2014, https://foreignpolicy.com/2014/09/04/indias-fake-love-jihad/.

26. Kapur, Ratna, 'Hecklers to power? The waning of liberal rights and challenges to feminism in South Asia', in Ania Loomba and Ritty Lukose (eds), *South Asian Feminisms*, Durham: Duke University Press, 2012, pp. 333–55.

27. Kapur, Ratna, 'The Ayodhya case: Hindu majoritarianism and the right to religious liberty', *Maryland Journal of International Law*, 29, 1 (2014), p. 331.

28. Thapar, Romila, 'Syndicated Hinduism', in *Cultural Pasts*, New Delhi: Oxford University Press, 2000, pp. 1025–54; see also Vajpeyi, Ashok, *India Dissents:3000 years of Difference, Doubt and Argument*, Delhi: Speaking Tiger Publishing Private Limited, 2017.

29. See *S. R. Bommai v. Union of India*, (1994) 3 Supreme Court Cases 1 (India). After the destruction of the mosque 1992 the supreme court unanimously affirmed the importance of secularism to the Indian constitution and emphasised the principle of equal treatment of all religions. It condemned those political forces committed to undermining more pluralistic instantiations of this constitutional ideal. The case suggested that the court was committed to holding back the tides of intolerance and Hindu majoritarianism in the name of secularism.

30. *Ismail Faruqui v Union of India*, All India Reports 1995 Supreme Court 605 (India).

31. Ibid. at 644–5.

32. Ibid. at 641. In September 2018, a three judge bench of the supreme court refused to revisit the *Ismail Faruqui* decision that upheld the government's acquisition of the land

where the mosque once stood and rejected a plea that the case should be heard by a larger bench: *M.Siddiq vs Mahant Suresh Das and Others*, Supreme Court of India, Civil Appeal Nos. 10866–10867 of 2010, order dated 27 Sep. 2018.

33. Ibid. at 634.
34. *Dr. Prabhoo, v. Union of India*, All India Reports 1996 Supreme Court at 1129 (India). In the course of one election campaign, many candidates campaigned on the Hindutva platform and argued that the protections afforded to Muslims under various legal provisions violated the constitutional mandate of the equal treatment of all religions on which Indian secularism is based.
35. Ibid. at 1130.
36. Ibid.
37. Thapar, Romila, 'Syndicated Hinduism', in *Cultural Pasts*, New Delhi: Oxford University Press, 2000, pp. 1025–54.
38. *Abhiram Singh v. CD Commachen*, (2017) 2 Supreme Court Cases 629, ruled that a political candidate or anyone with his/her consent, cannot appeal to the candidate's, his agent's, or voters'—religion, race, caste, community or language during elections. The court was interpreting the pronoun 'his' used in Section 123 (3) of the RPA, 1953. The question to be decided was whether it only means a bar on appeals made in the name of the candidate or his rival or his agent or others in his immediate camp; or did the word 'his' also extend to soliciting votes on the basis of religion caste, community, race, language of the electorate as a whole? (Feldman, 2017).
39. *Abhiram Singh v. CD Commachen* (delivered by the Supreme Court on 2 Jan. 2017), available at https://indiankanoon.org/doc/85515763/, Justice Chandrachud (dissent) para. 20.
40. Feldman, Noah, 'India's High Court Favors Nationalism over Democracy', Bloomberg View, 8 Jan. 2017, https://www.bloomberg.com/view/articles/2017-01-08/india-s-high-court-favors-nationalism-over-democracy

20. QUEER PRESENCE IN/AND HINDU NATIONALISM

1. McClintock, Anne, *Imperial Leather: Race, Gender and Sexuality in the Colonial Context*, New York: Routledge, 1995.
2. Yuval-Davis, Nira, *Gender and Nation*, London: Sage, 1997.
3. Peterson, V. Spike, 'Sexing political identities/ nationalism as heterosexism', in Sita Ranchod-Nilsson and Mary Ann Tétreault (eds), *Women, States, and Nationalism: At Home in the Nation?*, pp. 54–80, New York: Routledge, 2000.
4. Duggan, Lisa, *The Twilight of Equality?: Neoliberalism, Cultural Politics, and the Attack on Democracy*, Boston: Beacon Press, 2004.
5. Puar, Jasbir, *Terrorist Assemblages: Homonationalism in Queer Times*, Durham: Duke University Press, 2007.
6. Bacchetta, Paola and Jin Haritaworn, 'There are many transatlantics: Homonationalism, homotransnationalism and feminist-queer-trans of color theories and practices', in Kathy Davis and Mary Evans (eds), *Transatlantic Feminist Conversations*, pp. 127–44, Farnham: Ashgate, 2011. In a new book, *The Right to Maim* (2017), Puar mentions that it would

be useful to define homotransnationalism as the new deployment of the status of trans-gender people alongside models of national homosexuality for imperial objectives. In fact, in the global north we are seeing dual trends towards greater acceptance of mainly cisgender trans folks alongside continued anti-transgender violence. However, empiri-cally, the status of transgender subjects is often much better in the very global southern sites that the global north demonises than in the global north. For example, in India where homosexuality continued to be outlawed until 2018, transgender subjects now have third gender status. There is no such status in the US. In Iran, trans surgeries are reimbursed by the state. Such reimbursement, too, does not exist nationally in the US. This points to the necessity for a new theorisation of our present times wherein homonormativity continues to operate in homonationalist and homotransnationalist modes, but where in the global north, as Puar rightly observes, some new models for assimilate-able transnormativity are emerging (for example, Jenner, etc). Again, draw-ing upon Puar, we might also consider that this new expanded homonationalism, homo-transnationalism, and current global northern models for trans-acceptability are unfolding correspondingly against the backdrop of an extended cast of evermore demon-ised racialised and sexualised others. For instance, while Muslims and gender and sexu-ally nonconforming queers once served as the negative model, in the US now Mexican and other Latinx immigrants, and in France sub-Saharan African refugees and Roma peoples, are added in full force to the major, highly publicised, public enemy lists.

7. Foucault, Michel, *The History of Sexuality*. Vol I., New York: Vintage, 1980.
8. See Thadani, Giti, *Sakhiyani. Lesbian Desire in Ancient and Modern India*, London: Cassell, 1996; Kanchana, Untitled, unpublished paper circulated among lesbians and gays in Delhi, 1988; Khan, Shivananda, in *Khush*, directed by Pratibha Parmar, Kali Films, 1991; Vanita, Ruth (ed). *Queering India: Same-Sex Love and Eroticism in Indian Culture and Society*. New York: Routledge, 2002; and Vanita, Ruth and Saleem Kidwai (eds). *Same-Sex Love in India: Readings from Literature and History*, New York: Palgrave, 2000.
9. Thadani, *Sakhiyani. Lesbian Desire in Ancient and Modern India*; Cohen, Lawrence, 'The pleasures of castration', in Paul Abramson and Steven. D. Pinkerton (eds), *Sexual Nature/Sexual Culture*, Chicago: University of Chicago Press, 1995.
10. Patel, Geeta, 'Home, homo, hybrid: Translating gender', *College Literature*, 24, 1 (1997), pp. 135–9.
11. Bacchetta, Paola, *Gender in the Hindu Nation*, New Delhi: Women Unlimited, 2004.
12. Said, Edward, *Orientalism*, New York: Pantheon Books, 1978; see also Sprinkler, Michael (ed.), *Edward Said: A Critical Reader*, Cambridge: Blackwell Publishers, 1992.
13. Prakash, Gyan, 'Writing Post-Orientalist Histories of the Third World: Indian Historiography is Good to Think', Nicholas. B. Dirks (ed.), *Colonialism and Culture*, Ann Arbor: University of Michigan Press, 1995.
14. Chakravarty, Uma, 'Whatever happened to the Vedic Dasi?' in Kumkum Sangari and Sudesh Vaid (eds), *Recasting Women: Essays in Indian Colonial History*, New Delhi: Kali for Women, 1989; Nandy, Asish, *The Intimate Enemy*, Delhi: Oxford University Press, 1980.
15. Thadani, *Sakhiyani. Lesbian Desire in Ancient and Modern India*

16. Nandy, op. cit.

17. Sinha, Mrinalini, *Colonial Masculinity: The 'Manly Englishman' and the 'Effeminate Bengali' in the Late Nineteenth Century*. New Delhi: Kali for Women, 1997.

18. McClintock, *Imperial Leather*, p. 22.

19. Ballhatchet, Kenneth, *Race, Sex and Class Under the Raj*, London: Weidenfeld and Nicolson, 1980, p. 10 and 162.

20. Ballhatchet, *Race, Sex and Class Under the Raj*, p. 120.

21. Golwalkar, M.S., *Bunch of Thoughts*, second edition (revised and enlarged), Bangalore, Jagarana Prakashana,1980: 107, 208).

22. Irigaray, Luce, ed., *Sexes et genres à travers les langues*, Paris, Grasset, 1990, p. 12; Spender, Dale, *Man Made Language*, London, Routledge and Kegan Paul, 1980, p. 145.

23. McClintock, *Imperial Leather*.

24. Anderson, Benedict, *Imagined Communities*, London: Verso, 1991

25. Golwalkar, 1980: 291

26. Lane, Christopher, *The Ruling Passion: British Colonial Allegory and the Paradox of Homosexual Desire*, Durham: Duke University Press, 1995, p. 21.

27. Derrida, Jacques, 'The politics of friendship', *The Journal of Philosophy*, 85, 11 (1988), pp. 632–48.

28. Golwalkar, 1980: pp. 588, 449.

29. Golwalkar, M.S., *Bunch of Thoughts*, second edition (revised and enlarged), Bangalore: Jagarana Prakashana, 1980; Bangalore: Sahitya Sindhu Prakashana, 1996.

30. Shanin, Teodor, 'The idea of progress', in Majid Rahnema and Victoria Bawtree (eds), *The Post-Development Reader*, London: Zed Books, 1997.

31. Golwalkar, 1996, p. 372.

32. Bharatiya Janata Party (BJP), *BJP Election Manifesto*, New Delhi: BJP Publication, 1998, p. 41.

33. Ibid.

34. Ghosh, Deepshikha, 'Homosexuality no crime, says RSS leader, then calls it "psychological case"', NDTV, 18 Mar. 2016, https://www.ndtv.com/india-news/homosexuality-no-crime-its-a-psychological-problem-top-rss-leader-1288426.

35. Choudhary, Amit Anand, 'SC must review Sec 377 ruling, allow gay relationships: Jaitley, Chidambaram', *Times of India*, 29 Nov. 2015, https://timesofindia.indiatimes.com/india/SC-must-review-Sec-377-ruling-allow-gay-relationships-Jaitley-Chidambaram/articleshow/49965445.cms.

36. Ibid.

37. Nair, Harish V., 'Supreme Court reopens homosexuality debate, religious bodies unite to oppose LGBT rights', *India Today*, 3 Feb. 2016, https://www.indiatoday.in/mailtoday/story/supreme-court-reopens-lgbt-debate-religious-bodies-unite-to-oppose-decriminalisation-306794-2016-02-03.

38. Daily News & Analysis, 'Section 377: 14 times Subramanian Swamy made homophobic comments on Twitter', *Daily News & Analysis*, 8 Jan. 2018, http://www.dnaindia.com/india/report-as-long-as-they-don-t-create-gay-bars-to-select-partners-it-s-not-a-problem-subramanian-swamy-on-section-377-2573818; see also Times of India, 'Swamy backs Section 377 for gay people who "flaunt it"', *Times of India*, 8 Jan. 2018,

https://timesofindia.indiatimes.com/india/swamy-backs-section-377-for-gay-people-who-flaunt-it/articleshow/62416887.cms

39. Hindustan Times Correspondent, 'House panel led by BJP MP says no shame in being transgender', *Hindustan Times*, 22 July 2017, https://www.hindustantimes.com/india-news/house-panel-led-by-bjp-mp-says-no-shame-in-being-transgender-favours-right-to-marriage-divorce-for-community/story-U38T3TQpF3y3DJs6iQS4dP.html.

40. Pasquesoone, Valentine, 'Seven countries giving transgender people fundamental rights the U.S. still won't', *MIC*, 9 Apr. 2014, https://mic.com/articles/87149/7-countries-giving-transgender-people-fundamental-rights-the-u-s-still-won-t.

41. Guillaumin, Colette, *L'Idéologie raciste. Genèse et langage actuel*, Paris: Mouton, 1972.

42. Bacchetta, Paola, 'Communal property/sexual property: On representations of Muslim women in a Hindu nationalist discourse', in Zoya Hasan (ed.), *Forging Identities: Gender, Communities and Nations*, New Delhi: Kali For Women, 1994; Bacchetta, Paola, 'Hindu nationalist women as ideologists: Rashtriya Swayamsevak Sangh, Rashtra Sevika Samiti, and their respective projects for a Hindu nation', in Kumari Jayawardena and Malathi de Alwis (eds), *Embodied Violence: Communalizing Women's Sexuality in South Asia*, New Delhi: Kali For Women, 1996; Bacchetta, Paola, *Gender in the Hindu Nation*.

43. Golwalkar, 1980, pp. 234–5

44. Chandra, Bipin, *Communalism in Modern India*, Delhi: Vani Books, 1984; Pandey, Gyanendra, *The Construction of Communalism in Colonial North India*, Delhi: Oxford University Press, 1990.

45. Golwalkar, 1980, p. 413.

46. Golwalkar, 1980, p. 147.

47. Ramachandran, Smirti Kak, 'RSS to eulogize Bangladesh's poet Kazi Nazrul Islam as "good Hindu"', *Hindustan Times*, 23 Apr. 2017, https://www.hindustantimes.com/india-news/rss-to-eulogise-bangladesh-s-national-poet-kazi-nazrul-islam-as-good-hindu/story-a1RgOk3YlAh5sRoPLDXVnK.html.

48. Chatterjee, Tanmay, 'Muslim clerics in Bengal demand ban on RSS, say Ram Navami processions with weapons illegal', *Hindustan Times*, 23 Apr. 2017, https://www.hindustantimes.com/kolkata/muslim-clerics-in-bengal-demand-ban-on-rss-say-ram-navami-processions-with-weapons-illegal/story-9HAk6tKT2ngPa9HvsULxtK.html

49. Golwalkar, 1980, pp. 14–15.

50. Sinha, Rakesh, 'West's cultural laboratory', *Organiser*, 10 Jan. 1999, p. 17.

51. Bhatia, V. P., 'Raise tempers, lacerate and raise the whirlwind: The philosophy behind Deepa Mehta's kinky film "Fire"', *Organiser*, 27 Dec. 1998, p. 13.

52. Shabana Azmi is a widely acclaimed actress who played one of the (Hindu) lesbians in *Fire*. She is also a Muslim, an activist and has been a Congress Party Member of Parliament.

53. Golwalkar, 1980, p. 231.

54. Golwalkar, 1980, p. 197.

55. Golwalkar, 1980, pp. 197–8.

56. Somerville, Siobhan, 'Scientific racism and the invention of the homosexual body' in Roger N. Lancaster and Michaela di Leonardo (eds), *The Gender and Sexuality Reader: Culture, History, Political Economy*, New York: Routledge, 1997.

57. Seshadri, H. V. (ed.), *Dr. Hedgevar The Epoch-Maker*, Bangalore: Sahitya Sindu, 1981.
58. Unsigned, 'Shabana's swear, Rabri's roar, Teresa's terror? The three which sustain secularism', *Organiser*, 10 Jan. 1999, p. 8.
59. Golwalkar, 1980, p. 477.
60. Golwalkar, 1980, pp. 471, 476, 469.
61. Golwalkar, 1980, p. 473.
62. Sharma, Chandrika Prasad, *Poet Politician: Atal Bihari Vajpayee*, Delhi: Vikas, 1998, p. 25.
63. Sharma, *Poet Politician*, p. 49.
64. Shukla, Sangeeta, *Great Personalities of India: Narendra Modi*, Delhi: Diamond Books, 2014.
65. Makwana, Kishore, *Modi, the Common Man's P.M.*, Bangalore: Prabhat Prakashan, 2015.
66. Nolte, Ernst, *Three Faces of Fascism*, New York: Mentor 1965, p. 370.
67. Falasca-Zamponi, Simonetta, *Fascist Spectacle: The Aesthetics of Power in Mussolini's Italy*, Berkeley: University of California Press, 1997, pp. 15–17.
68. Patel, Geeta, 'Time tallied', unpublished paper presented at Harvard University, Nov. 1998.
69. Menon, Ritu and Kamla Bhasin, *Borders and Boundaries: Women in India's Partition*, New Delhi: Kali for Women, 1998; Human Rights Watch, *We Have No Orders to Save You. Human Rights Watch Report*, 14, 3 (Apr. 2002); Bacchetta, Paola, 'The (failed) production of Hindu nationalized space in Ahmedabad, Gujarat', *Gender, Culture and Place*, 17, 5 (2010), pp. 551–72.
70. Bacchetta, Paola, 'Extra-ordinary alliances: Women unite against religious-political conflict in India', in Kathleen Blee and France Winddance Twine (eds), *Feminism and Anti-Racism: International Struggles*, pp. 220–49, New York: New York University Press, 2001.

21. REMAKING THE HINDU/NATION: TERROR AND IMPUNITY IN UTTAR PRADESH

1. As told to Angana P. Chatterji, name withheld.
2. IANS, 'Army begins leaving Muzaffarnagar', *The Hindu*, 17 Sep. 2013, https://www.thehindu.com/news/national/other-states/army-begins-leaving-muzaffarnagar/article513 8208.ece; British Broadcasting Corporation, 'Muzaffarnagar: Tales of death and despair in India's riot-hit town', 25 Sep. 2013, https://www.bbc.com/news/world-asia-india-24172537.
3. Jaini, Bharti, 'Government releases data of riot victims identifying religion', *Times of India*, 24 Sep. 2013, http://timesofindia.indiatimes.com/india/Government-releases-data-of-riot-victims-identifying-religion/articleshow/22998550.cms.
4. Times of India, 'Muzaffarnagar violence: Over 10,000 displaced; 10,000 arrested', *Times of India*, 12 Sep. 2013, http://timesofindia.indiatimes.com/india/Muzaffarnagar-violence-Over-10000-displaced-10000-arrested/articleshow/22499187.cms.
5. Two Circles, 'Three years after Muzaffarnagar riots, no justice in sight for gang-rape survivors', *Two Circles*, 9 Feb. 2017, http://twocircles.net/2017feb09/404370.html.

6. United States Department of State [Bureau of Democracy, Human Rights and Labour], *2013 International Religious Freedom Report—India*. 2013, http://www.state.gov/j/drl/rls/irf/religiousfreedom/index.htm?year=2013&dlid=222329.

7. Rashtriya Swayamsevak Sangh (National Volunteer Association), a leading Hindu nationalist organisation. Rashtriya: National (Hindi); Swayam: Oneself (Hindi); Seva (Hindi): Service; Sevak (Hindi): One who offers service, male gendered, see Chatterji, Angana P., *Violent Gods: Hindu Nationalism in India's Present—Narratives from Orissa*, Gurgaon: Three Essays Collective, 2009, p. 40.

8. All India Democratic Women's Association (AIDWA), *Report of AIDWA visit to Muzaffarnagar*, 9 Oct. 2013. http://sacw.net/article6075.html.

9. The Amnesty International report of 2017 noted seven cases of gang-rape: Amnesty International, 2017, *Losing Faith—The Muzaffarnagar Gang-Rape Survivors' Struggle For Justice*, https://amnesty.org.in/losing-faith-muzaffarnagar-gang-rape-survivors-struggle-justice/.

10. All India Democratic Women's Association (AIDWA), 2013, op. cit.

11. Ibid.

12. 'Majoritarianism refers to cultural nationalism and political assertions by the majority and dominant community toward acquiring and maintaining social, economic, cultural, political, religious, legal, and state-nationalist power'. Chatterji, Angana P., Shashi Buluswar, Mallika Kaur, *Conflicted Democracies and Gendered Violence: The Right to Heal: Internal Conflict and Social Upheaval in India*, New Delhi: Zubaan, 2016, p. 24.

13. The article is premised on archival and secondary research and select primary interviews by the author.

14. The term, Hindutva, derived from Hindu Tatva—Hindu principles, 'Hindu-ness'—was popularised in 1923 by Vinayak Damodar Savarkar, a founding figure of the Hindu Mahasabha (literally, Great Assembly). The movement to create the Hindu Mahasabha ensued in 1906 and the Akhil Bharatiya (All India) Hindu Mahasabha was inaugurated in 1915, to compel a national movement for Hindutva and to sustain opposition to the Muslim League and the Indian National Congress.

15. Encyclopedia Britannica, *Britannica Encyclopedia of World Religions*, London: Encyclopedia Britannica, 2006, p. 128.

16. Indian Express, 'Chief Ministers of Uttar Pradesh', *Indian Express*, 15 May 2007, http://archive.indianexpress.com/news/chief-ministers-of-uttar-pradesh——/30945/0.

17. Freedom of religion sustains the freedom of individuals and communities to manifest and change their religion or belief. Freedom of religion or belief may be practiced in culture, society, economy and polity and across the domestic and public realm through acts of living, worship, observance, education, teaching and livelihood.

18. See United States Commission on International Religious Freedom, *Constitutional and LegalChallenges Faced by Religious Minorities in India*, Feb. 2017, http://www.uscirf.gov/sites/default/files/Constitutional%20and%20Legal%20Challenges%20Faced%20by%20Religious%20Minorities%20in%20India.pdf.

19. Adityanath founded the Hindu Yuva Vahini (Hindu Youth Force) in 2002, to promote combative Hindu nationalism. He was the head of the Gorakhpur Hindu sect at the time of the 2017 elections, Bal, Hartosh Singh, 'India's new face', *New York Times*,

24 Apr. 2017, https://www.nytimes.com/2017/04/24/opinion/indias-new-face.html, and Singh, Rajesh Kumar, 'Yogi Adityanath's Hindu Yuva Vahini splits amid struggle to stay significant', *Hindustan Times*, 25 May 2018, https://www.hindustantimes.com/india-news/relegated-to-the-margins-yogi-adityanath-s-hindu-yuva-vahini-struggles-to-stay-significant/story-K0wqv6e86VHzZK5XQ5uPgK.html.

20. 'Political society': see Chatterjee, Partha, *The Politics of the Governed: Reflections on Popular Politics in most of the World*, New York: Columbia University Press, 2004.

21, Including through the initiation and cultivation of minority community organizations that are supportive of Hindu nationalism, such as the Muslim Rashtriya Manch, and the creation of what has been termed a 'collaborator class'.

22. Ayodhya: In *Making India Hindu*, David Ludden writes: 'Holy men declared Monday, 6 December 1992 auspicious, and more than 300,000 people gathered that day in Ayodhya... At mid-day, a vanguard among them broke down police barricades around a mosque called the Babri Masjid, built in 1528 by the first Mughal emperor of India, Babar...and in five hours they hammered and axed it to the ground... Violence triggered by the demolition killed 1,700 people and injured 5,500 over the next four months'. See: Ludden, David (ed.), *Contesting the Nation: Religion, Community, and the Politics of Democracy in India*, Philadelphia: University of Pennsylvania Press, 1996, published in India as *Making India Hindu*, Delhi: Oxford University Press, 1996, p. 1; 'Reconversion': Hindutva organisations frame conversions to Hinduism as 'reconversions'. The victimised-subject of conversion who is of Adivasi, Dalit or caste descent is postulated by Hindu nationalists to be 'originally' Hindu, and their coercive conversion a 'return home' ('*ghar wapasi*') to their authentic/original/Hindu faith.

23. An unfounded conviction put forward by Hindu nationalists that propagate disinformation about conspiracies by Muslim men to lure Hindu girls to seduce and convert them to Islam, see: Suresh, Appu Esthose, 'Love jihad: UP's forbidden couples', *Hindustan Times*, 19 Oct. 2016, http://www.hindustantimes.com/static/uttar-pradesh-communal-riot/love-jihad-uttar-pradesh/.

24. Among minority communities and allies these acts are known as 'anti-conversion acts'. 'These laws usually state that the basis of conversion must be voluntary. Some of the laws require that the authorities be informed or give prior permission before conversion takes place'. These laws are currently in force in six of the twenty-nine states in India, in Arunachal Pradesh, Chhattisgarh, Gujarat, Himachal Pradesh, Madhya Pradesh, and Odisha, (Chatterji et al., *Conflicted Democracies*, op. cit., p. 90; Chatterji, *Violent Gods*, op. cit., p. 35; and Dasgupta, Manas, 'Bill violative of freedom of religion: Gujarat governor', *The Hindu*, 1 Aug. 2007, http://www.thehindu.com/todays-paper/bill-violative-of-freedom-of-religion-gujarat-governor/article1883582.ece).

25. For details, see section entitled, 'Recent History'.

26. 'Racialization seeks to ethnicize and religionize the self/Other. Race and racial difference remain pertinent, beyond the colonial and Western context, to understanding contemporary constructions of difference in the post/colony. Racialization creates representations of the Other through ascribing racial and ethnic identities to peoples in ways that defy their self-recognition. Within unequal relations of power and contexts of accommodation, racialized groups may begin to—be forced to—identify with

the ascribed identity for safety, assimilation, or access to resources'. Chatterji et al., 2016, op. cit., pp. 24–5.

27. 'Securitization is the establishment of policies, discourses, and practices that define the parameters of freedom, threats to national security, and mechanisms for national preservation. Securitization delimits the state's constantly shifting relations to its internal and external Others'. *Conflicted Democracies*, op. cit., p. 25.

28. For details, see sections entitled, 'Recent History' and 'Terror and Violence'.

29. I am grateful to Thomas Blom Hansen and Richard Shapiro for conversations that helped me elaborate on issues of Hindu cultural dominance, Hindu nationalism, and nationalist Hinduism this section.

30. For Christian cultural dominance, see Shapiro, Richard, 'Religion and Empire: Secular Christian cultural dominance in the United States', *International Journal of the Humanities*, 2, 3 (2006), pp. 2491–500.

31. Non western modernity/west-imbricated modernity, during colonialism

32. The 'post/colony' and the '(post)colonial' are constitutive of contested discursive and political spaces; see Afzal-Khan, Fawzia, and Kalpana Seshadri-Crooks, (eds.) *The Pre-Occupation of Postcolonial Studies*, Durham: Duke University Press, 2000; Guha, Ranajit, and Gayatri Chakravorty Spivak, (eds.) *Selected Subaltern Studies*, New York: Oxford University Press, 1988; Loomba, Ania. *Colonialism/Postcolonialism*. New York: Routledge, 1998; Said, Edward W. *Orientalism*. New York: Pantheon Books, 1978; Zein-Elabdin, Eiman, and S. Charusheela, (eds.) *Postcolonialism Meets Economics*. New York: Routledge, 2003.

33. The imaginary of *Bharat Mata* (prevalently a nationalistic and Hindu characterisation) was ideologically assimilated into state institutions, such as the paramilitary Central Reserve Police Force (CRPF), whose slogan states: 'CRPF *Sada Ajay; Bharat Mata Ki Jay*' (CRPF Always Victorious; Hail/Victory to Bharat Mata), see Chatterji, *Violent Gods*, op. cit., p. 48).

34. Hindutva-isation refers to the political and sociocultural processes via which majoritarian understandings and practices become pervasive within society, fostering their normalisation in the name of 'authentic' Hindu religion and culture. Such processes are aided by Sanskritisation, see Chatterji, *Violent Gods*, op. cit., p. 43; also, Srinivas, M. N., *Religion and Society among the Coorgs of South India*, Oxford: Clarendon Press, 1952; Srinivas, M. N., *Caste in Modern India and Other Essays*, Bombay: Asia Publishing House, 1962.

35. See Chatterjee, Partha, *The Nation and Its Fragments: Colonial and Postcolonial Histories*. Princeton: Princeton University Press 1993; Chatterjee, Partha, 'Beyond the Nation? Or within?', *Social Text*, 56 (Autumn 1998), pp. 57–69. doi: 10.2307/466770; Chatterji, Bhola, *Aspects of Bengal Politics in the Early Nineteen-Thirties*, Calcutta: World Press, 1969; Guha, Ranajit, *History at the Limit of World-History*, New York: Columbia University Press, 2002; also, Chatterjee, Indrani, 'Renewed and connected histories: Slavery and the historiography of South Asia', in Indrani Chatterjee and Richard M. Eaton (eds.), *Slavery and South Asian History*, Bloomington: Indiana University Press, 2006, pp. 17–43; Guha, Sumit, *Beyond Caste: Identity and Power in South Asia, Past and Present*, Boston: Brill, 2013.

36. See Anderson, Benedict, *Imagined Communities: Reflections on the Origin and Spread of Nationalism*, New York: Verso Books, 1991.

37. See Anderson, Perry, 'After Nehru', *London Review of Books*, 34, 15 (2012), pp. 21–36, https://www.lrb.co.uk/v34/n15/perry-anderson/after-nehru.

38. It is relevant to note that: 'a Stockholm International Peace Research Institute report records that between 2010 and 2014, India was the world's largest procurer of arms, with a 15 per cent share of the global arms imports (Wezeman and Wezeman, 2015: pp. 4–5). Between 2005 and 2014, India's import of arms increased by 140 per cent (Ibid., p. 5). Adjacently, India is home to one in three of the world's poorest people and ranked at 135 from a total of 187 countries in the Human Development Index for 2013 (United Nations Development Program, 2014). India ranked 143 (of 162 countries) in the Global Peace Index in 2014 (Institute for Economics and Peace, 2014: 29), see also Chatterji et al., 2016, p. 77. For sources in the above quote, see: Wezeman, Pieter D. and Siemon Wezeman, *SIPRI Fact Sheet: Trends in International Arms Transfers, 2014*, Solna: Stockholm International Peace Research Institute (2015), https://www.sipri.org/sites/default/files/files/FS/SIPRIFS1503.pdf; United Nations Development Program, *Human Development Report 2014*, New York: United Nations Development Program (2014), http://hdr.undp.org/en/content/human-development-report-2014, Institute for Economics and Peace, *Global Peace Index 2014*, New York: Institute for Economics and Peace (2014) http://economicsandpeace.org/wp-content/uploads/2015/06/2014-Global-Peace-Index-REPORT_0–1.pdf.

39. For fascisizing and majoritarianism, see Robinson, Andrew and Simon Tormey, 'Living in smooth space: Deleuze, postcolonialism and the subaltern', in Simone Bignall and Paul Paton (eds.), *Deleuze and the Postcolonial*, Edinburgh: Edinburgh University Press, 2010, p. 23.

40. Das, Veena, 'Language and body: Transactions in the construction of pain', in Nancy Scheper Hughes and Philippe Bourgois (eds), *Violence in War and Peace: An Anthology*, Part VIII: Gendered Violence, Oxford: Blackwell Press, 2004, p. 332; also see, Visweswaran, Kamala, eds, 2013, *Everyday Occupations Experiencing Militarism in South Asia and the Middle East*, Pennsylvania: University of Pennsylvania Press.

41. 'Geographicity', see Chatterjee, Indrani, *Forgotten Friends: Monks, Marriages, and Memories of Northeast India*, New York: Oxford University Press, 2013.

42. For 'conflicted democracy' and India, see Chatterji, Angana P., Shashi Buluswar, Mallika Kaur (eds), *Conflicted Democracies and Gendered Violence: The Right to Heal: Internal Conflict and Social Upheaval in India*, New Delhi: Zubaan, 2016.

43. Chatterji, *Violent Gods*, op. cit., p. 86; Chatterji et al., *Conflicted Democracies*, op. cit., p. 81.

44. Political violence in the current form since 1990.

45. Chatterji et al., *Conflicted Democracies*, op. cit.; Chatterji, Angana P., Parvez Imroz, Gautam Navlakha, Zahir-Ud-Din, Mihir Desai and Khurram Parvez, *Buried Evidence: Unknown, Unmarked and Mass Graves in Indian-administered Kashmir*, Srinagar: International People's Tribunal on Human Rights and Justice in Indian-administered Kashmir, 2009, http://www.kashmirprocess.org/reports/graves/BuriedEvidence Kashmir.pdf; Chatterji, Angana P., 'The militarized zone', in Tariq Ali, Hilal Bhatt,

Angana P. Chatterji, Pankaj Mishra and Arundhati Roy, *Kashmir: The Case for Freedom*, London: Verso, 2011.

46. Many Adivasi communities do not consider themselves 'Hindu' even as they may be counted upon as Hindus by majoritarian groups and the state, for example in the census. Hindu nationalists routinely term Adivasis as Vanavasis. Vanavasi: Forest dweller, derogatory naming of Adivasis (first dweller), who are routinely associated by Hindu nationalists with 'backwardness' and 'primitivity', as 'savage' (not as ennobling). 'Savage' ('wild' in Old French) is derivative of silvaticus in Latin, meaning 'of the woods'/'forest dweller,' also see Chatterji, *Violent Gods*, op. cit., p. 67.

47. Many Dalit groups do not consider themselves Hindu even as they may be counted upon as Hindus by majoritarian groups and the state, for example in the census.

48. Narmada Bachao Andolan: http://www.narmada.org; see the judgement delivered in *Nandini Sundar & Ors versus State of Chhattisgarh*, 2007, http://pudr.org/content/nandini-sundar-ors-versus-state-chattisgarh; also: Sundar, Nandini, 'Hostages to Democracy', *Verso* (blog), 30 May 2018, https://www.versobooks.com/blogs/3856-hostages-to-democracy

49. Civil and political rights and social, cultural, and economic rights.

50. Chakravarti, Uma, and Nandita Haksar, *The Delhi Riots: Three Days in the Life of a Nation*, New Delhi: Lancer International, 1987; Chatterji et al., *Conflicted Democracies*, op. cit.

51. 'During [Emergency], the writ of habeas corpus was held suspended by the Supreme Court of India. In India, states of emergency and states of exception are defined and decreed through distinct and overlapping apparatuses. The (Indian) states of emergency and exception are not so exceptional. For nearly seventy years now, the response of the postcolonial Indian state has been inconsistent with respect to the imposition of emergency through the presidential decree. In areas of [political] conflict, central governments have, in contradiction of individual states' rights, declared emergency for successive periods, legally contravening of myriad fundamental rights and freedoms', Chatterji et al., *Conflicted Democracies*, op. cit., pp. 227–9.

52. See, Foucault, Michel, *Security, Territory, Population, Lectures at the Collge De France, 1977–1978*, translation Graham Burchell, Michel Senellart (ed.), Franois Ewald and Alessandro Fontana (general eds.), Arnold I. Davidson (English series ed.), New York: Palgrave Macmillan, 2007.

53. See, also, the colonial, Orientalist construction, disciplining, and representation of Hinduism as a 'world religion', Guha, Ranajit, *History at the Limit of World-History*, New York: Columbia University Press, 2002. Further, the movement led by the intelligentsia in the nineteenth century initially focused on reforms in Hinduism and later shifted to the consolidation of nationalism, perforce imbricating one with the other. See also, King, Richard, *Orientalism and Religion: Post-colonial Theory, India and the 'Mystic East'*, New York: Routledge, 1999.

54. Thapar, Romila with Sundar Sarukkai, Dhruv Raina, Peter Ronald deSouza, Neeladri Bhattacharya, and Jawed Naqvi, *The Public Intellectual in India*, Delhi: Aleph Book Company, 2015, p. xxvi.

55. Singh, Gurharpal, *Ethnic Conflict in India: A Case-Study of Punjab*, New York: St. Martin's Press, 2000, p. 35.

56. Singh, *Ethnic Conflict in India: A Case-Study of Punjab*, op cit., p. 35; Smooha, Sammy, 'The model of ethnic democracy', EMI Working Paper #13, 1–95, European Centre for Minority Issues, Flensburg, Germany, 2001, https://www.ecmi.de/uploads/tx_lfpubdb/working_paper_13.pdf; Smooha, Sammy, 'Minority Status in an Ethnic Democracy: The Status of the Arab Minority in Israel', Ethnic and Racial Studies 13 (3), 2010, pp. 389–413, http://www.tandfonline.com/doi/abs/10.1080/01419870.1990.9993679.

57. Shackle, Christopher, Gurharpal Singh, and Arvind-pal Singh Mandair (eds), *Sikh Religion, Culture and Ethnicity*, Richmond: Curzon, 2001.

58. Panikkar, K.N., *Communalism in India: A Perspective for Intervention*, New Delhi: People's Publishing House, 1991; see also Mahmood, Saba, 'Religious freedom, minority rights, and geopolitics', *The Immanent Frame* (blog), 5 Mar. 2012, https://tif.ssrc.org/2012/03/05/religious-freedom-minority-rights-and-geopolitics/; Chatterji, *Violent Gods*, op. cit.

59. Chatterji et. al, *Conflicted Democracies*, op cit., p. 82; see also Puri, Jyoti, *Sexual States: Governance and the Decriminalization of Sodomy in India's Present*, Durham: Duke University Press, 2016.

60. JanMohamed, Abdul R., and David Lloyd, *The Nature and Context of Minority Discourse*, New York: Oxford University Press, 1990.

61. Chatterji et. al, *Conflicted Democracies*, op cit.

62. Singh, Gurharpal, 'The Limits of "Conventional Wisdom": Understanding Sikh Ethnonationalism', in Arvind-Pal S. Mandair et. al, *Sikh Religion, Culture, and Ethnicity*, op. cit., p. 155.

63. 'Minoritisation is the social, political, and economic exclusion and targeting of non-dominant peoples and groups through dehistoricization, marginalization, and stereotypification', Chatterji et. al, *Conflicted Democracies*, op cit., p. 45.

64. Hong, Grace Kyungwon and Roderick A. Ferguson (eds), *Strange Affinities: The Gender and Sexual Politics of Comparative Racialization*, Durham: Duke University Press, 2011.

65. Chatterji, *Violent Gods*, op. cit.; see also Loomba, Ania, 'Race and the possibilities of comparative critique', *New Literary History*, 40, 3 (2009), pp. 501–22. doi: 10.1353/nlh.0.0103.

66. Ghassem-Fachandi, Parvis, *Pogrom in Gujarat: Hindu Nationalism and Anti-Muslim Violence in India*, Princeton: Princeton University Press, 2012; Hansen, Thomas Blom, *The Saffron Wave: Democracy and Hindu Nationalism in Modern India*. Princeton: Princeton University Press, 1999; Jaffrelot, Christophe, 'Communal riots in Gujarat: The state at risk'? *Heidelberg Papers in South Asian and Comparative Politics*, Working Paper No. 17, 1–20. South Asia Institute, Department of Political Science, University of Heidelberg, Heidelberg, 2003, http://archiv.ub.uni-heidelberg.de/volltextserver/4127/1/hpsacp17.pdf.

67. Ibid.

68. Sarkar, Tanika, 'Semiotics of terror', *Economic and Political Weekly*, 37, 28 (13 July 2002), pp. 2872–6.

69. Chatterjee, Partha, *The Nation and Its Fragments: Colonial and Postcolonial Histories*, Princeton: Princeton University Press, 1993; Jaffrelot, 'Communal riots in Gujarat', op. cit.

70. Secularisation in India has functioned within varied contexts of Hindu cultural dominance. In Europe, as in the United States, secularisation has functioned within varied contexts of Christian cultural dominance, see Shapiro, 'Religion and Empire', op. cit.; Asad, Talal, *Formations of the Secular: Christianity, Islam, Modernity*, Stanford: Stanford University Press, 2003; Chatterjee, *The Nation and Its Fragments*, op. cit.

71. Chatterji et al, *Conflicted Democracies*, op. cit.

72. Press Trust of India, 'Bhima-Koregaon activists' arrest: Gautam Navlakha moves Bombay HC to quash FIR, says he's been "falsely implicated"', *Firstpost*, 22 Oct. 2018, https://www.firstpost.com/india/bhima-koregaon-activists-arrest-gautam-navlakha-moves-bombay-hc-to-quash-fir-says-he-has-been-falsely-implicated-5404301.html; Roy, Arundhati, 'We are living through history as fake news', *Indian Express*, 8 Oct. 2018, http://www.newindianexpress.com/nation/2018/oct/08/we-are-living-through-history-as-fake-news-arundhati-roy-1882794.html; Faleiro, Sonia, 'India's attack on free speech', *New York Times*, 2 Oct. 2015, https://www.nytimes.com/2015/10/04/opinion/sunday/sonia-faleiro-india-free-speech-kalburgi-pansare-dabholkar.html.

73. The shifts in religion and 'religious dimension' develop or deepen through time, whereby, for example, institutions that profess to be secular, including institutions of state, assume a religious tone and/or character' (Chatterji et al, *Conflicted Democracies*, op. cit., p. 24).

74. Chatterji, Angana P. and Lubna Nazir Chaudhry (eds), *Contesting Nation: Gendered Violence in South Asia—Notes on the Postcolonial Present*. New Delhi: Zubaan, 2012.

75. Das, Veena, *Life and Words: Violence and the Descent into the Ordinary*, Berkeley: University of California Press, 2007; Kabir, Ananya Jahanara, 'Double violation? (Not) talking about sexual violence in South Asia' in Sorcha Gunne and Zoë Brigley Thompson (eds), *Feminism, Literature and Rape Narratives: Violence and Violation*, pp. 146–63, New York: Routledge, 2010.

76. Chatterjee, *The Nation and Its Fragments*, op. cit.; Hinnells, John R., and Richard King, *Religion and Violence in South Asia: Theory and Practice*, New York: Routledge, 2007.

77. Navanethem Pillay in the *Washington Post*: 'From time immemorial, rape has been regarded as spoils of war... Now it will be considered a war crime. We want to send out a strong signal that rape is no longer a trophy of war'. Berkeley, Bill, 11 Oct. 1998, 'Judgement day', *Washington Post*, https://www.washingtonpost.com/archive/lifestyle/magazine/1998/10/11/judgement-day/3ae2490b-c3c7–4c17-b43c-e96bbfc064e5/?noredirect=on&utm_term=.15c7ce903a02; see Rwanda International Criminal Tribunal, 'Press Release: Rwanda International Criminal Tribunal pronounces guilty verdict in historic genocide trial', AFR/94 L/2895, 2 Sep. 1998, https://www.un.org/press/en/1998/19980902.afr94.html.

78. Bannerji, Himani, 'Demography and democracy: Reflections on violence against women in genocide or ethnic cleansing' in *Demography and Democracy: Essays on Nationalism, Gender, and Ideology*, Toronto: Canadian Scholars' Press, Inc., 2011, p. 90.

79. Chatterji, *Violent Gods*, op. cit., pp. 34, 147–8, 159, 174–6, 183.

80. Chatterji, *Violent Gods*, op. cit., pp. 83–5, 159, 165, 277–363.

81. Chatterji, *Violent Gods*, op. cit., pp. 157–211.

82. Chatterji, *Violent Gods*, op. cit., pp. 163–89.

83. Census of India [Ministry of Home Affairs, Government of India], *C-1 Population By Religious Community, 2011*, 2011, http://www.censusindia.gov.in/2011census/C-01/DDW00C-01%20MDDS.XLS.

84. Ibid.

85. Census of India [Ministry of Home Affairs, Government of India], *C-1 Population By Religious Community*, op. cit. Note: Adivasis and Dalits are routinely counted as Hindus.

86. Economics & Statistics Division, State Planning Institute, Uttar Pradesh, 'Advance estimates of State Domestic Product (State Income), 2014–15' 16 Feb. 2015, http://updes.up.nic.in/Press%20Release%20of%20advance%20Estimates%20of%20State%20Domestic%20Product%20(State%20Income)%202013–14%20Dated%2016.2.2015.pdf, p. 4.

87. Crore: ten million.

88. Calculated using data from National Institution for Transforming India, Government of India, *GSDP at Current Prices, 2004–05 Series (2004–05 to 2014–15)*, 2015, http://niti.gov.in/content/gsdp-current-prices-2004-05-series-2004-05-2014-15.

89. Rawat, Virendra Singh, 'UP clocks maximum food grain production in India', *Business Standard*, 7 Mar. 2014, https://www.business-standard.com/article/economy-policy/up-clocks-maximum-food-grain-production-in-india-114030700676_1.html

90. Papola, T.S., Nitu Maurya, and Narendra Jena, *Inter-regional Disparities in Industrial Growth and Structure*, New Delhi: Institute for Studies in Industrial Development, 2011.

91. India Brand Equity Foundation, *Uttar Pradesh: A Rainbow Land*, 2015, https://www.ibef.org/download/Uttar-Pradesh-August-2015.pdf, p. 3.

92. Press Trust of India, 'Rural Muslim poverty highest in Assam, WB, UP and Guj: UNDP', *Economic Times*, 18 Feb. 2013, https://m.economictimes.com/news/politics-and-nation/rural-muslim-poverty-highest-in-assam-wb-up-and-guj-undp/amp_articleshow/18561389.cms.

93. Economics & Statistics Division, 'Advance estimates of State Domestic Product', op. cit.

94. National minorities 'are prevalently subordinate groups, discriminated against by virtue of differences in race, caste, ethnicity, indigeneity, class, religion, language, gender, sexual identity, and other social markers' (Chatterji et al., *Conflicted Democracies*, op. cit., p. 52); and 'the classification of [ethnic and religious] national minority is often relational to the identification of a social majority that occupies a privileged position to social, economic, legal, and political power. The social power exercised by the majority community may be linked to majoritarian and nationalist aspirations. The formal classification of a 'minority' group and their capacity to secure rights within a state may involve highly contentious processes. Such classification by states both renders the minority group formally subordinate in the social hierarchy while potentially enabling access to resources for development and assimilation' (Chatterji et al., *Conflicted Democracies*, op. cit., p. 53).

95. Lesbian, Gay, Bisexual, Transgender/Transgender Association, Intersex, Questioning, and Ally.

96. In Uttar Pradesh, those who do not abide by heterosexual norms face systemic

harassment, surveillance, forced disclosure, exaction, loss of livelihood and home, expulsion, isolation, and violence. The National Crime Records Bureau reported that Uttar Pradesh had the highest number of arrests under the Indian Penal Code, Section 377, in 2015, at 239. The report found that minors were also being arrested under 377 when another law, the Protection of Children from Sexual Offices Act, should cover such crimes. The NCRB data does not differentiate sexual abuse and consensual sex acts between adults, see Thomas, Shibu, '14% of those arrested under section 377 last year were minors', *Times of India*, 29 Sep. 2016, https://timesofindia.indiatimes.com/city/mumbai/14-of-those-arrested-under-section-377-last-year-were-minors/articleshow/54573741.cms.

97. In writing this section, I have drawn extensively on research that I have undertaken for a report for which I am the lead author, which includes collaborative work undertaken by me with Mihir Desai, Teesta Setalvad, and Pei Wu. I am grateful for this work and to be able to draw on it. The research was undertaken between June 2016 and January 2018 with the objective of detailing issues in rural and urban hotspots in eastern and western Uttar Pradesh. 158 applications were filed in under the Right To Information Act and secondary sources, including reports, media, legal cases and other official and independent sources, were used and corroborated with records received from lawyers, local civil society leaders and victimised-survivor networks, together with a few select primary interviews.

98. Shuklal, Neha, 'UP state minorities commission says it never studied status of minorities in UP', *Times of India*, 17 Sep. 2014, http://timesofindia.indiatimes.com/india/UP-State-Minorities-Commission-says-it-never-studied-status-of-minorities-in-UP/articleshow/42711450.cms.

99. Ibid.

100. Vishwa Hindu Parishad, World Hindu Council, was formed in 1964 as Hindutva's ideological front.

101. See: NDTV, 'Muzaffarnagar riots: BJP MLA accused of inciting violence arrested from court', NDTV, 17 Oct. 2013, https://www.ndtv.com/india-news/muzaffarnagar-riots-bjp-mla-accused-of-inciting-violence-arrested-from-court-538027; Ali, Mohammad, 'Muzaffarnagar riots case: Bailable warrant against Union Minister, BJP leaders', *The Hindu*, 24 Oct. 2015, http://www.thehindu.com/news/national/muzaffarnagar-riots-bailable-warrant-against-union-minister-bjp-leaders/article7800251.ece; Mohan, Vishwa, 'Government bans 100 terror outfits', *Times of India*, 16 May 2010, https://timesofindia.indiatimes.com/india/Government-bans-100-terror-outfits/articleshow/5935393.cms; Ministry of Home Affairs [Government of India], 'Banned organisations', http://www.mha.nic.in/BO, accessed 5 Oct. 2015. However, no injunctions were imposed on these organisations. It is noteworthy that, 'in 2010, India banned approximately a hundred organisations under the Unlawful Activities (Prevention) Act (UAPA) of 1967, including Lashkar-e-Taiba and Hizbul Mujahideen (Mohan, 2010). They are among the thirty-eight groups currently on the banned list as of March 2015 (Ministry of Home Affairs, 2015)', see Chatterji et al., *Conflicted Democracies*, op. cit., p. 85. While majoritarian cadre and organisations have been implicated in numerous sites of social violence in India since 1947, no Hindu nationalist groups were among the thirty-eight listed in March 2015.

102. Human Rights Watch, *India: Stop Forced Evictions of Riot Victims*, 2014, https://www.hrw.org/news/2014/01/17/india-stop-forced-evictions-riot-victims.

103. Heise, Tammy, 'Religion and Native American assimilation, resistance, and survival', in *Oxford Research Encyclopedia of Religion*, http://religion.oxfordre.com/view/10.1093/acrefore/9780199340378.001.0001/acrefore-9780199340378-e-394.

104. Press Trust of India, 'RSS strengthening base in Kerala, number of shakhas rising', *Economic Times*, 14 Feb. 2017, https://economictimes.indiatimes.com/news/politics-and-nation/rss-strengthening-base-in-kerala-number-of-shakhas-rising/articleshow/57146535.cms.

105. Ibid.

106. Hindu nationalist discourse argues that all 'Indians' are 'originally' Hindus, even those who do not self-identify as such. This is contrary to the understandings and self-representations of certain minority, marginalised caste, tribal, and casteless peoples, who understand their right to conversion as an essential component in the practice of freedom of religion. Conversion out of Hinduism can act as a way to circumvent caste oppression even as the social, gendered, and economic hierarchies consolidated through the caste system often carryover, post-conversion, into other religions. Key Hindu nationalist strategies against conversions from Hinduism and for conversions to Hinduism include coercive induction of non-Hindus to Hinduism, advocacy to implement 'freedom' of religion acts to stall or stop conversions to Christianity and other religions, and campaigns for the denial of reservation benefits to those who convert to other religions.

107. Economic Times, 'Aligarh Muslim University Union asks Home Minister Rajnath Singh to ban ghar vapasi', *Economic Times*, 15 Dec. 2014, ProQuest (1635917535).

108. Figures pertain to the exchange rate available on 21 October 2018.

109. See Human Rights Watch, *India: Events of 2015*, 2016, https://www.hrw.org/world-report/2016/country-chapters/india; United States Commission on International Religious Freedom, *Annual Report—2015*, 2015, http://www.uscirf.gov/sites/default/files/USCIRF%20Annual%20Report%202015%20%282%29.pdf, op. cit., p. 151.

110. Ibid.

111. Singh, Ramendra, 'Riot-hit UP sees surge in cow slaughter cases', *Indian Express*, 11 Oct. 2015, http://indianexpress.com/article/india/india-news-india/riot-hit-up-sees-surge-in-cow-slaughter-cases/

112. Raj, Suhasini, 'Mob in India kills Muslim man over rumors of cow slaughter', *New York Times*, 30 Sep. 2015, ProQuest (1718092666).

113. Barstow, David and Suhasini Raj, 'Mob attack, fuelled by rumors of cow slaughter, has political overtones in India', *New York Times*, 4 Oct. 2015, http://www.nytimes.com/2015/10/05/world/asia/mob-attack-over-rumors-of-cow-slaughter-has-political-overtones-in-india.html.

114. Graff, Violette and Juliette Galonnier, 'Hindu-Muslim Communal Riots in India II (1986–2011)', *Online Encyclopaedia of Mass Violence*, 2013, http://www.sciencespo.fr/mass-violence-war-massacre-resistance/fr/document/hindu-muslim-communal-riots-india-ii-1986-2011.

115. Kumar, Sanjay, 'The hotspot of communal violence in India is not where you think it is', *Ultra News*, 2 Dec. 2015, https://ultra.news/s-k/15976/communal-violence-in-india-sees-an-increase-in-2015-dips-in-gujarat-rajasthan-crime-records.

116. Sethi, Abheet Singh, 'Uttar Pradesh, India's communal tinderbox', *The Wire*, 10 July 2015, http://thewire.in/2015/10/07/uttar-pradesh-indias-communal-tinderbox-12614/.

117. Ministry of Home Affairs [Government of India], *Statement Showing Communal Incidents, Number of Persons Killed/Injured Therein During the Years 2010, 2011, 2012, and 2013 (up to March)*, 2013, http://mha1.nic.in/par2013/par2013-pdfs/ls-070513/6502.pdf.

118. Ministry of Home Affairs [Government of India], *STATEMENT REFFERED TO IN REPLY TO PART (a to c) OF LOK SABHA UNSTARRED QUESTION NO. 2251 FOR 10.03.2015*, 2015, http://mha1.nic.in/par2013/par2015-pdfs/ls-100315/2251.pdf.

119. Ministry of Home Affairs [Government of India], *STATEMENT REFERRED TO IN REPLY TO PART (a) to (b) OF LOK SABHA UNSTARRED QUESTION NO. 849 FOR 07.02.2017 SHOWING NUMBER OF COMMUNAL INCIDENTS, NUMBER OF PERSONS KILLED/INJURED THEREIN DURING THE YEARS 2014, 2015 & 2016*, 2017, http://mha1.nic.in/par2013/par2017-pdfs/ls-072217/849.pdf.

120. Outlook, 'UP witnesses 60 communal incidents, 16 deaths in 2017, highest in the country', *Outlook*, 9 Aug. 2017, https://www.outlookindia.com/website/story/up-witnesses-60-communal-incidents-16-deaths-in-2017-highest-in-the-country/300193.

121. Indian Express, 'Highest growth ever: RSS adds 5,000 New shakhas in last 12 months', *Indian Express*, 16 Mar. 2016, http://indianexpress.com/article/india/india-news-india/rss-uniform-over-5000-new-shakhas-claims-rss/.

122. Ibid.

123. At its annual meeting in Nagpur, Maharashtra, in March 2016, the Akhil Bharatiya Pratinidhi Sabha, the decision-making unit of the RSS, determined to restyle the traditional and symbolic uniform of its workers from khaki shorts to brown trousers. To the older cadre, shorts evoked a readiness to march, to perform martial arts. To the younger generation, the change signified modernisation.

124. Press Trust of India, 'RSS strengthening base in Kerala, number of shakhas rising', *Economic Times*, 14 Feb. 2017, https://economictimes.indiatimes.com/news/politics-and-nation/rss-strengthening-base-in-kerala-number-of-shakhas-rising/articleshow/57146535.cms.

125. The figures cited here are derived from Sangh Parivar organisations and sources and require independent verification.

126. Ekal Vidyalaya Foundation. 2018. 'Our Schools'. https://www.ekal.org/our-schools.

127. Press Trust of India, 'RSS can prepare an army within 3 days: Mohan Bhagwat', *Times of India*, 12 Feb. 2018, https://timesofindia.indiatimes.com/india/rss-can-prepare-an-army-within-3-days-mohan-bhagwat/articleshow/62877231.cms.

128. See Mahaprashasta, Ajoy Ashirwad, 'Adityanath's 2014 article equating women with demons comes back to haunt him', *The Wire*, 19 Apr. 2017, https://thewire.in/gender/adityanath-womens-rights-triple-talaq.

129. Such targeting seeks to undermine kinship relations and community security and to disrupt the transmission of culture. Such disruption intends to assert the dominion of majority culture over 'resources', including minority women, see Bacchetta, Paola, 'Communal property/sexual property: On Representations of Muslim Women in a Hindu nationalist discourse', in Zoya Hasan (ed.), *Forging Identities: Gender, Communities, and the State*, pp. 188–225, New Delhi: Kali for Women, 1994; Chatterji and Nazir Choudhry, *Contesting Nation*, op. cit.; Loomba, Ania and Ritty Lukose, *South Asian Feminisms*, Durham: Duke University Press, 2012.

130. In writing this section, I have drawn extensively on research that I have undertaken for a report that is pending publication for which I am the lead author, which includes collaborative work undertaken by me with Mihir Desai, Teesta Setalvad, and Pei Wu.

131. Submission by a community leader/organisation to PCRes-Berkeley, 2017–18.

132. Indian Express, 'Parliament HIGHLIGHTS: Triple Talaq Bill to be tabled in Rajya Sabha tomorrow', *Indian Express*, 3 Jan. 2018, https://indianexpress.com/article/india/triple-talaq-bill-rajya-sabha-live-updates-instant-talaq-bjp-congress-narendra-modi-amit-shah-5008156/.

133. Submission by a community leader/organisation to PCRes-Berkeley, 2017–18. In 2005, a Muslim rights activist from Bhadrak, Orissa, had stated to Angana P. Chatterji: 'We must support the Muslim Women's Personal Law Board when they speak out and other progressive Muslim voices. But we cannot judge every Muslim man as— —'s [name withheld] father-in-law, as much as rape by a Hindu man does not link "all Hindus" with the crime. This puts fear in the Muslim community and makes the community withdraw. It isolates Muslims even more from the mainstream and increases conservative influence' (Chatterji, *Violent Gods*, op. cit., p. 110).

134. Schultz, Kai, 'India criminalizes instant "Talaq" divorces for Muslim men', *New York Times*, 20 Sep. 2018, https://www.nytimes.com/2018/09/20/world/asia/india-talaq-muslim-divorce.html.

135. Flavia Agnes, 'The politics behind criminalising triple talaq', *Economic and Political Weekly*, LIII, 1 (6 Jan. 2018), https://www.epw.in/journal/2018/1/commentary/politics-behind-criminalising-triple-talaq.html; Khan, Muniza Rafiq, *Socio-Legal Status of Muslim Women*, Delhi: Radiant Publishers, 1993.

136. Submission by a community leader/organisation to PCRes-Berkeley, 2017–18.

137. George, Nirmala, 'India records huge spike in 'honor killings' in 2015', *Associated Press*, 7 Dec. 2016, http://bigstory.ap.org/article/0e76638f1855421699050c168c6 36e96/india-records-huge-spike-honor-killings-2015.

138. Ibid.

139. Ibid.

140. Ibid.

141. Suresh, 'Love jihad', op. cit.

142. Raghavan, Pyaralal, 'Growing sway of inter caste marriages', *Times of India* (blog), 4 Dec. 2012, http://blogs.timesofindia.indiatimes.com/minorityview/growing-sway-of-inter-caste-marriages/.

143. National Council of Applied Economic Research, '5 per cent of Indian marriages inter-caste; in Mizoram, 55 per cent', 11 May 2016, http://www.ncaer.org/news_details.php?nID=188.

144. In writing this section, I have drawn extensively on research that I have undertaken for a report that is pending publication for which I am the lead author, which includes collaborative work undertaken by me with Mihir Desai, Teesta Setalvad, and Pei Wu.

145. https://www.hindustantimes.com/static/uttar-pradesh-communal-riot/love-jihad-uttar-pradesh/

146. 'Rape victims seek SIC probe, SC issues notices', *Indian Express*, 18 Jan. 2014, https://indianexpress.com/article/india/india-others/rape-victims-seek-sit-probe-sc-issues-notices/; Dixit, Neha, 'The Law is under Trial here', *Outlook*, 16 Feb. 2015, https://www.outlookindia.com/magazine/story/the-law-is-under-trial-here/293296.

147. Indo Asian News Service, 'SC notice on plea seeking probe into rapes in Muzaffarnagar', *Indo Asian News Service*, 17 Jan. 2014, ProQuest (1477993778).

148. Figures pertain to the exchange rate available on 21 October 2018.

149. Kashmir Times, 'Aftermath of Muzaffarnagar's riots: Women bear the brunt', *Kashmir Times*, 17 Mar. 2014, ProQuest (1507798795).

150. Associated Press, 'Two Indian sisters "gang-raped," killed and hanged from a tree', *The Guardian*, 29 May 2014, https://www.theguardian.com/world/2014/may/29/indian-sisters-gang-raped-hanged-tree.

151. Chowdhury, Sagnik, 'Badaun case: Cousins committed suicide after one caught in 'intimate' act, says CBI', *Indian Express*, 28 Nov. 2014, https://indianexpress.com/article/india/india-others/no-evidence-found-of-murder-rape-in-badaun-sisters-case/.

152. AIDWA national general secretary Jagmati Sangwan stated that: 'We strongly demand that that there should be an impartial re-investigation into the case as it appears that the CBI is trying to save people who are politically connected. First, it came out with the honour killing angle. Then they claimed it to be suicide by bringing in the love triangle theory', Chatterjee, Pritha, 'Badaun case: Why few are buying CBI's suicide story', *Indian Express*, 29 Nov. 2014, https://indianexpress.com/article/india/india-others/in-badaun-why-few-are-buying-the-cbis-suicide-story/; Agarwal, Priyangi, 'NGOs and locals question CBI's Badaun theory, seek fresh probe', *Times of India*, 8 Feb. 2015, http://epaperbeta.timesofindia.com/Article.aspx?eid=31808&articlexml=NGOs-and-locals-question-CBIs-Badaun-theory-seek-08022015014031.

153. Venkatesan, J., 'Don't disturb country's secular fabric, says SC', *The Hindu*, 8 Aug. 2014, http://www.thehindu.com/news/national/countrys-secular-fabric-should-not-be-disturbed-observes-supreme-court/article6296248.ece.

154. United States Department of State [Bureau of Democracy, Human Rights and Labor], *2014 International Religious Freedom Report—India*, 2014, http://www.state.gov/j/drl/rls/irf/religiousfreedom/index.htm?year=2014&dlid=238494.

155. Verma, Lalmani, 'Citing love jihad, Sangh groups in Uttar Pradesh unite to fight', *Financial Express*, 31 Aug. 2014, http://www.financialexpress.com/archive/citing-love-jihad-sangh-groups-in-uttar-pradesh-unite-to-fight/1284158/.

156. *Rakhi* = a band or bracelet tied around a person's wrists signifying a brother-sister bond.

157. Srivastava, Rajiv, 'In west Uttar Pradesh, Rashtriya Swayamsevak Sangh's launches rakhi drive to fight "love jihad"', *Economic Times*, 9 Aug. 2014, ProQuest (1552012553).

158. Ibid.

159. Times of India, 'VHP disowns UP "love jihad" leaflets', *Times of India*, 11 Sep. 2014, http://timesofindia.indiatimes.com/india/VHP-disowns-UP-love-jihad-leaflets/articleshow/42216235.cms.

160. Nair, Rupam Jain and Frank Jack Daniel, 'India at a hard line with 'love jihad' and religious conversion', *Hindustan Times*, 6 Sep. 2014, http://www.hindustantimes.com/india/india-at-a-hard-line-with-love-jihad-and-religious-conversion/story-Ap8V VuLF2dI2bFuwrv7rKP.html.

161. Hindustan Times, '"Love jehad" missing, but its ghost haunts west UP', *Hindustan Times*, 11 Feb. 2017, ProQuest (1867148333).

162. Rai, Sandeep, 'Muslim woman weds Hindu man, both killed', *Times of India*, 29 Nov. 2014, http://timesofindia.indiatimes.com/city/meerut/Muslim-woman-weds-Hindu-man-both-killed/articleshow/45321279.cms.

163. Ibid.

164. Ibid.

165. Figures pertain to the exchange rate available on 21 October 2018. Sharma, Pankul, 'UP to gift couples in intercaste marriages rs 50,000, medal and certificate', *Times of India*, 29 Jan. 2015, https://timesofindia.indiatimes.com/city/meerut/UP-to-gift-couples-in-intercaste-marriages-Rs-50000-medal-and-certificate/articleshow/46046914.cms.

166. Press Trust of India, '14-year-old Dalit girl gang-raped by four men in Uttar Pradesh', *Mid-Day*, 1 June 2015, https://www.mid-day.com/articles/14-year-old-dalit-girl-gang-raped-by-four-men-in-uttar-pradesh/16254195

167. Amnesty International, 2015, https://www.amnesty.org/download/Documents/ASA2023162015ENGLISH.pdf; Gopika Bashi, 2015, https://counterview.org/2015/09/11/ordered-rape-of-dalit-sisters-highlights-severe-caste-and-gender-discrimination-in-india/; Sharma, 'UP to gift couples in intercaste marriages', op. cit.

168. Ibid.

169. Deccan Herald, 'BJP, VHP, RSS nexus against "love jihad"', *Deccan Herald*, 6 Oct. 2015, http://www.deccanherald.com/content/504728/bjp-vhp-rss-nexus-against.html; also see, United States Department of State, *International Religious Freedom Report 2015—India*, 2016, https://www.state.gov/j/drl/rls/irf/2015/sca/256305.htm.

170. Bajrang Dal is the militant wing of Hindu nationalism. United States Department of State, *International Religious Freedom Report 2015—India*, 2016, https://www.state.gov/j/drl/rls/irf/2015/sca/256305.htm.

171. Seth, Maulshree, 'Uttar Pradesh govt considers relaxing norms to register Hindu marriages', *Indian Express*, 13 May 2016, http://indianexpress.com/article/india/india-news-india/
hindu-marriage-registration-rules-1973-uttar-pradesh-govt-considers-relaxing-norms-to-register-marriages-2797714/.

172. Haque, Amir, 'UP Assembly Polls: SP Sees Saffron in Bajrang Dal's Mock Ayodhya Drill', *India Today*, 24 May 2016, http://indiatoday.intoday.in/story/sp-sees-bjp-game-plan-in-bajrang-dal-self-defence-sessions-at-ayodhya/1/676425.html.

173. Rana, Uday, 'Man with RSS links allegedly stoked Bijnor clashes', *Times of India*,

16 Sep. 2016, http://timesofindia.indiatimes.com/city/meerut/Man-with-RSS-links-allegedly-stoked-Bijnor-clashes/articleshow/54396366.cms.

174. Angad, Abhishek, 'Bijnor violence: "Before firing, made 12 calls to cops, MLA but no action taken"', *Indian Express*, 18 Sep. 2016, http://indianexpress.com/article/india/india-news-india/bijnor-violence-before-firing-made-12-calls-to-cops-mla-but-no-action-taken-3036819/. Rana, 'Man with RSS links allegedly stoked Bijnor clashes', op. cit.

175. Siddiqui, Imran Ahmed, 'Muzaffarnagar echo in Bijnor', *The Telegraph*, 21 Sep. 2016, https://www.telegraphindia.com/india/muzaffarnagar-echo-in-bijnor/cid/1517696.

176. Suresh, 'Love jihad', op. cit.

177. Suresh, 'Love jihad', op. cit.

178. Sahu, Manish, 'Hindu Mahasabha by her side, Aligarh woman says "raped, converted forcibly"', *Indian Express*, 10 June 2018, https://indianexpress.com/article/india/hindu-mahasabha-by-her-side-aligarh-woman-says-raped-converted-forcibly-5211286/, and Jaiswall, Anuja, 'Hindu Mahasabha holds "ghar wapsi" amid tension', *Times of India*, 4 Nov. 2016, http://timesofindia.indiatimes.com/india/hindu-mahasabha-holds-ghar-wapsi-amid-tension/articleshow/55236114.cms.

179. Scroll.in, 'BJP will form an anti-Romeo squad to protect girls in Uttar Pradesh: Amit Shah', *Scroll.in*, 29 Jan. 2017, https://scroll.in/latest/828024/bjp-will-form-an-anti-romeo-squad-to-protect-girls-in-uttar-pradesh-amit-shah.

180. Ibid; Asian News International, 'Bajrangi Dal thrashes couples in Muzaffarpur in protest against V-Day', *Business Standard*, 14 Feb. 2017, http://www.business-standard.com/article/news-ani/bajrangi-dal-thrashes-couples-in-muzaffarpur-in-protest-against-v-day-117021401101_1.html.

181. Ibid.

182. Amnesty International, *Losing Faith*, op. cit.

183. Verma, Lalmani, 'Anti-Romeo & love jihad: Experiments in moral policing in Uttar Pradesh', *Indian Express*, 24 Mar. 2017, http://indianexpress.com/article/explained/anti-romeo-love-jihad-experiments-in-moral-policing-in-uttar-pradesh/.

184. Asian News International, 'UP ATS to launch 'ghar wapsi' campaign for deradicalisation of misguided youth', *Asian News International*, 27 Apr. 2017, ProQuest (1892234441).

185. Indian Express, 'Hindu Yuva Vahini harasses interfaith couple in Meerut', *Indian Express*, 12 Apr. 2017, ProQuest (1886710766).

186. Rai, Rajat, 'Leave now or face dire consequences: Hindu outfit to Kashmiris in UP', *India Today*, 23 Apr. 2017, https://www.indiatoday.in/mail-today/story/uttar-pradesh-navnirmaan-sena-kashmiris-973011-2017-04-23.

187. 'One dead, 25 houses torched as Thakurs, Dalits clash in UP's Saharanpur', *Hindustan Times*, 5 May 2017, https://www.hindustantimes.com/india-news/one-dead-25-houses-torched-as-thakurs-dalits-clash-in-up-s-saharanpur/story-5u5NBXaVnd-3jA2zm9jC2XM.html.

188. Aradhak, Purusharth, 'Prime accused in Bulandshahr "love jihad" lynching case arrested', *Daily News & Analysis*, 9 May 2017, ProQuest (1896111598).

189. Burqa, also burkha, a head-to-ankle outer garment used as a cloak. Indian Express,

'Woman asked to take off burqa at Yogi Adityanath rally in balia, probe ordered', *Indian Express*, 22 Nov. 2017, http://indianexpress.com/article/india/woman-asked-to-remove-her-burqa-at-cm-adityanaths-rally-in-balia-ap-4949177/.

190. Scroll.in, 'RSS affiliate plans to marry 2,100 Muslim women to Hindu men from next week', *Scroll.in*, 1 Dec. 2017, https://scroll.in/latest/859907/rss-affiliate-plans-to-marry-2100-muslim-women-to-hindu-men-from-next-week.

191. In defining the use of the term, Michel Foucault writes that a *dispositif* (apparatus) is a 'heterogenous ensemble consisting of discourses, institutions, architectural forms, regulatory decisions, laws, administrative measures, scientific statements, philosophical, moral, and philanthropic propositions—in short, the said as much as the unsaid. Such are the elements of the apparatus. The apparatus itself is the system of relations that can be established between these elements', Foucault, Michel, 'Confessions of the flesh', in Colin Gordon (ed.), *Power/Knowledge: Selected Interviews and Other Writings*, pp. 194–228. New York: Pantheon Books, 1980.

192. Bhatia, Ishita, 'Lawyers, drivers, students, waiters, kiosks in 'love-jihad' spy network', *Times of India*, 16 Jan. 2018, https://timesofindia.indiatimes.com/city/meerut/lawyers-drivers-students-waiters-kiosks-in-love-jihad-spy-network/articleshow/62514200.cms.

193. Sahu, Manish, 'Yogi Adityanath government initiates process on withdrawal of 131 riots cases', *Indian Express*, 22 Mar. 2018, https://indianexpress.com/article/india/yogi-adityanath-govt-initiates-process-on-withdrawal-of-131-riots-cases-muzaffarnagar-shamli-5106475/.

194. Carvalho, Nirmala, 'Uttar Pradesh pastor arrested for "forced conversions" freed on bail', *AsiaNews.it*, 26, June 2018, http://www.asianews.it/news-en/Uttar-Pradesh-pastor-arrested-for-%27forced-conversions%27-freed-on-bail-44267.html.

195. Pandey, Manish Chandra, 'BJP to focus on Dalit outreach, Hindutva ideology in UP as battle 2019 looms', *Hindustan Times*, 12 Aug. 2018, https://www.hindustantimes.com/india-news/bjp-to-focus-on-dalit-outreach-hindutva-ideology-in-up-as-battle-2019-looms/story-9m1MqMuwAiUasrA8lE46TK.html; Note: 'A crime is committed against Dalits every 15 minutes in India. And six Dalit women are raped every day, according to official statistics that register a 66% hike in atrocities in the past ten years 2007–2017. The situation has worsened, with a further spike in anti-Dalit violence, over the past four years': Sengupta, Rai, '2017 Timeline of Atrocities Against Dalits: UP, Rajasthan Top The List', *The Citizen*, 29 Nov. 2017, https://www.thecitizen.in/index.php/en/newsdetail/index/2/12381/2017-timeline-of-atrocities-against-dalits-up-rajasthan-top-the-list.

196. Wankhede, Harish S., 'The two faces of Hindutva's Dalit agenda', *The Wire*, 10 May 2018, https://thewire.in/caste/the-two-faces-of-hindutvas-dalit-agenda.

197. Srivastava, Piyush, 'UP priests thrashed', *The Telegraph*, 10 Sep. 2018, https://www.telegraphindia.com/india/up-priests-thrashed/cid/1667256.

198. India Today, 'Woman harassed in Meerut says cops asked her to frame her friend for rape but she refused', *India Today*, 27 Sep. 2018, https://www.indiatoday.in/india/story/woman-harassed-in-meerut-says-cops-asked-her-to-frame-her-friend-for-rape-but-she-refused-1350014-2018-09-27.

199. Hindu nationalist organizations have created a vast network of organizations and support among the Diaspora in the United States and the United Kingdom, for example, and used the same to raise considerable resources to fund majoritarianism in India, see: Agrawal, Girish, Angana Chatterji, Shalini Gera, Biju Mathew, Ali Mir, and S. Ravi Rajan.2002. *The Foreign Exchange of Hate: IDRF and the American Funding of Hindutva*. Sabrang Communications and South Asia Citizens Wire.http://www.sacw.net/2002/FEHi/FEH/. Anonymous.2014.*Hindu Nationalism in the United States: A Report on Nonprofit Groups*. South Asia Citizens Wire.http://www.sacw.net/article9057.html.

200. Agamben, Giorgio, *Remnants of Auschwitz: The Witness and the Archive*, New York: Zone, 1999; Agamben, Giorgio, *State of Exception*, Chicago: Chicago University Press, 2005.

201. Routinely homophobic, Queer-phobic, homo-normative.

202. Foucault, Michel, *Language, Counter-memory, Practice: Selected Essays and Interviews*, translated by Donald F. Bouchard and Sherry Simon, Ithaca: Cornell University Press, 1977.

203. Uttar Pradesh has a total of eighty Lok Sabha seats of a total of 552 Lok Sabha seats in India, and 403 assembly constituencies.

204. Sanyal, Anindita, 'BJP loses UP's Kairana in big win for opposition: 10 Points', NDTV, 31 May 2018, https://www.ndtv.com/india-news/on-counting-day-for-key-bypolls-test-for-opposition-bloc-in-up-10-facts-1860180.

205. See Ganguly, Meenakshi, 'The BJP's increasing authoritarianism may be eroding the support it enjoyed in 2014' *Scroll.in*, 7 Sep. 2018, https://scroll.in/article/893161/the-bjp-is-possibly-losing-the-support-it-enjoyed-in-2014-because-of-its-increasing-authoritarianism.

206. Deleuze, Gilles and Felix Guattari, *A Thousand Plateaus: Capitalism and Schizophrenia*, London: Continuum, 2004; Guattari, Félix, 'The Micro-Politics of Fascism', in *Molecular Revolution: Psychiatry and Politics*, R. Sheed (trans.), Harmondsworth: Penguin/Peregrine, 1984, pp. 217–32; Deleuze, Gilles and Michel Foucault, 'Intellectuals and Power', in David Lapoujade (ed.), Mike Taormina (trans.), *Desert Islands And Other Texts 1953–1974*, pp. 206–213, New York: Semiotext(e), 2004; Deleuze, Gilles and Félix Guattari, *Anti-Oedipus*. Robert Hurley, Mark Seem and Helen R. Lane (trans.), London and New York: Continuum, 1972; Foucault, Michel, 'Preface', in Deleuze, Gilles and Félix Guattari, *Anti-Oedipus*, op. cit., also, https://www.timesnownews.com/mirror-now/society/article/fascism-aadhaar-demonetisation-and-justice-loya-arundhati-roy-raises-concerns-about-state-of-the-country/215788

207. See social death and social disposability, Patterson, Orlando, 'Authority, alienation, and social death' in *Slavery and Social Death: A Comparative Study*, pp. 35–76, Cambridge and London: Harvard University Press, 1982, and Giroux, Henry A., 'Reading Hurricane Katrina: Race, class, and the biopolitics of disposability', *College Literature*, 33, 3 (2006), pp. 171–96. For biopolitics, see Foucault, Michel, *The History of Sexuality, Volume 1: An Introduction*, Robert Hurley (trans.), New York: Random House, 1978; Foucault, Michel, 'The birth of biopolitics' in Paul Rabinow (ed.),

Ethics: Subjectivity and Truth: Essential Works of Foucault, 1954–1984, Volume 1, Robert Hurley and others (trans.), Paul Rabinow (series ed.), pp. 73–80, New York: The New Press, 1997; Foucault, Michel, *Society Must be Defended, Lectures at the Collège de France, 1975–1976,* David Macey (trans.), Mauro Bertani and Alessandro Fontana (eds.), Franois Ewald and Alessandro Fontana (general eds.), Arnold I. Davidson (English series ed.), New York: Picador, 2003; and Foucault, Michel, *Security, Territory, Population, Lectures at the Collège De France, 1977–1978,* Graham Burchell (trans.), Michel Senellart (ed.), Franois Ewald and Alessandro Fontana (general eds.), Arnold I. Davidson (English series ed.), New York, Palgrave Macmillan, 2007. For necropolitics, see Mbembe, Achille, 'Necropolitics', *Public Culture* 15, 1 (Winter 2003), pp. 11–40.

208. Bhowmick, Nilanjana, 'Meet the militant monk spreading Islamophobia in India', *Washington Post,* 24 Mar. 2017, https://www.washingtonpost.com/news/global-opinions/wp/2017/03/24/meet-the-militant-monk-spreading-islamophobia-in-india/.

209. As told to Angana P. Chatterji in 2014, name withheld.

BIOGRAPHICAL BRIEFS FOR EDITORS AND AUTHORS

Biographical Briefs for Editors

Angana P. Chatterji is Co-chair, Political Conflict, Gender and People's Rights Initiative and Visiting Research Anthropologist at the Center for Race and Gender at University of California, Berkeley. Chatterji's scholarship bears witness to contemporary issues in political conflict and (post)colonial, decolonial conditions of grief, dispossession and agency. Chatterji co-founded the People's Tribunal on Human Rights and Justice in Kashmir (2008–2012). In Odisha, she founded the People's Tribunal on Religious Freedom (2005), and in the Narmada Valley, she served on a commission on displacement (2004). In 2015–16, Chatterji was a Visiting Scholar at the Institute for the Study of Human Rights, Columbia University. Previously Chatterji was Professor, Department of Social and Cultural Anthropology at the California Institute of Integral Studies, where she co-created a graduate curriculum in postcolonial anthropology and taught from 1997–2011. Chatterji was Adjunct Professor, University of San Francisco in 2013–14. Her publications include: Violent Gods: Hindu Nationalism in India's Present; Narratives from Orissa (Three Essays Collective 2009); *Land and Justice* (forthcoming); monograph, lead editor: *Conflicted Democracies and Gendered Violence: The Right to Heal* (Zubaan, U. Chicago distribution, 2016); *Contesting Nation: Gendered Violence in South Asia*, co-editor Lubna Nazir Chaudhry (Zubaan, 2012, U. Chicago distribution, 2013); *Kashmir: The Case for Freedom*, co-authors Tariq Ali, Hilal Bhat, Pankaj Mishra and Arundhati Roy (Verso, 2011); and reports, lead author: BURIED EVIDENCE: Unknown, Unmarked, and Mass Graves in Kashmir (2009), Communalism in Orissa (2006), and Without Land or Livelihood (2004). https://www.crg.berkeley.edu/angana-chatterji/

BIOGRAPHICAL BRIEFS FOR EDITORS AND AUTHORS

Thomas Blom Hansen is the Reliance-Dhirubhai Ambani Professor in South Asian Studies and Professor and Chair of the Department of Anthropology at Stanford University. Previously, Hansen taught at Roskilde University, University of Edinburgh, Yale University and University of Amsterdam, where he served as Dean of the International School for Humanities and Social Sciences. Much of Hansen's fieldwork in India was undertaken during the tumultuous and tense years in the beginning of the 1990s when conflicts between Hindu militants and Muslims defined national agendas and produced frequent violent clashes in the streets. More recently, Hansen has pursued a detailed study of religious revival, racial conflict and transformation of domestic and intimate life from the 1950's to the present in a formerly Indian township in Durban in South Africa. His publications include: *The Saffron Wave. Democracy and Hindu Nationalism in Modern India* (Princeton, 1999) which explores the larger phenomenon of Hindu nationalism in the light of the dynamics of India's democratic experience; *Wages of Violence: Naming and Identity in Postcolonial Bombay* (Princeton, 2001) which explores the historical processes and contemporary conflicts that led to the rise of violent socioreligious conflict and the renaming of the city in 1995; *Sovereign Bodies: Citizens, Migrants, and States in the Postcolonial World*, co-edited with Finn Stepputat (Princeton, 2005); and *Melancholia of Freedom: Social Life in an Indian Township in South Africa* (Princeton, 2012). https://anthropology.stanford.edu/people/thomas-blom-hansen

Christophe Jaffrelot is Senior Research Fellow at Centre d'Etudes et de Recherches Internationales at Sciences Po, Paris, Research Director at Centre National de la Recherche Scientifique, and Professor of Indian Politics and Sociology at the India Institute, King College, London. He is a part of the scientific councils of the Südasien Institut (Heidelberg), the ZMO (Berlin) and the CeMIS (Göttingen). Jaffrelot's work spans issues pertaining to politics of religion, class; theories of nationalism and democracy; and nationalist movements and ethnic conflicts in South Asia, in particular India and Pakistan. On India, his work on the Hindu Nationalist movement links history with the present, and he traces the continuities and discontinuities between nationalist discourse and the intellectual founding of Hindu nationalism from colonial time through independence from British rule to India's present. His publications include: *The Pakistan Paradox. Unstability and Resilience* (Oxford University Press, 2015); *Armed Militias of South Asia*, co-edited with L. Gayer (Hurst, 2010); *Rise of the Plebeians? The Changing Face* *of Indian Legislative Assemblies*, Co-Editor with S. Kumar (Routledge, 2009); *Patterns of Middle Class Consumption in China and India*, co-editor with Peter van der Veer (Sage, 2008); *Dr. Ambedkar and Untouchability. Analyzing and Fighting Caste* (Hurst, 2005); *India's Silent Revolution. The Rise of the Lower Castes in North India* (Hurst, 2003); Editor, *Pakistan, Nationalism Without a Nation?* (Manohar, 2002); *The Hindu Nationalist Movement and Indian Politics, 1925 to the 1990s* (Hurst 1999). http://www.sciencespo.fr/ceri/en/users/christophejaffrelot

Biographical Briefs for Individual Contributors

Flavia Agnes is co-founder of MAJLIS, a legal and cultural resource center in Mumbai. A women's rights lawyer, her work brings women's rights to the forefront within the legal system, contextualizing issues of gender and identity, and has focused on reforming Christian Personal Laws and advancing the rights of Muslim women. Her scholarship includes social trends and legal reforms and pluralism, minority law reforms, secularism and human rights. Her publications include, *Law and Gender Inequality*: The Politics of Personal Laws in India (Oxford University Press, 2012) and *My Story Our Story ... Of Rebuilding Broken Lives* (Forum Against Oppression of Women, 1988), and *Women and Law* (Oxford University Press, 2016, co-editor Sudhir Chandra).

Paola Bacchetta is Professor of Gender and Women's Studies and Co-chair, Political Conflict, Gender and People's Rights Initiative at Center for Race and Gender at University of California, Berkeley. Her scholarly interests span political conflict, transnational feminist and queer theory, decolonial and postcolonial theory and epistemologies of the south. Her publications include, *Co-Motion* (Duke University Press, forthcoming), *Global Racialities* (Routledge, co-edited with Sunaina Maira, forthcoming), *Gender in the Hindu Nation: RSS Women as Ideologues* (Women Unlimited, 2004) and *Trans-Q Fem: Elementi per una critica femminista queer e transnazionale* (Trans-Q Fem: Elements for a Queer Transnational Feminist Critique, Verona: Ombre Corte, 2015, co-editor Laura Fantone).

Pranab Bardhan is Professor of the Graduate School at the Department of Economics at University of California, Berkeley. He has held teaching appointments at MIT and the Delhi School of Economics and was the BP Centennial Professor at London School of Economics for 2010 and 2011 and held the Distinguished Fulbright Siena Chair at the University of Siena, Italy in 2008–9. Bardhan's publications include *Awakening Giants, Feet of Clay: Assessing the Economic Rise of China and India* (Princeton University Press, 2013), *The Contested Commons: Conversations between Economists and Anthropologists* (Blackwell, 2008) and *Globalization and Egalitarian Redistribution India* (Princeton University Press, 2006, with Samuel Bowles and Michael Wallerstein).

A.K. Bhattacharya has been an economic journalist with several publications including *The Financial Express* and *The Economic Times* for the last four decades and was the former editor of the *Business Standard* and the *Pioneer*. At present, he is the Editorial Director at the Business Standard. His fortnightly columns (New Delhi Diary and Raisina Hill) take a close look at implications of policy making and government affairs. A winner of Shriram Lifetime Achievement Award for Excellence In *Financial Journalism*, he is at present the General Secretary of the Editors Guild of India.

Ian M. Cook is Research Fellow at Central European University within the project 'Academic Podcasting: Digital Scholarship, Communities of Knowledge Production and the Elusive Search for the Public' at the Center for Media, Data and Society. With an interest in time and space, *South Asia Studies, Visual Anthropology and Urban Studies*, he has conducted ethnographic fieldwork in Mangaluru (India) and Budapest (Hungary) with research interests including: urbanization, morality, rhythm, informal economies, modes of learning, housing, land use, development, migration, infrastructure and intercommunity relationships.

Parvis Ghassem-Fachandi is Associate Professor of Anthropology at Rutgers University. He has taught at Princeton University in 2006 and held a postdoctoral fellow at the Center for Religion and Media, New York University in 2006–07. He was also a fellow at the *Institut d'Études Avancée de Nantes* (France) in 2012 and at the Indian Institute of Advanced Studies, Shimla, in 2016. He is the author of two monographs: *Pogrom in Gujarat: Hindu Nationalism and Anti-Muslim Violence in India* (Princeton University Press, 2012) and Muslimische Heilige in Gujarat: Sufismus, Synkretismus, und Praxis im westlichen Indien (Editio Cortis Aquilae, 2008), and the editor of Violence: *Ethnographic Encounters* (Berg Press, 2009).

Abdul R. JanMohamed is Professor, Department of English, University of California, Berkeley. His publications include *Reconsidering Social Identi-*

fication: Race, Gender, Class, and Caste (Routledge, 2011), *The Death-Bound-Subject: Richard Wright's Archaeology of Death* (Duke, 2005), *The Nature and Context of Minority Discourse* (Oxford University Press, 1990, co-editor David Lloyd), and *Manichean Aesthetics: The Politics of Literature in Colonial Africa* (University of Massachusetts, 1983). He was the founding editor (along with Donna Przybylowicz) of *Cultural Critique*. His current research, provisionally entitled, *Thick Love: Birthing the Death-Bound-Subject*, focuses on black feminist neo-slave narratives that depict the vicissitudes of giving birth to and nurturing life in a culture organized around the production of death-bound-subjectivity.

Pralay Kanungo is currently the ICCR Chair of Contemporary India Studies at International Institute for Asian Studies, Leiden University. He is also Guest Professor (2015–2020) at Sichuan University, Chengdu and Honorary Professor (2015–2018) at Australian Catholic University, Melbourne. Previously, he was Professor and Chair, Centre for Political Studies, Jawaharlal Nehru University, Delhi, a Fellow at Nehru Memorial Museum and Library, Delhi and Visiting Professor at Maison des Sciences De L'Homme, Paris. Kanungo is the author of *Cultural Entrenchment of Hindutva: Local Mediations and Forms of Convergence* (Routledge, 2011, with Daniela Berti and Nicolas Jaoul) and *The Politics of Ethnicity in India, Nepal and China* (Primus, 2014, with Marine Carrin and Gerard Toffin).

Ratna Kapur is Visiting Professor of Law, School of Law, Queen Mary University of London (2015–18) and **Senior Core Faculty**, International Global Law and Policy Institute, Harvard Law School (since 2013) and **Global Professor of Law**, Jindal Global Law School, Sonepat (on long term leave). Her publications include, *Human Rights and Liberal Freedom: Gender and Alterity* (book manuscript in progress), Makeshift Migrants and Law: Gender, Belonging and Postcolonial Anxieties (Routledge, Taylor and Francis Group, 2010), *Erotic Justice: Law and the New Politics of Postcolonialism* (Taylor and Francis, Cavendish: London, 2005) and *Secularism's Last Sigh? Hindutva and the (Mis)Rule of Law* (Oxford University Press, 2001, co-author Brenda Cossman).

Arkotong Longkumer is Lecturer in Religious Studies at the University of Edinburgh. He is the author of *Reform, Identity and Narratives of Belonging: The Heraka Movement of Northeast India* (Continuum, 2010) and has published in journals such as *Himalaya, Contributions to Indian Sociology, HAU:*

Journal of Ethnographic Theory, South Asia: Journal of South Asian Studies, and Religion. He is currently writing a book on Hindu nationalism in Northeast India and Hindu nationalists' engagement with indigenous peoples.

James Manor is the Emeritus Professor of Commonwealth Studies at the School of Advanced Study, University of London. He is acknowledged as one of the world's leading experts on Indian politics, especially how it is affected by caste, political economy—particularly poverty and its alleviation—regionalism and modes of political leadership. His publications include *Politics and the Right to Work: India's National Rural Employment Guarantee Act* (Oxford University Press, 2017, with Rob Jenkins) and *Against the Odds: Politicians, Institutions and the Struggle Against Poverty* (Hurst, 2012, co-edited with Marcus Andre Melo and Njuguna Ng'ethe), and *Broadening and Deepening Democracy: Political Innovation in Karnataka* (Routledge, 2009, with E. Raghavan).

C. Raja Mohan is Director of Carnegie India, the foreign affairs columnist for *Indian Express*, and Visiting Research Professor at the Institute of South Asian Studies, National University of Singapore. A former member of India's National Security Advisory Board, in 2009–10, Mohan was the Henry Alfred Kissinger Chair in Foreign Policy and International Relations at the Library of Congress. Mohan's publications include, *Modi's World: Expanding India's Sphere of Influence* (Harper Collins India, 2015) and *India's Naval Strategy and Asian Security* (Routledge, 2016, co-edited with Anit Mukherjee), *Samudra Manthan: Sino-Indian Rivalry in the Indo-Pacific* (Carnegie, 2012), and *Power Realignments in Asia: China, India and the United States* (Sage, 2009, co-edited with Alyssa Ayres).

Suhas Palshikar is Director of Lokniti and Professor in the Department of Politics and Public Administration at the University of Pune. He is also the Chief Editor of the journal *Studies in Indian Politics*. His teaching focuses on in India, on issues of political sociology, politics, the party system, political economy, and on political processes in Maharashtra. His publications include, *State of Democracy in South Asia* (Oxford University Press, 2008, with Yogendra Yadav, Peter deSouza, et. al.), *Jamatwad, Dharmanirapekshata ani Lokshahi* (Pratima Prakashan, 2006), *Samakaleen Bharatiya Rajkaran* (Pratima Prakashan, 2004), *Raajakaaranaach Taaleband: Bharatiy Lokashahichi Vaatachaal* (Sadhana, 2013), *Lokshahi: Arth ani Vyavahar* (Diamond, 2010, co-editor Rajendra Vora, Marathi translation by Chitra Lele).

Jyoti Puri is Professor of Sociology at Simmons College. She writes and teaches at the crossroads of sociology, sexuality and queer studies, and postcolonial feminist theory. Her publications include, *Sexual States: Governance and the Struggle against the Antisodomy Law in India's Present* (Duke University Press, 2016), *Woman, Body, Desire in Post-colonial India* (Routledge, 1999) and *Encountering Nationalism*, (Blackwell Publishers, 2004). Puri has co-edited a special issue on gender, sexuality, state, and nation for *Gender & Society* (2005) and another one on sexuality and the state for *Rethinking Marxism* (2012). She has also published numerous articles and book chapters. She is the recipient of fellowships and grants, including a Rockefeller Research Fellowship and a Fulbright Senior Research award.

Mridu Rai is Professor of History at Presidency University, Kolkata. In 2010–2011, she was a research fellow at the Shelby Cullom Davis Centre for Historical Studies at Princeton University, then taught at Trinity College, Dublin, where she taught until May 2014. She is the author of *Hindu Rulers, Muslim Subjects: Islam, Rights and the History of Kashmir* (Princeton University Press, 2004) and of several articles in academic and non-academic publications. Her current book project, expected to be completed by the end of 2016, examines why outright violence--as opposed to earlier patterns of violence accompanied by ideological suasion—has become the predominant mode of maintaining caste dominance in colonial and postcolonial north India.

Tanika Sarkar is Professor of History at Jawaharlal Nehru University in Delhi. She has also taught at the St. Stephen's College and Indraprastha College, Delhi University, and the University of Chicago. Her publications include *Bengal 1928–1934: The Politics of Protest*, (Oxford University Press India, 1987), *Words to Win: A Modern Autobiography* (Kali for Women, 1999), *Khaki Shorts and Saffron Flags: A Critique of the Hindu Right* (co-authors Tapan Basu, Pradip Datta, Sumit Sarkar and Sambuddha Sen; Orient Longman 1993), *Women and the Hindu Right* (co-edited with Urvashi Butalia, 1995), *Hindu Wife, Hindu Nation: Community, Religion, Cultural Nationalism* (Hurst, 2001), and *Caste in Modern India: A Reader* (Permanent Black, 2013, two volumes, co-edited with Sumit Sarkar).

Nandini Sundar is Professor of Sociology at the Delhi School of Economics, Delhi University. Her current interests relate to citizenship and politics in South Asia, the sociology of law, and inequality. Her publications include, *The*

Burning Forest: India's War in Bastar (Juggernaut Press, 2016); an edited volume, *The Scheduled Tribes and their India* (OUP, 2016) and *Civil Wars in South Asia: State, Sovereignty, Development*, (Sage, 2014, co-edited with Aparna Sundar), and *Subalterns and Sovereigns: An Anthropological History of Bastar* (Oxford University Press, 2007, 1997). She was awarded the Infosys Prize for Social Sciences—Social Anthropology (2010), and the Ester Boserup Prize for Development Research (2016).

Paranjoy Guha Thakurta is a journalist and an educator. He has worked with print, radio and television media, and documentary cinema. From April 2016 until July 2017, Thakurta was Editor of the *Economic and Political Weekly*. Between 1995 and 2001, he anchored "India Talks" on CNBC-India television channel. He is Visiting Faculty at various institutions, including the Jawaharlal Nehru University, University of Delhi, Jamia Millia Islamia, Indian Institute of Management, Indian Institute of Technology-Kanpur, and Lal Bahadur Shastri National Academy of Administration. Thakurta served as a member of the Press Council of India between January 2008 and January 2011. His publications include, *Media Ethics: Truth, Fairness and Objectivity, Making and Breaking News* (Oxford University Press, 2009).

Sukhadeo Thorat is Professor Emeritus, Centre for the Study of Regional Development, School of Social Sciences at Jawaharlal Nehru University, New Delhi; Distinguished Professor, Savitribai Phule University, Pune, Maharashtra; K.R. Narayanan Chair (Honorary) for Human Rights & Social Justice, Mahatma Gandhi University, Kerala; Chairperson, Indian Institute of Dalit Studies, New Delhi; Former Chairperson of University Grants Commission; and Former Chairperson of Indian Council of Social Science Research.

INDEX

INDEX

INDEX

INDEX